Wealth Management and Investment in Islamic Settings

Toseef Azid · Murniati Mukhlisin ·
Othman Altwijry
Editors

Wealth Management and Investment in Islamic Settings

Opportunities and Challenges

Springer

Editors
Toseef Azid
College of Business and Economics
Qassim University
Saudi Arabia, Saudi Arabia

Othman Altwijry
College of Business and Economic
Qassim University
Saudi Arabia, Saudi Arabia

Murniati Mukhlisin
Rector STEI Tazkia
Bogar, Indonesia

ISBN 978-981-19-3685-2 ISBN 978-981-19-3686-9 (eBook)
https://doi.org/10.1007/978-981-19-3686-9

This Springer imprint is published by the registered company Springer Nature Singapore Pte Ltd.
The registered company address is: 152 Beach Road, #21-01/04 Gateway East, Singapore 189721, Singapore

Foreword

For the last five decades, the epistemology of social, economic, management, business, psychological, and several theories in the Islamic framework have been developed based on the integration of this life and life hereafter. The development of these theories follows the injunctions of the two Divine sources, the *Qur'an* and the *Sunnah* of the Prophet (PBUH). Islamic theories focus on the development of societies which sustain the environment of virtues and discourage vices. This approach is in contrast to the understanding of theories in the conventional system, which is largely considered neutral toward moral and ethical values.

Accordingly, Islamic Wealth Management (IWM) takes a systems view of the relationship between worldly life and the hereafter. The wealth management process also follows the injunctions of the *Qur'an* and the *Sunnah*, in addition to detailed *shari'ah* sources such as *Fiqh* (Islamic jurisprudence) on practical matters related to wealth management. For the past fourteen hundred years, the *Qur'an* and the *Sunnah* have taught their followers how to behave vis-à-vis with the wealth they own, and the status of man in relation to this wealth. Both Divine sources provide principles and a broad view of wealth management-related phenomena. Epistemologically, these phenomena present the different dimensions that can develop the believers' personality and increase their *falah* (a broader concept of welfare), improve their moral and ethical values, upgrade the environment level, regulate the market and develop their social and economic values. These sources also recommend how believers should develop very prominent sectors of social life such as education and health through the institutions of zakat, *waqf*, and other forms of charity.

Literary, the definition of *al-mal* (wealth) has three attributes: it has value, has benefit, and must be possessed and owned. Furthermore, *al-mal* must meet the criteria of *halal* (lawful) and *Tayyib* (good or pure) [2:172], as opposed to *Haram* [unlawful] and *Khabith* (evil or impure) [5:100]. Hence, regardless of the quantity, good or pure, *al-mal* is preferred over the evil or impure one [5:100]. Impure *al-mal* is that which is unlawful or not permitted by the *shari'ah*. For example, wealth generated through *maysir* (gambling), *riba* (interest), or through the production of unlawful goods such as wine and pork. Here, the concepts of *halal* and *Tayyib* (lawful and pure) and *Haram* and *Khabith* (unlawful, impure) are clearly mentioned by the *shari'ah*.

Islamic literature discusses the different types of wealth, such as corrupt wealth (which is not generated by following the rules and regulations of *shari'ah*), impure wealth (earned through unlawful means), and pure wealth (earned by following the *shari'ah* injunctions).

Over the years, the development of the Islamic financial industry has opened doors for several opportunities for Muslim investors and households toward the IWM. Opportunities are also extended to academicians and policymakers to add to the discourse of IWM. There are two different opinions in the literature regarding the domain of Islamic wealth management. One opinion views IWM as the domain of the governments of the Muslim countries which are duty-bound to promote Islamic wealth management. In contrast, the other opinion grants the significant role of a wealth manager to IWM. The wealth manager is expected to have expertise in different fields of human psychology, sociology and know the different verdicts of *shari'ah* related to financial matters. Accordingly, the wealth management industry would promote and develop its norms and dimensions while taking into consideration the clients' psychological, social, and religious states. Nevertheless, the contributors of this volume are of the view that these two opinions should be considered simultaneously since market forces and the law of government affect each other.

The concept of IWM in the present work is oriented toward inter-generational and intra-generational justice. The former, intergenerational justice, is a long-term measure which is achieved in time series across generations. The common institutions used to achieve this form of justice is the law of inheritance and *waqf*. On the other hand, inter-generational justice is a short-term measure applicable at a point in time within each generation. The typical institutions used to achieve it are zakat and other forms of charity.

Wealth Management and Investment in an Islamic Setting: Opportunities and Challenges can be viewed as an alarm bell and catalyst for the gurus of the Islamic wealth management industry. Instead of replicating the system and product of conventional industry, they should develop their system and products guided by the fundamental sources of Islam. The authors of the current volume come from various countries and therefore enrich the work with varieties of experiences represented by these countries that include Pakistan, Egypt, Indonesia, Mauritius, Malaysia, Dubai, Brunei, Nigeria, and Turkey. This is a significant manifestation of the strength of diversity across the content of the chapters.

Wealth Management and Investment in an Islamic Setting: Opportunities and Challenges offers a variety of issues and their solutions in the domain of Islam to its readers and valuable views related to wealth management. The work is timely because of the development of Islamic finance around the globe, scholars in business, economics, and finance focusing on religion as a related field of study.

Wealth Management and Investment in an Islamic Setting also offers a mixture of subjects as a subset of wealth management in the context of different cultures with novel experiences. I am delighted to recognize the efforts of the authors in addressing the various contemporary issues related to the process of wealth management, the role of the believers in this process, and the extent of *falah* they would achieve in this worldly life and life hereafter.

The efforts of the brilliant scholars of this volume can increase mutual understanding across the different cultures of the globe. I hope secularly oriented schools of business, economics, and finance can benefit from such research without teaching Islam directly to their students. This will equip the students to learn about different cultures within the Islamic world in the wealth management context.

I hope that readers as academicians, policymakers, and financial advisors will benefit from the scholarly work of the contributors of this volume.

February 2022

Mustafa Omar Mohammed
Director
Center of Islamic Economics
International Islamic University Malaysia
Kuala Lumpur, Malaysia

Preface

The theory of wealth management suggested that investors and households always behave like rational economic agents and take rational decisions and maximize their utility. However, they have certain constraints based on their socio-economic environment. Their ultimate objective is to get economic, social, psychological, and religious security. Therefore, they expect that the market should behave efficiently to earn a good return. However, since 1987, the financial markets all over the world have suffered several financial crises; in the resultant outcome were numerous bankruptcies and huge fertilities. This posited rather market inefficiency, asymmetric information, or irrational behavior of the market agents. It is also leading to a major problem for the old retired individuals. These dysfunctions are a disposition effect, regret aversion, loss aversion, cognitive dissonance, anchoring, mental accounting, overconfidence, over- and under-reaction, reference-dependent preferences, confirmation biases, herding behavior, hindsight bias, and many other behavioral biases. All these attributes made the financial markets extremely complex. Over and above asymmetric information contributed more to this apathy due to moral hazards and adverse selection.

After observing the recent global financial crises, most of the experts in financial markets, economists, and bankers tried to apply those models suggested by Nobel Prize co-winner 2013 Robert Shiller (2000) in his book entitled *Irrational Exuberance*. However, another thought emerged during this period about Islamic finance. Several experts found that Islamic finance is more resilient because of its nature, i.e., Asset-based/backed. Therefore, they relooked the foundation of conventional finance and tried the different models. Among them, the most attractive was Islamic Finance. This opened other doors for researchers, policymakers, and academicians. Consequently, governments introduced the new rules and regulations, whereas investors changed their options and preferences orders. These endeavors have also reshaped the activities of the wealth management industry. Furthermore, it also improved the role of the wealth manager. In a nutshell, three major developments (recent financial crises, Shiller's thoughts, and development of Islamic Finance) improved the understanding of the major actors in the wealth management industry.

This volume tries to integrate behavior, religion, and finance, which is a generally neglected area in the current wealth management literature. And the major player in the wealth management industry did not pay too much attention to this perspective. In reality, this perspective started with the birth of human beings and simultaneously grew with the generations. In fact, it is an essential part of human beings' social, psychological, and economic life. We trust our humble effort would increase a better and deep understanding of the subject matter of wealth management. Our whole efforts are based on the assumption that religious and moral values are the central pillar of the building of human behavior. By following this assumption, we invited scholars from diverse social-cum-religious backgrounds to develop the different dimensions of wealth management and investment under the umbrella of *shari'ah*.

As editors of this volume, we aim to provide an opportunity to the scholars to start a discussion regarding the wealth management industry's social, behavioral, psychological, and financial issues. This was our endeavor to encourage them to develop some missing moral and religious issues of the wealth management industry and provide their empirical findings in this volume. We admit that contributors to this volume offered new avenues for further discussion on this subject. We acknowledged that credit goes to all contributors who tried to fill the gap and identified new issues in the current literature on wealth management and investment. We tried not to edit or change the contributor's scholarly work; therefore, readers would understand their views in the original form.

This volume, "Wealth Management and Investment in an Islamic Setting," invites its readers to think about the behavioral and religious issues related to the different dimensions of wealth management, particularly related to Islamic finance. Moreover, we expect that readers from diverse academic and professional backgrounds may find some interesting discussions related to their field of knowledge. We anticipate that this volume also opens new avenues for the followers of the conventional theories of finance and economics. However, we do not claim that this volume covers all the salient features of the understudied area. This volume does not include many critical areas, such as financial therapy, reference-dependent preferences, role of state, disposition effect, regret aversion, loss aversion, cognitive dissonance, mental accounting, and many others.

We believe that economic and financial activities are not achieving their targets if they are not integrated with religious and moral values. In our view, it is the religious and moral responsibility of everyone to manage their wealth as per divine guidance. Particularly, the followers of Abrahamic religions believe that they are accountable to God on the day of judgment. And they have very clear commandments about the management of wealth and resources. However, this current volume is only focused on Islamic wealth management.

This volume has five parts. After the introduction section, Part I discusses the theoretical framework of wealth management within the Islamic jurisdiction, the application of Islamic wealth management is presented in Part II, Part III provides the state of wealth management in different countries, and Part IV sketches Islamic social responsible investment in the *mode of waqf*. Finally, Part V discusses a particular issue related to the success of Muslim Households as true believers. In this volume, twenty-two chapters are selected covering the different research topics. The first chapter deals with basic wealth management issues in the Islamic domain.

Eight chapters are included in Part I. All these chapters developed the foundation of Islamic Wealth Management (IWM). For example, Chap. 2 discusses the salient points of Islamic Wealth Management from *Qur'anic* Texts. Chapter 3 covers the spiritual aspect of the IWM; Chap. 4 develops an exciting aspect of the subject which covers three dimensions, i.e., politics, warfare, and welfare; Chap. 5 focuses on wealth creation; Chap. 6 discusses the IWM through injunction of zakat. In contrast, Chap. 7 touches on the very crucial topic of debt management.

Part II has three chapters. These chapters cover the application side of the subject. For example, Chap. 8 suggests the financing model of small-medium property enterprises in the context of *maqasid al-shari'ah* (objective of Islamic Jurisprudence). Chapter 9 develops a stochastic mathematical model to measure the effects of fixed return instruments on investment decisions in the periphery of Islamic economics. In contrast, Chap. 10 presents the family financing management from the *sakinah* family perspective.

Part III has eight chapters. Among them, Chap. 11 analyzes the behavior of the Halal industry in Indonesia; Chap. 12 discusses the role of accounting, Islamic microfinance, and IWM while studying the three markets, i.e., Pakistan, Egypt, and Indonesia; Chap. 13 studies the Sukuk and *maslaha* perspective in Brunei; Chap. 14 presents the Malaysian experience based on religion and debt management; Chap. 15 discusses a fascinating case of Mauritius based on the prospects and challenges of Islamic investment wealth management; Chap. 16 discusses the case of the Jakarta Islamic index with the reference to sustainability, *shari'ah* governance, and financial performance. Chapter 17 presents a comparative analysis between *Sukuk* Better and Conventional Bonds. In contrast, Chap. 18 provides an interesting discussion related to COVID-19 and socially responsible practices of Islamic banks.

Part IV discusses the *waqf* as a special mode of social responsible investment; Chaps. 19 and 21 both throw the light on the social development goals and their relationship with the sustainable development goals, whereas Chap. 20 studies the role of *waqf* bank in Indonesia and the association between blended finance and sustainable development goals, whereas Chap. 22 in Part V summarizes the discussion in a novel way and posits how Muslim Households get success through the management of their wealth by following the guidance provided by *the Qur'an* and practices of the Prophet Muhammad (PBUH).

Saudi Arabia, Saudi Arabia — Toseef Azid
Bogar, Indonesia — Murniati Mukhlisin
Saudi Arabia, Saudi Arabia — Othman Altwijry

Contents

1 Wealth Management and Investment: An Islamic Epistemology 1
Nasim Shirazi, Othman Altwijry, Toseef Azid, and Muhammad Omer Chaudhry

Part I Principles of Islamic Wealth Management

2 Decoding Islamic Wealth Management from *Qur'anic* Texts 27
Nurizal Ismail, Zurina Shafii, and Nashr Akbar

3 Islam, Spirituality and Wealth: Islamic Framework of Wealth Management 43
Muhammad Abdullah

4 Islamic Investment-Cum-Wealth Management: Politics, Warfare and Welfare 57
Muhammad Iqbal Anjum

5 Wealth Creation and Management in Islam 73
Muhammad Ashfaq, Hanna R. Abdelwahab, Shahab Aziz, and Shahbaz Sharif

6 Investment and Wealth Management in Contemporary Times: *Zakat* as a Viable Approach 91
AbdulGafar Olawale Fahm

7 The Urgency of Debt Management in the Perspective of Islamic Wealth Management 103
Rizqi Zakiya and Achmad Firdaus

Part II Applications of Islamic Wealth Management

8 Project Financing Models for Small Medium Property Enterprises in the Framework of *Maqasid Al-Shari'ah* 115
Alia Gemala Alidinar, Ascarya Ascarya, Nurul Huda, and Abrista Devi

9 The Effects of Fixed Return Instruments on Investment Decisions in Islamic Economics: Using Stochastic Mathematical Model 135
Hasan Kiaee

10 Family Financial Management in Realizing *Sakinah* Family 151
Putri Apria Ningish, Murniati Mukhlisin, and Jumni Nelli

Part III Country Experiences

11 Measuring the Impact of Open Innovation on Firm Performance in Indonesia Halal Industry 167
Faried Kurnia Rahman

12 How Does Accounting Play a Role in Islamic Microfinance and Islamic Wealth Management Practices? Case Studies in Indonesia, Pakistan and Egypt 183
Murniati Mukhlisin and Sugiyarti Fatma Laela

13 Social Impact Sukūk: Implications from the Notion of *Maslaha* 201
Abu Umar Faruq Ahmad, Nurul Aini Muhamed, and Rashedul Hasan

14 Religion, Islamic Values and Debt Management, the Malaysian Experience 211
Wan Marhaini Wan Ahmad, Asmak Ab Rahman, and Azizi Che Seman

15 Prospects and Challenges for Islamic Investment and Wealth Management in Mauritius 227
Salma Sairally and Najmul Hussein Rassool

16 Sustainability, *Sharī'ah* Governance and Financial Performance: Evidence from Companies Listed on the Jakarta Islamic Index 249
Zuraida Zuraida and Asna Husin

17 When It Comes to Risk, is Sukuk Better Than Conventional Bonds? A Comparative Study of NASDAQ Securities 283
Ahmed-Nur Ali Farah, Alija Avdukic, and Fawad Khaleel

18 COVID-19 Pandemic and '*KITA JAGA KITA*': Appraisal of Social Responsible Practices of Islamic Banking Institutions in Malaysia 313
Noor Suhaida Kasri and Siti Fariha Adilah Ismail

Part IV *Waqf*: An Ethical Investment

19 *Waqf* as a Financing Tool and Its Role in Achieving SDGs and Foreseeing the Future 333
Eiman Ahmad Mohammad Khaleel Al Hashmi

20 Blended Finance and the Role of *Waqf* Bank: Shaping the SDGs in Indonesia 357
Gunawan Baharuddin and Bayu Taufiq Possumah

21 Waqf Contributions for Sustainable Development Goals: A Critical Appraisal 367
Omar Kachkar and Marwa Alfares

Part V Special Issue

22 A Path Towards Success for Muslim Households: Wealth Management and *Shari'ah* Rulings 395
Toseef Azid, Othman Ibrahim Altwijry, Osama Rewashadeh, and Nasim Shirazi

Editors and Contributors

About the Editors

Toseef Azid is a professor of Economics at the College of Business and Economics, Qassim University, Saudi Arabia. He holds a Ph.D. in Economics from University College of Wales, Aberystwyth, UK (1993). He received Overseas Research Scholarship from the British government, a Fulbright Award Scholar in Residence (2006). He taught in Pakistan, Brunei, the UK, the USA, and Saudi Arabia. His research focuses on technological change, labor economics, Islamic economics, and Islamic finance. His eight books have been published, one in Pakistan (Some Basic Principles of Islamic Economics), four by Routledge, UK (Labor in Islamic Setting: Theory and Practice; Social Justice and Islamic Economics: Theory, Issues and Practice; Foundations of a Sustainable Economy Moral, Ethical and Religious Perspectives; Labor Economics in an Islamic Framework Theory and Practice), two by Emerald (Corporate and Shari'ah Governance in the Muslim World: Theory and Practice; Monetary Policy, Islamic Finance, and Islamic Corporate Governance: An International Overview), and the eighth one, Women Empowerment in the Islamic World: Theory and Practice, by World Scientific Publishers, Singapore.

Murniati Mukhlisin is currently a Rector, Tazkia University College of Islamic Economics, Bogor, Indonesia. She earned her Bachelor's degree in Islamic accounting from International Islamic University of Malaysia, Master's degree from University of Indonesia (postgraduate), and Ph.D. from University of Glasgow, United Kingdom. Murniati has work experiences in banking, financial, and IT services. Murniati started her career as a lecturer in Islamic Accounting and Finance in 2002, and she is currently Islamic Accounting certified. She taught at University of Glasgow in 2014 and Essex Business School, University of Essex, Colchester, UK, from 2015 to 2017. Her research interest is in the areas of financial reporting, Islamic accounting, Islamic banking/finance, and Islamic financial literacy. She authored ten books and international journal papers, as well as hundreds of articles published in national and international media. Her book called *Sakinah* Finance concerns Islamic family finance. She currently assumes position as a Shari'ah Expert at BRI Corporate University, Board Member of Indonesian Economist Association, and Advisor to Association of Islamic FinTech Indonesia.

Othman Altwijry is Assistant Professor in the College of Business and Economics, Qassim University, Saudi Arabia. He holds his Ph.D. in Islamic Banking and Finance from International Islamic University, Malaysia (2013). He got his Bachelor of Islamic Law/*Shari'ah* from Qassim University (2003), and Master of Science in Islamic Banking and Finance from International Islamic University, Kuala Lumpur, Malaysia (2010). He presented several papers in the international conference held in different parts of the world. His papers are published in peer-reviewed international journals. Two of his papers won second prize in the International conference held in Malaysia and Dubai.

Contributors

Ab Rahman Asmak Universiti Malaya, Kuala Lumpur, Malaysia

Abdelwahab Hanna R. IU International University of Applied Sciences, Bad Honnef, Germany

Abdullah Muhammad Islamic Economics, Markfield Institute of Higher Education (MIHE), Leicestershire, United Kingdom

Ahmad Abu Umar Faruq Islamic Economic Institute, King Abdulaziz University, Jeddah, Saudi Arabia

Akbar Nashr Institut Agama Islam Tazkia, Jl. Ir. H. Djuanda No. 78, Sentul City, Bogor, Indonesia

Al Hashmi Eiman Ahmad Mohammad Khaleel Zayed University, Abu Dhabi, UAE

Alfares Marwa Istanbul Sabahattin Zaim University, Istanbul, Turkey

Alidinar Alia Gemala Jakarta Selatan, Indonesia

Altwijry Othman College of Buisness and Economics, Qassim University, Buraydah, Saudi Arabia

Altwijry Othman Ibrahim College of Buisness and Economics, Qassim University, Buraydah, Saudi Arabia

Ascarya Ascarya Bogor, Indonesia

Ashfaq Muhammad IU International University of Applied Sciences, Bad Honnef, Germany

Avdukic Alija Dundee, SPE, UK

Azid Toseef College of Buisness and Economics, Qassim University, Buraydah, Saudi Arabia

Aziz Shahab Bahria Business School, Bahria University, Islamabd, Pakistan

Baharuddin Gunawan Universitas Pancasila Indonesia, South Jakarta, Indonesia

Chaudhry Muhammad Omer Bahauddin Zakariya University, Multan, Pakistan

Che Seman Azizi Universiti Malaya, Kuala Lumpur, Malaysia

Devi Abrista Perumahan Haji, Jl. Tumenggung Wiradiredja, Cimahpar Bogor Utara, Jawa Barat, Indonesia

Fahm AbdulGafar Olawale Department of Religions, University of Ilorin, Ilorin, Nigeria

Farah Ahmed-Nur Ali Alfurqan Centre, Leicester, UK

Firdaus Achmad Institut Agama Islam Tazkia, Jl. Ir. H. Djuanda No. 78, Sentul City, Bogor, Indonesia

Hasan Rashedul Islamic Economic Institute, King Abdulaziz University, Jeddah, Saudi Arabia

Huda Nurul Cipinang Cimpedak Jatinegara Jakarta Timur, Indonesia

Husin Asna Department of Arabic, School of Tarbiyah and Education, Ar-Raniry State Islamic University, Darussalam, Banda Aceh, Indonesia

Iqbal Anjum Muhammad Assistant Professor of Economics, Internaional Institute of Islamic Economics, International Islamic University Islamabad, Islamabad, Pakistan

Ismail Nurizal Institut Agama Islam Tazkia, Jl. Ir. H. Djuanda No. 78, Sentul City, Bogor, Indonesia

Ismail Siti Fariha Adilah Maybank Islamic Bank, Dataran Maybank, Kuala Lumpur, Malaysia

Kachkar Omar Ibn Haldun University, Istanbul, Turkey

Kasri Noor Suhaida INCEIF University, Kuala Lumpur, Malaysia

Khaleel Fawad Rosyth, Kyth, UK

Kiaee Hasan Faculty of Islamic Studies and Economics Imam, Sadiq University, Tehran, Iran

Laela Sugiyarti Fatma Institut Agama Islam Tazkia, Bogor, Indonesia

Muhamed Nurul Aini Islamic Economic Institute, King Abdulaziz University, Jeddah, Saudi Arabia

Mukhlisin Murniati Institut Agama Islam Tazkia, Bogor, Indonesia

Nelli Jumni UIN Sultan Syarif Kasim, Riau, Indonesia

Ningish Putri Apria Faculty of Islamic Economics and Business (FEBI), Universitas Islam Negeri Sulthan Thaha Saifuddin, Jambi, Indonesia

Possumah Bayu Taufiq Institut Agama Islam Tazkia, Bogor, Indonesia

Rahman Faried Kurnia Institut Agama Islam Tazkia Jl. Ir. H. Djuanda No. 78, Sentul City, Bogor, Indonesia

Rassool Najmul Hussein Kuala Lumpur, Malaysia

Rewashadeh Osama College of Business and Economics, Qassim University, Buraydah, Saudi Arabia

Sairally Salma Kuala Lumpur, Malaysia

Shafii Zurina Universiti Sains Islam Malaysia, Bandar Baru Nilai, Nilai, Negeri Sembilan, Malaysia

Sharif Shahbaz IU International University of Applied Sciences, Bad Honnef, Germany

Shirazi Nasim College of Islamic Studies, Doha, Qatar

Wan Ahmad Wan Marhaini Universiti Malaya, Kuala Lumpur, Malaysia

Zakiya Rizqi Institut Agama Islam Tazkia, Jl. Ir. H. Djuanda No. 78, Sentul City, Bogor, Indonesia

Zuraida Zuraida Department of Accounting, Faculty of Economics and Business, Syiah Kuala University, Darussalam, Banda Aceh, Indonesia

List of Figures

Fig. 2.1	Dimensions of management	30
Fig. 3.1	Different States of Wealth. *Source* Al-Ghazali, (2004)	48
Fig. 4.1	Islamically sustainable human development: Ever expanding environmentally sustainable production possibilities in an Islamic universal economy	61
Fig. 5.1	Cycle of wealth creation, enhancement, protection, and distribution. *Source* Adapted from Shanmugam and Zahari (2009)	76
Fig. 5.2	Concept of Zakatul Maal. *Source* Ashfaq & Abdelwahab	80
Fig. 8.1	Project financing and work model	122
Fig. 8.2	The synthesis result of objective cluster related to Islamic financing project model	123
Fig. 8.3	The synthesis result of criteria cluster related to Islamic financing project model	123
Fig. 8.4	The synthesis result of the function of bank sub criteria cluster related to Islamic financing project model	124
Fig. 8.5	The synthesis result of collateral and SPV Sub criteria cluster related to Islamic financing project model	125
Fig. 8.6	The synthesis result of sharia compliance sub criteria cluster related to Islamic financing project model	126
Fig. 8.7	The synthesis result of external risk sub criteria cluster related to Islamic financing project model	127
Fig. 8.8	The synthesis result of internal risk sub criteria cluster related to Islamic financing project model	128
Fig. 8.9	The synthesis result of alternatives sub criteria cluster related to Islamic financing project model	129
Fig. 9.1	The optimal path of wealth in 3 different Islamic investment decision models	144
Fig. 9.2	The optimal path of consumption in 3 different Islamic investment decision models	144

Fig. 9.3 The optimal path of utility in 3 different Islamic investment decision models ... 145
Fig. 9.4 The optimal path of welfare in 3 different Islamic investment decision models ... 146
Fig. 10.1 Islamic perspective family financial planning model (Adopted from Tamanni and Mukhlisin, 2018) ... 163
Fig. 11.1 The composition of firms ... 175
Fig. 11.2 Open activities in agriculture, goods and consumption ... 177
Fig. 11.3 Innovation activities in Trade and Services ... 178
Fig. 13.1 *Maslaha* rate of return *Source* Alshelfan (2014) ... 206
Fig. 13.2 The structure of *Sukūk Ihsan*. *Source:* International Islamic Financial Market (2016) ... 207
Fig. 16.1 Conceptual framework of the sustainability study ... 254
Fig. 17.1 VaR confidence level. *Sources* Ahmed et al. (2016, p. 44) ... 289
Fig. 17.2 Distribution of average daily returns for Sukuk ... 292
Fig. 17.3 Distribution of average daily returns for conventional bonds ... 293
Fig. 17.4 VaR of Sukuk and Bonds using confidence level of 99% ... 294
Fig. 17.5 VaR of Sukuk and bonds in 10 days holding period and VaR estimates of (5000 repetitions) with 99% confidence level ... 296
Fig. 17.6 Sukuk distribution in line chart and histogram ... 297
Fig. 17.7 Conventional bonds distribution in line chart and histogram ... 298
Fig. 17.8 F-Test results for Sukuk and conventional bonds ... 299
Fig. 17.9 Sukuk for 10 Day Monte Carlo simulation and (5000 iterations) tabulated in a histogram ... 302
Fig. 17.10 Conventional bonds for 10 Day Monte Carlo simulation and (5000 iterations) tabulated in a histogram ... 306
Fig. 20.1 Waqf Bank model ... 362
Fig. 21.1 UN 17 SDGs. *Source* https://sustainabledevelopment.un.org/sdgs ... 368
Fig. 21.2 Poverty in OIC and non-OIC countries. *Source* SESRIC staff calculations based on World Bank, PovcalNet, COMCEC and SESRIC Technical Report (2015) ... 369

Fig. 21.3 Life expectancy at birth last 20 years. *Source* (COMCEC, 2019; Ahmed, 2019) http://www.comcec.org/en/wp-content/uploads/2019/04/2-OIC-Presentation_Access-to-Health-Services-1.pdf . . . 370
Fig. 21.4 Mortality rate under 5 (per 1000 births). *Source* (COMCEC, 2019; Ahmed, 2019) http://www.comcec.org/en/wp-content/uploads/2019/04/2-OIC-Presentation_Access-to-Health-Services-1.pdf . . . 370
Fig. 21.5 Mortality ratio (per 100,000 births). *Source* (COMCEC, 2019; Ahmed, 2019) http://www.comcec.org/en/wp-content/uploads/2019/04/2-OIC-Presentation_Access-to-Health-Services-1.pdf . . . 371
Fig. 21.6 Government spending on education as a percentage of GDP. *Source* (BAĞCI, 2019) https://www.sesric.org/imgs/news/1584_PRESENTATION_SESRIC_EN.pdf . . . 371
Fig. 21.7 Government spending on education per student. *Source* (BAĞCI, 2019) https://www.sesric.org/imgs/news/1584_PRESENTATION_SESRIC_EN.pdf . . . 372
Fig. 21.8 Sectoral distribution of ISFD projects 2008–2017. *Source* (ISFD Annual Report, 2017) . . . 381
Fig. 21.9 APIF projects. *Source* APIF Annual Report (2019) . . . 382

List of Tables

Table 1.1	Contrasts of gift and commodity exchange	19
Table 2.1	Verses on Kasb and Infâq in the Qur'an	32
Table 2.2	Framework of islamic wealth management	33
Table 2.3	Al-Kasb in islamic wealth management	34
Table 2.4	Infāq in islamic wealth management	35
Table 5.1	An overview of the comparison between Islamic zakat (tax) system and conventional taxation system	81
Table 5.2	Comparison of poverty alleviation tools in Islam	83
Table 5.3	Difference between Muslim and non-Muslim will	84
Table 6.1	Types of wealth	93
Table 9.1	The monthly hypothetic value for the parameters in 3 proposed model	143
Table 10.1	Divorce data in Indonesia	152
Table 11.1	Population and sample	172
Table 11.2	The dependent variable	173
Table 11.3	The independent variables	173
Table 11.4	Normality of the data	174
Table 11.5	Multicollinearity of the data	175
Table 11.6	Model summary	176
Table 11.7	Significance of the model	176
Table 11.8	Regression results	176
Table 12.1	Age range	195
Table 12.2	Education level	195
Table 12.3	Work	196
Table 13.1	The average rental yield by the *sukūk al-'Ijarah* during 2014–2018 in Brunei	204
Table 14.1	Confirmation of the dimensions of religiosity	218
Table 14.2	Mean and standard deviation of awareness about Islamic religious dictates regarding debt management	219
Table 14.3	Mean and standard deviation of actual debt management behaviour	219

Table 14.4 Profiles of respondents and the significant differences of their awareness of religious debt dictates and actual debt management behaviour ... 220
Table 14.5 Significant mean differences from Tukey HSD Post Hoc tests ... 221
Table 14.6 Pearson product-moment correlations between actual debt management behaviour, awareness of religious debt dictates and dimensions of religiosity ... 222
Table 14.7 Model summary for actual debt management behaviour ... 222
Table 14.8 Beta coefficient summary for actual debt management behaviour ... 223
Table 15.1 Mauritius' accolades vis-à-vis international benchmarks ... 229
Table 15.2 Industry initiatives in the development of Islamic banking and finance ... 231
Table 15.3 Regulatory milestones and facilitative measures to promote islamic banking and finance by government and regulators ... 233
Table 15.4 Awareness building initiatives ... 235
Table 16.1 Sample companies in the JII index 2015 to 2019 ... 257
Table 16.2 Variable measurements ... 259
Table 16.3 Panel A. Descriptive statistics for research variables. Panel B. Descriptive statistics for sustainability and islamic disclosure. Panel C. ESG disclosure by year. Panel D. ISR disclosure by year. Panel E. Pearson's correlation coefficient ... 260
Table 16.4 Results of Robust Multiple Least Square Regression of Sustainability Practice on Financial Performance ... 266
Table 16.5 Global Reporting Initiative (GRI) standard indicators ... 270
Table 16.6 The Islamic Social Reporting (ISR) index ... 275
Table 17.1 List of Sukuk instruments ... 286
Table 17.2 List of conventional bonds ... 287
Table 17.3 Descriptive characteristics of Sukuk daily returns ... 289
Table 17.4 Descriptive characteristics of conventional bonds daily returns ... 292
Table 17.5 Historical simulation for Sukuk and conventional bonds at 99% of VaR confidence ... 294
Table 17.6 Monte Carlo simulation for Sukuk and bonds in 99% of VaR confidence ... 295
Table 17.7 Maximum loss of Sukuk and conventional bonds' portfolios ... 298
Table 17.8 Main types of sukuk structures ... 301
Table 17.9 Test analysis for sukuk and conventional bonds ... 309
Table 21.1 Rankings in infrastructure progress, OIC and counterpart developing countries ... 372
Table 21.2 GDF activities in 2018 ... 376

Table 21.3 IHH projects in 2019 378
Table 21.4 Turkish Diyanet Foundation expenditure for the year 2019 in Turkish Lira 379
Table 21.5 ISFD projects 2008–2017. In US$ million 381
Table 21.6 List of APIF projects approved in 2019 (all figures are in $ millions) 383
Table 21.7 List of impact projects funded fully or partially by APIF 383
Table 21.8 Summary of challenges to full employment of waqf in socio-economic development 384
Table 21.9 Waqf good governance indicators (AAOIFI waqf governance standard 2018) 386

Chapter 1
Wealth Management and Investment: An Islamic Epistemology

Nasim Shirazi, Othman Altwijry, Toseef Azid, and Muhammad Omer Chaudhry

Social scientists raised several questions about the nature of wealth. For example, how we can define wealth, its nature, how one can get it (natural or unnatural way), its impact on man's behavior (good or bad), society's perception, and many others. But, more importantly, there is also a big question mark about the impact of wealth on the human soul; either it corrupts our souls or gives us power, etc.

Generally, textbooks define wealth as the capacity to produce and consume. So, it is a value-based but subjective term. However, one cannot define wealth in an absolute term. Munger (2007) discussed remarkably and said in this way, "There is a simple test for determining whether something is a resource (something valuable) or just garbage (something you want to dispose of at the lowest possible cost, including costs to the environment). If someone will pay you for the item, it's a resource. Or, if you can use the item to make something else people want, and do it at lower price or higher quality than you could without that item, then the item is also a resource. But if you have to pay someone to take the item away, or if other things made with that item cost more or have lower quality, then the item is garbage."[1]

It has a different perception in the eyes of various fields of knowledge; for example, religious dimensions do not match the socio-economic dimensions; it has a different perception in the psychological and religious framework. For instance, in Chap. 2 of the *Qur'an*, Allah (SWT) says in verse 261 as:

---

[1] https://www.econlib.org/library/Columns/y2007/Mungerrecycling.html retrieved on 7th February 2022.

N. Shirazi
College of Islamic Studies, Daha, Qatar

O. Altwijry · T. Azid (✉)
College of Buisness and Economics, Qassim University, Buraydah, Saudi Arabia
e-mail: toseefazid@gmail.com

M. O. Chaudhry
Bahauddin Zakariya University, Multan, Pakistan

T. Azid et al. (eds.), *Wealth Management and Investment in Islamic Settings*,
https://doi.org/10.1007/978-981-19-3686-9_1

> The example of those who spend their wealth in the Way of Allah is like that of a grain of corn that sprouts seven ears, and in every ear, there are a hundred grains. Thus Allah multiplies the action of whomsoever He wills. Allah is Munificent, All-Knowing (2:261)

However, one can assess the value of the assets at market prices. Therefore, one can estimate that one has more wealth than another. The textbooks also mention that wealth is created when resources move from a lower value to higher-value uses. Another version is as "voluntary transactions create wealth." Claar and Lingle (2020. p. 2) expressed that "you are wealthy when you possess the creative capacity and insight necessary to increase the utility of others through a mutually beneficial exchange." Schumpeter (1996) clearly explained that wealth is created through productive capacity. Religiously it is believed that everyone is born with some wealth. However, it is realized when he is involved in the exchange and can discover more value.

In the conventional literature, one can find two types of wealth, i.e., natural[2] and unnatural.[3] For example, Aquinas Thomas (1981) divided wealth into two kinds, i.e., natural and artificial wealth**.** Aquinas Thomas (1981) explained, "Natural wealth is that which serves as a remedy for his natural wants, such as food, drink, clothing, cars, dwellings, and such like; while the artificial wealth, such as money, is that which is not a direct help to nature, but is invented by man for the convenience of exchange and as a measure of all things saleable." In contrast, Polanyi (2001) differentiated two types of commodities, real and fictitious, where fictitious are labor, land, and money. Sowell (2015) stated "poverty occurs automatically. It is wealth that must be produced and must be explained." However, Augustine (1887) highlights the spiritual power of poverty.

On the other hand, Islam has different epistemology of wealth in terms of *halal* and *haram*. *Qur'an* mentioned that only those things that be used are permitted (halal); otherwise, those are not allowed to use (haram). As it is mentioned in Chap. 6 of *Qur'an:*

> Tell them (O Muhammad!): 'I do not find in what has been revealed to me anything forbidden for anyone who wants to eat unless it is carrion, outpoured blood and the flesh of swine, all of which is unclean; or that which is profane having been slaughtered in a name other than that of Allah. But whosoever is constrained to it by necessity—neither desiring to disobey nor exceeding the limit of necessity—your Lord is surely All Forgiving, All-Compassionate. (6: 145)

After creating one's wealth, his next task is to managing it. In the current literature, one can find a lot of discussion about wealth management and the role of wealth manager. However, in a nutshell, the management of wealth and assets of

---

[2] Define by Aristotle, "Natural wealth means: every authentic integral part of nature like plant, fungi, animal, mineral, fossil, water, soil, etc." (https://www.google.com/search?q=natural+and+unnatural+wealth&rlz=1C1GGRV_enSA844SA845&oq=natural+and+unnatural+wealth&aqs=chrome..69i57.11299j0j4&sourceid=chrome&ie=UTF-8 retrieved on 7th February 2022.).

[3] Define by Aristotle, " But when a human sustains herself in certain other ways — such as by the accumulation of coinage through trade, speculation, or usury, she is behaving unnaturally." (https://sniggle.net/TPL/index5.php?entry=30Nov18 retrieved on 7th February 2022).

any individual/organization is known as wealth management. Furthermore, financial planning and investment management services are part of it. This is the primary task of the wealth manager to provide those services which satisfy the need and requirements of his clients. The scope and purpose of the services of a wealth manager are to articulate those financial goals that are important in his clients' lives. Therefore he designs strategies for investment that achieve the financial goals of his clients. He provides a broad range of services, for example, "establishing retirement accounts to writing options to acquire individual stocks and bonds for their clients' portfolios." It is supposed that wealth managers must have the knowledge and deep understanding of the advanced financial techniques, all the dimensions of the different financial markets and the socio-psycho diemension of his clients. In resultant he will be able to provide the proper guidance to them (Abdullah, 2018; Abdullah et al., 2017, 2018; Al-Abbadi & Abdullah, 2017).

After the 70s, the development of Islamic economy ics and finance opened new doors for discussing wealth management and the role of a wealth manager in this industry. It is observed that Islamic economics and finance have unique characteristics, value-based with certain limitations, and different rules and regulations. The concept of wealth management and the role of wealth managers in the conventional literature is not compatible with the epistemology of Islamic economics and finance. Therefore, it is necessary to discuss the epistemology of wealth in the periphery of Islam and the concept of wealth management.

1.1 Epistemology of Wealth and Wealth Management in the Islamic Framework

According to Islamic epistemology, Allah (SWT) is the creator of everything in this universe. He is the owner of the entire universe, whereas man is the only trustee, and he is also accountable to Allah (SWT) for all of his actions. Therefore, he can maximize his utility only if he can perform his duties as a trustee (Shafii, Yusoff, & Noh, 2013; Qaseem, 2016). There are also some restrictions on the investors, they are not allowed to invest in specific projects, where *Riba*(usury), *Gharar*(ambiguity), *Maysir*(gambling), intoxicant, and pork are involved. Only those projects are permitted which are following the objectives of the *shari'ah*. Simultaneously, wealth management should be in the periphery of justice, cooperation, and avoidance of wealth wastage and greediness. *Shari'ah* provides guidance related to the different dimensions of wealth, such as its accumulation, protection, growth, consumption, purification, disposition, and distribution. Islam recommends that its followers should earn with an honorable way for themselves and their families. However, Islam also provides the guidance to the wealthy people about the concentration of wealth and the welfare of the society.[4] Simultaneously, Islam teaches how

[4] "Five necessities in Islam are religion, life, intellect, wealth, and honor".

one can protect his wealth. After all, wealth is one of the necessities that should be protected. Allah (SWT) says in chapter An Nisa as:

> And give not unto the foolish your property which Allah has made a means of support for you, but feed and clothe them therewith, and speak to them words of kindness and justice. (4: 5)

In this system, the purification of wealth is based on the payment of Zakah (obligatory duty) and charity. Moreover, Islam also guides regarding consumption, i.e., not to be a miser and not to be extravagant; a man must save for his future needs. Chapter *Al Furqan* of *Qur'an* defines the different characteristics/behaviors of the ⌜true⌝ servants of the Most Compassionate", among the one is how they are spending. Allah (SWT) says as:

> And [they are] those who, when they spend, do so not excessively or sparingly but are ever, between that, [justly] moderate (25: 67)

Further, Islam also provides a technical solution for the distribution of wealth through its law of inheritance and some other rules attached with the law of inheritance.[5]

1.2 Islamic Concept of Wealth

According to Islamic jurisprudence, if anything has material form and has value known as wealth, the constraint is that the rules of *shari'ah* must be followed. Islam recommends that someone use his abilities, productive capacities, and also appreciates Muslims to earn wealth for themselves, for their families, and for other needy members of the society. However, priority should be given to the needs of the family. As Prophet Muhammad (PBUH) said,

> ...leaving your heir in wealth (owning enough wealth) is better than leaving them in shortage, begging from others..... (5408 Sahih Bukhari).

However, the most critical aspect is the way of earning. It should be through the legitimate way.

(Known *halal* in Islamic jurisprudence), avoid hoarding[6] and spending in the way of Allah (SWT). If wealth is managed in this way, that will be better for their worldly life and the life hereafter. As a vicegerent of Allah (SWT) in this world, man is accountable for all of his actions, and he is also responsible for the earning and spending of his wealth. Therefore he should keep balance in returns of this worldly life and the life hereafter. Islam encourages everyone to work hard in this world

---

[5] Detail is available in Chapter An Nisa.

[6] "Who collects wealth and [continuously] counts it. He thinks that his wealth will make him immortal. No! He will surely be thrown into the Crusher. And what can make you know what is the Crusher? It is the fire of Allah, [eternally] fueled, Which mounts directed at the hearts. Indeed, it [i.e., Hellfire] will be closed down upon them. In extended columns." (104: 2–9).

and earn as much as possible. Yahaya and Azhar (2005) explained three sources of wealth accumulation, i.e., through natural resources, exchange, and gifts. Islam also guides its followers on how to accumulate and distribute wealth. There are three main guidelines that Islam provides, i.e.

i. Everyone has the freedom to participate in economic activities and earn as much as possible. *Qur'an* has guided in this verse as: *''We have distributed their livelihood among them in worldly life, and have raised some above others in the matter of social degrees, so that some of them may utilize the services of others in their work.*" (43: 32).
ii. In this system, Allah (SWT) is the owner of everything, whereas man is a vicegerent to him and his status is in this world is as a trustee. The *Qur'an* says, "*To Him (God) belongs that is in the heavens and all that is on the earth, and all that is between them, and all that is under the soil.*" (2: 86). The *Qur'an* also guides that wealth does not only for the earners but others have also right on it, as prescribed by *Qur'an* "*In their wealth there is a known right for those who ask for it and those who have a need for it*" (17: 24–25) and "*And pay what is rightfully due to Him on the day of harvesting*" (6: 142). *Qur'an* expressed the status of man as trustee, and Allah (SWT) is the absolute owner in this verse as: "*Lo! We offered the trust unto the heavens and the earth and the hills, but they shrank from bearing it and were afraid of it. And man assumed it. Lo! He hath proved a tyrant and a fool*" (33: 72).
iii. Islam also reduces the gap between the rich and poor through its injunctions and instruments. Therefore, there is a very low possibility of concentration of wealth. Allah (SWT) ordered in *Qur'an* as: "*So that this wealth should not become confined only to the rich amongst you*" (59: 7).

However, wealth must be for the benefit of human life and not for destruction. It all depends upon the behavior of society and individuals that how they manage their wealth and assets. The most important part is how we as humans follow the guidance provided by Allah (SWT). One can only use it properly if he believes in the reward and punishment in the life hereafter. Consequently, then this wealth may be used for the wellbeing of humankind. Islam does not negate the material acts which help in the creation of wealth, such as production, exchange, storage, consumption, and trade. It also promotes the redistribution of wealth and reciprocity (exchange of gifts). However, it classifies the different sources and their uses. It assigns them different meanings and terminologies, i.e., bitter wealth (earned through fair means but not purified), purified wealth, clean wealth, corrupt wealth, mental account, general purpose wealth, and special purpose wealth. Allah (SWT) says in chapter *Al Imran* about bitter wealth as:

> Those who are miserly with what God has granted them out of His grace should not think that it is good for them; on the contrary, it is bad for them. Whatever they meanly withhold will be hung around their necks on the Day of Resurrection. It is God who will inherit the heavens and earth: God is well aware of everything you do. (3: 180)

We can summarize the above discussion in the following way: It should be noted that man is not the owner of this wealth. He acts as a trustee and uses it as the guidance given by Allah (SWT) and his messenger Prophet Muhammad (PBUH). It is recommended in this system that whenever someone acquires wealth, he must follow the *shari'ah's* law. Islamic jurisprudence approved those parameters which are beneficial to human beings. Before discussing the different dimensions of wealth, explaining some salient points about profit in its system is necessary.

1.2.1 The Concept of Profit in Islam

In the system of Islam, there is no restriction on earning a profit. However, just profit is appreciated; risk is the prerequisite, whereas exploitation is not allowed. Moreover, all the transactions should be under the umbrella of *shari'ah*, for example, Ibn Al-Arabi (1957a, b) said that any increase which has not its equal counter value (*iwad*) will come under the category of interest (*riba*). Abdullah (2018) mentioned the components of *iwad* as; i. risk, ii. Liabilities, iii. Earnings. He further elaborated that anything which has the above three components is permitted. If any one of the three components is not present in the transaction, then it is forbidden and will come under the category of *haram* (not permitted). Generally, the risk is related to the market risk, earning is to put efforts for earning and accumulating the wealth, and ownership is the part of liability. Abdullah (2018) mentioned the two maxims from Majallah as: "Rewards begets risk" (*Al-ghurm bi al-ghunm*) and "benefit begets liability" (*al-kharaj bi al-daman*) and "burden is proportional to benefit, and benefit is proportional to burden" (Abdullah, 2018; Abdullah et al., 2017, 2018; Al-Abbadi & Abdullah, 2017).

1.3 Types of Wealth

Islam defines the different categories of wealth, which are explained in the following section.

1.3.1 Corrupt Wealth (Impure Wealth)

It is consensus among the Muslim scholars that wealth itself is not bad, but the way of its earning and spending make it corrupt or dirty, this is a religious understanding. If wealth is earned through unfair means, it is considered corrupt wealth, for example, through usury, fraud, gambling, taking the rights of others, etc. This wealth cannot be purified with any Islamic instrument like zakat or charity. It is not only related to this world, but the earner of this wealth will be punished in the life hereafter. In *Qur'an,* Allah (SWT) explained the ways which are not permitted. If corrupt wealth is used for moral, religious, or social purpose, it cannot be purified. It does not fulfill the *maqasid* (purpose) of *shari'ah*. It cannot be laundered through rituals. Once it is corrupt, it cannot be transformed into another form. The amount of corrupt wealth has not any significant value as mentioned in chapter *Al Maidah* of *Qur'an*:

> Say, Not equal are evil and the good, although the abundance of evil might impress you. So fear Allah, O you of understanding, that you may be successful. (5: 100)

Once it is corrupt, it is always corrupt, and only one thing can save if someone will repent with his good intention and try to seek forgiveness from Allah (SWT) and distribute it among the poor people. But it does not consider a charity. In chapter *Al Furqan*, *Qur'an* explained in this way:

> Except for those who repent, believe, and do righteous work. For them, Allah will replace their evil deeds with good. And ever is Allah Forgiving and Merciful. And he who repents and does righteousness does indeed turn to Allah with [accepted] repentance. (25: 70–71)

It is assumed that wealth has a significant impact on the behavior of individuals. If food and other eatable are purchased and consumed from this wealth, it will undoubtedly impact the blood and flesh of those individuals. And ultimately change the direction of their hearts. It is confirmed from the sayings of Prophet (PBUH) that the heart is shaping the people's actions and directing them which way they have to opt, i.e., right path or wrong path. Following the sayings of Prophet (PBUH) are explaining the above phenomenon as:

> Know that in human body there is a flesh. If it's good, so does the whole body and if it is damaged, so does the whole body. Surely it is the heart."[7] (cited in Kamri & Daud, 2011)
>
> on this earth, and more than that, on the Day of Judgment, he will be punished in hell.
>
> It is not wealth due to bountiful assets owned, rather real wealth are those that result in serenity and tranquility in life (Hadith narrated by Bukhari & Muslim)
>
> A person will not enter paradise, if his growth is derived from haram or illegal means/efforts (Hadith narrated by Imam Ahmad)

It should also be noted that the wealth someone earns from the business of pork, liquor, animal waste, or through illegal means like theft, robbery, bribery, gambling, or interest does not come under the category of *mutaqawwim*[8] (worthiness).

---

[7] "Al-Bukhari, Sahih al-Bukhari (Kaherah: Dar al-Hadith, n.d), hadith no. 50; Al-Nawawi, Sahih Muslim bi-Syarh al-Nawawi, hadith no. 2996".

[8] "According to the Hanafi school of thought (*mazhab*), a category of mal that is capable of legal (*shari'ah*-compliant) ownership and legal transfer. This category includes all things that possess value from the perspective of *shari'ah*, and therefore are subject to the full range of lawful transactions (shari'ah-compliant commutative and non-commutative contracts) such as sale *(ba'i)*, rent *(ijarah)*, pledge (*rahn*), and gift (*hibah*). *Mal mutaqawwim*, in general, can be traded at a price. Examples include commodities such as wheat, rice, and oil, and assets such as lands, houses, equipment, and shares of stock. Items such as loans and bonds are not *mal mutaqawwim* because *shari'ah* forbids trading borrowed funds for the purpose of making profit". (https://www.investment-and-finance.net/islamic-finance/a/al-mal-almutaqawwim.html#: ~ :text = Al%2Dmal%20al%2Dmutaqawwim%2C,the%20purpose%20of%20making%20profit. Retrieved on 7th February 2022).

1.3.2 Clean Wealth (Purified Wealth)

If someone is earning and accumulating the wealth without using unfair means, but he is not spending in the way of Allah (SWT), even then, his wealth is not clean. There are two types of spending in the way of Allah (SWT), one is obligatory, and the other is voluntary. The obligatory spending is known as Zakah. It is social security for the poor, purifies the wealth of the sahib-i-nisab, and develops their spirituality. When someone spends in the way of Allah (SWT), it is a symbol of his relationship to Allah (SWT) and the community. Through this, Muslims improve the community's well-being, reduce the hardship of the poor segment of society, and increase the link to Allah (SWT). Those who are spending in the way of Allah (SWT) will get the reward in the life hereafter. This is mentioned by Allah (SWT) in verse 261 of Chap. 2 of the *Qur'an*. Chapter *Al Fajar* also said about those who are not spending in the way of Allah (SWT) and accumulating the wealth through unfair means in this way:

> Absolutely not! In fact, you are not 'even' gracious to the orphan, nor do you urge one another to feed the poor. And you devour 'others" inheritance greedily and love wealth fervently. Enough! When the earth is entirely crushed over and over, and your Lord comes 'to judge' with angels, rank upon rank, and Hell is brought forth on that Day—this is when every 'disbelieving' person will remember 'their own sins'. But what is the use of remembering then? (89: 17–23)

This is a permanent and solid exchange, because it is trading with Allah (SWT) whereas redistribution of their wealth among the poor segments of the Islamic society. It is not based on the market forces, neither a transitory one, nor emphasizes the accumulation of wealth, whereas it creates the environment of brotherhood, kindness, and love. After spending in the way of Allah (SWT) under the guidance of *Qur'an* and *Sunnah,* after that it considers as *ma'al* or property. Consequently, it becomes a clean or purified wealth, and its technical term is *mutaqawwim,* as we explained above.

1.3.3 General Purpose Wealth

In this era of advanced technology, a market cannot function without general purpose wealth. In the market where the exchange takes place, the value of goods can be compared. The value of wealth is the scale where we can measure how much one owns his wealth. Therefore wealth is used for the different purposes of private and government evaluations. Owing to this, the concept of general purpose wealth is straightforward and used in every market, whether a moral or conventional market. In general, this type of wealth is neutral towards its transactions. However, Islam is not neutral towards its spending even though it was earned through permitted ways of *shari'ah*. The owner of this wealth has paid the compulsory and voluntary payments and disbursed some portion of his wealth in the way of Allah (SWT). Islam recommends that the transactions of this wealth should be according to the guidance which is provided by *Qur'an* and *Sunnah.* This wealth must not be spent on non-permitted activities like gambling, pornography, or the purchase of liquor, pork, etc. Therefore, the use of general purpose should not be considered in the conventional economic system. It is general purpose wealth, but it has some moral constraints imposed by Islamic jurisprudence. However, with these constraints, it follows the general rules of the market.

1.3.4 Special Purpose Wealth

As a trustee in this world, man has some responsibilities related to the wealth which he owns. He must follow the teachings of Islam about wealth management, i.e., how to acquire, how to spend, how to store, how to develop for the future, and how to transfer to the children. This concept is not only limited to this world but also extended to the life hereafter. It is supposed that this wealth is not only for personal needs but also for the needs of others. In this system, wealth has special purposes, such as charity, hibah (gifts), waqf, etc. For example, that amount of wealth is earmarked for the payment of Zakah and some other charities, or for waqf, which is for the needs (education, health or worship, or other welfare purposes of the society) of other segments of the society. It is allowed that people can earmark some portion of their wealth for some special purposes. And they have different nomenclature for different items. This type of special wealth is subject to particular religious dimensions, such as the money fixed for the dowry (*Mahar*) from the husband to his wife at the marriage contract.

Another excellent example is the bank account which Malaysians are opening in the Haji Tabung Bank[9] for haj, and they are not intended to consume, and this is only for the haj. Similarly, if someone has earmarked some portion of his wealth for sacrificing the animals at the event of *Eid-el Adha.* Or someone bought an animal with the intention that he would slaughter it on the day of *Eid*, then he must slaughter it. These are the special limits imposed on wealth converted into a special purpose wealth.

1.3.5 Mental Account and Wealth

The teaching of the *Qur'an* and the practice of Prophet Muhammad (PBUH) guide the followers of Islam about the mental account of their wealth. If someone has some units of currency in his pocket and spends on his daily expenditures, it has a different value, and the same units if he spends in the way of Allah (SWT), then it has an additional value. It is worth noting that both are equal in denomination, but their values are different. Which some one spends in the way of Allah (SWT) that gives more utility and value whereas *Qur'an* says in the following way:

---

[9] "Tabung Haji facilitates savings for the pilgrimage to Mecca through investment in Shariah-compliant vehicles".

> The example of those who spend their wealth in the Way of Allah is like that of a grain of corn that sprouts seven ears, and in every ear there are a hundred grains. Thus Allah multiplies the action of whomsoever He wills. Allah is Munificent, All-Knowing. (2: 261)

The former, which we spend, is only for this world, whereas the latter is for that forever life. So the feelings and willingness to pay are different for both spending. It is also interesting to mention that value is different for the different spending, even in the way Allah's way (SWT). For example, helping widows, orphans, and needy persons has a different value than constructing places for worship and so forth. Interest diminishes or destroys wealth, whereas, through charity, it grows. In chapter *al Baqrah* Allah (SWT) says in verse 276 as:

> Allah deprives interest of all blessing, whereas He blesses charity with growth.1 Allah loves none who is ungrateful and persists in sin .[10]

1.4 Islamic Wealth Management

Wealth management is the combination of two terms, i.e. wealth and management. Management deals with the organization and planning of all the resources to achieve the desired goals, whereas wealth is related to the ownership, controlling, and using the resources. Therefore, wealth management is planning and organizing those resources which we own, its control, and use. In the financial dictionary, "In general, wealth management is more than just investment advice, as it can encompass all parts of a person's financial life."

In the Islamic context, man is not the absolute owner of the wealth, he is only considered a trustee. However, this is his responsibility to manage this wealth in that way that is guided by *Qur'an and Sunnah.* And it is known as *tasarruf* of wealth. It is important to note that the universal set of Islamic wealth management has three sub-sets, i.e., how to get its ownership (*al-tamalluk*), how to acquire (*al-takasub*) it, and how to consume (*al-istihlak*) it. However, this management of wealth must be related to man's success in this world and life hereafter.

The main objective of any action in the Islamic *shari'ah* is to achieve the *falah* in both the lives of human beings, i.e., welfare in this world and in the life hereafter. Therefore, wealth management decisions should be based on the above mentioned criteria, i.e. every investment or project will be socially responsible. In economics and finance, several theories explained the behavior of rational investors, his level of satisfaction, the behavior of market and prices, for example, expected utility theory, efficient market hypothesis, the arbitrage principles, the portfolio principles, the

---

[10] Maududi (1972) explains as in *Tafheem ul Qur'an, Surah Al Baqrah,* Verse 276 "By God's decree, the law of nature is such that interest not only serves as a strain on moral and spiritual well-being, and social and economic growth, it also causes actual regression and decline. Charity, however, (including such acts as lending money to people with the stipulation that they should return it if they can. and at their convenience) leads to the growth and expansion of man's moral and spiritual qualities and to the growth of human society and economy. Looked at from moral and spiritual standpoints, it is evident that interest is not only the outcome of selfishness, miserliness and callousness but also encourages their growth."

capital asset pricing theory, and many others. However, Islam presents a very realistic model based on human beings' psychological, social, and moral norms under the umbrella of divine knowledge and guidance. It also provides him training on how he should behave in all the different aspects of life, particularly in the management process of his wealth. This differentiates Muslim investors from the conventional one, which shifts the whole scenario. However, as a believer, a Muslim investor's or wealth owner's level of satisfaction depends not only on the satisfaction what he achieves in this world but also on the expected reward in the life hereafter. This is also the responsibility of the Muslims to reduce the unequal distribution of wealth and decrease the degree of poverty in the society where they live. The value-based system of Islam has offered different instruments for achieving these objectives. Islamic financial theory explains the unique epistemology of Muslim investors, which polished individual investor behavior and overall market behavior and reduced the different cognitive and emotional biases, because life hereafter is more critical for Muslim investors (Abdullah, 2018; Abdullah et al., 2017, 2018; Al-Abbadi & Abdullah, 2017).

Evensky et al. (2011) and Jennings et al. (2011), while discussing wealth management, emphasized the customized solutions and mentioned four categories of the process of wealth management, i.e. "client relationship, client profile, investment policy, and portfolio management, monitoring, and market review." However, Islamic wealth management deals with these four categories differently due to its unique characteristics. For example, client relationship is based on professional as well as on brotherhood. The client profile is based on the knowledge which he has about wealth management. The important question is about the wealth which he earned. Is it pure or impure? And so forth, whereas investment policy and portfolio management must be based on the *shari'ah* compliant, which also follows the *maqasad of shri'ah*, these four are not value-neutral in the Islamic system. Moreover, zakat and charity are the essential ingredients of a Muslim's wealth management (Edbiz Consulting, 2016; Jennings et al., 2011). However, it is not sufficient only that form fulfills the *shari'ah*/legal injunctions but also the substance should also have the dimensions of social justice and social welfare (Ahmed, 2013; Tasdemir et al., 2017).

1.4.1 Islamic Wealth Management Industry

It is observed that most of the Islamic financial industry products are replicates of the conventional financial industry. Most of the wealthy Muslims are not taking too much interest in the products of this industry. Due to the above and other reasons, the Islamic Wealth Management Industry is not very well developed. It is also a well-known fact that Islamic wealth management is the sub-set of Islamic finance; therefore, it has the same advantages and disadvantages as contained by Islamic finance, particularly the conflict between *shari'ah* objectives and the practice of Islamic finance (Ahmed, 2013; Farooq, 2014). Ismail and Antonio (2012) and Sandwick (2011) argued that Islamic wealth management is not different than the conventional one except for its *shari'ah* compliance products and the purification of wealth through compulsory religious duty (Zakah). Farooq (2014) analyzed that Islamic wealth management is not providing socio-economic services to the Muslim *Ummah*. Asutay (2007) also criticizes Islamic finance because of the substance of its products those do not follow the true spirit of Islamic teachings.

However, keeping the above in view, financial planning, client education, and reinforcement of good financial behavior are required. Therefore, financial therapy and application of behavioral finance are needed, especially for client relationships and client profiling. It is also observed in most Muslim countries that most wealthy Muslim clients are not always interested in the high rate of returns. Several cultural dimensions of these countries have a significant impact on the preference order of these clients. Therefore, the managers of wealth management must consider their clients' financial and non-financial goals carefully. It is a consensus among the experts that financial and non-financial goals make each client's unique personality. Therefore, it is suggested by the experts that there is a dire need to develop and promote the Islamic wealth management industry (IWM) (Abdullah, 2018; Abdullah et al., 2017, 2018; Al-Abbadi & Abdullah, 2017). For the promotion of IWM industry, Malaysia Islamic Financial Center (2016) suggested that IWM should take new steps towards the new development phase of wealth (Abdullah, 2018; Abdullah et al., 2017, 2018; Al-Abbadi & Abdullah, 2017).

1.4.2 Role of Wealth Manager

From centuries to centuries, it is always realized that wealth gives the sense of security, improves the quality of life, achieves financial and non-financial goals, and leads to the satisfaction of the wealth holder (Britt et al., 2015a, b). A client doesn't need to be Muslim or non-Muslim; both have the exact requirements. Therefore, the wealth manager must consider all the above points with many other dimensions. However, Muslims have their own requirements, which are guided by the *Qur'an* and the practices of Prophet Muhammad (PBUH). As it is observed from the previous discussion that giving philanthropy is the central part of the Islamic teachings. Therefore, the wealth manager should consider the economic aspects of his Muslim clients and has also to see other social, spiritual, psychological, and religious factors. It is also observed that if a wealth manager is very sharp and has enough knowledge about factors other than economic, he will be able to give his clients the right and better advice. However, Muslim clients have always want to increase their financial life quality and uplifting the social welfare.

Furthermore, in the current literature of wealth management, wealth that is left after fulfilling the implicit and explicit liabilities is known as discretionary wealth (excess capital). Therefore, it is suggested in the literature that should be managed by the wealth manager for the social welfare projects and keep this above the zero level (Abdullah, 2018; Abdullah et al., 2017, 2018; Al-Abbadi & Abdullah, 2017).

It is proposed that the wealth manager be well equipped with the knowledge of *shari'ah* and integrate the needs of his clients which he has for this world and life hereafter. His excess capital should be managed to give him more utility and good financial life and propose those projects from which he will expect more reward in the life hereafter.

1.4.3 Wealth and Philanthropy, Free or Regulated Market

As we mentioned above, philanthropy in the Islamic system is the main ingredient that enhances social welfare. Therefore, the wealth manager as advisor and therapist should know that what *Qur'an* explains about the people who are a miser and have been involved in the love of wealth and not distributed among the needy members of the society. There are several verses in the different chapters of the *Qur'an* related to the subject mentioned above. For example, giving inferior goods to needy persons even that giver himself does not like it., such behavior is mentioned in Chap. 3, verse 92.

> You will never attain virtue until you spend something you are fond of, while Allah (God) is Aware of anything you may spend.

If someone behaves like a miser and does not feel comfortable when spending in the way of Allah (SWT), *Qur'an* warns him in Chap. 4 verse 37 as:

> Who are stingy and enjoin upon [other] people stinginess and conceal what Allah has given them of His bounty—and We have prepared for the disbelievers a humiliating punishment. (4: 37).

If anyone consumes the wealth of others in a wrong way, Allah (SWT) warns him in Chap. 9 verse 37 as:

> O, believers! Indeed, many rabbis and monks consume people's wealth wrongfully and hinder 'others' from the Way of Allah. Give good news of a painful torment to those who hoard gold and silver and do not spend it in Allah's cause. (9: 37).

On the other hand, if some asks the bounties of Allah (SWT) and promise that he will spend in the way of Allah (SWT but he does not. Then Allah (SWT) warns him, as in Chap. 9, verses 75–77.

> And among them are those who made a covenant with Allah, [saying], "If He should give us from His bounty, we will surely spend in charity, and we will surely be among the righteous." But when He gave them from His bounty, they were stingy with it and turned away while they refused. So He penalized them with hypocrisy in their hearts until the Day they will meet Him—because they failed Allah in what they promised Him and because they [habitually] used to lie. (9: 75–77)

And the same subject is discussed in chapter 47, verse 38, chapter 57:24, Chap. 17, verse 100. If some spends but does not remind recipients and does not injure them with his actions, Allah (SWT) gives him the good news:

> Those who spend their wealth in the way of Allah and then do not follow up what they have spent with reminders [of it] or [other] injury will have their reward with their Lord, and there will be no fear concerning them, nor will they grieve. (2: 262)

And also not be hatred by the giver, it is mentioned in chapter 24 verse 22 as:

> And let not those of virtue among you and wealth swear not to give [aid] to their relatives and the needy and the emigrants for the cause of Allah, and let them pardon and overlook. Would you not like that Allah should forgive you? And Allah is Forgiving and Merciful. (24: 22)

It is also important to note that wealth managers should also keep their clients from the bias of regret aversion. Therefore this is the responsibility of the wealth manager to explain to his clients the benefit and harms of the projects in the light of *Qura'nic* teachings, as explained by Allah (SWT) in verse 216 of Chap. 2.

> "Battle has been enjoined upon you while it is hateful to you. But perhaps you hate a thing, and it is good for you, and perhaps you love a thing, and it is bad for you. And Allah knows while you know not". (2: 216)
>
> And the saying of Prophet (PBUH) is: and that no one ever can benefit or harm him unless it is written by Allah Almighty (Al-Tirmithi: no. 2516)

This brainstorming will change the behavior of the clients from undesirable to desirable. Many examples can be quoted in front of Muslim clients. It is also necessary to teach them that everything is not related to the free market phenomenon, and we have to see beyond the boundaries of a free market. For example, gaps that are not filled by the market process can be filled by non-market activities. As we have observed, the objective of the market is to maximize its agents' profit, but the objective of non-market behavior is entirely different. There is no doubt that mainly Muslim clients are interested in the reward of life hereafter.

1.4.4 Financial Therapy

As we have seen in the conventional theory that the concept of financial therapy is founded on the psychological, social, cultural, and economic behavior of the investors, which ultimately leads to financial well-being and achieves financial goals. And consequently, that improves the quality of life at the micro as well as at macro level, the macro level is not as we have in the conventional theory, which discusses only the economy's performance in this world. In contrast, the macro-level is also connected with life hereafter. The quality of life can only be improved when Muslims manage their wealth according to the teachings of Islam, which is integrated with the life hereafter. Muslim investor believes that his financial health can only be protected and improved (as it was mentioned above) if he will spend in the way of Allah (SWT) with his pure intention to please Allah (SWT). Moreover, investors have different biases which have a negative or positive impact on the further investment, such as "the disposition effect, regret aversion, loss aversion, cognitive dissonance, anchoring, mental accounting, overconfidence, over-and under-reaction, confirmation biases, herding behavior, and hindsight bias" (Hens & Meier, 2016; Johnson & Horan, 2013; Pompian, 2012; Shiller, 1998). However, there is not a single universally accepted technique of psychotherapy; therefore, wealth managers should be acquainted with the different theories and models of psychotherapy, for more detals of these therapies see Britt et al. (2015b) and Grable et al. (2011).

Islamic social and psychological norms are universal, and they are not time and spatial specific, whereas their epistemology suits every culture. On the other hand, conventional physiotherapy is value-neutral, based on materialism, to some extent anti-religious, therefore not considering moral values as its primary tools. Consequently, it is assumed that technique of Islamic financial therapy should be different from conventional financial therapy. In the conventional literature, wealthy persons are ranked into three categories, i.e., "Ultra-High-Net Worth Individuals (UHNWIs), Very High-Net-Worth Individuals (HNWIs), and mid-tier millionaires" (Beaverstock et al., 2013). Generally, net worth is quoted in liquid assets; however, it varies, but, commonly, one million U.S dollars is considered as a net worth. However, Prophet Muhammad (PBUH) defined the richness as:

> Abu Dharr reported: The Messenger of Allah, peace, and blessings be upon him, said, "O Abu Dharr, do you say an abundance of possessions is wealth?" I said yes. The Prophet said, "Do you say a lack of possessions is poverty?" I said yes. The Prophet repeated this three times, then he said, wealth is in the heart, and poverty is in the heart. Whoever is wealthy in his heart will not be harmed no matter what happens in the world. Whoever is impoverished in his heart will not be satisfied no matter how much he has in the world. Verily, he will only be harmed by the greed of his soul." (Source: Al Tibrani and Al-Hafiz al-Mu'jam al-Kabīr 1643, 2016)

The wealth manager in Muslim society should have a different attitude towards their clients. They should also have different instruments that match the psychological state of clients. As discussed above, Muslim investors and consumers are linked with this worldly life and life hereafter. The Muslim clients are different from conventional clients regarding their thoughts, behavior, preferences, and values. Particularly their preferences are not only for this world but also for the life hereafter. This integrated approach changes the whole scenario, and it is the foundation of Muslims' goal-based investment (GBI). They are more cautious about life hereafter, conservative towards the guidance of *Qur'an* and *Sunnah* (the practice of Prophet Muhammad, PBUH). Although they are not neutral towards their financial matters yet the most important point is that how their financial accounts and assets will maintain and increase under the umbrella of *shari'ah*. One aspect is the most vital that Muslims must not have evil suspicions towards the wealth manager because Islam does not appreciate the evil suspicions. As *Qur'an* describes the evil suspicions in chapter 49 verse 12:

> O believers! Avoid many suspicions, 'for' indeed, some suspicions are sinful. (49: 12).

However, wealth managers should have sufficient knowledge about Islamic jurisprudence. He should know that how a Muslim client will make his financial plans. Therefore he should take optimal decisions which gives maximum satisfaction to his clients. Wealth managers should know the psychological state of the Muslim investors and also know the salient features of Islamic *fiqh* and *shari'ah;* therefore, they will be able to provide the consultancy within the divine knowledge because Muslim clients' beliefs, attitudes, and preferences are different in the Islamic world view. It is a well-known factor that Muslim clients also want to invest in the life hereafter. This unique character differentiates him from conventional investors and clients (Abdullah, 2018; Abdullah et al., 2017, 2018; Al-Abbadi & Abdullah, 2017).

The goal-based investment model in this environment has three risks mentioned by Chhabra (2005), i.e. personal risk, market risk, and aspirational risk. However, their nature is completely different than the conventional model. Personal risk is not only based on the poverty and life standard but also has fear from Allah (SWT) and desire to serve the Muslim *Ummah*, the income should be earned in a way which is guided by the *Qur'an* and *Sunnah* and it is the main ingredient of market risk. Whereas aspiration risk has a different dimension than the conventional model, it is how the behavior of investors sustain to earn the profit in this world and reward in the life hereafter. This is too some extent a complex model which is based on piousness (*Taqwa*). Therefore the most important aspect is the degree of piousness (*Taqwa*). Ubay Ibn Ka'ab explains taqwa as:

> "An incredible example that demonstrates this is when Umar Ibn Al-Khattab (may Allah be pleased with him) asked Ubay Ibn Ka'ab (may Allah be pleased with him) about Taqwa. Ubay said, "Have you ever taken a thorny path?" Umar replied, "Yes, I have." Ubay then asked, "So how did you travel along this thorny path?" Umar replied, "I rolled up my garment and was cautious as to where I would tread to avoid being pricked by the thorns." So Ubay responded and said, "This is Taqwa." (https://onepathnetwork.com/what-is-taqwa/)

Wealth managers must be well aware that where Muslim clients can invest and where cannot invest. In real terms, Muslim clients want to succeed in this life and life hereafter. *Qur'an* guides how Muslims should supplicate.

> Our Lord, give us in this world [that which is] good and in the Hereafter [that which is] good and protect us from the punishment of the Fire. (2:201)

It is interesting to know that expected returns are replaced by the expected reward in the life hereafter. There are several historical events where wealthy Muslims preferred the reward hereafter to the worldly returns, therefore, their risk, and returns have a unique path. Why Muslim client needs more income because he wants to spend more in the way of Allah (SWT). The psychological state of Muslim investors is different for risk tolerance. He prefers to observe loss instead of earning more through unfair means. He will not invest in the forbidden investment activities, instead of it he will keep his wealth with himself and then observe the discount of 2.5% in terms of Zakah payment. It will give him more satisfaction, whereas haram earnings are not acceptable. The wellbeing of the Muslim investors is also based on the life hereafter (Abdullah, 2018; Abdullah et al., 2017, 2018; Al-Abbadi & Abdullah, 2017).

1.5 Role of State

It is suggested by the social scientists that the issues related to the financial life of any individual have significant importance; therefore, they should be given more preferences. Generally, it is assumed that it is the responsibility of the state to look after the affairs of its citizens and particularly their financial matters. It is also observed from the different reports of the international organizations that this is the state's responsibility to manage the financial issues, such as their matters related to property and wealth of its citizens, besides solving the issues related to growth and development (World Bank, 1978). Moreover, the current public treasury of the governments in dealing with the different operations of the public funds, i.e., disbursement of the funds, raising funds, etc. It is also important to note that the various steps taken by modern governments related to finance have significant impact on the whole economy as well as on the public treasury. The public finance experts divide public institutions' roles into two major categories, i.e., law and power; culture and welfare. However, welfare is based on the creation and disbursement of wealth or income, i.e. it implies that how to increase the size of resources which will ultimately increase the welfare of the whole community.

Islamic state is the trustee of Allah (SWT) on this world and as an agent of Allah (SWT), its responsibility to realize the *falah* (welfare) of the community. The role of an Islamic state is to implement all the injunctions which were mentioned in *Qur'an* and explained by the prophet Muhammad (PBUH). Its morals and ethical values restrict the Islamic state. The Islamic State has to maintain justice, look after its citizens' interests, and implement those instruments that will redistribute the wealth on the equity basis among the different segments of the society. It is also the duty of the state to manage the public wealth for the welfare of the whole community. Islamic scholars believe that this is the responsibility of the government to safeguard the religion and manage worldly affairs. However, in the Islamic system, the concentration of wealth is not appreciated. On the other hand, preserving wealth and income is highly appreciated. Therefore it is the task of the government of the Islamic state to implement those tools which will help restrict the concentration of wealth and protect the wealth and income of its citizens (Kahf, 1990; Siddiqi, 1986).

1.6 Gift Economy and Gift Exchange in the Islamic Framework

A gift economy is the opposite of the market economy; anthropologists argue that the gift economy builds the community and the market economy damages the community and relationships among the members of society. In the gift economy, the exchange of objects takes place without buying and selling. There is no explicit agreement or expectations about any reward, either immediate or future. However, the exchange of objects in the gift economy is not a universal phenomenon. It varies from society to society, culture to culture, place to place, and time to time. There are also different modes of exchange in the gift economy, i.e. expecting an immediate reward, future reward, reciprocity, inalienable possessions, etc. The central concept behind gift-giving is transferring property rights over a specific item.

Malinowski (1920) and Mauss (1969) argued that gift-giving and returning are the main parts of the non-market economy. As Malinowski argued that gift exchange is based on reciprocity, and in his opinion, there is no free gift. On the other hand, Mauss argued that a relationship among the members of a specific society return gift is the gesture of maintaining the relationship; otherwise, there is an end of the relationship. He also added that if there is no return gift, then there is only one way to maintain the relationship that is promising of gift in the future. In the opinion of Mauss, it is a network of debtor-creditor. If there is no return, then no relationship will be developed. Gregory (1982, 1997) argued that in a non-market economy, the giving gift places one party in debt because there is always a lag between giving and returning debt. This phenomenon is for establishing the relationship among both parties. Gregory distinguished gift economy from the true gift economy where no expectation of receiving the gifts in return. Those gifts without return expectations are also known as "pure gifts" but this place the receivers are in debt, i.e., the poison of the gift. Sahlins (1963) introduced a new term, known as generalized reciprocity, i.e. not expecting the exact value of the gifts but expecting that in future it will be balanced out over time. It generally occurs among close relations. Balanced and Symmetrical reciprocity means that giver is expecting to return a specific amount in the future. If returning the same as a debt, it is known as strict reciprocity; however, if more than that, it is the the same as interest on investment. On the contrary, market or negative reciprocity means that each part is expecting the profit, even sometimes at the expense of others. It occurred among the more distant partner. It is also argued in the literature of gift economy that in most places, gift-givers are political leaders or known as "big men," and receivers are termed as "rubbish men." Rubbish men cannot return, and consequently, they are in the debt of these big men. Bloch and Parry (1989) argued that long-term social relations are separated from short-term market relations. Gregory (1982) narrated that gift exchange has five characteristics and commodity exchange has also five characteristics, which are epicted in Table 1.1.

Generally it does not look nice if gifts are converted into commodities (Appadurai, 1986). Many business organizations are offering gifts just to win the loyalty of their customers. Bird-David and Darr (2009) gave the name "mass-gifts" of these hybrid type gifts which are large in number and free with purchase. It is also argued that gift economy can be used as an instrument for reducing the poverty.

Islamic system, as we discussed above, has its unique characteristics. Theoretically and practically, all of its followers are considered brothers. Therefore the building of the Islamic society is founded on brotherhood. In Islamic society, kinship is not based on economic or political functions, but it is influenced by the nature of the practice of the Muslims, which is guided by the *Qur'an* and the practices of Prophet Muhammad (PBUH). Gift economy and gift exchange are also not based on the material objectives, whereas the giving gift (*hibah*) in the Islamic system is

Table 1.1 Contrasts of gift and commodity exchange

Commodity exchange	Gift exchange (in the conventional system)	Gift exchange (in Islamic system)
Immediate exchange	Delayed exchange	Reward expected in the life hereafter
Alienable goods	Inalienable goods	Ownership is transferred
Actors independent	Actors dependent	Actors independent
Quantitative relationship	Qualitative relationship	Brotherhood
Between objects	Between people	Between brothers

Source Gregory (1982) 3rd column was developed by the authors of this chapter

entirely a religious, spiritual, and moral phenomenon. Islam appreciates the exchange of a gift. Prophet (PBUH) once said that the exchange of gifts increases love among Muslims.

> Abu Hurayra reported that the Prophet (PBUH) said, '*Give gifts, and you will love one another*.' [Al-Adab Al-Mufrad]

However, if in the exchange of gifts motive is not good, then Prophet (PBUH) said:

> If anyone intercedes for his brother and he presents a gift to him for it, and he accepts it, he approaches a great door of the doors of usury. [Abu Dawud]

If someone gives a gift, then it should be accepted:

> Narrated Abu Huraira: The Prophet (PBUH) said, "*I shall accept the invitation even if I were invited to a meal of a sheep's trotter, and I shall accept the gift even if it were an arm or a trotter of a sheep.*" [Bukhari]

It is also guided that do not belittle someone's gift, as Prophet (PBUH) said:

> …Never belittle any gift you give your neighbor even if it is a hoof of a sheep. [Al-Bukhari and Muslim]

If someone receives a gift, he has to say, "May Allah reward you with good".

> Abu Hurairah narrated that the Messenger of Allah (PBUH) said: *Whoever is not grateful to the people, he is not grateful to Allah.* [Tirmidhi].

Giving a gift is based on justice if it is given to children, parents, and siblings. Prophet (PBUH) said:

> It was narrated from Nu'man bin Bashir that: his father gave him a gift of a slave, and he came to the Prophet (PBUH) so that he could witness the gift. He said: "Have you given something to all of your children?" He said: "No." He said: "Then take back (your gift). [Ibn Majah]

If someone gives a gift with love and kindness, then one has to accept:

Narrated Abu Huraira: The Prophet (PBUH) said, "*I shall accept the invitation even if I were invited to a meal of a sheep's trotter, and I shall accept the gift even if it were an arm or a trotter of a sheep.*" [Bukhari]

Who should be given more priority of gift:

Narrated Aisha: I said, *"O Allah's Messenger (PBUH)! I have two neighbors; which of them should I give a gift to?" The Prophet (PBUH) said, "(Give) to the one whose door is nearer to you.*" (Sahih al-Bukhari 2595)

Giving gifts is among the close circles and the different groups of the extended Islamic society. Allah (SWT) mentioned the recipients of gifts (charity) in Chap. 9 verse 60 as:

Surely donations are only for the poor, and the indigent, and the ones collecting them, (Literally: working (doing) upon them) and the ones whose hearts are brought together, (i.e., newly converted enemies, so as to reconcile their hearts) and the ransoming of necks, (i.e., captives and slaves) and the ones penalized (for debt), and in the way of Allah, and the wayfarer; an ordinance from Allah, and Allah is Ever-Knowing, Ever-Wise. (9: 60)

These donations are not only "pure gift" with no expectations of returns, but it is also the purification of wealth. It is worth noting that here recipients are not placed in debt, which is without "poisonous." Because the return (reward) is from Allah (SWT). This is the process of purification of the wealth instead of the poison of the gift. This is a relationship of brotherhood and not a creditor-debtor, as discussed by Mauss. It is the intention and dedication of the giver and how he is expecting the reward from Allah (SWT). How one is grateful to Allah (SWT) through giving in the way of Allah (SWT) and the amount of the gift is not the matter, the actual thing is which portion of the wealth has been given in the way of Allah (SWT). However, there is one restriction on the gift-givers; he should not repurchase it from the recipients. A saying of Prophet (PBUH) which is reported by Ibn Umar as follow:

"'Umar b. al-Khattib (Allah be pleased with him) donated a horse in the path of Allah, and (later on) he found it being sold, and he decided to buy that. So he asked the Messenger of Allah (may peace be upon him) about it. whereupon he (the Holy Prophet) said: Don't buy that and do not get back what you gave in charity." (Sahih Muslim Book 12 3952).

However, there is no other restriction, and recipients can consume it or invest it. However, on the event *Eid al Adha,* a festival where Muslims slaughter lambs, cows or camels, distribute their flesh among the Muslims, and only one-third they can store for themselves. *Waqf* is another example, once it is donated, the givers cannot repurchase it.

As mentioned above, Islam develops a society based on brotherhood; therefore, there is no rubbish or bigger man. All are equal (preferences are given to a more degree of piousness: *muttaqi*). However, their ranks are different. As Allah (SWT) explains in the following verses of various chapters of the *Qur'an.*

Surely the believers are none but brothers unto one another, so set things right between your brothers,1 and have a fear of Allah that you may be shown mercy. (49:10)

> O mankind, We have created you from a male and a female, and made you into races and tribes, so that you may identify one another. Surely the noblest of you, in Allah's sight, is the one who is most pious of you. Surely Allah is All-Knowing, All-Aware." (49: 13)

> "Is it they who distribute the Mercy of your Lord? It is We Who have distributed their livelihood among them in the life of this world, and have raised some above others in rank that some of them may harness others to their service. Your Lord's Mercy is better than all the treasures that they hoard. (43: 32)

Another crucial area is the inheritance law in this system which is related to the distribution of wealth. After the deceased person's demise, his property is distributed among his heirs as commanded by Allah (SWT). It is mentioned in a full detail in Chap. 4, verses 7–14 of the *Qur'an*. However, wills and gifts (*hibah*) also give the right to adopted children and some others those are not real heirs. Though there is a restriction on will and *hibah*, one cannot make it more than one-third of his whole property.

1.7 Conclusion

Allah (SWT) is the creator of everything. Therefore, ownership of everything belongs to him. Man is accountable for all of his actions, and he is considered a trustee of all these resources. He has the right to use these resources in the periphery of *shari'ah.* He has the right to own, earn, generate and spend wealth. However, he is not allowed to use it to destroy this earth. He is allowed to manage his wealth as per the orders of Allah (SWT). He is also guided that he has to spend this wealth for the sake of Allah (SWT). He has to disburse some portion of this wealth among the needy members of society and give to his Muslim brothers and sisters as gift. There are two types of gifts, i.e., one is obligatory and others which are not obligatory but they are also much appreciated. Wealth management is also based on the rules and regulations of *shari'ah.* On the other hand, wealth managers should have also religious responsibilities other than professional responsibilities.

The wealth-generating process is not as simple as in the conventional system. If wealth is pure, then it is considered wealth; if it is impure, then it does not come under the category of wealth; otherwise, it becomes a curse. In chapter *Al Maidah,* in verse 100, Allah (SWT) says as:

> Tell them, O Messenger, that the pure and the impure cannot be alike anyhow, although the abundance of the impure may allure you much. So, O people of understanding, refrain from the disobedience of Allah: it is expected that you will attain to true success.

We are concluding our discussion with the explanation of the above verse by Maududi (1972) in *Tafhim ul Qur'an* as:

> This verse sets up a new standard of values, which is quite different from the standard of those who look only at the outward aspect of things. Such people usually judge things by their quantity and not by their quality.......................... According to this standard, it is not the number or the quantity of a thing that increases or decreases its true worth but the

question of whether it has been obtained by fair means or foul. Obviously, a drop of rose scent has greater value than a heap of filth, and a cup of pure water is far greater in worth than a cistern full of impure urine. Therefore one who is wise will always remain content with the lawful, though it may appear to be very insignificant and worthless, and will never try to grab the unlawful. On the other hand, however, it might appear to be very alluring and grand.

References

Abdullah, A., Hassan, R., & Kassim, S. (2017). An Islamic wealth management investment appraisal of oil tankers. *International Journal of Economics and Financial Issues, 7*(5), 59–70.

Abdullah, A., Hassan, R., & Kassim, S. (2018). A conceptual framework for Islamic institutional and retail investment in maritime assets. *International Business Research, 11*(2), 176–188.

Abdullah, A. (2018). A life cycle approach to Islamic wealth management and risk tolerance. *Journal of Islamic Finance, 7*(2), 1–13.

Ahmed, H. (2013). Islamic wealth management: Goals and instruments. *Q Report*, 26–30.

Al-Arabi, I. (1957a). *Ahkam al-Qur'an.* 'Isa al-Babi al-Halabi, Cairo, Egypt.

Al-'Arabi, I. (1957b). *Ahkam al-Qur'an.* Cairo: 'Isa al-Babi al-Halabi.

Al-Tibrani, S., & Al-Hafiz A.A. (2016). *Al-Mu'jam al-Kabīr*. Millat Publications.

Aquinas Thomas, A. (1981). *Summa Theologica.* New York: English Dominican Fathers. pp. II–II, Q58, A1.

Appadurai, A. (1986). Introduction: Commodities and the politics of value. In A. Appadurai (Ed.), *The social life of things: Commodities in cultural perspective* (pp. 3–63). Cambridge University Press.

Al-Abbadi, A. H., & Abdullah, A. (2017). Modeling psychology in islamic wealth management. *International Journal of Economics and Finance, 9*(10), 64–85.

Asutay, M. (2007). Conceptulaization of the second best Solution in Overcoming the Social Failure of Islamic Banking and Finance: Examining The Overpowering of HOMOISLAMICUS by HOMOECONOMICUS. *IIUM Journal of Economics and Management, 15*(2), 167.

Augustine of Hippo (1887) [AD 392]. Schaff, Philip (ed.). *Acts or Disputation Against Fortunatus the Manichaean.* via Wikisource.

Beaverstock, J. V., Hall, S., & Wainwright, T. (2013). Servicing the super-rich: new financial elites and the rise of the private wealth management retail ecology. *Regional Studies, 47*(6), 834–849. https://doi.org/10.1080/00343404.2011.587795

Bird-David, N., & Darr, A. (2009). Commodity, gift and the mass-gift: On gift-commodity hybrids in advanced mass consumption cultures. *Economy and Society, 38*(2), 304–325.

Bloch, M., & Parry, J. (Eds.). (1989). *Money and the morality of exchange* (pp. 1–33). Cambridge University Press.

Britt, S. L., Klontz, B. K., & Archuleta, K. L. (2015a). Financial therapy: establishing an emerging field. In B. T. Klontz, K. L. Archuleta, & S. L. Britt (Eds.), *Financial therapy: Theory, research and practice* (pp. 3–13). New York: Springer.

Britt, S. L., Klontz, B. T., & Archuleta, K. L. (Eds.). (2015b). *Financial therapy: Theory*. Springer.

Chhabra, A. B. (2005). Beyond Markowitz: A comprehensive wealth allocation framework for individual investors. *The Journal of Wealth Management, 7*(4), 8–34.

Claar, V. V., & Lingle, C. (2020). Stock-market valuation is not wealth, and neither is happiness. *Journal of Market and Morality, 23*(1), 149–155.

Edbiz Consulting. (2016). Islamic wealth management in a global context. *Islamic Wealth Management Report*, 14–25

Evensky, H., Haron, S. M., & Robinson, T. R. (2011). *The new wealth management: The financial advisor's guide to managing and investing client assets.* CFA Institute Publications.

Farooq, M. O. (2014). Islamic wealth management and the pursuit of positive-sum solutions. *Islamic Economic Studies, 22*(2), 99–124.
Grable, J. E., Archuleta, K. L., & Nazarinia, R. R. (Eds.). (2011). *Financial planning and counseling scales*. Springer.
Gregory, C. A. (1982). *Gifts and commodities*. Academic Press.
Gregory, C. A. (1997). *Savage money: The anthropology and politics of commodity exchange*. Harwood Academic.
Hens, T., & Meier, A. (2016). *Behavioral finance and the psychology of investing*, BHFS, Credit Suisse AG, Zurich, Switzerland (www.credit-suisse.com).
Ismail, N., & Antonio. (2012). The Islamic wealth management: An analysis from IBN SĪNĀ'S perspective. *Journal of Islamic Thought and Civilization, 2*(1), 19–36.
Jennings, W. W., Horan, S. M., Reichenstein, W., & Brunel, J. L. P. (2011). Perspectives from the literature of private wealth management. *The Journal of Wealth Management, 14*(1), 8–40. https://doi.org/10.1080/13562517.2010.515024
Johnson, R., & Horan, S. M .(2013). Human capital and behavioral biases: Why investors don't diversify enough, *The Journal of Wealth Management, 16*(1), 9–21.
Kahf, M. (1990). Financing public sector in islamic perspective, Paper presented in the Third Islamic Economics Conference of the Association of Muslim Social Scientists of the U. S. Poor Man, Rich Man, Big-Man, Chief: Political Types in Melanesia and Polynesia.
Kamri, N. A., & Daud, M. Z. (2011). Islamic wealth management: A review on the dimension of values. *Shariah Journal, 19*(3), 187–212.
Malinowski, B. (1920). Kula: The circulating exchange of valuables in the archipelagoes of Eastern New Guinea. *Man, 20*, 97–105.
Maududi, A. A. S. (1972) *Tafheem ul Qur'an, Idara Tarjuman ul Qur'an*, Lahore, Pakistan.
Mauss, M. (1969). *The gift: Forms and functions of exchange in archaic societies*. Cohen and West Ltd. (first published 1950)
Mauss, M. (1990). *The gift: The Form and reason for exchange in archaic societies* (trans. Halls, WD). London; New York: Routledge.
Mauss, M. (1990). *[1924] The gift*. Routledge.
Malaysia Islamic Financial Center (2016). *Islamic wealth management: Growing stronger globally*. Kuala Lumpur: Malaysia Islamic Financial Center (MIFC).
Munger, M. (2007) Think globally, act irrationally: recycling, *Library of Economics and Liberty*. https://www.econlib.org/library/Columns/y2007/Mungerrecycling.html Accessed 7th Feb 2021.
Polanyi, K. (2001). [1944] *The great transformation: the political and economic origins of our time*. Boston: Beacon Press, pp. 45–80.
Pompian, M. M. (2012). *Behavioral finance and wealth management: How to build investment strategies that account for investor biases* (2nd ed.). New Jersey: Wiley.
Qaseem, M. (2016). Shariah perspective in wealth and its management. *Islamic Wealth Management Report*, 26–37.
Shiller, R. J. (1998). *Human behavior and the efficiency of the financial system* (NEBR Working Paper Series No. 6375). Cambridge.
Sahlins, M. l. (1963). Poor man, rich man, big-man, chief: Political types in Melanesia and Polynesia. *Comparative Studies in Society and History, 5*(3), 294–7. https://doi.org/10.1017/s0010417500001729
Sandwick, J. (2011). *Islamic wealth management*. Michael Gassner consultancy, Cologne, Germany.
Schumpeter, J. A. (1996).*History of economic analysis: With a new introduction* (2nd ed). Elizabeth Boody Schumpeter (Editor), Mark Perlman (Introduction), Oxford University Press.
Shafii, Z., Yusoff, Z. M., & Noh, S. M. (2013). *Islamic financial planning & wealth management*(1st ed.). IBFIM.
Siddiqi, M. N. (1986). Public expenditure in an Islamic State. Paper presented in the International Seminar on Fiscal Policy and Development Planning in an Islamic State, Islamabad, Pakistan.
Sowell, T. (2015). *Wealth, poverty and politics, an international perspective*. Basic Books, United States.

Tasdemir, M., Cobanoglu, M. M., & Iqbal, Z. (2017). Wealth in Islam. *Islamic Wealth Management Report, 2016*, 38–45.
World Bank. (1978). *World development report 1978*. Oxford University Press.
Yahaya, J., & Azhar, M. (2005). *Interaksi Harta Dalam Al-Qur'an*. Penerbit Universiti Teknologi Malaysia.

Nasim Shah Shirazi is a professor at the College of Islamic Studies (CIS), Hamad bin Khalifa University, Doha. Before joining CIS, he was working as Lead Economist and Acting Manager, Islamic Economics & Finance Research Division, IRTI, Islamic Development Bank. Previously, he worked Deputy Dean (Suleyman Demirel University, Almaty), Dean, Director Research and Director General, International Institute of Islamic Economics (IIIE), International Islamic University Islamabad (IIUI), Pakistan. Professor Shirazi served as a professor at International Islamic University Malaysia as well. He holds a Ph.D. in Economics from IIIE, IIUI. He has designed, developed, and taught courses at the graduate and post-graduate levels in Economics, Finance, Islamic Economics, and Decisions Sciences at the National and International Universities. With more than 76 publications, Professor Shirazi is well respected for his research in development economics, public finance, and Islamic.

Othman Altwijry is Assistant Professor in the College of Business and Economics, Qassim University, Saudi Arabia. He holds his Ph.D. in Islamic Banking and Finance from International Islamic University, Malaysia (2013). He got his Bachelor of Islamic Law/Shari'ah from Qassim University (2003), Master of Science in Islamic Banking and Finance from International Islamic University, Kuala Lumpur, Malaysia (2010). He presented several papers in the international conference held in the different parts of the world. His papers are published in peer reviewed international journals. Two of his papers won second prize in the International conference held in Malaysia and Dubai.

Toseef Azid is professor of Economics at College of Business and Economics, Qassim University, Saudi Arabia and International Visiting Scholar, Economics Department, Wayne State University, Detroit, Michigan, USA (2017). He holds Ph.D. in Economics from University College of Wales, Aberystwyth, UK. He received Fulbright Award as Scholar in Residence where he worked on a research project on "Economics of Middle Eastern Countries". His research focuses on technological change, development Economics, labour economics, Islamic economics and Islamic finance. His recent books as co-editor entitled "Labour in an Islamic Setting: Theory and Practice" and "Social Justice and Islamic Economics: Theory, Issues and Practice" published by Routledge, UK, "Corporate and Shari'ah Governance in the Muslim World: Theory and Practice" published by Emerald, UK and Economic Empowerment of Women in the Islamic World: Theory and Practice" published by World Scientific Publications, Singapore.

Muhammad Omer Chaudhry is Associate Professor at Bahauddin Zakariya University, Multan, Pakistan and holds Ph.D. in Logistics/Supply Chain Management with specialization in Transport Economics from Molde University College, Norway, MSc in Logistics from the same College, MPhil from BZU, Multan,. He published a number of academic papers in national and international journals, He presented many papers at peer reviewed conferences all over the globe. He also conducted some significant research in religious economics.

Part I
Principles of Islamic Wealth Management

Chapter 2
Decoding Islamic Wealth Management from *Qur'anic* Texts

Nurizal Ismail, Zurina Shafii, and Nashr Akbar

In the late 1990s, wealth management was recorded as the fastest-growing sector of the financial service industry.[1] Recently, Islamic wealth management is one of the new emerging financial service industries that attract many wealthy people to trust their wealth managed in accordance with Islamic values and principles. This is due to the increase of Muslim population which is expected to increase by 26% by 2030 to approximately 2.2 billion, and the growth of GDP per capita of Muslims (OIC Countries) about 4.3% Cumulative Annual Growth Rate (CAGR) to 2024.[2] Some countries attempt to grab the market of Islamic wealth management, such as Malaysia, Singapore, and Indonesia.

The development of Islamic wealth management as part of Islamic economics should be in line between practical and theoretical aspects. Indeed, the philosophical foundation concept of Islamic wealth management is essential to understand well—managing wealth from the Islamic perspective. Comparing with Conventional wealth management, Islamic wealth management has its philosophical foundation and operational framework. In the view of Shalleh (2012), Islamic wealth management has to redefine the meaning of wealth from its Islamic perspective.[3] This paper has a simple aim. It seeks to redefine the contemporary concept of wealth management from an Islamic perspective derived from Qur'anic texts and give a proposed framework of Islamic wealth management.

[1] Maude (2006).

[2] State of The Global Islamic Economy Report (2019/2020).

[3] Shalleh (2012).

N. Ismail (✉) · N. Akbar
Institut Agama Islam Tazkia, Jl. Ir. H. Djuanda No. 78, Sentul City, Bogor 16810, Indonesia
e-mail: nurizal@tazkia.ac.id

Z. Shafii
Universiti Sains Islam Malaysia, Bandar Baru Nilai, 71800 Nilai, Negeri Sembilan, Malaysia

T. Azid et al. (eds.), *Wealth Management and Investment in Islamic Settings*,
https://doi.org/10.1007/978-981-19-3686-9_2

2.1 The Qur'an as the Primer Source of Islamic Economic Thought

The Qur'an is the primary source in the epistemology of Islamic knowledge and science. It contains aspects of knowledge such as fiqh, history, family law, economics, and politics. As the primary source, the Qur'an also provides rules for human behavior that serve as guidelines for social, economic, and political aspects. One of the essential aspects of human life as the caliph of God who carries out the mandate is to seek God's gifts to meet their needs in this world and the Hereafter. So, it is not surprising that many great works of Islamic economics, such as *al-kharāj, al-amwāl,* and *al-Kasb,* were written from the spirit of the Qur'an.

In the history of the development of Islamic economic thought, the sources of economic thought are divided into 2, namely general and specific. According to Orman, the Qur'an is a particular reference source for the history of Islamic economic thought because it does not explicitly discuss economics. However, many aspects are helpful for human life. Because it is the primary source and guide for humankind in his life, it would also require extensive use of innovative thinking (*ijtihād*) to see and understand the relevance of the religious texts to the presentage (khan, 2018: p. 48). So, an exemplary method in developing Islamic economics exists by exploring economic ideas from the text of the Qur'an, which is used to answer problems and the realities of human economics from time to time.

2.1.1 *Previous Works of Literature*

Islahi and Ausaf (2010) edited the book entitled "Economic Problem and the Teaching of the Qur'an," containing 1. Economic Doctrine of the Qur'an: A System Framework; 2. Qur'anic Perspective of Compensation Principle; 3. Economic Justice: Islamic Economic System Versus. Capitalism; 4. Qur'an and the Scarcity Concept; 5. Informal Institutions and the Qur'anic Redistributive Scheme; 6. Economic Challenge and Its Qur'anic Solution; 7. A review on the Relationship between the Riba in the Qur'an and in the Hadith.[4] This book may be pretty complete in discussing economic problems from the point of view of the Qur'an. In essence, the Islamic economic system consisting of philosophy, principles, and institutions has been described in the Qur'an as a solution to economic problems.

One of the important issues discussed in economics is scarcity. The Qur'an also discusses it in depth. Zaman (2010), in his paper entitled Scarcity: East and West, said that instead of striving for more wealth, the Qur'an teaches humans to restrict their idle desires, endeavors to lead simple lifestyles, and contribute to others less fortunate.[5] It also teaches humans to be content with what they have and not envy those

---

[4] Islahi and Ausaf (2010).

[5] Zaman (2010).

who have more material wealth. In his study, Ahmed (2010) explains the scarcity of 2 types of letters, namely Makkiyah and Madaniyah. According to him, The Makkah verses of the Qur'an stress and build faith in God's power to create, provide, enlarge or restrict the provisions; the Madaniyah verses stress and expand the Divine rule in its principal forms –obligation, recommendation, permission, abhorrence, and prohibition.[6]

Another economic problem is poverty which the Qur'an also discusses in depth. Bonner (2005) mentions several terms related to poverty contained in the Qur'an, namely *dhu'āfa*, *faqîr*, and poor. In addition, he also mentioned that the Qur'an includes a distinctive set of economic prescriptions and norms in alleviating poverty.[7] According to Kaleem and Ahmed (2010), the basic principles of the philosophy of poverty alleviation in the Qur'an include the Islamic point of view regarding natural sources of wealth, the concept of brotherhood, the concept of family empowerment, Management selection criteria, encourage to spend money, prohibition of interest, and concept of charity and voluntary services.[8]

In the first point, wealth becomes an essential issue of all economic problems because actually, the object of the economy is wealth to meet human needs that can prosper. The term of wealth in Islam is known as '*māl*' which can be found in a primary source of Islam. The term mal or its derivatives has been mentioned in the Qur'an in more than 90 verses.[9] The core economic problem is wealth management at the micro and macro levels. Therefore, the study of Islamic wealth management from Qur'anic texts is important in this regard.

From 38 journal articles analyzed by VOSviewer, there is 8 clusters area of research. The central issues are term management. The first cluster focuses on personal issues to family finance related to Islamic wealth management, including aspects of causes and effects, consumerism, and physiology. The second cluster discusses the issue of the past and present history of IWM from the aspect of principles, gender, economic status, and institutions. The third cluster is about the awareness of giving a case study in Malaysia. The fourth cluster is more related to trust, which is also part of Islamic wealth management. Then the fifth cluster focuses on Islamic wealth planning from asset allocation, a risk, to the discussion of the life cycle approach. The sixth cluster focuses on the behavioral finance of Islamic wealth management. The seventh cluster discusses Islamic social finance, which is closely related to Islamic wealth management. The last cluster relates the development of Islamic wealth management to Islamic microfinance and efficiency.

The results of previous research mapping on Islamic wealth management explain that there is no study of Islamic wealth management with a review of the Qur'an that has studied it comprehensively from 2010 to 2021. Initial research on IWM was

[6] Ahmed (2010).

[7] Bonner (2005).

[8] Kaleem and Ahmed (2010).

[9] Islam (1999).

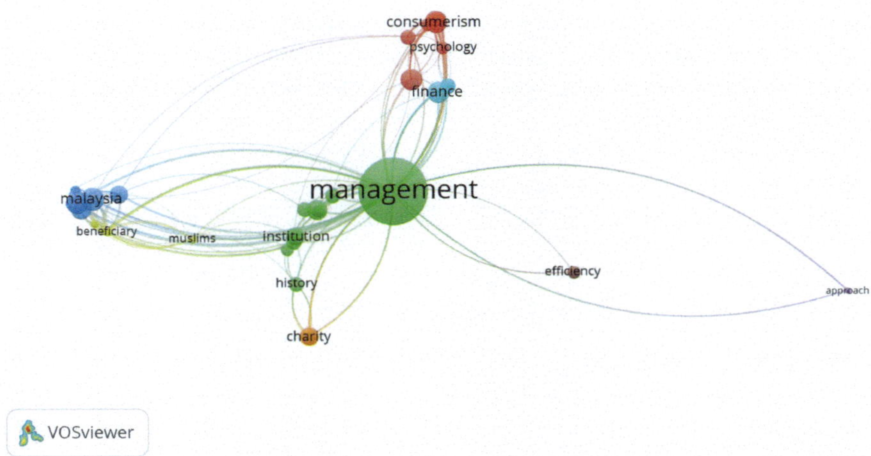

Fig. 2.1 Dimensions of management

conducted by Kamri and Daud (2011)[10], Shalleh (2012),[11] and Ismail and Antonio (2012)[12] tried to find ideas and principles of Islamic wealth management values sourced from the Qur'an, hadith, and the thoughts of scholars from their works related to Islamic economic thought sources. In subsequent developments, Farooq (2013 & 2014) tried to compare the principles of value between Islamic and Conventional wealth management.[13] As for discussing it with a historical approach, Cizakça (2014) discusses the development of Islamic wealth management in the past from today.[14] After that, the IWM study focused more on studying elements, institutions, and case studies. Therefore, the IWM study by looking at the words in the Qur'an, namely *al-kasb* and *al-infāq*, can be used as the basis or foundation in developing the IWM concept in the future (Fig. 2.1).

2.2 Methodology of the Study

This study is confined to wealth management as part of Islamic Economics and Finance studies, whereby the objective of Islamic economics is to identify and establish an economic order that is in line with Islamic Scripture and tradition (Addas,

---

[10] Kamri and Daud (2011).

[11] Shalleh (2012).

[12] Ismail and Antonio (2012).

[13] Farooq (2014).

[14] Basha and Tahir (2019); Amand et al. (2018); Mahadi et al. (2019); Al-Abbadi and Abdullah (2017); Nasution (2014); Wouters (2013); Halim (2011).

2008:32).[15] The study employs qualitative research to achieve the research objectives, referring to the meanings, concepts, definitions, characteristics, metaphors, symbols, and descriptions (BERG, 1989).[16] It will use content and descriptive analysis to get the finding of the study.

The data collection is generated from Islamic sources: the Qur'an and other Islamic literature such as journals, books, magazines, report documents, and the internet. These sources will be put into coding and analyzed using QDA miner Lite to answer the research problem of study, contributing to Islamic economics development, especially in Islamic wealth management.

Several stages were carried out in this research process—first, the stage of categorizing the verses of the Qur'an, which contain the words *al-kasb* and *al-infāq*. The second stage is to analyze the categorization of wealth management verses into several codings. Finally, the coding that has been obtained is adjusted to the current IWM development under the framework of the Qur'an.

2.3 Result and Discussion

2.3.1 Wealth Management in the Qur'an

2.3.1.1 The Essence of Wealth

There are several main objectives regarding the essence of wealth from the Qur'anic and Sunnah perspective.

Firstly, wealth is a trust from Allah. Allah Ta'ala owns the wealth, and human is given a trust to manage it, as mentioned in al-Hadid: 7. The message is that human as a trustee should be responsible for making the best and most effective use of wealth endowed in acceptable ways to Allah.

Therefore, according to Al-Ghazali: "Man is the driving force of economic activity and is the living creature responsible for the level of economic performance" (1994: 91). Human is responsible as a Khalifah on earth and a trust (Amanah) of government for themselves and the environment. It can be said that this is the philosophical foundation of Islamic economics that God is the absolute and the real owner of all resources in the universe that is endowed to humankind as trusteeship. Morever, Allah SWT has mentioned in Adz-Dzariyat: 19 that human should donate some part of their wealth as there are others' right in their wealth.

Secondly, wealth is the adornment of life as stated in Surah Al-Kahfi: 46. The human inclination to wealth gives depth insight to us that wealth becomes one of the essential things sustaining human life. In addition, since wealth is the adornment of life it will perish along with the death of the owners. The owner will not bring it to

[15] Addas (2008).

[16] Berg (1989).

the hereafter. Qurthubi reminds that one's heart should not be bound by his wealth as it will perish.[17]

Thirdly, wealth is a human trial, as mentioned in al-Anfal: 28 that human properties and their children are but a trial. Fourthly, wealth is means to the Hereafter. In Surah Al-Layl: 4–7, Allah SWT will guide those who gives and fears Allah, and believes in the best [reward].

2.3.1.2 A Framework of Wealth Management: Earning (*Al-Kasb*) and Spending (*Infâq*)

The terms *kasb* and *infâq* are related to wealth management by some early Muslim scholars such as al-Syaibâni and Ibn Sîna (Ismail & Antonio, 2012; Mohammed, 2011).[18] Both terms are explicitly mentioned in the Qur'an. The terms *kasb* and *infāq* are mentioned side by side, indicating that what humans get in income through work must be spent in good ways. In Table 2.1, the results of the categorization obtained through the QDA miner lite software consist of the words *al-kasb* and *al-infāq* related to IWM.

The early Muslim scholars in developing the Concept of Islamic wealth management indeed refer to the Qur'an as the primary reference source. It is argued that

Table 2.1 Verses on Kasb and Infâq in the Qur'an

No	Surah	Page	No	Surah	Page
1	Al-Baqarah	267	15	Al-Imran	134
2	Al-Nisa	32	16	Al-Nisa	34
3	Al- 'Araf	96	17	Al-Nisa	38–39
4	Al-Baqarah	2–3	18	Al-Anfal	3
5	Al-Baqarah	195	19	Al-Anfal	36
6	Al-Baqarah	215	20	Al-Anfal	60
7	Al-Baqarah	219	21	Al-Ra'd	22
8	Al-Baqarah	254	22	Muhammad	38
9	Al-Baqarah	261–262	23	Al-Hadid	7
10	Al-Baqarah	265	24	Al-Hadid	10
11	Al-Baqarah	270	25	Al-Munafiqun	7
12	Al-Baqarah	272–274	26	Al-Munafiqun	10
13	Al-Imran	92	27	Al-Tagabun	16
14	Al-Imran	117	28	Al-Talaq	6–7

Processed by QDA miner lite

[17] Qurthubi and Muhammad bin Ahmad (2003).

[18] Ismail and Antonio (2012); Mohammed (2011).

Table 2.2 Framework of islamic wealth management

Category	Code	Count	Surah
Islamic wealth Management	Framework IWM	2	1.Al-Baqarah 267 2.Al-Hadid 7

Processed by QDA miner lite

Surah al-Baqarah, 267 and al-Hadid, 7 can be put as the framework developing the concept of Islamic wealth management as mentioned in Table 2.2.

The first Surah explains to believers to spend (*Infāq*) their wealth through an effort (*kasb*) in a good way. Also, the second Surah explains the same thing as to spend wealth with what Allah has made humans as a trustee endowed by Allah on the earth and sky. The word trust and a good way reflect management that humans must seek and spend their wealth.

a. Al-Kasb

The term *al-kasb* is derived from *kasaba-yaksibu-kasban*, which means pursuing *rizq* (Sustenance) and livelihood (Ibn Manzur, 1/716). The meaning of al-kasb means explaining the existence of an effort made by humans both through their body and mind in producing sustenance and livelihood. Because there is also a livelihood obtained without going through an effort such as grants, alms, inheritance, and wills.[19] several ways to earn a living through *al-kasb* in the Qur'an:

i. Agriculture

[The let man look at his food (and how we provide it). For that, we pour forth water in abundance, and we split the earth in fragments, and produce therein corn, and grapes, and nutrition plans, and olive and dates, and enclosed gardens dense with lofty trees, and fruits and fodder for use and convenience to you and your cattle] (At-Taubah:24-32)

ii. Steel industry

[.....we sent down iron, in which is (material for) mighty warm, as well as many benefit for humankind, that God may test who it is that will help] (Al-Hadid: 25).

[O ye children of Adam! We have bestowed raiment upon you to cover your shame as well as to be an adornment to you] (Al-'Araf: 26).

iii. Trade

[O ye who believe! Eat not up to your property among yourselves in vanities: but let there amongst you traffic and trade by mutual good-will: nor kill yourselves: for verily God hath been to you Most Merciful] (An-Nissa: 29).

There are 2 Surahs related to the term al-kasb mentioned in the previous discussion, which is shown in Table 2.3.

---

[19] Ismail and Antonio (2012).

Table 2.3 Al-Kasb in islamic wealth management

Category	Code	Count	Surah
Kasb	Faith and piety based kasb	1	Al-A'raf, 96
Kasb	Different portion of earning	1	Al-Nisa, 32

Processed by QDA miner lite

Two Surahs produce these two codes, namely the importance of faith and Piety in seeking al-Kasb and the differences in the parts of human efforts. Surah al-A'raf explains the importance of faith and Piety that will lead to the blessings of human life, including human efforts in fulfilling their lives must be tied to faith and devotion to Allah. The meaning of faith and Piety is that their hearts believe and confirm what the Apostles brought; They follow the Apostle and become pious by obeying and leaving all prohibitions.[20]

It is in line with Surah al-Talaq verses 2–3 that Allah will appoint a way out for whosoever keepeth his duty to Him. And will provide for him from (a quarter) whence he hath no expectation. Moreover, Allah will suffice whosoever putteth his trust in Allah. So, looking for wealth accompanied by faith and piety results in the blessing of life.

The second Surah explains that each (male and female) gets a reward according to their deeds. If the deed is good, then the reward is good, and if the deed is bad, then the reward is bad. This is the opinion of Ibn Jarir.[21] There is no exception with seeking wealth; if it is intended as worship and done in a good way, you will be rewarded not only in this world but also in the Hereafter. This verse also explains for every human being not to envy the portion received over the others because it has become God's provision.

iv. Infâq

Infāq comes from the word *anfaqa-yunfiqu-infāqan,* which means to spend, to use, to spend. In the hadith of Rasulullah, peace be upon him narrated by Imam Bukhari, it is said that your wealth is what you spend, while what you keep is the property of your heirs (Bukhari). It can be said that the purpose of seeking treasure is to be spent. The Qur'an has explained the concept of Infaq as described in Table 2.4 below.

In the code of faith and piet, Surah contains ten verses that explain the importance of faith and piety in spending. With faith and piety, the pattern of spending will be under the teachings of Shari'ah. In Surah al-Baqarah, 4 verses explain the importance of faith and piety in spending. In Surah al-Baqarah, verse 3 describes a simultaneous relationship where spending on something good is similar to belief in God and performing shalat. Another form of faith is believing in the last day. Because of that, in verse 254, humans are also reminded to spend their sustenance on the good before the Day of Judgment comes, on the day when there will be no more buying and selling, no more friendship, and no more intercession. In verse 265, it is explained

[20] Ibnu et al. (2003).

[21] Ibid, Jilid 2, 293.

Tabel 2.4 Infāq in islamic wealth management

Category	Code	Count	Surah
Infaq verses	Faith and piety based Infaq	10	1. Al-Baqarah, 3 2. Al-Baqarah, 254 3. Al-Baqarah, 265 4. Al-Baqarah, 270 5. Al-Nisa, 38 6. Al-Nisa, 39 7. Al-Anfal, 3 8. Al-Anfal 36 9. Al-Ra'd, 22 10.Al-Tagabun, 16
Infaq verses	Type of spending	7	1. Al-Baqarah, 195 2. Al-Baqarah, 219 3. Al-Baqarah, 262 4. Al-Imran, 117 5. Al-Anfal, 60 6. Muhammad, 38 7. Al-Hadid, 10
Infaq verses	Priority of spending	3	1. Al-Baqarah, 215 2. Al-Baqarah, 273 3. Al-Imran, 92
Infaq verses	Time of spending	2	1. Al-Imran, 134 2. Al-Munafiqun, 10
Infaq verses	Different portion of spending	2	Al-Nisa, 34 Al-Talaq, 7
Infaq verses	Reward	7	1. Al-Baqarah, 261 2. Al-Baqarah, 265 3. Al-Baqarah, 272 4. Al-Baqarah, 274 5. Al-Anfal, 60 6. Al-Ra'd, 22 7. Al-Hadid, 7

(continued)

Tabel 2.4 (continued)

Category	Code	Count	Surah
Infaq verses	Opposite behaviour on spending	3	1. Muhammad, 38 2. Al-Munafiqun, 7 3. Al-Tagabun, 16
Infaq verses	Spending after divorce	1	1. Al-Talaq, 6

Processed by QDA miner lite

that when humans spend their wealth to seek the pleasure of Allah and peace of mind, Allah will multiply the reward. In verse 270, we must believe that what we spend Allah knows best because we do it in good ways that Allah has prescribed.

The second code is the type of spending that consists of 2 parts, namely infaq to meet the needs in the world and infaq in the way of Allah/needs of the Hereafter. Spending for worldly needs is mentioned in Surat al-Baqarah, 219, al-Imran, 117, and al-Hadid, 10. As for spending for the Hereafter, it is mentioned in Surat al-Baqarah, 195, al-Baqarah, 262, al-Anfal, 60, and Muhammad, 38). Spending for the Hereafter is always associated with Islamic charity in modern times. Interestingly, Surveys found that some things will remain familiar, and others may change. As stated in a 2010 survey by Barclays Wealth, almost a quarter of HNWIs globally say charity is a top spending priority.[22] This division was not later developed by scholars including Imam al-Syaibani and Ibn Sina. Imam al-Syaibani divides it into obligatory, recommended, and permissible spending,[23] and Ibn Sina divides it into 3, namely infaq for men himself and his family, infaq for the act of virtue, and infaq for saving (*al-iddikhār*).[24]

Next, the code of spending priority. Surah al-Baqarah verses 215, and 272 explain our spending priorities from the closest ones, namely parents, relatives, orphans, faqir, poor, and ibn al-sabil. Surah al-Imran verse 92 explains about spending the best thing on someone. The importance of spending on a priority scale because we know more about situations that are closer to us, whether they are in happy or difficult conditions, than those that are further away. Everything we spend on family and other people sincerely will be worth alms which will be rewarded with Allah. As supported by the narration of Al-Miqdam ibn Ma'dikarib heard the Messenger of Allah, may Allah bless him and grant him peace, say, "What you feed yourself is sadaqah for you. What you feed your child is sadaqah for you. What you feed your wife is sadaqah for you. What you feed your servant is sadaqah for you."[25]

Time of spending may be done in the field or the narrow as mentioned in Surah al-Imran, 134. In Surah al-Munafiqun verse 10, we are reminded to spend the sustenance that Allah has given us in a good way before death picks us up. Do not let regret

---

22 Barclays (2010).

23 Mohammed (2011).

24 Ismail and Antonio (2012).

25 https://sunnah.com/adab:82.

the happen as in the fragment of the verse "...so that he should say: "My Lord! If only You would respite me to a near term, so that I should have given alms and been of the improved ones". So the best time to spend is in the world with the allocation described in the previous discussion.

In the explanation of the code for different portions of spending, Allah has explained in His word, and those men are leaders for women because Allah has made some of them (men) more than others (women) and because they (men) have spent part of their wealth. In Islam, men have a greater responsibility than women in their families to provide a living.

In the explanation of the code for different portions of spending, Allah has explained in His word that those men are leaders for women because Allah has made some of them (men) more than others (women) and because of what they (men) have spent part of their wealth. Code of Reward contains 4 Surahs with 7 verses. In Surah al-Baqarah, verses 261, 265, 272, and 274, al-Anfal verse 60, al-Ra'd verse 22, and al-Hadid verse 7 have explained the reward that will be given to individual Muslims who spend their wealth with pleasure. Allah and in the way of Allah with tremendous and multiplied rewards.

Akhlaq is essential to Islamic wealth management. al-Qur'an mentions the behaviors contrary to Islamic teaching in Surah Muhammad verse 38, al-Munafiqun verse 7, and al-Tagabun verse 16, one of them is miserliness. Based on these verses, it is clear that being stingy/miserliness is one of the destructive behaviors that keep people from being generous.

The last code is about spending after divorce, explicitly mentioned in Surah al-Talaq verse 6, "Let them live where you live ⌜during their waiting period⌝, according to your means. And do not harass them to make their stay unbearable. If they are pregnant, then maintain them until they deliver. And if they nurse your child, 1 compensate them, and consult together courteously. But if you fail to reach an agreement, then another woman will nurse ⌜the child⌝ for the father". The issue of livelihood becomes a great concern in Islam even when husband and wife are divorced, and there are rules when a woman is divorced and is pregnant, then a man must spend her a living until she gives birth and breastfeeds her child. Because when a child is divorced, his parents are still the responsibility of his father to provide for him until he is mature and earns his living.

2.4 Proposed Concept of Islamic Wealth Management

The central foundation in Islamic wealth management is Tawhīd. The wealth that we will manage is trusted wealth that requires the responsibility of the trustee. It can be seen from the verses related to *al-kasb* and *al-infāq,* which have the same code; faith and piety, which are the manifestation of Tawhīd. By Tawhīd, a human may earn and consume according to His need while the the remain of his wealth or income should be allocated on charity in the cause of Allah or reinvested in business (Faruqi, 1998). His need can be found in the Shari'ah.

Shari'ah will better provide knowledge on the essence of wealth, type of al-kasb and spending, and priority of spending in human life. Also, it governs the man how to earn and spend the wealth just a way derived from the Qur'an and Sunnah. The last foundation to be embedded in the practice of Islamic wealth management is *akhlaq* (ethics). An example of the unethical behavior in Islamic wealth management mentioned in this study is miserly behavior that keeps people from spending their wealth on the path determined by the Shari'ah. The behaviors that must arise from human behavior in managing their wealth are *zuhud, qanā'ah*, and *tawakkal* to Allah. By then, in Islamic ways, earning and spending Muslims' wealth must benefit them in this world and the Hereafter.

Wealth creation in Islamic can be through *al-kasb* (earning), inheritance, will, and Islamic social finance instruments such as *hibah, waqf,* and *sadaqah. Al-kasb* is carried out through human effort to sustain life. For inheritance and will are acquired by the human from his father or ancestors enjoying a good living. Islamic social finance or wealth distribution instrument such as *hibah, waqf,* and *sadaqah* are using for helping others to obtain the good life. These kinds of wealth creation always exist in human life related to the fulfillment of *infaq* (spending) objective.

Moreover, *infaq* (spending) is firstly related to the world's need covering man and his family's spending through direct or indirect spending such as saving and investment. Secondly, spending for the need of Hereafter is related to Islamic social finance instruments such as *giving zakah, infaq, sadaqah,* and *waqf*. Hence, Islamic wealth management should be done in two steps based on the Qur; an *al-kasb* (earning) and *infāq* (spending) to achieve *Falah* (the success here and the Hereafter).

Then, there are three objectives of Islamic wealth management, and they are: First, individual purposes such as to sustain life on earth, to improve knowledge, and to strenghten the faith. Second, family purposes covering to fulfill the family's needs, allocate the wealth for education, and save for expected events. Third, the society's purposes including to promote growth, provide social activities, and reduce inequality of income distribution. These three are to achieve happiness and welfare by His blessing (*barakah*) here and the Hereafter. Allah SWT says in surah al-Qasas: 77 that every human should optimize the gift from Allah (wealth) to seek the blessing in the hereafter without leaving the wordly affairs by spending it in the way of Allah, fulfilling the need of him and his family, and doing charity as being grateful to Allah.

2.5 Conclusion

The Islamic conception of wealth management from Qur'anic framework is very comprehensive covering all philosophical foundation; epistemology, ontology, and axiology. Surah al-Baqarah is the most Surah covers the discussion of Islamic wealth management, followed by Surah al-Nisa, al-Imran, al-Anfal, al-Hadid, al-Tagabun, al-Ra'd, and Muhammad. Surah al-Baqaqah is Madaniyyah that contends explanation of the establishment of Shari'ah in the area of *ibādah*, mu'āmalat, and customs, which start from verse 177 to the end of Surah.[26]

Islamic wealth management must be based on *Tawhīd* as a central pivot, Shari'ah, and akhlaq as the rule and conduct for Muslim people. The Islamic wealth management process contends three aspects: (1) wealth creation, (2) spending, and (3) saving or investment. Wealth creation has a relationship with the fulfillment of the *infaq* (spending) objective. The objective is to promote *maqashid shari'ah,* promoting just and welfare in order to achieve *Falah.*

References

Al-Qur'an, A., & Waleed, A. J. (2008). *Methodology of Economics: Secular VS Islamic.* Malaysia: IIUM Press.

Ahmed, & Wahbalbari, A.(2010). The concept of scarcity and its implication on human behaviour: searching the qur'anic Perspective. *Review of Islamic Economics*, 14(1).

Al-Abbadi, A. H., & Abdullah, A. (2017). Modeling psychology in islamic wealth management. *International Journal of Economics and Finance, 9*(10), 64–85.

Al-Syaibani., Muhammad, b.,& al-Hasan. (2011). *Earning a livelihood.* Trans. Adi Setia. Kuala Lumpur: IBFIM.

Ash-Shiddieqy., & Teungku, M. H. (2000). *Tafsi Qur'anul Majid: Annur*, Jilid. Semarang: Pustaka Rizki Putra.

Amand, F. P., Taufiq, B., & Firdaus, A. (2018). Consumerism in personal finance: An Islamic wealth management approach. *Al-Iqtishad Journal of Islamic Economics, 10*(2), 325–340.

Aziz, F., Mahmud, M., & Karem, E. (2008). The nature of infaq and its effects on distribution of wealth. *KASBIT Business Journal, 6*(1), 44–48.

Basah., Sarimah., Tahir., & Putri Rozita. (2019). Towards Acceptance of Islamic Wealth Management. *Journal Of Islamic, Social, Economics and Development* (JISED), 4(24), 14–21.

Berg, B. L. (1989). *Qualitative Research Methods: For the Social Sciences.* Pearson Education Inc.

Bonner., & Michael. (2005). Poverty and Economics in the Qur'an. *Journal of Interdisciplinary History*, 35(3).

Farooq., & Mohammad, O. (2013) Islamic wealth management and some unconventional thoughts *Q Report*, 1.

Farooq, M. O. (2014). Islamic wealth management and the pursuit of positive-sum solutions. *Islamic Economic Studies, 22*(2), 99–124.

Halim., & Akmal, H. (2011). The legality of a living trust as an instrument for Islamic wealth management: A Malaysian perspective. *IIUM Law Journal*, 119(1).

Ibnu., Katsir., Tafsir, I. K., Trans, M., & Abdul Ghofar. (2003). Jilid 3 (Bogor: Pustaka Imam Asy-Syafi'I.

Islahi., Abdul, A., & Ahmad. (2010). Ausaf (eds.), *Economic Problems and the Teaching of the Qur'an*, India: Idarah Ulum al-Qur'an, 1–161.

Islam, M. W. (1999). Al-Mal: The concept of property in islamic legal thought. *Arab Law Quarterly, 14*(4), 361–368.

Islamic Wealth Management. (2012). The Rise of the Rice Investor. *Islamic Finance News*, 1–33.

Ismail., Nurizal., Antonio., & Syafi'I. (2012). The islamic wealth management: an analysis from ibn sīnā's perspective. *Journal of Islamic Thought and Civilization*, 2(1), 19–36.

Kamri., Nor 'Azzah., Daud., & Mohd Zaidi. (2011). Islamic wealth management: a review on the dimension of values. *Jurnal Syariah*, 19(1), 187–212.

[26] Ash-Shiddieqy and Hasbi (2000).

Kaleem., Ahmad., Ahmed., & Ahmad. (2010). The Quran and poverty alleviation: A theoretical model for charity-based Islamic microfinance institutions (MFIs). Nonprofit and voluntary sector quarterly 39(3).
Maude., & David. (2006). *Global private banking and wealth management: the new realities.* England: John Wiley & Sons Ltd.
Mahadi, N. A., Mazli, S. A., & Muneeza, A. (2019). Islamic financial wealth management: Empowering women in Islamic societies. *International Journal of Management and Applied Research, 6*(3), 116–129.
Mohammed., & Mustafa Omar. (2011). Economic consumption model revisited: Infaq based on al-shaybani's levels of Al-Kasb. *International Journal of Economics, Management and Accounting,* 1993).
Nasution., & Atiqi Chollisni. (2014). Efficiency of Baitul Maal Wa Tamwil (BMT): an effort towards Islamic wealth management in microfinance institution. *The Journal of Muamalat and Islamic Finance Research.*
Qurthubi., & Abu Abdullah Muhammad bin Ahmad. (2003). *al-Jāmi' li Ahkām al-Qur'ān*, Riyadh: Dār 'Ālam al-Kutub.
Shalleh, M. S. (2012). Rethinking wealth management: An Islamic Preliminary View. *International Journal of Business and Social Sciences., 3*(13), 232–236.
State of The Global Islamic Economy Report, 2019/2020.
The Hadits of the Prophet Muhammad. (2014). www. sunnah.com. Retrieved.
Wealth., & Barclays. (2010). Global giving: The culture of philanthropy. Barclays. Barclays Wealth.
Wouters., & Paul. (2013). Elements of islamic wealth management. *Contemporary Islamic Finance: Innovations, Applications, and Best Practices,* 147–164;
Zaman., & Asad. (2010) Scarcity: East and west. *Journal of Islamic Economics, Banking and Finance,* 6(1).

Nurizal Ismail is PhD Candidate in Economics and Mu'amalat at University Sains Islam Malaysia. He obtained a Master's degree in Islamic Civilization from International Institute of Islamic Thought and Civilization (ISTAC), International Islamic University of Malaysia. In 2017, he attended a short-course at Leiden University Centre for the Study of Islam and Society, Leiden University, The Netherlands. He is a lecturer of history and economics at Tazkia Islamic University College His work was published in the Journal of Islamic Thought and Civilization, Tsaqafah: Journal of Islamic Civilization and International Journal of Advanced Research in Islamic and Humanities. He also wrote some books related to the history and Islamic economics, such as Sejarah Pemikiran Ekonomi Islam (2021) published by the National Committee for Sharia Economics and Finance (KNEKS), Maqasid Syariah dalam Ekonomi Islam (2020) published by Tazkia publishing, and book chapter in Halal Governance and Management: Malaysia and ASEAN Countries—Intermediate to Advance (2020).

Zurina Shafii, PhD is associate professor at the Faculty of Economics and Muamalat and a research fellow in Islamic Finance and Wealth Management Institute (IFWMI) of Universiti Sains Islam Malaysia (USIM). She holds an Accounting Degree from Universiti Teknologi Mara (UiTM) and a Master's degree and PhD in Islamic Finance from Durham University, UK. She holds professional accounting qualification, ACCA and also a Certified Islamic Financial Planner. She co-authored two books on Islamic financial planning published by IBFIM. She also authored two books on Islamic finance titled 'Governance and Shari'ah Audit in Islamic Financial Institution' and 'State of Islamic Finance: A Retrospective Assessment and Looking Forward', published by Penerbit USIM.

Nashr Akbar is Head of Islamic Economic Department at Tazkia Islamic University College, Indonesia. He earned his master degree in Economics from International Islamic University of

Malaysia. He has authored two books. One of the books namely "Tafsir Ayat Ekonomi Kontemporer (Economic interpretations of the Qur'anic verses)" has been awarded as the best book in Islamic Book Fair, Indonesia 2018. He specialized in Islamic economics and history of economic thought. He participated in several conferences held in Turkey, Malaysia, and Indonesia. He also participated in the several joint research projects with Bank Indonesia and Financial Service Authority. Since 2015, he is assigned as managing editor of journal TIFBR (Tazkia Islamic Finance and Business Review).

Chapter 3
Islam, Spirituality and Wealth: Islamic Framework of Wealth Management

Muhammad Abdullah

There is little doubt that wealth constitutes backbone of a society as well as of a civilization (Ariff & Mohamad, 2017). Within the classical Islamic discourse, the issue of wealth has been treated with a rather cautious note (Al-Nabhani, 2004). The diligence of Islamic scholars in treating wealth is, apparently, informed by their perception that there is a dichotomy between the concept of spirituality and amassment of wealth (Al-Ghazali, 2004). Wealth, at occasions, is deemed as an antonym to spiritual richness. The Islamic literature provides a mixed stand-point on virtue of paucity vis-à-vis being wealthy (Al-Shaybani, 2015). The primary sources of *Shari'ah* i.e. *Qur'an* and *Sunn'ah* appear to criticize those who hoard wealth (al-Qur'an 9/34). In comparison, in different *Qur'anic* verses wealth has been referred as a blessing and bounty of God, which needs to be deployed in the righteous causes (al-Qur'an 2/267; Abdullah, 2015; Hasan, 2015).

From amongst the five pillars of Islam, at least, two directly relate to financial capacity of a believer. These two include *Zakat* (the annual obligatory charity) and *Hajj* (pilgrimage to Mecca), which cannot be performed without being financially capable. In addition, the Islamic emphasis and exhortation on *Sadaqah* (charity), *Infaq* (spending and alms-giving) *Waqf* (endowments) and *Wasiyyah* (Islamic will) cannot be duly responded except by those who enjoy affluence (Lev, 2005; Siddiqui, 1991; Singer, 2008). From an Islamic theological perspective, wealth may potentially lead to both directions i.e. to spiritual ascendance as well as to distraction of mind and soul (Al-Shaybani, 2015; Aydin, 2017).

There is a noted scarcity of literature on Islamic approach towards wealth and its management from an Islamic jurisprudential perspective. This study aims at addressing this lacuna in the available literature on wealth and its management from

M. Abdullah (✉)
Islamic Economics, Markfield Institute of Higher Education (MIHE), Markfield, Leicestershire, United Kingdom
e-mail: nadwi.ab@gmail.com

T. Azid et al. (eds.), *Wealth Management and Investment in Islamic Settings*,
https://doi.org/10.1007/978-981-19-3686-9_3

an Islamic perspective. The chapter attempts to critically analyze the Islamic position towards amassing wealth, followed by delineating its virtues and vices with the lens of Islamic theology and classical jurisprudential discourse. The resultant discussion leads to the analysis of Islamic framework of wealth management.

3.1 Wealth Within Islamic Purview

The Islamic philosophy of wealth is composed of several elements covering the definition, classification, treatment and utilization of wealth in a comprehensive manner (Farooq, 2013; Abdul-Rasul, 1980). In the classical Islamic literature, several aspects of wealth find manifest and scholarly exposition (Al-Shaybani, 2015). In the primary and secondary sources of *Shari'ah*, generally the term '*Maal*' (plural; *Amwal*) has been frequently used to refer wealth (al-Qur'an, 2:177; 18:46; 89:20). In the *Qur'anic* usage, another common term employed to denote wealth is '*Rizq*' which has been described and counted as one of the key blessings of Allah (SWT) (Al-Qur'an, 7:32; 13:26; 16:71). A deliberation on the background and context of a specific *Qur'anic* verse in which these two terms are used elucidates their nature and status in the sight of the Creator (Allah). In Qur'an, the purpose of wealth (*Maal*) has been plainly stated as a couch on which the human life reclines, and the same shall not be given away to a foolish or to an unintelligent as he may waste it (al-Qur'an: 4:5). The Islamic policy on wealth is best discernible through this *Qur'anic* injunction.

The classical Islamic literature is replete with discussion on wealth, its objectives and its treatment, though not in a systematically organized manner (Al-Ghazali, 2004; Al-Shaybani, 2015). The Islamic paradigm of wealth creation, its preservation, modes of its utilization along with the mechanism of its growth and progression is comprehensively covered in the Islamic literature (Salim et al., 2016; Retno, 2015). From a *Shari'ah* perspective, wealth needs to be created by proper utilisation of God-given resources in line with the prescription of the primary sources of *Shari'ah*[1] (Salim et al., 2016). Within the Islamic scheme of material well-being, there is an exhortation to earn and generate wealth, albeit, through *Shari'ah*-compliant means, mechanism and modes (Ahmed, 2013). The *Qura'nic* verse "for a human being is what he endeavors for" (al-Qur'an: 53/39) provides the key Islamic principle on how *Shari'ah* views making efforts towards earning and attaining a dignified life. There is hardly any reservation within the classical Islamic discourse on the merit of striving and putting efforts to obtain affluence and wealth. *Al-Qur'an* not only prescribes deployment of capabilities in the pursuit of earning, but it makes it a virtue meriting reward for it in Hereafter. On the one hand, the *Qura'nic* command "and strive to search for Allah's bounty" (*al-Qur'an*: 62:10) endorses the merit of striving for affluence; on the other, its instruction to "solicit Allah for His bounty" (al-Qur'an: 4:32) explains the value of supplication (*Dua*) in this regard. The *Shari'ah*

[1] Shariah refers to the Islamic rules, principles, norms and law.

injunctions on exploring the scope of bounties from Allah (SWT[2]) reveal the Islamic vision of employing one's capabilities to acquire wealth and affluence in order to enjoy them (Zaman, 1991).

In general, the Islamic framework of earning and generating wealth covers three key areas i.e. the subject matter to be earned, the adopted process and mechanism of earning and the behavioral aspects of the performer of the activities. *Shari'ah* prescribes a set of guidelines treating each of these areas (Usmani, 2008). To qualify for a *Shari'ah*-compliant earning, the performer is required to ensure that his/her activities are in compliance with the *Shari'ah* ethos, values and principles (AAOIFI, 2015).

Shari'ah considers a business activity impermissible if its subject matter is *Shari'ah* non-compliant (Sanusi & Rosly, 2008). In the list of *Shari'ah* non-compliant subject matters include, for example, *Shari'ah*-prohibited items such as pork, alcohol, tobacco and their derivatives (SCM, 2017). In transactional activities, involving in gambling, interest-based and exploitative transactions etc. are prohibited under *Shari'ah* norms (AAOIFI, 2015). The *Shari'ah*-impermissibility of involving in any such *Shari'ah* non-compliant business or transaction is universal (Usmani, 2008).

The other Islamic criteria dictate that the process and mechanism of a transactional activity needs to qualify for *Shari'ah*-compliance. The process and mechanism of a business activity is required to avoid *Shari'ah* prohibited elements such as interest (*Riba*), gambling (*Maysir*) and any ambiguity leading to dispute (*Gharar*) (Ayub, 2007; Usmani, 2008). By stipulating this criteria, *Shariah* aims at eliminating the potential means of exploitation in business dealings. The end-objective of this is to bring ease and long-term benefits to all while removing the hardship from the society (Habib, 2018).

3.2 Wealth and Spirituality: A *Shari'ah* Perspective

Shari'ah has laid a set of guidelines on creation of wealth as well as it has put forth a framework of its utilisation and preservation. Within the classical Islamic scholarship, there are junctures of dispute on the treatment of wealth. In general, the point of dispute is premised on different approaches and perspectives of scholars to interpret the texts and contexts of Islamic injunctions on wealth. Also, the divergence of opinions is caused by the Islamic jurisprudential versus Islamic mystical approaches of the interpreters towards wealth (Al-Ghazali, 2004; Al-Shaybani, 2015). In other words, the differences of interpretations arise based on whether *Shari'ah* injunctions on wealth and its treatment are construed in a formal or in a mystical way. While on one hand, wealth has been considered one of the worldly traps through which one is diverted from the purpose of life; on the other, by the proper usage of wealth, one is

---

[2] The abbreviation SWT denotes *Subhanahu wa Ta'ala* (The one Who is pure of shortcomings and is great).

promised to earn spiritual rewards in the Hereafter (Al-Ghazali, 2004; Al-Shaybani, 2015).

The classical Islamic scholarship appears to be caught in a dilemma so far as the matter of wealth along with its positional complexities is concerned in the life of a spiritually-charged ideal believer. While defining its exact position in helping or harming the spiritual excellence and ascendency, the divided opinions and voices of scholars propel the skepticism on the status of wealth in *Shar'iah*. The jurisprudential discussion on the pros and cons of wealth dragged to the extent that there are established points of dispute on the supremacy of material affluence over the state of poverty and paucity (Sabra, 2000). In this discussion, the sources of analogy and references remain almost the same, yet with differing inferences and interpretations.

To demystify the Islamic position on wealth and its treatment particularly with reference to attaining piety, there is a fine show of methodological variations among the Islamic scholars. As per the varying methodologies which served as tools to reach certain conclusion, the opinions of the scholars differed diametrically on *Shari'ah*-sanctity of generating material wealth and its accumulation. From the scholastic position of completely rejecting the idea of accumulating wealth, to the contentions of acquiring it to enjoy the bounties of Allah and for being able to financially contribute in righteous causes, there are piles of substantiating evidences to support the two claims (Al-Ghazali, 2004; Al-Shaybani, 2015).

Alongside the contentions of poverty alleviation and its virtues in the Islamic literature, there are arguments for the support and virtues of poverty adoption as well (Sabra, 2000). The nature of a multi-dimensional argumentation within the classical Islamic scholarship on the virtues and vices of wealth blurs the line of a clear-cut Islamic position on the topic. Possibly, there may be a fine-line which can help draw the superiority of one contention over the other, however, the line of demarcation between the two perspectives is dimly palpable in the mainstream Islamic literature. Whereas, the Islamic literature seems to prompt for seeking refuge of Allah from paucity and indigence, the practices of early Islamic society remain inconsistent with this supplication. As, at times a self-adopted lifestyle of destitution appears to be appreciated by early Islamic societies as a mark of spirituality, sagacity as well as a sign of piety and God-consciousness (Sabra, 2000).

Scholars such as al-Ghazali (d. 526) intensely argued for the merit and virtues of a complete abstinence from the worldly privileges, opulence or material wealth. The premises of argument for al-Ghazali are directly drawn from the Prophetic traditions. That the Prophet Muhammad (PBUH) was offered a choice between securing affluence or continuing with poverty, and he chose to remain from amongst the poor is clearly established within the Islamic traditions (Al-Ghazali, 2004). Thus, the practice of the Prophet (PBUH) in opting poverty over affluence is, according to Al-Ghazali (2004), indicative of the ideal Islamic position towards acquiring affluence or poverty. Based on the analysis of the prophetic traditions and the practices of the companions of the prophet (PBUH), Al-Ghazali (2004) sketched a pro-poverty and abstinence-leaning Islamic paradigm. The analytical discussion by al-Ghazali on the superiority of poverty versus affluence is vividly illustrative of his position on the topic. Not only that scholars such as al-Ghazali support the argument that poverty is nearer to Godliness, but they consider affluence and wealth counter to spiritual excellence (Sabra, 2000).

Dipping deep into the classical Islamic jurisprudential literature on the supremacy of poverty versus affluence reveals that the state and status of poverty has been sub-categorised into many forms, each having its own distinctive merit. Al-Ghazali (2004), for example, in his magnum opus namely *Ihya Uloom al-Din* classifies poverty into five key categories. According to Al-Ghazali (2004), poverty which has been referred as *'al-Faqr'* can be either caused by a choice or be fuelled by compulsion. While the state of poverty adopted by choice is sourced from the concept of *Zuhd*, a poverty by compulsion falls under the term *Iztirar*. Thus, one who abstains from wealth and affluence by choice is called *al-Faqir al-Zahid*, whereas the one who is poor by compulsion is termed as *al-Faqir al-Muztar*. For Al-Ghazali (2004: 258), *Faqr* is a result of worldly privileges being out of reach of one, while *Zuhd* refers to abstinence from the worldly privileges by choice. As per Al-Ghazali (2004), the two types of poor (*Faqir*) i.e. *al-Faqir al-Zahid* and *al-Faqir al-Muztar* have different status in view of *Shariah*.

With reference to *Maal* (wealth) and *Faqr* (poverty), Al-Ghazali (2004: 259–60) categorises the situation and their different status in *Shariah* into *Zuhd*, *Riza*, *Qana'at*, *Iztirar* and *Istigna'a*. While *Zuhd*—the one who adopts it, is called *Zahid*- is to detest and abhor wealth and worldly privileges for the fear of being engrossed in the same, *Riza*—the one who adopts it, is called *Razi*—holds back one from aspiring for wealth but it does not push to abhor it. However, a *Razi* prefers not to be engaged in worldly affluence and growth. Similarly, the concept of *Qana'at*—the one who adopts it, is called *Qane'*—propels one to prefer privileges and being blessed with wealth but it does not inspire the *Qane'* to strive and struggle to obtain it. Comparatively, *Iztirar*—the one who suffers from it is called *Muztar*—entails lack of basic necessities. Finally, *Istigna'a*—the one who enjoys this is called *Mustaghni*—drives one to treat wealth and affluence as a non issue. To explain this state, Al-Ghazali (2004) cites the story of Aisha (the beloved wife of the Prophet), whereby she received 1000 dirham as a gift and on the same day she distributed it in charity. On this, her maid solicited that you may have withheld at least one dirham for our food today. Aisha (R.A.) replied, oh you should have reminded me this a little earlier. By referring to this story of Aisha (R.A.), Al-Ghazali (2004) argues that since Aisha (R.A.) was in the state of *Istighna*, she was unaffected by the fact whether she retained a required sum of money to fulfill her own basic necessities or not.

In terms of determining the spiritual status of these states, Al-Ghazali (2004) considers *Zuhd* as being superior to other forms of *Faqr* (poverty). Nevertheless, if *Iztirar* is intermingled with *Zuhd*, it assumes a higher rank compared to all other states of poverty. Notwithstanding this, the highest rank of excellence that one can achieve in this context, as per Al-Ghazali (2004), lies in the state of *Istighna*, as being a *Mustaghni* one reaches at a higher status than being bothered about wealth, affluence or privileges of this worldly life. In other words, wealth and affluence from the perspective of *Istighna* constitutes one of the many blessings of Allah (SWT), and for a *Mustaghni* it does not matter whether it is in his hands or in the hand of others.

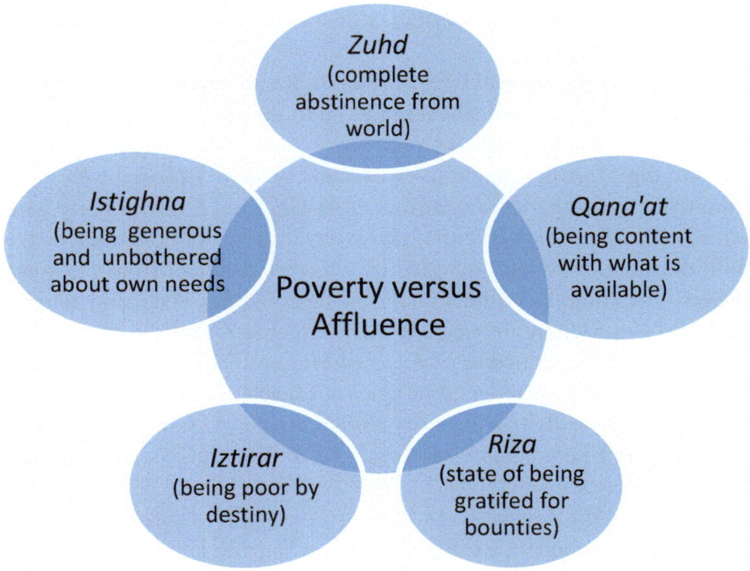

Fig. 3.1 Different States of Wealth. *Source* Al-Ghazali, (2004)

The Fig. 3.1 contains different states and approaches towards wealth as postulated by Al-Ghazali (2004);

In contrast to the argument of al-Ghazali in favor of poverty and its excellence over affluence, a majority of the mainstream Islamic scholarship adopts a somewhat different approach on the issue. The key point of departure for the mainstream scholarship, compared to the protagonist of the pro-poverty narrative, lies in disputing the basis of analogy to prove supremacy of poverty over affluence (Al-Shaybani, 2015). The majority approach postulates that it is not the state and condition of an individual which defines the spiritual supremacy or excellence, rather it is the composite of intention, behavior, actions and performance of the individual which determines the level of spirituality and the moral highness in *Shari'ah* (Al-Shaybani, 2015). As per the supporters of this approach, a poverty-stricken individual who is engaged in disobedience of Allah cannot be better than an obedient wealthy and rich person (Al-Shaybani, 2015). That the rich in this example is far better placed in the sight of *Shari'ah* is agreed by all. Similarly, in comparison to an obedient poor whose forms of worship and ladder of spirituality is restricted only to physical *Ibadat* (devotion), a generous and obedient wealthy who performs the physical *Ibadat* as well as spends his wealth in the way of Allah (SWT) is at a higher position for enjoying more than one way of doing good.

To substantiate this approach, it is argued that the Prophetic model on wealth is that he neither abhorred wealth nor did he accumulate or amassed it. Rather, he preferred to distribute and dispense whatever he received among the needy and deserving entities (Al-Shaybani, 2015). The key point is that wealth in itself is not something to be despised of per se, as had this been the case, the Prophet (PBUH) might have not encouraged to earn nor did he distribute the same among his companions from the booty and other gifts. Rather, he might have preferred to trash all the wealth. As, if the wealth is despised for the giver, it must be loathsome for the taker as well. Furthermore, had the state of poverty been desired in *Shari'ah,* the Prophet (PBUH) had never sought refuge of Allah (SWT) from poverty (Ahmad, 1991). However, those who hold the notion that the state of poverty is desirable in *Shariah* contend that the Prophet (PBUH) did seek refuge from the abject poverty, however, he as well supplicated to be among the poor and have-nots in this world and in Hereafter, which proves the superiority of poor over the affluent (Al-Ghazali, 2004).

Among the basis of argument for the anti-affluence group of scholars include the Prophetic traditions in which wealth and worldly privileges have been counted in a negative sense and are condemned by the Prophet (PBUH) as a distracter or a barrier between the believer and his Creator (Al-Shaybani, 2015). However, in practice, the lives of the rich and wealthy companions such as Othman (R.A), Abdul-Rahman Ibn al-Awf (R.A) as well as Anas Bin Malik (R.A) etc. are seemingly pitched in contrast to the position adopted by the pro-poverty group of scholars. It is argued that neither the companion Abdul Rahman Ibn al-Awf (R.A.) nor did the Othman al-Ghani (R.A.) abandoned their wealth, which indicates that there is no harm in holding wealth per se. In contrast, the Prophetic *Hadith* that there is no scope of envy except in two persons; 'a righteous wealthy, and a learned', substantiate the claim of those who argue that wealth per se is not an object of abhorrence in *Shari'ah.* As per this *Hadith*, the Prophet (PBUH) said that do not envy except in two; one whom Allah has granted wealth (*Maal*) and has guided him to spend in His way, and the one who has been blessed with knowledge and he utilizes his knowledge to teach and to do justice (Al-Bukhari, 1999).

In view of the above discussion, a balanced approach towards affluence and poverty can be developed by defining the parameters of the two juristic positions. The balance approach accommodates the two positions without rejecting out-rightly any of them (Ariff, 1988; Chapra, 2008). This is achieved by contextualizing back-grounds of the two approaches. To this effect, it is argued that the concept of *Zuhd* and *Istighna* as described by Al-Ghazali (2004) is possibly applicable at an individual level rather than being generalised. As, the excellence of *Zuhd* cannot be generalized to the society as a whole except by entailing several hindrances in the matters of *Deen* (religion) as well as in proper functioning of the society. If applied indiscriminately to all in the society, the harm of this approach may outweigh its claimed benefits. As, the building-blocks of the society and its different pillars may collapse if the wealth is collectively shunned. Without wealth, not only the practices of *Hajj*, *Zakat*, *Sadaqah* will fall defunct, other support institutions of a Muslim society such as *Masjid*, *Madrasa* etc. will also come to a standstill.

It is argued that wealth is desired so far as its utilization is rightly guided. Rather, wealth is potentially a means to achieve greater piety and spirituality provided it fulfills the *Shari'ah*-prescribed objectives in a proper manner (Kamali, 2017). Thus, once the objectives of wealth is synchronized with the objectives of *Shari'ah*, striving for wealth and planning for its management will automatically qualify for *Shari'ah*-validity and appreciation. The desirability of acquiring wealth and its management in *Shari'ah* is mirrored by the inclusion of wealth preservation among the five key constituents of *Maqasid al-Shari'ah* (the higher objectives of *Shari'ah*) (Abdullah, 2018a, b). To sum it up, having been termed as *Hifz al-Maal* (preservation of wealth) in the classical juristic discussion, the status of wealth becomes crucial in fulfilling the objectives of *Shari'ah* (Abdullah, 2020; Ibrahim et al., 2014). The subsequent section of this chapter delineates the Islamic framework of wealth management by analysing the concept, mechanism, process and structures of the wealth management in a *Shari'ah*-compliant manner.

3.3 An Islamic Framework of Wealth Management

In the classical Islamic literature preservation of wealth appears among the five key higher objectives of *Shari'ah* (Atiyah, 2007). The *Shari'ah* paradigm for preservation of wealth is built on a few key pillars. These constitute either ex-ante or ex-post building-blocks of safeguarding wealth (Kamali, 2017). Among these pillars include wealth creation, its accumulation, its protection, wealth purification and distribution. The concept of preserving wealth is untenable without its pre-existence. Thus, to preserve wealth, it becomes pre-requisite to generate wealth. The foregoing discussion in this chapter so far has focused on the *Shari'ah* approach and paradigm of wealth and its treatment from a mystic versus jurisprudential perspective. This section of the chapter aims at dissecting the fundamentals of wealth preservation along with its key pillars such as creation of wealth, its accumulation and maintaining its *Shari'ah*-complaint status by fulfilling the pertinent *Shari'ah*-prescribed obligations.

The wealth management framework from a *Shari'ah* perspective is composed of several dimensions (SCM, 2017). As a primary requisite, the source of wealth has to be compliant with the tenets and ethos of *Shari'ah* (Ansari, 1991). Generally, wealth is secured either by the action and activity of a person or is sourced from inheritance. *Shari'ah* has set rules and parameters in both the cases to filter out and ensure that the origin of wealth is from a legal and *Shari'ah*-permissible source (Khattak, 2018). Wealth seized through embezzlement, encroachment, usurpation, illegal means or illegitimate sources is sieved and excluded at this stage by application of relevant *Shari'ah* parameters. Under an ideal *Shari'ah* framework of wealth management falls only the wealth which is attained through legitimate sources (MIFC, 2016). In case, there is a mixed source of wealth generation or acquisition, whereby there is a blend of legitimate and illegitimate sources from which the wealth is acquired, the *Shari'ah*-prescribed purification mechanism has to be activated to purify such wealth (Gadhoum, 2017). A plain vanilla solution to purify wealth in such a situation is that any part of the wealth acquired through illegitimate sources is to be identified and eliminated. The treatment of such purification is possible only if there is a clarity on the parts or amounts of the wealth sourced through *Shari'ah* non-compliant means and mechanism.

In the wake of initial purification-exercise of wealth from all non-compliant elements, the residual wealth is considered as qualified for the next step of *Shari'ah* rulings and parameters. At this stage, the growth and increment of wealth in a *Shari'ah*-complaint manner is the primary focus of Islamic wealth management framework (MIFC, 2016). Without planning for growth and increment, there is a high risk of wealth-diminution; something not desirable under the *Shari'ah* paradigm. However, the objective of countering diminution and accomplishing growth in wealth needs to be aligned with the *Shari'ah* ethos and principles (Ariff, 2017). From the prism of *Shari'ah*, wealth in itself cannot be a tool to create further wealth. In other words, *Shari'ah* does not endorse the notion that wealth necessarily begets more wealth (Gadhoum, 2017). Rather, as per the *Shari'ah* framework, wealth is required to be put into an investment or be linked with a real activity; carrying its duly calculated and diligently managed risk (Derigs and Marzban, 2009). The *Shari'ah* paradigm envisages that any investment-related risk can be managed, however, cannot be completely shifted or eliminated (Tahir and Brimble, 2011). Planning and resorting to best strategies to manage wealth for its growth is appreciated in *Shariah* under the conceptual underpinning of the *Qura'nic* term *al-Ihsan* (seeking excellence with diligence) (Abdullah, 2020). The mainstream *Shari'ah* position on wealth is that it needs to be safeguarded from wastage and slippage. Rather, it requires proper management, diligent planning and deployment in avenues where it can grow and benefit different stakeholders (Abdullah, 2018a, b).

For investment and allocation of wealth with the purpose of growth, the principles and parameters of *Shari'ah* need to be complied with (Derigs and Marzban, 2009). In regard to investment in different segments, be it in equity, fixed income instruments, real estate, commodity market or in other avenues, to qualify for *Shari'ah*-compliance merit, all the *Shari'ah*-prohibited elements and mechanism such as involvement in interest, gambling, excessive ambiguity and any form of unfairness or unethical activity must be avoided (Khatkhatay and Nisar, 2007). The fusion of *Shari'ah* spirit in investment decision-making process safeguards against involving in excessively risky or hazardous dealing. Similarly, synthesizing ethos of *Shari'ah* within investment-strategy helps maintain the collective good of the society. The *Shari'ah* ethos dictate that the interest of the society gets precedence over the individual interest if there arise a conflict between the two (Kamali, 2017). Thus, if benefits of an individual is attainable only by sacrificing the interest and common benefit of the society or by harming the collective interest of the society, pursuing such individual interest is rejected by *Shari'ah* (Auda, 2008).

One of the defining features of *Shari'ah*-based wealth management framework, compared to its conventional counterpart, is that it requires purification of the part of wealth which represents a *Shari'ah* non-compliant income (Khatkhatay and Nisar, 2007). For example, an investment in a company which receives a little portion of its income from *Shari'ah* prohibited elements, such investment income must be purified by channeling the *Shari'ah* non-compliant portion to a charity. Not only this, the calculation and treatment of Islamic obligatory charity namely *Zakat* falls within the ambit of an Islamic wealth management scheme (Ayub, 2007). In this way, the concept of purification within the discussion of Islamic wealth management equally applies to two separate notions namely; purification of non-compliant income vis-à-vis Islamic obligatory purification as part of Islamic religious duty. Other than this, the voluntary dispensation and distribution of wealth among the needy and deserving entities is also one of the distinguishing features of Islamic wealth management practices. For this, the Islamic concepts of *Waqf* (Islamic endowment), *Wasiyya* (Islamic will) and *Hibah* (Islamic gift) are frequently employed by many Islamic wealth managers (Labuan, 2019).

There are various existing models of Islamic wealth management in different jurisdictions. For being well-established in *Shari'ah* and vastly flexible, the concept of *Waqf* has been garnering wider popularity and acceptance for the purpose of managing wealth in a *Shari'ah*-compliant manner (Labuan, 2019). *Waqf* exhibits a variety of possibilities and scope for its different characters (Abdullah, 2018a). The key characters of a *Waqf* include a *waqif* (endower), *mutawalli* (trustee), beneficiaries and the objectives of *Waqf*. For instance, a deed of *Waqf* can be made by an individual as well as by an institution (Abdullah, 2019). The subject matter of a *Waqf* may include real estate (including commercial, non-commercial and residential buildings), agricultural lands, cash, stocks, *Sukuk*, *Waqf* -share (certificate) and any other *Shari'ah*-compliant non-perishable property/valuable (Abdullah, 2018a). Similarly, the role of the *Mutawalli* can be played by the waqif himself or by any other qualified entity. Also, for the potential beneficiaries of a *Waqf,* there is a wider scope. For instance, the benefits of a *Waqf* can be allocated for the *Waqif*, his/her progeny, relatives, friends alongside allocating for poor, pauper and needy. Similarly, among the *Waqf* beneficiaries may include a rich, wealthy, affluent as well as any individual of a contrary financial background. In a nutshell, the *Shari'ah*-based paradigm of wealth management constitutes a comprehensive and multi-dimensional framework consisting of a blend of individual, societal as well as spiritual benefits (Khaleel & Abdullah, 2016).

3.4 Conclusion and Recommendations

This chapter attempted to provide a comprehensive overview of Islamic approach on wealth and its treatment within the *Shari'ah* paradigm. The chapter discussed the *Shari'ah* guidelines on earning and managing wealth. By delineating the process, mechanism and the subject matter of earning, it endeavored to draw *Shari'ah* parameters and criteria for wealth creation. The points of discussion included how wealth is generated in *Shari'ah*-compliant manner and the religious duties of individuals in relation to wealth. The chapter deliberated the Islamic jurisprudential vis-à-vis mystic approaches of discussion on wealth and its treatment for accomplishing spiritual richness versus material well-being.

The chapter found that within the classical Islamic literature there is neither unanimity of opinion nor a standard Islamic perspective on the status of wealth and its treatment in *Shari'ah.* To deduce a balanced approach on wealth and its treatment in *Shari'ah,* one needs to juxtapose the arguments and contentions of different approaches adopted by Islamic jurists versus Islamic mystics. Generally, the evidences supplied by the two categories of scholars are somehow similar in nature 'albeit, with their different interpretations. Capturing the contentions of one side along with its evidences in isolation of other side's arguments may blur the line of understanding for a lay man. As a balanced view, this chapter found that wealth and affluence in itself is neither desired nor is abhorred in *Shari'ah*, rather the intention, actions and performance of a wealthy or a poor is the true parameter to judge whether wealth is desired or loathsome in view of *Shari'ah*. This conclusion helps dispel the doubt over the state and status of wealthy vis-à-vis poor in *Shari'ah*. As the chapter argued that neither wealth and affluence nor poverty and abstinence per se is a factor for spiritual ascendance or reward, it recommends that the focus should be accorded to the treatment of an individual and his actions in different situations to judge his/her moral and spiritual status.

This study found that wealth is among the key blessings of Allah which has been frequently referred in the primary sources of *Shari'ah* as one of the bounties for the mankind. As per the Islamic literature, earning, accumulating and preserving wealth is among the key objectives of *Shari'ah*. This study argues that the wealth-related objective of *Shari'ah* can be fulfilled only if the wealth creation, its usage, preservation and its circulation is carried out in the manner as prescribed by *Shari'ah* itself. Thus, it is contended that the framework of Islamic wealth management requires that the wealth creation, its accumulation, allocation, purification, and distribution must be synchronized with the tenets and ethos of *Shari'ah*. In a nutshell, for being a multidimensional discipline, the *Shari'ah*-based wealth management framework covers a comprehensively wide spectrum of areas including the wealth-related consideration for the subject individual, his/her progeny, the society, poor and other deserving entities. Finally, the scope and objective of an Islamic wealth management paradigm is not restricted only to fulfilling the mundane aspirations of this world for the subject individual but ideally it includes the preservation of reward and excellence for him/her in Hereafter as well.

References

AAOIFI. (2015). *Shari'ah Standards for Islamic Financial Institutions*. Bahrain: Accounting and Auditing Organisation for Islamic Financial Institution.

Abdullah, M. (2015). a new framework of corporate governance of *Waqf*: A preliminary proposal. *Islam and Civilisational Renewal, 6*(3), 353–370.

Abdullah, M. (2018a). Waqf, sustainable development goals (SDGs) and Maqasid al-Shariah. *International Journal of Social Economics, 45*(1), 158–172.

Abdullah, M. (2018a). Evolution in *Waqf* jurisprudence and Islamic financial innovation. *Journal of Islamic Monetary Economics and Finance, 1*(4), 161–182.

Abdullah, M. (2019). *Waqf* and trust: The nature, structures and socio-economic impacts. *Journal of Islamic Accounting and Business Research, 10*(4), 512–527.

Abdullah, M. (2020). Waqf, social responsibility and real economy. In B. Saiti & A. Sarea (Eds.), *Challenges and Impacts of Religious Endowments on Global Economics and Finance* (pp. 23–36). USA: IGI Global.

Abdul-Rasul, A. (1980). *Al-Mabadi' al-Iqtisadiyyah Fi Al-Islam*. Cairo: Dar Al-Fikr Al-Arabi.
Ahmad, Z. (1991). *Islam, Poverty and Income Distribution*, Leicester, UK: The Islamic Foundation.
Ahmed, K. (2013). *Contemporary Islamic finance: Innovations*. London: Wiley.
Al-Bukhari, al- Sahih. (1999). *Kitab al-Ilm'*. In A. Salih (Ed.), *Mawsuah al-Hadith al-Sharif.* Riyadh: Darussalam.
Al-Ghazali, A. H. (2004). *Ihya Uloom al-Deen (Kitab al-Faqr wa al-Zuhd)* (Vol. 4. pp. 259–330). Cairo: Dar al-Afaq.
Al-Nabhani. (2004). *al-Nezam al-Eqtisadi Fi Islam*. Beirut: Dar Al ummah.
Ansari, M. (1991). Methodological foundations of Islam as an ethico economic paradigm. *Humanomics, 7*(3), 40–62.
Al-Shaybani, M. H. (2015). *al-Kasb,* Abu Dhabi, Abu Dhabi: Tourism and Cultural Authority.
Ariff, M. (1988). Comments on M.A. Mannan's "The economics of poverty in Islam with special reference to muslim countries." In M. Iqbal (Ed.), *Distributive Justice and Need Fulfilment in an Islamic Economy* (pp. 336–341). Islamabad, Pakistan: International Institute of Islamic Economics.
Ariff, M. (2017). Wealth management, its definition, purpose, structure. In M. Ariff & S. Mohamad (Eds.), *Islamic Wealth Management: Theory and Practice* (pp. 12–24). Gloucester: Edward Elgar.
Ariff, M., & Mohamad, S. (2017). Wealth as understood in economics and finance. In M. Ariff, & S. Mohamad, (Eds.), *Islamic Wealth Management: Theory and Practice* (pp. 3–11). Gloucester: Edward Elgar.
Atiyah, J. (2007). *Towards realization of the higher intents of Islamic law: Maqasid Al-Shariah: A functional approach*. London: The International Institute of Islamic Thought.
Auda, J. (2008). *Maqasid al-Shariah as philosophy of Islamic law: A systems approach*. London: The International Institute of Islamic Thought.
Aydin, N. (2017). Spirituality and subjective wellbeing living a fulfilled life without falling into the trap of consumer culture. *Humanomics, 33*(3), 300–304.
Ayub, M. (2007). *Understanding Islamic Finance*. West Sussex: John Wiley & Sons, Ltd.
Chapra, M. U. (2008). *The Islamic vision of development in the light of the Maqasid Al-Shari'ah*. Jeddah, Saudi Arabia: Islamic Research and Training Institute, Islamic Development Bank.
Derigs, U., & Marzban, M. (2009). New strategies and a new paradigm for *Shariah* compliant portfolio optimization. *Journal of Banking & Finance, 33*(6), 1166–1176.
Farooq, M. (2013). Islamic wealth management and some unconventional thoughts. *LIBFC Bi-Annual Report, 1*(1), 45–52.
Gadhoum, M. (2017). Wealth from the *Shariah* perspective. In M. Ariff & S. Mohamad (Eds.), *Wealth Management: Theory and Practice* (pp. 13–24). Gloucester: Edward Elgar.
Habib, F. (2018). *Fundamentals of Islamic finance and banking*. London: Wiley.
Hasan, S. (2015). *Human Security and Philanthropy: Islamic perspective and Muslim Majority Country Practices*. New York: Springer.
Ibrahim, A., Eltrash, J., & Farooq, O. (2014). Hoarding versus circulation of wealth from the perspective of Maqasid Al-Shari'ah. *International Journal of Islamic and Middle Eastern Finance and Management, 7*(1), 6–21.
Khaleel, F., & Abdullah, M. (2016). *Waqf* (Islamic endowment), human capital and humanitarian aid. *Interdisciplinary Journal of Economics and Business Law, 5*(2), 36–52.
Kamali, H. (2017). The Shari'ah purpose of wealth preservation in contracts and transaction. *Islam and Civilizational Renewal, 8*(2), 153–175.
Khatkhatay, M., & Nisar, S. (2007). *Shariah*-compliant equity investment: an assessment of current screening norms. *Islamic Economic Studies, 15*(1), 48–76.
Khattak, M. (2018). Protection and distribution of wealth, islamic commercial and financial transactions: A Maqasid Al-Shariah perspective. *European Journal of Islamic Finance, 10*, 1–8.
Labuan, IBFC. (2019). *Meeting the Unique Needs in Islamic Wealth Management*. Retrieved December 27, 2019, from https://www.labuanibfc.com/resource-centre/featured-articles/meeting-the-unique-needs-in-islamic-wealth-management.

Lev, Y. (2005) *Charity, Endowments and Charitable Institutions in Medieval Islam*, USA: University Press of Florida.
MIFC. (2016). *Islamic Wealth Management: Growing Stronger Globally*, Kuala Lumpur, Malaysia.
Retno, W. (2015). *Redistribution Adjusts Efficiency In Economy; Islamic Paradigm*. Retrieved December 25, 2019, from https://mpra.ub.uni-muenchen.de/67809/. MPRA Paper No. 67809.
Sabra, A. (2000) *Poverty and Charity in Medieval Islam: Mumluk Egypt. 1250–1517*. Cambridge: Cambridge University Press.
Salim, R., Hossain, R., & Mawali, N. (2016). Distribution of wealth and resources in Islam: Restoring social justice, peace and prosperity. *International Journal of Economic Research, 13*(2), 571–586.
Sanusi, M., & Rosly, S.A. (2008). *Fiqh Muamalat For Islamic Financial Practitioners*, unpublished, International Islamic University Malaysia, Kuala Lumpur.
SCM. (2017). *Islamic Fund and Wealth Management: Blueprint*, Securities Commission Malaysia, Kuala Lumpur, Malaysia.
Siddiqui, N. M. (1991) The role of the voluntary sector in Islam. In M. Ariff (Ed.), *The Islamic Voluntary Sector in Southeast Asia*. Singapore: Institute of Southeast Asian Studies.
Singer, A. (2008). *Charity in Islamic societies*. Cambridge: Cambridge University Press.
Tahir, I., & Brimble, M. (2011). Islamic investment behaviour. *International Journal of Islamic and Middle Eastern Finance and Management, 4*(2), 116–130.
Usmani, M. T. (2008). *An Introduction to Islamic Finance*. Karachi: Maktaba Ma'arifu Quran.
Zaman, H. S. M. (1991). *Economic Functions of an Islamic State: The Early Experience*. Leicestershire: The Islamic Foundation.

Mohammad Abdullah, Ph.D. is an expert of Islamic Sciences, Islamic Jurisprudence and Islamic finance. Abdullah is a well-trained and highly experienced *Shari'ah* Scholar, providing *Shari'ah* consultancy and advisory services to various Islamic financial institutions in Europe, South America and the UAE. He has produced research papers and Book chapters on the comparative study of *Waqf* and English trust, *Shari'ah* governance, Islamic finance and development studies. Abdullah holds a Bachelor degree in *Shari'ah* Sciences from Darul Uloom Nadwatul Ulama, Lucknow, India; M.A. in Islamic Banking, Finance and Management from the Markfield Institute of Higher Education, UK, and Ph.D. from University of Gloucestershire (UK). Abdullah is also a Certified *Shari'ah* Advisor and Auditor (CSAA) by the AAOIFI. Abdullah is a frequent speaker at International Conferences, and he has presented papers on Islamic banking and finance in different countries including Germany, Norway, Italy, Ireland, Scotland, UK, Trinidad & Tobago, Indonesia, Malaysia, India, Turkey and Dubai.

Chapter 4
Islamic Investment-Cum-Wealth Management: Politics, Warfare and Welfare

Muhammad Iqbal Anjum

In Islamic *Sharii'ah*, wealth—called *Mal* (*Amwaal* pl.ural of *Mal*) as well as *Al-mal Ma'ruf* (thing that is customarily well-known as wealth)—is defined as any nonhuman thing which is created for the interest and benefit of humanity to which humans are instinctively inclined and attracted and is materially and spiritually benficial/valuable/preservable for the time of necessity/possessable/investable/transactable by free will/subjectable to rules of possession/expenditure/regulation/restriction/prohibition (Islam, 1999). Therefore, *Mal*/wealth includes tangible and non tangible religious/personal/physical/ intellectual/economic/monetary/financial/material/environmental/universal/political/social/ strategic resources, assets and institutions. Here, it is pertinent to highlight that in the Islamic literature on wealth, the terms *Al-Mal*, *Qawwaam*, *Zari'ah* (mean), *Mata'alRizq* (sustenance), *Khair* (welfare, wealth and property), and *Fadl* (wellbeing/fortune) have been used interchangably [(Al-Fasi, 1981 (1402AH)].

Islam legally confers, defends/protects and promotes Muslims' inviolable rights of acquiring defending, protecting and increasing *Mal*/Wealth/property according to a Saying of the Holy Prophet Muhammad (pbuh): "*Kullu al-Muslim 'ala al-Muslim haramun damuhu wa maluhu wa 'irduhu*"—Muslims' blood, property and dignity are protected against each other. In this context, the Holy Prophet Muhammad (pbuh) said in his last sermon[1]:

> O People, just as you regard this month, this day, this city as Sacred, so regard the life and property of every Muslim as a sacred trust. Return the goods entrusted to you to their rightful owners. Hurt no one so that no one may hurt you. Remember that you will indeed meet your Lord, and that He will indeed reckon your deeds. Allah has forbidden you to take usury

[1] *The Arab News* 11 October 2013, The last sermon of the Holy Prophet Muhammad (*pbuh*)" Available from https://www.arabnews.com/news/467364 (Viewed 4 February 2021).

M. Iqbal Anjum (✉)
Assistant Professor of Economics, Internaional Institute of Islamic Economics, International Islamic University Islamabad, Islamabad, Pakistan
e-mail: miqbalanjum@iiu.edu.pk

T. Azid et al. (eds.), *Wealth Management and Investment in Islamic Settings*,
https://doi.org/10.1007/978-981-19-3686-9_4

(interest), therefore all interest obligation shall henceforth be waived. Your capital, however, is yours to keep. You will neither inflict nor suffer any inequity. Allah has judged that there shall be no interest and that all the interest due to Abbas ibn Abd Al-Muttalib (Prophet's uncle) shall henceforth be waived O people, listen to me in earnest, worship Allah, say your five daily prayers (Salah), fast during the month of Ramadan, and give your wealth in *Zakaat*. Perform *Hajj* if you can afford to.

All mankind is from Adam and Eve, an Arab has no superiority over a non-Arab nor a non-Arab has any superiority over an Arab; also a white has no superiority over black nor a black has any superiority over white except by piety (taqwa) and good action. Learn that every Muslim is a brother to every Muslim and that the Muslims constitute one brotherhood. Nothing shall be legitimate to a Muslim which belongs to a fellow Muslim unless it was given freely and willingly. Do not, therefore, do injustice to yourselves.[2]

While granting the ownership rights to humans as a matter of *Amaanah*—trust—Allah (*swt*) conditioned, moderated and balanced the the owners' behavior as well as the patterns of exercise of their ownership rights (Saud, 1989). For precluding the concentration of wealth among few wealthy people and for ensuring wider circulation of wealth among all humans in the society, Allah (*swt*) declared painful punishment for miserly humans involved in the practices of accumulating wealth in the forms of gold as well as silver and not spending their wealth in the way of Allah (*swt*).[3]

This is how universal teachings of Islam—a religion of peace—have institutionalized an ideal socio-economic environment of perfect peace, harmony and welfare-based interpersonal and international relations and, thereby, precluded the possiblities of unjust interpersonal violent conflicts and international warfare over wealth.

Against the background of both the long-term process of either weakening or elimination of the numerous Islamic institutions[4] after the earlier Golden Age of Islam (especially due to the West's dominance over the Islamic world as well as the consequent partial secularization of the Muslim societies of the Islamic world) and the recently launched processes of revival and reforms of the Muslim societies of the contemporary Islamic world, it is highly desirable for the current Muslim societies to accomplish their Islamically sustainable development-oriented processes of Islamic wealth's management-cum-investment in the possible three distinct stages of the development of Islamic institutions in the current Islamic world as explained in the next section.

---

[2] ibid.

[3] (See Qur'an Chapter *Al-Tauba*, 34–35).

[4] For example, the Islamic caliphate, Islamic courts, *al-Hisbah*—Islamic ombudsman—, Islamic society, Islamic police, Islamic entrepreneurships/proprietorships, Islamic financial/industrial/agricultural/business partnerships (*al-Mushariksaat* and al Mudarabah), *Hima* (Islamic enclosures for protecting public interests – *al-Masaaleh al-Aa'mmah*) individual a Islamic markets, Baitul Mal, *Waqf*, public ownership of the objects of common ownership such as lakes/pastures/rivers/oceans and the Islamic practices of the Islamic values such as justice, benevolence, trustworthiness, honesty, integrity, transparency of transactions, moderate freedom balanced by the Islamic sense of responsibility and the accountability of economic agents and implementation of social/economic/financial/political/strategic contracts in letter and spirit and protection of the Islamic rights of all economic agents, animals and natural environment.

4.1 Islamic Institutional Framework and Islamic Principles of Wealth Management-Cum-Investment

In the universal Islamic economy, generally the Islamically environmentally sustainable management, investment, production, and distribution of the rightful *Halaal* wealth will be accomplished in the perfectly cooperative-cum-competitive market, and discrimination-free and environment-friendly Islamic macroeconomic-cum-microeconomic institutional framework that is based on al-*Maqasid* al-*Shari'ah* and consists of private sector, public sector, voluntary sector, and natural/environmental sector, which constructively interact as well as function by applying/implementing the following Islamic principles:

I. Allah (*swt*) is the creator of the universe including mankind and man/woman is accountable to Him (*swt*) for all of his/her actions (Saud, 1989)
II. Welfare for all creatures [(Naqvi, 2003), (Chapra, 2000)]
III. Reward/punishment is in this world and life hereafter
IV. *La Darar Wa La Diraar* (neither harming himself/herself nor inflicting harm on others) (Saud, 1989)
V. *Amr Bil Ma'roof Wa Nahi Anil Mukar* (enjoining good and forbidding bad)
VI. Prohibition of injustice [(Islahi, 1996), (Naqvi, 2003)]
VII. Enforcement, protection and exercise of the Islamically acknowledged ownership rights
VIII. Implementation of the law of inheritance, imposition of *Zakat* as well as *Ushr* and the establishment of interest free *Halal* Islamic economy

In the institutional framework of this setting, Islam legally confers, and promotes Muslims' inviolable rights of acquiring defending, protecting and increasing *Mal* according to a Saying of the Holy Prophet Muhammad (*pbuh*), "*Kullu al-Muslim 'ala al-Muslim haramun damuhu wa maluhu wa 'irduhu*"—Muslims' blood, property and dignity are protected against each other." The set of the prime progressive Islamic institutional vehicles of the balanced growth in the Islamic universal wealth include purification-cum-growth (*Tazkiyah*)-oriented Islamic education and training of economic agents, Islamic entrepreneurships, Islamic partnerships—*Musharikah, Mudharabah*, Islamic corporations, *Baitul-Mal* and the Islamic banking system as the prime Islamic vehicles of the sustainable wealth management-cum-investment, production and distribution of the rightful *Halaal* Islamic wealth management on part of individuals, business firms, public corporate firms, and the Islamic state (Mannan and Ahmad, 1996).

Following is a menu of the potential Islamic instruments of Halaal Islamic financial instruments in the framework of the potential Islamic capital markets:

I. Equity-based instruments—stocks—of the public sector companies for open market operations (Chapra, 1996)
II. State Certificates issued by the Islamic state to get *al-Qardh al-Hassan* (Ansari, 1996)

III. Government *Mudarabah* Shares and Government Partnership Shares (Siddiqi, 1969)
IV. Central Deposit Certificates, Central Lending Certificates, Specific Investment Certificates, General Investment, Certificates, Profit-Sharing Certificates (al-Jarhi, 1981)
V. *Waqf* Certificates and *Waqf Qardh (Hassan)* Certificates (Sadeq, 2005)
VI. Profit Loss Sharing Securities for open market operations (Khan, 2002)

For ensuring the protection of interests of all economic agents in the current first stage of low levels of institutional development of an Islamic economy, socially/economically sustainable Islamic wealth's investment-cum-management must be required to be accomplished only and only through the institutional arrangements of Islamic individual entrepreneurships/proprietorships, *Awqaafs*, *Hima*, *Baitul Maal*, and Islamic public treasury's authorities having special responsibilities of management-cum-investment of objects of common ownership such as mineral resources, oceans, pastures etc.

In the second intermediate stage of institutional transition and development, an Islamic wealth's management-cum-investment is primarily required to be predominately accomplished through the institutional arrangements of Islamic individual entrepreneurships/proprietorships, *Awqaafs*, *Hima*, *Baitul-Mal*, and Islamic state's public treasury authorities having special responsibilities of management and investment of objects of common ownership such as mineral resources, oceans, pastures and only a very small part of the Muslim *Ummah*'s Islamic wealth's management-cum-investment is to be allowed to be accomplished by Islamic business/partnerships.

In the final stage of the perfectly developed Islamic institutions, the largest volume of the Muslim *Ummah*'s Islamic wealth's management-cum-investment will be required to be predominately accomplished through the institutional arrangements of Islamic individual entrepreneurships/proprietorships, Islamic business/investment partnerships, *Awqaafs*, *Hima*, *Baitul-Mal*, Islamic state's public treasury authorities having responsibilities of management and investment of objects of common ownership such as mineral resources/oceans/pastures and, the least possible Islamic wealth's investment and management will be required to be accomplished by the Islamic corporations for precluding the possibilities of emergence of extreme income and wealth inequalities and the potential principal-agent problems associated with the corporations in the context of conflict of interests of owners and managers of the corporations (Ragan et al., 1993).

4.2 Islamic Investment and Wealth Management Amidst the Islamic Sustainable Development

The Fig. 4.1 below illustrates the Islamic multidimensional phenomena of sustainable development represented by the continuously expanding circular production

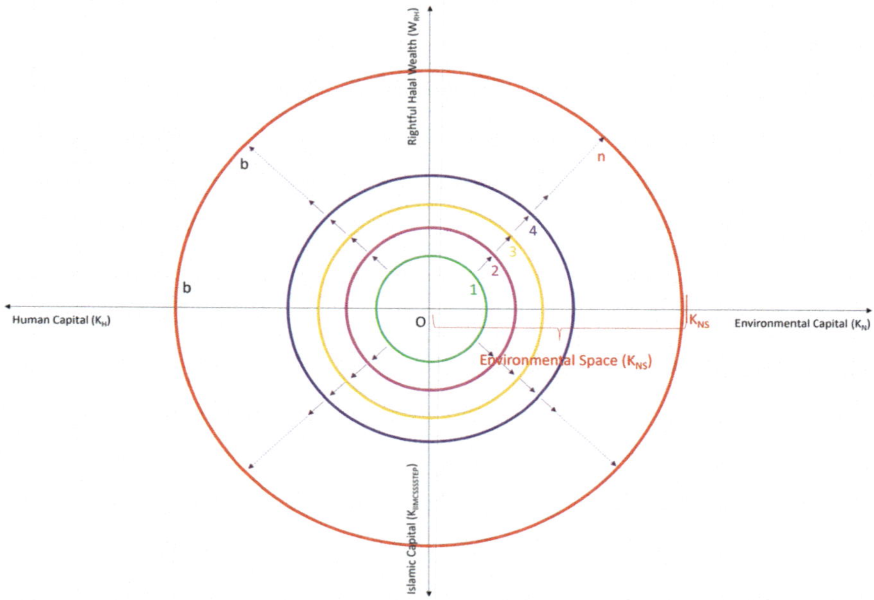

Fig. 4.1 Islamically sustainable human development: Ever expanding environmentally sustainable production possibilities in an Islamic universal economy

possibilities in light of the objectives of Islamic *Shari'ah* (*Maqasid al-Shari'ah*) in the dynamic frameworks of the intertwined Islamic economic system and the Islamic political economy, which are respectively defined by this author as following:

The Islamic Economic System is a functional whole of numerous constructive and cooperative economic partnerships among private, public and voluntary sectors for comprehensively solving genuine economic problems of both the entire humanity in general and the Muslim *Ummah* in particular in light of the progressive universal Islamic principles as well as teachings in the holistic ideal institutional framework of Islam (Anjum, 1995, 1996, 1998, 2006, 2008a, 2008b, 2021).

Islamic political economy is a realm of scientific inquiry into the nature and principles of Islamic universal political, economic, institutional, operational, behavioral, environmental, social, strategic and policy frameworks launched for ensuring peace, independence, freedom, empowerment, self-respect, development and bliss of all humans—the entire humanity—in general and all Muslims—the entire Muslim *Ummah*—in particular in the universal jurisdiction of *Khilafatul Khulafa* (Government of all governments) extending across all universal places, spaces, environments, resources and times (Anjum, 2021).

The Islamic economic system aims at maximizing the following universal Social Welfare (W_S) function of the Muslim *Ummah* in particular and the humanity in general on the basis of Islamic principle of justice and benevolence in case of existence of n individuals' having their respective utilities $U_1, U_2, U_3, \dots U_n$ (Anjum,

1996):

$$\mathrm{W_S} = \mathrm{W_S}\,(\mathrm{U_1}, \mathrm{U_2}, \mathrm{U_3}, \ldots \mathrm{U_n})\, \delta \mathrm{W_S}/\delta \mathrm{U_i} > 0 \ldots \mathrm{i} = 1, 2, 3, \ldots \mathrm{n}$$

W_S can generate Islamic social preferences, and, thereby, the social indifference curves that are used in welfare economics. This Islamic universal social welfare function implies that Islam ensures optimal increases in utilities of all individual members of the universal human society by achieving environmentally and socially equitable *Tazkiayh*-driven (purification-cum-growth-driven) balanced growth in the Islamically Rightful *Halal* Wealth (W_{RH}) in the framework of the following dynamic universal resource function and the corresponding universal natural resource growth function contributed by Anjum (1998):

$$R(t) = A(t)\,\mathrm{F}[H(t), N(t, L(t))] \tag{4.1}$$

$$G_R = G_A + \varepsilon_{R,H} G_H + \varepsilon_{R,N} G_N + \varepsilon_{R,N} \varepsilon_{N,L} G \tag{4.2}$$

The above dynamic universal natural resource function is conditioned by the universal truth that *Allah* (*swt*) has created all the natural resources with their natural potential to experience automatic growth and development overtime by His divine grace in order to continuously and steadily develop all humans to the higher and higher as well as better and better stages of human development as implied by the two *Qura'nic* verses.[5]

The above process of universal resource development in the Islamic system is centered around the development of humans as universizens—humans as universal citizens—via the human capital formation by instituting a continuous process of imparting Islamic education of religious and natural sciences, training and implementing Islamic ethics-based population development policy within the functional institutional framework of objectives of the Islamic system–*Maqasid al-Shari'ah*—which ensures protection-cum-development of Islam as the complete code of life for the humanity, the human life/personality, human intellect, human race/human generations through the Islamic marriage (*Nikah*)–based regeneration of humans and the Islamically rightful *Halal* wealth (*al-Mal*) including universal natural environmental resources. This Islamic model of the intertwined human development and universal natural resource development is premised in the fact that Islam acknowledges the leading role of human capital formation in accelerating the pace of the socially and environmentally sustainable universal development process.

In the above growth Eq. (4.2), $\epsilon_{R,H}$, $\epsilon_{R,N}$ *and* $\epsilon_{N,L}$ are the different elasticities. The Eq. (4.2) illustrates the possibility of decomposition of the rate of the geometric growth rate of universal resources into its four constituents: geometric growth rate of technology "A", the geometric growth rate of human resources—population growth—the geometric growth rate of non-human physical resources

[5] " [Qur'an Chapter Inshqaq verse 19 and Chapter Al-Fatir verse 1].

and the geometric growth rate of the quality of labor—human capital formation. Here it is pertinent to note that the quality of population means the degree of Islamic character of Muslim population/people. Keeping in view the fact of human capital formation being the cause of the technical progress, Eq. (4.2) implicitly and explicitly highlights the key roles of both the mutually beneficial progressive processes of the population growth and the human capital formation as drivers of economic development of the whole world including the Islamic world.

In short, following is the socially and environmentally sustainable automatic universal natural resource growth function Eq. (4.2) implied by the Eq. (4.3):

$$G_R = \mathrm{G}\,(G_A, G_H, G_N, G_L) \tag{4.3}$$

4.2.1 *The Islamic Transmission Mechanism for Realizing Sustainable Development*

Numerous Islamic institutional factors such as the Islamic law (*Shari'ah*), the Islamically acknowledged and entrusted rights of ownership of individuals/society/Islamic state and a large number of iterative Islamic distributive-cum-redistributive measures play their respective key roles in accelerating environmentally sustainable mutually integrated processes of management, consumption, saving, investment and creation/distribution/redistribution of the Islamically rightful *Halaal* wealth by triggering a distinct Islamic transmission mechanism involving constructive interactions of five sectors—clean natural environment, house-holds, private investors-cum-producers, the public sector and the voluntary social welfare sector, whose expenditures are financed voluntarily by Muslims in the form of *Zakat*, *Ushr*, *Sadaqaat*, *Infaq*, *Awqaaf*, gifts, inheritance and wills.

The Islamic macroeconomic transmission mechanism is a dynamic intertwined two-step transmission process such that the implementation of Islamic distributive and redistributive measures increase the magnitude of various constituent parts of the aggregate demand, which in turn results in an increase in equilibrium income. As a part of the first step, social welfare-oriented investments undertaken by the voluntary sector, along with the moderately increased private consumption as well as private investment in physical/human capital accomplished by entrepreneurships/proprietorships in environment-friendly labor-intensive projects, effectively increase employment opportunities for workers as well as moderately increase the people's income, wealth, consumption, aggregate demand, employment, equilibrium output, and the living standards of all participants of the production process. For example, *mudarabah* (a cooperative venture between the unemployed-non-capitalist-skilled worker and the unable-to-work capital owner) and *musharikah* (a cooperative venture among owners of small amounts of capital) lead to the employment of previously unemployed physical capital, human capital and environmental capital in environmentally sustainable ways. This scenario enables the investors, producers, and consumers to realize the potential benefits of economies of scale in production and leads the Islamic economy to a better macroeconomic equilibrium characterized by moderately higher levels of overall investment, employment, income, wealth, health, spiritual welfare and aggregate demand while preserving the quality of natural environment.

In the simultaneously accomplished second step of this transmission mechanism, the swift implementation of the Islamic redistributional measures enable the Islamic economy to experience a higher degree of equitable distribution of income and wealth because the numerous Islamic welfare institutions such as *Baitul Mal*, *Zakat*, *'Ushr'* and Sadaqat increase the income/wealth/consumption of the poor thereby empowering and improving their socioeconomic status. Because of the fact that, in general, the marginal propensity of the poor to consume is higher than that of the rich, payment of *Zakat/Sadaqaat/ 'Ushr* results in a net moderate increase in aggregate consumption, aggregate demand, and equilibrium output, employment, income, wealth and welfare thereby reinforcing the increase in investment, employment, and individual output/income/wealth/welfare that was triggered in the first step of this transmission mechanism.

Above all, this transmission mechanism achieves the goals of an efficient as well as equitable distribution of resources, elimination of extreme income and wealth inequalities, extreme poverty, zero emissions of pollution as well as zero flow of waste into environment, and, the eventual increase in levels of sustainable development of the universal Islamic economy, and sustainable development-cum-empowerment of all people of the whole universe while simultaneously ensuring the protection/conservation as well as enrichment of peaceful environment of the whole universe..

Islam ensures sustainability of the moderate acceleration of the above continuous universal natural resource growth G_R, which is represented and illustrated by the phenomena of the self-perpetuating process of outward shifting of the circular production possibilities curves as shown in Fig. 4.1 and explained below.

In contrast to the capitalists'/communists' continuous blind amoral unidirectional pursuit of growth in national monetary wealth by hook or by crook (measured along the Y-axis) based on the concept of weakest sustainability implying that the physical monetary wealth/assets/capital and environmental/human/social/ethical/religious/political/economic capital are perfect substitutes which eventually culminates in socially/environmentally/culturally/politically unsustainable dead-end economic growth and development, Fig. 4.1 illustrates the matchless Islamic concept of environmentally, socially, culturally, economically, politically and strategically sustainable human development which simultaneously achieves sustainable human development by continuously shifting the Islamic production possibilities—based on the concept of multidimensional the Islamically Rightful Halal Wealth—outwards from the green circle "1" to the pink circle "2", then to the yellow circle "3", then to the purple circle "4" and so on until eventually the most outward red circle "n" of production possibilities while ensuring the functioning of the system of Islamic sustainable human development within the natural limits of the Environmental Space[6] (NS) represented by a small red line NS on the X-axis used for measuring the stock of environmental capital (K_N) in the first quadrant.

In the Fig. 4.1, Environmental Capital (K_N) and the Islamically Rightful Halal Wealth (W_{RH})—monetary wealth—are respectively measured along X-axis and Y-axis in the first quadrant. Moreover, the human capital (K_H)—a composite index of size of human population, average level of attainment of education-cum-training-cum-experience (that is, experience is a composite index of the average work experience in the home country and the average global work-cum-travel/migration experience), and the health measured by the average life expectancy at birth—is measured along common X-axis of the second and third quadrants. In addition, the Islamic Capital ($K_{IIMCSSSSTEP}$)—a composite index of Islamic Institutional, Moral, Civilizational, Spiritual, Social, Scientific, Strategic, Trust, Entrepreneurial and Political Capital—is measured along common Y-axis of the third and fourth quadrants.

The Islamically inspired continuous dynamic progressive synergies and mutual productive interfaces among the four Islamically conditioned factors of the Islamic wealth creation-cum-management, namely, $K_{N,}$ W_{RH}, K_H and $K_{IIMCSSSSTEP}$ trigger socially, environmentally, politically, and strategically peaceful sustainable balanced continuous expansions of the production possibility curves of the Islamic universal economy by inspiring all humans to proactively assume progressive and creative individual Islamically permitted entrepreneurial roles and creative Islamically permitted entrepreneurial roles in the framework of diverse economic/business/financial/investment partnerships (for example, *Musaqah* and various forms of *Mudharabah* and *Musharakah*) as well as by continuously ensuring the perfect fulfillment of the following Islamic conditions of strong sustainability—a further improved and extended strong sustainability version of the Pearce-Atkinson strong sustainability rule (Anderson, 2014)—in their processes of both the creation and management of the wealth of the universe entrusted by Allah (*swt*) to humans:

$$\left[\text{Depreciation of Wealth}\right)/\text{Gross Universal Product}] \leq 0$$

$$\left[\text{Depreciation of } K_N\right)/\text{Gross Global Product}] \leq 0$$

$$\left[\text{Depreciation of } K_H\right)/\text{Gross Global Product}] \leq 0$$

$$\left[\text{Depreciation of } K_I\right)/\text{Gross Global Product}] \leq 0$$

[6] While throughput refers to the total volume of material resources flowing through the human production and consumption cycle, environmental space is that particular level of throughput, which can be tolerated by the nature without occurrence of serious damage to nature's capacities of resource-regeneration, pollution-absorption and performing other natural functions (Anderson, 2014).

4.3 Universal Islamic Divine Civilized Politics of Wealth-Welfare Nexus Versus the Secular Mundane Amoral Barbaric Nationalistic Politics of Wealth-Warfare Nexus

Historically, wealth's potentially wrongful blind pursuit/accumulation/management/investment/ consumption has always been the most dangerous pitfall for individuals, business enterprises/societies, dynasties, nations, empires and civilizations. In contrast, Islam ensures peaceful sustaianble universal human development, welfare and bliss—a perfect culmination of the simultaneously achieved balanced spiritual and material developmemt of humans—by institutionalizing and operationalizing a progressive instrumenntal role of wealth in the frramework of the five fundamental objectives of Islam—*Al-Maqasid Al-Shari'ah* (Objectives of the Islamic Law). In the context of Islamic investment and wealth, it is pertinent to note the ideal Islamic commitment to simultanously invest in all the Islamiclly valid diverse forms of capital/wealth—Islamic moral capital, spritual capital, physical capital, human capital, natural capital, social capital, political capital, environmental capital etc—which were originally used as the Islamic strategic means in the Islamic political economy for accelerating the pace of durable human bliss-oriented balanced Islamic universal sustainable development. In this setting, there emerges peaceful universakl Islamic civilization in complete haemony with the interests of protection as well as the qualitative development of the natiral universe and its constituent echosystems.

In contrast to the Islamic framework in which the ownership/management/investment of wealth and the Islam's constructive divine politics are inherently cointegrated for the purpose of ensuring empowerment and development of all humans, there has evovled secular capitalistic framework of ownership of wealth as a direct outcome of a divisive tensions/conflicts/warfare-based mundane political system, which has culminated in wealth's potentially thoughtless/irresponsible/wrongful blind pursuit, accumulation, management, consumption, investment, production, and distribution, which have always been the most dangerous pitfall of exploitation/extraction/tensions/conflicts/clashes/warfare/slavery through enslavement as a result of feudalism communism, enclosure movement/colonization/exploration campaigns/Nazism/colonialism/globalization for individuals, business firms, societies, dynasties, nations, dynasties, regions, empires and civilizations.

Originally, creation of both the universal wealth and the humanity in the framework of the matchlessly wisdomdful and all powerful Universal Order of Allah (*swt*) highlights the universal truth that universal wealth has been endowed by Allah (*swt*) to the humanity as a politico-economic-cum-strategic means to facilitate it for economically, politically, and strategically ensuring the dominance of His divine universal order as well as His divine Islamic system—"*al-Din*"– in His entire universe through the divine Islamic politics, which is inseparably integrated with the the universal

Islamic politicoeconomic system through the divinely institutionalized Islamic politics of humankind in the institutional framwork of *Khalifatullahi fil-Ardh.*[7] At the same time, universal wealth has been the key driver of mundane human politics and interpersonal-cum-global political and strategic conflicts, which have been shapping and conditoioning the mundane politics of humnity.

Unfortthately numerous ever-worsening patternof unsustainable development—global warming, climate change, extreme poverty, excessive taxation, stagflation, extreme wealth inequalities, deforestation, deterioration of human values, globalization of warfare, contamination of all environmental media, and culminationn of lopesided development into dead-end growth—prove the failure of the conventional economics to increase the universal wellbeing and happiness of majority of humans in the world as well as authenticates Nassau Senior's defectsw and myopic definition of economics—"Economics is a science of wealth, not of welfare."—based on an an extremey limited/narrow conception and scope of wealth.

Here it is pertinent to note the inherently self-destructive, limited process of wealth formation based on humans' relentless unidirectional pursuit of material wealth alone—a direct result of the wealth being entrusted to the billions of unwise people (investors, consumers, producers and policy makers) as well as their irrational rulers, whose macroeconomic policies of maximization of their material wealth have culminated in the global environmental disasters—the global warming and the global Climate change, blackening of the universal horizons/atmospheres/three environmental media (air, water and land) in Europe/America/Asia (China, Japan, and India) and the dawn of the New Global Dark Ages. The inevitable culmination of these patterns of unsustainable development into a perpetual holocaust for both the increasingly impoverished poor human masses and the increasingly extinguished numerous natural living species warrant Islamic research initiatives for contributing an alternative scheme of Islamic investment/management/production/distribution/redistribution, which precludes the the possibilities of handing over the multidimensional wealth to the unwise people and irrational economic agents and which moderates the excessive tendencies of material wealth creation by only permiting the moderate levels of production/acquisition/consumption/savings/investment/trade/distribution/redistribution of only and only the Islamically rightful Halaal wealth in light of the teachings of the Holy *Qur'an.*[8]

While acknowledging the apprehensions of potential conflicts and bloodshed among humans, Islamic *Shari'ah* most effectively moderates the potentially conflicts-oriented violent excessive inclination of humans in general and Muslims believers in particular towards excessive accumulation of material wealth by developing the highest levels of the quality of *Taqwa*—truly fearing from Allah (*swt*)—through its motivational system of good news (*Basharat*) and great rewards from Allah (*swt*) for those Muslims who obey the Islamic commandments about the Lawful (*Halaal*) and the Forbidden (*Haraam*) in the context of wealth and bad news in the

[7] (Quran Chapter *Al Shura'a* verse 13).

[8] [*Qur'an*: chapter *Al-Ma'idaha* verse 5, chapter *Al-Nisa* verse 5, chapter *Al-Adiyat* verses 6–8].

forms of warnings of painful punishments for those Muslims who do not obey the Islamic commandments about the Lawful (*Halaal*) and the Forbidden (*Haraam*) in the context of wealth. For example, some of the *Qur'anic* teachings most effectively moderate the socioeconomic behavior of the Muslims in the context of the Islamically rightful/just as well as balanced-cum-moderate consumption/investment of *Halaal* income/wealth[9]:

The *Qur'anic* teachings lead to the truthful universal Islamic paradigm of the multidimensional wealth management, which reminds the Islamic economic agents about the universal truth that only and only Allah (*SWT*) is all powerful and the absolute owners of the multidimensional universal wealth and that He (*SWT*) has entrusted the universal multidimensional wealth to the humans under the inviolable sacred terms and conditions of trusteeship of resources, which must be fulfilled by them for maximizing their welfare, and the violation of these terms and conditions warrants painful punishment for them by Allah (*SWT*).[10]

Historically, the political dimension of the conventional secular concepts of wealth, its ownership/management/investment emerged from the views of Chinese philosopher Confucius, Greek philosophers (for example, Xenophon, Plato and Aristotle) and English philosophers (for example, Thomas Hobbes (1588–1679)). Plato and Aristotle differed on the assignment of particular types of property rights to the different classes of the society. In this setting, theoretical-cum-politico-philosophical assertions of Hobbes highlight the creation of private property by the (power of the) state which existed before the creation of the property rights and that the private property was not created by natural law (Hobbes, 1651a, 1651b). Hobbes acknowledged the imperative of having instituted state and politics of the state for assigning as well as protecting property rights and wealth of the subjects of states in the framework of a social contract and claimed that in the absence of a social contract-based civil society, uncivil society/nation is characterized by perpetual violence and war of all men against all men, due to which uncivil societies/nations of the earlier (non-modern) ages were "then few, fierce, short-lived, poor, nasty, and destroyed of all that Pleasure, and Beauty of life... (Hobbes, 1651a, 1651b)" (Dupont, 2017).

However, practically the realization and existence of a Hobbesian social contract has not precluded civil warfare within the civil societies of nation states of the modern age such as Pakistan during 1970–1971 which culminated in separation of East Pakistan (now Bangladesh) as well as the international warfare—for example, long wars launched by the former Soviet Union and the West against Afghanistan as well as the long war between Iraq and Iran in the Middle East and global warfare (for example, the old and recent Cold Wars), in spite of the practical realization and existence of global social contract on the platform of the United Nations Organization. Above all, Hobbesian common wealth-based on social contract is itself involved

---

[9] [*Qur'an*: chapter *Al-Humaza* verses 1–9, chapter *Al Lahab* verses 1–5, chapter *Al- Ma'un* verses 1–7, chapter *al-Takathu*r verses 1–8, chapter *Al-Baqarah* verses 28–33, chapter *Al-Ra'd* verse 4, chapter *Al-Asr* verse 1–3].

[10] [*Qur'an*: chapter *Al-Mulk* verse 1–3, 15, 21 and 24, chapter *Al-Ra'd* verses 16–17 and 26, chapter *Al-Quraish* verses 1–4].

in warfare for colonization of the foreign lands through exploration-cum-military campaigns of the Hobbesian common wealth, which practically culminated in famous curse of natural resources—warfare for the capture and control of national mineral wealth—and decline in social welfare for nation states such as Congo (Todaro, 2000). Later Jeremy Bentham and Adam Smith endorsed the politics of the state for protecting the wealth of the rich. While Bentham believed in both the simultaneous birth as well as death of property and law, Adam Smith emphasized the interdependence of property and the civil government, which was originally formed for preservation of both the property and the inequality of possession (Dupont, 2017). These theoretical-cum-politico-economic contributions triggered pro-colonization theoretical contributions such as the theory of climatic determinism, which warrants the Western imperial warfare for colonization of the non-Western foreign territories by asserting that warmer climate zones produce less civilized, more degenerate peoples, who are in dire need of help for their salvation, education, civilization and socioeconomic-cum-political development to be provided by the Western imperial powers (McGregor, 2004). Against this theoretical background as well as historical background, it is not at all a matter of surprise that patterns of both the growth in the wealth—wealth creation—of capitalist and communist nations and their international trade, which is regarded as engine of growth and development according to the assertion of Adam Smith, have been determined by their respective military power—a historical fact highlighted by Findlay and O'rourke (2007):

> "As we point out below, the greatest expansions of world trade have tended to not come from the bloodless *tâtonnement* of some fictional Walrasian auctioneer but from the barrel of a Maxim gun, the edge of a scimitar, or the ferocity of nomadic horsemen."

4.4 Epilogue and Policy Implications-Cum-Recommendations

Wealth and politics have been complementary in both the competing Islamic and secular paradigms of wealth. The universally harmonious, peaceful, constructive, progressive and divine Islamic politics of humans as the vicegerents of Allah (swt), which has been aiming at ensuring the dominance of the blessed Universal Order of Allah (*swt*) and Islam as His revealed *Ad-Deen*—a complete code of successful and blissful life of all humans—in the whole universe, highlights the multidimensional wealth as a mainstay of the universally sustainable human development and bliss in this world and in the world-hereafter, Islam and the progressive divine Islamic politics of perfectly protecting and optimally developing the Islamically rightful *Halaal* multidimensional wealth of the whole universe peacefully integrates all humans as well as integrates the entire humanity and all other entities of the natural universe, precludes all the potential pitfalls [for example, division and disintegration of humanity into socioeconomic classes of rich (haves) and poor people (have-nots), class-conflicts, human enslavement, civil wars, extractive-cum-exploitative globalization, the international and global Hot Wars and the Cold

Wars, holocausts of humans and other living species as well as their ecosystems, impoverishment of humanity, destruction of environment, global warming, the global Climate Change etc.] of the multidimensional wealth as well as its investment/production/management by implementing the Islamic teachings and principles, and culminates in zenith of the matchless progressive Islamic blissful civilization and the ideal patterns of sustainable human development/empowerment/welfare/blissful happiness/thankfulness. This divine Islamic paradigm of the wealth-politics-welfare nexus was practically transformed into a historical glorious universal truth of the actual existence of the then matchless universal Islamic civilization in the Golden Age of Islam.

The secular amoral paradigm of the blind unidirectional pursuit of material wealth highlights maximization of investment/accumulation/consumption of wealth by hook or by crook as the only and only one goal of the lives of humans as individuals/families/human race in this world alone. This later paradigm of wealth gives rise to politics-cum-geopolitics of accumulation of material wealth, which leads to the allocation of rights of ownership of material wealth among individuals and communities of humans as well as to the creation of states for both the effective protection of private property rights of individual owners of wealth—preservation of inequality between wealthy and poor people—and the fresh allocation-cum-protection of rights of ownership of material wealth among individuals and communities of humans by means of political legislation. This secular mundane amoral politics and geopolitics of material wealth has been culminating in perpetuation and increase in income/wealth inequalities, political tensions/conflicts, civil wars, political revolutions, the Western culture of global warfare and human bloodshed/enslavement/feudalism/European and global enclosure movements—colonialism in Africa and Asia etc—the endless warfare in the forms of the World Wars that culminated in two explosions of atomic bombs in the open Japanese atmospheres of Hiroshima and Nagasaki, the Cold Wars, the historic international Space Race for the conquest and monopolistic control of the resources of planets other than earth as well, the strategic and logistic preparations for potential international Star Wars, the Great Depression, Global Financial Crisis, the Great Recession and above all the Global Warming as well as the Global Climate Change in the framework of the dazzling and glamorous globalization.

This chapter has exposed and exploded the numerous myths—the myth contributed by the father of modern economics Adam Smith that economics of the invisible hand of self-interest can lead to a sustainable growth in the socioeconomic welfare of humanity, that the monetary wealth creation-oriented unidirectional economic growth (the growth in national material wealth) in the framework of capitalist economics and communist-cum-socialist economics can culminate in socially/environmentally/politically/strategically peaceful sustainable human development, that the growth processes of capitalism and communism can automatically lead to socio-economic and strategic justice, peace, reduction in economic inequalities as well as increase in individual and social welfare and sustainable economic development, that comparative advantage is the basis of international trade, that the pattern of international trade is determined by the comparative advantage, that the international trade promotes peace and stability, that the peaceful international trade is engine of national wealth creation and growth, that the international terms of trade are determined by the market forces, and that the West is helpful for achieving global peace and environmentally sustainable development.

Above all, the global humanity has been confronting the inevitable strategic choice of either welcoming/embracing/establishing the matchless universal Islamic peaceful civilization and realizing the truly environmentally sustainable development of the entire humanity or welcoming/embracing the Western culture of perpetual global and universal warfare, extreme multidimensional poverty-cum-enslavement of the global masses, the universally disastrous Global Warming and the Climate Change, the universal wealth destruction, the COVID19-propelled pandemic, and the consequent socially/economically/politically/strategically unsustainable human development. In light of the indisputable facts that the secular amoral capitalist-cum-socialist political economy of the management of the national material wealth and its maximization via interest-based investment/foreign direct investment/manipulated foreign trade/trade wars/the system of the Hot wars and the Cold Wars management has been the real premier cause of the contemporary serious global crises of unsustainable development—globally widespread extreme income/wealth inequalities, extreme poverty and continuous global warfare—the universal truths of' the existence of huge potential of Islam's uniquely peaceful/egalitarian/constructive dynamics of wealth-politics-welfare nexus warrants the policy recommendation for all nations in general and for Muslim nations in particular to welcome and perfectly implement the universal Islamic political economy of investment and wealth management for realizing peaceful, equitable, and socially/environmentally/politically/strategically sustainable multidimensional Islamic wealth-politics-welfare nexus.

References

Al-Fasi, A. (1402). Islamic economic theory. In *Islam ki ma'ashi ta'leemaat* (*Islamic Economic Teachings*). Islamabad: Islamic Research Institute.

Al-Jarhi, M. A. (1981). A monetary and financial structure for an Interest-free economy: Institutions, mechanism and policy. In Z. Ahmad, M. Iqbal, & M. F. Khan (Eds.) [1983], Money and banking in Islam. In *Proceedings of the international seminar on monetary and fiscal economics* (pp.69–87). Islamabad (Pakistan): Institute of Policy Studies.

Anderson, D. A. (2014). *Environmental economics and natural resource management* (4th ed.). Routledge.

Anjum, M. I. (1995). An Islamic scheme of equitable distribution of income and wealth. *The American Journal of Islamic Social Sciences, 12*(2), 224–239.

Anjum, M. I. (1996). Eternal challenge of Islamic economics to capitalism and communism. *Humanomics, 12*(1), 53–90.

Anjum, M. I. (1998). Human capital formation as a locomotive of the Islamic world in the 21st century. *Annual Journal of International Islamic University Islamabad,* Issue, (6), 55-100.

Anjum, M. I. (2006). Globalization at crossroads of warfare, revolution and universalization: The Islamic panacea, stratagem and policy instruments. *Humanomics, 22*(3), 162–177.

Anjum, M. I. (2008a). Islamic world's development policy responses to the challenges of financial globalization. *Humanomics, 24*(1), 5–16.

Anjum, M. I. (2008b). Latest roles of Islamic financial institutions in enriching the structure and menu of financial instruments of the fast-globalizing Islamic capital markets in the 21st century. In S. S. Ali (Eds.), *Islamic capital markets: Products, regulation, and development* (pp.409–440). Jeddah (Saudi Arabia): Islamic Research and Training Institute, Islamic Development Bank.
Anjum, M. I. (2021). Islamic universal politico-economic institutional transmission mechanisms for global sustainable development. A paper presented in the 9th Islamic Economics Workshop organized by the Research Center for Islamic Economics (iKAM) at Istanbul in Turkey on 17–19.
Ansari, A. A.(1996). An institutional framework for capital formation in an Islamic Economy. In M. A. Mannan, & Ahmad, M. (Eds.). (1996). *Economic development in an Islamic framework* (pp. 115–149). International Institute of Islamic Economics.
Chapra, M. U. (1996). Monetary management in Islamic economy. *Islamic Economic Studies* 4(1), 1–34.
Chapra, M. U. (2000). *The future of economics: An Islamic perspective.* Leicester (U.K.): The Islamic Foundation.
Dupont, D. (2017). *The history of economic ideas.* Routledge.
Findlay, R., & Kevin, H. O. (2007). *Power and plenty: Trade, war, and economy in the Second Millennium.* Princeton University Press.
Hobbes, T. (1651a). *Léviathan.* London (UK): J. M. Dent and Sons. Viewed from: https://holybooks-lichtenbergpress.netdna-ssl.com/wp-content/uploads/Thomas-Hobbes-Leviathan.pdf.
Hobbes, T. (1651b). *De Cive.* London (UK): J.C. Viewed from: http://www.public-library.uk/ebooks/27/57.pdf
Islam, M. W. (1999). Al-Mal: The concept of property in Islamic legal thought. *Arab Law Quarterly, 14*(4), 361–368.
Islahi, A. (1996). *History of economic thought in Islam: A subjectwise survey.* Aligarh Muslim University.
Khan, W. M. (2002). *Transition to a riba-free economy*, Islamabad: The International Institute of Islamic Thought.
Mannan, M. A., & Ahmad, M. (1996). Economic development in an Islamic Framework. *Islamabad: International Institute of Islamic Economics.*
McGregor, K. M. (2004). Huntington and Lovelock: Climatic determinism in the 20th century. *Physical Geography, 25*(3), 237–250.
Naqvi, S. N. H. (2003). *Perspectives on morality and human well-Being:* A Contribution to Islamic Economics. Leicester (U.K.): Islamic Foundation.
Ragan, J. F., Thomas, L. B., & Roger, C. T. (1993). *Principles of Economics.* The Dryden Press.
Saud, M. A. S. (1989). Towards Islamization of knowledge. Virginia, USA: *International Institute of Islamic Thought.*
Sadeq, A. M. (2005). Socioeconomic development role of *waqf* in the 21st century and restructuring of its administration with special reference to Bangladesh. In M. Haneef, & M. Anwar (Eds.), *Studies in Islamic economics in the 21st century* (pp.269–299). Kuala Lumpur (Malaysia): International Islamic University Malaysia.
Siddiqui, M. N. (1969). *Ghair sudi bankari* (Urdu) (Interest Free Banking). Delhi (India): Markazi Maktaba Islami/Lahore (Pakistan): Islamic Publications,
The Arab News. (2013). The last Sermon of the Holy Prophet Muhammad (pbuh). *The Arab News* 11 October 2022. https://www.arabnews.com/news/467364
Todaro, M. P. (2000). *Economic development* (Ed. 5), New York: Addison-Wesley.

Chapter 5
Wealth Creation and Management in Islam

Muhammad Ashfaq, Hanna R. Abdelwahab, Shahab Aziz, and Shahbaz Sharif

The interest in global Islamic fund and wealth management industry is on the rise, which was triggered by a surge in demand as the Muslim communities around the world become more affluent. Bank Negara Malaysia (2016) reported that in 2015, the AuM (total global Islamic assets under management) stood at more than US$75 billion while the number of Islamic funds recorded was US$1,053. By the end of 2019, AuM is expected to reach US$77 billion with the number of Islamic funds projected to reach US$185 billion (Thomson Reuters, 2015).

Nowadays, Islamic banks and Islamic financial institutions are turning their attentions towards Islamic Wealth Management (IWM) and its prevalence is affecting the global financial market (Mubarak, 2010). Many standard commercial banks, such as Egypt's Misr Bank and Saudi Arabia's National Commercial Bank, have started operating "Islamic Windows", where "Islamic products" are being offered to customers through the regular networks in the banking systems (). The same is emulated by some Multinational Banks, through the establishment of wholly owned subsidiaries such as HSBC *Amanah* and Citi Islamic Investment Bank, by HSBC and Citibank in Bahrain respectively (Obaidullah, 2008a, b). The management of wealth in Islam focuses on capturing the UNHWI's (Ultra-High Net Worth Individuals) market segment from oil-rich and other wealthy countries.

It is often perceived that Islamic *Shari'ah* law has a narrow view of wealth management, but in actuality, it does not, nor does it prohibit Muslims from accumulating wealth. In fact, wealth management covers a large area of the *Shari'ah* law, and includes distribution of bequest, savings/investments management, realty planning, Islamic tax-related (*zakat*) matters matters as well as other charitable acts and contracts (Mubarak, 2010). It is pertinent to remind readers that the sole purpose of wealth creation in Islam is not just for the sole enjoyment and prosperity of the individuals, but also for a fair distribution of the wealth among fellow humans. This

M. Ashfaq (✉) · H. R. Abdelwahab · S. Aziz · S. Sharif
IU International University of Applied Sciences, Bad Honnef, Germany
e-mail: muhammad.ashfaq@iu.org

T. Azid et al. (eds.), *Wealth Management and Investment in Islamic Settings*,
https://doi.org/10.1007/978-981-19-3686-9_5

is where the beauty of the *Shari'ah* law comes in as it facilitates the distribution of wealth in a fair and just manner for the betterment of society and the sanctity of human life. It is also pertinent to understand that wealth distribution in Islam is not just considered as a charitable act but it actually incorporates a much more significant twofold dimension; eradication of poverty and gaining of spiritual benefit.[1]

5.1 Concept of Wealth in Islam

In Islam, the believers are taught that everything belongs to Allah, the One, True God. He has given wealth to people, not for the sole purpose of self-enjoyment, but as a test of how he manages it. Every Muslim will be asked by Allah on the Day of Judgement about their way of living, including wealth accumulation and distribution, as evident from the following verses of the Holy Quran and *Ahadith.*[2]

> And let not those who [greedily] withhold what Allah has given them of His bounty ever think that it is better for them. Rather, it is worse for them. Their necks will be encircled by what they withheld on the Day of Resurrection. And to Allah belongs the heritage of the heavens and the earth. And Allah, with what you do, is [fully] Acquainted. (Qur'an 3:180).
>
> The son of Adam will not pass away from Allah until he is asked about five things: How he lived his life, how he utilized his youth, what means he earned his wealth with, how he spent his wealth, and what he did with his knowledge (Sahih hadith reported by Imam Al-Tirmidhi, Vol. 4, Book 11, Hadith 2416).

Muslims are required to know that Allah gives wealth to man as a trust, and they are not the true owners of the provided wealth (Al-Shanqaiti, 2009; Salim, 2006). This means that, "*wealthy people are just custodians or trustees of wealth in this temporal world*" (Mubarak, 2010). As trustees, man is instructed to utilize the resources according to the terms and conditions that come with the trust (Ismail, et al., 2010). One misconception that needs to be debunked is that Islam does not censure wealth acquisition. Rather, it reminds the believers that "*obsessive preoccupation in accumulating and building wealth by an individual leads to the side-lining of the most essential part of the self - one's spirituality*" (Al-Shanqaiti, 2009). Allah says in the Qura'n, "*(Woe to him) who accumulates wealth and keeps counting it*!" (Quran, 102:1). Instead, Islam promotes the fair circulation of wealth and forbids the unfair withholding of wealth. Spending wealth extravagantly is also scorned, and instead, it enjoins the earning of money, spending and investing in approved (*halal*) ways (Al-Shanqaiti, 2009). Islam considers earning a *halal* living as obligatory and Man are instructed to be responsible to their family and community rather than relying on begging for charity.

---

[1] (Quran 3:92).

[2] Collections of traditions containing sayings of the prophet Muhammad (peace be upon him), with accounts of his daily practices (the Sunn'ah), and which constitute the major source of guidance for Muslims apart from the Holy Qur'an.

Islam forbids malpractices such as gambling, bribery, corruption, fraud, hoarding and interest (*riba*) as these are often addictive and lead to economic disparity and injustice. In the corporate world, such criminal acts include embezzlement, contractual fraud, insider trading and other white-collar crimes. Allah said in the Holy Qur'an, "*O ye who believe! Squander not your wealth among yourselves wrongfully, except it be a trade by mutual consent*" (Qur'an 4:29). Islam specifically permits trading and prohibits interest when lending money because not only is it unfair to the borrower but also becomes a burden to the debtor when he is not able to pay on time.[3] In Islam, wealth can be obtained through two legal ways: one's effort and through inheritance. By one's effort, it means the accumulation of wealth through jobs, or contemporary dynamic tools such as investments in shares, trusts, funds, capitals and many other instruments which are permissible under Islamic rules.

5.2 Islamic Wealth Management (IWM)

Islamic Wealth Management (IMW) is a field that seeks to provide customers with *Shari'ah*-compliant products and services (Maybank Singapore, 2020). It comprises of integrated services incorporating financial management and planning as well as portfolio management (Farooq, 2014). This is one form of a branch of a diverse advisory services on wealth management. *Shari'ah* in Islam means the Islamic canonical law (the legal system or the laws of Islam) which is "based on the teachings of the Quran and traditions of the Prophet Muhammad (pbuh)" (Rizvi, 1992). *Shari'ah*-compliant products and services refer to those that are governed by *Shari'ah* jurisprudence and the tenets of Islam (Chen, 2020). Entrepreneurs, business owners and basically High Net Worth Individuals (HNWI) and their families can benefit from wealth management services through the engagement of qualified specialists, proficient in the *Shari'ah* Law as well as banking, state law, tax, investment management, tax and estate laws and regulations. The marketplace for investments in *Shari'ah*-compliant products and services has seen a steady increase over the decades with private banks, financial institutions and investors becoming more interested. However, the international IWM industry continues to be largely untapped although it is predicted to grow within the next few years.

Under the *Shari'ah* law, Muslims are taught five fundamental necessities of human existence: faith (religion), life, progeny (children), intellect and property (wealth) (Bank Negara Malaysia, 2016). It is incumbent on every member of the society to preserve and protect these fundamentals. *Shari'ah* decrees the many purposes of wealth but warns that it should not be expended on unlawful products or activities or spent extravagantly without giving benefit to anybody or anything. Islam states that the desire to gain wealth by itself is a great motivation to work hard, thus eschewing laziness and idleness. The capability of an individual to gain wealth and distribute it equitably gives hope to the underprivileged people. Thus, this necessity for proper

[3] (Qur'an 16:92).

wealth management provides the discipline and foundation for the protection, support and betterment of family and society. Salim (2006) states that by abstention from lavish expenditure, a Muslim can help fight consumerism and inflation.

What is distinctive, in essence, about IWM as compared to conventional ones? The new discipline of Islamic finance is on *Shari'ah*-compliance. This means that wealth management in the context of Islam must ensure adherence to the *Shari'ah* law; for example, the avoidance of *riba* or interest in any dealings and contracts, *gharar*, playing with excessive risk and uncertainty and *maysir* or gambling. Furthermore, the items of contracts or business must not deal with prohibited items such as pork, intoxicants, pornography, human trafficking etc.

5.3 The Wealth Cycle

As shown in Fig. 5.1 below, the four elements of a wealth cycle are:

- Wealth Creation
- Wealth Enhancement
- Wealth Protection
- Wealth Distribution

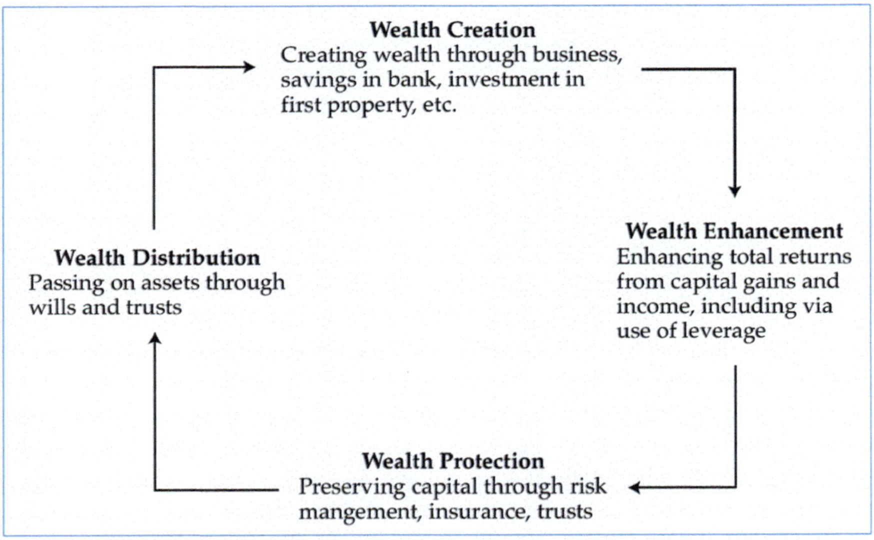

Fig. 5.1 Cycle of wealth creation, enhancement, protection, and distribution. *Source* Adapted from Shanmugam and Zahari (2009)

5.3.1 Wealth Creation

In Islam, *Allah* is the creator of the whole universe and He is the sole owner of everything that He creates (Javaid & AW, 2015). Qaseem wrote that human beings are created by Allah to be vicegerents on earth and his deeds and actions must be effected in accordance with Allah's commands. Wealth is considered as one of the blessings granted to humans and they should use it as a tool to seek *Allah*'s benedictions or approval. According to the Islamic principles, the accumulation of wealth can be through inheritance or bequests, gifts, hard work, investments, as well as business or partnership activities. Shanmugam and Zahari (2009) stressed that the creation of wealth can only be through permissible (*halal*) means.

5.3.2 Islamic Rules with Regards to Wealth Creation

Wealth creation in Islam is not merely getting more money through various means. It is subject to various *Shari'ah* rules. A Muslim is restricted from engaging in activities which create injustice or unfairness (e.g. discrimination, bias, inequality etc.) to all the parties concerned or to the general public. These activities include *riba* (usury), *maisir* (gambling), *gharar* (deception or uncertainty) and conducting business in prohibited products or services such as pornography, brewery, drugs, etc. (Al-Shanqaiti, 2009; Al-Ghazzali, early twelfth century). Usury refers to the extra amount paid by the debtor to the lender, as a condition for the loan or a deferment of payment. This is considered unjust because firstly, it puts a burden on the already needy borrower as he will not only have to pay the amount of money he had borrowed but also the premium owed. In conventional loan contracts, these interests are normally exorbitant and accumulative and can even add up to more than the loan itself. Islam promotes love and compassion, and preying on the needy in the community or scheming on them through fraudulent means is considered a big sin. Secondly, usury encourages people to be lazy and allows them to reap rewards without actual labour. *Maisir* or gambling is considered an injustice in Islam because one party wins at the expense of the other, in contrast with trade, in which both parties win. In gambling, there is the possibility of the individuals gaining easy money, without work, which is not acceptable in Islam. Being productive members of the society is what Islam enjoins and exploiting the weaknesses of other people for one's own gain is completely against God's will. *Gharar* has many meanings such as deception, risk or uncertainty. It technically refers to exposure to excessive, unnecessary risk or uncertainty in a business transaction. Examples include undefined quality of commodities traded or unspecified delivery date. Another important concept of injustice in Islam is exploiting those that are at a disadvantage such as orphans, widows, the disabled, elderly or the sick.

5.3.3 Wealth Enhancement

Wouters found that improvement, protection or the expansion of wealth is one of the most sought-after services by HNWI and their wealth management advisors. He further stated that these advisors who are basically contemporary asset managers or portfolio managers tend to focus too much on wealth enhancement and ignores the other three important aspects of the wealth cycle, especially wealth distribution. This is of course, contrary to the Islamic teachings, and is one of the root causes of the prevailing issue of poverty and income disparity around the world. These individuals are too engrossed in accumulating wealth for themselves and tend to ignore the needs of the society. To dwell on this issue is not the aim of this chapter, but it is worth mentioning at this juncture so that the readers are aware of the current practice in the world today, even among the Muslims. The Islamic financial system offers a variety of ways, instruments and products in which wealth can be enhanced. Examples include: (Shanmugam & Zahari, 2009).

- Stocks
- Investment funds
- *Sukuk* (Islamic financial certificate),
- *Takaful* (a type of Islamic insurance), and
- Other *halal* financial dealings

This topic is wide and encompasses many related subjects and is best dealt separately.

5.3.4 Wealth Protection

Wealth protection is of great significance in Islam and there are a variety of tools which can be utilized to serve this purpose such as *Takaful arrangement* (Shanmugam & Zahari, 2009). Protection of wealth means to preserve one's self, one's family, and one's property from uncertainties and financial losses (Othman & Subramaniam, 2013). Tasdemir et al. (2016) discussed the fact that Islam regards wealth as a precious blessing from Allah, and its preservation is of great importance for its growth. Just like wealth enhancement, this is another big topic which is not the main aim of this chapter. It is best to refer to other books if readers are interested in learning more about it.

5.3.5 Wealth Distribution

According to the principles of Islam, righteousness or moral uprightness is not related to the amount of wealth owned by a person. Rather, righteousness and piety are attributed to the believer who distributes his wealth in a just manner to the underprivileged people around him.[4] The basis for this is that wealth is a trust (or trial) endowed to man and he is answerable for it in the day of judgement.[5]

Wealth distribution means simply taking away from the well-off according to certain provisions and delivering it to the destitute to comfort and satisfy their needs, to solve the problem of poverty and to ensure economic and social justice. The ultimate goal is reciprocal social responsibility and to ensure that no one is left deprived. Reciprocal social responsibility leads to a stronger, tenacious society in which destitution, poverty and suffering are eliminated from the faces of the earth.

5.3.6 Wealth Distribution - Charity

When evaluating how wealth should be distributed, Islam takes into account the social perspective. Basically, Islam advocates the three-tier structure of importance: The household (i.e. immediate family); the kinfolk (relatives) and other members of society (the underprivileged) (Umair, 2015). This means that Islam prioritises the individual's own household as the primary beneficiaries when it comes to wealth distribution, before any other people. Following this are the kinfolk or other relatives. This helps to strengthen the family bond in the society and eliminates feelings of jealousy and vengeance. And finally, the last beneficiaries are those who are underprivileged in the society, which are clearly stated in the Qur'an (2:215), the orphans, widows, the poor and the wayfarers (travellers).[6] In what ways can wealth be distributed through charity? Wouters delineated four distinct tools through which individuals can contribute to the development of community and the poor and needy in Islam. They are:

- *Zakat* (wealth purification),
- *Sadaqah* (voluntary charity),
- *Qard Hasan* (benevolent loan) and
- *Waqaf* (charitable endowment).

i. Zakat (Wealth Purification)

Zakat is the third of the five pillars of Islam. It is a form of wealth purification in Islam and is equivalent to tax. Allah says in the Holy Quran, "*And establish regular prayer and pay the poor due (zakat) and bow down your heads with those who bow down (in worship)*" (Quran 2:43). Islamic history has proven that the payment of *zakat* has enhanced peace and harmony in the community and helped to reduce social and economic disparity (Hoque, et al., 2015). Dr. Pranam Dhar, a professor in West Bengal University says that *zakat* contributes to social justice.

---

[4] (Qur'an 3:92).

[5] (Qur'an 6:165).

[6] (Quran 2:215).

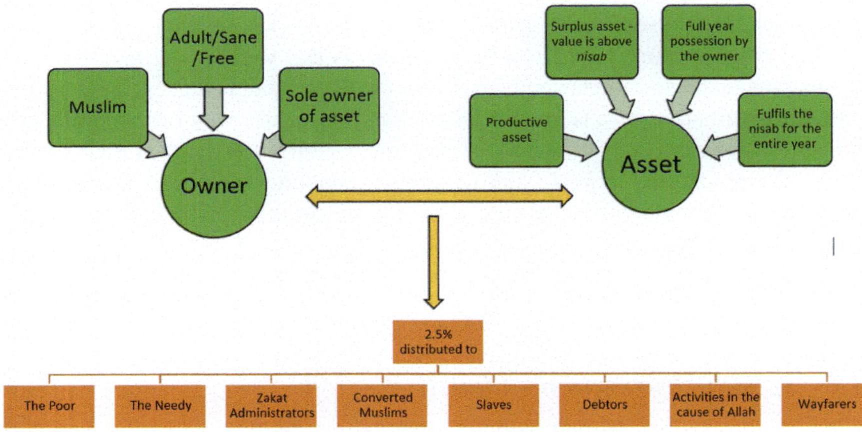

Fig. 5.2 Concept of Zakatul Maal. *Source* Ashfaq & Abdelwahab

Zakatul maal (Tax on Assets)

Zakatul maal is obligatory on the owner of agricultural/farm produce, reared animals, commodities of business, gold, silver, mines and buried treasure. When a Muslim's wealth reaches a prescribed amount (which is called '*nisab*' - the minimum amount), over and above his needs, it is obligatory upon him to pay a 2.5% *zakat* (tax) of it (Hossain, 2012). Besides the *nisab*, there are other conditions that must be met for example the owner must be sane/adult, he is the sole owner of the asset and he must have owned the asset for a full hijrah (Islamic) year or *Haul*. Refer to Fig. 5.2 for a full overview of *zakatul maal.*

The concept of zakatul maal can be represented by Fig. 5.2.

Zakatul Fitr

Zakatul Fitr is another tax obligation, which is applicable to all Muslims irrespective of their wealth, age, or dependency except those living in absolute poverty. Payment could be in the form of staple food or the equivalent in money. During the prophet's (pbuh) time, the Muslims were enjoined to give one saa' (equivalent to about 3 kg) of dates or one saa' of barley. Some of the scholars have interpreted that it is logical to give the staple food of the country as the *zakatul fitr* instead of cash.

Zakat in Islam: An Effective Poverty Alleviating Instrument

The Islamic concept of *zakat* has many positive impacts on society. It looks after the needs and welfare of the underprivileged, and removes economic hardship of the poor. This ultimately can help to narrow the inequality among the different groups in the society (Hossain, 2012). For more detail on this subject see Hassan and Ashraf (2010), Stirk (2015), Al-Shanqaiti (2009) and Dhar (2013).

Table 5.1 An overview of the comparison between Islamic zakat (tax) system and conventional taxation system

Islamic Zakat System	Conventional Taxation System
Sources of regulation include the Holy Quran, Hadis, *Ijtihad, Qiyas and Ijma* (consensus of Muslim scholars)	Source of regulation is determined by the current government
Tax is sanctioned by Allah on Muslims	Tax is authorised by government on citizens
Only wealth above the *nisab* is *zakatable*	There are some concept of exemption
Full ownership of the wealth must be one year (*haul*). For example, a property which has just been bought will need to be held by the owner for one full year, before it is *zakatable*	There is concept of yearly assessment, but ownership need not meet one full year. For example, a property which is bought just one day before the end of the financial year, is taxable
Rate and distribution are specified. Zakat can only be distributed to the specified eight categories—the poor, the needy, zakat administrators, newly converts, those in bondage and in debt, those who strive in the cause of Allah and the wayfarers	Rate and method of spending is relatively changeable. Tax money is used for public spending including provision of services, state administrative costs, education, health etc. including defence
Monetary basic needs of the individual is deducted from the wealth before the amount of *zakat* is calculated	Monetary basic needs of the individual or business is not deducted from the income
Zakat law is not open for amendments since it is based on revealed doctrines	Tax law is relatively open for debates and amendments since it is man-made and not based on revealed doctrines
For zakat to be paid, the taxpayer or wealth must satisfy various criteria	Tax law does not have strict criteria with regards to the taxable item or the taxpayer

Source Adapted from Abu Bakar (2008)

ii. A comparison between Islamic zakat tax system and conventional tax system

Hossain (2012) made a comparison between Islamic *zakat* tax system and conventional tax system. One of the similarities is that, just like tax, *zakat* is compulsory upon any eligible Muslim. As such, any Islamic state has the responsibility to follow this ruling to collect *zakat* from its residents and those who failed to pay the *zakat should be* penalized or fined. The main difference between *zakat* tax system and conventional tax system is that *zakat* is based on *nisab* (the required minimum amount) and anything below this minimum limit is exempted from the tax. Table 5.1 presents a simple overview of the comparison between Islamic *zakat* system and conventional tax system.

Besides *zakat*, three other wealth distribution charity instruments are discussed below. They are *sadaqah, qard hasan and waqf*.[7]

Sadaqah (Voluntary Charity)

Vera attributed the literal meaning of *Sadaqah* as to be truthful and since it is voluntary and not obligatory, the performance of this charitable act reflects empathy, kindness and love of a believer towards others. It also demonstrates true devotion of a Muslim to *Allah*. Islam enjoins its followers to give *Sadaqah* as it leads to community advancement. It is considered as a significant tool to eradicate poverty and instils equality and justice in the society. It is also commonly utilized to fund education, research, and social advancement. Islam regards charity as of high importance, and in societies where there is strong economic disparity, such benevolent acts should become obligatory (Hassan & Ashraf, 2010).

Qard Hasan (Benevolent Loan)

Qard Hasan, which literally means benevolent or generous (*hasan*) loan (*qard*) is the extension of loan to the poor (or needy) with no expectation of profitable returns. This is the only loan permissible in Islam and lenders or financial institutions are not allowed to charge interest or additional costs to cover their administrative costs when extending such loans (El-Zoghbi & Tarazi, Farooq and Jalil and Rahman.

Research done by Obaidullah (2008a, b:37) revealed that *qard hasan* is an effective microfinance tool as it facilitates the transfer of funds from people who have excess to those who are short of funds.

In Iran, a kind of system for *qard hasan* has been established. In this system, *qard* hasan is divided into four types of funds:

- Family *qard hasan*
- Workplace *qard hasan*
- Community *qard hasan*
- Large *qard hasan*

Just like in non-profit institutions, mutual funds are pooled and loans are provided to community members based on the above categories. Loans are provided by Islamic banks while funds are distributed to help low income groups in the country.

¦Waqf (Charitable Endowment)

Waqaf literally means the holding of a certain fixed property (buildings, land, office spaces etc.) for charitable purposes. Hassan stated that it could also include money, books, shares, stocks and other tangible assets. Examples of *waqf* could include gifting of land or building for the explicit use of orphanages, hospitals, *madrasah* (Islamic religious schools) (Housby, 2013:144) and other useful activities. In the *waqf* system, four conditions are necessary:

[7] In Chapter 8 these are discussed in detail.

- The donor
- The property or any tangible asset
- The beneficiary
- The declaration

5.3.7 A Comparative View of Poverty Alleviation Instruments in Islam

Table 5.2 gives a comparative overview of the variety of instruments in Islam to eradicate poverty. Among these instruments, *zakat* is the most distinctive as it is a compulsory obligation for those who have excess funds to transfer those funds to the poor. Although *zakat fitr* is imposed on every individual, *zakatul maal* is not imposed on every individual (as compared to the conventional tax system where all incomes are taxable) and there are certain conditions which must be met such as the *nisab* and the *haul*. On the other hand, *shadaqa* and *waqf* are voluntary acts given as a gift to the poor or needy.

Waqf is devoted to community benefits and it is the only wealth distribution instrument where re-investment of assets is permitted.

5.3.8 Wealth Distribution—Estate Management

The second type of wealth distribution is estate management. *Faraid* is the inheritance law of Islam and it is based on the Holy Quran, the *Hadith* and the consensus of the

Table 5.2 Comparison of poverty alleviation tools in Islam

	Zakat	Shadaqa	Waqf
Compulsory/Voluntary	Compulsory	Voluntary	Voluntary
Rate	Fixed rate	Any amount	Any amount
Spend	Generally spent in one year	Generally spent in one year	Generally capitalized
Investments	Generally, not invested-need to be discharged as soon as possible	Generally, not invested-may be according to need and mandate	Invested in social or economic asset
Time for payment	Generally paid in Ramadan	Can be paid any time	Can be paid any time
How payment is made	Generally paid in cash or stock	Can take the form of any asset	Can take the form of any asset-cash, land coins, jewelery

Source Adapted from Yumna and Clarke

Prophet's (pbuh.) companions and their *ijtihad*. Most of the Islamic law related to estate management or *Faraid* is explained in detail in the An-Nisa verse (The women) of the Qurán. Under the *Faraid* law, only the spouse, parents, and children (known as Quranic heirs) are true heirs to the decedent's estate. Others such as grandchildren, adopted children, illegitimate children, foster or non-Muslim parents/children/family members are not automatically considered as heirs (Al-Shanqaiti, 2009).

A Muslim is permissible to dispose of his/her estate as he/she wishes and to any person not among the heirs, but up to only one-third ($\frac{1}{3}$) of the total assets. This is to prevent the true heirs (Qur'anic heirs) from feeling betrayed or wronged for not getting what is rightfully theirs. In addition, the amount of the estate is calculated after the following disbursements have been completed first:

- Funeral expenses
- Debts/Loans of the deceased

Debts here encompass both debts to Allah such as *zakat,*[8] *kaffarah* (compensation for deliberately missing or breaking a fast without valid reason(s) during the month of Ramadan) or debts to human beings.

Table 5.3 below shows a comparison between a Muslim and a non-Muslim will.

Table 5.3 Difference between Muslim and non-Muslim will

Islamic Will	Non-Islamic Will
The disposal of the majority of a decedent's estate is determined by Islamic law	The disposal of all the decedent's estate is governed by the decedent
True heirs (Qur'anic heirs—spouse, children and parents) are determined by Islamic law. Distribution of the estate to these heirs are governed by Islamic Inheritance Law and changes are totally forbidden	A decedent has the full freedom and discretion to distribute his/her estate to spouse, children, parents and other heirs/individuals
Islamic Inheritance Law allows only one-third (1/3) of the decedent's estate to be distributed to other heirs and the consent of the Qur'anic heirs need not be obtained	A decedent has the freedom to dispose of 100% of his/her estate in any way he/she wishes

Source Al-Shanqaiti (2009)

[8] The majority view (of scholars is that *zakat* should be paid regardless whether it is mentioned in the will or not, although this view is still debatable among Muslim jurists (Al Shanqaiti, 2009).

5.4 The Future of Wealth Creation and Management in Islam

An Overview of Major Challenges towards expansion

Islamic finance has made great strides forward in the past few decades, but Islamic wealth management is still in its infancy, both in size and sophistication, and is lagging behind (Jersey Finance & Hubbis, 2019). Nevertheless, there is a huge potential for it to expand rapidly amongst the wealthy and rising middle- and higher-income persons in countries where Muslims are the majority such as those in the Middle East, Asia and Africa. There are great challenges in administering wealth management as well as products and services which are *Shari'ah*-compliant such as "getting a consensus on *Shari'ah* compliance, lack of product and shortage of expertise," (Jersey Finance & Hubbis, 2019, p. 8). A survey done by Jersey Finance & Hubis (2019) highlights the growing demand amongst the 25 to 50-year-olds generation, for *Shari'ah*-compliant products and services. According to the authors too, these younger generations, who are mostly Western-educated, "*possess a natural proclivity for Islamic wealth management because it represents a more socially-conscious model, given the tenets housed within Sharia compliant finance and solutions*" (Jersey Finance & Hubbis, 2019, p. 8). Some of the challenges are mentioned below:

Firstly, *Shari'ah*-compliant financial products as well as Islamic financial solutions are not easy to devise and manage. Among the reasons attributed to this is that they often fall under grey areas with regards to religious interpretations amongst scholars, protagonists from the industry as well as business clients (Jersey Finance & Hubbis, 2019). Secondly, there is a widespread lack of expertise available as it is really difficult to find individuals who are both knowledgeable in the Islamic laws as well as academic knowledge in finance, banking etc. Besides that, there are also complex interpretation issues from the legal and Islamic jurisprudence perspective, documentation and the lack of scale. Countries such as Malaysia, Dubai and Bahrain are at the top of the world as the pre-eminent Islamic finance markets and centres of excellence.

Malaysia is currently the third largest market in the world for *Shari'ah*-compliant assets, especially *takaful* and *sukuk*. In the past years, its government has stepped up efforts in boosting Malaysia as the centre of excellence in Islamic finance (Alfalah Consulting, 2014). With continuing efforts and better coordination between the government and the private sectors, the supply of IWM products and services may increase in the near future to fulfil increasing demands. Even non-Muslim countries like Singapore and London, where there is a significant number of Muslims and expertise in Islamic finance, are gearing up and working assiduously to work with one another and other centres in the world, creating onshore and offshore solutions for Islamic financial products and services (Maybank Singapore, 2020).

Islamic finance and wealth management system extol the merits of social unity and community growth and development. Thus, it is idealistically suited to align itself with the global drive towards socially responsible investing (SRI) and products offering high environmental, social and governance (ESG) as well as sustainable values (Jersey Finance & Hubbis, 2019). Leading market players, therefore, expect this to play an ever-larger role in the wealth management efforts of the industry and the clientele.

5.5 Conclusion

The concept of wealth management in Islam encompasses a holistic approach and it includes both physical and spiritual wealth. In contrast, conventional wealth management targets only on material wealth (Alfalah Consulting, 2014). Indeed, IWM is becoming increasingly an attractive sector and potentially, it is anticipated to bring good returns in the financial services industry.

There is a growing interest in Islamic finance and Islamic instruments in tandem with the technological and financial innovation in the conventional financial sector. Islamic finance is not only for Muslims, and any individuals, irrespective of their faiths or beliefs, can purchase/invest in *Shari'ah*-compliant products and services (Maybank Singapore, 2020).

The problem of global poverty is very much recognized by Islam and it is at the heart of its teachings. However, Islam does more than just recognizing the issue. It delves deeper in order to identify the root of the problem which causes poverty and social injustice and then providing practical solutions through various instruments such as *zakat*, *sadaqah*, *waqf* and other distribution tools.

Indeed, Islam is not just about theology or religious rules. It is a complete, all-encompassing religion that goes beyond worshipping the one true god. It provides humanity with comprehensive and compassionate legislations as well as guidelines in order to enable humans to live in harmony among fellow Muslims and non-Muslims. It is complete because it not only promotes peace and love among humanity but also provides wholesome guidance for different dimensions of life including the socio-political and economic aspects..

Accepting and following this guidance for wealth distribution would move the world a step closer towards poverty alleviation and eradication. The balance of wealth can be restored globally and will no longer be in favour of the rich. As according to Oxfam International (a global movement of people that aims to end the injustice of poverty), (2020), the total fortunes of the twenty-six (26) wealthiest people in the world is much greater than all of the possessions owned by world's poorest 3.8 billion people.

References

Abu Bakar, N. B. (2008). Zakat and taxation: A conceptual Comparison. *TAFHIM: IKIM Journal of Islam and the Contemporary World*, 2(3).

Alfalah Consulting. (2014). *Malaysia plans to be a pioneer of Islamic Wealth Management.* Retrieved 7 April, 2020, from http://www.alfalahconsulting.com/search/label/Islamic%20wealth%20management.

Al-Ghazzali, I. A. -H. Early 12th Century. *Revival of Religious Sciences (Ihy Ulum-ud-Din).* 1st ed. city in Persia (Iran): Maktabah Mujaddidiyah.

Al-Shanqaiti, E. (2009). Chapter 6. Islam and Private Wealth Management. In: *A Primer on Islamic Finance.* s.l.:The Research Foundation of CFA Institute.

Awang, R., & Mokhtar, M. Z. (2011). Technical Comparison between business zakat and tax on business income in Malaysia. *Malaysian Accounting Review, 10*(2), 13–25.

Bank Negara Malaysia. (2016). *Islamic Wealth Management: Growing Stronger Globally,* Kuala Lumpur: Bank Negara Malaysia.

Bukowski, A. (2014). Social Role of Alms (Zakat) in Islamic Economies. *Annales.etyka w Zyciu Gospodarczym, 17*(4), 123–131.

Chen, J. (2020). *Shari'ah-Compliant Funds.* Retrieved April 8, 2020, from https://www.investopedia.com/terms/s/Shari'ah-compliant-funds.asp.

Daly, S., & Frikha, M. (2015). Islamic finance in favor to development and economic growth: An illustration of the principle of "Zakat." *Arabian Journal of Business and Management Review, 5*(145), 2.

Dhar, P. (2013). Zakat as a measure of social justice in islamic finance: An accountant's overview. *Journal of Emerging Economies and Islamic Research,* 1(1).

Farooq, M. O. (2014). Islamic wealth management and the pursuit of positive-sum solutions. *Islamic Economic Studies, 22*(2), 99–124.

Hassan, M., & Ashraf, A. (2010). *An Integrated Poverty Alleviation Model Combining Zakat, Awqaf and Micro-Finance.* Bangi, s.n., pp. 261–281.

Hoque, N., Khan, M. A., & Mohammad, K. D. (2015). Poverty alleviation by Zakah in a transitional economy: A small business entrepreneurial framework. *Journal of Global Entrepreneurship Research,* 5(7).

Hossain, M. (2012). Zakat in Islam: A powerful poverty alleviating instrument for Islamic countries. *International Journal of Economic Development Research and Investment,* 3(1).

Housby, E. (2013). *Islamic and ethical finance in the United Kingdom.* Edinburgh University Press.

Ismail, A. G., Hassan, M. E. M., Ismail, N., & Shahimi, S. (2010). *The Tawhidi Epistemology: Zakat and Waqf Economy.* Universiti Kebangsaan Malaysia.

Javaid, O., & AW, S. (2015). Global financial capital vs. Islamic concept of wealth: The question of ideological dominance. *Journal of Islamic Business and Management, 219*(3327), 1–18.

Jersey Finance & Hubbis. (2019). *The Evolution of Wealth Management in the World of Islamic Finance: Views from the Islamic Finance Wealth Management Community,* s.l.: Jersey Finance.

Kaleem, A., & Ahmed, S. (2010). The quran and poverty alleviation: A theoretical model for charity-based Islamic microfinance institutions (MFIs). *Nonprofit and Voluntary Sector Quarterly, 39*(3), 409–428.

Maybank Singapore. (2020). *Wealth Management from a Shari'ah Perspective.* Retrieved April 4, 2020, from https://www.maybank2u.com.sg/en/personal/about_us/maybank-singapore/humanising-finance/wealth/wealth-management-from-a-Shari'ah-perspective.page.

Mubarak, M. (2010). *Islamic Wealth Management - A Paradigm Shift in Islamic Finance,* s.l.: Islamic Finance News.

Obaidullah, M. (2008a). *Introduction to Islamic Microfinance.* 1st ed. New Delhi: IBF Net (P) Limited, India.

Obaidullah, M. (2008b). *Introduction to Islamic Microfinance.* s.l.:IBF Net Limited.

Othman, A., & Subramaniam, P. (2013). Wealth Management from the *Shari'ah* Perspective. *Q Report,* pp. 94–99.

Qassem, A. (2016). *Afghanistan's political stability: A dream unrealised.* s.l.:s.n.
Rizvi, S. M. (1992). *The Shari'ah.* 1st ed. Toronto: s.n.
Salim, N. (2006). Wealth Management. *Islamic Finance News,* 3(42).
Shanmugam, B., & Zahari, Z. R. (2009). *A Primer on Islamic Finance.* s.l.:s.n.
Stirk, C. (2015). *An Act of Faith: Humanitarian Financing and Zakat,* s.l.: Global Humanitarian Assistance.
Tasdemir, M., Cobanoglu, M., Iqbal, Z. (2016). Wealth In Islam. *Islamic Wealth Management Report,* pp. 38–45.
Thmoson Reuters. (2015). *Thomson Reuters Releases Global Islamic Asset Management Outlook.* Retrieved April 8, 2020, from https://www.thomsonreuters.com/en/press-releases/2015/may/thomson-reuters-releases-global-islamic-asset-management-outlook-report.html.
Toor, I. A., & Nasar, A. (2001). Zakat as a Social Safety Net: Exploring the Impact. *Research Report,* Issue 53.
Umair, M. (2015). *Minhaj-Ul-Quran: Islam and the Distribution of Wealth.* Retrieved April 20, 2020, from https://www.minhaj.org/english/tid/36694/Islam-and-the-Distribution-of-Wealth-article-by-Muhammad-Umair.html.
United Nations. (2020). *Ending Poverty.* Retrieved April 5, 2020, from https://www.un.org/en/sections/issues-depth/poverty/.
Veen, R. C. (2009). Charitable Giving in Islam. In: *Islamic Relief Worldwide.* Birmingham: Reas Street South, pp. 4–5.
World Data Lab. (2020). *World Poverty Clock.* Retrieved April 5, 2020, from https://worldpoverty.io/headline.

Muhammad Ashfaq is a professor of finance and accounting at IU International University of Applied Sciences. He is a regular visiting faculty member at Wittenborg University of Applied Sciences in the Netherlands and the International MBA program at Coburg University in Germany. His research interests include international finance, digital transformation, FinTech, emerging markets, and the global financial system. He earned his doctoral degree on the topic of knowledge, attitude, and practices toward Islamic banking and finance from the University of Tübingen (Germany). He also received an MBA in financial management from Coburg University. He has played a key role in the conceptualization, development, and accreditation of study programs in various countries. He has most recently developed an extensive and innovative bachelor's degree program in digital business at IU International University.

Hanna R. Abdelwahab holds a Bachelor of Accountancy Degree from Nanyang Technological Institute, Singapore and an MBA Degree—Education Management (honors) from Wittenborg University of Applied Sciences, the Netherlands. She also holds a Post-Graduate Diploma in Education from Singapore and had been in the teaching profession for more than fifteen years in Singapore and Egypt, holding the post of Head of Science Department and Head of English Department (High School Section) respectively. Her MBA thesis entitled *"Business Students' Perceptions of Dutch Higher Educational Institutions in Preparing Them for AI Work Environments*" is due for publication in late 2022 by Sage Journal in Industry and Higher Education. At present, she is working at Wittenborg University of Applied Sciences as the Education Support Administrator, Secretary to the Graduation & Examination Board and a news article writer.

Shahab Aziz teaches Islamic finance, financial management and commercial banking at Bahira Business School, Bahria University, Islamabad Pakistan since 2019. He gained a Master's Degree in Islamic Banking and Finance from Loughborough University, UL (2005), MS in finance from Capital University of science and Technology Islamabad, Pakistan (2013) and Doctorate from universi Teknologi Malasyia, Kuala Lumpur, Malaysia (2019). Dr. Aziz has more than ten year's Islamic Finance industry experience and was serving in credit and risk management departments

(2007–2019) Dr. Aziz participates in conferences worldwide and conducts workshops and training related to research and data analysis.

Shabaz Sharif is a business management researcher, practitioner and trainer. He has conducted pieces of training on Smart PLS-SEM, AMOS, Mandalay, Endnote, SPSS and MPLUS. He is also a trainer of NVIVO and QUIRKOS qualitative tools and conducted training on them. He has published more than 20 research papers in the Scopus-Indexed and Web of Sciences Journals. The areas of his expertise are HRM, organizational behaviours and leadership theories. He has presented more than 25 research papers at national and international conferences and got awards and certificates.

Chapter 6
Investment and Wealth Management in Contemporary Times: *Zakat* as a Viable Approach

AbdulGafar Olawale Fahm

Among the key issues in effective investment and wealth management is whether there is a problem of over maintenance or under maintenance of wealth. However, maintenance is frequently seen as a business expense open to slicing like some other to maximize benefits. With these tensions, wealth managers are continually battling with how to offset the cost with the performance necessities for the investments. This article argues that a Muslim's venture and wealth management plan ought to incorporate the computation of zakat. As such, the cleansing of wealth through zakat is a critical piece of wealth management for a Muslim. The Qur'an, for instance, states the importance of fulfilling this financial obligation (Q17:26–27 & 29–30). Moreover, *zakat*, apart from, encouraging the preservation of investment and wealth, can also be seen as a way of optimal utilization of wealth through discouraging idle cash or hoarding excessive wealth.

The study does not approach this topic by analysing how *zakat* directly influences the socio-economic development of the community in terms of helping the poor or economically disadvantaged in the community or serving as a charity fund aimed at eradicating poverty, these are primary benefits embedded in *zakat* and have been well addressed by many researchers. Rather, this article illuminates wealth creation, Islamic investment, and wealth management through *zakat* which according to Mahomed (2016)

> …requires a review of *zakat* as a concept, its basic rules and objectives, the economic benefits it offers and the challenges facing zakat for effective wealth management. Often ignored, *zakat* planning is a necessary component in a Muslim's comprehensive wealth portfolio (p. 1).

This dimension of looking at *zakat* has been under-examined and should undergird the investment and wealth management plan of a Muslim in channelling financial obligation through religious institutions. Based on the issues often raised in

A. O. Fahm (✉)
Department of Religions, University of Ilorin, Ilorin, Nigeria
e-mail: fahm.ao@unilorin.edu.ng

T. Azid et al. (eds.), *Wealth Management and Investment in Islamic Settings*,
https://doi.org/10.1007/978-981-19-3686-9_6

contemporary times on assets and investment management ranging from insurance and protection strategies to liabilities and debts, this paper examines the concept of investment and wealth management from an Islamic perspective. While acknowledging the extant strategies in investment and wealth management for accomplishing extra pay or growth in value or reward, it is submitted that the features embedded in the institution of *zakat* as a socio-economic strategy can help in enhancing wealth as well as investment portfolio management. The paper ultimately recommends the examination of *zakat* institution in Islam by investment and wealth managers to serve as a way of attaining Islamic practices, ethics, and motivations in investment and wealth management especially when targeting Muslim clients and engaging the Islamic market. It is against the above backdrop that this article will proceed as follows: An overview of investment and wealth management; Islam, investment, and wealth management; what is *zakat*; *zakat* as investment and wealth management tool; and conclusion.

6.1 An Overview of Investment and Wealth Management

Investment implies the activity or process of putting away cash for benefit. All in all, it suggests every kind of resource, claimed or controlled directly or by implication for profit. This incorporates portable and steady property, contracts, shares in and stock and debentures of the organization, claims to cash, intellectual property rights, business concessions to look for, develop, concentrate or take advantage of natural resources (Douglas, 2009). According to Kaptan (2001).

> Investment is the employment of funds with the aim of achieving additional income or growth in value. The essential quality of an investment is that it involves waiting for a reward. It involves the commitment of resources which have been saved or put away from current consumption of resources in the hope that some benefits will accrue in future.

It is important to note that investment is a wide concept that embraces different categorisations from finance and economic experts. Investment from the finance point of view, for instance, entails assets that yield some positive return over a period and may range from safe to risky investment. Furthermore, financial investors contribute funds or capital to gain future pay as far as interest, profits, lease, charges, annuity benefits, or the appreciation for the worth of their capital. The main difference between financial investment and economic investment is that it does not matter to a financial investor regardless of whether cash is contributed for useful use or the acquisition of recycled instruments, for example, existing offers and stocks recorded on the stock trade (Kaptan, 2001). Whereas an economist's investment addresses the net increments to the economy's capital stocks as far as labour and products that are significantly utilised in the development of different labour and products. Subsequently, to the business analyst, venture includes the development of new and useful capital as new construction, new maker's tough gear like plant and hardware, inventories as well as human resources (Kaptan, 2001). From the Islamic perspective, the economist's understanding of investment is closer to the approach of how *zakat* funds should be seen, meaning, leading to more productive human and capital development.

Crucial to the notion of investment is the notion of wealth since "assets" lie at the core of investment concerns. This is why investment experts consider wealth management as something beyond investment exhortation, it includes other monetary administrations to address the requirements of prosperous clients. It is additionally a consultative interaction by which the counsel gathers data about the client's needs and tailors a bespoke procedure using fitting monetary items and administrations (Ganti, 2020). Wealth management is therefore seen as an investment advisory assistance that consolidates other monetary administrations to address the requirements of prosperous clients. Since wealth, according to Henry David Thoreau, "is the ability to fully experience life". Also, Edmund Burke once opined that "If we command our wealth, we shall be rich and free. If our wealth commands us, we are poor indeed." The present study suggests five components of wealth which include financial, social, intellectual, physiological, and spiritual (Table 6.1).

Based on the above, the following types, implications, and threats to wealth are identifiable:

In essence, wealth, which Investopedia (2018) defines as "the total market value of all physical and intangible assets owned, then subtracting all debts". Essentially, entails more than just physical but also intangible assets. The idea of wealth encompasses the accumulation of scarce resources and impinges on being ready to gather numerous significant assets or merchandise.

Although, there are writers who have noted other dimensions of wealth apart from the five types highlighted above. These are time or freedom; values or cultural capital; success, a memory of the Source, dignity, skill, friendliness, courage (Dahhaj, 2018; Forwardthinkingwm, 2019; Haylett, 2020; Shankar, 2016; TFOPhoenix, 2020; Wargent, 2020). However, for the present study, wealth management is understood in

Table 6.1 Types of wealth

Type	Implication	Threat
Financial wealth	Access to money, food, clothing, car, home, etc.	Poverty, unemployment, hunger, famine
Social wealth	Access to work, friends, gatherings, fun, etc.	Time, environmental degradation, natural disasters, pollution
Physiological wealth	Access to medical/health treatment, fitness, etc.	Lethal irresistible infections, absence of admittance to fundamental medical services
Intellectual wealth	Access to reading, knowledge, experience, travel, etc.	Lack of or limited access to opportunities and resources
Spiritual wealth	Access to self, people around one including loved ones, God	Repression, tensions, violence, crime, terrorism, abuses

its broadest sense as "the combining of personal investment management, financial advisory, and planning disciplines directly for the benefit of high-net-worth clients" (*Financial Times* Lexicon). There are several ways Islam confronts issues related to wealth management. One of such ways is the exact way that an individual's estate should be distributed on their passing, indicating who is qualified for acquiring and which share. Notwithstanding, the current study's attention is on zakat which is one of the mainstays of Islam with the dictate to offer a percentage of unused capital consistently as zakat to be used by the authorities for those in dire need.

6.2 Islam, Investment, and Wealth Management

The question this section will answer is how do Islam, Investment, and Wealth Management interface? This question is very important because of the assumption among some financial experts that contemporary investment and wealth management as little or no connection with Islam and its institutions; there are assumptions that Islam and Islamic Studies cannot contribute much in this area; there are assumptions that experts in Islamic Studies may not understand the intricacies of contemporary investment and wealth management outlooks.

The present study help address these misconceived assumptions. It should be noted that Islam aims to regulate all individual and collective behaviour. Islam's outlook from the outset is to integrate everything into its all-embracing vision, subjecting them to the same basic principles and same regulatory intuitions, the earthly and the heavenly, this world and the next world, *Dunya* and *Din*. In other words, in Islam faith and action go hand in hand, involved in and influencing each other.

According to Bouhdiba (1998), the Qur'an has about 203 verses (6,000 plus) that are directly or indirectly related to economics. Out of the 203 verses, 82 are connected to alms and *zakat*, 32 with food and prohibitions surrounding them, and 29 with wealth. Other verses can be linked to issues of ownership, trade, credit and debit, fraud, association, and contracts. All these go to show that Islam is a far-reaching system of life. It gives thoughtful attention to the economy, well-being, and prosperity of one and all that includes proprietors. This is because Islam guides man to have proper attitudes towards wealth and prosperity. The Qur'an says "Satan promises you poverty and commands you to indecency, and God promises you forgiveness from Him, and bounty" (Qur'an 2:268). In another verse, the Qur'an states "And when it is said unto them, 'Spend of that wherewith God has provided you,' those who disbelieve say to those who believe, 'Are we to feed one whom, if God willed, He would feed him? You are in naught but manifest error." (Q36:47).

This is a response to the individuals who laughed at the directive to spend in the way of God—to take care of poor people—found all through the Qur'an. Nasr (2015) notes about the verse that it emphasises how God is the One who takes care of and gives, that is to say, every one of the provisions that individuals get on earth is made by God. They cannot make any of that; for sure, they cannot make anything at all. It is God's will that individuals ought to have needs that they cannot accomplish without difficult work, like farming, separating earth natural substance to make things, shipping its products from one spot to another, giving such items as a trade-off for different items or cash, and so on. Nasr stated further that it is likewise God's will that individuals vary in their gifts and capacities to guarantee that everything expected to satisfy man's undertaking of building human existence on earth is accessible. The achievement of this task not just needs talents and capacities that bring in cash and produce wealth; it additionally requires others that can meet different human needs, without bringing in cash. This makes for a perplexing human culture, where individuals have various parts in a bustling world, and across ages. Nonetheless, the subsequent contrasts in the means accessible to various individuals do not prompt the ruination of life and society. It is a result of life's development. That is why the Qur'an mentions: "Allah has bestowed His gifts of sustenance more freely on some of you than on others: Those who are more favoured are not going to throw back their gifts to those whom their right hand possess (slaves or servant), so as to be equal in that respect. Will they then deny the favours of Allah" (Q16:71).

Thus, man is expected to strive in his earthly life to improve not only himself but also his family and society, what other way can one do that than to invest and judiciously manage one's wealth. A Muslim is urged to be self-supporting and to try not to be an obligation to anyone. To that end, Islam regards a wide range of work for earning one's livelihood since there is no foulness or bad behaviour included. The Prophet, for example, was reported to have said it is much better for one even to take his rope, cut wood, heap it up and offer it to eat and give charity than to ask others regardless of whether they give him. Hence, in Islam, one who invests and attempts to manage his wealth honestly cannot be regarded as useless. For every bit that a person does for himself and all others, he will be duly rewarded both in this world and the next as they will be regarded as righteous deeds.

Islamic principle is that as a person improves his wealth and income level, he shares some of his earnings with the community too. In this way, he helps to engineer and expand wealth and prosperity in society. The Islamic outlook is that in the wealth that a person makes, others have contributed their share to it, at least a part of the workforce even if nothing else. In other words, wealth and prosperity develop and propagate best in a society of skilled, honest, and dedicated workforce. It is thus only fair and reasonable to expect those who have benefited from such a society to put back into society by way of investment bits of what they make. In this way too, the economy will generate itself further.

From all that has been said above, it can be deduced that wealth management enjoys a lot of consideration from Islam. The genuine venture is allowed and favoured by God. Ventures can be carried out through people, organizations, offices, and so on. However, all ventures ought to be done with bluntness and genuineness. Cheating, concealing deformities of product from the sellers, taking advantage of the requirements of clients are viewed as corrupt and culpable. Furthermore, owners are continually reminded that the way that they are in all actuality simply agents designated by God to administer their possessions. Along these lines, there is nothing in Islam to prevent a Muslim from achieving riches and contributing to material enhancements. The idea of Real Ownership of things is to make owners prepared all the time to spend in the way of God and to add to noble motivations. It makes one receptive to the needs of society and gives one a significant job to carry out, a sacrosanct mission to satisfy. It likewise saves one from the pit of selfishness, greed, and foul play. This, indeed, is the concept of investment and wealth management in Islam.

Furthermore, the Qur'an speaks about ownership of wealth as a difficult test, and not a badge of righteous greatness or advantaged respectability or a means for abuse. The Qur'an says: "It is He Who has made you (His) agents, inheritors of the earth: He has raised you in ranks, some above others; that he may try you in the gifts He has given you. Verily, your Lord is quick in punishment, yet He is indeed Oft-Forgiving, Most Merciful" (Q6:165).

Moreover, in investment and wealth management among the things often sorted by proprietors is security and stability. These two are considered basic human needs in Islam, in fact, probably to the level as equal as food, apparel, and housing. This is because, without security and stability, a person cannot as expected lead his day-to-day existence and add to the turn of events and progression of society. To ensure security and stability, Islam encourages human beings to work, be allowed to contribute, and be qualified to earn and possess. Since one is simply a trustee that gives the essential measure of stability to guarantee the appropriate treatment of one's assets or one's trusts. Albeit, one has the power to procure, contribute, and spend. However, in this manner, one is guided by standards to keep the community secured. For instance, one is not unreservedly free to spend his or her wealth or manage properties the way one pleases. The Qur'an says: "And render to the kindred their due rights, as (also) to those in want, and the wayfarer. But squander not (your wealth) in the manner of a spendthrift. Verily, spendthrifts are brothers of the Evil Ones, and the Evil One is to his Lord (Himself) ungrateful" (Q17:26–27). "Make not your hand tied (like a niggard's) to your neck, nor stretch it forth to its utmost reach (like a foolish spendthrift); lest you become rebuked and destitute. Verily your Lord does provide sustenance in abundance for whom He pleases, and He provides in a just measure. For he does know and regard all His servants" (Q17:29–30).

That is why Ramadan (2003) opined that there are about four aspects of the moral meaning of wealth in Islam: (a) To please God and make gifts along the way He sets us (b) Giving fair measure (c) The struggle against egoism and acquisitiveness (d) Learning discretion. Thus, it can be submitted that the ultimate objective of Islam's concept of investment and wealth management is to get the required assistance needed by people and to ensure progress wherein each individual can reside in an environment of harmony, equity, and security. This is a human advancement that permits an individual to satisfy all his spiritual, scholarly, and material needs and develop each part of his being (Siddiqui & Murad, 2017).

6.2.1 What is Zakat?

Zakat is the third of the five mainstays of Islam. It is the main activity in Islam after the obligatory prayers. This is why it is mentioned throughout the Qur'an. It is referenced multiple times in the Qur'an and several times alongside prayer (Mahomed, 2016). The Qur'an says: "Take sadaqah (alms) from their wealth in order to purify them and sanctify them with it, and invoke Allah for them. Verily! Your invocations are a source of security for them, and Allah is All-Hearer, All-Knower" (Q9:103). In this verse, the verbal form of the word *zakat* (*tuzakiheem*) is used, and its meaning here is "to sanctify" or "to grow righteous".

Basically, *zakat* means "to grow" or "to increase". It means, "to increase" when used in conjunction with inanimate objects and "to grow" when used in conjunction with animate objects. However, since plants and animals will grow properly only when they are in a clean environment, the word has a further meaning of cleanliness. When the same sort of growth in an environment of cleanliness is applied to humans, the word takes on the meaning of spiritual purification or growth in righteousness.

One of the Quranic verses that give the complete meaning of *zakat* says, "The believers, men and women, are friends (*Auliya*') of one another, they enjoin (on the people) good and forbid (people) from evil; they perform as-salaat and give the *zakat*, and obey Allah and His Messenger. Allah will have His Mercy on them. Surely Allah is All-Mighty, All-Wise" (Q9:71). This verse introduced the notion of a believing community and how the giving of *zakat* is one of the main characteristics of that community. Also, paying *zakat* is obligatory for all kinds of people.

From the early period of Islam, the Prophet enjoined his followers to give their wealth to charity. Although the majority of the verses of *zakat* were revealed in Madina, some of them were revealed in Makkah (e.g. Q30:39) where the Muslims were a poor and persecuted minority. This shows that even when the community was very poor, the Muslims were still urged to practice charity. As mentioned earlier, everything that one owns belongs to Allah and we hold those things in trust for Allah. When one pays out a portion of what we hold, one purifies the remainder and encourages new growth, demonstrating the idea of investment and wealth management, albeit, in the spiritual sense. With the payment of *zakat*, wealth is purified but so also is the payer or the recipient because the verse quoted earlier says, "Take *sadaqah* (alms) from their wealth in order to purify them..." (Q9:103).

Just as people are created with various tones, perspectives, and levels of information, so too their deeds and provision vary. Certain individuals are rich and some poor. This, it is accepted, is to test the rich regarding whether they show appreciation, and to test the poor concerning whether they show restraint. The Prophet was reported to have said, "...He [Allah] has enjoined *sadaqah* upon their assets which will be taken from the rich of the (Muslim) community and distributed to the poor. If they accept that, refrain from laying hands upon the best of their goods..." (Bukhari). Hence, *zakat* refines and purifies riches, and filters the soul from parsimony and stinginess. It fortifies the affection between the rich and poor, removes disdain, makes security prevail, and gives joy to the community. All of these point to the Islamic understanding of the purpose of wealth and investment.

It is, however, pertinent to state that the payment of *zakat* is compulsory upon every individual who possesses the *nisaab* (least sum) for one year. The rate of *zakat* on gold, silver, different metals, and exchange merchandise is one-fourth of 10%. On rural produce and organic products the sum is one-10th if it is watered (by artificial means), and one-half of one-10th if it is not inundated (by artificial means, i.e., it is watered by precipitation or other normal means). Specific requirements can also be found on *an'aam* animals such as sheep, goats, cattle, and camels.

Also, the *Shari 'ah* does not require the payment of *zakat* on just any amount of wealth that is capable of growth, regardless of how little. Instead, it stipulates that wealth must exceed a certain minimum (*nisaab*). There are several *ahadith* from the Prophet in which minimums are delineated for different groups of assets. For instance, Ali ibn Abu Talib narrated that the Prophet said:

> When you possess two hundred dirhams and one year passes on them, five dirhams are payable. Nothing is incumbent on you, that is, on gold, till it reaches twenty dinars. When you possess twenty dinars and one year passes on them, half a dinar is payable. Whatever exceeds, that will be reckoned properly. [Then, the narrator said: "I do not remember whether the words 'that will be reckoned properly' were uttered by Ali himself or he attributed them to the Prophet".]

By and large, the Islamic teaches stipulates that whoever pays zakat, his or her sins are expiated thereby, wealth will be blessed and it will store up a great reward. The Qur'an says: "And perform as-salaat, and give *zakat*, and whatever of good (deeds that Allah loves) you send forth for yourselves before you, you shall find it with Allah. Certainly, Allah is All-Seer of what you do" (Q2:110).

6.3 *Zakat* as Investment and Wealth Management Tool

Although Islam is quite open as regard how *zakat* should be distributed, it is, however, our concern in this study in what way *zakat* can be linked to wealth management. The connection between *zakat* and wealth management can be viewed from various perspectives. Firstly, wealth management through *zakat* allows a fair distribution of wealth which is necessary to ensure that wealth is not confined only to a few, thereby discouraging hoarding. Secondly, *zakat* ensures that the proprietor practices good wealth management by helping out with the need of the less fortunate. Thirdly, *zakat* promotes efficient utilization of wealth to sustain the spirit of kinship within the society.

Indeed, wealth management in Islam is very important to the extent that it can be linked to one of the pillars of the religion, i.e. through *zakat*. This means that failure to properly manage one's wealth through *zakat* may lead one away from the fold of Islam. Furthermore, as mentioned earlier a purification mechanism for wealth can be achieved through *zakat* by ensuring the purification of a person, the wealth, and property. Besides investing wealth, one may unintentionally do things that are not proper, thus, *zakat* help makes reparations for it. In other words, it filters the wealth of the payer by eliminating the debasements that were amassed alongside the wealth.

In the spirit of proper investment and wealth management, Islam through *zakat* help to discourage the accumulation of wealth or hoarding. The Qur'an says: "What Allah has bestowed on His Messenger (and taken away) from the people of the township—belongs to Allah—to His Messenger and to relatives and orphans, the needy and the traveller; in order that it may not circuit between the wealthy among you. So take what the Messenger assigns to you, and deny yourselves that which he withholds from you. And fear Allah; for Allah is strict in punishment" (Q59:7).

Hence, Islam, in ensuring proper management of wealth discourages hoarding. According to Al-Jarhi (1985), storing over-the-top wealth or wealth that is not invested is irrational as *zakat* is charged on all monetary and real resources which regularly bring about a negative rate of return (*zakat* rate). Hoarding can also be seen interest that Islam disapproves of. This is because financially extorting a debtor to always having to repay so much more than what he originally borrowed (compound interest) since the debtor has to pay the accumulated interests too, and often the accumulated interests exceed the borrowed amount. Therefore, this means the creditor gathers exorbitant gains while the debtor is in penury. Islam forbids this form of "investment" when the says: "Those who devour usury will not stand except as stands one on whom the Evil One by his touch has driven into madness. That is because they say: "Trade is like usury," but Allah has permitted trade but forbidden usury. Those who after receiving direction from their Lord, desist, shall be pardoned for the past; their case is for Allah (to judge), but those who repeat (the offence) are Companions of the Fire; they will abide therein forever" (Q2:275).

It is also in the context of proper wealth management through *zakat* that Islam gives precise instructions on how to distribute and disperse wealth. Islam certainly does not condone the view that wealth should be restricted to a certain set of people due to blood or race or colour. Thus, *zakat* in Islam is indeed detailed to ensure equitable wealth utilization. It enables the recipient many of whom are classified among the less-favoured citizenry to play their role in society, even financially (Suhaib, 2009). Since the method of utilization of *zakat* is divinely ordained therefore no one can dispute its fairness. However, there is room for other genuine intentioned approaches to its utilization. The Qur'an says: "*Zakat* is for the poor and the needy and those who are employed to administer and collect it, and for those whose hearts are to be won over, and for the freeing of human beings from bondage, and for those who are overburdened with debts and for every struggle in Allah's cause, and for the wayfarers: This is a duty ordained by Allah, and Allah is the All-Knowing, the Wise" (Q9:60).

Also, measurement is important in *zakat* because of the requirement of *nisaab*, proper wealth management is needed by the proprietor that is willing to pay *zakat*. This helps to sustain fairness and protect the interest of the community. Hence, Islam insists that in investment and wealth management; justice, fair dealings, and accurate measurements should be considered. That is why several researchers (e.g. Al-Suhaibani, 1990; Ammani et al., 2014; Hassan, 2010; Hassan & Khan,

2007; Murinde, 1995; Norulazidah et al., 2010; Suprayitno et al., 2013) have noted that when *zakat* funds are collected and manage efficiently can lead to development through an increase in aggregate demand and consumption expenditure, debt burden reduction, employment, poverty reduction, increase investment and economic growth.

6.4 Conclusion

Investment and wealth management in Islam is both a responsibility and accountability and as such can be a source of joy or sadness. This is because with wealth a person can be closer to righteousness if one manages it well. However, if wealth is improperly managed or invested, or used for unbridled exploitation it would be a source of sorrow. That is why there are several references in the Qur'an to wealth and positions as well as the result of obsessions with them (e.g. Q28:76–83; Q7:103–137). Also, Islam guides to have a correct perspective of wealth, investment, and materialistic quests (e.g. Q17:18–21).

The study stresses that *zakat*, based on the Islamic perspective, is one of the essential Islamic socio-economic institutions through which an appropriate and balanced approach to investment and wealth management can be attained. Therefore, investment and wealth management experts should explore this institution when dealing with their Muslim clients. Having a correct understanding of *zakat* beyond its charity aspect is imperative for successful investment and wealth management. If *zakat* is understood as a mechanism or part of a mechanism that can help to regulate and drive investment and wealth management plans, the purpose of the study is achieved. It is proposed, therefore, that the concept of investment and wealth management should be gleaned from *zakat* for *zakat* funds to reach their fullest potential in society.

For *zakat* to achieve this goal, there is a need to see beyond its charity aspects but as a tool that drives investment and wealth management discipline in Muslim proprietors willing to follow the dictates of Islam. Through this, *zakat* can become a wealth-creating institution and be a long-lasting strategy to fight poverty. Although other Islamic socio-economic institutions exist, this paper recommends that investment and wealth management experts can also ruminant along the line of *zakat*. The study suggests that working along this line would lead to a far-reaching consolidation of the *zakat* institution more holistically.

Finally, it is worth saying that this study does not conflict with the socio-economic benefit inherent in *zakat* but is instead complementary to it. Although investment and wealth management are practiced the role of *zakat* is not fully appreciated, and is often, narrowed. Hence, this paper shows the various facets of *zakat* in sustaining investment and wealth management. This is of great value to Islamic finance experts, specifically investment and wealth managers because it will help them improve their financial planning as well as investment portfolio management or strategies especially when targeting Muslim clients and engaging the Islamic market.

References

Al-Jarhi, M. A. (1985). Towards an Islamic macro model of distribution: A comparative approach. *Journal of King Abdulaziz University: Islamic Economics, 2*(2).

Al-Suhaibani, M. I. (1990). *The effects of zakat on economics resources utilisation*. Al-Imam Mohammad Ibn Saud University.

Ammani, S. A., Abba, S. A., & Dandago, K. I. (2014). Zakah on employment income in Muslims majority states of Nigeria: Any cause for alarm? *Procedia-Social and Behavioral Sciences, 164*, 305–314.

Bouhdiba, A. (1998). Economic thought. In A. Bouhdiba & M. M. Al-Dawalibi (Eds.), *The different aspects of islamic culture: The individual and society in islam*. United Nations Educational, Scientific, and Cultural Organization.

Dahhaj, Z. K. (2018). *The 4 types of wealth that you must know about*. Medium.Com. Retrieved from https://medium.com/@zaiderrr/the-4-types-of-wealth-that-you-must-know-about-91350b421f1d

Douglas, Z. (2009). *The international law of investment claims*. Cambridge University Press. Retrieved from https://books.google.com.ng/books?id=8Bl-74IZRncC

Forwardthinkingwm. (2019). *Four types of wealth*. Forward Thinking Wealth Management. Retrieved from https://forwardthinkingwm.com/news-and-articles/four-types-of-wealth

Ganti, A. (2020). *Wealth management*. Investopedia. Retrieved from https://www.investopedia.com/terms/w/wealthmanagement.asp

Hassan, M. K., & Khan, J. M. (2007). Zakat, external debt and poverty reduction strategy in Bangladesh. *Journal of Economic Cooperation Among Islamic Countries, 28*(4).

Hassan, M. K. (2010). An integrated poverty alleviation model combining zakat, awqaf and micro-finance. In *The Tawhidi Epistemology: Zakat and Waqf Economy* (pp. 261–281). https://doi.org/10.1109/INCOS.2010.100

Haylett, D. (2020). *The four types of wealth*. TFP Financial Planning. Retrieved from https://tfp-fp.com/the-four-types-of-wealth/

Investopedia. (2018). *Wealth*. Investopedia.Com. Retrieved from https://www.investopedia.com/terms/w/wealth.asp

Kaptan, S. S. (2001). *Investment management*. Sarup & Sons.

Mahomed, Z. (2016). Zakat, islamic wealth management & wealth effects (pp. 1–2). *CIWM Special Edition*. Retrieved from https://www.inceif.org/archive/wp-content/uploads/2018/02/Zakat-Islamic-Wealth-Management-Wealth-Effects.pdf

Murinde, V. (1995). Is it prudent for Islamic banks to make investment decisions without the interest rate instrument? *Research in Accounting in Emerging Economies, 3*, 123–148.

Nasr, S. H. (Ed.). (2015). *The study Quran: A new translation and commentary*. HarperCollins Publishers.

Norulazidah, P. H., Omar Ali, D. H., & Myles, G. D. (2010). The consequences of zakat for capital accumulation. *Journal of Public Economic Theory, 12*(4), 837–856. https://doi.org/10.1111/j.1467-9779.2010.01476.x

Ramadan, T. (2003). *Western Muslims and the future of Islam*. Oxford University Press.

Shankar, S. S. R. (2016). *The 8 types of wealth*. Art of Living. Retrieved from https://wisdom.srisriravishankar.org/the-8-types-of-wealth/

Siddiqui, A. R., & Murad, K. (2017). *Treasures of the Qur'an: Surah al-Fatihah to Surah al-Mai'dah*. Kube Publishing Ltd.

Suhaib, A. Q. (2009). Contribution of zakat in the social development of Pakistan. *Pakistan Journal of Social Sciences (PJSS), 29*(2).

Suprayitno, E., Kader, R. A., & Harun, A. (2013). The impact of zakat on aggregate consumption in Malaysia. *Journal of Islamic Economics, Banking and Finance, 9*(1), 1–24.

TFOPhoenix. (2020). *The four types of wealth*. Tfophoenix.Com. Retrieved from https://tfophoenix.com/the-four-types-of-wealth/

Wargent, P. (2020). *4 types of wealth (and how to balance them)*. Michael Yardney's PropertyUpdate.Com.Au. Retrieved October 31, 2020, from https://propertyupdate.com.au/4-types-of-wealth-and-how-to-balance-them/

AbdulGafar Olawale Fahm teaches Islamic Studies at the University of Ilorin in Ilorin, Nigeria. He gained a Master's Degree in Islamic Spiritual Culture and Contemporary Society from International Islamic University Malaysia (2011) and his Doctorate from the same University (2015). He is a Senior Lecturer at the Department of Religions, University of Ilorin, Ilorin, Nigeria. His research interests also include Islamic Thought and Civilization; Philosophy, Ethics, and Contemporary Issues; Muslim World Issues; and interactions of Islamic culture and contemporary society. He participates in academic conferences worldwide on Islamic constructs, cultures and concerns.

Chapter 7
The Urgency of Debt Management in the Perspective of Islamic Wealth Management

Rizqi Zakiya and Achmad Firdaus

Debt on a macro scale becomes part of nation's income utilization tool. The approach used is in accordance with the function: Y = C + I + G + (X–M) (Wi: national income, C: national consumption, I: national investment, G: government spending, and X-M: export minus import. While government debt is included in I (national investment), both domestic debt and global debt.

Likewise, Individuals but also companies on a micro scale, choose debt as a business strategy to increase their level of economy. The positive impact of the debt is the acceleration of business progress. But if the debt is only used for consumptive needs without the positive reciprocity of debt expenditure that has been done, the result will be unresolved debt trap.

Consumptive lifestyle, described by Soman and Cheema (2002) with the phrase "borrow from future income". Willing to borrow to meet current needs. Nevertheless, Rapid development of technology and the changes in lifestyle in the community, provoked many people not to meet only their needs, but also try to fulfill their desires by debt.

Prophet (PBUH) taught his people to keep away debt.

> "(I seek refuge with Allah from Kufr and debt.)" A man said: "Are you equating debt with Kufr?" He said: "Yes." (Narated by Nasa'i & Hakim).

And

> Whoever takes the money of the people with the intention of repaying it, Allah will repay it on his behalf, and whoever takes it in order to spoil it, then Allah will spoil him. (Narated by Bukhari).

This paper will try to reveal: How Islam provides solutions to debt management, refers to the concept of Islamic Wealth Management (IWM). The findings is

R. Zakiya (✉) · A. Firdaus
Institut Agama Islam Tazkia, Jl. Ir. H. Djuanda No. 78, Sentul City, Bogor 16810, Indonesia
e-mail: rizqi@tazkia.ac.id

T. Azid et al. (eds.), *Wealth Management and Investment in Islamic Settings*,
https://doi.org/10.1007/978-981-19-3686-9_7

revealed by developing several research questions, namely: debt, needs or lifestyle, how the position of debt in wealth management, how Islam views debt, what is the condition of debt that is allowed, how does Islam provide a solution to the debt trap.

7.1 Debt, Need or Lifestyle

Economy is how people behave to fulfill unlimited desires by utilizing limited resources (Lipsey, 1991). Potential resources owned by each individual must be optimized to achieve the expected economic level. Thus, everything related to human interaction in fulfilling their desires is part of economic activity. Including debt as part of it. Debt is one of economic activities that applied globally in the society (Aziz, 2016). Debt is often chosen to meet the needs of life (Shohib, 2015).

At a macro level, no country without debt. The United States, Japan and China each has 31.8, 18.8 and 7.9% among total global debt. Moreover, Libanon has become the third largest debt ratio to gross domestic product which is reaching 149% of its GDP (Desjardins, 2018). The Greece even proven bankrupt in 2015. It was unable to pay a maturity of Rp. 22 trillion. Reciprocally, Zimbabwe, Jamaica, Argentina feel the negative impact caused by it (Daniel, 2015).

Indonesia as developing country inevitably adopt the same economy system. On July 2018, Indonesian government debt reached Rp. 4,253.02 Trillion. Debt received from bilateral loans reached Rp. 323.79 Trillion, from multirateral assets reached Rp. 411.19 trillion, commercial debt reached Rp. 43.32 trillion, supplier supply reached Rp. 1.04 trillion, domestic debt reached Rp. 5.79 trillion, and Government Securities reached Rp. 3,467.52 Trillion (Laucereno, 2018).

Government credit triggers an increase in household individual debt. Renanita and Hidayat (2013) revealed, based on data and information from the Directorate of Credit, Rural Banks and MSMEs of Bank Indonesia; In 2010, consumption loans, working capital loans and investment loans reached Rp. 47.1 Trillion (46.1%), Rp. 35.8 trillion (35%), and Rp. 19.3 Trillion (18.9%) of the total credit funds channeled to the population of Indonesia. The largest credit is allocated in consumptive purposes, more than working capital and investment credit. The high consumption credit has the potential to bring up new individuals who are unable to pay off debt in the future.

Consumptive debt is usually used to support a family, buy clothes, get married, provide treatment, build a house, buy crafts, marry off a child and so on. Imam Qatadah classifies them into gharim, that is, those who borrow without excessive. The leaders are responsible for paying off their debts. Source of funds form Baitul Mal (Tabari in Al-Qardawi, 2006).

Among them are those who struck by the disaster. Mujahid explained in Al-Qardawi (2006), three gharim groups namely (1) people whose property was flooded. (2) people who have lost their assets due to a fire accident. (3) A person responsible for his, owing no wealth, thus he has to borrow to support his family. Imam Malik, Imam Shafi'i and Imam Ahmad classify them all as gharim from what occurred on them.

Nevertheless, there are some people who borrow as to satisfy their unlimited desire based on their lifestyle. Hanudin (2012) revealed that lifestyle is the most powerful factor influencing a person in deciding to borrow. A person's lifestyle is influenced by the world view attached to it. This includes a consumptive lifestyle by utilizing debt as an option to fulfill it. But on the other side, groups who are trapped in debt not because of fulfilling their lifestyle, but in order to fulfill daily needs or other Muslims needs whom are called gharim and considered as one group among eight groups zakah receivers.

Al-Qurtubi (W: 595 H) steted:

> As for Gharim, just what on what is needed as their responsibility, if the debt is in obedience motives and not to overdo it, especially on important matters.

Al-Qurtubi explained that people who borrow on immoral motives are not considered as gharim. He also explained that even when facing an urgent case, debt is prohibited caused by immoral motives, excessive, and things that are considered futile. Al-Qurtubi's opinion is in line with the opinion of Syihabuddin (d: 684 CE). Syihabuddin said on his statement:

> Gharim is a person who owes not in pointless and harm motives, and he does not have the wealth to pay it off, or has property but does not meet his debt, so he has right to receive zakah to pay off his debts.

Furthermore Syihabuddin (d: 684 CE) explains that a person who is in debt for not for worthless nor harm motives is counted as gharim. Thus, all of debts made with the aim of futility are not included in the category of motives that caused him to become mustahiq gharim. Likewise with harm motives, both individually and socially.

7.2 Debt in Wealth Management

People decides to have debt usually caused by not having enough money to buy something they wanted (wants) or needed (needs). Possibly, something that is desired or needed is the goal of his personal finance. In financial management, debt that is used for consumptive purposes is classified as bad debt. Commonly debt used for consumption will be threaten as the long-term goals of financial management. It can be understood that when taking consumption debt, people who has a debt, must allocate payments including interest (usury) regularly. Of course this disturbs other financial management goals.

A debt for purchasing of new household furniture while the old one still functioning properly is considered as a bad debt. Also debt to buy a new car even though the old car is no running well. Furthermore, a new car is not bought for investment purpose to gain more business profit, but to increase personal prestige. Including the use of credit cards for luxury trips, as tourism is a tertiary need. It is wiser if tertiary needs are met from budgets that are within their capabilities. Forcing a luxury tour with a loan from a credit card is unwise.

Bad debt urgent limit ratio according to Tyson (2010) is calculated by the formula of bad debt/annual income. Tyson explained that financial health can be achieved if the ratio of bad debt ratio is 0. The safe ratio of bad debt ratio is between 10 to 20% of annual income. Tyson explained, once we start a bad debt, it will grow like a cancer. Growing up eating away the body. Bad debt is also like snowball. Starting from a small one, it enlarges simultaneously with the snowball rotation.

Conversely, good debt is debt made for investment. Debt to gain future value. Debt for education, home ownership, or for business, are classified as good debt. Indeed there is no guarantee that good debt will work well to create value in the future. Loans for education, education outcomes may not produce the expected value. Salary received from the work does not match the education being undertaken. The business that was run from the results of the loan went bankrupt. Houses built from the proceeds of loans struck by a fire or other disaster.

Islam views asset management as something that has a very important role. Billah (2010: 33) states that asset management is one way of managing one's personal assets or ownership in accordance with Islamic values. While Shafii et al. (2013) views the management of Islamic assets as a financial industry that regulates two things, namely Islamic financial planning and investment portfolio management.

Furthermore Shafii et al. (2013) explained the four principles of asset management according to Islamic sharia, namely: (1). Islam as a way of life. Islam is the foundation in all aspects of life including economic and business activities. (2). Everything belongs to God. The treasure that is managed by mankind in principle is the fortune given by God to humans. Therefore, humans are commanded to obtain and spend property in accordance with what God has entrusted to humans. (3). Humans as khalifah (representative of Allah) on earth. The task of man as the caliph of Allah on earth is to use all of these gifts for the benefit of himself, his family, the environment, and the prosperity of the world. (4). Financial planning is part of worship. Obtain property in a halal and thoyib (good) way. Spending wealth for things that are useful, both for yourself, family, and society. Saving for a future that has uncertainty. Managing debts wisely.

7.3 Debt on Islamic Perspective

Islam views debt as a trust that must be well cared for. Rasulullah—peace be upon him-as the best role model, seeks Allah's refuges toward excessive debt. Whereas, Islam encourages every Muslim to help people who in need to borrow. But also advocates debt exemption for fellow Muslims who are burdened with debt and find it difficult to settle it.

To avoid the debt trap, Allah in Q. S Al Baqarah (2): 282, regulates how the provisions of debt for every Muslims. "*O you who have believed, when you contract a debt for a specified term, write it down. And let a scribe write (it) between you in justice*" Make notes, witnesses, and commitments are needed to ensure that the debt can be fulfilled properly. So that debt becomes a joint commitment between the debtor and the recipient of the debt, to then remind each other so that it can be settled in accordance with the agreement. However, some people are unable to pay off debt because of the economic conditions they are facing. So he was in debt and unable to fulfill it.

Furthermore, there are several concerns that must be noted due to the consequence of excessive debt. First; excessive debt is able to trigger dishonesty and breaking promises. As stated by Rasulullah—be upon him- narrated by Bukhari (No. 2397) "*In fact, if someone is in debt, they often lie when they talk and break when they promise*". This is occurred when the debtor tries to get the loan as easy as possible by promising unprepared time of fulfillment. When the due date of his promise come, the debtor try all of the possible ways as the reason to legitimate his mistakes, even it costs his integrity.

Second; Soul of *mu'min* mortgaged due to his debt. As the hadith narrated by Bukhari "The believer's soul is suspended by his debt until it settled for him," even a martyr is mortgaged because of debt, Rasullah—peace be upon him- said "Shaheed is forgiven except debtors" Narrated by Muslim.

Third; Rewards reduction in the afterlife. Rasulullah—peace be upon him- said "Whoever dies by leaving the debt, his rewards will be taken to resolve it" Narrated by Ibn Majah. Four; Who are reluctant to pay off the debt will be considered as a thief in the hereafter. As hadits narrated by Ibnu Majah "Whoever is in debt and intends not to pay off his debts, he will meet Allah in a state of thieves".

Islam attention to debt is not only in the part of preventive aspect as initial anticipation when facing the conditions that must be met when deciding to have a debt. Islam also provides a solution for those who are in debt and put the status of gha rim as one of the eight asnaf (groups) who are entitled to receive zakah. As Allah states in Q. S. Al-Taubah (9): 60:

> The alms are meant only for the poor and the needy and those who are in charge thereof, those whose hearts are to be reconciled, and to free those in bondage, and to help those burdened with debt, and for expenditure in the Way of Allah and for the wayfarer. This is an obligation from Allah. Allah is All-Knowing, All-Wise.

The great attention is given by Islam to those who are entwined with excessive debt. As Allah states before that there is gharim as one of the eight asnaf (groups) who are entitled to receive zakah.

7.4 Conditions Permitted to Have Debts

Debt is permitted as long as Islamic rule kept well on every process following it. Thus, the debt could be forbidden for some cases depend on the motives accompanying it, as what stated "The law (for something) changes with the reasons for that" Al Maqdisi (d: 620 CE). Including debt, it could be allowed as long as the process done well based on the rule of Islam.

The rules offered could refer to the criteria of gharim who is entitled as one of Zakah receivers with accordance unto four aspects:

First, Definition of debtor. Or in Arabic word; "التعريف". Anis (1972) defined it in *Al-Mu'jam Al-Wasith* as "Limiting something by stating specific criteria" Gharim refer to Al-Kasani (d 587 CE) stated that gharim is "People who are in debt more than their possessions". Here Al-Kasani explain that everyone who intend to borrow must be considering their possessions as the first sources to fulfill their needs, as long as the wealth enough for him no need for him to borrow. Furthermore, Sirajuddin (d 1005 CE) explained that gharim is not just debitor but also creditor who has less possession to fulfill their needs as he said "Gharim is a person who has credit for someone he cannot take, whereas he has no more part to fulfill his needs" from both explanations refer to definition part of gharim, stated that the point of view is focused on the needs on every person to borrow.

Second, Motives of the debtor. Or in Arabic word; "السبب" Anis (1972) defined it in *Al-Mu'jam Al-Wasith* as "Everything that stood as the reason for acquiring something ". These are the motives should be noted by the debtors: (1) Not in immoral ways (Al-Aini: d 855 CE), (2) Allowed by Islam (*Mubah*) (Al Yamani: d 558 CE), (3) No harm motives, (4) No intention to become gharim (Syihabuddin: d 684 CE), (5) in obedience ways, (6) Not in excessive ways (Al Qurtubi: d 595 CE), meet personal and family needs (Ubaid, 1986). Those motives must be noted as to make sure the debt not breaking the rule of Islam.

Third, Purposes of the debtor. Or in Arabic word; "الهدف" Anis (1972) defined it in *Al-Mu'jam Al-Wasith* as "The targetted direction". The purposes meant here is whom the debt given to. Which Al-Aini (d 855 CE) explained that the purposes could be meant for personal purpose or reconciliation the disputes among others.

Fourth, Circumstances of the debtors. Or in Arabic word; "الحال" Anis (1972) defined it in *Al-Mu'jam Al-Wasith* as "The specifics of the alternating cases can be felt or known". The circumstance which is related with the debtor at least meets these conditions: (1) Having less wealth (Abidin: d 1252 CE), (2) urgent (Al-Qurthubi: d 595 CE), (3) Needy, (4) The debt must be not in *kafarat* matter (Al Lakhami: d 478 CE), (5) Poor (Al-Yamani: d 558 CE).

7.5 Islam Solution Toward Debt Trap

Heavy debt with its worldly consequences also displeases Allah, contaminates the purity of religiosity and disturbs personal spirit values (Bensaid et.al, 2013). Hence, Allah make the longest verse in Quran talks about it (Al-Baqarah: 282) and the only sin punished by war threat versus Allah and His messenger for usury sin as consecutive consequences charged to the debtors (Al-Baqarah: 279). Therefore, Islam has provided the solutions toward people who will to avoid the negatives side of debt.

First, personal support; Seek Allah's refuge from excessive debt as what stated by Rasulullah narrated by Bukhari: "*O, Allah I seek refuge from the sin (ma'tham) and excessive debt (maghram)*". This to strengthen self-alarm and awareness toward following potential problems caused by debt.

Second, Social support: Providing required shari'ah accounting standard refer to Al-Baqarah: 282: "*O you who have believed, when you contract a debt for a specified term, write it down. And let a scribe write (it) between you in justice*" and the point "*And bring to witness two witnesses from among your men*" the verse clearly states the importance of writing down due date of the debt and bringing the witnesses as preventive solution towards future potential matters.

Third, Institutional Support: Zakah for gharim. As Allah stated in Al-Taubah: 60: "*The alms are meant only for the poor and the needy and those who are in charge thereof, those whose hearts are to be reconciled, and to free those in bondage, and to help those burdened with debt, and for expenditure in the Way of Allah and for the wayfarer. This is an obligation from Allah. Allah is All-Knowing, All-Wise.*" This verse stated that those who burdened with debt are having right to receive zakah. But zakah must be asked institutionally by special authority organization focused on it.

As implementation of Al-Taubah: 103: "*Take of their riches a donation to purify them and to cleanse them thereby; and pray for them; surely your prayer is sereneness (i.e.; tranquility) for them; and Allah is Ever-Hearing, Ever-Knowing.*" Allah instruct Rasulullah –peace be upon him—to take alms as his position of the highest author among Muslim society. Therefore, by concerning on the solutions before, people are aware personally about the required circumstances to have a debt and avoiding it while it breaks the rules mentioned in definition, motives, purposes, and circumstances related with debtor to decide wethere to borrow or not.

7.6 Conclusions

Debt management is a must in Islam. Debt trap has become unsolved matter with no understanding about Islamic Wealth Management. By understanding Islamic view on debt, people are aware more that no ease without consequences. Debt as what kept away by Rasulullah SAW in his pray, could be the last solution to acquire fund for daily needs. But not least by paying attention on rules arranged in Islam. Hence, people are in need to know the definition, motives, purposes & circumstances related with gharim whom considered as one of eight groups of zakah receivers. Thus, in inevitable circumstances, the debtor has a right to be helped from zakah fund.

Therefore, people need to prioritize their wealth to fulfill their needs and put the goodwill not to borrow except for urgent needs. And paying attention on the motives such as in good, permissible, obedience (mubah) motives, with no harm, excessive and no intention to receive zakah by having the debt. Those motives are to meet personal or others needy needs but not for *kafarah* matter as it is punishment from Allah, caused by his personal mistake.

Accordingly, Islam has provided the solutions by suggesting all of muslem to seek Allah's refuge from excessive debt, providing required shari'ah accounting standard, and support from authority part by giving zakah for gharim as a care from Islam for those who paid attention on the rules set before deciding to have debt.

Some conclusions that can be drawn from the discussion above are:

1. Debt is part of wealth management. If it's inevitable, it should be allocated for the needs, to meet basic human needs rather than to meet the desires for consumptive purposes.
2. Bad debt is a debt to fulfill wants with consumptive purposes. It is not recommended choice, both from the perspective of non-Islamic wealth management or Islamic wealth management.
3. Islam views debt as a trust that must be well cared for. Debt is considered as a matter that must be accounted for in the afterlife. Therefore, debt affairs must be resolved before death. Freeing others from debt affairs, becomes an act of good value.
4. On Islamic view, indebted terms refer to the definition of gharim. Gharim is "People who are in debt more than their possessions". Gharim is one of the Asnaf who is entitled to receive zakat.
5. Three important things in assessing gharim namely: Motives of the debtor, Purposes of the debtor, and Circumstances of the debtors.
6. Islam solution to avoid the negatives side of debt: personal support, Social support, Institutional Support.

References

Al-Aini. (2000). Al-Binayah Syarh Al-Hidayah. Libanon: Darul Kutub Al-Ilmiyyah.

Abidin, I. (1992). Radd Al-Mukhtar ala Ad-Dur Al-Mukhtar. Libanon: Dar Al-Fikr.

Al-Yamani. (2000). Al-Bayan fi Madhhab Al-Imam Al-Syafi'i. Jeddah: Dar Al-Minhaj.

Al-Bukhari. (2002). Sahih Bukhari. Beirut: Dar Ibnu Katsir Al-Imam Ahmad ibn Hambal. Libanon: Muassasah Al-Rayyan.

Al-Kasani. (1986). Badai Ash-Shanai fii Tartib Asy-Syarai. Libanon: Darul Kutub Al-Ilmyyah.

Al-Lakhami. (2011). At-Tabshirah. Qatar: Wizarah Al-Awqaf wa Al-Syuun Al-Islamiyyah.

Al-Maqdisi. (2002). Raud{atu Al-Nadir wa jannati Al-Manadir ti usuli Al-Fiqh Ala madzhabi.

Al-Qardawi, Y. (2006). Hukum Zakat. Salman Harun, Didin Hafidhuddin dan Hasanuddin, Translator. Bogor: Pustaka Litera Antar Nusa.

Al-Qurt{ubi. (2004). Bidayah Al-Mujtahid wa Nihayah Al-Muqtashid. Mesir: Dar Al-H{adits.

Anis, I. (1972). Mu'jam Al-Wasith, Qahirah: Majma' Al-Lughah Al-Arabiyyah

Aziz, A., & Ramdansyah. (2016). Esensi utang dalam konsep ekonomi Islam. *Islamic Management and business Journal*, 4(1),124–135.

Bensaid., Benaouda., Grine, F., Mohd Nor., Mohd, R., & Yusoff. (2013) M.Y.Z.M. Enduring financial debt: An islamic perspective. *Middle-East Journal. Sci. Res*, 13(2), 162–170.

Billah, M. M. (2010). *Penerapan manajemen aset Islami*. Sweet & Maxwell Asia.

Desjardins, J. (2018), $63 Trillion of World Debt in One Visualization, http://www.visualcapitalist.com/63-trillion-world-debt-one-visualization/.

Daniel, W. (2015). Cerita Awal Bangkrutnya Yunani Karena Terlilit Utang https://finance.detik.com/berita-ekonomi-bisnis/d-2961543/cerita-awal-bangkrutnya-yunani-karena-terlilit-utang.
Hanudin, A. (2012). Explaining intention to use the islamic credit card: An Extention of The TRA Model. Munich: MPRA No. 36957.
Laucereno, S. F. (2018). Utang pemerintah naik lagi Jjdi rp. 4.253 Triliun. https://finance.detik.com/beritaekonomi-bisnis/d-4166308/utang-pemerintahnaik-lagi-jadi-rp-4253-triliun. Diakses pada tanggal 16/9/2018.
Lipsey, R. G., Steiner, P. O. (1991). Pengantar Ilmu Ekonomi I. Edisi Keenam. Jakarta: Rineka Cipta.
Renanita, T., & Hidayat, R. (2013). Faktor-faktor Psikologi Berutang pada Karyawan Berpenghasilan Tetap. *Jurnal Psikologi*, 40(1), 92–101.
Shafii, Z., Yusoff, Z. M., & Noh, S. M. (2013). Islamic financial planning and wealth management. Kuala Lumpur: IBFTM.Credit Limit and Credibility. *USA: Marketing Science 2002*, 21(1), 32–53.
Shohib, M. (2015). Sikap Terhadap Uang dan Perilaku Berutang. *Applied Physiology Journal, 3* (01), 132–143.
Soman, D., & Cheema, A. (2002). The effect of credit on spending decisions: The role of the muslim. (2006) Sahih Muslim. Riyadh: Dar Al-Tayyibah.
Sirajuddin. (2002). An-Nahr Al-Faiq Syarh Kanz Ad-Daqaiq. Libanon: Darul Kutub Al-Ilmiyyah.
Syihabuddin. (1994). Adz-Dzakhirah. Libanon: Dar Al-Garb Al-Islami.
Tyson., & Eric. (2010). *Personal finance for dummies*. 6th editio. Indianapolis: Wiley Publishing Inc.
Ubaid, K. (1986). Fiqh Al-Ibadat ala Al-Madhhab Al-Maliki. Suria: Maktabah Al-Insya.
Wibowo, D. (2015). Pengaruh pendapatan per kapita, Economic growth rate, Economic structure, dan Tax Rate Ratio pada Negara-negara OECD dan Indonesia. *Jurnal Akuntansi Universitas Jember. 11*(1), Hal. 45–61.

Rizqi Zakiya earned his bachelor degree and master degree from Tazkia Islamic University College, Indonesia. His research focus on zakah and Islamic wealth management. He also has a keen interest in youth development, Islamic studies and Islamic classical literature. He has delivered numerous talk shows and written articles in the areas which he focuses on.

Achmad Firdaus earned Ph.D. in Islamic economics from Syarif Hidayatullah State Islamic University, Jakarta. He is an associate professor of Islamic economics at Tazkia Islamic University College. His primary research interests are Islamic wealth management, Islamic performance management, Islamic strategic management, Islamic marketing, Islamic finance/banking/insurance. His works have been published in ISRA International Journal of Islamic Finance, Journal of Islamic Marketing, Al-Iqtishad Journal of Islamic Economics, Ikonomika, Russian Journal of Agricultural and Socio-Economic Sciences. He serves as reviewer for the International Journal of Islamic and Middle Eastern Finance and Management, Tazkia Islamic Finance and Business Review, Al-Tijary Jurnal Ekonomi & Bisnis Islam, Ulumul Syar'i, At-tijaroh Jurnal Ilmu Manajemen dan Bisnis Islam.

Part II
Applications of Islamic Wealth Management

Chapter 8
Project Financing Models for Small Medium Property Enterprises in the Framework of *Maqasid Al-Shari'ah*

Alia Gemala Alidinar, Ascarya Ascarya, Nurul Huda, and Abrista Devi

The projected population of Indonesia shows that over the next twenty-five years it continues to increase from 238.5 million in 2010 to 305.6 million in 2035 (Statistik and Bappenas, 2013). This will affect the amount of demand for housing commodities for the community, both for the purpose of meeting primary needs in meeting the needs and also for short- and long-term investment devotions. Therefore, nowadays there are increasing property entrepreneurs both small-medium class and also big companies are trying to fulfill requirement of housing for society in Indonesia.

Property entrepreneurs face obstacles especially small and medium scale businessmen with limited capital that is in access to funding. Henceforth, sometimes they have difficulty to develop their business. Issues in small construction projects include liquidity problems, working capital problems and the speed of business development (Nesan, 2012). In addition, the access to financing implemented by banks is still focused on lending to property businesspersons. Among the types of financing provided by sharia banks for property projects, which provided by the State Savings Bank Syariah (BTN Syariah, 2016) are (1) working capital financing; (2) investment financing; and (3) construction financing.

Another type of sharia financing which newly issued by BNI Syariah Bank was named Griya Swakarya, using a buying and selling scheme caleed Murabaha. This

A. G. Alidinar
Komplek DDN 2 blok i no. 16 pondok labu, Jakarta Selatan 12450, Indonesia

A. Ascarya
Jl. Seroja Raya no.1, Taman Yasmin Sektor 3, Bogor 16113, Indonesia

N. Huda
Jl kebon Nanas Selatan II Rt 10 Rw 05 No 1 A Otista III, Cipinang Cimpedak Jatinegara Jakarta Timur, Indonesia

A. Devi (✉)
Perumahan Haji, Jl. Tumenggung Wiradiredja, Blok B6 No 4, Cimahpar Bogor Utara, Jawa Barat, Indonesia
e-mail: abristasmart@gmail.com

T. Azid et al. (eds.), *Wealth Management and Investment in Islamic Settings*,
https://doi.org/10.1007/978-981-19-3686-9_8

scheme can be used for financing project development and housing purchase (BNI Syariah, 2016). This financing is not in the form of a loan but a contract of sale between the contractor/developer in purchasing the property inventory for BNI Syariah and the sale and purchase agreement (murabaha) between BNIS and the customer in the property marketing. Property purchased by BNIS is not included in the accounts receivable item but becomes an inventory of murabahah/ijarah assets for BNIS.

There are other types of financing that also involve banking but not in the form of loans but in the form of project financing or known as Project Financing. In this project financing model scheme, Islamic banks will act as agents (wakalah) from customers who want to invest in the property business. According to CIDB (The Construction Industry Development Board) data, countries that have successfully implemented project financing model are USA, Brazil and India (CIDB, 2011). South Africa, through NCDP (National Contractor Development Program) driven by CIDB realizes the need for financial support for new contractors and collaborates with financial institutions (banking) to develop financial models to bridge capital needs for employers (CIDB, 2011). Then in early 2011 government was introduced several financing model projects involving several financial institutions such as NURCHA (National Urban Reconstruction and Housing Agency) and ECDC (Eastern Cape Development Corporation) (CIDB, 2011).

For large contractors, project financing can be done in the form of issuance of sukuk or bonds that can be traded in the capital market. While for medium or small contractors, the scheme that can be used is a project financing model (Project Financing) which is done with profit sharing patterns that can be done by sharia commercial banks.

The sharia bank acting as an agent will provide supervision and monitoring services of the project being financed, thus investors be able to build confidence in the investment in a particular for property project. The offered rate of return will certainly outweigh the interest on deposits and bonds and with measurable risks.

Research on Islamic Project Financing has been undertaken by previous studies such as those conducted by Javed and Fida (2014) examining project financing with sharia contracts for infrastructure projects in Pakistan. The study is linked to sharia financing with a key focus on exploring the role of sharia financing in funding infrastructure development projects especially in the Pakistani context.

Ebrahim (1999) conducted a study by analyzing the traditional model of financing an Islamic project by considering modern financial techniques. The instruments or contracts described include debt instruments, hybrids, and equities. The goal of the maqoshid Al Shariah is to reach falah and provide maslahah or benefit. From the maqoshid side, the role of sharia banking with the financing pattern of this project is to be one of the solutions in the improvement of the maslahah in the state's economy. Islamic banks not only provide working capital loans (its role as sahib-ul-maal) to entrepreneurs but also can develop its function as a customer agent in the provision of capital to developers or contractors who have a track record and good credibility.

This chapter will discuss the current type of financing in Islamic banking and proposed a financing model in the form of fund raising from third parties (investors) by involving the bank as a trustworthy institution by investors (investors). In this case the bank performs its function as agent (representative) of the customer. This research will also provide an overview of the results of research, what contracts can be used as an alternative financing than the existing financing today.

8.1 Project Financing

The definition of project financing as stated by CCBCAF and SMP (Committee for Capacity Building of CA Firms and Small and Medium Practitioners) is as follows:

> Project Finance is a vast area encompassing law, accounting, management, finance, taxation, engineering and many other related subjects. There is no universally accepted definition of "project financing". Sometimes it is identified with firming up various sources of finance for a given project which may be setting up a manufacturing unit or an infrastructure project or a trading unit. Sometimes it is identified only with arrangement of funds through banks and financial institutions for a given project. In common parlance it also includes arrangement of working capital funds for a given project. However, with the increasing complexities of the business it would be more appropriate if the term "project financing" is given a wider and more comprehensive meaning to include all finance related activities and decisions starting from identification and conception of the project to the implementation and running of a project

The term project financing refers to the financing of an economic unit in which a lender looks initially to the cash flows and earning of that economic unit as the source of funds from which a loan will be repaid and to the assets of the economic unit as collateral for the loan (Nevitt & Fabozzi, 1989).

The ultimate goal in project financing is to arrange a borrowing for a project which will benefit the sponsor and at the same time be completely non-recourse to the sponsor, in no way affecting its credit standing or balance sheet. Project financing is sometimes called off-balance sheet financing. This is done using the credit of a third party to support the transaction (Nevitt & Fabozzi, 1989).

In project financing, the bank or sponsors share the risk not to the company but to the funded project. In case of recording in the company's financial system, project financing will have its own post and also called off balance sheet financing.

8.1.1 Fundamental Elements in Project Financing

Financing is basically given on the basis of trust, the provision of financing is the provision of trust. This means that the accomplishment is absolutely to be believed to be returned by the beneficiary in accordance with the time and terms agreed upon. Based on this, the elements of financing include (Ali & Mahmood, 2015):

1. The existence of two parties, namely financiers and recipients pembiyaan.
2. Trust, i.e. the belief of the lender that the recipient will repay the loan it receives in accordance with the terms and conditions agreed by both parties.
3. Agreement, i.e. agreement between the financier and the beneficiary
4. Duration, i.e. the repayment period of the loan has been agreed.
5. Risk, i.e. the existence of a grace period of return will result in an uncollected risk of non-performing loan.
6. Remuneration is an advantage over the granting of a loan, the service that we are familiar with the profit sharing or margin.

Furthermore, Ali & Mahmood (2015) also explained about the main purpose of lending of financing, among others:

1. Looking for profit (profitability) that is with the aim to obtain the results of financing disbursed in the form of profit gained from the profit sharing obtained from the business managed by the customer.
2. Safety or security is the security of the achievements or facilities provided must be absolutely guaranteed so that the purpose of profitability can be really achieved without significant obstacles.
3. Helping the customer's business, which is helping the business customers who need funds, either investment funds or in the form of financing.
4. Helping the government, that is, the more financing channeled by the bank, the more development will increase in various sectors.

8.1.2 Project Finance within the Maqasid Al-Shari'ah Framework

The language of Maqasid is derived from qashada, which means strong desire, firm, and deliberate. This meaning can also be interpreted by intentional or intended (qashada ilaihi). While shari'ah in language shows to three meanings, that is source of drinking water, straight and bright road and the beginning of doing a job (Wibowo, 2004).

The five elements of Maqasid Al-shari'ah are Maintaining religion (hifzh al-dîn), Maintaining the soul (hifzh al-nafs), Maintaining the mind (hifzh al-'aql), Keeping the family (hifzh al-nasl) and Maintain the wealth (hifzh al-mâl). By not involving the element of interest in financing and increasing the role of the community in financing of potential projects undertaken by entrepreneurs who can be proven trustworthy and professionalism is the way (wasilah) to create justice and improve the level of economic community (maslahah).

The concept of maqasid al-shari'ah affirms that Islamic law is prescribed to manifest and preserve the maslahat of mankind. The core of the concept of maqâshid al-syari 'ah is to realize the good at the same time avoid the bad or benefit and refuse harm. Maqâshid al-syari'ah is maslahat, because the establishment of law in Islam must lead to maslahat.

Project financing within the framework of Islam is financing undertaken by investors or sponsors who want to invest their money in a particular project and expect a revenue share from the project's revenue. Project financing on a profit-sharing basis will be able to assist the contractor in fulfilling the working capital needed to finance a particular property development project.

The privilege of project financing involves bank customers in financing the real sector and at the same time assisting in the distribution of income to improve the people's economy. This is in accordance with the purpose of maqoshid al-syari'ah in creating benefit (maslahah).

Large-scale industrial infrastructure or real estate projects present unique financing challenges. This requires the deployment of necessary resources through equity investors (often project sponsors) and the availability of debt financing (Gabbani, 2012). Islamic Project Financing can be interpreted as project financing that can be done in accordance with the rules of Islam by using a contract in accordance with sharia (Ebrahim, 1999). Two basic principles are given by Sharia in Islamic finance: share risks and promote welfare (Javed & Fida, 2014). The sharing of profits and losses arising from business in accordance with Sharia law, that is, in sharia transactions must be supported by assets, since the money itself has no intrinsic value, and investments must be made in businesses not prohibited by Sharia.

There are five main rules in Islamic finance that affect project financing: (1) usury, or interest, is prohibited; (2) gharar, or excessive risk taking, is prohibited; (3) the gain or loss of the transaction shall be divided; (4) a transaction must be asset-backed because money has no intrinsic value; And (5) investment should only support activities that are not forbidden by Islamic religion. This rule clearly has profound implications for the traditional structure of project financing activities, thus requiring the examination of each regulation in more detail (Khan, 1997; Gabbani, 2011). Shari'ah financial institutions through project financing, are expected to contribute significantly to the achievement of socio-economic goals especially for Muslims (Chapra, 1985; Hassan & Lewis, 2007).

Islamic Project Finance is an area that is conceptually conducive to Islamic finance and adheres to the basic Islamic economic philosophy. Islamic finance can configure itself as an ideal solution and able to meet the economic needs of the project. Remuneration of Islamic lenders is not based on an interval but on the actual income generated from the project. The lender will act as a partner and also be responsible for the risks as well, which in addition resemble the philosophy of Islamic project financing (Javed & Fida, 2014).

8.2 Method

This research uses Analytical Network Process (ANP) method which will be done in the form of in-depth interview to get information from sharia banking practitioner and property and also fiqh muamalah expert about financing of sharia construction. ANP is the developed from the previous method AHP (Analytic Hierarchy process), where ANP is chosen because of its capability to prioritise the elements in a more stable way than AHP does (Tanjung & Devi, 2013). In doing research using ANP method, there are two stages of data collection and the population consists of a group of sharia banking practitioners from BTN Syariah, two property practitioners and one muamalah fiqh expert from IIUM. At this early stage, the technique used to collect data and information is by conducting an interview with several selected respondents. This initial interview to obtain in-depth information on the problem and as a source of initial data in preparing the ANP framework model.

The next step after the ANP framework is structured, the next step is to design the questionnaire in accordance with the ANP framework that has been created. The questionnaire will be disseminated to the respondents who agreed to be an informant in this study of banking practitioners, property business practitioners and muamalah fiqh experts. The spread of this questionnaire is required to perform measurements using a scale ratio. In this data collection is done separately for each respondent.

In order to obtain the aggregate value among respondents, a geometric mean was used, which is calculated as follows:

$$GMk = \sqrt[n]{(R1 * R2 * \cdots * Rn)}$$

where, GM = geometric mean; R = judgement of individual respondent; n = number of respondents; and k = number of pairwise comparisons.

8.3 Result and Discussion

Study literature and in-depth interview have been conducted to obtain the network model of project financing from small medium property enterprises in the framework of Maqasid Al-Shariah. Decomposition of ANP model generates some project financing model, namely:

(1) Mudharabah lending model (BTNS): financing product which is served to fulfill the need of customer toward working capital by using mudharabah aqad principle (profit and lost sharing).

(2) Musyarakah lending model (BTNS): financing product which is served to fulfill the need of developer toward working capital in order to build regency project by using musyarakah aqad principle (profit and lost sharing), with the payback plan based on the ability of customer cashflow projection.

(3) Griya Swakarya financing model (BNIS): the financing of regency purchasing by using mudharabah aqad, BNIS served asset based on murabahah and sell to the customer.

(4) Project financing mudharabah (proposed): bank plays a role as agent (wakalah) from shohibul maal who is invested their money specifically on property project using mudharabah aqad.

(5) Project financing musyarakah (proposed): bank plays a role as agent (wakalah) from the customer who is being the partner (syirkah) from contractor/developer by using musyarakah aqad.

Five purposed project financing model as mentioned above is directed to achieve *al-falah* based on maqasid syariah. Therefore, the decomposition also generates some objectives of this study, namely:

(1) *Hifz Ad-Din*. Islamic project financing product could run the financing based on sharia compliance.
(2) *Hifz An*-Nafs. Islamic project financing is expected to blead into a blessing and kind soul.
(3) *Hifz Al*-'Aql. Financing impelementation appropriate with sharia and expected to keep society from interest minded.
(4) *Hifz An*-Nasl. More blessed income is expected that Indonesia people development is more prosperous.
(5) *Hifz Maal*. Socio-economic goal achievement, sharing equal income to all parties and equality distribution of income.

In order to achieve the goals based on maqasid sharia, some critera need to be considered. There are five main criteria obtained from study literature and indepth interview to some expert, namely:

1. The function of banking; (a) bank as mudharib (Antonio, 2001), (b) bank as sahibul maal (Antonio, 2001), (c) bank as investment manager (Antonio, 2001), (d) bank as agent (Antonio, 2001; Raharjo, 1999), (e) bank as social fund managers (Antonio, 2001).
2. Collateral and SPV; (a) financing based on lending with company asset as collateral (BNIS, BTNS), (b) Project financing, Project as collateral (Nevitt & Fabozzi, 1989; Roger, 1990), (c) Project financing using minimum collateral (Nesan, 2012; Fatony, 2010), (d) Asset is limited only owned by project (Finnerty, 2013; Parra, 2003), (e) Off balance sheet (Nevitt & Fabozzi, 1989).
3. Sharia Compliance; (a) the controversy of implementation because of mazhab diversity (Robbins, 2009), (b) prohibit riba but allow all revenue on capital (Alkhaldi, 2011), (c) income is coming from halal business, (d) transactions refer to tangible asset (Alkhaldi, 2011), (e) risk profit sharing, leasing and trading aqad (Alkhaldi, 2011).
4. External risk; (a) market risk (ICRA, 2004), (b) inflation and interest rate risk (Banaitiene & Banaitis, 2012), (c) political and regulation risk, (ICRA, 2004) (d) Force Meijer Risk (UCRA, 2004; Joni, 2012; Banaitiene & Banaitis, 2012) and (e) Fiscal Policy (Banaitiene & Banaitis, 2012).
5. Internal risks; (a) design risk (Banaitiene & Banaitis, 2012), (b) completion risk (L&R, 1998; ICRA, 2004), (c) funding risk (ICRA, 2004), (d) operational and technological risk (ICRA, 2004; Banaitiene & Banaitis, 2012), and (e) competence risk/project management risk (Joni, 2012; Banaitiene & Banaitis, 2012).

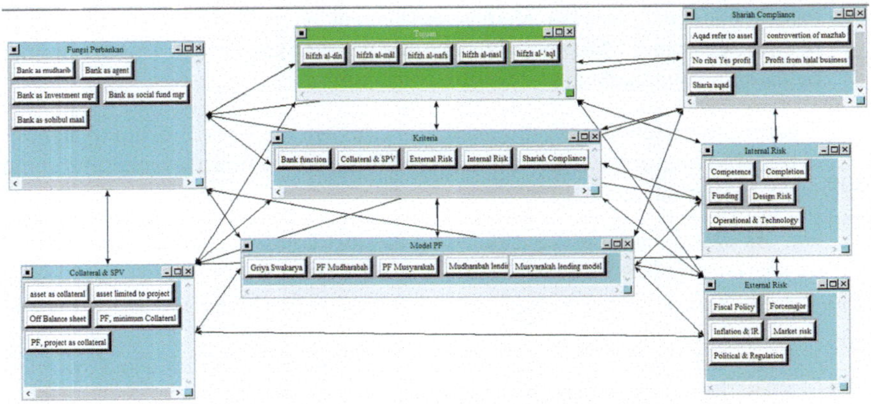

Fig. 8.1 Project financing and work model

Project financing ANP network model can be seen through Fig. 8.1:

Synthesis Results

Synthesis Results of Objectives

The results obtained show a statistical consensus of the experts and practitioners in relation to objectives, criteria, and alternatives of Islamic project financing model for small medium property enterprises in the framework of maqasid al-shari'ah. Figure 9.2 displayed the priority of the elements in objective cluster. The figure also displayed the priority result of each informant and the synthesis result which was calculating by geometric mean formula. There are three informants employed in this study to obtain the number of priority. R1 indicates the first respondent, R1 indicates the second respondent, and R3 indicates the third respondent, while geomean indicates the aggregate value of all respondents. There are five elements in objective cluster consist of *hifzh al-din, hifzh al-mal, hifzh an-nafs, hifzh an-nasl,* and *hifzh al-'aql.*

Figure 8.2 showed the individual valuation and consensus result of the objective priority of Islamic project financing model. The consensus results indicated that the *Hifz al maal* is the highest priority objective of Islamic project financing model (33%). This is followed by *hifz al-din* (23.1%), *hifz an-nafs* (16.6%), *hifz al-nasl* (13.3%) and the last priority is *hifz al- 'aql* (10.1%). The results of the rater agreement for objective cluster show that W = 80%, which means that the informants are highly agree to the objective priority of Islamic project financing model where *Hifz al maal* would be the main priority goal when people decide to do *muamalah* (transaction) with the bank, in case of property transaction. Informants argued that *hifz al- 'aql* is being less important objective in this case.

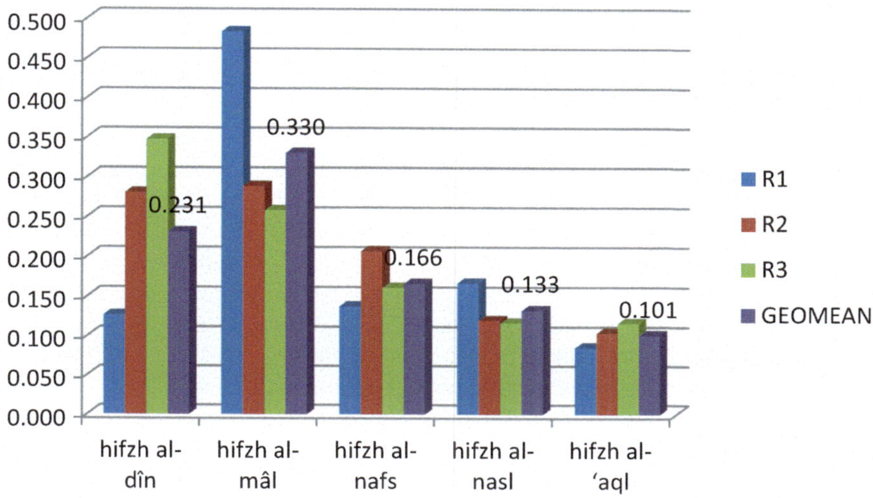

Fig. 8.2 The synthesis result of objective cluster related to Islamic financing project model

Synthesis Results of Criteria

Figure 8.3 displayed the priority of the elements in criteria cluster. The figure also displayed the priority result of each informant and the synthesis result which was calculating by geometric mean formula. There are three informants employed in this study to obtain the number of priority. R1 indicates the first respondent, R1 indicates the second respondent, and R3 indicates the third respondent, while geomean

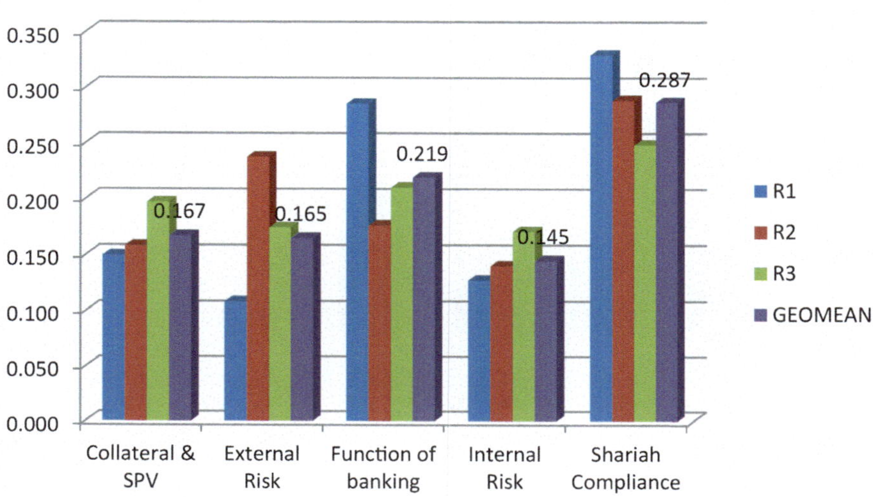

Fig. 8.3 The synthesis result of criteria cluster related to Islamic financing project model

indicates the aggregate value of all respondents. There are five elements in criteria cluster consisting of collateral and SPV, external risk, function of bank, internal risk, and sharia compliance.

Figure 8.3 showed the individual valuation and consencus result of the criteria priority of Islamic project financing model. The consensus results indicated that the *sharia compliance* is the highest priority criteria of Islamic project financing model (28.7%). This is followed by *function of bank* (21.9%), *collateral and SPV* (16.7%), *external risk* (16.5%) and the last priority is *internal risk* (14.5%). The results of the rater agreement for criteria cluster show that W = 77.77%, which means that the informants are highly agree to the criteria priority of Islamic project financing model where *sharia compliance* would be the main priority criteria when people decide to do *muamalah* (transaction) with the bank, in case of property transaction. Informants argued that *internal risk* is being less important criteria in this case.

Synthesis Results of the function of bank Sub-Criteria.

Figure 8.4 displayed the priority of the elements in function of bank sub criteria cluster. The figure also displayed the priority result of each informant and the synthesis result which was calculating by geometric mean formula. There are three informants employed in this study to obtain the number of priority. R1 indicates the first respondent, R1 indicates the second respondent, and R3 indicates the third respondent, while geomean indicates the aggregate value of all respondents. There are five elements in sub-criteria cluster (the function of bank) consisting of bank as agent, bank as investment manager, bank as mudharib, bank as fund social manager, and bank as shohibul maal.

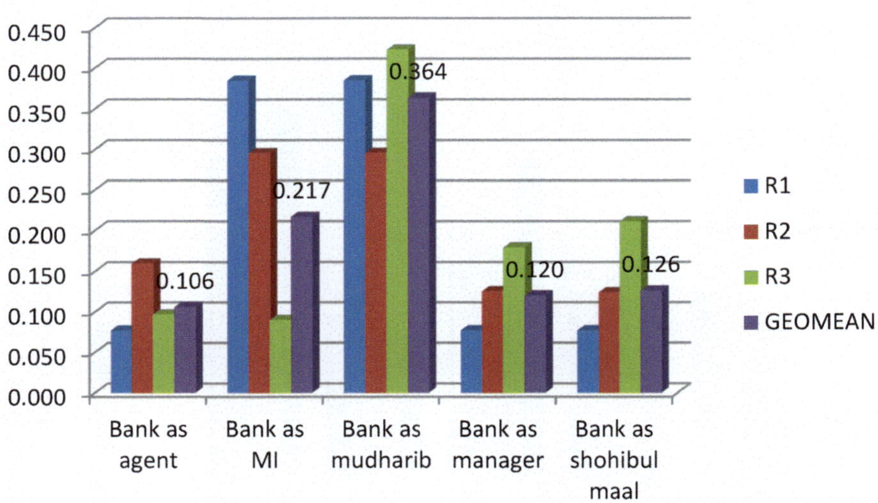

Fig. 8.4 The synthesis result of the function of bank sub criteria cluster related to Islamic financing project model

Figure 8.4 showed the individual valuation and consensus result of the function of bank priority of Islamic project financing model. The consensus results indicated that the *bank as mudharib* is the highest priority the function of bank of Islamic project financing model (36.4%). This is followed by *bank as investment manager* (21.7%), *bank as sahibul maal* (12.6%), *bank as manager* (12.0%) and the last priority is *bank as agent* (10.6%). The results of the rater agreement for this sub-criteria cluster show that W = 37.77%, which means that the informants agreement to the sub-criteria the function of bank priority of Islamic project financing model is low, where *bank as mudharib* would be the main priority sub-criteria the function of bank when people decide to do *muamalah* (transaction) with the bank, in case of property transaction. Informants argued that *bank as agent* is being less important sub-criteria in this case. It is true that the agent function is not a priority of the respondents but the result of the priority function of the sharia bank as mudharib or the holder of the trust for investors and depositors of sharia banks actually shows that the bank is expected to implement its role to secure investor funds for businesses that can bring better results, and it is actually part of agency roles. What is happening now for shariah banks there are no difference between sharia banks and conventional banks in terms of function and type of businesses, consequently Muslims are still reluctant to invest in Islamic banks as they do not see the fundamental difference between sharia banks and conventional banks.

Synthesis Results of the Collateral and SPV Sub-Criteria

Figure 8.5 displayed the priority of the elements in collateral and SPV sub criteria cluster. The figure also displayed the priority result of each informant and the synthesis result which was calculating by geometric mean formula. There are three

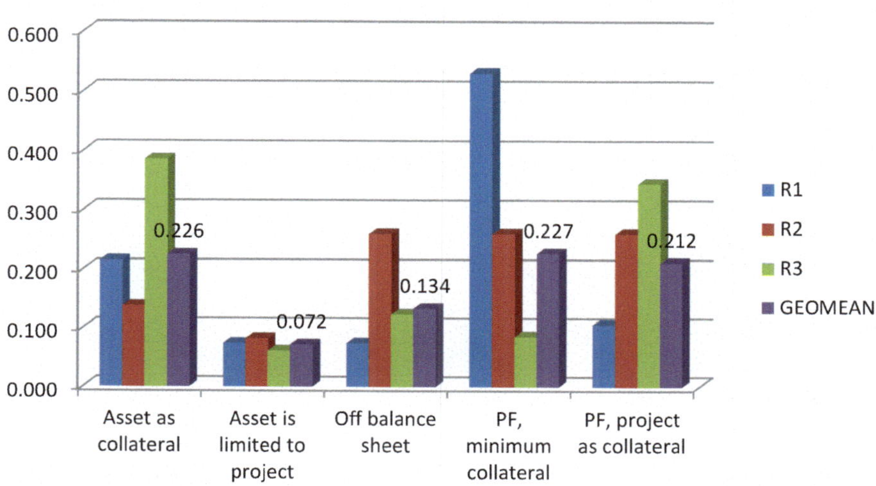

Fig. 8.5 The synthesis result of collateral and SPV Sub criteria cluster related to Islamic financing project model

informants employed in this study to obtain the number of priority. R1 indicates the first respondent, R1 indicates the second respondent, and R3 indicates the third respondent, while geomean indicates the aggregate value of all respondents. There are five elements in sub-criteria cluster (collateral & SPV) consisting of asset as collateral, asset is limited to project, off balance sheet, project financing with minimum collateral, and project financing with project as collateral.

Figure 8.5 showed the individual valuation and consensus result of collateral and SPV priority of Islamic project financing model. The consensus results indicated that the *PF, minimum collateral* is the highest priority the function of bank of Islamic project financing model (22.7%). This is followed by *asset as collateral* (22.6%), *PF, project as collateral* (21.2%), *off balance sheet* (13.4%) and the last priority is *asset is limited to project* (7.2%). The results of the rater agreement for this sub-criteria cluster show that W = 77.77%, which means that the informants are highly agree to the sub-criteria priority of Islamic project financing model where *PF, minimum collateral* would be the main priority sub-criteria when people decide to do *muamalah* (transaction) with the bank, in case of property transaction. Informants argued that *asset is limited to project* is being less important sub-criteria in this case.

Synthesis Results of the Sharia Compliance Sub-Criteria

Figure 8.6 displayed the priority of the elements in sharia compliance sub criteria cluster. The figure also displayed the priority result of each informant and the synthesis result which was calculating by geometric mean formula. There are three

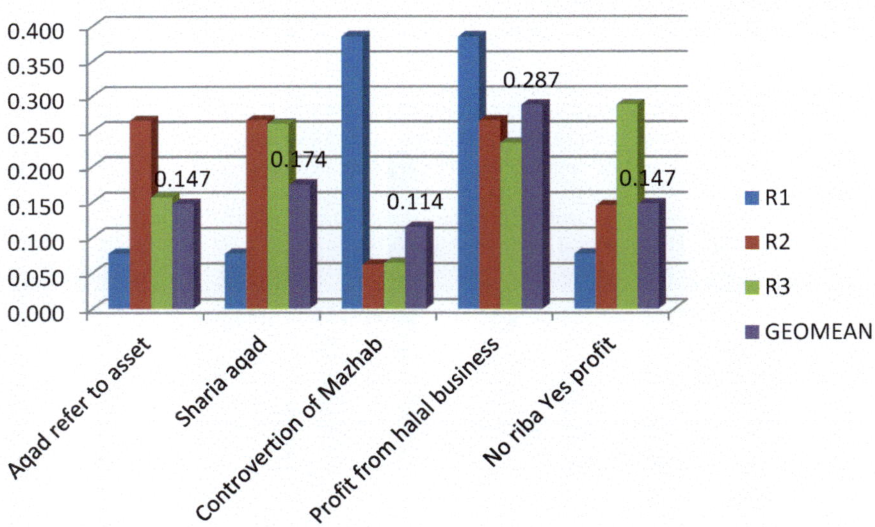

Fig. 8.6 The synthesis result of sharia compliance sub criteria cluster related to Islamic financing project model

informants employed in this study to obtain the number of priority. R1 indicates the first respondent, R1 indicates the second respondent, and R3 indicates the third respondent, while geomean indicates the aggregate value of all respondents. There are five elements in sub-criteria cluster (sharia compliance) consisting of aqad refer to asset, shari'ah aqad, controvertion of mazhab, profit from halal business, and no riba yes profit.

Figure 8.6 showed the individual valuation and consensus result of sharia compliance priority of Islamic project financing model. The consensus results indicated that the *profit from halal business* is the highest priority the sharia compliance of Islamic project financing model (28.7%). This is followed by *sharia aqad* (17.4%), *aqad refer to asset* (14.7%), *no riba yes profit* (14.7%) and the last priority is *mazhab controvertion* (11.4%). The results of the rater agreement for this sub-criteria cluster show that W = 78.89%, which means that the informants are highly agree to the sub-criteria priority of Islamic project financing model where *profit from halal business* would be the main priority sub-criteria when people decide to do *muamalah* (transaction) with the bank, in case of property transaction. Informants argued that *mazhab controvertion* is being less important sub-criteria in this case.

Synthesis Results of the External Risk Sub-Criteria

Figure 8.7 displayed the priority of the elements in external risk sub criteria cluster. The figure also displayed the priority result of each informant and the synthesis result which was calculating by geometric mean formula. There are three informants employed in this study to obtain the number of priority. R1 indicates the first respondent, R1 indicates the second respondent, and R3 indicates the third respondent, while geomean indicates the aggregate value of all respondents. There are five elements in

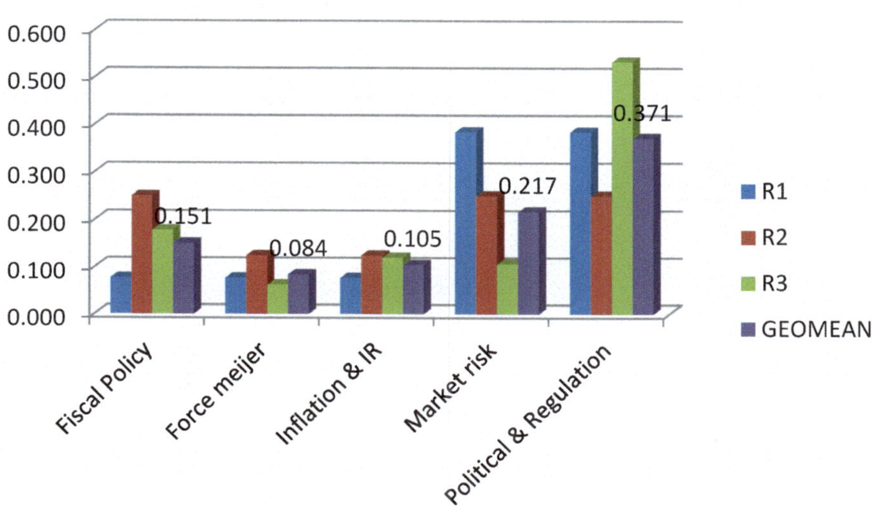

Fig. 8.7 The synthesis result of external risk sub criteria cluster related to Islamic financing project model

sub-criteria cluster (external riks) consisting of fiscal policy, force maijer, inflation and IR, market risk, and political and regulation.

Figure 8.7 showed the individual valuation and consensus result of external risk priority of Islamic project financing model. The consensus results indicated that the *political and regulation* is the highest priority the external risk of Islamic project financing model (37.1%). This is followed by *market risk* (21.7%), *fiscal policy* (15.1%), *inflation and IR* (10.5%) and the last priority is *force major* (8.4%). The results of the rater agreement for this sub-criteria cluster show that W = 64.44%, which means that the informants agreement to the sub-criteria priority of Islamic project financing model is fairly high, where *political and regulation* would be the main priority sub-criteria when people decide to do *muamalah* (transaction) with the bank, in case of property transaction. Informants argued that *force major* is being less important sub-criteria in this case.

Synthesis Results of the Internal Risk Sub-Criteria

Figure 8.8 displayed the priority of the elements in internal risk sub criteria cluster. The figure also displayed the priority result of each informant and the synthesis result which was calculating by geometric mean formula. There are three informants employed in this study to obtain the number of priority. R1 indicates the first respondent, R1 indicates the second respondent, and R3 indicates the third respondent, while geomean indicates the aggregate value of all respondents. There are five elements in sub-criteria cluster (internal risk) consisting of competence, completion, design risk, funding and operational and technology.

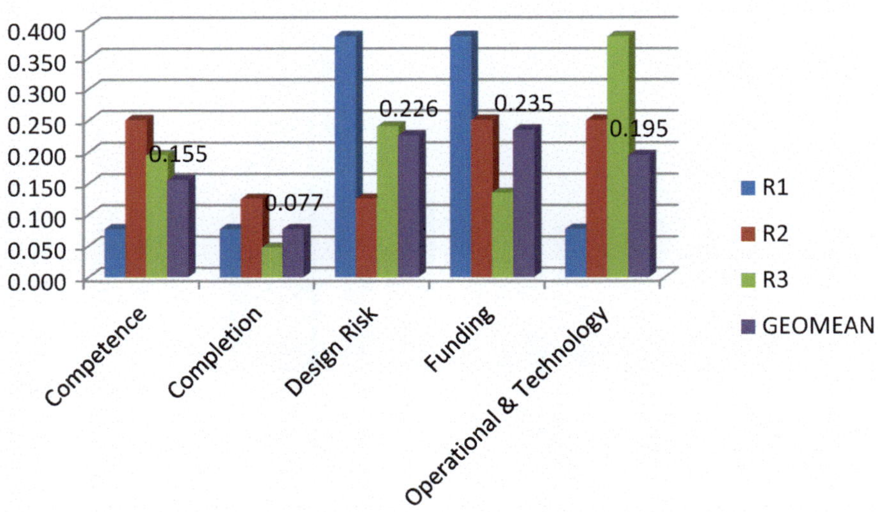

Fig. 8.8 The synthesis result of internal risk sub criteria cluster related to Islamic financing project model

Figure 8.8 showed the individual valuation and consensus result of internal risk priority of Islamic project financing model. The consensus results indicated that the *funding* is the highest priority the internal risk of Islamic project financing model (23.5%). This is followed by *design risk* (22.6%), *operational and technology* (19.5%), *competence* (15.5%) and the last priority is *completion* (7.7%). The results of the rater agreement for this sub-criteria cluster show that W = 24.44%, which means that the informants agreement to the sub-criteria priority of Islamic project financing model is low, where *funding* would be the main priority sub-criteria when people decide to do *muamalah* (transaction) with the bank, in case of property transaction. Informants argued that *completion* is being less important sub-criteria in this case.

Synthesis Results of the Islamic Project Financing Model Alternatives

Figure 8.9 displayed the priority of the elements in alternatives sub criteria cluster. The figure also displayed the priority result of each informant and the synthesis result which was calculating by geometric mean formula. There are three informants employed in this study to obtain the number of priority. R1 indicates the first respondent, R1 indicates the second respondent, and R3 indicates the third respondent, while geomean indicates the aggregate value of all respondents. There are five elements in alternative cluster consisting of Griya Swakarya, mudharabah project financing, musharakah project financing, mudharabah lending model, and musharakah lending model.

Figure 8.9 showed the individual valuation and consensus result of alternatives priority of Islamic project financing model. The consensus results indicated that the *mudharabah project financing* is the highest priority the alternatives of Islamic

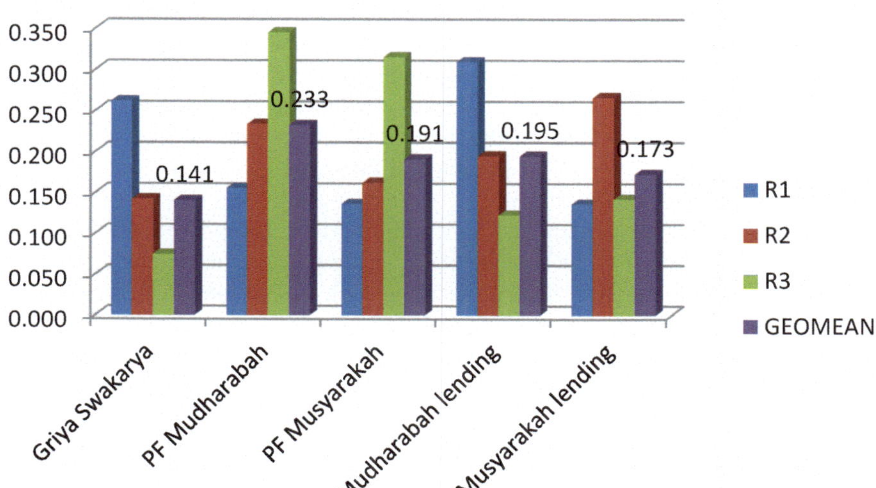

Fig. 8.9 The synthesis result of alternatives sub criteria cluster related to Islamic financing project model

project financing model (23.3%). This is followed by *mudharabah lending* (19.5%), *musharakah project financing* (19.1%), *musharakah lending* (17.3%) and the last priority is *Griya Swakarya* (14.1%). The results of the rater agreement for this sub-criteria cluster show that W = 22.22%, which means that the informants agreement to the alternatives priority of Islamic project financing model is low, where *mudharabah project financing* would be the main priority alternative when people decide to do *muamalah* (transaction) with the bank, in case of property transaction. Informants argued that *Griya Swakarya* is being less important alternative in this case. This is understandable because not many practitioners and communities understand the murabahah financing mechanism of BNI Syariah Bank. The product is new and it has not been implemented seriously by BNI Syariah itself. This is evidenced from interview with property entrepreneur(s) who become respondents of this research, who proposed financing at BNI shariah with Griya Swakarya scheme. Till to date there is no feed back to implement this scheme to property entrepreneurs who wish to take sharia financing by Griya Swakarya mechanism.

8.4 Conclusion

There are five main criteria of Islamic project financing model for small medium property enterprises, namely, collateral and SPV, external risk, function of bank, internal risk, and sharia compliance. Of those five, *sharia compliance* takes the highest priority. This means that the project financing model which is purposed to help property enterprises in getting friendly capital must be followed by sharia compliance.

There are five main functions of bank sub-criteria of Islamic project financing model for small medium property enterprise, namely, bank as agent, bank as investment manager, bank as mudharib, bank as fund social manager, and bank as sahibul maal. Of those five, *bank as mudharib* takes the highest priority. This finding is in-line with the next-alternative result where mudharabah project financing model is being the highest priority of Islamic project financing model for small medium property enterprises.

There are five main collateral and SPV sub-criteria of Islamic project financing model for small medium property enterprises, namely, asset as collateral, asset is limited to project, off balance sheet, project financing with minimum collateral, and project financing with project as collateral. Of those five, *project with minimum collateral* takes the highest priority. This main reason of this finding is because small medium property enterprises feel mind for the collateral regulation that are imposed on them so far.

There are five main sharia compliance sub-criteria of Islamic project financing model for small medium property enterprises, namely, aqad refer to asset, sharia aqad, the controvertion of mazhab, profit from halal business, and no riba yes profit. Of those five, profit from halal business takes the highest priority. There are five main external sub-criteria of Islamic project financing model for small medium property enterprises, namely, fiscal policy, force maijer, inflation and IR, market risk, and political and regulation. Of those five, political and regulation takes the highest priority, because of property business is closely related to the politic and regulation aspect. There are five main internal sub-criteria of Islamic project financing model for small medium property enterprises, namely, competence, completion, design risk, funding and operational and technology. Of those five, funding takes the highest priority.

Finally, there are five alternatives model that can be implemented to give the financing of small medium property enterprises, namely, Griya Swakarya, mudharabah project financing, musyarakah project financing, mudharabah lending model, and musyarakah lending model. Of those five, *mudharabah project financing* takes the highest priority. This means that business people of small medium property enterprises need a financing model to improve their business size which is based on profit and lost sharing with mudharabah aqad.

Recommendations

There should be a mutual agreement among decision-makers in supporting the existence of friendly project financing model for small medium property enterprises. Financial service industry (in this case refers to bank; the institution who gives the financing to the property enterprises) need to implement the project financing product by considering maqasid Al-Sharia for the entire activity, such as considering the *hifzh al-din, hifzh al-mal, hifzh an-nafs, hifzh an-nasl,* and *hifzh al-'aql* of the financing product. In order to implement the findings of this study, it needs a commitment and a high support from practitioners and government to implement the friendly model for small medium property enterprises project financing.

This study should help to broaden academic studies related to Islamic project financing model for small medium property enterprises where this study is rarely to found before. Further studies using a similar approach (ANP) with more respondents or adopting another approach, such as Interpretive Structural Modelling, are suggested.

References

Antonio, M. S. (2001). *Bank Syariah: Dari teori ke praktik*. Gema Insani.

Ali, U., & Mahmood, A. (2015). Proposing a KIBOR-free home financing model based on diminishing musharakah for Islamic Banks. *Pakistan Journal of Social Sciences* (PJSS), 35(2).

Alkhaldi, A. (2011). Risk and riba, Islamic banking Indonesian Credit Rating Agency (ICRA), (2014), *Metodologi Pemeringkatan untuk Transaksi Pembiayaan Proyek*. Journal

Banaitiene, N., & Banaitis, A. (2012). Risk management in construction projects. In *Risk management-current issues and challenges*. InTec.

BNI Syariah. (2016). *Surviving The Turbulence, PT. BNI Syariah*. Divisi Konsumer dan Kartu Pembiayaan, Jakarta.

Construction Industry Development Board (CIBD). (September 2011). Construction industry financial modelling options for contractor support and development, Afrika Selatan.

Chapra, U. (1985). *Towards a just monetary system; A discussion of money, banking, and monetary policy in the light of Islamic teaching* (p. 55). Islamic foundation.

Data Bank BTN Syariah. (2016). *Marketing tool kit*. Jakarta.

Ebrahim, M. S. (1999). Integrating Islamic and conventional project finance. *Thunderbird International Business Review, 41*(4–5), 583–609.

Fatony, M. G. (2010). *Analisa Kelayakan Investasi Proyek*. Bioethanol Di Jawa Timur, Universitas Indonesia.

Finnerty, J. D. (2013). *Project financing: Asset-based financial engineering*. Wiley.

Gabbani, M. (2012). Islamic project finance. In *Wednesday seminar* 2010–2011.

Hassan, M. K. dan Lewis, M. K. (2007). Islamic banking: An introduction and overview. In *Handbook of Islamic Banking* (p. 5). Edward Elgar Publishing limited.

Javed, A., & Fida, B. A. (2014). Islamic project financing in Pakistan: Current challenges and opportunities ahead. *Iranian Journal of Management Studies, 8*(1), 47.

Khan, M. F. K., & Parra, R. J. (2003). *Financing large projects: Using project finance techniques and practices*. Pearson Prentice Hall.

Khan, M. H. (1997). Designing an Islamic model for project finance. *International Financial Law Review, 16*, 13.

Nesan, J. (2012). Project finance model for small contractors in USA. *Construction Economics and Building, 6*(1), 25–41.

Nevitt, P. K., & Fabozzi, F. J. (1989). *Project financing, 5th*. Edition.

Rossi, E. (2015). Project finance. In infrastructure project finance and project bonds in Europe (pp. 7–24).

Roger, S. (1990). *Eurotunnel: An innovative approach to project financing*. S.M thesis, Civil Engineering, IT.

Sahruddin, S. (2006). Pelaksanaan pembiayan proyek dengan prinsip musyarakah pada perbankan syariah di Nusa Tenggara Barat Barat (Doctoral dissertation, Program Pasca Sarjana Universitas Diponegoro).

Statistik, B. P., & Bappenas, U. N. F. P. A. (2013). *Proyeksi penduduk Indonesia 2010–2035* (pp. 1–472). Jakarta: Badan Pusat Statistik.

Tanjung, H., & Devi, A. (2013). *Metodologi Penelitian Ekonomi Islam*. Gramata Publishing.

Wibowo, A. (2004). *Maqoshid Asy Syariah: The ultimate objective of Syariah*. Jurnal Islamic Finance.

Alia Gemala Alidinar earned her undergraduate degree in accounting from Andalas University, Indonesia, master degree in commerce from University of South Australia and second master degree from Tazkia Islamic University College in the area of Islamic Wealth Management. She is also a registered Indonesian Accountant. Alia is a member of Islamic Woman Entrepreneur Indonesia (WPMI), small medium enterprises organization with members approximately 800 in

Jakarta. Acting as a member of capital cooperation between third parties and the SMEs WPMI members. She presented her paper on Project Financing Models for Small Medium Property Enterprises in The Framework of *Maqasid Al-Shari'ah*, in the Thematic Workshop on Enhancing Poor's Capability and Financial Inclusion From Islamic Perspective, International Seminar, Islamabad, Pakistan, 11–12 December 2017.

Ascarya Ascarya, PhD is a senior lecturer at University of Darussalam, Gontor, Indonesia and Institut Agama Islam TAZKIA, Bogor, Indonesia. He is an Editor In-Chief of International Journal of Islamic Economics and Finance (IJIEF) Muhammadiyah University of Yogyakarta and a Co-managing editor of Journal of Islamic Monetary Economics and Finance (JIMF), at Bank Indonesia Institute, Bank Indonesia. He serves as editorial team member of several international scientific journals (SCOPUS indexed) and editorial board member of other international scientific journals. He has produced 40 international journals and books, 70 international papers, 25 national journals, 23 national papers, 41 working papers, 3 occasional papers, 22 books, 4 proceedings, 12 periodical publications, and 6 research notes. He has received four International Best Paper Awards in 2013, 2014, 2015 and 2016. He has also received BAZNAS Award 2018 as "Tokoh Pendukung Kebangkitan Zakat".

Nurul Huda, PhD He is a professor in the Faculty of Economics and Business, Yarsi University and holds a position as Vice Chancellor IV in the same university. He was granted Cum laude for Doctoral and master's degree in Islamic Economics from Airlangga University and University of Indonesia. Currently, he is trusted some important positions in organizations, Indonesian Islamic Economics Experts Association (IAEI) / Islamic Economic Community (MES), ILUNI PSKTTI UI, BWI, PKEBIS, LSP EKBISI, MASEI, DPP BP4, ADESy, LSP BWI and Elsya MES Program. Despite of publishing 19 books, he also conducted some research activities financed by several institutions. The research works were successfully published in reputable international and national journals. In addition, he is also an active speaker at national and international forums.

Abrista Devi is a PhD Student at INCEIF (International Centre for Education in Islamic Finance), Malaysia. Currently, she is a lecturer at Ibn Khaldun University, Indonesia. Abrista has written numerous academic papers and presented some of them in both national and international conferences. Her book with the title "Islamic Economic Research Methodology" has been sold more than 4000 copies. Abrista received the "Best Paper" award at the 4th International Islamic Monetary Economic and Finance Conference held by Bank Indonesia in 2018. In 2022, she is included as one of Indonesian Top 5000 scientists based on AD Scientific Index 2022 Version 1.

Chapter 9
The Effects of Fixed Return Instruments on Investment Decisions in Islamic Economics: Using Stochastic Mathematical Model

Hasan Kiaee

Investment decisions are those in which people make every day when they try to choose between different options available for consuming and investing their income and wealth. Two important questions raise in a typical investment decision problem: (1) what proportion of income should be consumed and how much should be invested and (2) how to allocate investing proportion of income into different investment opportunities.

In the conventional economics, when we look at the investment opportunities, two main categories are available: (1) risky assets and (2) risk free assets. The best way for considering the volatility characteristics of risky assets, in a mathematical model, is to use stochastic processes. So, almost all of the researchers who studied portfolio choice and investment decision used the stochastic mathematical approach. Merton (1969) is the first study which examined the combined problem of optimal portfolio selection and consumption decision for an individual investor in a continuous-time model. There are many studies in the mainstream economic literature, which tried to extend the Merton's model (for example: Chacko & Viceira, 2005; Kallsen & Muhle-Karbe, 2017; Putschogl & Sass, 2008).

From theoretical point of view, Islamic financial system was established on the profit and loss sharing investment decisions, but, practically Islamic financial institutions offer different types of fixed return instruments more than risk sharing contracts (Dar & Presley, 2000). So, even in Islamic economics, we would face the same question, as conventional economics, that what proportion of wealth should be allocated to risky assets and what proportion to fixed income instruments. Many researchers like Tahir and Brimble (2011) tried to examine the investment behaviors in the Islamic economic and finance.

H. Kiaee (✉)
Faculty of Islamic Studies and Economics Imam, Sadiq University, Modiriat Bridge, 1465943681 Tehran, Iran
e-mail: kiaee@isu.ac.ir

T. Azid et al. (eds.), *Wealth Management and Investment in Islamic Settings*,
https://doi.org/10.1007/978-981-19-3686-9_9

But there are a few number of researches which used stochastic mathematical approach to Investment decisions in the economic and finance. Hachloufi et al. (2013), by using stochastic mathematics present a new approach for modeling the Murabahah margin. Their model estimates the value of Murabahah margin that the Islamic banks usually set to make profit. Omar and Jaffar (2016), used the model of stochastic Mudarabah investment which can be used in forecasting the profit gains by both two parties when the capital is invested in the stock market.

Isa and Shafie (2017), used Islamic banks data in Malaysia from 1999 to 2014 and stochastic forecasting method to determine a profit benchmark for home financing and also to find an optimum price. They found that the exponential Brownian motion model with drift is one of the stochastic forecasting models which has been identified as the best model to forecast the profit of Islamic home financing. Masri (2018), considering the idea of mean–variance model of Markowitz (1952), has developed a Shari'ah-compliant optimization model for portfolio selection in an Islamic security market. He proposed a model which follows Shari'ah principles by avoiding excessive risk and providing an ethical and socially responsible approach for portfolio selection.

Reviewing the current literature about modeling investment decisions in Islamic economics reveal that there is no research which uses the stochastic investment-consumption model for analyzing the investment behavior in the Islamic framework. In the Islamic economic framework, the portfolio selection problem differs from conventional ones since the risk free asset is not available and the investor should choose between risky assets and fixed return instruments like Murabahah and Ijarah Sukuk. Although, theoretically, Islamic fixed return instruments and conventional risk free bonds are completely different from each other, but in practice, in Islamic financial institutions, Islamic fixed return instruments provide in such a way that they are very similar to conventional bonds. It is usually believed that if the investor of Sukuk faces the ownership risk of these products, the investor's satisfaction level will be declined and so financial institutions use different methods to cover almost all of these risks to make Sukuk similar to conventional bonds.

In this chapter, we try to examine the effects of fixed return instruments on the investment decisions in the Islamic economic framework. To consider Sukuk, as Islamic fixed return instruments, in our model, we will analyze three different scenarios: (1) Sukuk with no risk as conventional bonds, (2) Modeling investment decisions without Sukuk and (3) considering both risk and return for Sukuk in the model.

9.1 Stochastic Modeling of Investment Decisions

In the simple two assets model provided by Merton (1969), the investor allocates Q_t percent of her wealth in time t,w_t, in risky asset and $1 - Q_t$ percent in risk free asset. The price of risky asset,p_t, is assumed to follow Ito stochastic process as follows:

$$dp_t = \alpha p_t dt + \sigma p_t dz_t$$

where, α and σ represent average and standard deviation of risky asset return, respectively and z_t is a standard Brownian motion stochastic process. Risk free asset is assumed to provide r percent constant interest rate, where $r < \alpha$ and so its price, s_t, is as follows:

$$ds_t = rs_t dt$$

If we denote the amount of consumption in time t, by c_t then the change in total wealth in each period could be presented by a stochastic differential equation as:

$$dw_t = Q_t w_t \alpha dt + Q_t w_t \sigma dz_t + (1 - Q_t) rw_t dt - c_t dt \tag{9.1}$$

Utility function in this problem is a function of consumption and is assumed to be in logarithmic form. The discount rate of ρ is used to show the time preference for consumption. The investor, in the optimization problem, maximizes her welfare which is total utility during [0.T] as follows:

$$\max E\left[\int_0^T e^{-\rho t} \ln c_t dt\right] \tag{9.2}$$

The changes of wealth during time which were indicated as stochastic differential equation in (9.1) is the constraint for this optimization problem and has rearranged as Eq. (9.3):

$$dw_t = (\alpha - r)Q_t w_t dt + (rw_t - c_t)dt + \sigma Q_t w_t dz_t \tag{9.3}$$

To solve the optimization problem, as proposed by Sheldon (2006), we define a value function,$V(w)$, and obtain the Hamilton–Jacobi–Bellman (HJB) equation of the problem as:

$$\rho V(w) = \left[u_{(c_t)} + [(\alpha - r)Q_t w_t + (rw_t - c_t)]V_w + \frac{1}{2}\sigma^2 Q_t^2 w_t^2 V_{ww}\right], \tag{9.4}$$

where, V_w and V_{ww} are the first and second derivatives of the value function with respect of wealth, respectively. To find optimal path of control variables c_t^* and Q_t^* the following derivative should be calculated.

$$\frac{\partial}{\partial c_t} = \frac{1}{c_t} - V_w = 0 \rightarrow c_t^* = \frac{1}{V_w} \tag{9.5}$$

$$\frac{\partial}{\partial Q_t} = w_t(\alpha - r)V_w + \sigma^2 Q_t w_t^2 V_{ww} = 0 \rightarrow Q_t^* = \frac{(r - \alpha)V_w}{\sigma^2 w_t V_{ww}} \tag{9.6}$$

The details of the derivation of the value function is provided in Appendix 1. So, after calculating the two derivatives V_w and V_{ww}, the path of variables c_t^* and Q_t^* as a function of w_t could be obtained as Eqs. (9.7) and (9.8):

$$c_t^* = \rho w_t \tag{9.7}$$

$$Q_t^* = \frac{(\alpha - r)}{\sigma^2} \tag{9.8}$$

To find the optimal path of wealth, we should substitute c_t^* and Q_t^* into the Eq. (9.3). The resulted stochastic differential equation is given in Eq. (9.7) which is a function ofw_t.

$$\frac{dw_t}{w_t} = \frac{(\alpha - r)^2}{\sigma^2} dt + (r - \rho)dt + \frac{(\alpha - r)}{\sigma} dz_t \tag{9.9}$$

Equation (9.11) is a standard geometric Brownian motion. Solving this equation provides the optimal path of wealth during time which is showed in Eq. (9.10):

$$w_t = w_0 e^{\left(\frac{(\alpha - r)^2}{\sigma^2} + r - \rho\right)t + \frac{(\alpha - r)}{\sigma} z_t} \tag{9.10}$$

9.2 Investment Decisions in Islamic Economics

Prohibition of Riba is the main characteristic of Islamic finance. For a typical investor, in the original Islamic economic framework, entering into risk sharing activities like buying stocks was the only option available for the investment. But, Islamic finance has been rapidly developed in recent years in such a way that Islamic fixed return instruments like Murabahah and Ijarah Sukuks are used in many Islamic countries as financing instruments. Nowadays, when an investor tries to choose her investment portfolio, in addition to risky assets, she could select some securities which offer fixed return income and are compatible with Shariah rules too.

These instruments, in their nature, bring some risks to their holder since they are almost based on the buying of an asset and reselling it with a higher price or rent it and receiving contractual rent. But, in practice, financial institutions use different methods to reduce and transfer the ownership risks and make them very similar to conventional risk free instruments. When we want to analyze the effects of Islamic fixed return instruments on the investment decisions, we should first determine the type of Sukuk that we are dealing with. Whether we want to analyze the effects of practical Sukuk which are similar to conventional bonds or we use the theoretical Sukuk which have some risks according to their original design.

In this section, we construct an investment-consumption optimization problem to examine the effect of Islamic fixed return instruments on the investment decisions of the investor. To consider the effect of Sukuk on the investment decisions, we will analyze three different scenarios: (1) Sukuk, as a fixed return instrument, which is completely similar to a risk free bond, (2) the investor choses no fixed return instrument in her portfolio and (3) the investor would face the risks which are available in the Sukuk and consider them in her portfolio selection problem.

9.2.1 *Modeling Sukuk as a Fixed Return Bond*

Islamic fixed return instruments like Murabahah and Ijarah Sukuks differ from interest based bonds in their contractual nature, but since practically offer riskless and fixed return to their holders, some investors look at them the same as conventional bonds. So, it could be predicted that, for these investors, the optimization problem for investment decisions is the same as what we have examined in the previous section expect that we should put Sukuk rate in place of the interest rate of conventional risk free instrument.

In this case, the constraint of the optimization problem which was introduced in Eq. (9.3) will be changed as follows:

$$dw_t = (\alpha - m)Q_t w_t dt + (mw_t - c_t)dt + \sigma Q_t w_t dz_t \tag{9.11}$$

where, m is the rate of return in the fixed return Sukuk. This rate could be the difference between spot and deferred transaction in the Murabahah Sukuk or the leasing rate in the Ijarah Sukuk. As it is clear, in this case the optimal path of variables are similar to the conventional ones just we should substitute r with m. Equation (9.10) could be rewritten as:

$$w_t = w_0 e^{\left(\frac{(\alpha - m)^2}{\sigma^2} + m - \rho\right)t + \frac{(\alpha - m)}{\sigma} z_t} \tag{9.12}$$

9.2.2 *Portfolio Choice with no Fixed Return Instrument*

One extreme case is that the investor chooses no fixed return securities, even Sukuk, in her portfolio. She should either invest her money in the risky asset or pay it for consumption expenditure. The investment decision in this case is very close to the original version of Islamic finance which was established on the risk sharing contracts like Musharakah and Mudarabah. In this case, the objective function is the same as Eq. (9.2), but the stochastic constraint of Eq. (9.3) will be changed to,

$$dw_t = Q_t w_t \alpha dt + Q_t w_t \sigma dz_t - c_t dt \tag{9.13}$$

According to Eq. (9.13), the investor, uses Q_t percent of her wealth for investing in risky assets and consume c_t in each period. By solving the optimization problem of this case, we could rewrite Eq. (9.7) and (9.8) for the optimal path of control variables as:

$$c_t^* = \rho w_t \tag{9.14}$$

$$Q_t^* = \frac{\alpha}{\sigma^2} \tag{9.15}$$

Appling Eqs. (9.14) and (9.15) into the Eq. (9.13) and solving the stochastic differential equation gives us the optimal path of wealth as follows:

$$w_t^* = w_0 e^{\left(\frac{\alpha^2}{\sigma^2} - \rho\right)t + \frac{\alpha}{\sigma} z_t} \tag{9.16}$$

9.2.3 Investment Decisions Considering Sukuk Characteristics

The case that we have examined is just based on the risk sharing instruments and so ignored the vast number of achievements which are provided in recent years by the Islamic finance. The fixed return instruments in Islamic finance like Ijarah and Murabahah Sukuk offer specified return to their holders, but, in their nature, are completely different from risk free assets like bond in conventional economics. In both types of Sukuk, investors actually buy all or a part of commodity and resell it or rent it to make income, but in the risk free assets like bond, investors just lend money and receive it back after a period in addition to its interest.

As we examined in previous section, in practice, the Sukuk contracts, in some cases, are designed in such a way that when the investor buys it, she may not be aware of the underlying assets and their risk. So, in this case, the Sukuk investment modeling has no significant difference with the conventional risk free assets. In this section, we would suppose that the characteristics of Sukuk, which make it different from conventional bond, are applied and the investor would consider these characteristics when she is choosing her portfolio of assets.

For this purpose, first we try to bring the characteristics of Sukuk into the mathematical modeling. Then, by solving the optimization problem, we would see that if Sukuk contracts are designed based on their theoretical characteristics, not similar to risk free bonds, what would be the choice of the investor in the portfolio choice problem. The same as original problem, we assume that the investor allocates Q_t percent of her wealth in the risky asset in which its price follows Ito stochastic process as follows:

$$dp_t = \alpha p_t dt + \sigma p_t dz_t$$

Risk free instruments are unavailable to the investor but she could put s_t amount of her wealth in Sukuk instruments and buy a commodity and resell it or rent it to gain m percent income. The same as before, c_t is the amount of consumption in periodt. The change of total wealth in each period, which is the stochastic constraint of optimization problem could be written as Eq. (9.17).

$$dw_t = Q_t w_t \alpha dt + Q_t w_t \sigma dz_t + m s_t dt - c_t dt \tag{9.17}$$

It is clear that buying Sukuk instrument differs from lending a proportion of wealth in return of receiving interest, as it happens in conventional bonds. So, in Eq. (9.17), buying Sukuk is treated as one type of consumption, since investor actually buys underling asset and resell it or lease it by the profit rate of m. But, in reverse ofc_t which brings utility to the investor, buying s_t, as Sukuk underlying asset, brings uncertainty and risk for its holder in addition to m present income. To deal with this risk in our model, we have revised the utility function and considered this as a disutility that occurs to the Sukuk holder as the owner of the underlying asset. Our proposed utility function in Eq. (9.18) has a logarithmic form, similar to Eq. (9.2), in such a way that is directly related to c_t and is inversely related tos_t. The power of m for s_t shows the relationship between risk and return, since we expect the higher return Sukuk to bring more disutility to its holder.

$$u(c_t, s_t) = \ln(\frac{c_t}{{s_t}^m}) \tag{9.18}$$

By this utility function, we could form objective function as Eq. (9.19) for the optimization problem. The stochastic constraint for this problem is Eq. (9.17) which shows the wealth changes during time.

$$\max E\left[\int_0^T e^{-\rho t} \ln(\frac{c_t}{{s_t}^m}) dt\right] \tag{9.19}$$

For solving this optimization problem, we could write HJB equation as Eq. (9.20) and take derivatives with respect toc_t, Q_t and s_t to find optimal path of these variables as Eqs. (9.21), (9.22) and (9.23).

$$\rho V(w) = \left[u(c_t, s_t) + [\alpha Q_t w_t + m s_t - c_t]V_w + \frac{1}{2}\sigma^2 Q_t^2 w_t^2 V_{ww}\right] \tag{9.20}$$

$$\frac{\partial}{\partial c_t} = \frac{1}{c_t} - V_w = 0 \rightarrow c_t^* = \frac{1}{V_w} \tag{9.21}$$

$$\frac{\partial}{\partial Q_t} = w_t \alpha V_w + \sigma^2 Q_t w_t^2 V_{ww} = 0 \rightarrow Q_t^* = \frac{\alpha V_w}{\sigma^2 w_t V_{ww}} \tag{9.22}$$

$$\frac{\partial}{\partial s_t} = -\frac{m}{s_t} + mV_w = 0 \rightarrow s_t^* = \frac{1}{V_w} \quad (9.23)$$

Substituting Eqs. (9.21), (9.22) and (9.23) in Eq. (9.20) we could find the functional form of the value function, $V(w)$, by the same method provided in Appendix 1 for the original problem. So, we could have the optimal path of c_t, Q_t and s_t as a function of w_t as are given in Eqs. (9.24), (9.25) and (9.26).

$$c_t^* = \frac{\rho}{1-m} w_t \quad (9.24)$$

$$Q_t^* = \frac{\alpha}{\sigma^2} \quad (9.25)$$

$$s_t^* = \frac{\rho}{1-m} w_t \quad (9.26)$$

It should be noted that Eqs. (9.24) and (9.26) are completely the same. So, in this case, the optimal path of Sukuk investment is similar to the optimal path of consumption and both variables are directly related tom. By putting optimal path of variables in Eqs. (9.24), (9.25) and (9.26) into the Eq. (9.17), we could derive the stochastic differential equation as a function of w_t. Solving this stochastic differential equation leads to the optimal path of w_t as Eq. (9.27).

$$w_t^* = w_0 e^{\left(\frac{\alpha^2}{\sigma^2} - \rho\right)t + \frac{\alpha}{\sigma} z_t} \quad (9.27)$$

The interesting point is that Eq. (9.27) is similar to the Eq. (9.16). It shows that when we consider Sukuk characteristics in our model, the optimal path of wealth is the same as we just have risky assets. In the other word, when we deal with Sukuk as an instrument which brings both risk and return to its holder, the fixed return of Sukuk, m, dose not have any effect in the wealth accumulation of the investor.

9.3 Comparing Optimal Path of Different Models

In previous section, we have proposed 3 different models for analyzing the portfolio selection of a typical investor in the Islamic finance framework and found the optimal path of variables in each model. In this section, we could assume some values for the model parameters and compare the numerical optimal path for variables in different models. For the numerical calculation, we have assumed that the model variables have monthly changes for a period of 10 years. The hypothetical values for the model parameters are shown in the Table 9.1 for each model. In the rest of the chapter, we call the model in Sect. 9.2.1, "Sukuk as bond" (SAB), the model in Sect. 9.2.2,

Table 9.1 The monthly hypothetic value for the parameters in 3 proposed model

Parameters\Models	Sukuk as Bond (SAB)	Modeling without Sukuk (MWS)	Real Sukuk Modeling (RSM)
Risky return drift (α)	0.2%	0.2%	0.2%
Risky return volatility (σ)	5.0%	5.0%	5.0%
Sukuk rate (m)	0.5%	–	0.5%
Discount rate (ρ)	0.1%	0.1%	0.1%
Initial wealth ($)	1000	1000	1000

"Modeling without Sukuk" (MWS) and the model in Sect. 9.2.3, as "Real Sukuk modeling" (RSM).

Since all of the variables in 3 models are stochastic variables, we should perform some simulations for the path of Winner processz_t. For this purpose, as Hanson (2007) proposed, we construct dz_t by the average values of 500 series generated from normal distribution with zero mean and the variance equal to Δt^2. The accumulated values of dz_t up to the time t could be used as z_t for the calculation of numerical path of variables.

Before calculating the optimal path of variables, it would be useful to point out that the optimal value for the share of risky asset,Q_t, in all three models are independent of time. Using the parameter's value of Table 10.1 into Eqs. (9.8), (9.15) and (9.25), gives us the values of 20, 80 and 80 percent for the share of risky asset in the SAB, MWS and RSM models respectively. It is clear that the optimal share of Sukuk in the investment portfolio in SAB model, which does not consider the risks of Sukuk, is greater than RSM model.

9.3.1 *Optimal Path of Wealth*

The comparison of the optimal path of wealth in different models is illustrated in Fig. 10.1. For this comparison, the numerical path of Eqs. (9.12), (9.16) and (9.27) are calculated. As were mentioned in Sect. 9.2.3, the path of wealth in the MWS and RSM models are completely similar to each other. It is clear that the optimal path of wealth when we consider Sukuk as fixed return instrument without any risk (SAB model), is smoother and less volatile than the two other models. The other point is that, in almost all time the value of wealth in MWS and RSM models are greater than the value of wealth in SAB model (Figs. 9.1).

Fig. 9.1 The optimal path of wealth in 3 different Islamic investment decision models

Fig. 9.2 The optimal path of consumption in 3 different Islamic investment decision models

9.3.2 Optimal Path of Consumption

Consumption path has a critical role in the investment decision models since its value has direct effect on the utility and welfare of the investor. Figure 9.2 compares the optimal path of consumption in the 3 different models of Islamic portfolio selection. It is clear that our proposed RSM has higher level of consumption than the two other models. We could also see that SAB model has the smaller level of consumption comparing with the two other models.

To find the reason for higher level of consumption in RSM model, we should compare Eq. (9.24) with Eq. (9.14). The existence of a coefficient containing the Sukuk return, m, in Eq. (9.24), leads to higher level of consumption from the beginning period of time but for the two other models the consumption path is independent from Sukuk return.

9.3.3 Optimal Path of Utility

Calculating utility values of the investor in each model, enables us to compare the level of satisfaction of the investor in the different models. This comparison is illustrated in Fig. 9.3. According to this Figure, the level of satisfaction of the investor in RSM is higher than the two other models. The level of utility in the MWS also is higher and more volatile than SAB model. It should be noticed that in RSM model, which has highest satisfaction level, the risk of ownership in the Sukuk has also been considered as disutility factor in the utility function of the model. So, it seems that, the reason for higher utility level is the higher level of consumption in, RSM model, from the first period of time.

This fact is very important since it is usually believed that when we design Sukuk structure in such a way that the investor faces Sukuk risk, the utility level of investor would decline. So, in practice, the financial institutions do their best to cover all risks by different methods and keep the investor of Sukuk away from any risk. According to the model result, we could now claim that these efforts have no positive effect

Fig. 9.3 The optimal path of utility in 3 different Islamic investment decision models

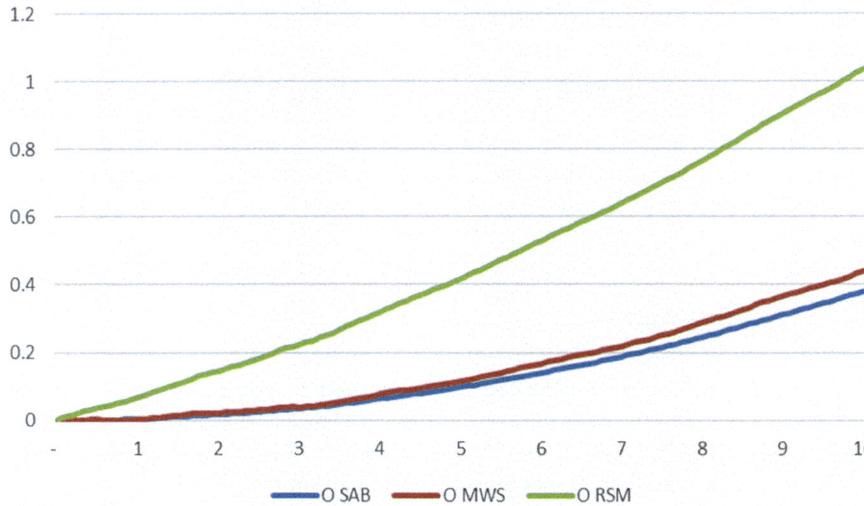

Fig. 9.4 The optimal path of welfare in 3 different Islamic investment decision models

on the investor utility level and just lead the financial market activist to this general perception that there is no practical difference between Sukuk and conventional bond.

9.3.4 Optimal Path of Welfare

The value of objective function or accumulation of discounted utility is the level of welfare of investor at each period of time. The value of welfare is important since, in the optimization problem, we have maximized this function with respect to stochastic constraint. The optimal value of welfare path for the 3 models are shown in the Fig. 9.4. According to this Figure, the welfare of investor in RSM model is greater than the two other models and SAB model has the smallest value of welfare. As we expect from the utility level in Fig. 9.3, the Fig. 9.4 shows that when we consider Sukuk characteristics in the model, the welfare of the investor would be increased comparing to the situation that just fixed return of Sukuk enter to the model as conventional fixed return bond.

9.4 Conclusion

To analyze investment decisions, in conventional economics, we should distinguish between two different questions. The first one is the amount of wealth to be allocated to consumption and investment in each period of time and the other question is that how much is the share of risky assets and risk free assets in the investment portfolio of the investor. In the current economic literature, the stochastic investment-consumption models are very popular to analyze the investment decisions since these models consider the stochastic nature of risky assets and at the same time try to answer two former questions. Although, there are a few number of studies in the Islamic economic and finance which have used the stochastic mathematical modeling, but there is no research in the literature that use stochastic investment-consumption modeling to analyze investment decisions in the Islamic finance framework.

Islamic financial system originally was established on the profit and loss sharing types of finance, but, in recent years many fixed return instruments have been introduced and used by Islamic financial institutions. So, even in Islamic economics, when we want to deal with investment decisions, we should determine that what proportion of wealth should allocate to risky asset and what proportion to fixed income instruments. The Islamic fixed return instruments have two main Shariah characteristics which make them different from conventional risk free instruments: (1) Islamic investor dose not lend the money, instead, buy a commodity and resell it or lease it to make income (2) the ownership of that commodity brings some risk and uncertainty for the investor.

In this paper, for the first time, we have tried to construct a stochastic investment-consumption model and analyze the effect of fixed return instruments on the investment decisions in the Islamic economic framework. To examine the effect of sukuk in the investment decisions, we have considered 3 different senarios: (1) Sukuk, as fixed return instrument, which is completely similar to a risk free bond, (2) the investor choses no fixed return instrument in her portfolio and (3) the investor would face the risks which are available in the Sukuk and considers them in her portfolio selection problem.

To analyze the risky characteristic of Sukuk in the model, we have assumed Sukuk as a type of consumption, since investor actually buys underling asset and resell it or lease it to make income. But, in reverse of usual consumption, which brings utility to the investor, buying Sukuk underlying asset, brings uncertainty and risk for its holder in addition to income. To deal with this ownership risk in our model, we revised the utility function and considered this risk as a disutility factor in the utility function of investor.

Finally, to compare the optimal path of variables in each models, after solving the optimization problems, we have assumed some hypothetical values for the parameters and calculated the numerical path of variables over time. The numerical results showed that, the model that considers the risky characteristics of Sukuk brings more utility and welfare to the investor comparing to the model that considers Sukuk as a risk free instrument.

Appendix 9.1 Finding the Form of Value Function

If we consider the value function with unknown coefficients A and B in the following form then we could calculate the first and second derivatives of this function with respect to w.

$$V_{(w)} = A l n w_t + B$$

$$V_w = \frac{A}{w_t}$$

$$V_{ww} = -\frac{A}{w_t^2}$$

Substituting this function and its derivatives in the Eq. (9.4), we could find the unknown coefficients from the equality of two sides.

$$\rho A \ln w_t + \rho B = \left[\ln \frac{w_t}{A} + (\alpha - r) \frac{(r-\alpha)\frac{A}{w_t}}{\sigma^2 w_t \left(-\frac{A}{w_t^2}\right)} w_t + \left(r w_t - \frac{w_t}{A}\right) \right] \frac{A}{w_t}$$

$$+ \frac{1}{2}\sigma^2 \left(\frac{(r-\alpha)\frac{A}{w_t}}{\sigma^2 w_t \left(-\frac{A}{w_t^2}\right)} \right)^2 w_t^2 \left(-\frac{A}{w_t^2}\right)$$

If we define $\gamma = \frac{(\alpha - \mathrm{r})}{2\sigma^2}$ so the above equation could be written as:

$$\rho \mathrm{Alnw_t} + \rho \mathrm{B} = \gamma \mathrm{A} + \left(\gamma \mathrm{w_t} - \frac{\mathrm{w_t}}{\mathrm{A}}\right) \frac{\mathrm{A}}{\mathrm{w_t}} - \ln \frac{\mathrm{A}}{\mathrm{w_t}} = \gamma \mathrm{A} + \gamma \mathrm{A} - 1 - \mathrm{lnA} + \mathrm{lnw_t}$$

$$\mathrm{A} = \frac{1}{\rho}$$

$$\mathrm{B} = \frac{\mathrm{r} - \rho + \gamma}{\rho^2} + \frac{\ln \rho}{\rho}$$

Finally, substituting coefficients A and B in to first and second derivatives and putting the results in to Eqs. (9.5) and (9.6) leads to:

$$\mathrm{c_t^*} = \frac{1}{\mathrm{V_w}} = \rho \mathrm{w_t}$$

$$\mathrm{Q_t^*} = \frac{(\mathrm{r} - \alpha)\frac{1}{\rho \mathrm{w_t}}}{-\sigma^2 \mathrm{w_t} \frac{1}{\rho \mathrm{w_t^2}}} = \frac{(\alpha - \mathrm{r})}{\sigma^2}$$

References

Chacko, G., & Viceira, L. M. (2005). Dynamic consumption and portfolio choice with stochastic volatility in incomplete markets. *Rev. Financ. Stud., 18*(4), 1369–1402.

Dar, H. A., & Presley, J. R. (2000). Lack of Profit Loss Sharing in Islamic Banking: Management and Control Imbalances, *Economic Research Paper,* Department of Economics, Loughborough University, No. 00/24.

Hachloufi, M. E., Hamza, F., & Janssen, J. (2013). A Mathematical Approach for Modeling Marge of Murabaha Islamic Banking Product. *Journal of Applied Statistical Science, 21*(4), 389–399.

Hanson, F. B. (2007). *Applied Stochastic Processes and Control for Jump-Diffusions: Modeling.* University of Illinois, Chicago, USA.

Isa, Z., & Shafie, N. A. (2017). A Stochastic Approach for Determining Profit Rate of Islamic Financing Products. *International Journal of Economics and Financial Issues, 7*(1), 154–163.

Kallsen, J., & Muhle-Karbe, J. (2017). The general structure of optimal investment and consumption with small transaction costs. *Mathematical Finance, 27*(3), 659–703.

Markowitz, H. M. (1952). Portfolio selection, *The. Journal of Finance, 7*(1), 77–91.

Masri, H. (2018). A Shariah-compliant portfolio selection model. *Journal of the Operational Research Society, 69*(10), 1568–1575.

Merton, R. C. (1969). Lifetime Portfolio Selection Under Uncertainty: The Continuous-Time Case. *The Review of Economics and Statistics, 51*(3), 247–257.

Omar, A., & Jaffar, M. M. (2016). The Continuous Model of Stochastic Mudharabah Investment. *Social Sciences & Humanities, 24*, 101–110.

Putschogl, W., & Sass, J. (2008). Optimal consumption and investment under partial information. *Decisions in Economics and Finance, 31*, 131–170.

Sheldon L. X. (2006). *Introductory Stochastic Analysis for Finance and Insurance*, John Wiley Sons.

Tahir, I., & Brimble, M. (2011). Islamic investment behavior. *International Journal of Islamic and Middle Eastern Finance and Management, 4*(2), 116–130.

Hasan Kiaee is Assistant Professor of economics at faculty of Islamic Studies and Economics at Imam Sadiq University and specially focused on quantitative area of Islamic economics and finance. He earned his master in 2008 and PhD in 2013 from University of Tehran, his PhD thesis was about using stochastic optimal control theory in modeling the Islamic banking behavior. In addition to contributing in some papers and books in this field, he actively participates in the Islamic banking and finance conferences inside and outside of Iran. Beside this academic background, he has a good practical knowledge in Islamic finance, as he has.

Chapter 10
Family Financial Management in Realizing *Sakinah* Family

Putri Apria Ningish, Murniati Mukhlisin, and Jumni Nelli

10.1 Background of the Problem

Improper household financial management is often a dispute in the family.[1] This causes a rift in household relations, many of which end in divorce. The number of divorces in Indonesia continues to increase every year. It can be seen from the data from several big cities in Indonesia below (Table 10.1).

From the data above, it can be seen that almost every year in all major cities in Indonesia there is an increase in the number of divorce decisions. One of the causes of this divorce is financial problems.[2] Financial problems are not only about the amount of property, but what is more dominant is because of the ignorance of managing finances in the family.

Good family financial management can resolve economic disparities in the household, thereby reducing the increase in divorce rates.[3] Especially when the level of knowledge and tenacity of housewives is quite high. The higher the knowledge of housewives about family financial management, the higher the economic survival

[1] This is based on the author's conclusion in reading and analyzing several local newspapers in big cities in Indonesia.

[2] Dyah Kusumawati, *Pengelolaan Keuangan Dalam Keluarga dari Sudut Pandang Islam,* online journal that is accessed at https://media.neliti.com/, page.175.

[3] Efrita Norman and Ermi Suryani, "*Managemen Keuangan Keluarga Pascaperceraian*", As-Syar'i: Jurnal Bimbingan & Konseling Keluarga. Vol. 1 no. 1, 2019, page. 25.

P. A. Ningish (✉)
Faculty of Islamic Economics and Business (FEBI), Universitas Islam Negeri Sulthan Thaha Saifuddin, Jambi, Indonesia
e-mail: putriapria8@gmail.com

M. Mukhlisin
Institut Agama Islam Tazkia, Bogor, Indonesia

J. Nelli
UIN Sultan Syarif Kasim, Riau, Indonesia

T. Azid et al. (eds.), *Wealth Management and Investment in Islamic Settings*,
https://doi.org/10.1007/978-981-19-3686-9_10

Table 10.1 Divorce data in Indonesia[4]

No.	Location of religious court	Number of divorce verdict			
		2016	2017	2018	2019
1	Jakarta Barat	556,246	577,085	646,347	763.019
2	Bandung	1,484	909	650	1,601
3	Surabaya	1,387	1,265	2,254	3,711
4	Medan	1,817	1,114	2,894	3,505
5	Tangerang	675	797	981	2,642

rate of their family. The author sees that there is still a lack of special literature that discusses family financial management. There are several, but they have not been neatly documented and not comprehensive. Seeing how important a special discussion is on Islamic wealth management or personal finance, for that the author wants to study and explore more in terms of family financial management, so this article is entitled: "Family Financial Management in Realizing *Sakinah* Family", with main research problem: how reconstruction of family financial management can be carried out in Islam? This research is a type of library research and field research that aims to examine method of family finance in an Islamic household. This research is qualitative by using descriptive method. *Maqasad al Shari'ah* is used as a guide in analyzing the data then categorized and interpreted using a thematic analysis perspective.

The next section delineates the literatures on eight principles in managing family finance. Then the paper discusses model of family finance. The final section concludes the study and suggests recommendations for future research.

10.2 Literatures on Eight Principles

The economic practices applied by the Prophet Muhammad in his family, society and the state are like the principles that Allah SWT mentions in the Qur'an. The financial management of the family of the prophet Muhammad SAW is never separated from the following things:

(1) Tawhid

The main foundation of all Islamic teachings is monotheism. Tawhid is the basis for all concepts and activities of Muslims, whether economic, political, social or cultural. The essence of monotheism is a complete surrender to the will of God, both concerning worship and *muamalah*, in order to create a pattern of life that is in accordance with God's will.

[4] The five big cities were deliberately chosen because from 2016 to 2019 they experienced a significant increase. And four years from 2016 to 2019 were taken because that was the most recent year issued by the Supreme Court, https://ujungan3.mahkamahagung.go.id/.

The concept of monotheism, which is the philosophical basis, teaches two main teachings in economics, including the financial management system.

First, all the resources that exist in nature are creations and belong to Allah in absolute terms (absolute and essential). Every financial management and effort to seek must be in accordance with the rules of Allah SWT as well as spending it.

Second, Allah SWT provides abundant natural resources to meet human needs. These resources are God's countless (infinite) blessings. However, humans as vicegerents of Allah should not be wasteful and greedy in using them.

In addition to believing that the treasure is a gift from Allah SWT, every Muslim family must also believe that all these treasures will be deliberately questioned by Allah later on the Day of Judgment, as the Prophet Muhammad SAW said:

لَا تَزُولُ قَدَمَا عَبْدٍ يَوْمَ الْقِيَامَةِ حَتَّى يُسْأَلَ عَنْ عُمُرِهِ فِيمَا أَفْنَاهُ، وَعَنْ عِلْمِهِ فِيمَ فَعَلَ، وَعَنْ
مَالِهِ مِنْ أَيْنَ اكْتَسَبَهُ وَفِيمَ أَنْفَقَهُ، وَعَنْ جِسْمِهِ فِيمَ أَبْلَاه

Meaning: *The feet of a servant will not move on the Day of Resurrection until he is asked: about his age, in what way he spends; about his knowledge, in what way he practiced; about his wealth, where did he get it and what did he spend it; and about his body, in what way does he make use of* (HH at-Tirmidhi, ad-Darimi, al-Baihaqi. Editor at-Tirmidhi).[5]

(2) Worship

Muslim families in managing their finances cannot be separated from the spirit and intention of worshiping Allah SWT. The purpose of trying is not only to get material wealth but also because of the encouragement to get the reward and forgiveness of Allah SWT, as the words of the Prophet Muhammad SAW:

من طلبَ الدُّنيا حَلالًا ، إِسْتِعْفَافًا عَنِ الْمَسْأَلَةِ ، وَسَعْيًا عَلَى أَهْلِهِ وَتَعَطُّفًا عَلَى جَارِهِ جَاءَ
يَوْمَ الْقِيَامَةِ وَوَجْهُهُ كَالْقَمَرِ لَيْلَةَ الْبَدْرِ وَمَنْ طَلَبَ الدُّنيا حلالًا مُكاثِرًا لَقِيَ اللهَ وَهُوَ عَلَيْهِ
غَضْبَانُ

Meaning: *Whoever seeks the world lawfully, keeps himself from begging, strives for his family and is compassionate to his neighbors, then he meets Allah with a face like the full moon, And whoever seeks the world in a lawful way, but because of the intention of piling up, then later he will meet Allah with a condition that is hated by Him.*[6]

---

[5] Abu Zakariya Muhyiddin Yahya An Nawawi, *Riyadhus Shalihin*, Cairo: Dar Dakwah Al Islamiyah, Page. 131.

[6] Al-Qalami, Abu Fajar *Ringkasan Ihya' Ulumiddin,* First Printing. (Surabaya: Gitamedia Press, 2003).

(3) Morals

The key in Islamic economic transaction is a good personality, such as; *siddiq* (truthful), *amanah* (trustworthy), *fathonah* (ingenious), and *tabligh* (advocacy), and these are the characters of the Prophet SAW. So he was famous in the city of Mecca as *Al Amin* (trusted peson). Everyone was happy to deal with him.[7]

(4) Halal and Good

Prophet Muhammad SAW exemplified perfectly throughout his life that he never eats, gets and spends his wealth except lawful and good. In the Qur'an, surah al-Baqarah verse 172:

يَا أَيُّهَا الَّذِينَ آمَنُواْ كُلُواْ مِن طَيِّبَاتِ مَا رَزَقْنَاكُمْ وَاشْكُرُواْ لِلّهِ إِن كُنتُمْ إِيَّاهُ تَعْبُدُونَ -١٧٢-

Meaning: *O you who believe! Eat of the good sustenance that We have given you and be grateful to Allah, if you only worship Him.*[8]

(5) Priority Scale

This is in accordance with the maqashid Sharia, Rasulullah SAW taught the people to pay attention to the priority scale in their lives. In accordance with maqashid shariah, the priority in financial arrangements for Muslim families are: needs classified as *Daruriyyat* then *Hajiyyat* then *Tahsiniyyat*. Daruriyyat is divided into five parts sequentially are; *hifdz ad din* (protect religion), *hifdz an-nafs* (protect soul), *hifdz al-aql* (protech intellectuality), *hifdz an-nasl* (protect offspring), and *hifdz al-mal* (protect wealth).

(6) Not stingy and not extravagant

Muslim families must be balanced between giving and withholding, meaning that they should not be too generous so as to cause regret and should not be too stingy, as mentioned by Allah SWT in Surah Al Furqan verse 67:

وَالَّذِينَ إِذَا أَنفَقُوا لَمْ يُسْرِفُوا وَلَمْ يَقْتُرُوا وَكَانَ بَيْنَ ذَلِكَ قَوَاماً -٦٧-

Meaning: *And (including the servants of God the Most Merciful) those who, when they spend (wealth), they are not excessive, and are not (also) stingy, between the two naturally.*[9]

Also there is a saying of the Prophet SAW:

كلوا واشربوا والبسوا وتصدقوا في غير إسراف ولا مخيلة

[7] Dodik Siswantoro, *ibid*, page. 21–24.

[8] Mujamma' Al Malik Fadh Li Thiba'et al. Mush-haf Asy-Syarif, page. 42.

[9] Ibid, page.568.

Meaning: *Eat you, and drink, and dress yourselves, and give charity without being excessive and not arrogant.*[10]

(7) Separating the husband's property with the wife's property

As in the case of the division of inheritance, men and women have their own ownership, both have the right to inherit or pass on inheritance.

(8) Work hard

The Prophet Muhammad SAW also motivated every Muslim to work hard and seek wealth, as narrated from *Shokhr Al Ghomidiy*, the Prophet Sallallaahu 'alaihi wa sallam said:

اللَّهُمَّ بَارِكْ لأُمَّتِى فِى بُكُورِهَا

Meaning: "*O Allah, bless my people in the morning.*"

That is, since the morning work hard because the morning is a time of blessing to get sustenance. As the prophet Muhammad SAW routinely prays so that he is far from being lazy. So, it can be said that the financial management of the Rasulullah family consists of nine pillars, including: monotheism, worship, morals, lawful and good, priority scale, not being stingy and not extravagant, separating husband and wife's property, working hard.

10.3 Discussion on Model of Family Finance

Financial Management is an activity of planning, budgeting, checking, managing, controlling, seeking and storing funds. Islamic perspective family financial management is as follows:

(1) Make a plan (planning)

In planning, it is necessary to have a solid initial foundation. The foundation for every Muslim in planning family finances is;

a. Tawhid

Tawhid is the foundation of Islam, all actions, behavior and even worship will have no value without being based on monotheism to Allah SWT, and conversely all actions, behavior and worship based on monotheism to Allah SWT will be worth worship and bring blessings to all. Likewise, in managing family finances, a monotheistic family will manage their family finances better and bring more comfort to the family compared to those who do not have good monotheism.

[10] The editor of this hadith was mentioned by Imam Bukhari and Imam An-Nasa'i.

فَإِذَا قُضِيَتِ الصَّلَاةُ فَانتَشِرُوا فِي الْأَرْضِ وَابْتَغُوا مِن فَضْلِ اللَّهِ وَاذْكُرُوا اللَّهَ
كَثِيراً لَّعَلَّكُمْ تُفْلِحُونَ

Meaning: *When the prayer has been performed, then you are scattered on the earth; seek the bounty of Allah and remember Allah a lot so that you are lucky.*[11]

The essence of monotheism is a complete surrender to the will of God, both concerning worship and *muamalah*, in order to create a pattern of life that is in accordance with God's will. The concept of monotheism, which is the philosophical basis, teaches two main teachings in economics, including the financial management system.

Furthermore, the concept of monotheism teaches that everything starts from Allah, aims at the end to Allah, uses the means and resources according to law of Allah. The activity of finding and managing family finances is useful for achieving the pleasure of Allah SWT. With the right monotheism, family financial planning will be optimal and efficient and on target.

b. Right intention

This intention will determine the direction of work, everyone tries to make a living for his life, especially the head of the family. If from the beginning the work has been intended for Allah SWT, the work or routine to earn a living will be worth the reward in the sight of Allah SWT. Likewise in planning family finances. The planning will be carried out with enthusiasm, as well as the results obtained, regardless of the amount and whatever the form will be gratefully accepted to Allah SWT, then there Allah will give blessings to everyone who is bestowed upon His servants, so as to create comfort for the family.

10.4 Managing Income

Revenue management is very important in financial planning because good financial planning comes from clean and halal income. Allah has guided his servants to seek sustenance and consume *halal & thayyib* because the household economy is said to be successful if the income received is halal and thayyib. In Usul Fiqh, the legal basis for muamalah is that it is permissible or permissible unless it is forbidden, so something that does not have any unlawful provisions is permissible.[12] Several criteria in managing family income, including:

a. Halal and Good

The basic concept for obtaining and spending wealth is "Halal and Good". Livelihood is earned through business and lawful work, regardless of fraud, corruption or usury.

[11] Mujamma' Al Malik Fadh Li Thiba'et al. Mush-haf Asy-Syarif, hlm. 933.

[12] Luqyan Tamanni dan Murniati Mukhlisin, Sakinah Finance, (Solo: Tinta Medina, 2018), page. 34.

After it is obtained in a lawful way, it is then spent or used in a way and for halal purposes as well. Not to be used for gambling, to be used for immorality or to facilitate immoral activities, not to be bought for unlawful clothing, food and shelter.

In addition to the halal concept, *thayyib* must also be, according to the word of God in the letter al-Baqarah 168 above. All respondents agreed that the sustenance or income earned and used is a good livelihood. "Good" here means that it does not cause harm to those who use it. Food that is eaten does not contain substances that harm the body, does not harm health, as well as clothing, shelter and also the activities carried out are good activities.

Wealth obtained by illegal means, such as corruption, stealing, usury, the results of being a prostitute and others, will not be a blessing and will quickly disappear without realizing it. How many people used to not care about the lawful and unlawful wealth, after they repented and said; *"I used to have a lot of wealth, but it quickly ran out somewhere, without me realizing it. Day and night I worked late looking for a lot of treasure, but the treasure disappeared quickly, the saddest thing, I was not happy with the treasure. Now that I have migrated and repented, I am looking for lawful wealth, my wealth is enough to live on and I feel happiness."*

A little lawful but blessed wealth is much better than a lot of unlawful wealth. This illicit treasure quickly disappears and Allah destroys it. Lots of rich people in an instant turn into bankrupt and poor, or rich but can't enjoy any of their wealth due to illness or other reasons. What we need to look for from rizki is not only the amount, but also the blessing. With blessed treasures, our lives become easier and easier to face various trials of life. The way to get blessings is through piety by staying away from what is haram and focusing on what is lawful and what is good.

b. Mujahadah

Some scholars say: "*Mujahadah is not obeying the will of lust*", and there are others who say: "*Mujahadah* is restraining lust from its pleasures." The best wealth is from one's own efforts even though the effort is quite difficult, on the other hand the worst wealth is property that is obtained by someone without any effort or given for free is not from a hard enough effort. The Prophet Muhammad, when he lived with his uncle Abu Talib, although he was a ruler in the city of Mecca, but he did not want to depend on his uncle.[13]

A Muslim must always work hard in earning a living, one indication of hard work is eager to work from the beginning of the day, namely from the morning, because morning time is a blessed time to get sustenance, in the morning Allah distributes good sustenance for his servants.

c. Friendship

Prophet Muhammad SAW once said:

---

[13] Dodik Siswantoro, Wealth Management (Manajemen Harta) Rasulullah SAW, Metode Pembelajaran Dari Hal Yang Belum Pernah Dibahas, (Yogyakarta: Phoinix Publisher, 2020), page. 14.

عَنْ ابْنِ شِهَابٍ قَالَ أَخْبَرَنِي أَنَسُ بْنُ مَالِكٍ أَنَّ رَسُولَ اللهِ صَلَّى اللهُ عَلَيْهِ وَسَلَّمَ قَالَ مَنْ
أَحَبَّ أَنْ يُبْسَطَ لَهُ فِي رِزْقِهِ وَيُنْسَأَ لَهُ فِي أَثَرِهِ فَلْيَصِلْ رَحِمَهُ

Meaning: *From Ibn Shihab he said; Anas bin Malik reported to me that the Messenger of Allah -peace and prayer of Allah be upon him- said: "Whoever wants to widen the door of sustenance for him and prolong his life, let him connect the ties of kinship."* (HR. Bukhari).

By staying in touch, there will be many acquaintances so as to increase the network and colleagues, with the number of work and business opportunities networks getting wider, so the risk is wide. The same applies to age, that by having frequent relationships with many people will be good, the heart will be at peace, people who intend to harm it are also absent so that their safety is maintained and eventually they will live a long life. So friendship can expand sustenance and prolong life.

10.5 Managing Needs

Need is something we really need to survive if we don't get it our life will suffer. Such as food, drink, clothing, and shelter. In Islam, the need is *dharurriyat* (principal). A person is willing to do anything so that these basic needs are met both in religion, soul, lineage, reason (science), and property. Managing this need is also very important because if it is not managed properly, desires will also be spent, resulting in budget swelling or a deficit.

There are several principles that need to be considered by Muslim families in managing their family needs, including:

a. Not stingy and not wasteful

In interpreting verses 29 and -30 of the words of Allah SWT in the letter al-Isra 'Imam Ibn Kathir mentions in his commentary: Allah SWT commands (to His servants) to be economical in life, and denounces miserliness; and at the same time prohibiting exaggeration; وَلا تَجْعَلْ يَدَكَ مَغْلُولَةً إِلَى عُنُقِكَ "*And do not make your hands shackled around your neck*".[14] In other words, don't be a stingy person and always refuse people who ask and never give anything to someone. The Jews, may Allah's curse be upon them, say that Allah's hands are shackled. What they mean is that Allah is miserly, when in fact Allah is Most High, Most Holy, Most Exalted and Most Giving.

Allah SWT said: وَلا تَبْسُطْهَا and don't stretch it too much. This means that you do not overspend in spending your wealth by giving beyond your means and spending more than your income. كُلَّ الْبَسْطِ فَتَقْعُدَ مَلُومًا مَحْسُورًا because of that you become despicable and regretful.[15]

---

[14] QS. Al Isra':29, Al-Quran dan Terjemahannya, Mujamma' Al Malik Fadh Li Thiba'et al. Mushhaf Asy-Syarif, 1418 H, page. 428.

[15] Ibid.

The command of Allah SWT in verses 29 and 30 of Surah al-Isra is an order to spend wealth in a "balanced" manner. When spending money, keep in mind the budgeting of current and future needs. Don't be too generous in giving alms to make it difficult for yourself.

Nor should it be stingy, there are at least two disadvantages for a miser. First, the loss while in the world, which causes enmity and hatred among close people and local residents where he lives. At least miserliness has caused displeasure in others. Besides, a stingy person is a weary person. He put all his might into amassing wealth, but he did not enjoy his wealth. Because, it's the heirs who will enjoy it.

b. *Infaq*

Infaq is meant here is obligatory infaq in the form of zakat and family income as well as sunnah *infaq*, namely in the form of ordinary alms. To achieve a happy life in the world and the hereafter, the Prophet Muhammad SAW based on revelations from Allah SWT has laid the basic framework for building an economy and financial system that is truly standard, systemic, and eternal.

Whoever has the breadth of sustenance and does not want to give it to the needy, then this is the kind of person whom the angels pray every morning and evening so that Allah SWT will get away his sustenance. There are various forms of extinction, it can reduce the amount of sustenance he receives, or he suffers from a disease, so that a lot of funds are spent on treatment, or it can also become extinct in the form of loss of goods, such as motorbikes, cars and other parts of it, also in the form of matters that become difficult and difficult to solve.

Infaq can create a peaceful feelings that eventually can make the family atmosphere more harmonious, this is what creates *mawaddah, warahmah* in the family. By giving charity, Allah SWT forgives the sins of those who donate. Sin is directly proportional to the narrowness of sustenance, meaning that the perpetrators of sin have their sustenance narrowed by Allah SWT, then sins also cause many disputes in a family, so that it can disrupt life.

c. Keep a record of all daily expenses

Although making notes is necessary, the application in the Muslim family community is not much. For this reason, this point also needs to be socialized to the community, especially Muslim families so that God's commands are carried out properly especially obligations related to property, so they need to maintain their own financial records. The record in question is a record of cash inflows and outflows or income and expenses.

d. Avoid debt

Rasulullah SAW was very afraid of debt and was very worried if it became his habit. It was narrated from Aisyah RA that she reported, "The Messenger of Allah used to pray in his prayers:

اللَّهُمَّ إِنِّي أَعُوذُ بِكَ مِنْ عَذَابِ الْقَبْرِ وَأَعُوذُ بِكَ مِنْ فِتْنَةِ الْمَسِيحِ الدَّجَّالِ وَأَعُوذُ بِكَ مِنْ فِتْنَةِ
الْمَحْيَا وَفِتْنَةِ الْمَمَاتِ ,اللَّهُمَّ إِنِّي أَعُوذُ بِكَ مِنَ الْمَأْثَمِ وَالْمَغْرَمِ

Meaning: *"O Allah! Verily, I seek refuge in you from the punishment of the grave, from the slander of Al-Masiih Ad-Dajjaal and from the slander of life and the slander of death. Dear Allah! Verily, I seek refuge in you from things that lead to sin and from debt."*

If the family's finances run into a deficit, try to stay away from debt. Because debt is an act that is not liked by the Prophet.

e. Save and invest

The command to save and invest in order to prepare for future needs, says Allah SWT in Surah An-Nisa. 9:

وَلْيَخْشَ الَّذِينَ لَوْ تَرَكُوا مِنْ خَلْفِهِمْ ذُرِّيَّةً ضِعَافًا خَافُوا عَلَيْهِمْ فَلْيَتَّقُوا اللَّهَ وَلْيَقُولُوا
قَوْلًا سَدِيدًا

Meaning: *And be anxious when you leave your children weak and worried for their welfare, and fear Allah, say noble words.*[16]

10.6 Managing Dreams

Needs and wants are very different. Needs are what we have to fulfill in order for life to go on while wants are what we want to complete life. Human needs are basically the same consisting of food, drink, clothing, and shelter. While the desires of every human being must be different from cars, motorbikes, computers, and so on. Human desires are various and many, maybe even exceeding needs, this is what is often called a dream.

Dreams in Muslim families must follow the maqashid shariah concept, meaning that the family's financial dreams / desires must be in line with maqashid shariah. The priority of family finances must be directed to maintaining religion, guarding the soul, maintaining reason, protecting descendants and protecting wealth.

a. Keeping Religion

In terms of working for sustenance, work with the intention of seeking the pleasure of Allah, do not sacrifice worship because of a job. Working is a must with the intention of seeking Allah's pleasure, in order to avoid immoral ways or not according to shariah. Accompanied by the spirit of worshiping Allah, God willing, always enthusiastic, not complaining a lot when there is a problem, returning all problems back to Allah so that there is no wrong way for the solution and praying for things to be eased.

[16] Mujamma' Al Malik Fadh Li Thiba'et al. Mush-haf Asy-Syarif, *Al-Qur'an and Terjemahannya,* (Madinah:1424 H). page.116.

b. Keeping Life

Maintenance of life safety covers nine main areas: a. Staple food and serving equipment, side dishes and spices, clean water and salt. b. Equipment for body maintenance. c. Clothes. d. Housing e. Health care f. Transportation and telecommunications and communication tools. g. Security for individuals and society. h. Comfortable working conditions. i. Care for the elderly, orphans.

c. Keeping Descendants

To maintain the safety of offspring, it is necessary: (1) preparation before marriage such as; pre-wedding preparation, insight into post-wedding household development, and others. (2) Routine check-ups to ensure the health and safety of the fetus for pregnant women. (3) Child care: health guidance and education for children, basic programs for children's health and nutrition, cultivation of the right faith and basic principles of Islam.

d. Keeping Property

Wealth is a mandate that must be developed in a planned manner for the purpose of eliminating poverty, meeting the basic needs of each individual, making life comfortable and encouraging the creation of an even distribution of income and wealth. In acquiring and developing assets, it is required to be based on Islamic values. There must be a moral filter in its management.

e. Keeping your mind

Among the things that are dangerous in corrupting the mind are drugs and all kinds of illegal drugs. On the orders of religion, everything that destroys the mind must be avoided and avoided, many young people have been involved in this drug vortex as users or dealers. While the maintenance of reason can consist of: a. Education; children's school fees and all children's educational needs from uniforms to learning tools and so on b. religious studies; budgeted to be able to follow religious studies.

10.7 Monitoring

There are several principles in controlling the financial management of Muslim families, including:

a. Audit

Muslim families are required once a year to audit the assets collected and if it reaches one nisab, it is obligatory for the family to pay zakat. So from this audit, we will find out how much and how much of our assets have been collected for one year. So that we know our rights and obligations to the assets we have. Because in our property there are other people's rights, especially for the weak. And because in that treasure there are two who are asked in the hereafter, where did you get the treasure and where did you spend the treasure.

b. Gratitude (Syukur)

A very strong medicine and factor so that a person can be grateful for the blessings of Allah SWT, that is, every servant should pay attention to those who are lower than him in terms of reason, lineage, wealth, and other favors. If a person continues to do this, then this will lead him to be much grateful to his Lord and praise Him. Because he always see people who were far below him in these things. Many of them hope to reach or at least approach what has been given to them from the blessings of health, wealth, sustenance, physical, and morals. Then he will much praise Allah SWT who has given him many gifts. This is what becomes self-control in managing lust that tends to be greedy.

c. Evaluation

Evaluation of *muhasabah* in family financial planning means to re-audit all income and expenses that have been made in a family, whether there is sustenance that is forbidden to be obtained or used so far. So when doing self-reflection for mistakes and sins committed, what is expected is to immediately seek forgiveness or ask forgiveness from Allah SWT. With *istighfar* to Allah may Allah erase all sins and mistakes that have been done. Because *istighfar* can expand sustenance.

Rasulullah SAW was sent by Allah SWT to perfect good morals, as the words of the prophet Muhammad SAW:

إِنَّمَا بُعِثْتُ لأُتَمِّمَ مَكَارِمَ الأَخْلَاقِ

Meaning: *Verily I was sent only to perfect the glory of morality.*[17]

As a good Muslim, we should imitate the morals of the Prophet SAW, including in terms of meeting the needs of family life. So that good morals become our protection in carrying out economic activities.

In a simple way, Islamic perspective family financial planning can be described in the model below (Fig. 10.1):

10.8 Conclusion and Recommendation for Future Research

The ability to manage finances is very important and absolutely necessary in addressing and managing household finances. On the other hand, the inability to manage household finances can have an impact on disrupting harmony in the family.

Islamic perspective family financial management is as follows:

(1) Making plans (planning), where the foundation in making this plan is monotheism and intention.

[17] HR Al-Baihaqi from Abu Hurairah Radhiyallahu 'Anhu.

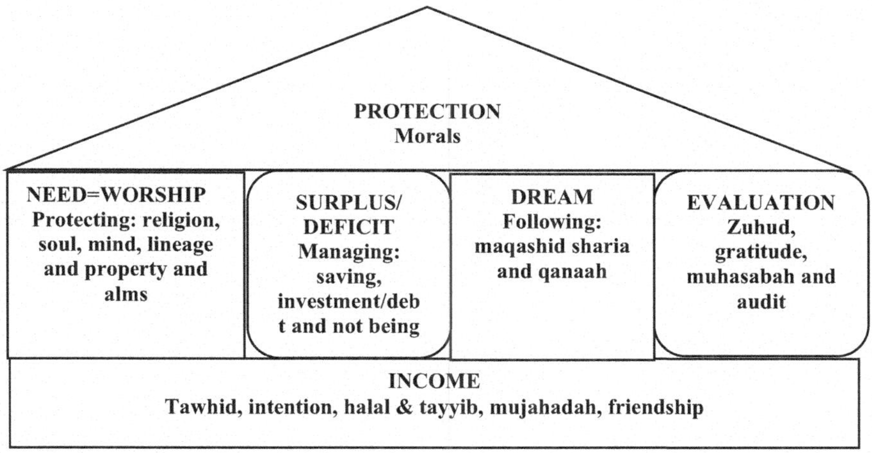

Fig. 10.1 Islamic perspective family financial planning model (Adopted from Tamanni and Mukhlisin, 2018)

(2) Managing Income, the basic concept for obtaining and spending wealth is "Halal and Good", completed with *mujahadah* and *silaturrahim.*
(3) Managing Needs; Not wasteful and not stingy (proportionate), donate, make records of income and expenses (cash flow), manage debt and save or invest.
(4) Managing dreams/wants (managing dreams); protecting religion, guarding life, guarding reason, guarding offspring, maintaining honor.
(5) Evaluation (Controlling); audit, gratitude and muhasabah.

If these five principles are applied in the family, then with Allah's permission the family will reach the stage of *sakinah*, always receives the blessing and mercy of Allah SWT.

Seeing the importance of family financial management, the authors suggest to all related parties to provide massive guidance to all Muslim families so that they can implement good financial management in their families. The importance of implementing Muslim family financial management is not only for the family concerned but will also have an impact on the peace of the wider community and even the country.

This paper also would like to propose to Ministry of Religious Affairs to include include Islamic family financial management materials in pre-marital courses for young couples not only in theory but also a guide to practice. It is hoped that married couples who build their households with healthy and shariah-compliant financial guidelines will be able to maintain family harmony so that they can create a *sakinah* family.

The authors would like to recommend a further research on family finance by taking consideration of theories surrounding family finance to be discussed both from classic Muslim scholars and modern scholars.

References

Al-Qalami, A. F. (ed. and pen). (2003). *Ringkasan Ihya' Ulumiddin*, First Printing. Gitamedia Press.
dan Ermi Suryani, E. N. (2019). Managemen Keuangan Keluarga PascaperceRaian. *As-Syar'i: Jurnal Bimbingan & Konseling Keluarga,* 1(1).
dan Murniati Mukhlisin, L. T. (2018). *Sakinah Finance.* Tinta Medina.
Katsir, I. (2015). *Tafsir Al Qur'anul Adhim.* Dar Al Hadits, M/1426H.
Kusumawati, D. *Pengelolaan Keuangan dalam Keluarga dari Sudut Pandang Islam.*Universitas Sulthan Fatah.
Mahkamah Agung. (2021). Direktori Putusan. https://putusan3.mahkamahagung.go.id/.
Mujamma' Al Malik Fadh Li Thiba'at Al Mush-haf Asy-Syarif, *Al-Qur'an dan Terjemahannya,* (Madinah:1424 H).
Siswantoro, D. (2020). *Wealth Management (Manajemen Harta) Rasulullah SAW, Metode Pembelajaran Dari Hal Yang Belum Pernah Dibahas.* Phoinix Publisher.

Putri Apria Ningsih is a lecturer in Islamic financial management at the Islamic University of Sutan Thaha Saifuddin Jambi. She earned a Ph.D. with the predicate of cum laude at the postgraduate degree at UIN Sutan Syarif Kasim Riau. In addition, she is also active in writing in the field of Islamic finance.

Murniati Mukhlisin Ph.D. earned her bachelor degree in accounting from International Islamic University Malaysia, master degree in accounting from Universitas Indonesia, and Ph.D. in accounting from University of Glasgow, UK. She taught at University of Glasgow and Essex Business School, University of Essex, UK. Murniati published her works on critical perspective in the areas of financial reporting, Islamic accounting, Islamic banking and finance, and Islamic financial literacy. She is a certified Islamic financial planner, halal supervisor and trainer. She is a founder of Sakinah Finance and Sobat Syariah and currently serves as a Rector at Tazkia Islamic University College, Bogor, Indonesia.

Jumni Nelli earned her Ph.D. in Islamic Family Law from the Postgraduate Program at UIN Suska Riau, Indonesia. She is a Postgraduate Lecturer in the Faculty of Shari'ah and Law at UIN Suska Riau with her area of expertise in Islamic Law and Family Law. She is an active writer with her works published in journal of women and gender. Topics of her publications among others are: Acts of Violence against Wives in the Perspective of Islamic Law, Islamic Women in Socio-Cultural Reality in Indonesia, Ihdad Career Women (Normatic Considerations and Moral Ethics), Al Paradigm-Mashlahah in the Global Era, and the Position of Women in Islamic Law: The Perspective of Gender Analysis. Her ongoing research includes: Empowerment of Oil Palm Farmers in Sialang Indah Village who are Marginalized by the Industrialization System of the Plantation Sector and Empowered Women: Empowerment Model of Islamic State Pension Savings Bank.

Part III
Country Experiences

Chapter 11
Measuring the Impact of Open Innovation on Firm Performance in Indonesia Halal Industry

Faried Kurnia Rahman

Business industry has been getting more aware on innovation for the past few decades. It becomes the main element of business' competitiveness and profitability (Vithessonthi & Racela, 2016). Cruickshank (2010) argued that a number of studies have given more attention on innovation from the different fundamental of knowledge, such as management studies, economics, entrepreneurship, psychology, sociology, and also broader innovation studies (Cruickshank, 2010). The attention and implementation of the research are increasing in line with the need of knowledge transfer.

Innovation is the development of knowledge aimed to improve social and economic life (Savrul & Incekara, 2015) which is expected to have significant impacts to the firm (Saatçıoğlu, 2013). Innovation is considered as an important instrument for the firms to adapt with global changes (Saatçıoğlu, 2013) and to improve the performance in the long-term (Calantone et al., 2002; Uzkurt et al., 2013) through the expansion of the current market or the creation of new market (Savrul & Incekara, 2015). Uzkurt et al (2013) argued that innovation and firm performance are crucial factors in economic growth.

Innovation can be perceived from economic and social viewpoints (Saguy, 2016). Economic viewpoint will emphasize its effect on the government to enhance economic growth and business sustainability. Social standpoint will be seen as the guidance in the relationship among the stakeholders. Saguy (2016) also discussed on how essential innovation in contemporary condition referring to the high competition in business nowadays. From those two viewpoints, innovation is an important factor to survive from economic turbulence, environmental challenges, diminishing resources, and knowledge development. Another viewpoint on innovation is that innovation is seen as a new form of capital (Abouzeedan & Hedner, 2012). It can also be treated as a measurement of business creativity environment.

F. K. Rahman (✉)
Institut Agama Islam Tazkia Jl. Ir. H. Djuanda No. 78, Sentul City, Bogor 16810, Indonesia
e-mail: faried@tazkia.ac.id

T. Azid et al. (eds.), *Wealth Management and Investment in Islamic Settings*,
https://doi.org/10.1007/978-981-19-3686-9_11

Rønning and Knutagård (2015) stated the most prominent definition of innovation is Joseph Schumpeter's definition in 1934. Schumpeter defined innovation as "*the introduction of a new good; the introduction of an improved or better method of production; the opening of a new market; the discovery of a new source of supply or raw materials or half- manufactured goods*" (Rønning & Knutagård, 2015). Innovation is "firm's activity in researching, developing, and introducing new product based on new technology" (Sood & Tellis, 2009). Other authors define it as "the process that application new ideas into commercial or creating new value"(Archibald & Archibald, 2013; Johannessen, 2013), "as ideas, successfully applied, and explains why it has the ability to affect us so profoundly" (Dodgson & Gann, 2010), and "new standards or new establishment" (Mangiarotti & Riillo, 2014).

Innovation is an exciting and uncertain business, particularly when the flows of knowledge and information are escalate (Chesbrough, 2011). It is a strategic mission to improve the performance of the firm rather than just the development of new products and services (Rosenbusch et al., 2011). The new products and services enter the market with high frequency, and its lifetime becomes shortly. The firms should provide more investment in their innovation to sustain. Therefore, there is a necessity to have appropriate combination of innovation and investment ability (Cruickshank, 2010).

Firms can depend on external linkages to promote the innovation "openness", and there are many ways to implement its development (Villasalero, 2014). Firms can establish innovation linkages based on geographical, industrial, size, or combination cluster. These linkages aim to implement innovation practices ensuring sustained performance (Breunig et al., 2014). Those practices can be implemented from different methods. Cruickshank (2010) stated that there are five methods, such as: Schumpeterian (identification of creative destruction), economic, managerial, psychological, and marketing.

These 5 "openness" methods can prevent the firms from mistakes of losing opportunities in recognizing the values of new ideas. In the past, many firms depended on internal R & D department to innovate a new product or service, and did market research on its feasibility study. Innovation has shown as the main driver for industrial revolution since the mid-twentieth. In the early stages of innovation paradigm, it still refer to "closed innovation" which means as the exploration of internal resourcing in finding new innovation where internal Research and Development (R & D) centre as the central element. There is no guarantee that firms can continuously have ideas, resources, capacities, and capabilities to perform well (Munsch, 2009). The firms should be able to manage all the challenges which are encountered in innovation phases. Now, it is starting to move into what we called as "open innovation paradigm" (Schenker-Wicki & Inauen, 2011).

This research aims to measure the impact of open innovation on shariah compliant firms in Indonesia Halal industry. To reach this objective, this research raises the following research question: Do inbound innovation indicators of open innovation paradigm influence firm's corporate value in halal industry?

11.1 Innovation and Performance

11.1.1 Open Innovation

Since its presence in high-tech sector, nowadays open innovation paradigm has span to many industries, such as: engineering, medical, consumer goods, food and beverages, architecture and logistic (Gassmann, Enkel, & Chesbrough, 2010). Open innovation (OI) paradigm was proposed by Henry Chesbrough in 2003. He described OI as an "*..the use of purposive inflows and outflows of knowledge to accelerate internal innovation and expand the markets for external use of innovation, respectively*" (Chesbrough, 2003). Chesbrough developed the theory from the perspective that important ideas or knowledge can be generated from internal or external of the firms and can be delivered to the market from internal or external of the firms as well. In OI paradigm, the firms focus on recognizing, exploring and combining external knowledge with internal R&D activities (West & Gallagher, 2004).

OI paradigm is not a straightforward the exploration of external resources, but slightly it is a combination of internal and external capacities and capabilities of R&D (Buganza & Verganti, 2009). It can be recognized as opposite of "old style" innovation paradigm when the firms depend on their internal R&D to produce new products and their resources to access the market (Chesbrough, 2006; Laursen & Salter, 2004). The success key how to do open innovation is the appropriate integration system of internal and external resources. The integration should be done systematically through the exploration of firms' dynamic capabilities on their management of technology along the innovation process (Lichtenthaler, 2009). When OI paradigm is not done systematically and it is implemented excessively, the firms will generate negative impact on their performance (Laursen & Salter, 2004).

The combination process will meets three challenges, such as maximization, incorporation, and motivation (West & Gallagher, 2006). Maximization of innovation refers to the optimalization of firms' approaches to earn maximum returns. Incorporation refers to firms' effort in identifying external the knowledge, absorb and understand the knowledge, and incorporate the knowledge into firms' innovation activities. The last challenge is motivation. It refers to firms' ability to encourage external parties to produce the knowledge. External parties in innovation are customers, suppliers, competitors, cross-sector firms, consulting firms, and universities (Inauen & Schenker-Wicki, 2011; West, 2006).

Chesbrough (2003) argued that internal R&D personnel should adopt with the paradigm changes where the firms then should consider the knowledge from those external parties. He proposed the four new roles of internal R & D:

1. To identify, understand, select from, and connect to the wealth of available external knowledge
2. To fill in the missing pieces of knowledge not being externally developed
3. To integrate internal and external knowledge to form more complex combinations of knowledge, to create new system and architectures

4. To generate additional revenues and profits from selling research outputs to other firms for use in their own systems

Through this four new roles, Chesbrough stated that internal R&D personals should have the ability to recognize and explore external knowledge that can be utilized for internal purposes. They also should have the ability to commercialize any unemployed internal knowledge to external users.

Open innovation derives in many shapes and characteristics. A set of open innovation structure in an industry can be different with other set of open innovation structure in different industry (Huizingh, 2011). Huizingh argued that to develop the structure or model from empirical approach, it is better to use the aspects of inbound versus outbound open innovation and pecuniary versus non-pecuniary interactions. Open innovation paradigm requires firms' internal R & D to be open from outside ideas, where it can be generate from external stakeholders which has solutions to improve firms' innovation that has designed (Breunig et al., 2014; Huizingh, 2011). This paradigm also enable firms to achieve benefits from the utilization its technologies and ideas by external parties (Villasalero, 2014).

In the last decade, the research on open innovation paradigm has got more attention. It reflects that the research on firms behavior and performance is recommended to investigate the interaction between the firms and external stakeholders (Laursen & Salter, 2004). The implementation of Open Innovation paradigm in firm level can contribute significant effect to the firm (Sisodiya et al., 2013), both form inbound or outbound dimensions (Hung & Chou, 2013).

According to Sisodiya et al (2013), at least there are two significant effect of open innovation for the firm. First, it will support the firm to have a sustainable system of new products development. Open innovation will give many option to the firms to obtain various inputs and to improve their innovation activities. Second, it can make the firms more efficient through the exploration of external resources. Based on these two arguments, Sisodiya et al. argued that the implementation of open innovation paradigm will improve firms' financial performance. And, any innovation efforts will be rewarded by the market through the stock markets even though the firm has not start the commercialization stage (Rubera & Kirca, 2012).

The exploration of external resource is the best approach to improve firm performance when the uncertainty of market condition is high (Stolwijk et al., 2012). Although it is carried out in informal way, open innovation still can give significant effect to the firm performance (Stefan & Bengtsson, 2014). Open innovation paradigm also can be utilized not only to improve firm's knowledge in developing new product, but also to improve firm's revenue (Caputo et al., 2016). Caputa et al. (2016) argued that open innovation can be used as a new approach for the firm to increase its performance. Open innovation also found as a significant approach to improve firm performance through its commercialization of innovation (Greco et al., 2016).

11.1.2 Firm Performance

In general, there are two norms why the firms are measured by financial performance (Hasan, 2007). The first is economic efficiency. It means that firms aim to produce maximally with given resources. The second is allocative efficiency. It means that the firms should produce given outcome using minimum resources. Firm performance is an outcome of firm's objectives that were developed previously (Bedoui, 2012) to measure the efficiency and the effectiveness of the usage of firm's resources (Al-Matari et al., 2014; Gatsi, Okpoti, Gadzo, & Anipa, 2016).

It can be generated from firm's financial statements that is reported periodically (Al-Matari et al., 2014; Gatsi et al., 2016). Al-Matari et al (2014) argued that it also can reutilized as an identification tool of the firm's success in particular period of time. Bedoui (2012) argued that the firm's theoretical model is mostly based on economic indicators, including the measurement of firm performance. There are numerous approaches to measure the performance (Chen & Liang, 2016; Masa'deh, Tayeh, Al-Jarrah, & Tarhini, 2015). And, economic variables are vital factors to the measurement of firm performance (Mirza & Javed, 2013).

Many research refers to financial performance when they are discussing firm performance. Financial performance more interesting for the stakeholders since the objective of the firm is to maximize the profit for the shareholders and minimize the cost (Bedoui, 2012; Road, 2007). In an efficient market, mostly firm performance is measured from two approaches, profitability approach and market perception approach (Ascarya & Edmans, 2012; Sukmana, 2014).

The firm can utilize financial performance ratios for three advantages, such as (Moyer, McGuigan, & Rao, 2005):

1. As analytical instrument. It aimed to support the firms in recognizing their strengths and weaknesses.
2. As monitoring instrument. It aimed to assist the firms in discovering any problems in a particular aspect
3. As benchmark in designing future planning. It aimed to help the firms in developing future plan.

Profitability approach refer to the measurement of firms' performance using profitability ratios, commoly known as accounting-based measurement (Al-Matari et al., 2014). The most prominent ratios are Return on Asset (ROA) and Return on Equity (ROE). Second approach is market perception. It means that firms' performanced measured using its share market value (Edmans, 2012). Firm's performance also can be measured with a subjective scale such as the Likert-Scale (Calantone et al., 2002; Cruz-González et al., 2014; Xu, Ribeiro-Soriano, & Gonzalez-Garcia, 2015).

Market performance is measured by market ratios which reflecting the firm's stock value (Moyer et al., 2005). Moyer et al (2005) stated that market firm performance as "*..an assessment of performance as perceived by the financial market*". There are some advantages to measure firm perfomance using market-based indicators (Agarwal & Taffler, 2006):

1. it provides a sound theoretical model for firm bankruptcy,
2. in efficient markets, stock prices will reflect all the information contained in accounting statements and will also contain information not in the accounting statements,
3. market variables are unlikely to be influenced by firm accounting policies,
4. market prices reflect future expected cashflows, and hence should be more appropriate for prediction purposes, and
5. the output of such models is not time or sample dependent.

Market performance measurement also indicates shareholders' expectations on the firms' future performance (Al-Matari et al., 2014). It represents future growth opportunities (Al-Matari et al., 2014), that also encompasses sustainable development (Bedoui, 2012). It also considers intangible values, instead of solely tangible values (Clarke, Seng, & Whiting, 2011), especially the effect or R&D (Ayadi et al., 1996).

11.2 Method

11.2.1 Data and Sample

Although there are 521 Indonesian firms which are listed in each capital market, only 301 Indonesian firms that can be categorized as *Shari'ah* Compliant Firms. In Indonesian case, 210 out of 301 firms are consistently listed as *Shari'ah* compliant firms the during past five years. Therefore, this research will explore 36 out of 91 listed-*Shari'ah* compliant firms in Indonesia which comply with the definition of "halal industry". The 36 firms were selected since these firms are the firms disclosing the practice that can be categorized as the practice of open innovation in their annual report. These firms consistently comply with *Shari'ah* benchmarks for the last five years (Table 11.1).

The data will be collected from the published annual reports of listed *Shari'ah* compliant firms in Indonesia. Altogether, this research will conduct the analysis of 36 listed *Shari'ah* compliant firms. The 2015 examination will give a current picture of performance and open innovation in Indonesian *halal* industries. The selection of sample was restricted to the firms that are listed in *Daftar Efek Syariah* to represent

Table 11.1 Population and sample

Listed firms	Total number
Listed firms in Indonesian Islamic capital market	301
Cluster which comply with "halal industry"	91
The selected sample	36

Table 11.2 The dependent variable

Variables	Measurement
Market Value	MV = (Stock price at year t x outstanding share price of year t)

shari'ah compliant firms in Indonesia Halal industry. The method for sampling is cluster random sampling since the sample is not as varied as it would be in a simple random sampling (Yusof, Rokis, & Jusoh, 2013) (Tables 11.2 and 11.3).

11.2.2 Data Measurement

The statistical model for this research are as follow:

- $MV = a + b_1\ IOI + b_2R\&Dint + b_3\ SIZE + b_4EMP$

It is expected that IOI, R&D, SIZE and EMP give positive impact on the market share. Therefore, it is hypothesized that :

Ha: IOI, R&D, SIZE and EMP have a significantly positive influence on market share.

To analyze the data, this research will employ regression. Econometric analysis has some advantages. It can explain the different statistical impacts of independent variables. Other than that, it can also show how much the independent variables influence the dependent variable (Cooper & Schindler, 2011). For the data, annual reports are mainly used in this type of research (Guan et al., 2015; Hassan et al.,

Table 11.3 The independent variables

Variables	Measurement	Sources
InBound Efforts (IOI)	InBound pecuniary expenses (Open Costs; patent cost, Intellectual Property Cost; Additions; Intangibles)	(Caputo et al., 2016; Michelino et al., 2015)
Firm Size (SIZE)	The log of total assets at the end of the fiscal year	(Asdemir, Fernando, & Tripathy, 2013; Gul et al., 2010)
R&D Intensity (R&Dint)	Log of (research and development expenses/sales)	(Arora & Sharma, 2016; Caputo et al., 2016; Hwang & Lee, 2010; Inauen & Schenker-Wicki, 2011; Laursen & Salter, 2006; Michelino, Cammarano, et al., 2014; Michelino, Caputo, et al., 2014)
Employee (EMP)	Total salaries	(Michelino, Cammarano, et al., 2014; Michelino, Caputo, et al., 2014)

2011; Keupp & Gassmann, 2009). This research will explore annual reports data from selected firms which are listed in Islamic capital market in Malaysia and Indonesia.

11.3 Result and Discussion

Test of Normality

Several preliminary tests should be conducted in regression analysis. The first test that applied in this research is normality test. This test was performed to confirm that the data are normally distributed (Table 11.4).

To measure the normality of the data, we refer to the result of its 'skewness' and 'kurtosis' values. The normally distributed data should have the value between + 1 to -3. The table above shown that the data in this research are not normally distributed. This could be affected by the small number of data observed in the research.

Test of Multicollinearity

Collinearity (or multicollinearity) problem is the situation when one independent variable is a linear function of other independent variables. The problem of multicollineaity can be identified through the value of tolerance and VIF (Variance Inflation Factors). The VIF value should less than 10 and the tolerance value must be more than 0.1. The collinearity diagnostics confirm that there is no problem with multicollinearity (Table 11.5).

Table 11.4 Normality of the data

Statistics

		Market Value	Inbound Innovation	Research Development	Total Assets	Salaries Expense
N	Valid	36	36	36	36	36
	Missing	0	0	0	0	0
Mean		18,966.3697	136,507.9722	8411.8056	7,291,245.4444	434,568.4722
Skewness		4.411	5.367	4.928	4.702	2.576
Std. Error of Skewness		0.393	0.393	0.393	0.393	0.393
Kurtosis		21.904	30.522	26.178	24.846	7.887
Std. Error of Kurtosis		0.768	0.768	0.768	0.768	0.768
Minimum		72.24	478.00	0.00	156,998.00	15,867.00
Maximum		270,864.60	2,590,127.00	163,364.00	89,748,236.00	3,204,476.00

Table 11.5 Multicollinearity of the data

Model		Collinearity Statistics	
		Tolerance	VIF
1	(Constant)		
	Inbound Innovation	0.702	1.424
	Research Development	0.607	1.648
	Total Assets	0.186	5.380
	Salaries Expense	0.141	7.086

Analysis

From the 36 firms, most of the firms, 58%, are from cluster of goods and consumption industry. 25% are from agriculture firms, and 17% are trade and services firms (Fig. 11.1).

To measure the open innovation activities in these firms, this study explores three indicators that represent the involvement of external resources. The indicators include external expert involvement, royalty payment, and trademarks purchasing. These are treated as the independent variables. The costs that the firms spend in these activities are considered as the firms effort in implementing open innovation strategies.

Regression analysis is used to examine the relationship between a dependent variable and one or more independent variables (Table 11.6).

Adjusted Rsquare shows the value of 0.955 which means that 95% of independent variables describe the dependent variable.

The Table 11.7 above confirms that the proposed model is significant. It reveals that market value is affected by the independent variables. The following table explains which variables significantly affect market value (Table 11.8).

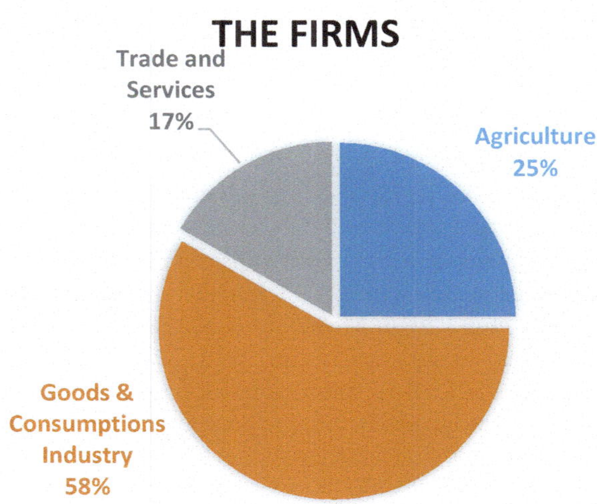

Fig. 11.1 The composition of firms

Table 11.6 Model summary

Model Summary				
Model	R	R Square	Adjusted R Square	Std. Error of the Estimate
1	0.980[a]	0.960	0.955	10,253.25685

[a] Predictors: (Constant), Salaries Expense, Research Development, Inbound Innovation, Total Assets

Table 11.7 Significance of the model

ANOVA[a]						
	Model	Sum of Squares	Df	Mean Square	F	Sig
1	Regression	78,692,565,373.843	4	19,673,141,343.461	187.133	0.000[b]
	Residual	3,259,007,554.142	31	105,129,275,940		
	Total	81,951,572,927.984	35			

[a] Dependent Variable: Market Value
[b] Predictors: (Constant), Salaries Expense, Research Development, Inbound Innovation, Total Assets

Table 11.8 Regression results

Model		Unstandardized Coefficients		Standardized Coefficients		
		B	Std. Error	Beta	t	Sig
1	(Constant)	-696.396	2060.701		-0.338	0.738
	Inbound Innovation	0.102	0.0005	0.923	21.599	0.000
	Research Development	0.297	0.078	0.176	3.817	0.001
	Total Assets	0.001	0.000	0.279	30,354	0.002
	Salaries Expense	-0.007	0.007	-0.101	-1.063	0.296

The results reveal that the Inbound innovation, R&D, and total assets (size) positively and significantly associate with market value. However, Salaries expense does not show any significant impact. The empirical evidence strongly supports the previous research stating that Inbound innovation affects firm performance positively (Caputo et al., 2016; Michelino et al., 2015; Michelino, Cammarano, et al., 2014; Michelino, Cammarano, et al., 2014; Michelino, Caputo, et al., 2014; Michelino, Caputo, et al., 2014). This can be an opportunity for halal industry to improve the innovative strategies in order to compete in the industry.

Referring to the characteristics of the firms, this study found that the listed shari'ah compliant firms (SCFs) in Indonesia have different pattern in their open innovation activities (Fig. 11.2).

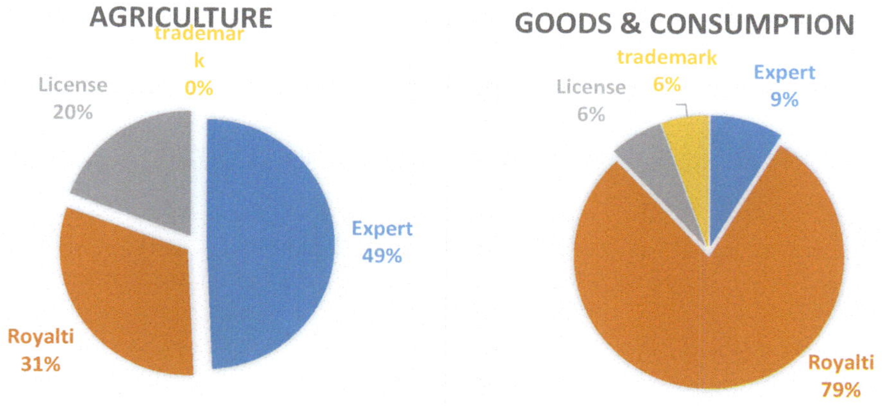

Fig. 11.2 Open activities in agriculture, goods and consumption

For agriculture firms, the implementation of open innovation strategy is dominated by the involvement of external expert in their production process. It can be recognized that the firms are exploring external knowledge to support their sustainability. The dominance of external expert involvement can be considered that the firms focus more on the development or the management process. The agriculture firms also take benefit from external innovation and through the utilization of the innovation. It is shown by the significant activities of the firms in paying royalties.

In goods & consumption firms, royalty payment is the most dominant activity as compared to the other two indicators. It is along with the expectation where the firms in this cluster focus on the products compared to the internal innovation process. While in the trade and services firms, the payment of trademark activity is the most dominant activity in their open innovation indicators. It also in line with the characteristics of the firms where they focus more on selling than the development or the innovation process of their products (Fig. 11.3).

The exploration of open innovation strategies is different among each cluster. The characteristics of the core business of the firms give the significant impact on the choice of the strategy. The external expert involvement in the three clusters play significant impact of the strategy in general. It shows that the firms should collaborate their internal expert with the internal expert in the innovation process. Nevertheless, the choice of the strategy also should be in line with their internal innovation effort through the optimization on their R&D.

11.4 Conclusion

The objective of open innovation is to improve social and economic life which at the end it is expected to have significant impacts to the firms' sustainability. The

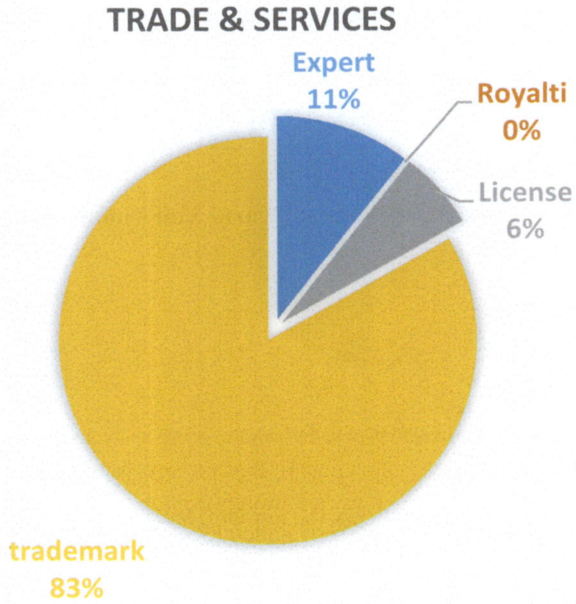

Fig. 11.3 Innovation activities in Trade and Services

discussion of innovation continues in almost all sectors including halal industry which has been growing tremendously in the global industry. This research aims to measure the impact of open innovation on shariah compliant firms in Indonesia Halal industry. This study found that inbound innovation through open costs; patent cost, and intellectual property costs have significant impacts on market value of the firms in "halal industry". These significant impacts should encourage so called halal firms to innovate more by involving external resources.

This research possesses several weaknesses such as the limited number of observations due to the limited number of the firms categorized as halal firms listed in Islamic Capital Market. Secondly, many Indonesian firms are categorized as sellers rather than innovators. The future studies should highlight those issues. The future studies can also compare among different markets.

References

Abouzeedan, A., & Hedner, T. (2012). Organization structure theories and open innovation paradigm. *World Journal of Science, Technology and Sustainable Development, 9*(1), 6–27. https://doi.org/10.1108/20425941211223598

Agarwal, V., & Taffler, R. (2006). Comparing the performance of market-based and accounting-based bankruptcy prediction models. *Journal of Banking & Finance, 44*(0), 0–37. Retrieved from /citations?view_op=view_citation&continue=/scholar?hl=en&start=40&as_sdt=0,5&scilib=1

&scioq=Selecting+and+weighting+features+using+a+genetic+algorithm+in+a+case-based +reasoning+approach+to+personnel+roster\n/citations?view_op=view_citation&continue=/schol.

Al-Matari, E. M., Al-Swidi, A. K., & Fadzil, F. H. B. (2014). The measurements of firm performance's dimensions. *Asian Journal of Finance & Accounting, 6*(1), 24. https://doi.org/10.5296/ajfa.v6i1.4761

Archibald, R. D., & Archibald, S. C. (2013). Leading and managing innovation: What every executive team must know about project, program and portfolio management, 144. Retrieved from https://books.google.es/books?id=GbugmQEACAAJ

Arora, A., & Sharma, C. (2016). Corporate governance and firm performance in developing countries: Evidence from India. *Corporate Governance, 16*(2), 420–436. https://doi.org/10.1108/CG-01-2016-0018

Ascarya, & Sukmana, R. (2014). *Formulating Islamic Bank Performance Measurement Based on Shari Ah Objectives.*

Asdemir, O., Fernando, G. D., & Tripathy, A. (2013). Market perception of firm strategy. *Managerial Finance, 39*(2), 90–115. http://dx.doi.org/10.1108/03074351311293972.

Ayadi, O. F., Dufrene, U. B., & Obi, C. P. (1996). Firm performance measures: Temporal roadblocks to innovation? *Managerial Finance, 22*(8), 18–33.

Bedoui, M. H. E. (2012). Shari'a-based ethical performance measurement framework. In *The Chair of Ethics and Financial Norms [CENF]* (pp. 1–12).

Breunig, K. J., Aas, T. H., & Hydle, K. M. (2014). Incentives and performance measures for open innovation practices. *Measuring Business Excellence, 18*(1), 45–54. https://doi.org/10.1108/MBE-10-2013-0049

Buganza, T., & Verganti, R. (2009). Open innovation process to inbound knowledge: Collaboration with universities in four leading firms. *European Journal of Innovation Management, 12*(3), 306–325. https://doi.org/10.1108/14601060910974200

Calantone, R. J., Cavusgil, S. T., & Zhao, Y. (2002). Learning orientation, firm innovation capability, and firm performance. *Industrial Marketing Management, 31*(6), 515–524. https://doi.org/10.1016/S0019-8501(01)00203-6

Caputo, M., Lamberti, E., Cammarano, A., & Michelino, F. (2016). Exploring the impact of open innovation on firm performances. *Management Decision, 54*(7), 1788–1812. https://doi.org/10.1108/MD-02-2015-0052

Chen, D.-N., & Liang, T.-P. (2016). Knowledge diversity and firm performance: An ecological view. *Journal of Knowledge Management, 20*(4), 671–686. https://doi.org/10.1108/JKM-10-2015-0377

Chesbrough, H. (2003). *Open innovation: The new imperative for creating and profiting from technology (First).* Harvard Business School Publishing Corporation

Chesbrough, H. (2006). Open innovation and open business models : A new approach to industrial innovation, 38. Retrieved from http://www.oecd.org/science/inno/37915612.pdf.

Chesbrough, H. (2011). Open services innovation: Rethinking your business to grow and compete in a new Era. *Presentation, 37*. https://doi.org/10.1017/CBO9781107415324.004.

Clarke, M., Seng, D., & Whiting, R. H. (2011). Intellectual capital and firm performance in Australia. *Journal of Intellectual Capital, 12*. . https://doi.org/10.1108/14691931111181706.

Cooper, D. R., & Schindler, P. S. (2011). *Business Research Method (11th Editi).* McGraw-Hill.

Cruickshank, L. (2010). The innovation dimension : Designing in a broader context. *Design Issues, 26*(2), 17–26.

Cruz-González, J., López-Sáez, P., Emilio Navas-López, J., & Delgado-Verde, M. (2014). Directions of external knowledge search: Investigating their different impact on firm performance in high-technology industries. *Journal of Knowledge Management, 18*(5), 847–866. https://doi.org/10.1108/JKM-06-2014-0243

Dodgson, M., & Gann, D. (2010). Innovation: A very short introduction, 163. http://doi.org/https://doi.org/10.1093/actrade/9780199568901.001.0001.

Edmans, A. (2012). The link between job satisfaction and firm value, with implications for corporate social responsibility. *Academy of Management Perspectives, 26*(4), 1–19. https://doi.org/10.5465/amp.2012.0046

Gassmann, O., Enkel, E., & Chesbrough, H. (2010). The future of open innovation. *R & D Management*, 1–9.

Gatsi, J. G., Okpoti, C. A., Gadzo, S. G., & Anipa, C. A. A. (2016). Determinants of market and book based performance of manufacturing companies in ghana: An empirical study. *International Journal of Economics, Commerce and Management, IV*(1), 392–411.

Greco, M., Grimaldi, M., & Cricelli, L. (2016). An analysis of the open innovation impact on firm performance. *European Management Journal, 1–33.* https://doi.org/10.1016/j.emj.2016.02.008.

Guan, J., Zhang, J., & Yan, Y. (2015). The impact of multilevel networks on innovation. *Research Policy, 44*(3), 545–559. https://doi.org/10.1016/j.respol.2014.12.007

Gul, F. A., Kim, J. B., & Qiu, A. A. (2010). Ownership concentration, foreign shareholding, audit quality, and stock price synchronicity: Evidence from China. *Journal of Financial Economics, 95*(3), 425–442. https://doi.org/10.1016/j.jfineco.2009.11.005

Hasan, Z. (2007). Evaluation of Islamic banking performance: On the current use of econometric models, (3920).

Hassan, M. K., Sanchez, B., & Yu, J.-S. (2011). Financial development and economic growth: New evidence from panel data. *The Quarterly Review of Economics and Finance, 51*(1), 88–104. https://doi.org/10.1016/j.qref.2010.09.001

Huizingh, E. K. R. E. (2011). Open innovation: State of the art and future perspectives. *Technovation, 31*(1), 2–9. https://doi.org/10.1016/j.technovation.2010.10.002

Hung, K. P., & Chou, C. (2013). The impact of open innovation on firm performance: The moderating effects of internal R&D and environmental turbulence. *Technovation, 33*(10–11), 368–380. https://doi.org/10.1016/j.technovation.2013.06.006

Hwang, J., & Lee, Y. (2010). External knowledge search, innovative performance and productivity in the Korean ICT sector. *Telecommunications Policy, 34*(10), 562–571. https://doi.org/10.1016/j.telpol.2010.04.004

Inauen, M., & Schenker-Wicki, A. (2011). The impact of outside-in open innovation on innovation performance. *European Journal of Innovation Management, 14*(4), 496–520. https://doi.org/10.1108/14601061111174934

Johannessen, J. A. (2013). Innovation: A systemic perspective - developing a systemic innovation theory. *Kybernetes, 42*, 1195–1217. https://doi.org/10.1108/k-04-2013-0069

Keupp, M. M., & Gassmann, O. (2009). Determinants and archetype users of open innovation. *R and D Management, 39*(4), 331–341. https://doi.org/10.1111/j.1467-9310.2009.00563.x

Laursen, K., & Salter, A. (2004). Open for innovation : The role of openness in explaining innovation performance among UK manufacturing firms. In *the DRUID Academy Winter 2004 PhD Conference.*

Laursen, K., & Salter, A. (2006). Open for innovation: The role of openness in explaining innovation performance among U.K. manufacturing firms. *Strategic Management Journal, 27*(2), 131–150. https://doi.org/10.1002/smj.507.

Lichtenthaler, U. (2009). Outbound open innovation and its effect on firm performance: Examining environmental influences. *R and D Management, 39*(4), 317–330. https://doi.org/10.1111/j.1467-9310.2009.00561.x

Mangiarotti, G., & Riillo, C. A. F. (2014). Standards and innovation in manufacturing and services: The case of ISO 9000. *International Journal of Quality & Reliability Management, 31*(4), 435–454. https://doi.org/10.1108/IJQRM-06-2012-0077

Masa'deh, R., Tayeh, M., Al-Jarrah, I., & Tarhini, A. (2015). Accounting vs. market-based measures of firm performance related to information technology investments. *International Review of Social Sciences and Humanities, 9*(1), 129–145. Retrieved from http://www.irssh.com/yahoo_site_admin/assets/docs/12_IRSSH-1114-V9N1.115111327.pdf..

Michelino, F., Cammarano, A., Lamberti, E., & Caputo, M. (2014). Measurement of open innovation through intellectual capital flows: Framework and application. *International Journal of Intelligent Enterprise, 2*(August), 213–235. https://doi.org/10.1504/IJIE.2014.066679
Michelino, F., Caputo, M., Cammarano, A., & Lamberti, E. (2014). Inbound and outbound open innovation: Organization and performances. *Journal of Technology Management and Innovation, 9*(3), 65–82. https://doi.org/10.4067/S0718-27242014000300005
Michelino, F., Lamberti, E., Cammarano, A., & Caputo, M. (2015). Measuring open innovation in the bio-pharmaceutical industry. *Creativity and Innovation Management, 24*(1), 4–28. https://doi.org/10.1111/caim.12072
Mirza, S. A., & Javed, A. (2013). Determinants of financial performance of a firm: Case of Pakistani stock market. *Journal of Economics and International, 5*(2), 43–52. Retrieved from http://www.academicjournals.org/journal/JEIF/article-abstract/C229C2A27911.
Moyer, R. C., McGuigan, J. R., & Rao, R. P. (2005). Evaluation of Firm Performance. In *Contemporary Financial Management Fundamentals*, pp. 91–129. Thomson/South-Western.
Munsch, K. (2009). Open model innovation. *Research-Technology Management, 6308*(May-June), 48–52. https://doi.org/10.1016/j.cub.2010.01.021.
Road, E. H. (2007). Theory of the firm, management and stakeholders: An islamic perspective. *Islamic Economic Studies, 15*(1), 1–30.
Rønning, R., & Knutagård, M. (2015). *Innovation in social welfare and human services.* Routledge.
Rosenbusch, N., Brinckmann, J., & Bausch, A. (2011). Is branding always beneficial? A meta-analysis of the relationship between branding and performance in SMEs. *Journal of Business Venturing, 26*, 441–457. https://doi.org/10.1016/j.jbusvent.2009.12.002
Rubera, G., & Kirca, A. H. (2012). Firm innovativeness and its performance outcomes: A meta-analytic review and theoretical integration. *Journal of Marketing, 76*(3), 130–147. https://doi.org/10.1509/jm.10.0494
Saatçıoğlu, Ö. Y. (2013). Barriers in partnerships in open innovation process. *Journal of Entrepreneurship and Innovation Management, 2*(3), 99–119.
Saguy, I. S. (2016). Challenges and opportunities in food engineering: Modeling, virtualization, open innovation and social responsibility. *Journal of Food Engineering, 176*, 2–8. https://doi.org/10.1016/j.jfoodeng.2015.07.012
Savrul, M., & Incekara, A. (2015). The effect of R&D intensity on innovation performance: A country level evaluation. *Procedia - Social and Behavioral Sciences, 210*(1194), 388–396. https://doi.org/10.1016/j.sbspro.2015.11.386
Schenker-Wicki, A., & Inauen, M. (2011). The impact of outside-in open innovation on innovation performance. *European Journal of Innovation Management, 14*(4), 496–520. https://doi.org/10.1108/14601061111174934
Sisodiya, S. R., Johnson, J. L., & Grégoire, Y. (2013). Inbound open innovation for enhanced performance: Enablers and opportunities. *Industrial Marketing Management, 42*(5), 836–849. https://doi.org/10.1016/j.indmarman.2013.02.018
Sood, A., & Tellis, G. J. (2009). Do innovations really pay off? Total stock market returns to innovation. *Marketing Science, 28*(3), 442–456. https://doi.org/10.1287/mksc.1080.0407.
Stefan, I., & Bengtsson, L. (2014). Appropriability mechanisms, openness and firm performance. In *1st World Open Innovation Conference*, pp. 1–30.
Stolwijk, C. C. M., Vanhaverbeke, W. P. M., Ortt, J. R., Pieters, M. W., den Hartigh, E., & van Beers, C. (2012). The effect of internal and external technology sourcing on firm performance throughout the technology life cycle. *Technology Analysis and Strategic Management, 24*(10), 1013–1028. https://doi.org/10.1080/09537325.2012.723687
Uzkurt, C., Kumar, R., Kimzan, H. S., & Eminoglu, G. (2013). Role of innovation in the relationship between organizational culture and firm performance: A study of the banking sector in Turkey. *European Journal of Innovation Management, 16*(1), 92–117. https://doi.org/10.1108/14601061311292878

Villasalero, M. (University of C. -L. M. (2014). University knowledge, open innovation and technological capital in Spanish science parks. *Journal of Intellectual Capital, 15*(4), 479–496. https://doi.org/10.1108/JIC-07-2014-0083.

Vithessonthi, C., & Racela, O. C. (2016). Short- and long-run effects of internationalization and R&D intensity on firm performance. *Journal of Multinational Financial Management, 34*, 28–45. https://doi.org/10.1016/j.mulfin.2015.12.001

West, J. (2006). Does appropriability enable or retard open innovation? In H. Chesbrough, W. Vanhaverbeke, & J. West (Eds.), *Open innovation: researching a new paradigm*. Oxford: Oxford University Press.

West, J., & Gallagher, S. (2004). *Key challenges of open innovation : Lessons from open source software*. Retrieved from http://www.cob.sjsu.edu/west_j/Papers/WestGallagher2004.pdf..

West, J., & Gallagher, S. (2006). Open innovation : The paradox of firm investment in open source software. *R & D Management*, (3).

Xu, Y. B., Ribeiro-Soriano, D. E., & Gonzalez-Garcia, J. (2015). Crowdsourcing, innovation and firm performance. *Management Decision, 53*(6), 1158–1169. https://doi.org/10.1108/MD-06-2014-0408.

Yusof, S. A., Rokis, R. A., & Jusoh, W. J. wan. (2013). Financial Fragility of Malaysians in Urban Households. In *2nd Applied International Business Conference (AIBC2013) Emerging Megatrends in Asian Market*, pp. 193–204.

Faried Kurnia Rahman is a lecturer in Islamic Business and Management Department, Tazkia Islamic University College. He got his degree from Tazkia Islamic University College, his master degree (M.Sc. Fin) from International Islamic University Malaysia. Currently, He is pursuing his Ph.D at Malaysia-Japan International Institute of Technology (MJIIT) – Universiti Teknologi Malaysia. His primary research interests are halal industry, Islamic finance, Islamic banking, and Islamic business and management. His works were published in some Scopus and WOS indexed journals and proceedings. He has served as editor for a national indexed Islamic journal, TIFBR. His academic teachings focus on Islamic Banking, Islamic Investment, Financial Management, and Advanced Financial Management.

Chapter 12
How Does Accounting Play a Role in Islamic Microfinance and Islamic Wealth Management Practices? Case Studies in Indonesia, Pakistan and Egypt

Murniati Mukhlisin and Sugiyarti Fatma Laela

Indonesia experienced economic turmoil following the 1997 financial crisis and political instability which saw the currency depreciate by 80% of its original value and put half of the population into unemployment. Indonesia's poverty rate based on the national poverty line reached a record low of 9.2% in September 2019. The proportion of Indonesia's population living below the national poverty line has more than halved since 1993. In 2017, the proportion of individuals living in extreme poverty (under Purchasing Power Parity (PPP) 2011 of USD 1.90 per day) was 5.7%, and the proportion of individuals living in moderate poverty (PPP was USD 3.2 per day in 2011) was 27.3%. Despite this progress, the rate of poverty reduction after 2010 is about half (0.3 percentage points per year) from 2003 to 2010 (0.6 percentage points per year). Vulnerability remains high; in 2018, 73.9 million people (30% of the population) were in poverty and could easily fall back into poverty. The COVID-19 outbreak could exacerbate existing challenges and reverse recent achievements in poverty reduction. The government has announced several packages to reduce the impact on the poor, such as the Flagship Conditional Cash Transfer (CCT) program and additional food stamps. But the main challenge it faces is identifying, reaching, and providing assistance to people over the age of 40 who are not covered by the social assistance target database (World Bank, 2020a, b, c).

The World Bank reports that the political turmoil in Egypt in 2013 that nearly increased the fiscal deficit and gross public debt by 100% led to a high unemployment rate of more than three quarters among the productive group aged 15–19 years to date for the first time in twenty years. Egypt has recently seen a decline in poverty levels, which analysts attribute to the success of its economic reform program and therefore the accompanying social protection policies. Consistent with the country's official statistical agency report on December 3, Egypt's poverty rate fell to 29.7 percent in the 2019–20 financial year, down from 32.5 percent two years earlier. This is the

M. Mukhlisin (✉) · S. F. Laela
Institut Agama Islam Tazkia, Jl. Ir. H. Djuanda No. 78, Sentul City, Bogor 16810, Indonesia
e-mail: murniati@tazkia.ac.id

T. Azid et al. (eds.), *Wealth Management and Investment in Islamic Settings*,
https://doi.org/10.1007/978-981-19-3686-9_12

first time Egypt has experienced a decline in poverty levels since 1999. At the peak of 2016 Egypt adopted a program of economic reforms that included the release of the local currency, the gradual lifting of fuel and electricity subsidies, as well as the passage of a package of economic laws. the government launched social policies and initiatives such as "Live with Respect" that directly improve the lifestyle of citizens in terms of housing quality, sanitation and health services.

Like many countries in the Middle East and North Africa, only about 3.2% of Egyptians live below the international poverty line of USD 1.90 per day (see PPP in 2011); only 4.1% of Egyptians are considered multidimensional poverty. The low proportion of international poverty and multidimensional poverty reflects Egypt's strong performance compared to other countries in terms of consumption, education and access to basic utilities. Given the high inflation during this period, the increase in poverty rates was not unexpected. COVID-19 control measures may impact future poverty reduction prospects through the labor market, food prices and remittance channels. Future trends in poverty will depend on subsequent policy responses. Expanding targeted cash transfer programs and increasing food subsidies can help curb rising poverty and real income losses (World Bank, 2020a, b, c).

While in Pakistan, In the 14 years from 2001 to 2015, Pakistan's poverty rate continued to fall significantly. The number of people using the national poverty line fell from 64.3 to 24.3%. Increased employment opportunities outside the agricultural sector were the main drivers of poverty alleviation during this period. Two self-reinforcing economic dynamics are the reasons for progress in poverty reduction: (i) Expansion of economic opportunities beyond the agricultural sector, particularly with growth in male non-agricultural employment; (ii) Increased emigration and related remittances. The latter not only promotes the consumption of beneficiary households, but also promotes the informal sector and increases real wages for the demand for locally produced internal goods and services. Between 2001 and 2015, about two-thirds of poverty reduction was driven by increases in labor incomes in the non-agricultural sector, an actual increase of 74%. However, since 2015, due to the macroeconomic crisis and the associated slowdown in growth, the pace of poverty reduction may have stopped. In this context, the recent outbreak of the COVID19 pandemic and containment measures put in place by the government are expected to increase poverty in several countries. The capacity of the informal non-agricultural sector to recover from the current crisis is critical to getting Pakistan back on the path of poverty reduction. From this perspective, the duration of the current crisis and the ability of government interventions to protect the material and human capital investments of the most vulnerable population groups are critical to averting the long-term consequences of the current crisis (World Bank, 2020a, b, c).

Several poverty alleviation programs such as the Islamic microfinance model were introduced in these three countries, but poverty rates remain high. Therefore, there must be a better mechanism to ensure the success of the Islamic microfinance mission. Availability of funds requires accounting administration skills to supervise Islamic microfinance participants, so the research objectives are to: 1. Critically analyze the Islamic microfinance model that has been introduced in Indonesia, Egypt and Pakistan to assess the level of accounting involvement in participants' activities;

2. Propose financial books and records for wealth management purposes that participants and their families can use to provide better insight into their business and community projects so as to improve their standard of living.

The majority of participants were women and it has been proven that their involvement in microfinance is the key for the success of poverty alleviation programs in countries where group-based programs operate. Group-based programs in microfinance are widespread such as the Grameen Model in Bangladesh which has recruited 7.06 million borrowers of which 97% percent are women (Yunus, 2007). Empowering women in the economy contributes to the achievement of shared prosperity in society and the enhancement of social cohesion which is essential for economic development and sustainability.

Paper is structured as follows. Part Two describes microfinance, Islamic microfinance, accounting and wealth management practices. While Part Three outlines the ethnographic approach adopted in the study, Part Four discusses the ethnographic findings. Finally, this paper suggests the conclusions and implications of Section Five.

12.1 Islamic Accounting, Microfinance and Islamic Wealth Management

Poverty remains a highly integrated phenomenon with the United Nations reporting that one in eight people worldwide remain hungry (UN, 2013). Indonesian economy grew 5.2% with an unemployment rate of 5.17% and a poverty rate of 9.8% or 25.95 million people (BPS, 2018). According to the World Bank, people who fell into the poverty line in 2018 were measured by an income of less than USD 1.9 per day or USD 87 per month, which means almost 40% or 100 hundred million Indonesians are poor. Furthermore, the CGAP report reveals that there are more than 600 million Muslims in the world living on less than USD 2 per day, of whom almost half are not even bankable (can receive financial support or loans) from interest-based institutions (El-Zoghbi & Tarezi, 2013). Indonesia experienced economic turmoil following the 1997 financial crisis and political instability which saw the currency depreciate by 80% of its original value and put half of the population into unemployment.

Some poverty alleviation programs such as the Islamic microfinance model have been implemented in these three countries, but poverty rates remain high. Therefore, there must be a better supporting tool and procedures to ensure the success of the Islamic microfinance mission. Availability of funds requires accounting administration skills to supervise and monitor participants or members. Hence the research objectives are to:

1. critically analyze the Islamic microfinance model introduced in Indonesia and Pakistan,
2. assess the level of accounting involvement in the activities of female participants,

3. propose bookkeeping for management practices a wealth of resources that participants and families can use to give them a better insight into their community businesses and projects,
4. communicate effectively with the government and non-government representatives.

Woman involvement in microfinance program began a few decades, although the program has developed since the seventeenth century· The large population of women belonging to microfinance groups was first initiated by Muhammad Yunus who initiated the Grameen Bank in Bangladesh in the 1970s. The program has risen to become one of the most well-known policies to tackle poverty in developing and transition countries (Bateman, 2017). Indonesia has implemented the first microfinance program initiated by Bank Rakyat Indonesia in 1895. However the similar program with the Grameen Bank model involving women participants was introduced in the late 1980s, initiated by Karya Usaha Mandiri (LPPI, 2013). The Grameen approach seems promising not only to lift millions (especially women) out of poverty and bring hope to the world's poverty alleviation (Korth et al., 2012).

In Pakistan, there is a lot of research being done on poverty and microfinance. Hussain (2003) points out between participants and non-participants in microfinance programs there are significant differences in capital expenditure, living conditions, literacy rates and also income levels. Montgomery (2005) argues that in terms of economic and social welfare indicators, the microcredit program has a positive impact. What's more, especially for the very poor participants in this program can help them obtain income-generating activities. This is supported by Shirazi and Khan (2009). They found that microfinance programs have reduced poverty in Pakistan. Members of the program have a better financial condition over a certain period. The multidimensional aspect of poverty happened in Pakistan. They have low income levels which led to lack access to basic services such as clean drinking water, adequate sanitation and health facilities, proper education, financial services and job opportunities (World Bank, 2007).

Agbola et al. (2017) survey of 211 microfinance clients and household non-clients in Northeastern Mindanao, Philippines: Microfinance has a slightly positive impact on poverty reduction with household income and savings of microfinance clients being higher than non-poor households, -client. Client household. Zhang (2017) adopts a unique cross-country panel dataset from 106 countries for the period 1998–2013 and shows that microfinance has a negative effect on poverty. Samer et al. (2015) interviewed 780 existing and new clients in the Malaysian states of Selangor and Melaka and found that microfinance had a positive impact on the household income of female borrowers who spent three years in the scheme. compared to new borrowers who have not received treatment. Miled and Rejeb (2015) employ 596 microfinance institutions in 40 developing countries while Mahmood et al. (2014) focus on women entrepreneurs in Pakistan (Leikem, 2012). While microfinance is definitely not a panacea for poverty, it can prove itself to be a useful tool in the fight against poverty.

However, research conducted by Donou-Adonsou and Sylwester (2016) argues that microfinance does not appear to have an impact on poverty regardless of the poverty measure used. The results confirm that while banks have some ability to reduce poverty, the microfinance model does not, at least at the aggregate level.

Kyophilavong et al. (2014) evaluated 361 households in 15 villages in the rural district of Sukhuma Champasak in Laos. They found a non-significant impact on poverty reduction. Viada and Gaul (2011) While the MFI's ambitious outreach goals should be appreciated in principle, the reality is that overzealous lending activities can override systems of governance and control, leading to less stringent credit standards and damaging and unintended consequences. Nawaz (2017) argues that microfinance has resulted in moderate reductions in borrower poverty, but has not yet reached many of the poorest in Bangladeshi villages.

Islamic microfinance is also growing rapidly in line with the boom of Islamic Financial Institutions (IFIs), especially Islamic banks in Indonesia in the 1990s. Most of the Islamic microfinance with a women's group have legal status as a shari'ah rural bank or shari'ah cooperative. The number of shari'ah rural banks in Java had reached 1.603 per March 2015 (OJK, 2103) while shari'ah cooperatives had reached a total of nearly 4,500 entities (DepKop, 2016). As for the Islamic community-based Islamic group loan, they are organized under various institutions such as zakat institutions, NGOs, and shari'ah cooperatives. There is no official number of groups but the member of each institution can reach 10,000 households with mostly women participants.

Several research papers show increasing results in Islamic microfinance models such as Usman and Tasmin (2016) which document that Islamic microfinance has been considered an important tool for empowering the poor, especially women, towards the development of micro-enterprises. Adnan and Ajija (2015) argue that BMT financing is effective in reducing poverty where most respondents can increase their income after receiving BMT financing.

The institution selected as the case study provides funds and loans to cover the necessities of life. In most cases, institutional members or participants have not expanded their business to a larger scale. According to a survey from Indonesia, this is because the business does not have a good financial record. This action research tries to improve their ability in wealth management to keep a good financial record to support them to grow their business.

There are several principles that must be obeyed by Muslim families in their finances which involve accounting as a family skill as stated by Syahatah (1998) as follows: (1) Maintaining a balance between income and expenses; (2) Spend wealth for good purposes based on Al-Qur'an Al-Baqarah (2): 172 and Al Maidah (5): 4 which emphasizes on permissible income and expenses; (3) Prioritizing spending according to *Maqāsidul-Syariah* in fulfilling five principles such as protection of religion (*dn*), protection of life (*nafs*), protection of reason (*'aql*), protection of property (*māl*), and protection of property. lineage (*ansab*); (4) Escape from excessive spending instead of destruction as indicated in the Qur'an Al-Isra (17): 16; (5) Avoiding non-halal expenditures to prevent people from living in luxury; and (6) Be moderate in spending as shown in the Qur'an Al-Furqon (25): 67 and Al-Isra (17):

29, also based on the hadith which says that Allah will give His mercy to those who spend moderately (HR Ahmad).

Keeping these principles in mind, family-run accounting is useful for guiding them towards a better family with records. Accounting is shaped by the environment it operates, including the political and economic factors. Similarly, accounting also shapes the behavior of people, including how they plan, act and control their lives, especially related to finance. Eventually, accounting will more or less affect people's mindsets in managing their finances. It can be a powerful tool in alleviating poverty, which parallels the overall goals of microfinance. Haqqi (2016) believes that acquiring financial knowledge is the basis for building a society, not the moral truth and healthy functioning of Islam. Salleh (2016) outlines the importance of not only Islamic finance but also personal finance and when making financial decisions such as retirement, planning, debt management, accepting loans, etc., you must not only know (knowledge) but also be confident. Mukhlisin and Tamanni (2016) in the manuscript they study the right model to empower the poor with accounting knowledge so that they can make good economic decisions. The results show that different countries have different results, namely the initial awareness of families and customers does not exist, but the media for obtaining literacy is guidance and information sharing from users and Islamic microfinance institutions. Clearly, this is one of the most powerful weapons that institutions can use to promote Islamic financial literacy. Take advantage of this—families and clients can easily benefit from participating in poverty alleviation. The best tools for poverty alleviation are those that enable companies and communities to better understand their ability to communicate effectively with stakeholders.

Accounting dictates the depiction of a deprived society through formal procedures, routines, measurement, classification, control and reporting. It is an essential tool for practicing wealth management. In addition, Ismail and Cahyo (2017) assert that wealth management is not only limited to the rich but also the poor, not only for the creation and accumulation of wealth, but also for the distribution of wealth. There are five components of wealth management such as wealth creation, wealth accumulation, wealth protection, wealth distribution, and wealth purification (Syafii et al., 2013).

12.2 Participatory Action Research (PAR) Approach

According to Kindon et al. (2008) PAR includes various participatory approaches to action-oriented research. It engages researchers and participants to solve problems and take action on how to change them for the better (Wadsworth, 1998). PAR has several cycles such as planning, action, reflection, and evaluation with the characteristics of active participation, open goals and a high level of commitment from researchers and participants (Kindon et al., 2008). The end goal is to provide solutions to research problems and achieve active learning. The expected outcome of this Participatory Action Research (PAR) is to instill basic accounting skills that will be used by participants to record and plan their financial activities for both family and business. The workshops and training took place in 1. Bogor, Indonesia, 2. Giza, Egypt, and 3. Lahore, Pakistan, followed by 4 months of accounting supervision involving 130 participants (mostly group leaders). Research with this PAR approach was started from August to March 2018. At the first level, the researchers conducted training on how to fill out records and continued with monitoring and supervision during that period.

12.2.1 Research Instruments

The expected result of this financial record is to instill discipline in the lives of participants which will improve their standard of living. To answer the two research objectives, a questionnaire instrument was used which was divided into four parts. The first questionnaire is about general information about participants in the Islamic microfinance program. The second part is a financial note that contains information about: family dreams, plans to realize dreams, family financial position at the beginning and end of the program, household debt records, savings and investments, initial and final cash projections. Streams, notes for the purpose of zakat, inheritance and wills.

The third part of the questionnaire is about daily cash records, which contains details of daily expenses such as primary, secondary and tertiary expenses. The main expenses include expenses for zakat/infaq/sodaqoh, debt payments, student fees and medical expenses. The main expenses are also expenses related to household needs such as rent for housing and utilities, food and clothing. Secondary expenses can include investments in savings, insurance, and emergency needs, while tertiary expenses include vacations, accessories, toys, and similar expenses. This record requires participants to record all expenses periodically (daily/weekly). The fourth part of the questionnaire was dedicated to participants who had their own businesses. This includes general information on their business, types of merchandise, cost of goods purchased/cost of goods sold, projected revenues and revenues (pro forma income statement) and pro forma cash flows.

There were three activities carried out for participants from October 2018 to January 2019, including: (1) classical training for participants and field assistant training on instruments, (2) weekly monitoring of instrument implementation, (3) random check of instrument implementation directly by researcher.

12.3 PAR Findings

12.3.1 Program Realization

In most cases, the level of accounting involvement among participants in the Islamic microfinance program is still relatively low, especially for participants with low levels of education and who do not own their own businesses. They only rely on the accounting system of Islamic microfinance institutions, which include debt payment accounts, mandatory and voluntary savings as well as infaq and sodaqoh. At Giza Egypt, the participants were slightly better in terms of their accounting knowledge, as they all run their own businesses. Indonesian and Pakistani participants exhibited similar patterns of accounting and wealth management.

Because the participants are not used to doing financial bookkeeping for their families, most of them have difficulty doing the bookkeeping. However, with the assistance of field workers, they begin to feel comfortable doing financial records and feel the benefits, especially in controlling daily expenses. In general, they have dreams that they want to achieve, such as owning their own house, performing Umrah and Hajj, but they cannot imagine how to save money to pursue their dreams. Their participation in the Islamic microfinance program has helped them in forcing themselves to manage their limited funds for life and business. By having a measurable financial plan supported by family financial records, it will help participants to train themselves in managing their wealth at least to survive or even more to develop their business.

12.3.1.1 BTTM (Baitut Tamkin Tazkia Madani), Indonesia

Baitut Tamkin Tazkia Madani (BTTM) is an institution founded in 2008 under the Andalusia Islamic Center Sentul City and Tazkia Group, an institution that cares about empowering the poor through shari'ah-based microfinance. They receive funds from donor agencies such as Qatar Charity, several CSR unit under Local Stated-Owned enterprises and individual donors. The initial goal of BTTM is to encourage the fulfillment of the economic needs of low-income families through microfinance entry points. Therefore they are able to have a decent economic life by today's economic standards. The pattern of BTTM development is almost the same as the Grameen Bank concept. BTTM had 2,007 members by 2018 in the Bogor. Majority of them are farmers, cake sellers, craft makers, etc. (TMFC, 2018). As of July 2018, BTTM had allocsted IDR 35 billion (USD 2.4 million) and had an outstanding financing portfolio of IDR 1.6 billion (USD 100,000).

The research team arranged a marked all-participant meeting on 17 August 2018. The purpose of this meeting was to inform the participants about the project and how to participate. There are 170 people from various villages around Babakan Madang, Bogor. There was a short exercise conducted on the day to familiarize the participants with the research instrument. The participants brought back the research instrument (exercise book) and began to record their financial activities. On October 18 2018, the research team briefed BTTM field officers on how to conduct PAR-based research in the next three months· On the same day, the research team visited the two groups where the participants lived and taught them how to fill out a questionnaire and book exercises. Fieldwork was repeated from 29 October to 5 November 2018. In between this period, we held a consolidation meeting with all BTTM field officers to ensure that the research instrument was understood by the participants. After that, we collected research instruments on December 10, 2018, to analyze the output.

The researchers collected data from 200 participants from BTTM in Indonesia. Of the 200 participants, only 68 participants returned the question instruments. They are divided into four groups: 1. Primary education/dropout/no school and do not have a business. This group consists of 8 participants; B. Elementary education/dropout/no school and do not have a business. (Selling fried foods, children's toys). This group consisted of 35 participants, only 5 provided sufficient information; 3. Middle/high school education and no business. This group consists of 10 people, only 4 people have sufficient information; 5. Junior/high school education and owning a business (sales, grocery shop, groom). This group contains 15 people, 4 people have sufficient information.

In general, the quality of the data did not meet our expectations. The three findings were: (1) they did not complete all three modules (financial plan, daily cash and business proposal), (2) handwriting was illegible (too many zeros, rupiah column was filled with alphabetical writing, etc.), and some content incomprehensible (for example in their financial position they write their assets, but assets are also written in their dreams). Participants who did not go to school/had not finished elementary school/only finished elementary school, most of them had limited writing skills. They also didn't understand the instructions properly (written in Latin script, misclassified expense accounts). The majority of the income comes from husbands (750 thousand to 1.5 million per month), they allocate most of BTTM's financing for daily needs, especially food with food costs: IDR 50,000–IDR 70,000 (family members of 4 or more). Most of them do not have their own house.

12.3.1.2 Impact Analysis After Treatment in Group A

1. In this group 2 people were relatively consistent in recording: savings, debt payments, infaq (most of the liabilities from BTTM) IDR 1,000–3000 for infaq, IDR 5,000 for savings;
2. Limited education & lack of mentoring can lead to a lack of understanding of the benefits of bookkeeping;
3. The data doesn't tell their dreams, so we can't calculate the required funding needs;
4. Recommendations: (1) reduce consumptive spending such as "snacks" and transfers to savings accounts; (2) determine the monthly and annual targets to be achieved; (3) BTTM must offer a fixed deposit mode so that participants cannot withdraw their funds at any time;

5. interviews are needed about the benefits of following an Islamic wealth management practice program.

12.3.1.3 Impact Analysis After Treatment in Group B

1. Five participants regularly recorded: savings, debt repayments, infaq (obligations from BBTM) with an amount greater than A (Rp 5000 for savings);
2. Limited education & lack of assistance, lack of understanding of the benefits of bookkeeping, can be covered by cultural efforts to increase socialization in the community and can absorb the experiences of others because of their efforts;
3. We can see implicitly in their dreams (although they don't write them down), perhaps because they are not confident enough with the small savings they have. Culturally, low-income people usually live as they are, without grandiose dreams. Slightly different from Group A who don't have dreams because of all the money they spend on food and other basic needs;
4. Recommendations: (1) determine the monthly and annual targets to be achieved; (2) provides two types of bookkeeping: personal & business. At least 10–15% of business profits can be allocated for business development (reinvesting). (3) BTTM must offer a fixed savings mode so that participants cannot withdraw their funds at any time. Some findings show that they can allocate IDR 10,000–IDR 15,000 daily for savings needed by their children's schooling;
5. interviews are needed about the benefits of following an Islamic wealth management practice program.

12.3.1.4 Impact Analysis After Treatment in Group C&D

1 Eight people routinely recorded: savings, debt repayments (to BTTM), infaq needed by BTTM also with a larger amount than group B, around Rp. 7000 for savings);

2 Because the majority of junior high school/high school education;

3 They write down the dreams they want to achieve clearly;

4 Recommendations: (1) determine the monthly and annual targets to be achieved; (2) for BTTM, must offer a fixed savings product mode (3) Need further interviews about the benefits after joining this program.

12.3.2 Akhuwat, Pakistan (25–30 November 2018 and 11–15 March 2019)

Akhuwat, Pakistan is a non-profit company, founded in 2001. Akhuwat aims to eradicate poverty by creating bonds of solidarity between the rich and the marginalized. The aim is to develop and maintain a social system based on mutual support by providing interest-free loans so that members can start businesses and become self-reliant. According to data provided by its official website in 2017, Akhuwat has distributed 2.6 Million Pakistani Rupees (USD 21,240) and 1.1 Million Pakistani Rupees (USD). 8,986) and an outstanding loan portfolio of 14.5 Million Pakistani Rupees (USD 118,454), with a total family benefit of 2.6 Million families.

The research team conducted a second fieldwork in the Akhuwat group, Lahore, Pakistan, between 25 and 30 November 2018. Due to limitations in understanding Urdu, the team recruited five students from Nur International University, Lahore to help. The same approach was adopted by the team such as briefing, small exercises and homework. Akhuwat is a different case from Indonesia and Egypt because 75% of the participants were male. Therefore, the treatment is slightly different because the male group is not strongly recommended to participate in gymnastics. On March 14th, the exercise books were collected and ready for analysis.

12.3.3 Rizqi Chapter Jameel, Egypt (3–8 February 2019 and 11–15 March 2019)

Rizqi Chapter Jameel (BRJ) is known as the leading job recruiter in Middle East founded by Mohammed Abdul Latif *Jameel*. Rizqi Chapter Jameel (meaning "beautiful gateway to prosperity" in Arabic) helps promising young men and women across the Arab world find a brighter future through lucrative work. Jameel Community started as a job creation initiative, Bab Rizq Jameel (BRJ) is now a full-fledged employment center combining, job placement, career counselling, vocational training as well as entrepreneurial initiatives. When BRJ started in 2003, they dreamed of creating 10 jobs. As of 2015, BRJ has created more than 720,000 job opportunities of which more than 490,000 are in Saudi Arabia. In addition to provide employment and training needed by industry, BRJ also contributes to minimizing the gap between university education and the needs of the private sector.

In 2009 BRJ announced officially its first branch in Egypt. BRJ has also provided 6,910 job opportunities in that year. The number of branch offices continues to increase, followed by an increase in job opportunities. The number of job opportunities created by BRJ was recorded at 25,862 in 2012 and this number represents 75% of all job opportunities created internationally. According to Dr. Moaz Al Farammy, Director of BRJ, geographically, BRJ is growing rapidly by providing job opportunities in five branches, namely Giza, Shobra, Banha, Shobra Al Khaima and Bolaq Al-Dakor. The payback ratio for all BRJ programs reached 99.32% at the end of 2012 and increased to 99.995% in 2018. Following are the financial data of BRJ EGYPT: Total Receivables EGP 27 Million; Workers in Egypt 200 employees; and 10,000 subscribers.

The research team carried out the third fieldwork at BRJ's headquarters and group located in Giza, Egypt, between 3 and 8 February 2019. The approach was not the same as the other two institutions because there was no good response from BRJ to us. Research team. After negotiating with the director during the team visit, we finally managed to meet the participants. However, due to local culture, photo-taking is limited during fieldwork. As per the questionnaire, our local team distributed and collected it between 11 and 15 March 2019. The data collected from BRJ, Egypt is only to answer the first research instrument, which is about the experience of participants in dealing with the BRJ program. Therefore, the analysis is only on the demographics of the participants.

12.4 Comparison_Analysis

From the latest data provided by GIEI (2017) we find that Pakistan and Indonesia have some similarities, especially in the financial sector. First in the financial sector, Indonesia leads Pakistan in the total assets of Islamic Financial Institutions (IFIs), as well as the number of institutions, the outstanding value of Sukuk, the number and value of Islamic mutual funds with a difference in the GIEI (Global Islamic Economy Index) score of around three index points. While other sections such as governance, awareness and social value to support the Islamic finance sector, Pakistan has a higher level. Pakistan has higher literacy and awareness for the Islamic finance sector, and the gap is very high, almost 50%. However, for government's support between Indonesia and Pakistan there are seven different index numbers. Regarding the field case, we took two similar economic empowerment programs involving women in Indonesia and Pakistan, namely BTTM (Baitut Tamkin Tazkia Madani) in Indonesia and Akhuwat in Pakistan. They practice group lending methods, apply Islamic contracts, with a majority of women as members.

12.4.1 Indonesian and Pakistani Respondents

Data collection through this questionnaire was carried out using a hardcopy questionnaire. This study involved 20 0 respondents from the BTTM population. The following is the profile of the respondents in this study:

12.4.2 Age Range

Researchers divided the age of the respondents into 5 parts of the age range, namely under 25 years, 26–35 years, 36–45 years, 45–55 years and over 55 years. From the following table, it can be seen that more than half of Akhuwat respondents in this study were in the productive age ranging from 36 to 45 years or 71 people (35.5%), followed by an age range of 2 6–3 5 years as many as 6 4 people (33%) and 38 respondents had a life span 45–55 years (19%), and <25 years as many as 20 people

Table 12.1 Age range

Age	Brothers		BTTM	
	Total	Percentage	Total	Percentage
<25 years old	20	10%	1 4	7%
26–35 years old	64	32%	45	23%
36–45 years old	71	35.5%	76	38%
45–55 years old	38	19%	45	23%
>55 years old	7	3.5%	17	9%

Table 12.2 Education level

Level of education	Brothers		BTTM	
	Total	Percentage	Total	Percentage
No education	114	5 7%	101	5 0%
Intermediate/Junior	35	17.5%	64	31%
Senior	0	0	35	17%
Diploma	51	25.5%	4	2%

(10%) and the rest are in the above range 55 years or 7 people (3.5%). Likewise with BTTM respondents, there are more than half of the respondents in the productive age ranging from 36 to 45 years or 76 people (3 8%), followed by the age range 26–35 years as many as 45 people (23%) and 45 respondents have an age of 45–55 years (23%), over 55 years as many as 17 people (9%) and the rest are in the range of up to 25 years or 14 people (7%). The following Table 12.1 summarizes the age level of the respondents:

12.4.3 Level of Education

From the data collected, it shows that there are 114 Akhuwat respondents who have no school experience, 52 respondents have a bachelor's degree, and 35 respondents attended junior high school. Meanwhile, 101 BTTM respondents did not have school experience, followed by 64 junior high school respondents, 35 high school respondents, and only 4 respondents who had diplomas. The following Table 12.2 summarizes the education level of the respondents.

12.4.4 Profession

From Table 12.3 shows that most (78) BTTM respondents have a job (39%), 6 2

Table 12.3 Work

Profession	Brothers		BTTM	
	Total	Percentage	Total	Percentage
Businessman	149	74.5%	5 5	2 7%
Work	21	10.5%	78	39%
Business and work	2	1%	5	3%
Not a business not even working	28	14%	62	31%

respondents do not run a business or work (31%), 55 respondents have a business (27%), and 5 respondents have a business and work (3%). While most of the Akhuwat respondents (149) have a business (74.5%), followed by respondents who do not have a business or work (28%), respondents have a job (21%), and 2 respondents have a business and work (1%).

12.4.5 Conclusions and Recommendations for Further Research

This participatory action research seeks to achieve the following research objectives: 1. Critically analyze the Islamic microfinance model that has been implemented in Indonesia, Egypt as well as Pakistan to evaluate the contribution of accounting knowledge and skills in participants' activities; 2. Suggest a simple bookkeeping for wealth management purposes that participants and their families can use to provide better insight into their business and community projects so as to improve their standard of living. By drawing their financial position, the participants realized that they had something in their life, changed their mindset that they were poor and always depended on others. Therefore, they become more grateful people. When writing down their financial dreams, participants agreed that they could achieve them as long as they worked with their family members towards the plan through investing and running their business. This exercise is transformed as motivation for the lower class groups on how they can achieve their life dreams. We found that the majority of respondents listed home renovation, home business expansion, children's education, Umrah and Hajj as their financial dreams.

The findings showed that 95% of the participants had no knowledge of accounting and wealth management practices such as recording their financial affairs and preparing their financial plans. After three months of training, participants in Indonesia (35%) actively participated and found the exercise useful. As per Pakistan, only 30% of all participants filled out the research instrument.

Overall, the three countries have different characteristics from each other. This is shown from the data analysis and group observations. BTTM-Indonesia is more structured in terms of learning exposure because the groups hold weekly meetings supervised by dedicated field officers. Akhuwat-Pakistan deals with Muslims and

Non-Muslims and male participants who already have business as their core job. BRJ-Egypt is not very open to public research and the male participants refused to actively interact with our male research team because of cultural differences. Only completed questionnaires were collected from the examined groups and showed mixed results on their understanding of accounting and wealth management. In short, accounting and wealth management is a new skill for the participants. Although accounting and wealth management are considered a burden but they are willing to learn when they need it to analyze their business and deal with external parties who need accounting details about their business.

Since the findings of this study are tentative, further research is necessary. We strongly recommend ethnography or PAR-based research for similar countries to educate accounting and wealth management in the wider society. A large number of participants and countries can be examined from different perspectives to reveal more valid empirical results.

References

Adnan, M. A., & Ajija, S. R. (2015). The effectiveness of baitul maal wat tamwil in reducing poverty in the case of Indonesian Islamic microfinance institutions. *Humanomics, 31*(2), 160–182. https://doi.org/10.1108/H-03-2012-0003

Agbola, F. W., Acupan, A., & Mahmood, A. (2017). Does microfinance reduce poverty? New evidence from Nertheeastern Mindanao, Philippines. *Journal of Rural Studies* , *50* , 159–171. https://doi.org/10.1016/j.jrurstud.2016.11.005

Bateman, M. (2010). *Why doesn't microfinance work? The destructive rise of local neoliberalism.* Zed Books.

BPS. (2018). *Publication.* Retrieved March 11, 2019, from https://www.bps.go.id/publikasi.html.

Donou-Adonsou, F., & Sylwester, K. (2016). Development Finance and Poverty Reduction in Developing Countries: New Evidence from Banks and Microfinance Institutions. *Development Financing Review* , *6* (1), 82–90. https://doi.org/10.1016/j.rdf.2016.06.02

El-Zoghbi, M., & Tarezi, M. (2013). Trends in Shari'ah-Compliant Financial Inclusion. *Focus Notes*, (March), 1–12.

GIEI. (2017). Thomson Reuteurs Report on the State Report of the Global Islamic Economy. 2016–2017. Retrieved August 20, 2018, from https://ceif.iba.edu.pk/pdf/ThomsonReuters-stateoftheGlobalIslamicEconomyReport201617.pdf.

Haqqi, A. R. A. (2016). The role of Islamic Universities in disseminating Islamic financial literacy for the community: UNISSA experience book chapter in Islamic Financial Literacy.

Hussain, A. (2003) Pakistan national human development report 2003: Poverty, growth and governance (Pakistan: United Nations Development Program (UNDP)). http://planipolis.iiep.unesco.org/upload/Pakistan/Pakistan%20HDR.pdf.

Ismail, N., & Cahyo, EN (2017). The Role of Islamic Banks as providers of Islamic wealth management in increasing the potential of Waqf funds. *Al-Iktisab: Journal of Islamic Economic Law,* 1(1), 35–54.

Kindon, S., Pain, R., & Kesby, M. (2008). Participatory action research. In the international encyclopedia of human geography. (pp. 90–95). other.

Korth, M., Stewart, R., Van Rooyen, C., & De Wet, T. (2012). Microfinance: Development intervention or just another bank? *Journal of Agrarian Change, 12*(4), 575–586. https://doi.org/10.1111/j.1471-0366.2012.00375.x

Kyophilavong, P., Rasphone, A., Sayvaya, I., & Vannalath, B. (2014). Factors influencing the performance of SMEs in Laos. *International Journal of Business Research and Applied Economics, 12*(4), 1267–1276.

Leikem, K. (2012). Microfinance: A tool to reduce poverty? viewcontent.cgi. Retrieved from http://digitalcommons.uri.edu/cgi/viewcontent.cgi?article=1308&context=srhonorsprog.

LPPI. (2013). Center for the Study and Development of Microfinance. Retrieved from http://www.lppi.or.id/index.php/module/Pages/sub/81/id/profil-koperasi-karya-usaha-mandiri-kopkum388.

Mahmood, S., Hussain, J., & Matlay, H. Z. (2014). Optimal size of microfinance loans and poverty reduction among women entrepreneurs in Pakistan. *Journal of Small and Enterprise Development, 21*(2), 231–249. https://doi.org/10.1108/JSBED-03-2014-0043.

Miled, K. B. H., & Rejeb, J.-E. (2015). Microfinance and poverty reduction: A review and synthesis of empirical evidence. *Procedia - Social and Behavioral Sciences, 195*(July), 705–712. https://doi.org/10.1016/j.sbspro.2015.06.339

Montgomery, H. (2005). Serving the poorest of the poor: the poverty impact of Khushhali Bank Microfinance loans in Pakistan. Tokyo: Asian Development Bank Institute. http://www.dbi.org/files/2005.09.28.book.khushhali.microfinance.study.pdf.

Mukhlisin, M., & Tamanni, L. (2016). Accounting literacy and poverty eradication—Early case studies in Egypt and Indonesia. Islamic Financial Literacy Book Chapter.

Nawaz, T. (2017). Investment strategy momentum, corporate governance and corporate performance: Analysis of Islamic banks. *Corporate Governance: International Journal of Business in Society, 17*(2), 192–211. https://doi.org/10.1108/CG-03-2016-0052

OJK. (2103). *Shari'ah Banking Statistics 2013* . Retrieved from http://www.ojk.go.id/dl.php?i=2689.

Salleh, Ak Md Hasnol Alwee Pg Md. (2016). Developing Islamic financial literacy from a personal finance perspective. Islamic Financial Literacy Book Chapter.

Samer, S., Majid, I., Rizal, S., Muhamad, MR, Sarah-Halim, & Rasyid, N. (2015). The impact of microfinance on poverty reduction: Empirical evidence from a Malaysian perspective. *Procedia - Social and Behavioral Sciences, 195* (January 2016), 721–728. https://doi.org/10.1016/j.sbspro.2015.06.343.

Shirazi, N. S., & Khan, A. U. (2009) The role of Pakistan's microcredit poverty alleviation fund in poverty alleviation: A case of Pakistan. *Pakistan Economic and Social Review, 47*(2).

Syafii, Z., Yusoff, Z., & Noh, S. M. (2013). Islamic financial planning and wealth management. Kuala Lumpur: IBFIM.

Syahatah, H. (1998). *Muslim home economics*. Jakarta: Human Echo. 101284-2.

TMFC. (2018). Tazkia micro finance center unpublished yearly report, p. 2.

UN. (2013). The millennium development goals report. Retrieved August 1, 2021, from http://www.un.org/millenniumgoals/pdf/report-2013/mdg-report-2013-english.pdf.

Usman, A. S., & Tasmin, R. (2016). The role of Islamic microfinance in improving human development in muslim countries. *Journal of Islamic Finance, 5*(1), 053–062. https://doi.org/10.13140/RG.2.1.3233.1762.

Viada, L., & Gaul, S. (2011). *The tipping point: over-indebtedness and investment in microfinance, microbanking bulletin.*

Yunus, M. (2007). Credit to the poor: Poverty as a distant history. *Harvard International Review, 29*(3), 20.

Wadsworth, Y. (1998). What is participatory action research? Retrieved November 5, 2006, from http://www.scu.ed.au/schools/gcm/ar/ari/p-ywadswoth98.html.

World Bank. (2007). Pakistan: Promoting rural growth and poverty reduction (Washington, DC: World Bank).

World Bank. (2020a). Overview of poverty and equity in Indonesia. https://databank.worldbank.org/data/download/poverty/33EF03BB-9722-4AE2-ABC7-AA2972D68AFE/Global_POVEQ_IDN.pdf.

World Bank. (2020b). Poverty and justice at a glance in the Arab Republic of Egypt. https://databank.worldbank.org/data/download/poverty/33EF03BB-9722-4AE2-ABC7-AA2972D68AFE/Global_POVEQ_EGY.pdf.
World Bank. (2020c). Poverty and Justice in Pakistan at a Glance. https://databank.worldbank.org/data/download/poverty/33EF03BB-9722-4AE2-ABC7-AA2972D68AFE/Global_POVEQ_PAK.pdf.
Zhang, Q. (2017). Does Microfinance Reduce Poverty? Some International Evidence. *BE Journal of Macroeconomics*, *17* (2), 1–13. https://doi.org/10.1515/bejm-2016-0011.

Murniati Mukhlisin earned her bachelor degree in accounting from International Islamic University Malaysia, master degree in accounting from Universitas Indonesia, and PhD in accounting from University of Glasgow, UK. She taught at University of Glasgow and Essex Business School, University of Essex, UK. Murniati published her works on critical perspective in the areas of financial reporting, Islamic accounting, Islamic banking and finance, and Islamic financial literacy. She is a professor in Islamic accounting, a certified Islamic financial planner, halal supervisor and trainer. She is a founder of Sakinah Finance and Sobat Syariah and currently serves as a Rector at Tazkia Islamic University College, Bogor, Indonesia.

Sugiyarti Fatma Laela obtained her PhD in Accounting from University of Indonesia. She is an Associate Professor of Islamic Accounting at Tazkia Islamic University College. She holds Certified Management Accountant and active in the profession from Institute of Certified Management Accounting Australia. Her research interest includes Management Accounting and Islamic Corporate Governance, especially in Islamic Banking. She published papers in national reputable journals and providing consultations in Islamic Accounting for local new papers. Her works have been published in Journal of Economic Issues, International Journal of Islamic and Middle Eastern Finance and Management, Journal of Islamic Accounting and Business Research, Journal of Islamic Monetary Economics and Finance , Journal of Islamic Finance, Jurnal Akuntansi Multiparadigma The University of Brawijaya, Jurnal Akuntansi dan Dinamika Bisnis The University of Syiah Kuala, Jurnal Akuntansi dan Keuangan Indonesia—University of Indonesia.

Chapter 13
Social Impact Sukūk: Implications from the Notion of *Maslaha*

Abu Umar Faruq Ahmad, Nurul Aini Muhamed, and Rashedul Hasan

Sukūk are required to ensure that no *haram* (unlawful) ingredients especially, *riba* (an unjustified increase of money), *gharar* (excessive uncertainty or risk), *qimar* (gambling) and *maysir* (financial gain comes from chance or speculation), and elements of unethical investments are embedded in their structure and commercial transactions (Ahmad, 2015).

Islamic finance industry witnessed unprecedented growth in the Sukuk issuance in the last decade. The total volume of global sukuk issuance increased from 64 billion USD in 2018 to 87.4 billion USD in 2019, representing an impressive 37 per cent growth (Moody, 2019). Several factor have attributed to such growth and specific countries (for example Malaysia and Saudi Arabia) has established themselves as the market leader in innovative Sukuk issuance. For example, we have witnessed the issuance of Socially Responsible Investment (SRI) Sukuk to find government projects in both South Asia and the GCC region (Ahmad, 2017).

Sukūk are currently getting momentum in ICM with some direction to include other elements of SRI such as environment, social and governance (Dawkins, 2016). The SIS is one of the unique and innovative financial instruments that are currently issued in the global ICM. Since 2006, Brunei Darussalam has issued a total of 130 *Sukūk* with a combined USD 9.71 in short-term offerings (Miglietta & Forte, 2007). This chapter endeavours to explore the area of SIS in Islamic finance industry about potential and challenges of adopting this instrument in ICM, specifically in Brunei Darussalam as a case study due to the recent significant development of ICM in this jurisdiction. Although Brunei is considered as the richest among the ASEAN Member countries being the fourth-largest oil and gas producer in this region and the ninth-largest exporter of liquefied natural gas in the world, the ICM has remained underdeveloped for some reasons. However, in recent years the Brunei government has intensified its efforts to capitalise on the growth of its ICM in the global Islamic finance

A. U. F. Ahmad (✉) · N. A. Muhamed · R. Hasan
Islamic Economic Institute, King Abdulaziz University, Jeddah, Saudi Arabia
e-mail: aufahmad@gmail.com

T. Azid et al. (eds.), *Wealth Management and Investment in Islamic Settings*,
https://doi.org/10.1007/978-981-19-3686-9_13

industry to make it as a hub in this region. Given that, this chapter seeks to explore the potential impact of SIS issuance on economic development of Brunei through identifying the challenges *inter alia* that might have an impact on the successful issuance of SIS. Socio-economic problems have always been ongoing issues globally, especially in a number of Muslim countries (Louche & Lydenberg, 2006).

Forty per cent of the Organization of Islamic Cooperation (OIC) countries' population earn under the poverty line, with 192 million people live below the poverty line in Sub-Saharan Africa only (Hoepner et al., 2011). Based on this fact, it becomes a necessity that the issue of social finance is included in Islamic finance agenda. There are several Islamic charitable contracts such as *Waqf* (perpetual charity) and *Sadaqah* (voluntary charity) are workable as important mechanisms for philanthropic purposes. These plain contracts are suitable for part of the *Sukūk* structure under the SIS. This type of *Sukūk* however, is not only applicable for developing or under developing countries, but it can also be launched in developed countries. As can be seen from the examples of Social Impact Bond (SIB) in the UK, *Sukūk* are also applicable in the situation where the government's budget for public projects is somehow limited. Malaysia is among the earlier issuers that are interested in issuing this type of *Sukūk*, to support its public education system.

13.1 The Principle of *Maslaha* in Islamic Finance

Although the practice of *Maslaha* started in the lifetime of the Prophet (pbuh) its theory was only methodically compiled during the 1500th and eighteenth centuries. The classical scholars al-Juwaynī, al-Ghazalī and ʿIzz ibn ʿAbd al-Salam were among the key innovators who introduced the doctrine of *Maslaha*, while Ibn Qayy īm, al-Qarafī and al-Shatibī have added *Maslaha* as a standalone topic in the sciences of'Usul al-Fiqh or the Principles of Islamic Jurisprudence. In fact, Al-Shatibi, along the line with Al-Ghazzali's classification, singles *Maslaha* out as being the only superseding Sharī'ah objective broad enough to include all actions deemed beneficial to mass people. He further categorises *Maslaha* into main three types: "*Daruriyat* (the essentials), *Hajiyat* (the complementary), and *Tahsiniyat* (the embellishments)". Some contemporary scholars such as Kamali, Chapra, Nyazee and Hallaq, assert that the above categorisation is deeply rooted in *Maqasid Sharī'ah* (the objectives of Sharī'ah) to safeguard community's interests in the best way possible. They view that such a categorisation suggests forming a *Maslaha*-based methodology that helps derive new rulings from the sources of the Sharī'ah in order to solve the emerging issues related to socioeconomic endeavours (Kamali, 2008).

The practice of *Maslaha* as a significant secondary source of Sharī'ah can play an incredible role in reforming Islamic practices to harmonise between revelations and realities or letters and spirit (Ibn Ashur, 2006). Given that, it should be understood that the rulings contain in the Sharī'ah must not merely be determined from the forms, from their substance also to reflect upon the fact how Sharī'ah emphasises the significance of considering the interests of the community at large rather than merely concentrating on individual benefits. From the *Maqasid Sharī'ah* perspectives, Islamic finance is not all about to cater for bringing benefits for financial institutions alone. It extends to the behaviour of the relevant industry players and stakeholders in the ICM, and how these propensities can create an impact on their economic activities (Renneboog et al., 2012). It is on this premise that the *Sukūk* issuance be it SIS or any other type is not a distinct matter having limited impact on the community, but it involves a greater public interest that has a far-reaching impact on a mass people who have stake in the *Sukūk* market, especially when they expand to markets beyond the boundary of the country in any jurisdiction (Dunfee, 2003). The investors in *Sukūk* may be free to choose the structure according to their own interpretation of the rules of the Sharī'ah within the permissible *'Ijtihad*, but the control of a part of the nation's wealth by any Islamic bank and investment channel have to have conscientiousness and doctrinal deference.

The major essence of Islamic finance, i.e., risk-sharing and social responsibility are missing in practice (Marwan & Engku, 2016). SIS instruments should allow investors to make an impact on the social *Maslaha* and thus institutions offering such products should go back to the roots (*Maslaha*) to assess the ability of the Social Impact *Sukūk* (SIS) in contributing to social development through its structure and mechanism.

13.2 The Current Status of *Sukūk* Instruments and the Market

The modern Islamic finance started in the 1960s with the establishment of two Islamic financial institutions (IFIs), one is in Egypt named Mit Ghamr Local Saving Banks, and the other is in Malaysia called Lembaga Tabung Haji/Pilgrim's Saving Corporation (Cebeci, 2012). Brunei as a majority Muslim country (being 82.70% of the population is Muslim) joined Islamic finance market in 2005 with the establishment of Bank Islam Brunei Darussalam (BIBD) as the flagship of Islamic financial institution. BIBD is a merger of two previously established local IFIs, Islamic Bank of Brunei and Islamic Development Bank of Brunei (Asian Development Bank, 2017).

The indirect financing in ICM includes Islamic unit trust, Islamic exchange-traded funds, Islamic real estate funds, where the funds are managed by the intermediary institutions. *Sukūk* are seen as alternatives for issuers (such as government, business corporations and non-government organisations) to gain long-term capital at a lower cost and lower financier or creditors' intervention (Morales, 2016). The first *Sukūk* issuance is the Malaysian corporate *Sukūk* issued by Shell MDS in 1990, followed sovereign *Sukūk* issued by the government of Malaysia in 2002 (Zulkhibri, 2015). Malaysia and Gulf Cooperation Council countries (GCC) remain the main worldwide *Sukūk* issuers. Both of these issuers dominate 72.2% of total global issuance (GSIA, 2016). The Brunei government through its regulatory authority, Autoriti Monetari Brunei Darussalam (AMBD), issued its BND 50 million 164th series of *Sukūk* on 6

Table 13.1 The average rental yield by the *sukūk al-'Ijarah* during 2014–2018 in Brunei

Series issued in 2018	Days (Tenor)	Maturity date	Total value in million (Brunei dollar)
153	91	April 12, 2018	100
154	91	May 10, 2018	100
155	364	March 07, 2019	50
156	91	July 12, 2018	100
157	91	August 09, 2018	100
158	364	June 06, 2019	50
159	91	October 11, 2018	100
160	91	November 08, 2018	100
161	364	September 05, 2019	15
162	91	January 07, 2019	100
163	91	February 07, 2019	100
164	364	December 05, 2019	32.5

Source: Autoriti Monetari Brunei Darussalam

December 2018, which made it to issue over BND 12.41 billion worth of short-term *Sukūk al-'Ijarah* securities since its maiden offering on 6th April 2006 (IIFM, 2016). Table 13.1 shows the average rental yield by the Brunei Government *Sukūk al-'Ijarah* between Quarter 1, 2014 and Quarter 1, 2018.

13.3 *Sukūk* Structure—From Generic to SRI

The preference from Sharī'ah perspective, however, is intangible assets. Relying only on intangible assets (such as financial obligations) will lead to issues of trade ability in the secondary market (Eurosif, 2003). There are four parties commonly involve in its structure: originator/obligor, special purpose vehicle (SPV), trustees and *Sukūk* holders/investors. Depending on the complexity of *Sukūk* structure, there may be more parties involved in the structure such as agents of originators/obligors and guarantor (Eurosif, 2006).

Originators/obligors are entities that issue *Sukūk* to raise funds. These entities can be a government, business firms and NGOs. The decision to issue *Sukūk* and arrange for underlying assets depends on originators' objectives (Eurosif, 2008). Based on issuers' category, *Sukūk* are structured and arranged as sovereign *Sukūk*, quasi-sovereign *Sukūk* and corporate *Sukūk*. SPV is an entity that is set up as an intermediary between originators and investors. Some of its roles (by steps) are purchasing the underlying assets from originator, issuing *Sukūk* to investors, collecting proceeds of *Sukūk* from investors and transferring them to originators (as payment on *Sukūk*), and transfer periodic coupon to investors (types of payment depends on types of contracts between the originators and investors).

Trustees act to ensure the conduct of issuers would not breach the rules and regulations. These roles will protect the rights of investors. *Sukūk* holders/investors consist of those who buy *Sukūk* for investment purposes. By purchasing *Sukūk*, they have the ownership of the undivided underlying assets and are entitled to receive the periodical coupon from issuers. The payment can be in the form of lease/rent (in '*Ijarah* contract), profit from the partnership (in partnership contract and profit on sales (in sales-based contracts) (Qaed, 2014). Stable return from the investment is important to those *Sukūk* investors who are concerned with financial aspects while at the same time follows the Sharī'ah principles (IFSB, 2017). The usage of the proceeds in the specifically targeted sectors (such as green sectors) may not become the main concern for these investors as long as the expected rate of return is achieved.

From the Sharī'ah perspective, *Sukūk* can be structured using several types of a single contract or the combination of various contracts (hybrid *Sukūk*). *Sukūk* according to their types of contracts can be divided into sales-based contracts (*Bai' Bithaman Ajil/BBA, Murabahah, Salam* and *Istisna'*), leased-based contracts (*'Ijarah, 'Ijarah Muntahiyah Bittamlik, 'Ijarah Mawsufah fi al-Dhimmah*), partnership contracts (*Mudharabah and Musharakah*) and agency based contracts (*Wakalah bi al-Istihmar*) (Said & Grassa, 2013). There are some evolutions on *Sukūk* structure since their establishment. Among the earliest *Sukūk* structure are the *Murabaha* and BBA *Sukūk*. The structure of BBA *Sukūk* was firstly introduced in 1996 and was heavily used as the main structure in Malaysia several years later (Guyot, 2011). The status of the BBA *Sukūk* structure gained extensive discussion and can be viewed as a classic case in the *Sukūk* market. The main issue behind the BBA *Sukūk* structure is the use of the debatable *Bay' al-'Inah* contract (Iqbal & Tsubota, 2006). The usage of this contract happens at the first tranche of sales transactions between the originator/issuer and SPV (prior to the second tranche of issuing the *Sukūk* to investors by SPV). As such, the underlying assets for the *Sukūk* are receivables, which leads to another issue of *Sukūk* trade ability. With the underlying assets consist of debt, the *Sukūk* trigger the controversial contract of *Bay' al-Dayn* (Ahmad et al., 2018). This happened when the BBA *Sukūk* are sold to another investor prior to their maturity date in the secondary market. This practice is not recognised by the global Sharī'ah circles and leads to global rejection of BBA *Sukūk*.

From the Islamic finance landscape, SIS are listed as few innovations in Islamic finance together with green *Sukūk*, SIS and SRI *Sukūk*. The terms SIS, green *Sukūk* and SRI *Sukūk*, however, are used interchangeably by the industry (Khazanah Nasional, 2015). Azman and Engku (2016) Provide the conceptual model for the definition of SRI *Sukūk* and SIS and proposed that SRI *Sukūk* should be part of SIS (Eurosif, 2010). Within the same model, the SIS are justified as part of the large picture of SRI. This perspective is different from the OECD's perspective, which highlights those types of investment alternative according to investors' interest and tolerance in return on investment. In this case, the SRI investors consider a competitive return, while SIS investors have more tolerance towards their return (Eurosif, 2012).

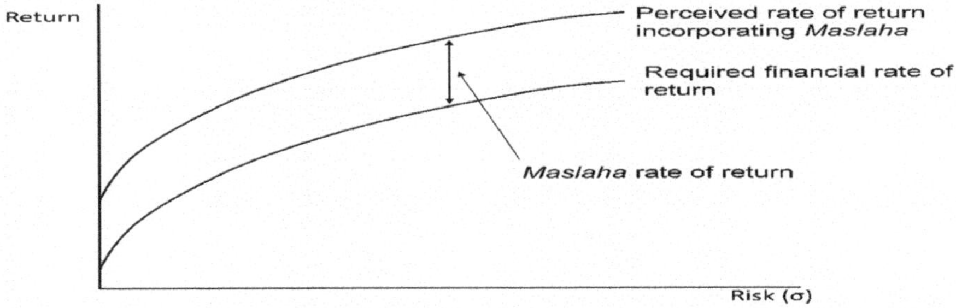

Fig. 13.1 *Maslaha* rate of return *Source* Alshelfan (2014)

Since there are some inconsistencies in the definition of SRI and SIS *Sukūk* in comparison to SRI bond and SIB, the definition of these Islamic instruments is placed under the same category (IFSB, 2016). Malaysian SRI *Sukūk* issued by Khazanah and Vaccine *Sukūk* under the International Finance Facility for immunisation are referred to as SRI *Sukūk* cum SIS (Al-Amine, 2013). Khazanah *Sukūk Ihsan* are structured using the structure of *Wakalah Bi al-Istihmar* and formed to support and improve the quality of education in Malaysia. Figure 13.1 shows the structure of the *Sukūk Ihsan* by Khazanah Nasional (Eurosif, 2014). Stakeholders of the *Sukūk* include government responsible to set the objective of the *Sukūk*, SPV/intermediary playing the roles to sell the *Sukūk* instruments and channels the proceeds to the service providers (Eurosif, 2016). Service providers acting to perform the programs to the selected schools, whereas, investors consisting the individuals and other private entities that provide funds and beneficiaries receiving the benefits (Fig. 13.2).

13.4 Discussion and Conclusions

The compliance with the principles of Sharī'ah is a mandatory requirement for any Islamic financial product, especially the SIS, which represent potential crossover with convention of Socially responsible investments such as SIB. In addition to the Sharī'ah requirements, socially responsible investments are also guided by an ethical and more code of environmental, social and governance investment. Conventional bonds represent interest-bearing debt, which is unlikely in the case of *Sukūk* as it creates participation rights in assets or ventures based on various types of contracts recognised under the principles of Islamic Law (Bennett & Iqbal, 2013). The vaccine *Sukūk* launched in 2014 by the International Finance Facility for Immunisation (IFFIm) has provided evidence of Sharī'ah compliance (Marwan & Engku, 2015). In recent years, SRIs are no longer relying on negative screening and focusing on promoting social change through investing in activities and industries they support (Hasan et al., 2018). However, Islamic finance has traditionally been relying heavily on negative screening. Although negative screening ensures that

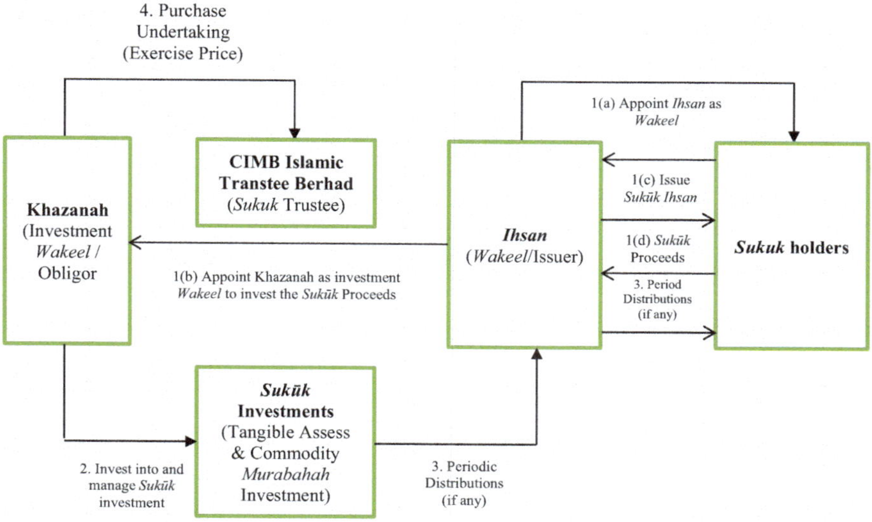

Fig. 13.2 The structure of *Sukūk Ihsan*. *Source:* International Islamic Financial Market (2016)

the investment satisfies Sharī'ah compliance, it also provides investors with limited investment opportunities (Elias, 2012).

References

Ahmad, A. U. F. (2015). Legal, regulatory and other key issues pertaining to sukuk. In *ICISEF 2015 Proceedings* (pp. 91–138). Sakarya, Turkey.

Ahmad, A. U. F. (2017). Regulation, performance and future challenges of *Sukūk*: The evidence from Asian markets. In D. Mutum (Ed.), *Advances in Islamic finance, marketing and management: An Asian perspective* (pp. 27–48). Bingley.

Ahmad, A. U. F., Muneeza, A., Farooq, M., & Hasan, R. (2018). Post-default Sukūk restructuring: An appraisal of Sharī'ah issues. *Management of Islamic Finance: Principle, Practice, and Performance (International Finance Review), 19*, 113–128.

Al-Amine, M. A. (2013). Managing liquidity risk in Islamic finance. In K. H. Ahmed (ed.), *Contemporary Islamic finance: Innovations, applications, and best practices* (p. 131). Wiley.

Alshelfan, A. I. (2014). *Maslaha: A new approach for Islamic bonds*. PhD thesis submitted to Victoria University, Melbourne, Australia.

Asian Development Bank. (2017). The Brunei Sukuk market. *ASEAN+3 Bond Market Guide 2017: Brunei Darussalam*. Retrieved November 6, 2019, from https://doi.org/10.22617/TCS178920-2

Azman, S. M. M., Bin S. A., & Engku, E. A. (2016). Potential role of social impact bond and socially responsible investment *Sukūk* as financial tools that can help address issues of poverty and socio-economic insecurity. *Intellectual Disclosure*, 343–364.

Bennett, M. S., & Iqbal, Z. (2013). How socially responsible investing can help bridge the gap between Islamic and conventional financial markets'. *International Journal of Islamic and Middle Eastern Finance and Management, 6*(3), 211–225.

Cebeci, I. (2012). Integrating the social *maslaha* into Islamic finance. *Accounting Research Journal, 25*(3), 166–184.
Dawkins, C. E. (2016). Elevating the role of divestment in socially responsible investing. *Journal of Business Ethics,* 1–14.
Dunfee, T. W. (2003). Social investing: Mainstream or backwater? *Journal of Business Ethics, 43*(3), 247–252.
Elias, E. (2012). The performance of socially responsible investment: Evidence from Sharī'ah—Compliant stocks'. *Ethonmed,* 1–40.
Eurosif. (2003). *SRI study 2003*. Retrieved October 29, 2019, from http://www.eurosif.org/research/#
Eurosif. (2006). *SRI study 2006*. Retrieved October 29, 2019, from http://www.eurosif.org/research/#
Eurosif. (2008). *SRI study 2008*. Retrieved on 29 October 2019, from http://www.eurosif.org/research/#
Eurosif. (2010). *SRI study 2010*. Retrieved October 29, 2019, from http://www.eurosif.org/research/#
Eurosif. (2012). *SRI study 2012*. Retrieved October 29, 2019, from http://www.eurosif.org/research/#
Eurosif. (2014). *SRI study 2014*. Retrieved October 29, 2019, from http://www.eurosif.org/research/#
Eurosif. (2016). *SRI study 2016*. Retrieved October 29, 2019, from http://www.eurosif.org/research/#
GSIA. (2016). Retrieved October 29, 2019, from http://www.gsi-alliance.org/wp-content/uploads/2017/03/GSIR_Review2016.F.pdf
Guyot, A. (2011). Efficiency and dynamics of Islamic investment: Evidence of geopolitical effects on Dow Jones Islamic market indexes'. *Emerging Markets Finance and Trade.*
Hasan, R., Ahmad, A. U. F., & Parveen, T. (2018). *Sukūk* risks: A structured review of theoretical research. *Journal of Islamic Accounting and Business Research, 10*(1), 35–49.
Hoepner, A. G. F., Rammal, H. G., & Rezec, M. (2011). Islamic mutual funds' financial performance and international investment style: Evidence from 20 countries. *The European Journal of Finance, 17*(9–10), 829–850.
Ibn Ashur, I. (2006). *Treatise on Maqasid al-Shariah* (1st ed., pp. 489). International Institute of Islamic Thought.
International Islamic Financial Market. (2016). *Sukuk report: A comprehensive study of the global sukuk market.*
Iqbal, Z., & Tsubota. (2006). Emerging Islamic capital market-a quickening pace and new potential. In *The Euromoney international debt capital management handbook*. Retrieved November 4, 2019 from http://www.worldbank.or.jp/debtsecurities/cmd/pdf/Euromoney_2006_Handbook_International_Debt_Capital_Markets.pdf
Islamic Financial Services Board. (2016). *Islamic financial services industry stability report*. Kuala Lumpur.
Islamic Financial Services Board. (2017). *Guiding principles on disclosure requirements for Islamic capital market products.* Ṣukūk and Islamic Collective Investment Schemes.
Kamali, M. H. (2008). *Maqasid al-Sharī'ah Made Simple.* International Institute of Islam Thought.
Khazanah Nasional. (2015). *Khazanah issues world's first ringgit-denominated sustainable and responsible investment sukuk*. Retrieved November 4, 2019, from www.khazanah.com.my
Louche, C., & Lydenberg, S. (2006). Socially responsible investment: Differences be-tween Europe and United States. In *Vlerick Leuven Gent working paper series* (p. 22). Vlerick Leuven Gent Management School.
Marwan, S. A., & Engku, E. R. (2015). Sustainable and responsible investment (SRI): Trends and prospects. In *Muzakarah Penasihat Syariah Kewangan Islam.*

Marwan, S. A., & Engku, E. R. A. (2016). The potential of innovative financial tools: Social impact bond (SIB) and sustainable and responsible investment (SRI) *Sukūk*, towards the sustainable growth of the Islamic finance industry. *European Journal of Islamic Finance, 4*, 1–9.
Miglietta, F., & Forte, G. (2007). Islamic mutual funds as faith-based funds in a socially responsible context. *Journal of Financial Economics*, 12.
Moody. (2019). Retrieved October 29, 2019, from https://www.thenational.ae/business/sukuk-issuance-set-to-rise-to-130-billion-in-2019-1.903609
Morales, Y. R. (2016). *Maslaha* as a guide and basis for governance of society. In *3rd Bitiala sa Maguindanao Series (conversations in Maguindanao*. Retrieved November 4, 2019, from https://ssrn.com/abstract=2714669
Qaed, I. Q. (2014). The structures and application of Sukuk. *International Journal of Management Sciences, Research Academy of Social Sciences, 4*(5), 218–224.
Renneboog, L., Ter Horst, J., & Zhang, C. (2012). Money-flows of socially responsible investment funds around the world. In H. K. Baker & J. R. Nofsinger (Eds.), *Socially responsible finance and investing: Financial institutions, corporations, investors, and activists* (pp. 455–477). Wiley.
Said, A., & Grassa, R. (2013). The determinants of *Sukūk* market development: Does macroeconomic factors influence the construction of certain structure of *Sukūk*? *Journal of Applied Finance & Banking, 3*(5), 18.
Zulkhibri, M. (2015). A synthesis of theoretical and empirical research on *Sukūk*. *Borsa Istanbul Review, 15*(4), 237–248.

Abu Umar Faruq Ahmad is currently an Adjunct Professor of Islamic Finance at Guidance College, Texas, USA and the United International University, Dhaka, Bangladesh respectively. He has a significant number of published peer-reviewed refereed journal articles, books, chapters in edited books, conference proceedings, and other intellectual contributions to his credit on *Shari'ah* compliance of Islamic banks' products and structures, Islamic economics, the opportunities and challenges of Islamic finance, case studies of Islamic banks and financial institutions, Islamic insurance and reinsurance, Islamic microfinance, *Sukuk*, and dispute resolution in Islamic banking and finance, among others. He presented papers at international conferences held in the USA, Ireland, Australia, UAE, Saudi Arabia, Turkey, Brunei, Qatar, Sudan, Nigeria, Malaysia, Indonesia, Bangladesh and Pakistan. His current editorial roles include serving as founding editor, senior editor, editorial advisory board member of a plethora of internationally reputed refereed journals including some of those published by Emerald Group Publishing, UK.

Dr. Nurul Aini Muhamed is an Associate Professor in the Faculty of Economics and *Muamalat*, Universiti Sains Islam Malaysia (USIM) and a research fellow in the Institute of Halal Research and Management (*IHRAM*). Currently, she is also a Deputy Director for the Centre for *Awqaf* and *Zakat*, USIM. Previously, she was a Deputy Dean (Academic and Research) and a Head Program of Bachelor Degree of *Muamalat* Administration of the Faculty. She obtained her Master of Islamic Finance Practice (MIFP) from INCEIF (2021) and PhD (Business and Management) from University of South Australia (2009). Her research interests include the Islamic Transaction Law, Islamic Banking and Finance, Halal Compliance and *Shari'ah* Governance. She is also a *Shari'ah* Committee member of Hong Leong MSIG Takaful and BNP Paribas Malaysia Berhad. She is the editor of 'Halal Governance and Management: *Malaysian & Asean Countries*', and author of '*Hutang Malaysia daripada Perspektif Ekonomi dan Islam*'

Rashedul Hasan is a Senior Lecturer in the Faculty of Business, Communication and Law at INTI International University, Malaysia. His BBA (Accounting and Finance) and MBA (Finance) from American International University Bangladesh (AIUB) with Summa Cum Laude distinction and PhD in Accounting from International Islamic University Malaysia (IIUM). His research interests include Islamic Finance, Corporate Governance, Voluntary Disclosure, Intellectual Capital and Sustainability. His papers are appeared in Thunderbird International Business Review, Islamic Quarterly, Journal of Economic Development and Cooperation, Journal of Islamic Economics, Banking and Finance, Journal of Islamic Economic Studies and International Journal of Public Sector Performance Management. He served as guest editor for the Journal of Business and Globalization. He has served as the editor of the Book of Proceedings for Asian Conference on Entrepreneurship. Dr. Hasan is actively involved in applied research and has worked on projects under the funding of the South-Korean and the Malaysian government.

Chapter 14
Religion, Islamic Values and Debt Management, the Malaysian Experience

Wan Marhaini Wan Ahmad, Asmak Ab Rahman, and Azizi Che Seman

The trend of the Malaysian household debt of recent years indicated that the Malaysian household are very much facing acute financial vulnerabilities. The Malaysian household debt to Gross Domestic Product (GDP) at the end of 2015 was 88.4% one of the highest among Asia's developing economies (BNM, 2016; Barua, 2015).

For an economy, even though household debt is a necessity to drive growth, it would however, become an impending threat once the debt has reached a level that is unsustainable. Private consumption, savings and investment are decreasing due to higher rate of household debt (Debelle, 2004; Hull, 2003). Obligation of the household to pay their increasing outstanding loans shall lead to a stifle in the aggregate demand and therefore, the economic growth might be retarded.

These vulnerabilities, furthermore, shall induce a negative impact to the national's financial stability (Charpe & Flaschel, 2013). Unnecessary debt can cause default in payment of outstanding due which leads to a bankruptcy if borrowings become non-payables. There is also an implication of credit bubble, similar to the sub-prime crisis in the US in 2008, which caused foreclosures of many home mortgages and the collapse of several major financial institutions (Demyanyk & Hemert, 2011). These are the reasons behind the acknowledgement of household debt as one of the best predictors of financial crisis and economic recession (Mian & Sufi, 2010).

More alarming is when the household debt is contributed by unmanageable consumerism. A report by Khazanah Research Institute on household debt in Malaysia concluded that consumerism was relatively high with many middle and low income households owning discretionary durable goods. Worryingly, most of these purchases were made by credit due to low income or shortages of cash as evidenced by the average borrowings of approximately 7 times of the annual income for those earning below RM3,000 monthly (KRI, 2016).

W. M. Wan Ahmad (✉) · A. Ab Rahman · A. Che Seman
Universiti Malaya, Kuala Lumpur, Malaysia
e-mail: wmarhaini@um.edu.my

T. Azid et al. (eds.), *Wealth Management and Investment in Islamic Settings*,
https://doi.org/10.1007/978-981-19-3686-9_14

Given the detrimental effects of uncontrolled and excessive household debts, the monitoring and control of the debt have become an important national agenda for many countries involving government agencies, financial institutions, credit bureaus, utility companies and research institutions. Pre-emptive and comprehensive measures have be undertaken by the governments to reduce households' repayment burden and to tighten standards in the loan approval screening process (KFSM, 2015; Sivos et al., 2011).

From both pragmatic and logical perspectives, the appropriate approach is to control the burgeoning debt from the start prior to the debt acquisition until full settlement. Guidelines provided by the relevant public and private agencies regarding debt management measures typically start with an advice where household is asked not to jump blindly into debt but to first consider various variables like the available alternative payment and financing, repayment terms, and the future earnings and situations. An individual should only commit to credit purchases or borrowings after much consideration of its necessity, benefits, productiveness, and foremost the affordability to pay the debt in the future. A realistic assessment must be conducted of how much income that one would have to service the future owing. Preferably, one should only acquire a debt that will leave him with a positive net disposable income after meeting the debt payment requirements and other expenses during the period (AKPK, 2011).

Basically, the advice is to ensure that the debt is manageable and the level of debt would not unduly constrain the life choices of the debtors in the future. After the acquisition of the debts, it is important for the household to maintain and regularly update the information on its indebtedness. Knowing the amount of debt incurred, and the timing of its payment will let the debtors know of the expected amount to be paid in each regular period. With proper budgeting, the impending default on payment can be avoided.

Studies that examined the factors that influence households' good debt management practices were aplenty. Among the known factors include financial literacy (Hilgert et al., 2003) psychological characteristics of the debtors (Wang & Lv, 2011), and their socio-economic background like age, employment status (Canner & Luckett, 1990), health problems (Grafova, 2007), financial soundness (Alfaro & Gallardo, 2012), and financial distress (Moorman & Garasky, 2008).

Some studies also examined the impact of religiosity on the debt management behaviour of certain religious disciples. Disciples from certain areas with high religious social norms were found to manage their debts better than other areas with low religious social norms. In addition, individuals located in areas with higher levels of religiosity exposed themselves to less financial risk and displayed higher ethical standards (Hess, 2012). These religious values were found to play a significant role in reducing the cost of debt through constraining opportunistic behaviour of debtors even in weak legal environment (Chen et al., 2016).

Studies on religiosity and debt behaviour have also found a significant relationship between the levels of financial debts with the level of religiosity of the subjects. Those who were religious were more inclined to borrow less given the social stability accorded by their religions and the religious reprimands on negligence and default on payments (Baele et al., 2014; Berggren, 1997; Sipon et al., 2013). Incidences of over indebtedness as well are avoided due to the teachings of thrift and responsibility (Guiso et al., 2003).

Theoretically, the relationship between religion and individual behaviour could be explained by the socialization within the family that transmitted these religious values. A social network between non-religious and religious individuals enable a wider influence of religion in a society (Greeley, 1963). Sources for the knowledge regarding their debt management awareness were likely to be picked from education, experiences, friends, family and the media (Hilgert et al., 2003). Religion has also been known to be a source of their morality to shape their attitudes and behaviours (Thornton & Camburn, 1989) for the experiences for those who associated themselves with certain religion are derived mainly from their religious teachings (Kennedy & Lawton, 1998).

The association between morality and religiosity is expected to be more pronounced among the Muslims. For in Islamic teachings, there was never a contentious of the correlation between a Muslim's theological rationalization, ritualistic participation and his/her morality. The teachings of Quran itself are dotted with the directives regarding these three components and their inter-relatedness to each other (Al-Mu'minun 23: 1–11; Al-Maidah 5: 1, 9; Al-Humazah 104: 1–2).

A good Muslim is one that embraces the Islamic teachings in all aspects of his undertakings enjoining the rightful and forbidding the unlawful (Al-A'raf 7: 157; As-Sajdah 32: 18). Similarly, it has always been expected that the Muslims endeavour to be aware and informed of the religious provisions pertaining to their undertakings. The importance of religious awareness and knowledge has been adeptly summed by the Quran in various verses depicting the differences between those learned and ignorant of the religious guidelines. "Are those who know and those who do not know alike? Only the men of understanding are mindful." (Al-Zumar 39: 9), "And it does not beseem the believers that they should go forth all together; why should not then a company from every party from among them go forth that they may apply themselves to obtain understanding in religion, and that they may warn their people when they come back to them that they may be cautious?" (Al-Anfal 9: 122). Given these sacred directives, a Muslim's actions and behaviour are defined collectively by his religion or belief. The level of an individual's religiosity is predicted to have considerable impact on his life including his social, economic and financial behaviour since those who are religious shall be more inclined to observe the religious commitments. Similarly, those who were knowledgeable of the religious dictates are postulated to be more inclined to behave accordingly.

Empirically, the association of Muslims' religiosity and their social-psychological outcomes have been proven by various studies including on personality (Elias et al., 2005; Johnstone et al., 2012), well-being, health and quality of life (Sahraian et al., 2013; Tiliouine & Belgoumidi, 2009) and political attitudes (Gonzalez, 2011). A vast and growing literature has also established direct impact of Islamic teachings as mirrored by religiosity towards Muslim behaviour in multiple fields of consumer behaviour like philanthropic behaviour (Carabain & Bekkers, 2012), enviromentally friendly consumption (Islam & Chandrasekaran, 2015), advertisement of controversial products (Fam et al., 2004), purchasing decisions (Alam et al., 2011), selection of Shari'ah compliant financial services (Metawa & Almossawi, 1998; Wan Ahmad et al., 2008; Lee & Ullah, 2011), and choice of halal consumer products (Mukhtar & Butt, 2012).

Among these studies, only a few were found to have examined the debt management behaviour among Muslims. Baele et al. (2014) examining more than 150,000 loans in Pakistan over a period of two years found that default rate of conventional loans is double than the default rate of Islamic loans. This is in tandem with the Islamic principle of contractual responsibility which obliges Muslims to pay their dues. Likewise, due to restriction on excessive consumption, practising Muslim and strong believers have lower level of financial debt (Sipon et al., 2013). The direct effect of religiosity on debt acquisition, however, may not last and diminishes as the religious group become the new economic elite who often materialize their class struggles through consumption (Yeniaras, 2016) or the new generation who tread the fine line between living by the tenets of their religion with consumptive demands of the modern economy (Abdul-Muhmin, 2008).

In explaining the burgeoning household debt both at the micro and macro level, Zakaria et al. (2012) concluded that the main reason was the violation of debt principles according to Islam which abhors debt accumulation and the usage of credit to create profit. Notably, the echoes of these studies have always been the importance of the effect of the religion on the debt management behaviour of Muslim households. The result of ignorance of Islamic principles for Muslims is expected to negatively impact the relationship between debtors and lenders as Islam capitalizes on the spiritual and morality reservoir to sustain harmony and justice (Bensaid et al., 2013).

14.1 Islam and Debt Management Behaviour

Debt *(dayn)* in Arabic the preferred language of Islamic sacred texts is derived from the root verb of *dayana* similar to the word of *diin* that signifies religion of submission. The shared origins is non-accidental given the connotation of submission as well for a debtor whose debt is a liability to be fulfilled. This is the responsibility of the borrowers to repay the principle.

As a religion that considers itself as a complete guide for mankind to conduct their life, there are abundance of sacred textual evidences as well as academic literatures regarding debt and its management among the households. Most often Islam takes a negative stance against debt and encourages its disciples to avoid it as much as possible due to the heaviness of its social implications, hence, the extended liability to the hereafter. This is clearly conveyed by a hadith of Prophat (PBUH) as: "*All the sins of a Shahid (martyr) are forgiven except debt.*" (Sahih Muslim, Book 20 Hadith 4649). Even from the consumption perspective, one is urged to live within one's means and debt becomes the last financial resort to fulfil the basic needs (Farooq, 2015).

Notwithstanding this, Islam does not forbid debt in totality due to its necessity in certain scenarios of man's life. The acquisition of debt, however, should be preceded with due regard given both to the upcoming benefits and the future risks that it brings (Al-Baqarah 2:195). Debt is only allowed for fulfilling the basic necessities or for legal business ventures. Prophet (PBUH) stated: "*During the journey of Mi'raj, I saw written on the door of Jannah: The one who gives charity is rewarded tenfold. The one who gives a loan is rewarded 18 folds. I asked Jibrail: Why does the one who gives a loan get rewarded more?' Jibrail replied 'The one who gets charity (they usually have some already) and the one who seeks a loan only does so when he is in dire necessity.*" (Sunan Ibn Majah, P175) By virtue of these hadiths, it can be concluded that lenders are considered as people of rectitude as supplying financing to help those in need is a way to seek Allah's (SWT) blessing.

Various researches have examined the relationship between personal characteristics and consumption. In is a norm of today where consumers leverage on debt to purchase luxurious items and unnecessary things. Thus, debt level were found to correlate positively with consumers pleasure in spending (Livingstone & Lunt 1992) and the more materialistic a person is the more likely the relationship (Watson, 2003). Islam instils a different perspective regarding consumption and debt. Consumption on the first place is deemed not solely for the fulfilment of one's pleasure but a religious duty that encompasses the responsibility to spend for the dependants and those in needs as well as in the way of Allah SWT. The principle of moderation in consumption (Zakaria et al., 2012) and avoidance of replacing God with materials in worship (Al-Tawbah 9: 24) imply that borrowings due to consumerism in pursuit of excessive material possession has always been condemned in Islam (Belk, 1983).

Even in the sphere of the business world, Islam prohibits creditor using credit as a tool to generate profit as reflected in the basics of Islamic finance principles—the prohibition of riba—in all loan giving. The mechanics of choice are through trades and investments where debt if necessary shall be minimized or collateralized with existing or foreseeable assets and services. This is in complete contrast with the conventional view of the attainment of higher profits with higher debt leverages based on interest-based loans.

Before the formation of any debt, the prospective debtors and creditors must be aware and take the necessary measures against the perceived risk of default and fraud. The Quran encourages the documentation of the loan agreement and when necessary to be furnished with witnesses and collaterals as security (Al-Baqarah 2: 282–3). Once the debt is acquired, more diligent and conscientious principles have been outlined regarding the settlement and extension of debt.

Of utmost importance is the responsibility to pay the debt as pledged. The borrower has a moral and contractual obligation to repay the loan. The *Qur'an* says, "O ye who believe! When ye deal with each other, fulfil what has been promised. The Quran even advocates the urgency to pay off a deceased's debt prior to the disbursement of his wealth to the heirs" (Quran 4: 11). Moreover, the fulfilment of the obligation itself is promised with blessings from the God. A tradition of the prophet Muhammad

(PBUH) says, "Whoever takes people's money (by debt) with the intention of paying it back, God will pay it back on his behalf and whoever takes it with the intention of usurping it, God will destroy him" (Al-Bukhari, 1984).

In Islam, defaulting debtors who have no source of payment (the *gharim*) are entitled a share from the *Bait ul M'al* (Bensaid, et al. 2013). The verse 60 of Surah Al-Tawbah in Qur'an explained it very well. Another striking dictate is the commendation to act with kindness and charity towards those in financial distress. The Quran states, "If the debtor is in distress, then let there be postponement until he is in ease" (Al-Baqarah 2: 280). A creditor that forgoes his right is considered performing a recommendable and praise-worthy action. This is exemplified by a tradition narrated by Abu Qatadah that Prophet Muhammad stated, "That person who desires that Allah relieves him of difficulty and worry on the Day of Judgement, let him grant respite or forgive a debtor." (Al-Naysaburi, 1967).

Amidst the above discourse and considerations, the study hypothesizes that religiosity is an important predictive factor of positive debt payment behaviour among Muslims. We postulate that those who are religious shall be more reluctant to take debt beyond their capabilities and are always prudent in ensuring a timely payment of any debt due as mandated by the religion. Our expectation is that those who are highly religious would have higher religious values, thus, are more inclined to demonstrate higher awareness and more religious compliant orientation in their debt management behaviour. For being religious means a person who submit wholly and comprehensively his being and conducts to a divine God.

Drawing on a sample of 757 urbanite respondents from employed Muslims that live in Kuala Lumpur, the study examines the impact of religiosity on debt management behaviour. In achieving this, the paper is structured as follows. The first few sections dealt with the statistics on the Malaysian household debt and the proposed measures for the households to manage their debts both in contemporary works and the Islamic teachings and literatures. The proceeding sections deal with the data and methodology used in developing and testing the religiosity, debt awareness and debt management scales. The later part discusses the findings and the conclusion of the study.

This study advances the consumer financial behaviour literature in three important ways. First, we examined the role of religiosity as a mean to predict customers with positive debt management behaviour in which measurements of religiosity that are compatible to Muslims were employed. Secondly, our contribution to understanding positive debt management behaviour is not limited to their religiosity levels but also through investigating whether or not consumers are influenced by their religious teachings in the decisions made related to their debts. And thirdly, we also examined the relationship between having positive debt management behaviour and other socio-economic variables such as age, marital status, education level and household income. For behaviours relating to debt management were also known to be influenced by one's surroundings and environment.

Data and Methodology

Data for this study were working age Malaysian Muslims living in the city of Kuala Lumpur and its suburbs. Malaysia is a country where about 60% of the population are Muslims and by default Islam is the religion of the Malays which are the dominant Bumiputras (the original settlers). The respondents were selected by purposive sampling methods to provide a wide range of subjects' differences in socio-economic variables particularly gender, marital status, highest level of education and monthly household income.

The questionnaires were self-administered by appointed and trained enumerators over a three weeks period, thus, only about three percent of the questionnaires were withdrawn from analysis due to the missing values and outliers.

14.2 Religiosity Measurement

Studies on Muslims' religiosity and behaviour have adopted multiple measures of religiosity whether based on the psychological orientation of the subject matters or the theological aspects of the religion. For this study, we chose to adopt the scales developed by Wan Ahmad et al. (2008), Tiliouine and Belgoumidi (2009) with slight modifications. These scales were developed based on the assumptions that Islam is a religion that composes three main components of faith, law and guideline as well as morality. Thus, the Islamic religiosity scale encompasses constructs representing the dogmatic and practical aspects as well as the moral and ethical values promoted by Islamic teachings.

Principal Component Factor Analysis was used to test for validity and reliability of the religiosity measures adopted. Correlation matrix revealed the presence of many coefficients of 0.3 and above. The Kaiser–Meyer–Olkin value was 0.835 exceeding the recommended value of 0.6 (Kaiser & Rice, 1974). The factor loading of each item was positive and ranged between 0.551 and 0.865. The factor analysis confirmed that four significant dimensions can be derived from the twenty two constructs examined where almost 58.0% of the total variance was explained by nineteen of the extracted factors. The four dimensions results confirmed the 4-factor model introduced by Wan Ahmad et al. (2008) representing the three main components of Islamic teachings. The practical aspect or participatory religious commitments were further divided into obligatory and optional participation in congruent with the Islamic rituals some of which are mandatory in nature while others are recommendable. These results can be accepted as proof for the validity of the items, and thus, of the scale. The internal consistency reliability of the measures were indicated by the high Cronbach's Alpha ranging from 0.701 to 0.829 for each dimensions. This result suggested that the inner consistency of the scale was high as well.

Based on equal percentiles of the scores of religiosity, we further divided the respondents into three layer variables. Individuals who scored more frequently are classified in the high religiosity category, followed by moderate and low religiosity categories. The decomposition should further throw lights on the relationship between religiosity and debt management behaviour (Table 14.1).

Table 14.1 Confirmation of the dimensions of religiosity

Factors	Constructs	Loadings
Religious Faith *Reliability (0.805)* *Average variance extracted (1.779)* *Composite reliability (0.878)*	I believe in Allah	0.757
	"Islam is the way of life"	0.860
	"*Qura'nic* teachings are applicable in today's life"	0.865
	"Rasulullah's traditions are applicable all times"	0.786
	"All deeds will be judged and rewarded accordingly after death"	0.551
Religious Participation (Obligatory) *Reliability (0.756)* *Average variance extracted (1.120)* *Composite reliability (0.817)*	"I pray five times a day"	0.729
	"I fast the whole of Ramadhan"	0.763
	"I pay zakat *fitrah* every year"	0.633
	"I make sure that my dressing covers my *aurat*"	0.634
	"I avoid food that are forbidden by my religion"	0.671
Religious Participation (Optional) *Reliability (0.701)* *Average variance extracted (0.800)* *Composite reliability (0.761)*	"I go to mosque to pray"	0.782
	"I give religious charity"	0.714
	"I read *Qur'an* and perform *zikr*"	0.654
Religious Behaviour *Reliability (0.829)* *Average variance extracted (1.530)* *Composite reliability (0.859)*	"I am honest at all times"	0.685
	"I worry if cannot pay debt on time"	0.702
	"I fulfil all that I promise"	0.794
	"I care about neighbours and their wellbeing"	0.720
	"I advise others to do perform good and avoid evil deeds"	0.749
	"I visit my family/friend when they are bed ridden"	0.598
Reliability (0.836) *Average variance extracted (5.187)* *Composite reliability (0.954)*		

14.3 Measurements for Debt Management Awareness and Behaviour

From the above literatures, the study identified seven Islamic principles regarding debt acquisition and management as illustrated in Table 14.2 below. Likert scale of 4 ranging from strongly do not agree to strongly agree was employed to measure the respondents' awareness of the main Islamic principles regarding debt. Recorded reliability score for the scales at 0.495 was below the recommended level but this was compensated by the extant Islamic religious dictates on debt management behaviour above.

In measuring the actual debt management behaviour of the respondents, similar items were used but with slight modifications to capture the actual behaviour. Likert scale of 4 ranging from never to always was employed to test originally 6 items. However, due to the low corrected item-total correlation value for the recoded construct of 'I have taken interest (riba)', this item was dropped from the scale. The remaining 5-items scale as shown in Table 14.3 reported a Cronbach alpha coefficient as 0.744 indicating good internal consistency, thus, was considered acceptable.

Table 14.2 Mean and standard deviation of awareness about Islamic religious dictates regarding debt management

	Mean	Std. deviation
Paying debt is religious obligation	3.592	0.610
It is not a sin if I choose not to pay even if can afford to pay (−)	2.805	1.075
It is sinful if I purposely choose not to settle a debt	3.434	0.743
Paying debt on time is a religious obligation	3.237	0.723
For a delayed debt, I can be charged an interest by lender (−)	2.535	0.911
It is compulsory on debtor to pay interest on late payment charge (−)	2.225	0.785
Creditor has a right to waive my debt	3.119	0.665

Table 14.3 Mean and standard deviation of actual debt management behaviour

	Mean	Std. deviation
I failed to pay my debt on time (−)	3.176	0.690
I pay my debt on time	3.320	0.687
I know when my debt is due	3.496	0.634
I would only take debt if know can pay on time	3.412	0.711
I would only take debt if can afford to pay only	3.512	0.678

14.4 Findings

The variations of the respondents were as illustrated in Table 14.4. Given that the respondents were chosen among those who were working and had at least an outstanding debt with a financial institution, the majority of them were holders of at least a bachelor degree and earned a monthly income of more than RM3,000.

Analyses of significant differences of the means of the demographic variables showed no significant differences between males ($n = 319$) and females ($n = 419$) in both their awareness of religious dictates ($t = 0.295$) and actual debt management behaviour ($t = 191$). Similar non-significant results were also recorded for the means between those who were single and married. On the other hands, results of one way ANOVA for highest level of education, monthly household income and level of religiosity showed significant mean differences at the $p < 0.05$ level as illustrated in Table 14.4 above. Further examination through Post-hoc comparisons using Tukey

Table 14.4 Profiles of respondents and the significant differences of their awareness of religious debt dictates and actual debt management behaviour

		Awareness of religious dictates			Actual debt management behaviour		
	N	Mean	SD%	Mean statistic	Mean	SD%	Mean statistics
Gender							
Male	319	2.975	2.975	t = 0.295	3.357	2.413	t = 0.191
Female	419	3.006	2.677		3.403	2.386	
Marital status							
Single	305	3.024	2.846	t = 0.067	3.346	2.441	t = 0.079
Married/Divorced/Widowed	433	2.970	2.719		3.409	2.362	
Highest education							
Secondary level	44	2.935	2.601	F = 0.018*	3.341	2.502	F = 0.007*
Certificate/Diploma	169	2.934	2.765		3.304	2.585	
Bachelor Degree	380	2.996	2.768		3.383	2.297	
Master/PhD	145	3.069	2.797		3.490	2.327	
Monthly household income							
Below RM3,000	207	3.023	2.837	F = 0.000*	3.325	2.624	F = 0.000*
RM3,000—RM5,999	192	2.886	2.476		3.363	2.271	
RM6,000—RM8,999	164	2.937	2.785		3.340	2.517	
RM9,000 and above	175	3.124	2.733		3.515	2.007	
Religiosity							
Low	247	2.899	2.451	F = 0.000*	3.206	2.389	F = 0.000*
Moderate	249	3.033	2.903		3.410	2.326	
High	242	3.045	2.850		3.536	2.191	

Table 14.5 Significant mean differences from Tukey HSD Post Hoc tests

	Awareness of religious dictates	*Actual debt management behaviour*
	Significant mean difference at 0.05 level	
Highest education level		
Certificate/Diploma—Master/PhD	−0.944	-0.928
Household income		
(Below RM3,000)—(RM3,000 - RM5,999)	0.962	
(Below RM3,000)—(RM9,000 and above)		−0.954
(RM3,000—RM5,999)—(RM9,000 and above)	−1.665	−0.765
(RM6,000—RM8,999)—(RM9,000 and above)	−1.308	−0.876
Religiosity		
Low—Moderate	−0.938	−1.020
Low—High	−1.023	−1.645
Moderate—High		−0.625

HSD revealed that the significant mean differences materialized as the respondents received higher education, earned higher income and were more religious (See Table 14.5).

The impact of religiosity on debt management behaviour was further highlighted by the correlation coefficients between awareness of religious debt dictates, actual debt management behaviour and the four dimensions of religiosity. The positive debt management awareness and behaviour were found to be significantly correlated with religious faith, obligatory religious participation and religious behaviour of the respondents (Table 14.6).

Hierarchical Multiple Regression

Hierarchical multiple regression was used to assess the ability of religiosity to predict the debt management behaviour of Muslims. Preliminary analyses were conducted to ensure no violation of the assumptions of normality, linearity, multicollinearity and homoscedasticity. Religiosity as presented by all four dimensions of religiosity as extracted by the factor analysis as shown in Model 1 below explained almost 18% of the variance in debt management behaviour. The variance increased by 5.3% when the Awareness of Religious Debt Dictates was entered into the model. All of the measures in the final model were statistically significant, with Optional Religious Participation Scale recording the highest value ($beta = -0.279$, $p < 0.000$) followed by Religious Behaviour Scale ($beta = 0.263$, $p < 0.000$) (Tables 14.7 and 14.8).

Table 14.6 Pearson product-moment correlations between actual debt management behaviour, awareness of religious debt dictates and dimensions of religiosity

		DMB	RDD	RF	ObRP	OpRP	RB
DMB	Pearson correlation	1					
	Sig. (2-tailed)						
RDD	Pearson correlation	0.304**	1				
	Sig. (2-tailed)	0.000					
RF	Pearson correlation	0.181**	145**	1			
	Sig. (2-tailed)	0.000	0.000				
ObRP	Pearson correlation	0.252**	0.164**	0.189**	1		
	Sig. (2-tailed)	0.000	0.000	0.000			
OpRP	Pearson correlation	0.21	0.059	0.107**	0.436**	1	
	Sig. (2-tailed)	0.288	0.056	0.002	0.000		
RB	Pearson correlation	0.333**	0.125**	0.136**	0.355**	0.401**	1
	Sig. (2-tailed)	0.000	0.000	0.000	0.000	0.000	

** Correlation is significant at the 0.01 level (2-tailed)
Note DBM—Actual Debt Management Behaviour, RDD—Awareness about Religious Debt Dictate, RF—Religious Faith, ObRP—Obligatory Religious Participation, OpRP—Optional Religious Participation and RB—Religious Behaviour

Table 14.7 Model summary for actual debt management behaviour

Model	R	R square	Adjusted R square	Std. error of the estimate	R square change	Change statistics			Sig. F change	Durbin-Watson
						F Change	df1	df2		
1	0.423[a]	0.179	0.174	2.180	0.179	39.898	4	733	0.000	
2	0.481[b]	0.232	0.226	2.110	0.053	50.355	1	732	0.000	1.812

[a] Predictors: (Constant), Religious Belief, Obligatory Religious Participation, Optional Religious Participation and Religious Behaviour
[b] Predictors: (Constant), Religious Belief, Obligatory Religious Participation, Optional Religious Participation, Religious Behaviour and Awareness about Religious Debt Dictate
Dependent Variable: Actual Debt Management Behaviour

14.5 Conclusion

Undoubtedly, increases in debt taking have significant impact on economies and household spending. The growth in debt taking especially when becomes uncontrollable creates pockets of financial vulnerabilities in the society. Even if the profitability of the financial institutions depends much on successfully attracting customers to borrow, adverse selection due to asymmetric of information could create unnecessary losses through loan defaults. As such, it becomes necessary for the financial providers to look into the quality of the loan applicants.

Table 14.8 Beta coefficient summary for actual debt management behaviour

Model		Unstandardized coefficients		Standardized coefficients	T	p-value	Collinearity statistics	
		B	Std. error	Beta			Tolerance	VIF
1	(Constant)	3.854	1.602		2.406	0.016		
	RF	0.274	0.078	0.120	3.505	0.000	0.959	1.043
	ObRP	0.260	0.049	0.206	5.337	0.000	0.756	1.323
	OpRP	−0.293	0.053	−0.214	−5.502	0.000	0.740	1.351
	RB	0.279	0.032	0.330	8.785	0.000	0.796	1.257
2	(Constant)	1.721	1.580		1.089	0.276		
	RF	0.213	0.076	0.093	2.797	0.005	0.947	1.056
	ObRP	0.220	0.047	0.174	4.636	0.000	0.745	1.342
	OpRP	−0.279	0.052	−0.204	−5.407	0.000	0.739	1.353
	RB	0.263	0.031	0.311	8.540	0.000	0.791	1.264
	DebtDic	0.203	0.029	0.235	7.096	0.000	0.954	1.048

The chapter offers significant theoretical implications through highlighting the importance of religiosity in influencing debt management behaviour of consumers. Religiosity, as measured by the religiosity scale as well as represented by the awareness regarding Islamic religious dictates on debt management behaviour were shown to have significant influences on the likelihood of positive debt management behaviour of the respondents. This finding provides additional inputs in substantiating the distinction between the impacts of Muslims with high and low religiosity and their debt management behaviour as confirmed by previous literature. For customers with high religiosity were found to be more likely to pay their debt on time and do not delay when the debt is expected to be paid. The study also confirms that the impacts of demographic factors especially education, and monthly household income should not be taken lightly in assessing customers' creditability.

Furthermore, the results from this study could provide the financial service providers with additional information for customers' loan score card decision. As religiosity clearly contributed to the debt management behaviour, the practical implication here is that loan assessment by the financial service providers should consider to include religiosity and the applicants' understanding of the religious debt dictates as part of the score marks to determine their eligibility to be awarded with loans. Consequently as well, it would be recommendable that the financial service providers to put some efforts in adding the religious dictates regarding debt in their promotional materials. For awareness of these dictates among Muslims could avoid to some extent the unwanted negative debt defaults.

References

Abdul-Muhmin, A. G. (2008). Consumer attitudes towards debt in an Islamic country: Managing a conflict between religious tradition and modernity? *International Journal of Consumer Studies, 32*, 194–203.

Agensi Kaunseling dan Pengurusan Kredit (AKPK) (2011). Power! Pengurusan Wang Ringgit Anda, Kuala Lumpur, pp. 24–37.

Alam, S. S., Mohd, R., Hisham, B. (2011). Is religiosity an important determinant on Muslim consumer behaviour in Malaysia? *Journal of Islamic Marketing, 2*(1), 83–96

Alfaro, R., & Gallardo, N. (2012). The determinants of household debt default. *Revista De Analisis Economico, 27*(1), 55–70.

Al-Naysaburi, M. (1967), Sahih Muslim, translated by Siddiqi, A.H., Sh Muhammad Ashraf, Lahore.

Al-Qazwini, M. (n.d.), *Sunan Ibn Majah.* Cairo: Isa al-Babi al-Halabi.

Baele, L., Farooq, M., & Ongena, S. (2014). Of religion and redemption: Evidence from default on Islamic loans. *Journal of Banking and Finance, 44*, 141–159.

Bank Negara Malaysia. (2016). *Financial Stability and Payment Systems Report 2016*, Kuala Lumpur.

Barua, A. (2015). Malaysia: On the path of fiscal reform. In I. Kalish, R. Majumdar, A. Barua, & L. Gunnion (Eds.), *Asia Pacific Economic Outlook—1st Quarter 2015* Deloitte University Press: United Kingdom

Bensaid, B., Grine, F., Mohd Nor, M. R., & Mohd Yusoff, M. Y. Z. (2013). Enduring financial debt: An Islamic perspective. *Middle-East Journal of Scientific Research, 13*(2), 162–170.

Berggren, N. (1997). Rhetoric or reality. An economic analysis of the effect of religion in Sweden. *Journal of Socio-Econmics, 26*(6), 571–596.

Canner, G. B., & Luckett, C. A. (1990). Consumer debt repayment woes: Insights from a household survey. *Journal of Retail Banking, 12*, 55–62.

Carabain, C. L., & Bekkers, R. (2012). Explaining differences in philanthropic behavior between Christians, Muslims, and Hindus in the Netherlands. *Review of Religious Research, 53*(4), 419–440.

Charpe, M., & Flaschel, P. (2013). Workers' debt, default and the diversity of financial fragilities. *Structural Change and Economic Dynamics, 27*, 48–65.

Chen, H., Huang, H. H., Lobo, G. J., & Wang, C. (2016). Religiosity and the cost of debt. *Journal of Banking and Finance, 70*, 70–85.

Conroy, S. T., & Emerson, T. L. N. (2004). Business ethics and religion: Religiosity as a predictor of ethical awareness among students. *Journal of Business Ethics, 50*(4), 383–392.

Debelle, G. (2004). Macroeconomic implications of rising household debt, BIS Working Paper, No. 153. http://www.bis.org/publ/work153.htm

Demyanyk, Y., & Hemert, O. V. (2011). Understanding the subprime mortgage crisis. *The Review of Financial Studies, 24*(6), 1848–1880.

Department of Statistics Malaysia (DOSM). (2012). *Household Income and Basic Amenities Survey Report 2012.*

Duygan-Bump, B., & Grant, C. (2009). Household debt repayment behaviour: What role do institutions play? *Economic Policy, 24*(57), 108–140.

Elias, N., Awang, A., & Mahmood Nazar, M. (2005). Examining religiosity and its relationship to self-control, procrastination and academic achievement. *Malaysian Journal of Learning and Instruction, 2*, 1–16.

Fam, K. S., Waller, D. S. & Erdogan, B. Z. (2004). The influence of religion on attitudes towards the advertising of controversial products. *European Journal of Marketing, 38*(5/6), 537–555.

Farooq, M. O. (2015). Islamic finance and debt culture: Treading the conventional path? *International Journal of Social Economics, 42*(12), 1168–1195.

Gonzalez, A. L. (2011). Measuring religiosity in a majority Muslim context: Gender, religious salience, and religious experience among Kuwaiti college students—A research note. *Journal for the Scientific Study of Religion, 50*(2), 339–350.
Grafova, I. B. (2007). Your money or your life: Managing money, managing health. *Journal of Family and Economic Issues, 28*, 285–303.
Greeley, A. M. (1963). A note on the origins of religious differences. *Journal for the Scientific Study of Religion, 3*(1), 21–31.
Guiso, L., Sapienza, P., Zingales, L., et al. (2003). People's opium? Religion and economic attitudes. *Journal of Monetary Economics, 50*(1), 225–282.
Hess, D. W. (2012). The impact of religiosity on personal financial decisions. *Journal of Religion and Society, 14*, 1–13.
Hilgert, M. A., Hogart, J. M., & Beverly, S. G. (2003). Household financial management: The connection between knowledge and behaviour. *Federal Reserve Bulletin, 89*(7), 309–322.
Hull, L. (2003). Financial deregulation and household indebtedness. *Reserve Bank of New Zealand Discussion Paper No. DP2003/01.*
Islam, T., & Chandrasekaran, U. (2015). Religiosity and ecologically conscious consumption behaviour. *Asian Journal of Business Research, 5*(2), 18–30.
Johnstone, B., Yoon, D. P., Cohen, D., Schopp, L. H., McCormack, G., Campbell, J., & Smith, M. (2012). Relationships among spirituality, religious practices, personality factors, and health for five different faith traditions. *Journal of Religion and Health, 51*(4), 1017–1041.
Kaiser, H. F., & Rice, J. (1974). Little Jiffy, Mark IV. *Journal of Educational and Psychological Measurement, 34*(1), 111–117.
Kennedy, E. J., & Lawton, L. (1998). Religiousness and business ethics. *Journal of Business Ethics, 17*(2), 163–175.
Khazanah Research Institute (KRI). (2016). *The State of Households II*, Kuala Lumpur.
Korean Financial Services Commission. (2015). Household Debt management Measures, July 22, Retrieved February 17, 2017, from http://www.fsc.go.kr/eng/new_contact/150722_household_debt_management_measures.pdf.
Lee, K., & Ullah, S. (2011). Customers' attitude toward Islamic banking in Pakistan. *International Journal of Islamic and Middle Eastern Finance and Management, 4*(2), 131–146
Livingstone, S. M., & Lunt, P. K. (1992). Predicting personal debt and debt repayment: Psychological, social and economic determinants. *Journal of Economic Psychology, 13*(1), 111–134.
Metawa, S. A., & Almossawi, M. (1998). Banking behavior of Islamic bank customers: Perspectives and implications. *International Journal of Bank Marketing, 16*(7), 299–313.
Mian, A., & Sufi, A. (2010). Household leverage and the recession of 2007–09. *IMF Economic Review, 58*(1), 74–117.
Moorman, D. C., & Garasky, S. (2008). Consumer debt repayment behavior as a precursor to bankruptcy. *Journal of Family Economic Issues, 29*, 219–233.
Mukhtar, A., & Butt, M. M. (2012). Intention to choose halal products: The role of religiosity. *Journal of Islamic Marketing, 3*, 108–120.
Sahraian, A., Gholami, A., Javadpour, A., & Omidvar, B. (2013). Association between religiosity and happiness among a group of Muslim undergraduate students. *Journal of Religion and Health, 52*(2), 450–453.
Sipon, S., Othman, K., Abd Ghani, Z., and Mohd Radzi, H. (2013). The impact of religiosity on financial debt and debt stress. *Procedia—Social and Behavioral Sciences, 140*, 300–306.
Szivos, P., Bernat, A., & Koszeghy, L. (2011). Managing household debt: Hungarian country report, TARKI Social Research Institute, Budapest, pp. 12–25.
Thornton, A., & Camburn, D. (1989). Religious participation and adolescent sexual behavior and attitudes. *Journal of Marriage and Family, 51*(3), 641–653.
Tiliouine, H., & Belgoumidi, A. (2009). An exploratory study of religiosity, meaning in life and subjective wellbeing in Muslim students in Algeria. *Applied Research Quality Life, 4*, 109–127.

Wan Ahmad, W. M., Ab Rahman, A., Che Seman, A., & Ali, N. A. (2008). Religiosity and banking selection criteria among Malays in Lembah Klang. *Jurnal Syariah, 16*(2), 99–130.
Wang, L., & Lv, W. (2011). The impact of attitude variables on the credit debt behavior. *Nankai Business Review International, 2*(2), 120–139.
Watson, J. J. (2003). The relationship of materialism to spending tendencies, saving, and debt. *Journal of Economic Psychology, 24*(6), 723–739.
Worthington, E. L., Jr., Wade, N. G., Hight, T. L., Ripley, J. S., McCullough, M. E., Berry, J. W., et al. (2003). The religious commitment inventory—10: Development, refinement, and validation of a brief scale for research and counseling. *Journal of Counseling Psychology, 50*, 84–96.
Yeniaras, V. (2016). Unpacking the relationship between materialism, status consumption and attitude to debt: The role of Islamic religiosity. *Journal of Islamic Marketing, 7* (2), 232–247.
Zakaria, R. H., Abdul Kader, R., Mohd Jaafar, N. I., & Marican, S. (2012). Burgeoning household debt: An Islamic economic perspective. *Middle-East Journal of Scientific Research, 12*(9), 1182–1189.

Wan Marhaini Wan Ahmad Ph.D. is currently a Senior Lecturer at the Department of Finance, Faculty of Business and Economics, Universiti Malaya, Malaysia. She obtained her Bachelor of Syariah (Hon.) from the Universiti Malaya, Kuala Lumpur. Further, she acquired her Master in Economics from the International Islamic University Malaysia and a doctoral degree in Islamic Finance from the University of Edinburgh, Scotland. She also holds a Certificate of Shari'ah Advisory from the Association of Shari'ah Advisors Malaysia. She has been a member of Shari'ah Advisory Panel for several local Islamic financial institutions and a registered Shari'ah Advisor for the Malaysian Islamic Capital Market. Her main research interests are Islamic finance, waqf and zakat. She has written, reviewed and edited articles and books as well as has more than two decades of experiences teaching and supervising students' works in these areas.

Dr. Asmak Ab Rahman Ph.D. is currently an Associate Professor at the Department of Shari'ah and Economics, Academy of Islamic Studies, University of Malaya. Her areas of specialization are Takaful, Islamic Economics, Islamic Law and Waqf. She has been teaching at the University of Malaya since 2005. Dr. Asmak has published a few books (which also includes chapters in books) and she has also published some of her works in the internationally recognized refereed journals such as Arab Law Quarterly, Humanomics, Journal of Islamic Marketing, International Journal of Islamic and Middle Eastern Finance and Management and Jurnal Syariah, She has presented papers at local and several international conferences. She has been awarded a number of government and university research funds as a principal investigator and co-investigator such as LRGS, FRGS and UMRG.

Azizi Che Seman is a Senior Lecturer at the Department of Shari'ah and Economics, Academy of Islamic Studies, Universiti Malaya. Topics of his research include Islamic transactions, Islamic economics and finance. He has a long involvement in the Islamic financial industry as Shari'ah committee in various Islamic financial institutions in Malaysia, namely Bank Muamalat, Agrobank and Sun Life Takaful, besides other institutions Islamic financial industry.

Chapter 15
Prospects and Challenges for Islamic Investment and Wealth Management in Mauritius

Salma Sairally and Najmul Hussein Rassool

Mauritius, a small island in the Indian ocean, is evolving into an important international investment and wealth management centre (Rassool, 2011). It is ranked seventh among the top-ten financial centres in the Middle East and Africa and 64th among global financial centres (Z-Yen and China Development Institute, 2020). It is also classified as an 'evolving centre' along with other financial centres such as Malta, Cape Town and Isle of Man by the Global Financial Centres Index 27 (Z-Yen and China Development Institute, 2020). Mauritius' geographical position makes it an ideal platform for doing business with the rest of the world. Overtime, the jurisdiction has grown to be recognised as a trusted international financial centre (IFC), compliant with international standards of good governance, transparency and taxation.

While the jurisdiction boasts a sophisticated and unparalleled platform for cross-border investments, it recognizes that no IFC can be complete without the offerings of Islamic finance. To complement the existing products and services of the Mauritius IFC, therefore, the government has taken a number of initiatives since 2007 with respect to regulations, tax, and overall policies to facilitate the development of the Islamic banking and finance industry. A few Islamic investment and wealth management (IIWM) products have been launched in the country with the aim to attract both local and foreign investors.

After more than a decade of the country's initiatives to broaden its array of financial services to encompass Islamic banking and finance, the following questions are asked:

What are the Islamic investment offerings offered so far in Mauritius?
What are the prospects for structuring Shari'ah-compliant investment and wealth management vehicles and products in the jurisdiction?

S. Sairally (✉) · N. H. Rassool
Kuala Lumpur, Malaysia
e-mail: salma.sairally@yahoo.com

T. Azid et al. (eds.), *Wealth Management and Investment in Islamic Settings*,
https://doi.org/10.1007/978-981-19-3686-9_15

What are the challenges and opportunities of positioning Mauritius as an IIWM destination?
How can Mauritius brighten its future as an IIWM platform?

So far, studies on the development of the Islamic finance industry in Mauritius have mainly focused on the Islamic banking component, examining patronage behaviour and bank criteria (e.g., Ramdhony, 2013; Abduh and Ramjaun, 2015; Abduh et al., 2018; Omran et al., 2018), prospects and challenges (e.g., Lallmahamood, 2014; Rassool, 2018), governance and financial reporting (Beebeejaun, 2020), and legal and regulatory aspects (e.g., Joharris, 2012; Mooneeram-Chadee, 2020). There is limited research carried out within the Islamic capital market segment, specifically on the positioning of Mauritius as an IIWM centre. Past researches, mainly short magazine articles, have focused on the attractive location of Mauritius to develop Shari'ah-compliant products such as Shari'ah-compliant trusts, funds, sukuk (Islamic investment certificates), and others (Uteem, 2009; Rassool, 2011; Tamano, 2020).

This chapter seeks to contribute to the literature on Islamic finance, especially in the IIWM area, by studying the case of a small island offshore jurisdiction such as Mauritius which has ventured into Islamic financial services in view of its ambition to develop into a worldclass financial services hub. To undertake the study, first, a literature-based analysis of current and potential offerings of IIWM products and services is carried out. Second, a survey structured on open-ended questions has been conducted in the first quarter of 2020 among professionals and academics to gauge their views on the challenges and opportunities for IIWM in Mauritius. The respondents included representatives from the regulators, operators, legal practitioners and academics. Based on the literature and survey analysis and the authors' own experience of Islamic finance in Mauritius, recommendations for a brighter future of the Mauritius jurisdiction as an IIWM centre are suggested.

15.1 Mauritius as an International Financial Centre

Mauritius emerged as an IFC in the 1990s and since, it has developed as a specialist IFC of substance, integrity and excellence. The Mauritius IFC has been built upon three core areas of specialisation: "cross-border investments and related fund administration activities; cross-border corporate banking; and private banking and wealth management" (FSC Mauritius, 2018). The jurisdiction is reputed for domiciling and routing funds into Asia and Africa, particularly India and China (Ocra Worldwide Mauritius, n.d.). It is today gearing up its strategy to attract more African funds in its domicile and establish holding structures for African foreign direct investments as the African continent seeks funding from global investors for its development and expansion (Rassool, 2011).

The country offers several advantages as an offshore centre for fund structuring and administration, including a substantial network of 46 double taxation avoidance agreements (DTAAs) (including 15 with African states), a growing number of "Investment Promotion and Protection Agreements" (IPPAs) with key emerging markets, cost-efficient professional services, as well as a robust legal and regulatory framework (EDB Mauritius, n.d.; Mauritius Revenue Authority, 2020). Mauritius also follows best practices in terms of good governance, transparency and ethics. Its legal system is mostly based on British common law and, to some extent, the French Napoleonic Code, although banking and commercial practices fall under British common law (Domaingue, 2002; EDB Mauritius, n.d.).

Table 15.1 shows the accolades earned by Mauritius as compared to international benchmarks. Other measures were taken to enhance and facilitate a sustainable business environment, such as the establishment of "the Competition Commission of Mauritius in 2009 and the Mauritius International Arbitration Centre Limited" in collaboration with the London Court of International Arbitration in 2010.

Table 15.1 Mauritius' accolades vis-à-vis international benchmarks

No.	Index	Global rank	Africa rank
1.	World Bank Doing Business 2020	13 out of 190 countries	1st
2.	Global Competitiveness Index 2019—World Economic Forum	54 out of 140 countries	1st
3.	Corruption Perceptions Index 2019—Transparency International	52 out of 180 countries	3rd
4.	International Property Rights Index 2019	40 out of 128 countries	1st
5.	Mo Ibrahim Index of African Governance 2019	–	1st
6.	Press Freedom Index 2019—Reporters without Borders	58 out of 180 countries	5th
7.	The A.T. Kearney Global Services Location Index 2019	30 out of 50 countries	2nd
8.	2018 Index of Economic Freedom—Heritage Foundation	25 out of 180 countries	1st
9.	Economic Freedom of the World 2019—Fraser Institute	8 out of 162 countries	1st
10.	Human Development Index 2019	66 out of 188 countries	2nd
11.	Democracy Index 2019—The Economist Intelligence Unit—Full Democracy	17 out of 167 countries	1st
15.	Mercer's 2019 Quality of Living Survey	83 out of 230 countries	1st
19.	Forbes Survey of Best Countries for Business 2019	39 out of 161 countries	1st
20.	The Travel and Tourism Competitiveness 2019	54 out of 136 countries	1st
21.	Social Progress Index 2019	44 out of 149 countries	1st

Source EDB Mauritius (2020)

The investment sector is backed by 51 Investment dealers who execute clients' orders and 335 Investment Advisors who provide advice on securities transactions to clients as of 30 June 2018. As of 30 June 2018, there were five investment banking license holders. The number of Authorised Funds as at 30 June 2018 stands at 1024, of which are 495 "Collective Investment Schemes" and 529 "Closed-end Funds" (FSC, 2019).

During the period 2008–2018, Mauritius ranked at the top in the African continent for HNWIs, with a growth in total wealth held of 124% (Afrasia, 2019). The growth is likely to continue over the next decade, with an expected increase of more than 100%. On the worldwide wealth market for the period 2008–2018, Mauritius is the second-fastest-growing wealth market worldwide, following China (Afrasia, 2019). Over and above, there are some other benefits, for example permanent residence permit to non-citizen investors (minimum of US$500,000), relatively low tax incentive, ownership rights, low corporate and personal income tax, five year tax holidays and necessary framework to protect the interests of foreign investors, etc.

To complement the existing products and services of the Mauritius' IFC, the government has taken several bold initiatives since 2007 concerning regulations, tax and overall policies to facilitate the development of the Islamic banking and finance industry in the country.

15.2 Historical Development of Islamic Finance in Mauritius

According to Lallmahamood (2014), the history of Islamic finance in Mauritius dates back to 1871 when Muslim traders contracted a partnership with some non-Muslims' group who faced economic problems. At that time, the banking system was not well established and the Muslims had surplus funds that were available for investment. In the modern age, there have been more recent developments of Islamic finance in the country, as discussed in the subsequent paragraphs.

i. ***Industry Initiatives***

The earliest initiative to provide Islamic financial services facilities to Muslims was in the form of an Islamic cooperative set up in 1998, as reflected in Table 15.2.

ii. ***Islamic Investment Offerings***

As indicated in Table 15.2, a few Islamic investment offerings have been initiated in Mauritius, in the form of both short and long term *sukuk* (Islamic investment certificates), Islamic funds (equity and *sukuk*), equity investment, and *takaful* contribution investment. To facilitate Islamic investment, laws and regulations have been amended on a piecemeal basis to meet the requirements of the market (as shown in Table 15.3). The Finance Act 2008 allows global investments and Shari'ah-compliant funds. The domiciliation of the fund in Mauritius is the result of government's

Table 15.2 Industry initiatives in the development of Islamic banking and finance

Year	Institution	Details	Remarks
1998	Al Barakah Multi-Purpose Co-operative Society Limited	Islamic cooperative opened to Muslims only	*Hajj* Savings, *Mudarabah*, *Musharakah*, *Murabahah*, *Istina*, *Qard*
1999	Authorized Long-term Ethical Equity Fund Ltd	Ethical Mutual Fund	Open-ended Fund
2007	International Islamic Financial Services Ltd (IIFS)	The first Consulting, Advisory, and Training firm in Islamic Banking & Finance	Set up by Najmul Hussein Rassool—Owner & CEO
2008	British American Insurance	The launching of a *Takaful* Unit-Linked product	
2009	HSBC, in collaboration with HSBC Amanah	Launching of an Islamic banking window	Current Account & Term Investment Account targeting offshore investors
2009	The Mauritius Leasing Co	The launching of *Ijarah*	*Ijarah* (leasing) was offered, including both operational and financial lease
2010	Tata Asset Management (Mauritius) Private Limited	Tata Indian Shari'ah Equity Fund	Investment in Shari'ah compliant equity listed Indian Companies
2011	Century Banking Corporation	Licensed as a full-fledged Islamic bank	Initially Qatari & local investors
2011	HSBC	Distribution of Shari'ah Global Equity Fund	
2012	Century Banking Corporation	Issue of Islamic Commercial Certificates	Iframac Limited. *Wakala*—3 months
2013	Century Banking Corporation	Issue of Islamic Investment Certificates	Le Warehouse Ltd—Stock *Murabaha*—3 years
2014	Habib Bank Ltd	Islamic Banking Window	Islamic Current Account

(continued)

Table 15.2 (continued)

Year	Institution	Details	Remarks
2016	Barak Fund Management Ltd	Global Sharia Trade Finance Fund	Short-term financing to SMEs in Africa
2019	SBM Capital Markets & Principal Islamic Asset Mgt	The launching of Global Islamic Funds	Islamic Asean Equity Fund and Global *Sukuk* Fund
2019	MUA Life Ltd	*Takaful* Unit-Linked	
2019	Skybound Capital	Global Islamic Trade Finance Fund	Facilitating trade across jurisdictions

Source Compiled by authors themselves from various sources

efforts to position the island as a Shari'ah-compliant hub. Only one local Shari'ah-compliant fund has been established, and two Shari'ah-compliant global funds are being distributed primarily to target the local market. Published materials also make mention of a couple of offshore Shari'ah-compliant funds that have been established in the Mauritius offshore sector (Rassool, 2018; Uteem, 2009).

iii. ***Regulatory Developments***

On the government and regulators side, proactive measures have been taken since the early 2000 to establish the sector as part of the financial services industry and encourage stakeholders to participate in the industry. Key regulatory milestones and major facilitative measures at the level of Government of Mauritius, "Bank of Mauritius (BOM) and the Financial Services Commission (FSC)" are provided in Table 15.3.

It is also worth noting that the Government of Mauritius took bold steps to join the International Islamic Financial Services Support Institutions such as the IFSB, IILM, AAOIFI) and requires accounting standards in the industry to follow the AAOIFI standards.

iv. ***Awareness Efforts***

Table 15.4 lists some key seminars, workshops and conferences organised from 1999 to 2014 by both private and governmental organisations. Courses on Islamic banking and finance were even introduced at the University of Mauritius and the University of Technology Mauritius (UTM). Since 2014, however, Islamic banking and finance awareness programmes have stalled as a result of slow progress being recorded in the development of the industry in the country.

Table 15.3 Regulatory milestones and facilitative measures to promote islamic banking and finance by government and regulators

Year	Institution	Details	Remarks
2006	Government of Mauritius—Bank of Mauritius	Steering committee on Islamic banking	Towards introducing Islamic banking products
2007	Government of Mauritius	"Amendment to the banking act 2004 and the bank of Mauritius act 2004"	"To allow banks to either operate as full-fledged Islamic banks or offer Islamic banking services through window operations"
2008	Bank of Mauritius	"Guideline for institutions conducting Islamic banking business"	"Issued under section 100 of the Banking Act 2004 and section 50 of the Bank of Mauritius Act 2004"
2008	Government of Mauritius	"Amendment to the registration duty act and stamp duty act"	"Removal of levy of multiple payments of duties payable under the Islamic mode of financing land and property"
2008	Government of Mauritius	"Amendment to income tax act"	"Interest and return on Islamic financing aligned"
2008	Government of Mauritius	"Inclusion of *sukuk* issuance in the budget speech"	
2009	Government of Mauritius	"Amendment to the public debt management act 2008"	"To allow the government to issue sovereign *sukuk*"
2009	Government of Mauritius	"Amendment to the value added tax act 1998"	"Exempt *murabahah* deals from double VAT"
2009	Bank of Mauritius	"BOM admitted as a member of the Islamic financial services board (IFSB)"	
2010	Bank of Mauritius	"BOM became a member of international Islamic liquidity management (IILM) corporation"	"BOM participated in the capital & became a member of IILM"
2010	Bank of Mauritius (BOM) and Bank Negara Malaysia (BNM)	"MOU between BOM and BNM"	"Capacity building and human capital development in the financial services industry, including Islamic financial services"

(continued)

Table 15.3 (continued)

Year	Institution	Details	Remarks
2017	Government of Mauritius	"Amendment of The Companies Act 2001 (Amended Act No. 10 of 2017 Government Gazette No. 70 of 24.07.17)"	"Islamic financial institutions and Islamic banks may adopt accounting standards issued by the accounting and auditing organization for Islamic financial institutions (AAOIFI) instead of those issued by the international accounting standards board (IASB)"
2018	Financial Services Commission (FSC)	"FSC joined IFSB"	"FSC became an associate member of the IFSB"
2018	Bank of Mauritius	"Guideline for Institutions Conducting Islamic Banking Business"	"Amended"
2019	Government of Mauritius	"Amendment of the Bank of Mauritius Act 2004"	"Securities include Shari'ah-compliant tools"

Source Compiled from various sources

15.3 Prospects for Developing Mauritius as an IIWM Destination

IFCs are increasingly attracting worldwide investors with significant foreign capital flows. Because of their tax and financial regulatory policies, they are under increasing international scrutiny over the years (Sairally et al., 2012). Some IFCs have developed various types of Islamic capital market instruments and provided a wide range of services, including offshore Shari'ah-compliant funds such as hedge funds, real estate funds, private equity funds, and endowment (waqf) funds, among others (Parker, 2007).

Mauritius is well poised to become an active player in the global Islamic finance industry due to its strategic position in the Indian Ocean. It is a stable democratic country, coupled with fiscal and non-fiscal benefits that make it an ideal destination for structuring IIWM products and services in both its onshore and offshore markets (Rassool, 2011). Islamic finance has the potential to bring diversity to the Mauritius financial markets, enhance business opportunities, and have a high impact on the economy (Bheenick, 2009, 2011). The following are some of the prospects for structuring IIWM products in Mauritius.

Table 15.4 Awareness building initiatives

Year	Institution	Details	Remarks
1999	Islamic Institute of Education and Training (IIET)	The first seminar on Islamic banking and finance	Participation of Dr Umar Chapra and Mr Ismail Mahiyuddin
2005	Islamic Cultural Centre—Ministry of Arts & Culture	Mauritius Islamic finance Forum	First national Islamic finance conference
2008	International Islamic Financial Services Ltd (IIFS)	The launching of the first website on Islamic banking and finance	www.iifs-mauritius.org
2008	IIFS, Cim Financial Services Group (Mauritius) and First International Consulting (Malaysia)	The organization of an Islamic finance week	Organisation of workshops to create more awareness and provide a better understanding of Islamic Finance
2008	LM Institute, a private training centre in Mauritius	Workshops on accounting for Islamic banks and financial institutions and risk management in Islamic banking and finance	Held in Mauritius
2009	IFSB, BOM and FSC Mauritius	Seminar on Islamic capital markets	Held in Mauritius
2009	Landmark Mgt & Technology Consultants Ltd	Islamic finance master class	In collaboration with Islamic Finance Consulting, Malaysia
2010	The University of Mauritius Trust in collaboration with ACCA Mauritius	Workshop on accounting for Islamic finance	
2010	LM Institute, a private training centre in Mauritius	Workshops on Islamic Wealth and Investment Management and Islamic Product Development	Held in Mauritius
2012	BOM and IFSB	The role of Islamic finance in Africa	Seminar held in Mauritius
2012	IFSB and FSC Mauritius	Facilitating the Implementation of IFSB Standards	Workshop held in Mauritius
2014	BOM and IFSB	Workshop on Islamic capital markets	Annual summit of the IFSB hosted by BOM

Source Compiled from various sources

15.3.1 Islamic Product Development

Mauritius' global business vehicles are commonly used for project finance, asset/investment holdings, securitization, aircraft/ship financing or leasing, international trading, joint ventures, or wealth management, among others. Similarly, cross-border *mudarabah*, *murabahah*, *musharakah*, *ijarah* and *sukuk*, among others, can be structured using these offshore investment vehicles (Tegally, 2009). A few offshore Shari'ah-compliant transactions that can be structured are briefly explained below.

i. ***Cross-Border Musharakah***

Cross-border *musharakah* transactions can be carried out between an Islamic financial institution (IFI) and the client investor for investment in a Shari'ah-compliant business. It can be structured using either a Limited Life Company (LLC) or a Limited Partnership (LP). Whereas an LLC can be used only for offshore transactions, an LP can carry out transactions both in and outside Mauritius. The LLC is a kind of partnership embodied under a corporate structure with two shareholders (partners). One of the shareholders (partners) will be the IFI and the other will be the shareholder, the client under *musharakah* principles. The constitution of an LLC will specify its lifespan. The IFI will usually own a share having only a right to the profits and capital of the LLC, whereas the client will have a share that carries the right to profits and capital with an additional right to manage the LLC (Tegally, 2009). In an LP, there will be both general partner/s and limited partner/s. The liability of the limited partner/s will be limited to the partner/s capital and will have no right in the management of the partnership. The IFI will be the limited partner while the client will be the general partner. The LLC constitution and the LP agreement govern the joint venture between the IFI and the client investor in conformity with Shari'ah rules and principles.

ii. ***Ijarah Financing***

In a simple *ijarah* financing such as aviation financing or leasing, Shari'ah-compliant trusts can be used as SPVs to act as the owner and lessor of the aircraft. These SPVs could be either in the form of charitable trusts or purpose trusts. The IFI will set up the trust in Mauritius and will finance the purchase of the aircraft through the SPV that will act as the owner and lessor of the aircraft. The SPV (lessor) will lease the aircraft to the client (lessee), collect the rentals and distribute the income to the IFI. In the case of a finance lease (*ijarah wa iqtina*), a purchase undertaking may be exercised at the end of the lease period (Tegally, 2009). The lessor will usually bear the insurance and significant maintenance costs. He would choose to establish such a trust in a neutral offshore jurisdiction to register the asset and to mitigate its additional risk exposures including lease term recovery, repossession upon default, war risks as well as reduce bureaucratic difficulties (McLean et al., 2009).

iii. ***Sukuk Structuring***

Mauritius now provides for the issuance of sovereign *sukuk*. The Public Debt Management Act 2008, as subsequently amended, includes sovereign *sukuk* in its definition of securities. Section (3A) gives power to the Minister of Finance to "enter into such agreement, sell, purchase or otherwise acquire any immovable property or any right therein, lease movable or immovable property and generally engage in such transactions and perform such activities as may be reasonably necessary for the purpose of issuing Sovereign Sukuks in Mauritius" (MOF, 2019).

Sukuk structures made in the Mauritius offshore sector carry many advantages to foreign investors. The SPV in Mauritius could be set up as a company holding a Global Business Licence (GBL) or as a trust. A GBL company is resident in Mauritius and investors can benefit from the advantages of double-taxation agreements signed by Mauritius with other countries. Trust in Mauritius is governed by English Common Law. The trust can elect to be established as a non-resident trust provided that its settlor and beneficiaries are non-residents and will be exempted from income tax. No withholding tax will be applicable on the periodic payments and the reimbursement of capital to non-resident *sukuk* holders.

iv. ***Funds Structuring***

Mutual funds were first established in the early 1990s in Mauritius. They can be structured as close-ended funds or open-ended funds. Global Funds licensed by the FSC will have a Global Business Licence (GBL Shari'ah-compliant funds, including mutual funds, can be established in Mauritius within the conventional framework by inserting in the by-laws, shareholders' agreements, or relevant business contracts specific for Shari'ah-compliance (Selvam, 2018). Global Shari'ah-compliant funds established in other jurisdictions can be distributed in Mauritius through a distributor of financial products (conventional or Islamic).

If an international IFI wishes to establish different types of Shari'ah-compliant funds such as *mudarabah, murabahah, ijarah, salam, istisna'*, among others, the IFI may use a Protected Cell Company (PCC) structure to house all these funds instead of creating a different GBL company for each type of fund. The company will be established under the Mauritius Protected Cell Companies Act 1999, as amended. The PCC is made up of a core (non-cellular) and many cells (cellular). Each cell is independent of each other with proper seggregation of assets and liabilities. Therefore, the liabilities of one cell cannot be discharged from the assets of other cells. The purpose of the company is to facilitate a structure of separate authorised cells, with each cell having its own distinct business, investment objectives, restrictions, and risk profile that are engaged in the overall business activity of the company. The PCC may be established as a GBL company to benefit from the advantages of double-taxation agreements.

A company resident in Mauritius is subject to tax on its worldwide income at the rate of 15%. However, a company holding a GBL will qualify for a 80% partial exemption concerning specific foreign-source income, such as foreign dividends not allowed as a deduction in the source country. The maximum effective tax rate is 3% for specific income streams (PwC, 2020).

v. ***Captive Insurance***

Captive insurance is mainly available in offshore jurisdictions to cater for wealth and risk management. Captive insurance is an insurance company formed to insure or reinsure the risks of enterprises that have substantial risks location and condition, whether locally and/or abroad.

A Shari'ah-compliant Captive Insurance (Captive Takaful) can be established in Mauritius within the same law. It can be set up as a GBL company or set up as a cell captive under the PCC structure. The Mauritius captive insurance offers many benefits, including an annual fee of only US$2,000 payable yearly to the regulator if set up as a GBL company and is free for a cell captive as the fee is levied on the PCC. Furthermore, if the PCC is a GBL company, as mentioned above, it will benefit from the advantages of double-taxation agreements and will qualify for a 80% partial exemption concerning specific foreign-source income, such as dividends, and will end up paying a maximum effective tax rate of 3%. For pure captives, they are entitled to a 10-year tax holiday for setting up in Mauritius, and there are no capital gains tax and withholding tax on dividends.

15.4 Challenges and Opportunities in Positioning Mauritius as an IIWM Destination

Positioning Mauritius as a destination of choice for IIWM products poses several challenges. These challenges can however be turned into opportunities if necessary steps are taken to address the issues. The following paragraphs discuss the issues, challenges and opportunities from both demand and supply side considerations.

15.4.1 Demand Side

i. ***Prevailing strong conventional finance mindset***

At the institutional level, Mauritius enjoys a strong conventional sovereign bond market. It has a very active government securities market whose sources of funds are used to partly finance the government's budget. It is also relatively easy for the government to avail of financing from friendly foreign governments (e.g., India, China, Japan) and international organisations (e.g., the World Bank, African Development Bank (AfDB), Agence Francaise de Development (AFD), etc.) at cheap rates and with other alluring facilities. Hence, the need for the government to raise funding through the *sukuk* market, either on the local or international market, is barely considered a viable economic option, unless there is a deliberate choice taken by the government to engage in Islamic finance to promote the sector.

Even at the retail level, conventional banking is much ingrained as the system of banking within the mindset of the population. As mentioned above, the Mauritian financial system is mainly bank-based, representing about 70% of the country's total financial assets, with commercial banks being largely responsible for the financing of private as well as partly public investments. The reliability, efficiency, profitability and long existence of conventional banks in the country contributed to the confidence and trust of the population in the system. The two largest commercial banks, namely the Mauritius Commercial Bank established in 1838 and the State Bank of Mauritius established in 1973 garner more than 60% of total market share. Moreover, despite the small population of 1.2 million, there are 19 commercial and investment banks in the country. Hence, for a new bank that endorses a new concept—that of Islamic banking—to compete in such a highly competitive environment is quite challenging.

ii. ***Limited market awareness***

Awareness of Islamic banking and finance is deficient among investors, issuers and other stakeholders in the country. Though much efforts were spent in creating awareness among market participants in the early years of Islamic finance development in the 2000s by both private and public sectors, the slow evolution of Islamic finance in the country caused interest in the sector to wane over time.. However, as none of the commercial banks came forward with Islamic retail banking and investment products to service the small Muslim population, expectations that the industry could take off at the retail level plummeted among Muslim individuals. It was mainly believed that the industry could develop at the global business level under the Mauritius IFC agenda to attract foreign and high net worth investors. As a result, most efforts geared towards creating awareness about Islamic finance among the population ceased. It was only at the global business level that some attempts at promoting Islamic finance remained to attract investment in the few Islamic capital market products developed by the private sector.

Therefore, an attempt to position Mauritius as an IIWM centre that would be of interest to both local and foreign investors and issuers would need major awareness building efforts at different stakeholder levels, including government, business and the general population.

iii. ***Negative image of Islamic finance***

Another major hindrance in the development of Islamic finance in Mauritius is the few cases of failures that led to a negative image being created on the sector, namely:

a. In the early 1990s, a first Shari'ah-compliant fund was initiated, however, without the necessary legal registration of the business with the regulatory bodies. Nonetheless, the initiative attracted much interest among the Muslims and the number of investors is reported to have grown exponentially within the first year (Lallmahamood, 2019). As the funds were mostly invested in long term real estate projects and trade assets, the initiative suffered from liquidity issues and finally defaulted on investors' requests for early withdrawals of their funds. Hence, the first attempt at offering a retail alternative failed at its very start as the venture was not carried out with the necessary professionalism and expertise required in Islamic fund management.

b. In 2015 the government closed the British American Investment (BAI) company, one of the largest conglomerates in the country which offered a *takaful* unit-linked product under the British American (BA) Insurance Company and *ijarah* (Islamic leasing) under the Mauritius Leasing Company. The closure of the company was however not associated to the group's Islamic finance operations; it was rather due to its other products, namely the Super Cash Back Gold policy offered by BA Insurance and the Bramer Property Fund Preference Shares issued by Bramer Bank which promised high returns to investors, apparently being paid from the money of other investors instead of from profits. These activities were associated to a Ponzi scheme and led to the revocation of Bramer Bank's licence and the ultimate collapse of the whole group, including the sale of its international operations. This badly damaged the image of the financial group, including Islamic finance, as the group was largely Muslim-dominated and was supporting Islamic finance.
c. In 2020, the banking licence of Century Banking Corporation, the only full-fledged Islamic bank in the country which was launched in 2011, was revoked by the Bank of Mauritius on account of non-compliance of the bank with banking laws relating to capital requirements, internal control systems, anti-money laundering and combatting the financing of terrorism (AML-CFT) requirements, and record keeping obligations (Bank of Mauritius, 2020). Again, it was not Shari'ah non-compliance issues which led to the closure of the bank; rather it was more a matter of poor corporate governance and legal non-compliance that caused the institution to fail. These are responsibilities that even non-Islamic firms have to fulfil, and as an Islamic bank, the ethical aspects of transparency, good governance and legal compliance were expected to be upheld as top-priority to safeguard the image of Islam and Islamic finance. This caused irreparable damage to the local Islamic finance industry's reputation.

There is a need to re-awaken Muslims from their complaisance in being involved in interest-based businesses and for the Muslim community to demand a sustainable Islamic retail banking and finance alternative from the banking sector. Government could also contribute significantly by building confidence in the market if it ventures into a debut *sukuk* issuance.

iv. ***Small investor base***

In Mauritius Muslims represent about 17% of its total population, i.e., about 200,000 Muslims. The Muslim community, though small, represents the rich merchants community from Kutch and Surat province of Gujarat in India, called the Memons and Surtees, as well as the 'Calcattias' community who originally came to Mauritius as indentured labourers from Bihar. With a large majority of the Muslims being traders, they hold a large proportion of wealth in their hands. This makes a case for the provision of Islamic banking and finance in the country to allow Muslims to live according to their faith. Promoting the Islamic financial system as an ethical and socially responsible mode of finance will motivate not only Muslims but also the larger population in Mauritius to invest the Islamic way. This will help build the investor base for Islamic investments in the country.

As regards ways to attract foreign Islamic investments in Mauritius, promotional campaigns in the form of roadshows, awareness programmes, conferences and seminars should be organised by both public and private sectors in collaboration with recognised international Islamic organisations such as the IFSB and IILM to showcase the investment-friendly framework of Mauritius for Islamic finance. The assistance of the Economic Development Board of Mauritius (EDB) may also be sought to promote Mauritius as a potential jurisdiction for Islamic finance.. Thus, in line with its mandate, the EDB can promote Mauritius as a destination of choice for both conventional and Islamic financial investments. It can, in collaboration with Mauritius embassies, target countries forming part of MENA, African Muslim-majority countries, as well as other Muslim countries in Europe, such as Turkey and Iran and the far-east countries such as Malaysia, Indonesia, and Brunei.

15.4.2 Supply Side

i. ***Low confidence of industry players***

Despite all the necessary legal and regulatory amendments initiated by the government to promote the sector, few minor players attempted at entering the market. Many of the respondents surveyed believed that the Islamic finance sector in Mauritius did not kick off successfully for reasons other than legal and regulatory issues. The BAI group, which was a big conglomerate, made big strides in supporting the development of the local Islamic finance industry; however it faced major setbacks in taking the concept further as the group was closed down by the government, as explained earlier.

For the concept of developing Mauritius as an IIWM centre to work, it is foremost essential that local players believe in the concept first. As long as major players do not appear convinced in the success of Islamic finance in the country, it will be difficult to promote same to both local and foreign investors. Industry players need to be ready to adapt to the Islamic way of doing business and incur the necessary additional costs related to Shari'ah compliance and Shari'ah governance to implement the system. Until they are satisfied with the already established conventional financial system which brings profitable and sustainable returns to their businesses, it would be unlikely that the major players would venture into Islamic finance. A mindset change is required not only at the investor level, but also at the issuer and industry players' level for the success of Islamic investments in Mauritius.

ii. ***Poor corporate governance policies***

Earlier cases of failures of Islamic finance initiatives were largely due to poor corporate governance policies and lack of transparent and ethical business practices, as noted above. To promote Mauritius as a destination of choice for IIWM, the good governance image of Islamic financial institutions and the country in general should be enhanced. Accordingly, there should be stringent supervisory role of the regulatory authorities to ensure that strong corporate governance policies are adopted since the early stage of setting up the Islamic financial institution. The issue of non-compliance to best industry practices with regard to corporate governance and other legal requirements should not be highlighted at the last stage when damage to the industry has already been done, as in the case of the revocation of the Century Banking Corporation licence.

iii. ***High Shari'ah governance cost***

Shari'ah compliance and Shari'ah governance are two key prerequisites of the Islamic financial system. To ensure Shari'ah compliance usually Islamic financial institutions set up a Shari'ah committee comprising mostly of Shari'ah scholars and other professionals in Islamic finance to vet through the processes and ensure that all transactions are in compliance with Shari'ah principles at all times.

In Mauritius, as there is no centralised Shari'ah advisory board at the regulators' level, it is expected that each Islamic financial institution will have to establish its own Shari'ah committee or recruit a Shari'ah advisor. It is to be highlighted that in the banking sector the appointment of Shari'ah advisors must meet the approval of the BOM. The FSC is however silent on this requirement. Furthermore, the FSC does not certify that the investment vehicle is suitable for persons seeking to invest in accordance with the Shari'ah, nor does it provide assurance of the company's compliance with the Shari'ah. Such a disclaimer is expected to be part of the Private Placement Memorandum (PPM) or any other constitutive investment documents. The onus of Shari'ah compliance thus rests with promoters and administrators of the Shari'ah-compliant investment.

The establishment of a Shari'ah committee adds to the cost of Islamic financial products. Usually, the more renowned the Shari'ah scholars the more they tend to charge in terms of retainer fees. In addition, Islamic financial institutions also have to incur additional costs in the form of internal Shari'ah review and external Shari'ah audit, over and above the normal financial audit processes, to ensure that the operations of the entities comply with Shari'ah.

All in all, for the success of Islamic financial businesses in Mauritius, industry players must be ready to bear the Shari'ah costs involved in implementing Islamic finance. These form part of the process of Islamic banking and finance operations. The role of regulators on this matter could be two fold: (a) to set a minimum requirement that Shari'ah assurance be provided by market players, (b) to facilitate the Shari'ah assurance process by instituting an independent Shari'ah committee that market players can call upon to approve and vet through their products and services at a reasonable cost.

iv. ***Enhancing legal processes***

Islamic capital markets and *takaful* in Mauritius do not have special regulations, however these follow the Securities Act 2005, Insurance Act 2005, Captive Insurance Act 2015 and relevant rules and regulations enacted under the said laws.

The banking sector in Mauritius is regulated by the Bank of Mauritius (BOM), while the non-banking sector is regulated by the Financial Services Commission (FSC). The Companies Act 2001 defines Islamic banks as banks licensed as such by the BOM and Islamic financial institutions as financial institutions licensed as such by the FSC. While the BOM has issued guidelines for financial institutions (both conventional and Islamic) carrying out Islamic banking business, the FSC has so far not issued any guidelines or framework for Islamic financial transactions in the non-banking and offshore sectors. There are as such no specific laws and regulations that govern Islamic banking and finance in Mauritius. In other words, Islamic finance products are regulated on the same scale as conventional finance products as they are perceived as 'other' financial products. The approach adopted by the government is to ensure a level playing field for Islamic finance and conventional finance instruments (Lallmahamood, 2019).

Despite the non-provision of Islamic finance regulations in the Islamic capital market sectors, some Islamic investment products have been structured within the same legal framework that have met the regulatory requirements. They complement the existing products and services of the Mauritius IFC. Still, it is believed that to be able to promote Mauritius as a IIWM centre, it is essential that the FSC comes up with necessary industry guidelines to provide more clarity on Islamic capital market operations in Mauritius.

It is further noted that the Court in Mauritius does not recognize Shari'ah as the governing law and in the event of Islamic finance disputes, it will hear these disputes based on Mauritian laws. In such cases, out of court settlements may need to be encouraged. Nonetheless, one of the advantages of the legal system in Mauritius is that it allows disputing parties to have recourse up to the Privy Council in England. This will play in favour of foreign issuers and investors when they partake in Islamic investments in Mauritius.

v. ***The need to offer attractive investment products***

For Mauritius to be able to venture into Islamic investments, it is important that the products are as attractive as their conventional counterparts, if not better in terms of rewards to investors, while at the same time not being too costly for the supplier. Other areas of attractiveness may also come into play for that particular niche. It is important that regulators look into various initiatives that will encourage Islamic product development and ensure greater variety to suit the risk appetite of Islamic investors.

It is to be highlighted that Mauritius has an attractive local tax regime and in view of its robust foreign trade relations it can positively attract Islamic investors to the jurisdiction. Furthermore, similar to countries like Malaysia, special tax incentives can be considered to further attract investments in the emerging Islamic finance sector.

vi. ***Lack of high-calibre industry professionals***

One of the challenges facing the development of IIWM in Mauritius is the lack of suitably qualified Islamic finance professionals who have knowledge in the operations of the sector as well as specific knowledge of Shari'ah application in Islamic finance. While in the early developmental years of Islamic finance in the country some Islamic finance courses were offered at the university level as part of mainstream banking and finance programs, these were discontinued over time with the growing disinterest of the population in Islamic finance. As mentioned in the early paragraphs, even workshops, seminars and short courses offered by private training institutions were stopped post-2010 as these no longer attracted participation of industry stakeholders. For a revival of the Islamic finance industry in Mauritius, it will require a refocus of both academic and training institutions on Islamic finance training to develop the needed qualified and competent professionals required for the sector. Experts will be required in a wide range of specialization including legal, banking, finance, accounting, auditing and Shari'ah.

vii. ***Competition from other Islamic financial centres and international financial centres***

Mauritius is known as a specialist IFC that focuses on countries within its geographical region.. If Mauritius would like to promote itself as an IIWM centre, it would clearly face strong competition from other IFCs in the region that are already promoting themselves as Islamic finance hubs (e.g., Singapore and Hong Kong) as well as key Islamic financial centres which are renowned leaders in Islamic finance (e.g., Bahrain, Dubai, Qatar and Malaysia). As mentioned above, even a number of African countries have made a headway start in their development of Islamic finance, including Islamic banking and the *sukuk* market, as compared to Mauritius. Mauritius in fact finds itself last in the list of countries with Islamic banking assets vis-à-vis all other countries with Islamic banking practice, including such African countries like South Africa, Kenya, Nigeria, Senegal and Egypt.

Thus, Mauritius has to rely on its strong position as a sound and credible investment jurisdiction to attract potential investors in Islamic finance. It can leverage on its existing relationship with Muslim-majority countries to undertake promotional campaigns to attract investors.

15.5 Conclusion and Way Forward in Brightening the Future of Mauritius as an IIWM Centre

Mauritius has a strong track record as a sound and credible IFC. The positive reputation of the country as an investment destination can be leveraged upon to brand the country as an Islamic finance destination as well. A few initiatives can be taken by key stakeholders to brighten the future of Mauritius as an IIWM centre. Three important recommendations are made in the discussion below.

i. ***Government to penetrate the market as a market maker***

The Government of Mauritius like Singapore and Hong Kong (Wico, 2010) can also play the role of a market maker to kickstart *sukuk* development in the country. It can pursue the issuance of a debut sovereign *sukuk* that will attract both local and foreign investors in the market. The issuance of sovereign *sukuk* will help consolidate the position of Mauritius as a global financial centre by developing an Islamic finance/*sukuk* platform. Different types of *sukuk* can be considered, for example, green sukuk to fund environmental projects, sustainable and responsible investment (SRI) sukuk, humanitarian sukuk, diaspora sukuk, retail sukuk, and etc.

The issuance of government *sukuk* will also help to develop pricing benchmarks against which all other Islamic debt instruments in the same market can be priced. It will further represent an essential starting point to encourage the development of corporate *sukuk* and other government issues. Already a number of African countries, such as South Africa, Senegal and Nigeria, among others, have opted for the issuance of *sukuk* to finance their budgets, especially for funding capital expenditure projects. Mauritius is already lagging behind as compared to its African counterparts in developing its *sukuk* market. To become an Islamic finance hub, in particular an Islamic wealth management platform, Mauritius should be able to provide a wider variety of investment products that will attract investors of different risk appetite. Thus, it should seek to develop both the Islamic debt market as well as the Islamic equity market.

ii. ***Developing a list of Shari'ah-compliant securities and an Islamic index***

To develop the Islamic equity market, the government through the Stock Exchange of Mauritius can look into the possibility of developing Shari'ah screening benchmarks that can be used to screen out listed companies that meet the requirements of the Shari'ah.

Mauritius can also learn from the experience of key Islamic finance leaders to develop a list of Shari'ah-compliant companies that form part of the All ordinary shares index, the SEMDEX, and publish this list to encourage Islamic investment on the stock exchange. Although this list may comprise only few companies at the start, it will encourage more companies to meet the Shari'ah screening requirements so that they could also form part of this list. The publication of the list of Shari'ah-compliant securities will also help promote Islamic equity investments in Mauritius to international investors. The Stock Exchange of Mauritius is a recognized exchange given that it is a member of the World Federation of Exchanges and has been awarded the 'Most Innovative African 2017 Stock Exchange Award'. Development of new products is aligned to the exchange's vision of supporting further innovation and attracting different types of investors onto its platform.

In the long term, it is also expected that an Islamic index could be developed that would constitute these Shari'ah-compliant equities. The development of an Islamic index that will meet Shari'ah principles will complement the SEMSI by offering a useful tool to investors looking for another brand of responsible investments, i.e., those that meet Shari'ah-compliance criteria. The Islamic index will add to the list of indices it produces and help in enhancing market liquidity and size.

iii. ***Developing the SRI brand***

The United Nations Development Programme (UNDP) is already partnering with a number of Islamic finance organisations in different countries to assist them to align with the SDGs, monitor, report and communicate development impact (UNDP, 2020). For example, the UNDP supported the Indonesian Ministry of Finance in the issuance of its first US$1.25 billion sovereign green *sukuk* (UNDP, 2020). Mauritius can also collaborate with international organisations in its endeavor to mobilise Islamic finance for sustainable and green investments. It should engage in leveraging Islamic finance for promoting the sustainable and responsible investment (SRI) brand so as to attract socially responsible green investors and issuers within its jurisdiction.

To create an ecosystem that promotes investment in *sukuk*, including SRI *sukuk*, by issuers and investors, the FSC could envisage the development and issuance of a 'Guidelines on Sukuk'. The FSC could also consider issuing a 'Guidelines on SRI Funds' to encourage investment in green, social and sustainable purposes.

Tax incentives could also be envisaged to attract investors and issuers in the Islamic SRI market. Embracing the SRI brand will be an innovative way to differentiate Mauritius from other African countries which have already entered the Islamic finance market. It also represents a viable strategy to advance the sustainability agenda.

Overall, given the nascent stage of Islamic finance development in Mauritius, targeted efforts to spur Islamic investment in the country are required to motivate both demand and supply sides. On the demand side, increased market awareness and efforts to build the investor base are required. On the supply side, increased efforts from market players, including government and the private sector, as well as greater guidance and clarity from the Islamic capital market regulator are expected. With Islamic finance slowly spreading in Africa and Mauritius' ambition to diversify its offerings within its IFC, it has no choice but to develop its own niche market in the industry and strive to become a region hub in Islamic finance in the region.

References

Abduh, M., & Ramjaun, S. (2015). The role of religion in Islamic bank patronizing behaviour: A survey in Mauritius. *Journal of Islamic Finance, 3*(2), 70–76.

Abduh, M., Ramjaun, S., & Mustaquim, M. (2018). Bank selection criteria and SERVQUAL survey among Muslims in Mauritius. *Qudus International Journal of Islamic Studies, 6*(2), 221–250.

Afrasia. (2019). *Africa Wealth Report 2019*, AfrAsia Bank and NWWealth.

Bank of Mauritius. (2020). Revocation of banking licence of Century Banking Corporation Ltd and appointment of a Receiver. Retrieved October 20, 2020, from https://www.bom.mu/media/media-releases/revocation-banking-licence-century-banking-corporation-ltd-and-appointment-receiver.

Beebeejaun, A. (2020). Governance and Financial Reporting of Islamic Banks: Evidence From Mauritius. In A. Rafay (Ed.), *Growth and emerging prospects of international Islamic banking*, IGI Global, Hershey, Pennsylvania, USA, pp. 245–262. Retrieved 28 October 2020, from https://www.igi-global.com/chapter/governance-and-financial-reporting-of-islamic-banks/249043.

Bheenick, R. (2009). Putting Mauritius on the world's Islamic finance map. *BIS Review*, No. 55. Retrieved 28 October 2020, from https://www.bis.org/review/r090507e.pdf.

Bheenick, R. (2011). Speech at launching ceremony of the Century Banking Corporation Ltd. Retrieved 19 August 2019, from https://www.bom.mu/media/speeches/address-mr-rundheersing-bheenick-governor-bank-mauritius-launching-ceremony-century-banking.

Domaingue, P. R. (2002). The historical development of the mixed legal system of Mauritius during the French and British colonial periods. *University of Mauritius Research Journal, 4*, 61–93.

EDB Mauritius. (n.d.). *Overview of the financial services sector*. Retrieved 28 October 2019, from https://www.edbmauritius.org/opportunities/financial-services/fs-overview/.

EDB Mauritius. (2020). *Why Mauritius*? Retrieved 9 September 2020, from https://www.edbmauritius.org/why-mauritius/.

FSC Mauritius. (2018). Innovating and transforming the Mauritius IFC of 2030: a blueprint for success. Retrieved 26 October 2020 https://www.fscmauritius.org/media/67408/highlights-of-blueprint.pdf.

FSC Mauritius. (2019). *FSC annual report 2017–2018*. Retrieved 9 September 2020, from https://www.fscmauritius.org/media/77954/fsc-mauritius-annual-report-2017-18.pdf.

Joharris, N. (2012). The legal aspects of Islamic finance and banking. *Mauritius Business Law Review, 4*, 5–8.

Lallmahamood, M. (2014). Islamic finance in Mauritius: Prospects and challenges. *Journal of Islamic Business and Management, 4*(1), 99–124.

Lallmahamood, M. (2019), *Islamic finance & markets in Mauritius—Lexology*, Century Banking Corporation Ltd. Retrieved 10 September 2020, from https://www.lexology.com/library/detail.aspx?g=6a5d2709-cc25-4b52-80a7-6ce0b1c44582.

Mauritius Revenue Authority (2020), *Double Taxation Agreements*, available at https://www.mra.mu/index.php/taxes-duties/international-taxation/double-taxation-agreements (accessed 9 September 2020).

McLean, J., Briant, R., Butler, K., & Richard, N. (2009). *Aviation financing and leasing*, Conyers Dill & Pearman.

MOF. (2019). *Public debt management Act 2009*. Ministry of Finance, Economic Planning & Development, Mauritius. Retrieved 4 March 2020, from http://mof.govmu.org/English/Legislation/Pages/default.aspx.

Mooneeram-Chadee, V. (2020). The regulation of Islamic banking in Mauritius. *ISRA International Journal of Islamic Finance, 12*(2), 151–166.

Ocra Worldwide Mauritius (n.d.). A guide to the Mauritius offshore fund. Retrieved 28 October 2019, from https://www.ocra-mauritius.com/solutions/mauritius-offshore-funds/.

Omran, M., Ramdhony, D., Khallaf, A., & Gleason, K. C. (2018). Home country bias and majority outgroup consumption: evidence from the introduction of Islamic banking in Mauritius. Retrieved 4 March 2020, from SSRN: https://ssrn.com/abstract=3318104, https://doi.org/10.2139/ssrn.3318104.

Parker, M. (2007). Offshore Hubs Lure Islamic Finance Business. *Islamic Banking and Finance News*, Retrieved 2 March 2020, from http://www.alhudacibe.com/newsletter/15-31july/article_10.html.

PwC. (2020). *Mauritius corporate taxes on corporate income*. Retrieved 4 August 2020, from http://taxsummaries.pwc.com/ID/Mauritius-Corporate-Taxes-on-corporate-income.

Ramdhony, D. (2013). Islamic banking awareness attitude and bank selection criteria. *International Journal of Humanities and Applied Sciences, 2*(2), 29–35.
Rassool, N. H. (2011). Mauritius—An emerging centre for Islamic finance. *New Horizon*, No. 180, July–September.
Rassool, H. N. (2018). Towards establishing an Islamic retail bank in a Muslim minority country: Prospects and challenges in Mauritius. *ISRA International Journal of Islamic Finance, 10*(1), 78–84.
Sairally, S. B., Muhammad, M., Hasan, S. (2012). Development of Islamic capital markets in offshore jurisdictions: A cross-country analysis. *ISRA Research Paper* No. 43/2012, International Shari'ah Research Academy for Islamic Finance.
Selvam, D. M. (2018). Mauritius: Still a small market. *Islamic Finance News*, April 2018.
Tegally, S. K. (2009). International Islamic finance vehicles. *Islamic Finance News*. Retrieved 28 February 2020, from https://www.islamicfinancenews.com/international-islamic-finance-vehicles.html.
Tamano, N. (2020). IFN Country Analysis. *Islamic Finance News*. Retrieved 28 October 2020, from https://www.islamicfinancenews.com/ifn-country-analysis/mauritius.
UNDP. (2020). *Islamic finance partners*. Retrieved 29 October 2020, from https://www.undp.org/content/undp/en/home/partners/islamic-finance.html.
Uteem, M. (2009), Mauritius Shari'ah. *International Finance Law Review*. Retrieved 29 February 2020, from https://www.iflr.com/article/b1lv1qqrcxndpf/mauritius-shariah.
Wico, Y. (2010). *Singapore: Monetary Authority of Singapore Sukuk Program*, Allen & Gledhill, first published in Islamic Finance News Deals of the Year Handbook 2009. Retrieved 14 September 2020, from https://www.mondaq.com/commercial-law/104716/monetary-authority-of-singapore-sukuk-program.
Z-Yen and China Development Institute. (2020). The global financial centres index 28. Retrieved 28 October 2020, from https://www.longfinance.net/media/documents/GFCI_28_Full_Report_2020.09.25_v1.1.pdf.

Salma Sairally is a Research Consultant at the ISRA Research Management Centre, International Centre for Education in Islamic Finance (INCEIF), Kuala Lumpur, Malaysia. She is also the Editor of the *ISRA International Journal of Islamic Finance*, a Scopus and ESCI-Indexed journal published by the International Shari'ah Research Academy for Islamic Finance (ISRA) in collaboration with Emerald Publishing Services. She holds a PhD in Economics from Loughborough University, UK; Masters in Islamic Studies from Portsmouth University, UK; BSc in Economics and Finance, University of New South Wales, Australia; and is an AAOIFI Certified Shari'ah Adviser and Auditor (CSAA).

Najmul Hussein Rassool is a freelance Business Management/Islamic Finance Consultant, Lecturer and Trainer. He holds a PhD in Islamic Banking & Finance with Al-Madinah International University, Malaysia; an MBA in Finance (WITS, South Africa), and a Post-Graduate Diploma in Economic Principles (London). He is a Chartered Islamic Finance Professional from INCEIF, Malaysia, an AAOIFI Certified Shari'ah Adviser and Auditor, and a Certified Islamic Finance Executive.

Chapter 16
Sustainability, *Sharīʿah* Governance and Financial Performance: Evidence from Companies Listed on the Jakarta Islamic Index

Zuraida Zuraida and Asna Husin

Sustainability has become a mainstream concern in both the business and academic settings in recent decades. Professional bodies and Institutional investors also recognize the importance of sustainability factors as a driving force for improving company values (Bernow, Klempner, & Magnin, 2017). In addition, sustainability issues have become even more significant for long-term investors. Similarly, academic institutions and scholars devoted a long list of studies examining the impact of sustainability performance on companies. Researchers interested in Islamic finance and *Sharīʿah* governance have also contributed to the richness of sustainability studies. The latter focus primarily on the role of Islamic financial institutions and Muslim entrepreneurial activities in advancing sustainability.

Our study on sustainability, *Sharīʿah* governance and financial performance in the context of the Indonesian financial market explores two sets of relationships: sustainability practices and the financial performance of companies under consideration, as well as their *Sharīʿah* compliance and financial performance connecting the second set with sustainability concerns. We seek to answer the main research question of whether sustainability, Islamicity and profitability together work complementarily or adversely. Numerous studies have positively linked sustainability practices and financial performance (Ali, Danish, & Asrar-ul-Haq, 2020; Buallay, 2019; Fauzi & Idris, 2009; Lukman, Suhendah, & Evan, 2020; Waddock & Graves, 1997; A. J. Wibowo, 2012). However, research on *Sharīʿah* governance in relation to financial performance is limited (Jan, Marimuthu, & Hassan, 2019a, b; Zyadat, 2017), while

Z. Zuraida
Department of Accounting, Faculty of Economics and Business, Syiah Kuala University, Darussalam, Banda Aceh, Indonesia
e-mail: zuraida@feb.unsyiah.ac.id

A. Husin (✉)
Department of Arabic, School of Tarbiyah and Education, Ar-Raniry State Islamic University, Darussalam, Banda Aceh, Indonesia
e-mail: asna.husin@ar-raniry.ac.id

T. Azid et al. (eds.), *Wealth Management and Investment in Islamic Settings*,
https://doi.org/10.1007/978-981-19-3686-9_16

an inquiry combining sustainability, Islamic principles and financial performance is even rarer, especially when it is applied to the Indonesian context. This study fills this gap.

16.1 Sustainability and Corporate Financial Performance

Since the term 'sustainability' has not yet received a univocal definition, our review therefore draws on studies linking corporate financial performance with sustainability utilizing several terms, often used interchangeably by researchers to indicate this concept. The most common are: corporate social responsibility (CSR); 'environmental, social and governance' (ESG); 'corporate social performance' (CSP); and 'socially responsible investment' (SRI), in addition to the term 'sustainability' itself.

One can observe some inconsistencies in the current literature, however most of them are related to the measurement technique. Corporate social performance (CSP) is a multi-dimensional construct whose behavior starts from the internal (e.g. treatment of women and minorities) to external behavior (environmental strategy). However, the measure used in some empirical works was often one-dimensional (such as corporate governance only). This problem is exacerbated when this one-dimensional procedure is applied to a small sample size.[1] It becomes even more problematic when it is utilized on a survey methodology which usually has inherent problems with the response rate. To address the above measurement problems, Waddock and Graves (1997) proposed a self-constructed index. It measures CSP and corporate financial performance attributes based on the Kinder, Lydenberg, and Domini (KLD) database which provides consistent scores across the entire Standard and Poors 500. They find that CSP is positively related to both previous and future financial performances.

However, much consensus has been established on the positive impact of sustainability practice on financial performance. Ali et al. (2020) find that corporate social responsibility has a significant effect on the company's financial performance. They suggest that this positive correlation stems from a positive image created among stakeholders, thereby lowering overall costs as a result of disclosing sustainability factors. Buallay (2019) shows a significant positive impact of aggregate ESG disclosure on corporate financial performance, while the environmental disclosure specifically has a positive effect on the 'Return on Assets' and 'Tobin's Q'. In contrast, social disclosure demonstrates a negative effect on ROA, ROE and Tobin's Q, while corporate governance disclosure has a negative effect on ROA and ROE, but a positive effect on Tobin's Q. This reveals on the one hand, the complexity of issues being studied, and on the other hand that the results are being affected by measurement proxies. The inconsistencies can also occur because 'Return on Assets' and 'Return on Equity' have different exposures to the economic environment. ROA—being the

[1] The small sample size provides lower statistical power thus reducing the likelihood of detecting the true effect and replication of study results (Button et al., 2013).

income earned per dollar deployed—may be less influenced by the capital structure, and thus by the economic circumstances. In contrast, ROE—being the net profit realized by the shareholders for every dollar invested—may be more susceptible to economic pressure. This is due to the fact that a portion of the company's capital may have come from borrowing in addition to investment by shareholders; therefore there is leverage involved when measuring ROE. In a good economic condition ROE is high due to the leverage effect, while in a declining economy it tends to be low. This effect can also lead to inconsistencies in research findings.

Research on sustainability issues in relation to financial performance in Indonesia is still rare, but a few have investigated this matter based on data collected from sub-segments of sustainability. Lukman et al. (2020) explore forty-five manufacturing companies listed on the Indonesia Stock Exchange, looking at the effect of their environmental performance reporting (EPR) and CSR activities on their financial presentation as measured by 'Return on Assets'. Their study assesses the data provided by the Indonesian Ministry of Environment and Forestry through its Environmental Management Rating Program (PROPER) that measures corporate sustainability practices. The forty-five firms during 2014–2015 are rated according to the PROPER rating system from best to worst as gold, green, blue, red, and black. This shows that corporate CSR activities produce no effect on financial performance, while sustainability disclosure does have a positive consequence.

The inconsistencies in such studies may alternatively be explained from the perspective of modern 'portfolio theory', which maintains that the objective of investment is to maximize profits and wealth. This theory emphasizes the importance of reducing risk for better returns, which can be achieved through diversification and other means. It further asserts that any restrictions imposed on investments have the potential for a lower performance, implying that sustainability practices by companies reduce their ability to choose certain profitable business strategies or pursue tactical risks. Thus, the mixed results shown in previous studies are consistent with this theory's belief that firms implementing sustainable practices have restricted themselves from choosing more profitable strategies and thereby suffer in their financial performance. Daugaard (2019, p. 15) and Barnett and Salomon (2006) stated as: "The returns initially fall as a fund manager increases their [his or her] screening intensity from weak to medium, but then returns rise again as the screening intensity becomes higher."

In contrast to the above analyses, Wibowo (2012) analyzed twenty-five companies from the SRI-Kehati index on the Indonesia Stock Exchange (2005–2010) and finds a significant relationship between CSR and profitability. Employing ROA as a proxy for financial performance, Wibowo discovers that there is a positive relationship between CSR disclosure and corporate profitability, and vice versa. Likewise, positive results were also demonstrated by the inquiry conducted by Fauzi and Idris (2009) on the relationship between corporate financial performance (CFP) and corporate social performance (CSP). Using a questionnaire-based survey with respondents consisting of managers from state-owned enterprises (Badan Usaha Milik Negara—BUMN) and from private companies, their research found a positive relationship between financial performance and social consciousness.

Despite such lingering inconsistencies, a number of researches investigating the relationship between sustainability and financial performance presented here have reported positive findings. These optimistic results are in line with several other theories such as 'agency theory', 'legitimacy theory' and 'signaling theory'. These three theories imply that sustainability disclosure by a company produces a positive image, shields it from negative public scrutiny and lawsuits, and enhances public acceptance, which in turn augments the company's attraction and sales. Since efficiency, acceptability and legitimacy can also have an impact on financial performance. On the basis of above arguments we develop our first hypothesis as:

> H1: Sustainability practice has a significant positive relationship with financial performance of the companies listed on the Indonesia Stock Exchange under the Jakarta Islamic Index. This relationship is moderated by the level of Islamic practice.

16.2 *Sharīʿah* Compliance and Corporate Financial Performance

This segment reviews the literature on Islamic Finance in relation to corporate sustainability practices, with reference to Muslim majority nations. The text sources in this specific field are still scanty, based, however, researchers tried to establish a solid alliance between sustainability practice and *Sharīʿah* application on the corporate financial outlook. They explained this three-dimensional relationship (sustainability, *Sharīʿah*-compliance, and profitability) utilizing various performance measures. Jan et al. (2019a, b) explore the relationship between sustainability practice and financial performance of Malaysian Islamic banking for the period of 2008–2017. Looking from the three different perspectives of management, shareholder and market, they argued that company financial performance can be measured by various financial ratios to indicate its business outlook: 'Return on Assets' points to the nature of the management; 'Return on Equity' to the benefits of the shareholders; and 'Tobin's Q' from the market view point. They find a significant and positive relationship between sustainability practices and financial indicators, suggesting good management practices by the banking industry as well as healthy returns for the shareholders. This study found that the impact of sustainability on the market is insignificant. Conducting an in-depth analysis to learn the reason for the above inconsistencies, they learnt that market participants are not appreciative of the bank's appropriation of its resources to fulfill its social and environmental efforts. The market views that the bank is institutionalized to make profits and to maintain its own economic sustainability without regard to social and ecological responsibility. Zyadat (2017) analyzes the effect of sustainability on the financial performance of Jordanian Islamic banking during the period 2008–2014. He collects the data from the country's two major Islamic institutions, namely the Jordan Islamic Bank and the Arab Islamic Bank. This study finds a statistically significant positive effect of sustainability on financial performance as measured by ROA and Earnings per Share (EPS), but demonstrates a negative outcome when measured by ROE. Ur Rehman et al. (2020) investigate the impact of corporate social responsibility disclosure on financial performance in the Islamic banking industry in Pakistan from 2012 to 2017. They find a significant negative relationship between aggregate sustainability disclosure and corporate financial performance. Nevertheless, when observed individually the disclosure of the environmental and economic dimensions reveals a meaningful positive effect on the bank's financial performance, while the disclosure of social practices does not positively affect its financial performance. Listyaningsih and Krishnamurti (2015) examine the performance of shares in the Indonesia Stock Exchange by dividing the data into two periods: the 2005–2007 phase consisting of JII and non-JII groups, and the 2008–2012 period comprising three groupings of JII, *Sharīʻah* and non-*Sharīʻah*. This study finds no difference in financial gains between investing in conventional or in Islamic stocks.

Given the inconsistencies of these research findings, several points should be considered. First, the different measurements of input variables, such as aggregate and individual sustainability disclosures, and of outcome variables, such as different performance measures, may have contributed to inconsistent results in previous studies. Secondly, incomplete reporting on sustainability and *Sharīʻah* practices by corporations could also be another reason for the limited association between these two practices (sustainability and Islamicity) and financial performance. Peng and Isa (2020) pull ESG scores from the Thomson Reuters ASSET4 database that provides a higher degree of robustness, accuracy, consistency, and validity of information. They examine the impact of sustainability practices on the financial performance of four hundred sixty-one Islamic companies from 20 different countries listed on the MSCI World Islamic Index during the period 2010–2017. Their analysis reveals that the ESG aggregate and its individual components are positively related to the firms' financial performance and suggest that ESG and *Sharīʻah* screening could increase the firm's value, promote more ethical, responsible and transparent practices, and thereby create new markets for potential investors. In addition, both sustainability practices and *Sharīʻah* performances have recently become business strategies for several global large companies due to high demand from their stakeholders. This suggests that companies that comply with these requests will provide good signals to stakeholders, who will eventually value their corporate sustainability and Islamic practices. Therefore, our second hypothesis is:

H2:Islamic practice has a significant and positive relationship with financial performance of companies listed on the Indonesia Stock Exchange under the Jakarta Islamic Index. Islamic practice also moderates the relationship between sustainability practice and financial performance.

16.3 Conceptual Framework

Figure 16.1 illustrates the the relationship between sustainability and Islamic practice, and the financial performance of selected companies listed on the Jakarta Islamic Index for the period of 2015–2019. In this model, one independent (ESG scores

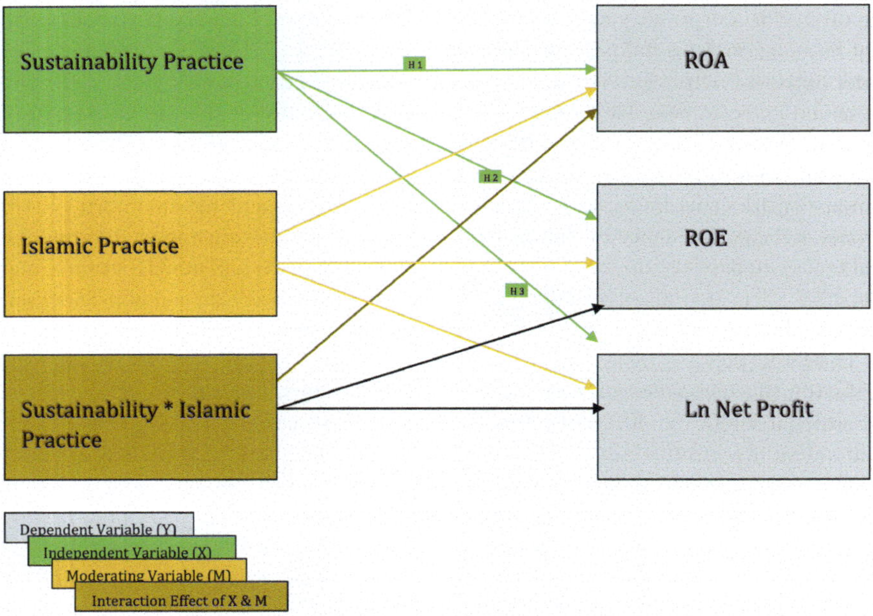

Fig. 16.1 Conceptual framework of the sustainability study

based on the Global Reporting Initiative (GRI) standards), three dependent (Return on Assets', 'Return on Equity' and 'Ln Net Profit'), one moderating (Islamic Social Reporting (ISR) scores) and one interaction variable is selected. A more detailed explanation of the operationalization of the variables is provided in the Methodology section.

16.3.1 Methodology

16.3.1.1 Sampling Procedure

The sample of this study consists of seventy-five firms, year observations derived from the fifteen companies listed on the Indonesia Stock Exchange (IDX) under the Jakarta Islamic Index for 2015–2019. The selection of 2015 as the beginning of our research period is because in that year the Indonesian Financial Services Authority (OJK) issued the Regulation Number 15/POJK.04/2015 concerning the application of *Sharīʻah* principles in the capital market.

The Jakarta Islamic Index (JII) is a *Sharīʻah* stock index consisting of the thirty most liquid Islamic stocks listed on the IDX, and these shares derive from the List of *Sharīʻah* Securities (Daftar Efek Syariah—DES) issued by the OJK. The JII constituents are reviewed by the IDX twice a year following the DES review by the OJK. The selection criteria involve two stages. First, sixty shares listed on DES that have sat on the ISSI index for the past six months are selected according to the order of the highest average market capitalization for the past one year. Secondly, of these sixty stocks, thirty are selected based on the highest average daily transaction value in the regular market. Consistent with the selection criteria, some stocks are removed from the index while other new shares enter the system to complete the number of thirty stocks at every review period. Thus, the Indonesia Stock Exchange is only responsible for selecting the JII list based on its market capitalization and market liquidity, whereas OJK is the organization responsible for issuing the List of *Sharī'ah* Securities or DES (Summarized from https://www.idx.co.id/idx-syariah/indeks-saham-syariah/).

The DES review is carried out by the OJK periodically and incidentally. Periodic evaluation is executed twice a year on fixed dates and the shares meeting the criteria according to OJK Regulation Number 35/POJK.04/2017 remain on the list. Incidental assessment is performed when the need to revise the DES list outside the fixed dates arise. The necessity for such revision occurs either when a new company is being added to the DES list as a result of an Initial Public Offering (IPO); or when the existing shares on the platform no longer meet *Sharī'ah* requirements according to OJK regulations. There are two main conditions for stocks to meet the DES criteria. First, the IDX listed companies perform no business activities prohibited by the *Sharī'ah*, such as gambling and *ribāwi* financial services. Second, public companies do not have more than 45% of the total interest-based debt (*ribā*) when compared to their total assets, and their total interest income and other non-*ḥalāl* income is not more than 10% of their total operating revenue.[2]

The above information indicates that the criteria for shares to be on the DES list are not completely *Sharī'ah* wheraes there is still a proportion of business activities contravening Islamic law. Allowing non-compliant transactions to be part of the *Sharī'ah* shares may have three implications for the development of Islamic Finance in Indonesia. First, it provides an opportunity for the corporate management to design business activities that meet only the minimum DES requirements. Second, the companies on the DES list are not motivated to become *Sharī'ah*-driven enterprises in the same way as sustainable companies are. The latter strive to tick every box of sustainability requirements. Had those companies been *Sharī'ah*-driven, they would have endeavored to make significant changes to their operations so that their *Sharī'ah* compliance would get better over time. Third, allowing the DES companies to be not fully Islamic could provide a setback for Muslim investors who might expect the firms under the Islamic index to be completely *Sharī'ah* compliant. However, a similar policy with a lower percentage is also being implemented in Malaysia (Firmansyah, 2017). In spite of a moderate level of *Sharī'ah* requirements stipulated by the Indonesian Government, a number of companies were unable to meet these requirements and were removed from the JII index, and thus from our sample.

---

[2] Summarized from https://www.ojk.go.id/id/kanal/syariah/data-dan-statistik/daftar-efek-syariah/default.aspx.

The sample companies comprise seven business sectors from the nine segment areas available on the Indonesia Stock Exchange. The IDX classifies the businesses of stock issuers into nine sectors following the Jakarta Stock Industry Classification (JASICA[3]) Index: (1) agriculture, (2) basic industry & chemical, (3) consumer goods, (4) construction & property & real estate, (5) finance, (6) infrastructure, (7) utilities & transportation, (8) mining miscellaneous industries, and (9) trade & services & investment. The two segments not included in our sample companies are agriculture and finance, because none of the companies under these two segments meets the sampling criteria outlined above.[4] Our sample companies have been listed on the IDX for various times ranging from five to thirty-seven years according to their IPO dates. Thus our selection of sample companies is random. The list of these firms and their seven sectors is presented in Table 16.1.

16.3.1.2 Data and Variables

The Dependent variable in this study is financial, measured by three proxies: 'Return on Assets', 'Return on Equity' and 'Ln Net Profit'. A Study by Firescu (2015) shows that managers are interested in the overall performance of the company, while investors in the profitability of their investments. Therefore, managers concentrate on the accounting return, commonly known as 'Return on Assets', and investors on the return of their investments, widely referred to as 'Return on Equity'. Both these ratios are rooted in the net profit, and therefore we also utilize 'Ln Net Profit' as our third performance measure. The data to assess performance measures are collected from the companies' annual reports. This study measures sustainability practice by ESG disclosure scores based on the ninety-two items of the Global Reporting Initiative (GRI) standards. Content analysis is performed manually to extract ESG disclosure scores from sample companies' annual and sustainability reports (see Appendix 1 for GRI Standard Items). Moderating variable is *Sharīʻah* practice measured by the disclosure of *Sharīʻah* items based on the Islamic Social Reporting (ISR) To assess *Sharīʻah* performance by the sample companies, we adopt the ISR 43-item disclosure index developed by Haniffa and Hudaib (2002), and modified by Othman et al. (2009) who added corporate governance to the index. This modified ISR index consists of six themes: (1) finance and investments, (2) products and services, (3) employees, (4) society, (5) the environment, and (6) corporate governance. We perform content analysis manually to extract ISR disclosure scores from the companies' annual reports (see Appendix 2 for ISR Items).

---

[3] JASICA refers to the Indonesian Business Classification adopted by the Central Bureau of Statistics from the International Standard Industrial Classification (ISIC).

[4] Although the banking sector is the most prominent segment of global Islamic finance, none of the banks in Indonesia was listed on the Jakarta Islamic Index during the period 2015–2018. During the course of 2019, Bank BTPN Sharia (BTPS) entered the system, making it the only bank thus far sitting on the Index. This shows that none of the banking companies meeting the sampling criteria to have been successively on the JII Index for the consecutive five-year period of 2015–2019.

Table 16.1 Sample companies in the JII index 2015 to 2019

No	Code	Company name	Business sector	IPO date
1	SMGR	Semen Indonesia (Persero) Tbk	Basic industry and chemicals	08/07/1991
2	ICBP	Indofood CBP Sukses Makmur Tbk	Consumer goods industry	07/10/2010
3	INDF	Indofood Sukses Makmur Tbk	Consumer goods industry	14/07/1994
4	KLBF	Kalbe Farma Tbk	Consumer goods industry	30/07/1991
5	UNVR	Unilever Indonesia Tbk	Consumer goods industry	11/01/1982
6	TLKM	Telekomunikasi Indonesia (Persero) Tbk	Infrastructure, utilities, and transportation	14/11/1995
7	ADRO	Adaro Energy Tbk	Mining	16/07/2008
8	INCO	Vale Indonesia Tbk	Mining	16/05/1990
9	ASII	Astra International Tbk	Miscellaneous industry	04/04/1990
10	BSDE	Bumi Serpong Damai Tbk	Property, real estate and building construction	06/06/2008
11	PTPP	PP (Persero) Tbk	Property, real estate and building construction	09/02/2010
12	WIKA	Wijaya Karya (Persero) Tbk	Property, real estate and building construction	29/10/2007
13	AKRA	AKR Corporindo Tbk	Trade, service & investment	03/10/1994
14	LPPF	Matahari Department Store Tbk	Trade, service & investment	10/10/1989
15	UNTR	United Tractors Tbk	Trade, service & investment	19/09/1989

The several variables in this study are controlled to avoid scale and spurious bias estimates in our research results. First is the company size as measured by the logarithm of total assets (Arayssi et al., 2016; Duque-Grisales & Aguilera-Caracuel, 2019; Lourenço et al., 2012). Second is leverage, we measure leverage by the ratio of total debts to total assets, known as 'financial leverage ratio', to describe the extent of loans used by the company to finance its assets (Baird et al., 2012; Carini & Chiaf, 2015; Khan et al., 2016). Third variable is inventory turnover. This variable describes the level of corporate sales activity, which is another determinant of financial performance, we measure inventory turnover using cost of goods sold divided by average inventory. Fourth control variable is the age of company, it is measured by the length of time it has been listed on the stock market. Data for control variables are collected from the companies' annual reports. The variable measurements are described in Table 16.2.

16.3.1.3 Data Analysis Technique

In this study data is analyzed by employing 'Robust Multiple Least Square Regression' models with the statistical software Stata. We apply robust regressions in order to avoid estimation bias from potential outliers in the data. Given the small sample size we chose not to remove the potential outliers.

$\text{FinPerf}_1 = \alpha_0 + \alpha_1\text{Sustain} + \alpha_2\text{ISR} + \alpha_3\ \text{Sustain*ISR} + \alpha_4\ \text{Size} + \alpha_5\text{Lev} + \alpha_6\text{InvTurn} + \alpha_7\text{Age} + \varepsilon$. (**Model 1**)

$\text{FinPerf}_2 = \alpha_0 + \alpha_1\text{Sustain} + \alpha_2\text{ISR} + \alpha_3\ \text{Sustain*ISR} + \alpha_4\ \text{Size} + \alpha_5\text{Lev} + \alpha_6\text{InvTurn} + \alpha_7\text{Age} + \varepsilon$. (**Model 2**)

$\text{FinPerf}_3 = \alpha_0 + \alpha_1\text{Sustain} + \alpha_2\text{ISR} + \alpha_3\ \text{Sustain*ISR} + \alpha_4\ \text{Size} + \alpha_5\text{Lev} + \alpha_6\text{InvTurn} + \alpha_7\text{Age} + \varepsilon$. (**Model 3**)

Where:

FinPerf:	ROA (Model 1); ROE (Model 2); Ln Net Profit (Model 3)
Sustain:	Sustainability practice
ISR:	Islamic practice
Size:	Company size
Lev:	Company leverage
InvTurn:	Inventory turnover
Age:	Company age

16.4 Results and Discussions

Table 16.3, Panel A provides descriptive statistics of the research variables. Both ROA and ROE are ratio variables with a mean value of 0.1130551 (11.30%) and 0.2696375 (26.96%) respectively; whereas net profit is a continuous variable so we

Table 16.2 Variable measurements

No	Label	Variable	Proxy	Measurement	Data type
1	FinPerf	Financial performance	ROA (model 1)	Net profit/total assets	Ratio (numerical)
			ROE (model 2)	Net profit/total equity	
			Ln net profit (model 3)	*Logarithm* of *net profit*	
2	Sustain	Sustainability practice	GRI consolidated set consists of 92 items	The GRI standard consisting of 92 items of environmental, social and governance (ESG) factors	Ratio (numerical)
3	ISR	Islamic practice	Islamic Social Reporting index	The Islamic Social index (ISR) proposed by Othman et al. (2009) that consists of 43 items and six themes	Ratio (numerical)
4	Size	Company size	Ln total assets	*Logarithm* of total assets	Ratio (numerical)
5	Lev	Company leverage	–	Total debt/total assets	Ratio (numerical)
6	InvTurn	Inventory turnover	–	Cost of goods sold divided by the average inventory for the same period	Ratio (numerical)
7	Age	Company age	– Ln age	*Logarithm* of age, the period from the time the company conducted its IPO until 2015, the beginning of this research period	Ordinal (categorical)

Table 16.3 Panel A. Descriptive statistics for research variables. Panel B. Descriptive statistics for sustainability and islamic disclosure. Panel C. ESG disclosure by year. Panel D. ISR disclosure by year. Panel E. Pearson's correlation coefficient

Panel A

Stats	Financial performance			Sustain	ISR	Sustain*ISR	Size	Lev	InvTurn	Age
	ROA	ROE	Ln_Net_Profit							
Min	−0.00696	−0.00835	0	0	0.395349	0	3.589.838	0.144675	0.20999	5
Max	0.457701	1.609.403	4.514.561	0.780488	0.534884	0.363018	5.546.491	2.909.504	64.97181	37
Mean	0.113055	0.269638	3.466.945	0.154797	0.465116	0.072744	4.617.849	1.074.351	11.25262	20.46667
P50	0.075637	0.142539	3.465.829	0.146342	0.465116	0.064663	4.620.989	0.876778	6.247174	24
Sd	0.110277	0.369479	0.661063	0.166717	0.039548	0.076067	0.446206	0.741173	14.50421	9.196552
Variance	0.012161	0.136515	0.437004	0.027795	0.001564	0.005786	0.1991	0.549338	210.3721	84.57658
N	75	75	75	75	75	75	75	75	75	75

Panel B

Stats	GRI ESG disclosure, consists of 92 items of Environmental, Social and Governance (ESG) factors	Islamic social reporting, consists of 43 items of disclosure of Islamic Social factors
Min	0	17
Max	64	23
Mean	12.69333	20
P50	12	20
Sd	13.67081	1.700.556
Variance	186.8912	2.891.892
N	75	75

Panel C

ESG disclosure

(continued)

Table 16.3 (continued)

Year	Observation	Mean	Standard deviation	Minimum	Maximum
2015	15	13.06667	18.08498	0	64
2016	15	9.133333	10.77608	0	33
2017	15	8.266667	7.401416	0	18
2018	15	12	10.26088	0	30
2018	15	21	16.59604	0	53
Panel D					
ISR disclosure					
Year	Observation	Mean	Standard deviation	Minimum	Maximum
2015	15	19.8	1.656157	17	22
2016	15	19.8	1.656157	17	22
2017	15	1.986.667	1.726543	17	22
2018	15	20.02	1.780851	17	23
2018	15	20.02	1.838737	17	23

Panel E

Stats	ROA	ROE	Ln_Net_Profit	Sustain	ISR	Sustain*ISR	Size	Lev	InvTurn	Age
ROA	1.0000									

(continued)

Table 16.3 (continued)

ROE	**0.9578*** (0.0000)	1.0000								
Ln_Net_Profit	**0.9578*** (0.0000)	0.1871 (0.1081)	1.0000							
Sustain	**2623*** (0.0230)	−0.0960 (0.4126)	0.0653 −0.5777	1.0000						
ISR	−0.1607 (0.1684)	0.0278 (0.8131)	**0.9594*** 0	0.1145 (0.3280)	1.0000					
Sustain*ISR	**0.0148*** (0.8995)	−0.0736 (0.5304)	0.1083 −0.3549	**0.9556*** (0.0000)	0.1800 (0.1222)	1.0000				
Size	−0.1377 (0.2386)	**0**	**0.5560*** 0	0.1639 −0.16	**0.6073*** (0.0000)	0.2024 −0.0817	1.0000			
Lev	**0**	**0.5800*** (0.0000)	**0.0622*** −0.5727	**0.2318*** (0.0453)	−0.0383 (0.7444)	**0.2409*** −0.0373	−0.2138 (0.0655)	1.0000		
InvTurn	**0.4094*** (0.0003)	−0.0125 (0.9154)	**0.3860*** −0.0006	0.1128 (0.3352)	0.0492 (0.6752)	0.1167 −0.3187	**0.4171*** (0.0002)	−0.0410 (0.7269)	1.0000	
Age	0.0130 (0.9117)	**0.4602*** (0.0000)	0.105 −0.3702	0.0257 −0.827	**0.3128*** (0.0063)	0.0611 −0.6027	−0.0976 (0.4048)	−0.0257 (0.8287)	0.9578 −0.7181	1.0000

Notes Table 16.3 Panel A presents descriptive statistics for all variable proxies used in this study. Table 16.3. Panel B provides descriptive statistics for the disclosure of sustainability and Islamic factors. In this study we used GRI based on ESG disclosure that consist of 92 items of ESG type

This table describes the Pearson's correlation coefficients for the main variables of the study. Significant correlations are indicated in Bold and *. All variables are defined in Table 16.2

transform this variable using log 10. The log net profit or Ln Net Profit has a mean value of 3.466945. Independent variable denoting Sustain is the weighted average of ESG disclosure index based on the GRI standards, so it is also a ratio variable. The minimum ESG disclosure index is 0 and the maximum net score is 0.7804878 (78.05%). The mean value of Sustain (ESG disclosure index) is 0.1547971 (15.48%), indicating that on average, the companies only have 15.48% disclosure of the 92 total items (100%) of the Global Reporting Initiative (GRI) standards. The percentage of average disclosure is significantly low. This limited disclosure can be seen more clearly when we look at the ESG disclosure value shown in Panel B, where the average value is just 12.69333 items of the 92 total disclosure standards. Considering sustainable disclosure is voluntary in nature, its level of disclosure is left to the discretion of the company. Usually, the more the company focuses on sustainability, the better the disclosure level becomes. Thus, the low level of disclosure by our sample companies indicates the lack of their commitment towards sustainability agenda.

The moderating variable of *Sharīʻah* practice measured by the Islamic Social Reporting index is also a ratio variable. The mean value of sample companies' ISR is 0.4651163 (46.51%), with the minimum value of 0.3953488 (39.53%) and the maximum of 0.5348837 (53.48%). Considering that there are only 43 items (100%) in the ISR index, this average value of about 50% (46.51% of 43 items) also reflects the relatively low level of Islamic practice, although comparatively higher than that of Sustain. This subdued score becomes even more apparent when we look at the average score of 20 in Panel B. The depleted level of ISR disclosure reflects the companies' meager commitment to meeting *Sharīʻah* requirements. Considering the Indonesian Financial Services Authority (OJK)'s prerequisites to be considered "Islamic", the companies' limited commitment to *Sharīʻah* obligation is not surprising. As discussed earlier, companies must meet certain criteria to be on the DES list, which is a steppingstone to enter the Jakarta Islamic Index. Low requirements could be the reason for the limited level of commitment. It suggests that these companies are motivated by a business opportunity to be placed on the *Sharīʻah* platform, rather than by Islamic ethics or both. Therefore, the companies are not inspired to faithfully fulfill ISR standards and engage in better disclosure—instead, they observe the bare minimum. Given the relatively low ESG and ISR disclosures by the companies under consideration, the interaction variables of the two are also not high with an average value of 0.0727436 (7.27%), a minimum value of 0 and a maximum of 0.3630176 (36.30%).

As for control variables, the mean values are 4.617849 for Size (firm size); 1.074351 for Lev (firm leverage); 11.25262 for InvTurn (inventory turnover); and 20.46667 for Ln_Age (firm age), implying that sample companies' differences in size and leverage structure are relatively insignificant. This is not surprising because the overall JII companies are based on market capitalization and market liquidity, so that the company size measured by total assets does not differ much from one another. Likewise, the leverage structure of sample firms is not far removed from each other since JII companies are prohibited from appropriating high debt. However, a high variety in the value of inventory turnover and company age is observed. Regarding years of existence, samples have had a minimum life-span on the stock market of five years and the maximum of thirty-seven. Age gaps represent the different stages of corporate maturity in sample companies.

The following panels demonstrate three key areas of inquiry: Sustainability, Islamic performance and moderating factor. Panel C exhibits the corporations' ESG disclosure by year and the results show an insignificant trend from year to year. The maximum value of 64 out of 92 items occurred in 2015, which declined thereafter reaching its lowest point of 18 in 2017. From there, the disclosure increased to the value of 30 in 2018 and 53 in 2019. Several reasons can be suggested for this inconsistent sustainability performance by our sample companies. First, sustainable practice is a voluntary effort and the decision to implement it is left to the discretion of the company. Second, awareness of sustainability practices in the country's business world remains relatively low and therefore there is limited culture of mimicking a role model in sustainability practice. The awareness issue also points to the lack of investors' demand for sustainability information, thus less pressure for the companies to produce it. Finally, the lack of pressure from the investors, the government and the public at large makes corporate sustainability remote from mainstream discourse. However, the situation has improved since 2017 when the Indonesian Financial Services Authority issued the Regulation Number 51/POJK.03/2017 regarding the Implementation of Sustainable Finance. This regulation requires financial service institutions, stock issuers, public companies and others to publish their sustainability reports: banking sector companies have to meet this requirement by 2019, and other issuers by 2020 (Woodhead 2020). This regulation may explain the improved sustainability disclosure by our sample companies in 2018 and 2019 as described above.

Panel D also displays the ISR disclosure by year, and the scores are rather static over the study period with a slight increase in the last two years (2018–2019). Yet, the level of disclosure remains below 50%. A number of reasons appear to explain the low Islamic application. First, perhaps *Sharīʻah* practices are not yet embedded in the operational strategies of the JII companies since they become constituents of the index based on a rather lax DES criteria and this tolerance may be the reason for their low commitment to *Sharīʻah* principles. Second, the companies sitting on the JII index seems not to possess a clear incentive to perform beyond the DES *Sharīʻah* requirements despite having an opportunity to attract potential Islamic investors. Third, lack of expertise of Islamic finance among the banking practioners seems to be another reason for our companies' low *Sharīʻah* compliance. A study by Iswanaji (2018) on the growth of Islamic banking in Indonesia shows the problem of skill proficiency and argues that the second major challenge encountered by its *Sharīʻah* industry, in addition to an inadequate regulatory framework, is the lack of qualified human resources, i.e. ninety percent of the workforce of Islamic banking having no prior Islamic Finance training. Taktak and Farooq (2014) demonstrates that recommendations by experts and analysts have no value-relevance to the *Sharīʻah* compliant companies in a similar fashion to non-*Sharīʻah* counterparts. Their study supports our argument that *Sharīʻah* companies have not been properly considered by investors in making investment decisions. This could be due to a lack of investor confidence or poor awareness of the lucrative potential of *Sharī'ah* stocks.

It is clear that disclosure of both sustainability and Islamic performance by sample companies remains at the lower end of the scale (below 50%). We argue that these firms have not fully committed to either ESG or to *Sharī'ah* obligations. We also assert that their sustainability practices have not gone hand-in-hand with their Islamic activities to seriously improve their financial performance. The slightly positive trend with regards to their Islamic compliance indicates that these corporations meet the *Sharī'ah* requirements prescribed by OJK in order to stay on the *Sharī'ah* index. By contrast, they have not found the niche to fully embrace sustainability, with this being reflected in their curvy performances throughout the course of study period. One explanation for such lack of commitment could be that these companies are still following the old school of thought: business for profit making. It also suggests that they have not transformed themselves to the level of high corporate ethics promoted by the United Nations and the world community. In addition, their practice is also a reflection of the country's overall relatively weak commitment to sustainability.[5] One weakness of Indonesian public institutions is the level of implementation and legal enforcement: a sound legal standing is not necessarily translated into good policy and action.

In addition to the above descriptive statistics and analysis, we also analyze the correlations of the variables. Panel E provides Pearson's correlation coefficients among the variables used in regression models. Patterning on this model, statistical analysis indicates that one of predictor variables Sustain is highly correlated with the interaction terms Sustain*ISR. Otherwise, there is no high correlation between the main predictor variables (including independent, moderating and control variables), indicating that multicollinearity is not a serious concern in regressions. Molala (2019) asserts that multicollinearity occurs when an absolute correlation coefficient higher than 0.7. In our results only Sustain and Sustain*ISR have correlation above 0.7 which is at 0.9556. To address the multicollinearity issue, we ran the generalized linear method (GLM) regression as a sensitivity test, and the results (not reported here) are consistent with the main regression tests.

The above descriptive statistics demonstrate that sample companies' sustainability practice and Islamic performance are still at their infancy, with a great deal of room for improvement. We are convinced that the corporations have to make additional long-term efforts to experience a significant impact of the sustainability practices on their financial performance. The Government and the *Sharī'ah* supervising board also have to be more attentive in supervising these firms, not only to ensure their compliance but also to provide a clear incentive to encourage an uptrend performance.

Table 16.4 reports the results of the estimating equations (Models 1, Model 2 & Model 3). The estimated coefficients for Sustain are −2.78717, −6.899427 and −

[5] Just last December, Indonesia along with a few other countries, was singled out by the UN Secretary General Antonio Guterres for its lack of commitment to carbon net zero emission (https://www.bbc.com/news/science-environment-55147647 https://www.theguardian.com/environment/2020/dec/09/rich-failing-help-fund-poor-countries-climate-fight-warns-un-chief-antonio-guterres).

Table 16.4 Results of Robust Multiple Least Square Regression of Sustainability Practice on Financial Performance

Variable	*Predicted sign*	*Model 1*		*Model 2*		*Model 3*	
		$FinPerf_1$		$FinPerf_2$		$FinPerf_3$	
		ROA Estimates (p value)	t-stat	ROE Estimates (p value)	t-stat	Ln_Net_Profit Estimates (p value)	t-stat
Sustain	+	−2.78717 (0.000)	−3.90	−6.899427 (0.001)	−3.42	−11.18781 (0.000)	−4.68
ISR	+	0.6658164 (0.047)	2.02	2.005176 (0.035)	2.16	2.499856 (0.026)	2.27
Sustain*ISR	?	5.714075 (0.001)	3.59	13.9844 (0.003)	3.11	23.15008 (0.000)	4.35
Size	+	−0.1914766 (0.000)	−6.74	−0.5223544 (0.000)	−6.51	0.2850459 (0.004)	3.00
Lev	?	0.0386704 (0.001)	3.38	0.2458493 (0.000)	7.60	−0.0271723 (0.481)	−0.71
InvTurn	+	0.0026603 (0.000)	4.40	0.0070884 (0.000)	4.15	0.0111066 (0.000)	5.50
Age	+	0.0027706 (0.007)	2.79	0.011035 (0.000)	3.93	0.0088847 (0.009)	2.67

(continued)

Table 16.4 (continued)

Variable	*Predicted sign*	*Model 1*		*Model 2*		*Model 3*	
		$FinPerf_1$		$FinPerf_2$		$FinPerf_3$	
		ROA Estimates (p value)	t-stat	ROE Estimates (p value)	t-stat	Ln_Net_Profit Estimates (p value)	t-stat
N		75		75		75	
Intercept		0.5697183 (0.000)	-	1.215801 (0.003)	-	0.8365665 (0.077)	-
N		75		75		75	
F (7, 67)		24.50 (0.0000)		36.36 (0.0000)		40.53 (0.0000)	
R-Square		0.71911778		0.79163192		0.80896373	
Adjusted R-Square		68.97%		76.98%		78.90%	

This table presents the results of investigations on the relationship of sustainability practices and financial performance with Islamic practice as moderating variable. All variables are defined in Section III. One-tail t-test is performed for directional predictions. Significant levels 1%, 5% & 10% denote as ***, **, * respectively. Model used are:

$FinPerf_1 = \alpha_0 + \alpha_1 Sustain + \alpha_2 ISR + \alpha_3\ Sustain*ISR + \alpha_4\ Size + \alpha_5 Lev + \alpha_6 InvTurn + \alpha_7 Age + \varepsilon$. (**Model 1**)

$FinPerf_2 = \alpha_0 + \alpha_1 Sustain + \alpha_2 ISR + \alpha_3\ Sustain*ISR + \alpha_4\ Size + \alpha_5 Lev + \alpha_6 InvTurn + \alpha_7 Age + \varepsilon$. (**Model 2**)

$FinPerf_3 = \alpha_0 + \alpha_1 Sustain + \alpha_2 ISR + \alpha_3\ Sustain*ISR + \alpha_4\ Size + \alpha_5 Lev + \alpha_6 InvTurn + \alpha_7 Age + \varepsilon$. (**Model 3**)

11.18781 respectively, and the results are statistically significant at the 0.01% level with t-statistics −3.9 (Model 1); −3.42 (Model 2) and −4.68 (Model 3). It is observed from the regression results, that t-statistics values in the three models are above critical value, it can be concluded that results are highly significant and support initial hypothesis. Results show that the companies with higher sustainability practices experience lower financial performance. These findings contradict our hypothesis which predicted that sustainability practice is positively associated with financial performance. These results also conflict with those of prior studies by Waddock and Graves (1997) and (Buallay, 2019). In addition, our outcomes contradict the three theories that support sustainability disclosures, namely agency, signaling and legitimacy theories discussed in the literature review. However, our results are in line with modern 'portfolio theory' which defies strategic limitations in portfolios. Our predictions for the unexpected results in this analysis are twofold. First, the small sample size in our study may have contributed to the negative results. Second, the minimum average ESG disclosure by our sample companies could be another reason.

Our analysis of Islamic performance by the sample companies is also tested with the same model. The estimated coefficients of the ISR is at 0.6658164 (t-stat 2.02); 0.6658164 (t-stat 2.16); 2.005176 (t-stat 2.02) in Model 1, Model 2 & Model 3 respectively; these results are statistically significant at the 0.5% level. Consistent with our predictions, Islamic practice is positively associated with financial performance. Likewise, the estimated coefficient of the interaction variable, Sustain*ISR was at 5.7140 (t-stat 3.59); 13.9844 (t-stat 3.11); and 23.15008 (t-stat 4.35) across the three models; the results were statistically significant at the 0.01% level. The positive coefficient for the interaction variable indicates that the presence of ISR positively moderates the relationship between sustainability practices and financial performance. These findings strongly support second hypothesis, which posits that better Islamic disclosure leads to improved financial performance; and likewise *Sharīʿah* compliance moderates the relationship between sustainability practice and financial performance. These outcomes support our initial prediction that ISR disclosure is positively associated with financial performance and acts as a positive moderator for the relationship between sustainability practice and financial performance. These results are also in accordance with the findings of several other studies by Jan et al., (2019a, b); Peng and Isa (2020); Ur Rehman et al. (2020). Our research findings are also in line with the three agency, signaling and legitimacy theories, thereby highlighting the importance of disclosure for better financial performance.

The models are robust with an adjusted R Square of 68.97% in Model 1; 76.98% in Model 2; and 78.90% in Model 3. These results show that the variables used in this study explain by about 70% financial performance in the three models.

16.5 Conclusion

This research explores the relationship between sustainability practices and financial performance in the Indonesian context. We reviewed fifteen sample companies listed on the Jakarta Islamic Index during the course of five years (2015–2019) utilizing the three proxies: ROA, ROE and Ln Net Profit. We first hypothesizes that sustainability practices improve financial performance of the companies under consideration, and secondly that *Sharīʿah* compliance has a significant positive impact on their financial performance. We further predict that Islamic practice moderates the relationship between sustainability practices and financial performance. Contrary to our first expectation, we find that sustainability practice has a negative and significant effect on these companies' financial performance. Meanwhile, *Sharīʿah* compliance demonstrates a significantly positive relationship with their financial performance, and that this measure also positively moderates the relationship between sustainability and profitability proxies.

Our research contributes to sustainability literature and Islamic Finance in three different ways. First, to the best of our knowledge no previous research has investigated the research models proposed in this study, so this analysis enriches the empirical conceptual model. Second, this inquiry contributes to the current literature by providing evidence of a three-dimensional relationship between sustainability, Islamic practice and financial performance. Third, this study provides new empirical insights to regulators regarding *Sharīʿah* compliance as a moderator of the relationship between sustainability practice and financial performance. As such it can be used as a basis for policy formation in advancing and regulating sustainability and *Sharīʿah* practices by companies.

Our study is subject to several limitations. First, due to our content analysis methodology, we are unable to establish a high level of data validity. However, we have attempted to use several verification approaches during the data mining process. Second, we focus on a small number of *Sharīʿah*-oriented companies, which makes our findings in need of careful consideration when they are generalized for understanding other research contexts. Third, we rely on an established set of company performance measures that may not adequately capture all the performance effects of sustainability and Islamic reporting practices. These limitations suggest important directions for further research. Future studies may explore our research questions by using alternative and broader data-sets from such databases, e.g. Bloomberg, Datastream, and others. This type of replication can help establish the applicability of our results.

Appendix

See Tables 16.5 and 16.6.

Table 16.5 Global Reporting Initiative (GRI) standard indicators

No	GRI standard	GRI standard title	Disclosure number	Disclosure title
	Governance indicators (G):			
1	GRI 102	Governance	102–18	Governance structure
2	GRI 102	Governance	102–19	Delegating authority
3	GRI 102	Governance	102–20	Executive-level responsibility for economic, environmental, and social topics
4	GRI 102	Governance	102–21	Consulting stakeholders on economic, environmental, and social topics
5	GRI 102	Governance	102–22	Composition of the highest governance body and its committees
6	GRI 102	Governance	102–23	Chair of the highest governance body
7	GRI 102	Governance	102–24	Nominating and selecting the highest governance body
8	GRI 102	Governance	102–25	Conflicts of interest
9	GRI 102	Governance	102–26	Role of highest governance body in setting purpose, values, and strategy
10	GRI 102	Governance	102–27	Collective knowledge of highest governance body
11	GRI 102	Governance	102–28	Evaluating the highest governance body's performance
12	GRI 102	Governance	102–29	Identifying and managing economic, environmental, and social impacts
13	GRI 102	Governance	102–30	Effectiveness of risk management processes
14	GRI 102	Governance	102–31	Review of economic, environmental, and social topics
15	GRI 102	Governance	102–32	Highest governance body's role in sustainability reporting
16	GRI 102	Governance	102–33	Communicating critical concerns
17	GRI 102	Governance	102–34	Nature and total number of critical concerns

(continued)

Table 16.5 (continued)

No	GRI standard	GRI standard title	Disclosure number	Disclosure title
18	GRI 102	Governance	102–35	Remuneration policies
19	GRI 102	Governance	102–36	Process for determining remuneration
20	GRI 102	Governance	102–37	Stakeholders' involvement in remuneration
21	GRI 102	Governance	102–38	Annual total compensation ratio
22	GRI 102	Governance	102–39	Percentage increase in annual total compensation ratio
	Environmental sustainability indicators (E):			
1	GRI 301	Materials	301–1	Materials used by weight or volume
2	GRI 301	Materials	301–2	Recycled input materials used
3	GRI 301	Materials	301–3	Reclaimed products and their packaging materials
4	GRI 302	Energy	302–1	Energy consumption within the organization
5	GRI 302	Energy	302–2	Energy consumption outside of the organization
6	GRI 302	Energy	302–3	Energy intensity
7	GRI 302	Energy	302–4	Reduction of energy consumption
8	GRI 302	Energy	302–5	Reductions in energy requirements of products and services
9	GRI 303	Water and effluents	303–1	Interactions with water as a shared resource
10	GRI 303	Water and effluents	303–2	Management of water discharge-related impacts
11	GRI 303	Water and effluents	303–3	Water withdrawal
12	GRI 303	Water and effluents	303–4	Water discharge
13	GRI 303	Water and effluents	303–5	Water consumption
14	GRI 304	Biodiversity	304–1	Operational sites owned, leased, managed in, or adjacent to, protected areas and areas of high biodiversity value outside protected areas
15	GRI 304	Biodiversity	304–2	Significant impacts of activities, products, and services on biodiversity
16	GRI 304	Biodiversity	304–3	Habitats protected or restored

(continued)

Table 16.5 (continued)

No	GRI standard	GRI standard title	Disclosure number	Disclosure title
17	GRI 304	Biodiversity	304–4	IUCN Red List species and national conservation list species with habitats in areas affected by operations
18	GRI 305	Emissions	305–1	Direct (Scope 1) GHG emissions
19	GRI 305	Emissions	305–2	Energy indirect (Scope 2) GHG emissions
20	GRI 305	Emissions	305–3	Other indirect (Scope 3) GHG emissions
21	GRI 305	Emissions	305–4	GHG emissions intensity
22	GRI 305	Emissions	305–5	Reduction of GHG emissions
23	GRI 305	Emissions	305–6	Emissions of ozone-depleting substances (ODS)
24	GRI 305	Emissions	305–7	Nitrogen oxides (NO_X), sulfur oxides (SO_X), and other significant air emissions
25	GRI 306	Effluents and waste	306–2	Waste by type and disposal method
26	GRI 306	Effluents and waste	306–3	Significant spills
27	GRI 306	Effluents and waste	306–4	Transport of hazardous waste
28	GRI 307	Environmental compliance	307–1	Non-compliance with environmental laws and regulations
29	GRI 308	Supplier environmental assessment	308–1	New suppliers that were screened using environmental criteria
30	GRI 308	Supplier environmental assessment	308–2	Negative environmental impacts in the supply chain and actions taken
	Social sustainability indicators (S):			
1	GRI 401	Employment	401–1	New employee hires and employee turnover
2	GRI 401	Employment	401–2	Benefits provided to full-time employees that are not provided to temporary or part-time employees
3	GRI 401	Employment	401–3	Parental leave
4	GRI 402	Labor/management relations	402–1	Minimum notice periods regarding operational changes
5	GRI 403	Occupational health and safety	403–1	Occupational health and safety management system

(continued)

Table 16.5 (continued)

No	GRI standard	GRI standard title	Disclosure number	Disclosure title
6	GRI 403	Occupational health and safety	403–2	Hazard identification, risk assessment, and incident investigation
7	GRI 403	Occupational health and safety	403–3	Occupational health services
8	GRI 403	Occupational health and safety	403–4	Worker participation, consultation, and communication on occupational health and safety
9	GRI 403	Occupational health and safety	403–5	Worker training on occupational health and safety
10	GRI 403	Occupational health and safety	403–6	Promotion of worker health
11	GRI 403	Occupational health and safety	403–7	Prevention and mitigation of occupational health and safety impacts directly linked by business relationships
12	GRI 403	Occupational health and safety	403–8	Workers covered by an occupational health and safety management system
13	GRI 403	Occupational health and safety	403–9	Work-related injuries
14	GRI 403	Occupational health and safety	403–10	Work-related ill health
15	GRI 404	Training and education	404–1	Average hours of training per year per employee
16	GRI 404	Training and education	404–2	Programs for upgrading employee skills and transition assistance programs
17	GRI 404	Training and education	404–3	Percentage of employees receiving regular performance and career development reviews
18	GRI 405	Diversity and equal opportunity	405–1	Diversity of governance bodies and employees
19	GRI 405	Diversity and equal opportunity	405–2	Ratio of basic salary and remuneration of women to men
20	GRI 406	Non-discrimination	406–1	Incidents of discrimination and corrective actions taken
21	GRI 407	Freedom of association and collective bargaining	407–1	Operations and suppliers in which the right to freedom of association and collective bargaining may be at risk
22	GRI 408	Child labor	408–1	Operations and suppliers at significant risk for incidents of child labor

(continued)

Table 16.5 (continued)

No	GRI standard	GRI standard title	Disclosure number	Disclosure title
23	GRI 409	Forced or compulsory labor	409–1	Operations and suppliers at significant risk for incidents of forced or compulsory labor
24	GRI 410	Security practices	410–1	Security personnel trained in human rights policies or procedures
25	GRI 411	Rights of indigenous peoples	411–1	Incidents of violations involving rights of indigenous peoples
26	GRI 412	Human rights assessment	412–3	Significant investment agreements and contracts that include human rights clauses or that underwent human rights screening
27	GRI 412	Human rights assessment	412–2	Employee training on human rights policies or procedures
28	GRI 412	Human rights assessment	412–1	Operations that have been subject to human rights reviews or impact assessments
29	GRI 413	Local communities	413–1	Operations with local community engagement, impact assessments, and development programs
30	GRI 413	Local communities	413–2	Operations with significant actual and potential negative impacts on local communities
31	GRI 414	Supplier social assessment	414–1	New suppliers that were screened using social criteria
32	GRI 414	Supplier social assessment	414–2	Negative social impacts in the supply chain and actions taken
33	GRI 415	Public policy	415–1	Political contributions
34	GRI 416	Customer health and safety	416–1	Assessment of the health and safety impacts of product and service categories
35	GRI 416	Customer health and safety	416–2	Incidents of non-compliance concerning the health and safety impacts of products and services
36	GRI 417	Marketing and labeling	417–1	Requirements for product and service information and labeling
37	GRI 417	Marketing and labeling	417–2	Incidents of non-compliance concerning product and service information and labeling
38	GRI 417	Marketing and labeling	417–3	Incidents of non-compliance concerning marketing communications

(continued)

Table 16.5 (continued)

No	GRI standard	GRI standard title	Disclosure number	Disclosure title
39	GRI 418	Customer privacy	418–1	Substantiated complaints concerning breaches of customer privacy and losses of customer data
40	GRI 419	Socioeconomic compliance	419–1	Non-compliance with laws and regulations in the social and economic area

Source GRI Resource Centre (https://www.globalreporting.org/how-to-use-the-gri-standards/resource-center/)

Table 16.6 The Islamic Social Reporting (ISR) index

Disclosure items	
A	*Finance and investment theme*
1	*Ribā* activities
2	*Gharar*
3	*Zakāt*: method used, zakatable amount, beneficiaries
4	Policy on late repayments and insolvent clients/bad debts written-off
5	Current value balance sheet (CVBS)
6	Value added statement (VAS)
B	*Product and service themes*
7	Green product
8	*Ḥalāl* status of the product
9	Product safety and quality
10	Customer complaints/incidents of non-compliance with regulation and voluntary codes (if any)
C	*Employee themes*
11	Nature of work: working hours, holidays, other benefits
12	Education and training/ human capital development
13	Equal opportunities
14	Employee involvement
15	Health and safety
16	Working environment
17	Employment of other special-interest-group (i.e. handicapped, ex-convicts, former drug-addicts)

(continued)

Table 16.6 (continued)

Disclosure items	
18	Higher echelons in the company perform the congregational prayers with lower and middle level managers
19	Muslim employees are allowed to perform their obligatory prayers during specific times and fasting during Ramaḍan on their working day
20	Proper place of worship for the employees
D	*Society themes*
21	*Ṣadaqah*/Donation
22	*Waqf*
23	*Qarḍ al-Ḥasan* (benevolent lending or interest free-loan)
24	Employee volunteerism
25	Education-school adoption scheme: scholarships
26	Graduate employment
27	Youth development
28	Underprivileged community
29	Children care
30	Charities/gifts/social activities
31	Sponsoring public health/recreational projects/sports/cultural events
E	*Environment themes*
32	Conservation of environment
33	Endangered wildlife
34	Environmental pollution
35	Environmental education
36	Environmental products/process related
37	Environmental audit/independent verification statement/governance
38	Environmental management system/policy
F	*Corporate governance themes*
39	*Sharī'ah* compliance status
40	Ownership structure: number of Muslim shareholders and their shareholdings
41	Board structure: Muslim vs non-Muslim
42	Forbidden activities: monopolistic practices, holding necessary goods, price manipulation, fraudulent business practices, gambling
43	Anti-corruption policies

Source Othman et al., (2009)

References

Ahmed, H. (2013). Financial inclusion and Islamic finance: Organizational formats, products, outreach, and sustainability. In Z. Iqbal & A. Mirakhor (Eds.), *Economic Development and Islamic Finance* (Vol. 203).

Ahmed, H., Mohieldin, M., Verbeek, J., & Aboulmagd, F. (2015). On the sustainable development goals and the role of Islamic finance. The World Bank.

Ahmed, H. I., & Barikzai, S. A. K. (2016). Objectives of islamic finance achieved by islamic banks. *Al-Adwa, 45*(31), 45–65.

Al-Jarhi, M. A. (2002). *Islamic Finance: An Efficient and Equitable Option.*

Al Ansari, R., & Alanzarouti, F. (2020). ESG and islamic finance: An ethical bridge built on shared values. *Journal of Islamic Financial Studies, 6*(1).

Algaoud, L. M., & Lewis, M. K. (2007). Islamic critique of conventional financing. In K. Hassan & M. Lewis (Eds.), *Handbook of Islamic Banking* (Vol. 38). Edward Elgar Publishing.

Ali, H. Y., Danish, R. Q., & Asrar-ul-Haq, M. (2020). How corporate social responsibility boosts firm financial performance: The mediating role of corporate image and customer satisfaction. *Corporate Social Responsibility Environmental Management, 27*(1), 166–177.

Ali, M. (2020). Impact of leverage on financial performance (evidence from pakistan food and fertilizer sector). *Journal of Critical Reviews, 7*(13), 447–456.

Allouche, J., & Laroche, P. (2005). A meta-analytical investigation of the relationship between corporate social and financial performance.

Anggaini, E. T. (2020). Sejarah dan perkembangan bank syariah di Indonesia. https://blog.amartha.com/sejarah-dan-perkembangan-bank-syariah-di-indonesia/.

Aouadi, A., & Marsat, S. (2018). Do ESG controversies matter for firm value? Evidence from International data. *Journal of Business Ethics, 151*(4), 1027–1047.

Arayssi, M., Dah, M., & Jizi, M. (2016). Women on boards, sustainability reporting and firm performance. *Sustainability Accounting, Management and Policy Journal, 7*(3), 376–401.

Baird, P. L., Geylani, P. C., & Roberts, J. A. (2012). Corporate social and financial performance re-examined: Industry effects in a linear mixed model analysis. *Journal of Business Ethics, 109*(3), 367–388.

Balatbat, M., Siew, R., & Carmichael, D. (2012). *ESG scores and its influence on firm performance: Australian evidence.* School of Accounting Seminar SeriesAustralia: UNSW.

Barnett, M. L., & Salomon, R. M. (2006). Beyond dichotomy: The curvilinear relationship between social responsibility and financial performance. *Strategic Management Journal, 27*(11), 1101–1122.

Barone, G. J., & Hickman, L. (2019). Agency problems, information asymmetry, and socially responsible investing in the wake of citizens united: A call for the disclosure of political contributions in the United States. *Journal of Accounting, Ethics and Public Policy, 20*(2), 225–235.

Bernow, S., Klempner, B., & Magnin, C. (2017). From 'why' to 'why not': Sustainable investing as the new normal. https://www.mckinsey.com/~/media/McKinsey/Industries/Private%20Equity%20and%20Principal%20Investors/Our%20Insights/From%20why%20to%20why%20not%20Sustainable%20investing%20as%20the%20new%20normal/From-why-to-why-not-Sustainable-investing-as-the-new-normal.ashx.

Blasi, S., Caporin, M., & Fontini, F. (2018). A multidimensional analysis of the relationship between corporate social responsibility and firms' economic performance. *Ecological Economics, 147*, 218–229.

Board, I. F. S. (2013). *Islamic Financial Services Industry Stability Report, 2013–2015.*

Board, I. F. S. (2020). *Islamic Financial Services Industry Stability Report 2020.*

Buallay, A. (2019). Is sustainability reporting (ESG) associated with performance? Evidence from the European banking sector. *Management of Environmental Quality: An International Journal, 30*(1), 98–115.

Button, K. S., Ioannidis, J. P., Mokrysz, C., Nosek, B. A., Flint, J., Robinson, E. S., & Munafò, M. R. (2013). Power failure: Why small sample size undermines the reliability of neuroscience. *Nature Reviews Neuroscience, 14*(5), 365–376.

Carini, C., & Chiaf, E. (2015). The relationship between annual and sustainability, environmental and social reports. *Corporate Ownership and Control, 13*, 979–993.

Chang, R.-D., Zuo, J., Zhao, Z.-Y., Zillante, G., Gan, X.-L., & Soebarto, V. (2017). Evolving theories of sustainability and firms: History, future directions and implications for renewable energy research. *Renewable Sustainable Energy Reviews, 72*, 48–56.

Chapra, M. U. (1985). *Towards a Just Monetary System* (Vol. 8). International Institute of Islamic Thought (IIIT).

Cho, S. J., Chung, C. Y., & Young, J. (2019). Study on the relationship between CSR and financial performance. *Sustainability, 11*(2), 343.

Choudhury, M. A. (2007). Development of Islamic economic and social thought. In K. Hassan & M. Lewis (Eds.), *Handbook of Islamic Banking* (Vol. 38). Edward Elgar Publishing.

Çizakça, M. (2013). *Islamic Capitalism and Finance: Origins, Evolution and the Future*: Edward Elgar Publishing.

Coad, A., Holm, J. R., Krafft, J., & Quatraro, F. (2018). Firm age and performance. *Journal of Evolutionary Economics, 28*(1), 1–11.

Damak, M., & Roy, D. (2020). Environmental, social, and governance: Islamic finance and ESG: Sharia-compliant instruments can put the S in ESG.

Dang, C., Li, Z. F., & Yang, C. (2018). Measuring firm size in empirical corporate finance. *Journal of Banking Finance, 86*, 159–176.

Daugaard, D. (2019). Emerging new themes in environmental, social and governance investing: A systematic literature review. *Accounting & Finance.* doi:https://doi.org/10.1111/acfi.12479.

Drizane, H., & Al-Malkawi, H.-A. (2020). Profit and loss sharing (PLS) modes of financing in Islamic financial institutions.

Duque-Grisales, E., & Aguilera-Caracuel, J. (2019). Environmental, social and governance (ESG) scores and financial performance of multilatinas: Moderating effects of geographic International diversification and financial slack. *Journal of Business Ethics*, 1–20.

Eccles, R. G., Ioannou, I., & Serafeim, G. (2014). The impact of corporate sustainability on organizational processes and performance. *Management Science, 60*(11), 2835–2857.

Fatemi, A., Glaum, M., & Kaiser, S. (2017). ESG performance and firm value: The moderating role of disclosure. *Global Finance Journal.*

Fauzi, H., & Idris, K. (2009). The relationship of CSR and financial performance: New evidence from Indonesian companies. *Issues in Social Environmental Accounting, 3*(1).

Finance, R. (2014). The emerging convergence of SRI, ESG and Islamic finance. https://ceif.iba.edu.pk/pdf/ThomsonReuters-ResponsibleFinanceReport2015TheEmergingConvergenceofSRIESGandIslamicFinance.pdf.

Firescu, V. (2015). Comprehensive income, a new dimension in performance measurement and reporting. *Procedia Economics Finance, 20*, 218–223.

Firmansyah, E. A. (2017). Seleksi Saham Syariah: Perbandingan antara Bursa Efek Indonesia dan Malaysia. *Jurnal Inspirasi Bisnis Dan Manajemen, 1*(1), 1–10.

Global Reporting Initiative. (2013). *G4 Sustainability Reporting Guidelines: Reporting Principles and Standard Disclosures.* https://www.globalreporting.org/resourcelibrary/grig4-part1-reporting-principles-and-standard-disclosures.pdf.

Gómez-, F., Przychodzen, W., & Przychodzen, J. (2017). Bridging the gap: How sustainable development can help companies create shareholder value and improve financial performance. *Business Ethics: A European Review, 26*(1), 1–17.

Gutsche, R., Schulz, J. F., & Gratwohl, M. (2017). *Firm-value effects of CSR disclosure and CSR performance.* Paper presented at the EFMA-Conference proceedings.

Hagel, J., Brown, J. S., Samoylova, T., & Lui, M. (2013). *Success or struggle: ROA as a true measure of business performance.*

Haider, J., & Azhar, M. (2010). *Islamic Capital Market* (Master), Umea University, Sweden.

Haniffa, R., & Hudaib, M. A. (2002). A theoretical framework for the development of the Islamic perspective of accounting. *Accounting, Commerce Finance: The Islamic Perspective Journal, 6*(1/2), 1–71.
Haniffa, R., & Hudaib, M. (2007). Exploring the ethical identity of Islamic banks via communication in annual reports. *Journal of Business Ethics, 76*(1), 97–116.
Hassan, K., & Lewis, M. (2007a). *Handbook of Islamic Banking*. Edward Elgar Publishing.
Hassan, K., & Lewis, M. (2007b). Islamic banking: An introduction and overview. In K. Hassan & M. Lewis (Eds.), *Handbook of Islamic Banking* (Vol. 38): Edward Elgar Publishing.
Helfaya, A., & Moussa, T. (2017). Do board's corporate social responsibility strategy and orientation influence environmental sustainability disclosure? UK evidence. *Business Strategy and the Environment, 26*(8), 1061–1077.
Ho, V. H. (2017a). Comply or Explain and the future of nonfinancial reporting. *Lewis Clark L. Rev.*
Ho, V. H. (2017b). *How a "Comply or Explain" rule would improve nonfinancial disclosure*. https://clsbluesky.law.columbia.edu/2017/03/14/how-a-comply-or-explain-rule-would-improve-nonfinancial-disclosure/.
Hsu, F. J., & Chen, Y.-C. (2015). Is a firm's financial risk associated with corporate social responsibility? *Management Decision, 53*(9), 2175–2199.
Hummel, K., & Schlick, C. (2016). The relationship between sustainability performance and sustainability disclosure–reconciling voluntary disclosure theory and legitimacy theory. *Journal of Accounting and Public Policy, 35*(5), 455–476.
Iatridis, G. E. (2013). Environmental disclosure quality: Evidence on environmental performance, corporate governance and value relevance. *Emerging Markets Review, 14*, 55–75.
Indahl, R., & Jacobsen, H. G. (2019). Private equity 4.0: Using ESG to create more value with less risk. *Journal of Applied Corporate Finance, 31*(2), 34–41. doi:https://doi.org/10.1111/jacf.12344.
Iswanaji, C. (2018). Challenges inhibiting Islamic banking growth in Indonesia using the analytical hierarchy process. *Journal of Islamic Economics Lariba, 4*(2), 97–107.
Jamaldeen, F. (2012). *Islamic Finance for Dummies*. Wiley.
Jan, A., Marimuthu, M., Marimuthu, M. P., & Isa, M. (2019a). The nexus of sustainability practices and financial performance: From the perspective of Islamic banking. *Journal of Cleaner Production, 228*, 703–717.
Jan, A., Marimuthu, M., & Hassan, R. (2019b). Sustainable business practices and firm's financial performance in Islamic banking: Under the moderating role of Islamic corporate governance. *Sustainability, 11*(23), 6606.
JawaPost.com. (2021). *Merger 3 bank syariah efektif 1 Februari 2021 dengan Nama BRISyariah*. https://www.jawapos.com/ekonomi/21/10/2020/merger-3-bank-syariah-efektif-1-februari-2021-dengan-nama-brisyariah/.
Källum, M., & Sturesson, H. (2017). *Financial leverage: The impact on Swedish companies' financial performance* (Bachelor), Linnaeus University, Sweden. https://www.diva-portal.org/smash/get/diva2:1136627/FULLTEXT01.pdf.
Kamla, R., & Rammal, H. G. (2013). Social reporting by Islamic banks: Does social justice matter? *Accounting, Auditing Accountability Journal.*
Kao, E. H., Yeh, C.-C., Wang, L.-H., & Fung, H.-G. (2018). The relationship between CSR and performance: Evidence in China. *Pacific-Basin Finance Journal, 51*, 155–170.
Khan, M., Serafeim, G., & Yoon, A. (2016). Corporate sustainability: First evidence on materiality. *The Accounting Review, 91*(6), 1697–1724.
Khan, S. (2020). *Growth of global Islamic finance industry to slow in 2020–21 due to pandemic.* S&P says.
Kidd, C. V. (1992). The evolution of sustainability. *Journal of Agricultural Environmental Ethics, 5*(1), 1–26.
Komite Nasional Ekonomi dan Keuangan Syariah. (2019). *Indonesian govt in best efforts to boost Islamic economy*. https://knks.go.id/berita/11/indonesian-govt-in-best-efforts-to-boost-islamic-economy?category=2.

Lehner, O. M., & Harrer, T. (2019). Accounting for economic sustainability: Environmental, social and governance perspectives. *Journal of Applied Accounting Research.*

Li, C. (2016, January). Islamic finance in Asia: Recent developments and regulatory issues. *Asia Focus.*

Listyaningsih, E., & Krishnamurti, C. (2015). How performance of Jakarta Islamic Index (JII) stocks relative to other stocks? *Jurnal Dinamika Manajemen, 6*(2).

Lokuwaduge, C. S. D. S., & Heenetigala, K. (2017). Integrating environmental, social and governance (ESG) disclosure for a sustainable development: An Australian study. *Business Strategy and the Environment, 26*(4), 438–450.

Lourenço, I. C., Branco, M. C., Curto, J. D., & Eugénio, T. (2012). How does the market value corporate sustainability performance? *Journal of Business Ethics, 108*(4), 417–428.

Lukman, H., Suhendah, R., & Evan, J. (2020). *Analysis corporate social responsibility and environmental performance report forward financial performance on proper ranking companies in Indonesia.* Paper presented at the International Conference on Management, Accounting, and Economy (ICMAE 2020).

Martínez, J., Banerjee, S., & García, I. M. (2016). Corporate social responsibility as a strategic shield against costs of earnings management practices. *Journal of Business Ethics, 133*(2), 305–324.

Michaels, A., & Grüning, M. (2017). Relationship of corporate social responsibility disclosure on information asymmetry and the cost of capital. *Journal of Management Control, 28*(3), 251–274.

Minutolo, M., Kristjanpoller, W., & Stakeley, J. (2019). Exploring environmental, social, and governance disclosure effects on the S&P 500 financial performance. *Business Strategy and the Environment, 28*(6).

Molala, R. (2019). *MLmuse: Correlation and collinearity—How they can make or break a model.*

Ng, A. C., & Rezaee, Z. (2012). *Sustainability disclosures and cost of capital.* Available at SSRN 2038654.

Orsagh, M., Allen, J., Sloggett, J., & Dehman, N. A. (2019). *ESG integration and Islamic finance: Complementary investment approaches.* https://www.unpri.org/download?ac=9578.

Othman, R., Thani, A. M., & Ghani, E. K. (2009). Determinants of Islamic social reporting among top Shariah-approved companies in Bursa Malaysia. *Research Journal of International Studies, 12*(12), 4–20.

Peng, L. S., & Isa, M. (2020). Environmental, social and governance (ESG) practices and performance in Shariah firms: Agency or stakeholder theory? *Asian Academy of Management Journal of Accounting and Finance (AAMJAF), 16*(1), 1–34.

Ping, F. B. (2020). Greater engagement among exchanges on ESG disclosure and products. https://www.wealthandsociety.com/updates-and-articles/greater-engagement-among-exchanges-on-esg-disclosure-and-products.

Pullman, M. E., Maloni, M. J., & Carter, C. R. (2009). Food for thought: Social versus environmental sustainability practices and performance outcomes. *Journal of Supply Chain Management, 45*(4), 38–54.

Puri-Mirza, A. (2020). *Islamic financial sector—Statistics & facts.* https://www.statista.com/topics/6345/islamic-financial-sector/#:~:text=The%20total%20value%20of%20all,Islamic%20law%20or%20the%20Shariah.

Que, A., Lau, C., Chan, E., Wong, G., Cheung, K., Leung, M., ... (2020). *Tougher ESG reporting requirements to take effect from July 2020.*

Rahman, R. (2020). *Indonesia's ranking in Islamic finance jump six spots but major challenges remain.* https://www.thejakartapost.com/news/2019/11/13/indonesias-ranking-in-islamic-finance-jump-six-spots-but-major-challenges-remain.html.

Said, R., Abd, K., Mohd, N. Z., Ilias, N. F., & Omar, N. (2018). Corporate social responsibility disclosure index of Malaysian Shariah–compliant companies. *International Journal of Ethics and Systems, 34*(1), 55–69.

Sairally, B. S. (2015). Integrating environmental, social and governance (ESG) factors in Islamic finance: Towards the realisation of maqasid al-shari'ah. *ISRA International Journal of Islamic Finance, 7*(2), 145.

Salma, B. (2013). Evaluating the corporate social performance of Islamic financial institutions: An empirical study. *International Journal of Islamic and Middle Eastern Finance and Management, 6*(3), 238–260. https://doi.org/10.1108/IMEFM-02-2013-0026

Sarker, M. N. I., Khatun, M. N., & Alam, G. M. (2019). Islamic banking and finance: Potential approach for economic sustainability in China. *Journal of Islamic Marketing.*

Schacht, J. (1995). Law and justice. In A. K. S. L. P. M. Holt, and V. Bernard Lewis, 2B (Ed.), *The Cambridge History of Islam* (Vol. 2, pp. 539–568). Cambridge University Press.

Schoon, N. (2008a). Islamic finance-A history. *Financial Services Review, 1,* 10–12.

Schoon, N. (2008b). Islamic finance—An overview. *European Business Organization Law Review, 9*(4), 621–635.

Services, B. P. (2020). Does Shariah-compliant finance have the power to change the world? Retrieved November 03, 2020, from https://www.bloomberg.com/professional/blog/does-shariah-compliant-finance-have-the-power-to-change-the-world/.

Siddiqi, M. N. (2004). *Riba, bank interest and the rationale of its prohibition.* Islamic Research and Training Institute Jeddah.

Sitorus, R. (2021). Resmi! Merger Bank Syariah BUMN Kantongi Izin dari OJK. https://finansial.bisnis.com/read/20210127/90/1348702/resmi-merger-bank-syariah-bumn-kantongi-izin-dari-ojk.

Subramaniam, R. K., Samuel, S. D., & Mahenthiran, S. (2015). Liquidity implications of corporate social responsibility disclosures: Malaysian evidence. *Journal of International Accounting Research, 15*(1), 133–153.

Sun, W., & Cui, K. (2014). Linking corporate social responsibility to firm default risk. *Journal of Asian Economics, 32*(2), 275–287.

Taktak, N. B., & Farooq, O. (2014). Shariah-compliance and value of analysts' recommendations: Evidence from the MENA region. *Journal of Islamic Accounting Business Research.*

Taqi, U. M. (1998). *An introduction to Islamic finance.* Karachi: Idaratul Ma'arif.

Tarmuji, I., Maelah, R., & Tarmuji, N. H. (2016). The impact of environmental, social and governance practices (ESG) on economic performance: Evidence from ESG score. *International Journal of Trade, Economics and Finance, 7*(3), 67.

UCLA. (2020). *What is sustainability?* https://www.sustain.ucla.edu/what-is-sustainability/.

Ur, Z., Zahid, M., Rahman, H. U., Asif, M., Alharthi, M., Irfan, M., & Glowacz, A. (2020). Do corporate social responsibility disclosures improve financial performance? A perspective of the Islamic banking industry in Pakistan. *Sustainability, 12*(8), 3302.

Uyar, A., Kuzey, C., & Kilic, M. (2020). Sustainable stock market and sustainability reporting propensity of the public sector: Mediating role of the private sector. *International Journal of Public Administration,* 1–14.

Waddock, S. A., & Graves, S. B. (1997). The corporate social performance–financial performance link. *Strategic Management Journal, 18*(4), 303–319.

Wang, D.H.-M., Chen, P.-H., Yu, T.H.-K., & Hsiao, C.-Y. (2015). The effects of corporate social responsibility on brand equity and firm performance. *Journal of Business Research, 68*(11), 2232–2236.

Wibowo, A. J. (2012). *Interaction between corporate social responsibility disclosure and profitability of Indonesia firms.* Paper presented at the UMT 11th International Annual Symposium on Sustainability Science and Management.

Wibowo, S. S. A., & Rohyati, E. (2018). The effect of working capital turnover and profitability of inventory turnover manufacturing companies listed in Indonesia stock exchange. *Journal of Applied Accounting Taxation, 3*(3), 95–98.

Woodhead, J. (2020). *Sustainability reporting in Indonesia.* https://www.challengesustainability.com/Sustainability-reporting-in-Indonesia_53.html.

Zuraida, Z., Houqe, M. N., & Van Zijl, T. (2018). *Value relevance of environmental, social and governance disclosure.* Edward Elgar Publishing.

Zyadat, A. A. H. (2017). The impact of sustainability on the financial performance of Jordanian Islamic banks. *International Journal of Economics Finance, 9*(1), 55–63.

Zuraida Zuraida, Ph.D. is a senior lecturer in Accounting at the Faculty of Economics and Business, Syiah Kuala University (USK), Banda Aceh, Indonesia. She earned her first degree in Economics majoring in Accounting from USK; an MBA from Edith Cowan University, Australia and a Ph.D. in Accounting from Victoria University of Wellington, New Zealand. She was a Fulbright Visiting Scholar at the New York University Stern Center for Sustainable Business in 2019 with a research focus on environmental, social and governance (ESG) factors. Zuraida has presented papers in major academic conferences held in the different parts of the globe. Academic publications in recent years include papers in Indonesian Journal of Sustainability Accounting and Management; Journal of Finance and Banking and in Edward Elgar book section of Handbook of Finance and Sustainability.

Asna Husin, Ph.D. teaches Philosophy of Education & Islamic Civilization at Ar-Raniry State Islamic University (UIN Ar-Raniry) scholar at the McLean Center for the Study of Culture and Values, The Catholic University of America (Washington D.C.). She received Fulbright Scholarship for Master's Degree in Middle Eastern Studies at Harvard University (1990–1992), and for Doctorate in Religious Studies at Columbia University (1993–1998). She was granted Fulbright Scholarship for 'Access to Muslim World' as visiting scholar at Santa Fe Community College in Gainesville, Florida (2006). She served as an Associate Fellow at the 'Center for the Study of Human Rights' at Columbia University (1998), while teaching Introduction to Islam as Adjunct Professor at the State University of New York (SUNY) – Old Westbury. She worked as 'Director of Women's Program' for the World Conference on Religion and Peace in New York when she organized in 1998 the 'World Women Assembly' in Amman, Jordan, attended by women's religious organizations from thirty-three countries. Dr. Husin founded and directed the NGO 'Peace Education Program' (Program Pendidikan Damai, an independent affiliate of Nonviolence International). She actively participates in scholarly conferences worldwide, and publishes on Islamic peace studies, human rights and gender equity, Ulama institutions, educational philosophy as well as civilizational resources.

Chapter 17
When It Comes to Risk, is Sukuk Better Than Conventional Bonds? A Comparative Study of NASDAQ Securities

Ahmed-Nur Ali Farah, Alija Avdukic, and Fawad Khaleel

Sukuk provides an alternative source of funding, especially for large-scale projects and investments. Here, differences in Sukuk financing modes in comparison to conventional instruments are considered regarding the extent to which risk levels yield significant similarities. The investors of *Sukuk* possess undivided beneficial ownership of the underlying assets, which entitles the certificate holders to shares in revenues generated from them Afshar (2013). Whereas, conventional bonds represent a contractual debt obligation in which the issuer is obliged to pay interest to the debt holder at an appointed date.

The first convertible Sukuk was issued in Dubai in 2007, in the same year, Malaysia's Khazanah National issued exchangeable *Sukuk* with an option to exchange them for the existing shares of the originator's subsidiaries. These issues attracted high interest both from investors as well as potential issuers of *Sukuk*, due to a narrative of risk reduction alternatives. Financial experts discussed the possibility of further innovation in *Sukuk*, such as contingent convertible *Sukuk* and reserve convertible *Sukuk*. Nevertheless, most of Shari'ah scholars have restricted these kinds of innovations due to their similarity with derivatives and excessive uncertainty (Al-Sayed, 2013).

This chapter is part of a thesis titled "*Comparative Risk Analysis of Sukuk and Conventional Bonds Issuances: Case Study of United Arab Emirates' Nasdaq Dubai Listed Companies*" submitted to Markfield Institute of Higher Education by Farah, A. A., as part of M.A Islamic Banking, Finance and Management.

A.-N. A. Farah
Alfurqan Centre, 1 Kamloops Crescent, Leicester L1 2HX, UK

A. Avdukic
24 Blackness road, Dundee D1, SPE, UK

F. Khaleel (✉)
15 Cromwell road, Rosyth, Kyth 2LD, UK
e-mail: dhiraar@gmail.com

T. Azid et al. (eds.), *Wealth Management and Investment in Islamic Settings*,
https://doi.org/10.1007/978-981-19-3686-9_17

Since the zero-coupon *Sukuk* is not tradeable in an Islamic secondary market, *Sukuk* investors hedge risk exposures applying embedded options by converting the *Istisna Sukuk* into real assets or usufructs. Investors are not forced to wait for the *Sukuk's* maturity before converting the *Sukuk* into cash. Whereas, investors avoid exposing the following market risks, such as, re-investment, credit, and interest-rate risks, particularly, where market volatility exists.

This study aims at empirically analysing the risk levels of sukuk portfolio compared to conventional bonds, using a sample data that is extracted from daily closing prices of *Sukuk* and bonds that are traded in Nasdaq Dubai's security market. In doing so, this study employs Value at Risk (VaR) method to analyse and compare the risk level of *Sukuk* and conventional bonds portfolio.

This paper contributes to the literature on comparative analysis of *Sukuk* and conventional bonds by elaborating on their risk elements and challenges of *Sukuk* and bonds in the light of risk management. In the light of available large literature, this paper provides the insight to riskiness of *Sukuk* for potential investors as an alternative financial tool and also aims to bridge the gap in Sukuk risk analysis compared to conventional bonds.

The rest of the paper is organised as follows: the Sect. 17.2 presents a literature review to contextualise the subject matter, followed by the previous studies about the implementation of VaR models in portfolio risk measurements. The following section highlights the method of the research and data analysis, followed by VaR model application to *Sukuk* and conventional bonds and discussion on the empirical results. Finally, conclusion presents the summary of the findings and emphasizes recommendations for future research on the same characteristic studies.

17.1 Data and Method

Quantitative research methodology is applied, creating a statistical model analysing data through the Value at Risk method. A case study on United Arab Emirates' *Sukuk* and conventional bonds issuances listed on Nasdaq Dubai's financial market is analysed. Secondary data is obtained from listed *Sukuk* and conventional bonds issuance in Nasdaq Dubai's financial market. The data details daily closing prices of *Sukuk* and conventional bonds for a period of one-year from 18th January 2016 to 17th January 2017. Relevant data used for analysis, the *Sukuk* and conventional bonds issuance satisfies the following two criteria: firstly, data excludes any *Sukuk* and bonds issuances traded in the market for less than one year. Secondly, it only considers a maturity period of 3–10 years from the listed *Sukuk* and conventional bonds issuances. Sale based *Sukuk* were purposly excluded from the analysis, as they have very short maturity, and therefore they does not align for the comparitive analysis with the bonds. The sample data of 30 (15 *Sukuk* and 15 bonds) *Sukuk* and conventional bonds are selected randomly from a listed 70 Sukuk and conventional bonds that have satisfied those criteria. For example, there were only 15 samples of traditional bonds which satisfied the above-mentioned criteria. Therefore, we selected equal samples of 15 from each site. The lists of *Sukuk* and conventional bonds and their descriptions are illustrated in Tables 17.1 and 17.2.

As demonstrated in the above Table 17.1, the range of Sukuk issue size differs between the amount of USD 178.1 million to USD 1.5 billion, while the total combined amount of *Sukuk* issuance is USD 12.38 billion. The *Ijarah* finance model was the most popular mode of financing a total of USD 6.23 billion, presenting a total percentage of 50.3% when compared to other financing modes. Secondly, the largest *Sukuk* issuances was the *Mudarabah* model offering a value of 28.3%, a total amount of USD 3.5 billion, and *Wakalah* asset financing was a percentage of 21.4%.

As shown in Table 17.2 above, the range of conventional bonds issue size varies between USD 124.9 million to USD 20 billion, a total of USD 43.1 billion altogether. Whereas, Bonds and Notes amount to a value of 48.8% equating to a total of USD 21 billion, while the second largest issued conventional bonds are Medium Terms Note at 38.6%. Euro Medium Notes was 10.3% and Perpetual Security has a value of 2.3%.

Sukuk and conventional bonds have a limited range of maturity from 3 to 10 years, except Emirates NBD Tier 1 Ltd- PRP, which is a perpetuity security with no limited time of maturity. Since there is limited available information on firms issuing both *Sukuk* and conventional bonds, attempts were made to find the *Sukuk* and bonds issuances from the same country to give an adequate comparison while eliminating state and industry risks.

17.1.1 Data Analysis

As previously mentioned, data analysis applied is quantitative in nature and involves several research methods. The study uses the Value at Risk (VaR) method as a main statistical tool by employing the Historical simulation and Monte Carlo simulation models to analyse risk levels of *Sukuk* and conventional bonds. An F-test is used to evaluate any differences between *Sukuk* and conventional bonds. Firstly, the log-normal daily returns are calculated from the daily closing prices of Sukuk and conventional bonds, and descriptive analysis through Excel calculating the expected average returns, variance, standard deviation, and skewness is applied. This descriptive statistic measures the central tendency and spread of data which allows a summary of data analysis. Historical simulation is then applied to examine the risk level of Sukuk and conventional bonds for the holding period of one year.

Secondly, the Monte Carlo simulation (MCS) model is applied to simulate the expected future returns distribution randomly to analyse possible losses of portfolio for *Sukuk* and conventional bonds. However, due to the literature recommendations and limited information on *Sukuk* and conventional bonds in the UAE's financial market, the MCS is a more effective method to check the VaR risk level of *Sukuk* and conventional bonds since it allows the repeated simulations of daily returns of portfolios, using a random process of NORMSINV (RAND) function of Excel. The study employs two VaR estimates of MCS; firstly, the 10 days holding period of the VaR estimates with 99% confidence level, as per recommendations of the Basel Committee. Another reason behind the 10 days VaR estimates is because *Sukuk* are

Table 17.1 List of Sukuk instruments

List of Sukuk	Issue date	Maturity	Tenor	Amounts	Type
Dar Al Arkan Sukuk Co	18.05.2014	24.05.2018	5	USD450 mln	Wakala
DIB Sukuk Limited	0/06/2015	03.06.2020	6	USD750 mln	Ijarah
DIB Tier 1 Sukuk Ltd	02.04.2013	20.03.2019	6	USD1 bln	Mudarabah
DIB Tier 1 Sukuk 2 Ltd	15.01.2015	20.01.2021	6	USD1 bln	Mudarabah
DIP Sukuk Ltd	23.02.2014	20.02.2019	5	USD300 mln	Ijarah
DP World Sukuk Ltd	03.07.2007	02.07.2017	10	USD1.5 bln	Mudarabah
EMG Sukuk Limited	19.06.2014	18.06.2024	10	USD750 mln	Wakala
Hong Kong Sukuk Ltd	04.06.2015	03.06.2020	5	ISD1 bln	Ijarah
Hong Kong Sukuk Ltd-Reg S	21.09.2014	18.09.2019	5	USD980 mln	Ijarah
ICD Sukuk Co. Ltd	22.05.2014	21.05.2020	6	USD700 mln	Ijarah
IDB Trust Services Ltd	25.02.2014	26.06.2017	3	USD800 mln	Wakala
INDONESIA III-144A	31.05.2015	10.09.2024	10	USD178.1 mln	Ijarah
INDONESIA III	31.05.2015	10.09.2024	10	USD1.32 bln	Ijarah
JAFZ Sukuk Limited	20.06.2012	19.06.2019	7	USD650 mln	Wakala
RAK Capital	01.04.2015	31.03.2025	10	USD1 bln	Ijarah

Sources Nasdaq Dubai; http://www.nasdaqdubai.com/listing/listed-securities

Table 17.2 List of conventional bonds

List of bonds	Issue date	Maturity	Tenor	Amounts	Type
Agri Bank of China	15.09.14	11.9.17	3	USD15 bln	Medium Term Notes
Bank of China Ltd AD	01.07.15	30.6.17	3	USD20 bln	Notes
DP World Ltd GMTN—RegS	10.06.15	18.05.20	5	USD375.1 mln	Bond
DP World Ltd- 144A	10.06.15	18.05.20	5	USD124.9 mln	Bond
Dubai Holding C.O. Ltd	01.02.07	01.02.17	10	USD500 mln	Notes
Emirates NBD PJSC2015	24.03.15	23.3.22	6	USD550 mln	Euro Medium Notes
Emirates NBD PJSC 2015	07.05.15	06.05.20	5	USD350 mln	Euro Medium Notes
Emirates NBD PJSC 2014	20.11.14	19.11.19	5	USD1 bln	Euro Medium Notes
Emirates NBD PJSC 2013	31.03.13	28.03.23	10	USD750 mln	Euro Medium Notes
Emirates NBD PJSC 2014	20.11.14	19.11.19	5	USD1 bln	Euro Medium Notes
Emirates NBD Tier 1 Ltd—PRP	02.06.13	30.5.19	6	USD1 bln	Perpetual Security
ICD Funding Ltd	22.05.14	21.5.24	10	USD300 mln	Euro Medium Notes
Ind. & Com. Bank of China	27.05.15	26.05.2020	5	USD400 mln	Euro Medium Notes
MAF Global Securities-14	08.05.14	7.5.2024	10	USD800 mln	Medium Notes
MAF Global Securities-2013	31.07.13	5.7.2019	6	USD800 mln	Medium Notes

Source Nasdaq Dubai

not very liquid products and require enough time to be traded on security markets. Secondly, the study generates (5000 repetitions) possible paths for the VaR estimates using randomly generated numbers to analyse the risk level of *Sukuk* and conventional bonds over the holding period.

17.1.2 Value at Risk Method

The Historical simulation method uses real data and reflects actual behaviour of the sample data. It provides a more reliable level of VaR estimation if the real distributions of sample data are 'at tails'. In addition, it is easier to estimate unlike other methods of VaR models (Mentel, 2013). Drawbacks to the model include: it assumes the historically simulated distribution can represent the future distributions; it possesses higher variation compared to other models; and needs considerable number of data to estimate the quantiles of the empirical distribution (Hassan, 2006).

Whereas, the Monte Carlo simulation (MCS) model simulates the risk factors randomly rather than being analytically obtained, such as, in the Delta-Normal model. The MCS has several advantages making it the most comprehensive model to measure market risks, if accurately implemented including: it is flexible to incorporate time variations in the returns or the volatility of the returns and can be implemented in the presence of fat tails; it can also be applied to any type of portfolios. On the other hand, the MCS details disadvantages such as: it is more complex to compute, and system implementation is costly; and it relies on specific stochastic processes for the risk factors, which can lead to inaccurate results when the stochastic process used are wrong (Hassan, 2006).

17.1.2.1 VaR Calculations

In this section, the study derives general formulas of VaR models, including both Historical and Monte Carlo simulations. The basic concept of calculating VaR along with its probability and density function is shown in Table 17.3, which demonstrates the maximum loss of portfolios over a given time span where the chosen confidence level of VaR lies on a horizontal axis in a particular time. If the returns are normally distributed, the VaR confidence level of 95%'s Z-value is 1.645; and VaR at 99% confidence level, Z-value is 2.326. For example, the maximum loss of portfolio over a given time horizon is an amount of y-axis with a probability of 95% (see Boxed section) as shown in Fig. 17.1 (Ahmad et al., 2015, pp. 43–44).

In calculating historical simulation, the model uses the calculated log-normal daily returns of Sukuk and conventional bonds over the holding period of 250 trading days and the daily returns are calculated as follows:

$$\text{Daily returns} = \text{LN}\ (P_t/P_{t-1}) \tag{17.1}$$

Table 17.3 Descriptive characteristics of Sukuk daily returns

List of Sukuk	Mean of daily returns (%)	Variance (%)	Standard deviation (%)	Skewness (%)
Dar Al Arkan Sukuk Co	0.035	0.008	**0.899**	−124
DIB Sukuk Ltd	0.030	0.005	**0.722**	156
DIB Tier 1 Sukuk Ltd	0.025	0.002	0.445	57
DIB Tier 1 Sukuk 2 Ltd	0.017	0.004	**0.643**	−1
DIP Sukuk Ltd	0.006	0.000	0.123	−231
DP World Sukuk Ltd	−0.010	0.000	0.221	−59
EMG Sukuk Limited	0.021	0.004	0.603	−73
ICD Sukuk Co. Ltd	0.002	0.000	0.169	−30
IDB Trust Services Ltd	−0.002	0.000	0.083	199
INDONESIA III -144A	0.011	0.003	0.553	−275
INDONESIA III	0.029	0.001	0.374	−19
JAFZ Sukuk Ltd	0.001	0.008	**0.882**	−3
Hong Kong Sukuk Ltd	−0.005	0.000	0.164	−76
Hong Kong Sukuk Ltd -Reg S	0.000	0.001	0.276	17
RAK Capital	0.016	0.001	0.321	−64
Average	**0.012**	**0.003**	**0.432**	**−35**

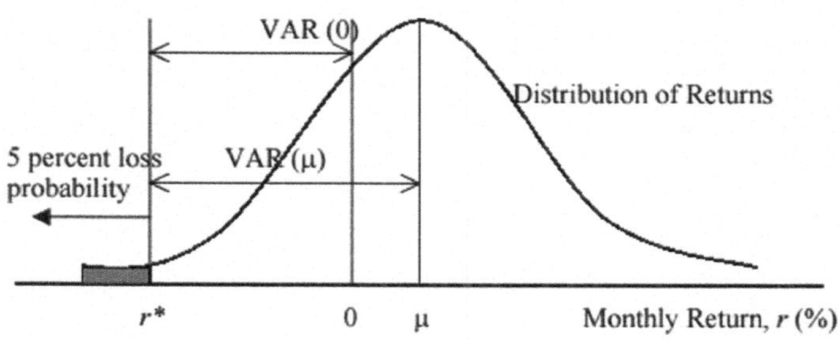

Fig. 17.1 VaR confidence level. *Sources* Ahmed et al. (2016, p. 44)

where P_1 is the price for today on Sukuk and conventional bonds and P_0 is the price of Sukuk and conventional bonds for day before, and 0, 1…t, is the holding period of portfolios. Here, to calculate the VaR using the Historical simulation model with 99% of confidence level, the Excel function of Percentile on daily returns are applied as follows:

$$\text{VaR} = \text{PERCENTILE}((r_{1\ldots t}), Z_{\alpha}) \quad (17.2)$$

$$\text{VaR} = \text{PERCENTILE}(\text{RETURNS RANGE}, 1\%) \quad (17.3)$$

where $r_{1...t}$ is the periodic daily returns of Sukuk and conventional bonds in "t" for holding period over the time, Z_{α} is the VaR confidence level of 99%.

In the case of Monte Carlo simulation, the study uses a geometric Brownian motion process to describe future returns on Sukuk and conventional bonds. The method uses two component parameters; drift which is a constant directional movement and random shock that presents the market volatility as shown below:

$$\text{Future daily returns} = \textit{drift} + \sigma * Z \tag{17.4}$$

$$\text{Future daily returns} = (\mu - (\sigma^2/2) * t + \sigma * Z \tag{17.5}$$

The drift is calculated from the mean (μ) minus half of the variance over time as shown in Eq. 17.5, σ is the volatility, and Z is the random variable from standard normal distribution N (0.1) using Excel function of NORMSINV (RAND), which will generate a simulated value of normal random variables having the parameters of mean (μ) and standard deviation (σ). Hence, the future expected daily returns are calculated by employing Monte Carlo simulation as follows:

$$\text{Future daily returns} = \textit{NORMIN}\,V(\textit{RAND}(), \mu, \sigma) \tag{17.6}$$

In this study, future daily returns are simulated using the above formula and the simulated daily returns use as 10 days for a holding period with a 99% confidence level of VaR estimates to analyse the risk level of *Sukuk* and conventional bonds portfolios. Also, to increase the accuracy of calculations 5000 simulations of *Sukuk* and conventional bonds daily returns will be run. According to Dowd (2005), 'Monte Carlo simulation procedures, accuracy will vary with square root of number of trial', so the more simulation, the better the result outcomes. In addition, the study presents the expected daily returns of *Sukuk* and conventional bonds in line chart and frequency, Histogram, to plot the simulated future returns to examine the normality distribution of the expected returns both *Sukuk* and conventional bonds.

F-Test Analysis

F-Test is used to test if the variance of two populations are equal. The test can be a two-sided test or one-tailed test. Whereas, the two-tailed version tests against the alternative hypothesis that the variances are not equal. On the other hand, the one-tailed version only tests in one direction that is the variance from the first population is either greater than or less than (but not both) the second population variance. Also, the F-test uses the Chi square test as combined method to find the p-value. Therefore, the F-test hypothesis is defined for a two-tailed test as follows NIST (2013):

$$\begin{aligned} H_0 &= \sigma_1^2 = \sigma_2^2 \\ H_1 &= \sigma_1^2 \neq \sigma_2^2 \\ F &= s_1^2/s_2^2 \end{aligned} \tag{17.7}$$

where σ_1^2 and s_2^2 are the sample variances. The more this ratio deviates from 1, the stronger the evidence for unequal population variances. The study will apply the two-tailed test, which tests against the alternative that the variance is not equal with a 99% confidence level. Therefore, this method will test if there is difference between *Sukuk* and conventional bonds risk level.

17.2 Analysis

The study presents VaR application to *Sukuk* and conventional bonds and discusses the empirical results that are obtained from the Historical and Monte Carlo simulation models and then presents the assessment and discussion of the results.

17.2.1 Descriptive Statistics of Sukuk and Conventional Bonds

As illustrated in Table 17.3 and Fig. 17.4, they report the descriptive statistics for the sample data of *Sukuk* and conventional bonds, using the Excel data tool which calculates daily returns' mean of 250 daily returns, variance, standard deviation, and skewness of the returns distribution for *Sukuk* and conventional bonds.

As shown in the Table 17.3, most of the Sukuk issuances have a positive mean 0.012%, except for DP World *Sukuk* Ltd IDB Trust Services Ltd, and Hong Kong *Sukuk* Ltd which shows a negative of expected daily returns. Also, Dar Al-Arkam *Sukuk* and JAFZ *Sukuk* Ltd dispense the highest volatility of 0.899 and 0.882% in which their daily returns are more volatile than the others. In addition, DIB *Sukuk* Ltd has a higher volatility of 0.722% too.

Furthermore, the above Fig. 17.2 indicates that the expected daily returns are not normally distributed around the mean but inclined more towards negative values in the left tail. Whereas, the return distribution of *Sukuk* are skewed and falls in the left tail. Also, there are some extreme daily return outliers that effects overall daily return distributions. More precisely, the expected returns of *Sukuk* are more left skewed as presented in Fig. 17.2. This means that daily returns of *Sukuk* are in negative outcome which clusters more in left tail.

As shown in Table 17.4, most of the conventional bonds also have a positive mean, except for Dubai Holding C.o. Ltd, Emirates NBD PJSC 2015, and ICD Funding Ltd that shows a negative mean of daily returns as well as ICD Funding Ltd which provides a higher standard deviation of 0.760%, this shows that the expected of ICD Funding has a higher spread of returns when compared to other bonds. In general, conventional bonds daily returns are less volatile compared to Sukuk except ICD Funding Ltd and MAF Global Securities 2014.

On the other hand, the overall mean of returns on Sukuk is 0.012% is slightly higher than conventional bonds' mean of 0.010% were as the descriptive statistics result

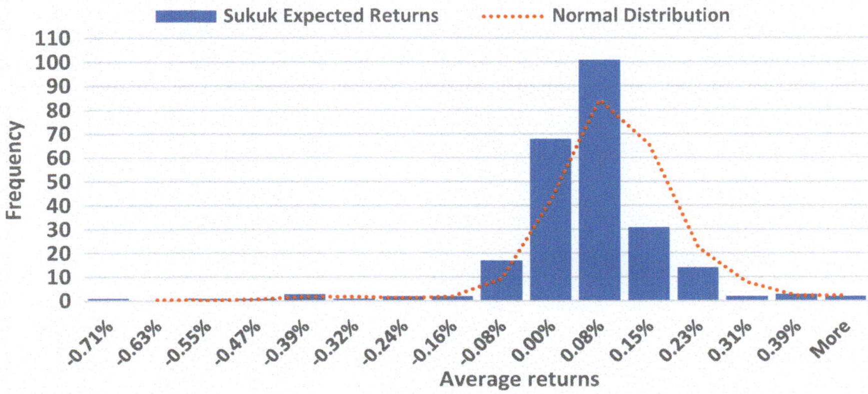

Fig. 17.2 Distribution of average daily returns for Sukuk

Table 17.4 Descriptive characteristics of conventional bonds daily returns

List of bonds	Mean of daily returns (%)	Variance (%)	Standard deviation (%)	Skewness (%)
Agri Bank of China	0.002	0.000	0.105	−68
Bank of China Ltd	0.004	0.000	0.090	22
DP World Ltd GMTN- RegS	0.018	0.000	0.198	172
DP World Ltd- 144A	0.008	0.001	0.245	−48
Dubai Holding C.O. Ltd	−0.002	0.001	0.273	16
Emirates NBD PJSC2015	0.011	0.000	0.148	−150
Emirates NBD PJSC 2015	−0.004	0.000	0.131	−23
Emirates NBD PJSC 2014	0.028	0.000	0.203	−31
Emirates NBD PJSC 2013	0.008	0.000	0.084	−78
Emirates NBD PJSC 2014	0.009	0.000	0.101	−264
Emirates NBD Tier 1 Ltd- PRP	0.012	0.000	0.165	−90
ICD Funding Ltd	−0.004	0.006	**0.760**	−9
Ind. & Com. Bank of China	0.035	0.001	0.309	514
MAF Global Securities 2014	0.017	0.004	0.606	−26
MAF Global Securities 2013	0.004	0.000	0.098	−122
Average	**0.010**	**0.001**	**0.235**	**−12**

points out that *Sukuk* instruments are more volatile and riskier than conventional bonds.

The sample skewness of conventional bonds shows that daily returns are not distributed equally around the mean and there are some outliers of daily returns as illustrated the above Fig. 17.3. Also, the chart shows that the average daily returns of

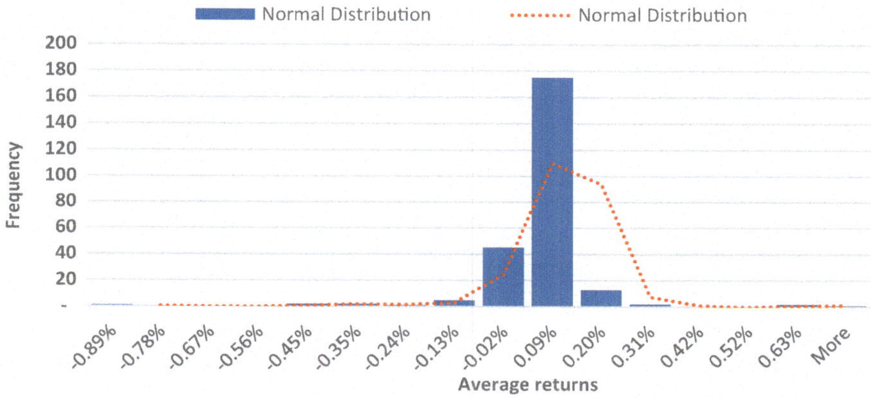

Fig. 17.3 Distribution of average daily returns for conventional bonds

conventional bonds are skewed to the left tail. However, the expected daily returns are more skewed to the left tail but it shows that they are slightly less skewed compared to Sukuk daily average returns as presented in the histogram charts of Figs. 17.2 and 17.3. This means that daily returns of *Sukuk* are in negative outcome which clusters more in left tail.

17.2.2 Historical Simulation Results

Historical simulation is implemented by using log-normal daily returns of *Sukuk* and bonds issuances taking 250 trading days in a year. The VaR with confidence of 99% is simply calculated as 1% percentile of hypothetical loss or gain of probability density function, but mainly we concern the left tail of the bell curve values which are the worst loss in a time.

Table 17.4 illustrates the value of VaR on *Sukuk* and conventional bonds with the VaR confidence of 99% level over a period of a given time. Whereas, the riskiest *Sukuk* are Dar al-Arkam *Sukuk* with the VaR of (−3.54%) and Indonesia III-144A with VaR of (−2.04), while the lowest VaR is the DP World *Sukuk* (−0.20%). On the other hand, the average VaR on *Sukuk* is (−0.90%), while the conventional bonds average VaR is (−0.48). This shows that *Sukuk* are twice as risky as conventional bonds detailed in the above table. In addition, the riskiest bonds are from MAF Global Securities-14 and Dubai Holding Co. VaR values of (−1.12% and −0.75%), while the lowest VaR on bonds is Emirates NBD PJSC 2014 for (−0.19) (Table 17.5).

As illustrated the above in Fig. 17.4, Sukuk has a higher risk level of daily returns than conventional bonds which shows that bonds are less risky than a *Sukuk*. Whereas, the average VaR on *Sukuk* is almost twice as high as the average VaR on conventional bonds as shown in Fig. 17.4. Furthermore, the bonds daily returns are more stable

Table 17.5 Historical simulation for Sukuk and conventional bonds at 99% of VaR confidence

List of Sukuk	VaR (%)	List of bonds	VaR (%)
Dar Al Arkam Sukuk Co	**−3.54**	Agri Bank of China	−0.35
DIB Sukuk Limited	−1.17	Bank of China Ltd AD	−0.22
DIB Tier 1 Sukuk Ltd	−0.62	DP World Ltd GMTN- RegS	−0.60
DIB Tier 1 Sukuk 2 Ltd	−1.27	DP World Ltd- 144A	−0.41
DIP Sukuk Ltd	−0.33	Dubai Holding C.O. Ltd	−0.75
DP World Sukuk Ltd	**−0.20**	Emirates NBD PJSC2015	−0.53
EMG Sukuk Limited	−0.62	Emirates NBD PJSC 2015	−0.19
ICD Sukuk Co. Ltd	−0.28	Emirates NBD PJSC 2014	−0.19
IDB Trust Services Ltd	−0.22	Emirates NBD PJSC 2013	−0.25
INDONESIA III -144A	−2.04	Emirates NBD PJSC 2014	−0.39
INDONESIA III	−1.14	Emirates NBD Tier 1 Ltd- PRP	−0.52
JAFZ Sukuk Ltd	−0.41	ICD Funding Ltd	**−0.73**
Hong Kong Sukuk Ltd	−0.51	Ind. & Com. Bank of China	−0.61
Hong Kong Sukuk Ltd -Reg S	−0.26	MAF Global Securities-14	−1.12
RAK Capital	−0.88	MAF Global Securities-13	−0.39
Average	**−0.90**	**Average**	**−0.48**

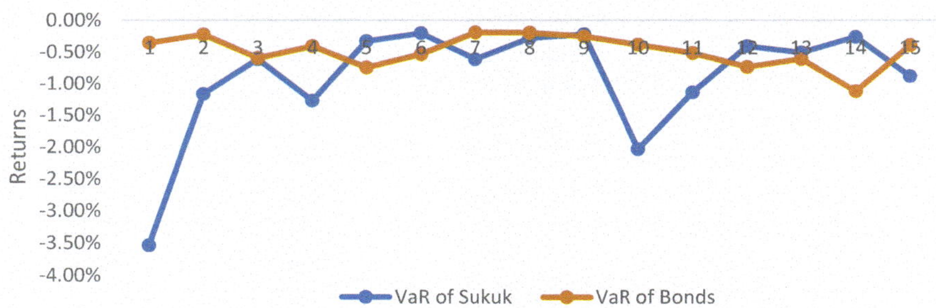

Fig. 17.4 VaR of Sukuk and Bonds using confidence level of 99%

than the *Sukuk* over the period. Therefore, this shows that *Sukuk* daily returns are more volatile and riskier than conventional bonds.

17.2.3 Monte Carlo Simulation Method

Here, the risk level of *Sukuk* and bonds using Monte Carlo simulation (MCS) model with the VaR 99% confidence level are described. To compute VaR, the study applies two VaR estimations: firstly, the study estimates 10 business days of holding period for randomizing daily returns, as per recommendations of the Basel Committee. In addition, *Sukuk* are not very liquid products and require time to be traded. Secondly, the study estimates randomly the VaR by simulating daily returns into (5000 repetitions) where the model applies to two parameters: drift which is a constant directional movement and random shock for volatility as presented in Eq. 17.3. Table 17.6 presents the value of VaR on *Sukuk* and conventional bonds using Monte Carlo simulation with the VaR of 99% confidence level. Hong Kong *Sukuk* Ltd and Dar Al Arkam *Sukuk* provide the highest VaR risk levels of (−0.165% and −0.162) in 10 days holding period and the highest VaR values of (−2.13%) for Dar Al Arkam and (−1.99%) for Hong Kong *Sukuk* Ltd. Whereas, the lowest VaR values are provided by Indonesia III-144A in both the 10 days and 5000 runs of VaR estimates.

In the case of bonds, MAF Global Securities-14 and ICD Funding Ltd have the highest VaR Values of (−1.18% and −0.86%) in 10 days, as well as, the highest VaR estimates of (−1.73% and −1.42%) in the VaR estimates of 5000 repetitions. While the lowest VaR on bonds is Emirates NBD PJSC 2014 for (−0.11%). In summarising, the VaR values of *Sukuk* are higher than conventional bonds VaR values in both the day VaR and 5000-iterations as shown the above Table 17.6. Therefore, the model shows that the expected average for the daily returns loss of value cannot exceed (−0.68%) for Sukuk and (−0.34%) for bonds with 99% confidence level in 10 days VaR estimates. Whereas, the expected average of daily returns loss of value cannot

Table 17.6 Monte Carlo simulation for Sukuk and bonds in 99% of VaR confidence

List of Sukuk	VaR [a]	VaR [b]	List of bonds	VaR [a]	VaR [b]
Dar Al Arkam Sukuk Co	**−1.52**	**−2.13**	Agri Bank of China	−0.22	−0.24
DIB Sukuk Limited	−0.29	−0.54	Bank of China Ltd AD	−0.20	−0.20
DIB Tier 1 Sukuk Ltd	−0.83	**−1.47**	DP World Ltd GMTN- RegS	−0.32	−0.45
DIB Tier 1 Sukuk 2 Ltd	−1.05	−1.44	DP World Ltd- 144A	−0.21	−0.57
DIP Sukuk Ltd	−0.33	−0.28	Dubai Holding C.O. Ltd	−0.47	−0.67
DP World Sukuk Ltd	−0.22	−0.55	Emirates NBD PJSC2015	−0.30	−0.34
EMG Sukuk Limited	**−1.34**	−1.37	Emirates NBD PJSC 2015	−0.18	−0.31
ICD Sukuk Co. Ltd	−0.81	−1.18	Emirates NBD PJSC 2014	−0.38	−0.43
IDB Trust Services Ltd	−0.32	−0.39	Emirates NBD PJSC 2013	−0.14	−0.19
INDONESIA III -144A	**−0.16**	**−0.20**	Emirates NBD PJSC 2014	−0.11	−0.22
INDONESIA III	−0.06	−1.38	Emirates NBD Tier 1 Ltd- PRP	−0.07	−0.39
JAFZ Sukuk Ltd	−0.95	−1.30	ICD Funding Ltd	**−0.86**	**−1.73**
Hong Kong Sukuk Ltd	−0.40	−0.39	Ind. & Com. Bank of China	−0.15	**−0.66**
Hong Kong Sukuk Ltd -Reg S	**−1.65**	**−1.99**	MAF Global Securities-14	**−1.18**	**−1.42**
RAK Capital	−0.24	−0.71	MAF Global Securities-13	−0.29	−0.22
Average	**−0.68**	**−1.02**	**Average**	**−0.34**	**−0.54**

[a] VaR of 10 days holding period simulations
[b] VaR of 5000 randomly iterations

exceed more than (−1.02%) for *Sukuk* and (−0.54%) with 99% confidence level in the second VaR estimates of 5000 iterations.

Figure 17.5 reveals clearly that VaR risk level of *Sukuk* are greater than conventional bonds in both the 10-day holding period and the VaR estimates of (5000 iterations) as shown in the above figure. This illustrates that expected daily returns of *Sukuk* are almost double those of conventional bonds in both the Historical and Monte Carlo simulation models. Therefore, Monte Carlo simulation strongly supports the results of Historical simulation, which means that *Sukuk* has more risk than conventional bonds and we can conclude that *Sukuk* risk levels are strongly higher than conventional bonds which indicates that *Sukuk* instruments are different and riskier than conventional bonds.

In addition, a line chart and frequency histogram are used to simulate the expected daily returns of *Sukuk* and conventional bonds as shown in Fig. 17.6, by selecting the highest and the lowest VaR values of *Sukuk* and conventional bonds. In the case of Dar Al Arkam *Sukuk*, the line chart in 10 days VaR estimates shows that the expected daily returns of the Dar Arkam are volatile in the 10 days' period, indicating more risk. Whereas, expected returns are more stable and normally distributed after performing 5000 simulations as shown in Fig. 17.7. For the lowest *Sukuk* VaR values, the expected daily returns of Indonesian III *Sukuk* are less volatile and normally distributed, illustrated in Fig. 17.8 (see Appendix 2).

With conventional bonds, the expected daily returns of ICD Funding provides a changing trend in the10 days' holding period applying the Monte Carlo simulation, which means that its daily returns are not stable compared to others. On the other hand, its expected returns appear stable and normally distributed in 5000 runs' VaR estimates as presented in Fig. 17.7, while Emirates NBD BJSC-14 are more stable and normally distributed after performing 5000 simulations (see Appendix 3).

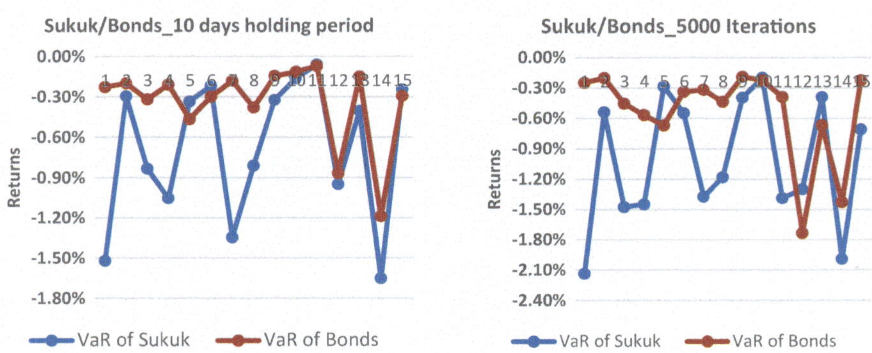

Fig. 17.5 VaR of Sukuk and bonds in 10 days holding period and VaR estimates of (5000 repetitions) with 99% confidence level

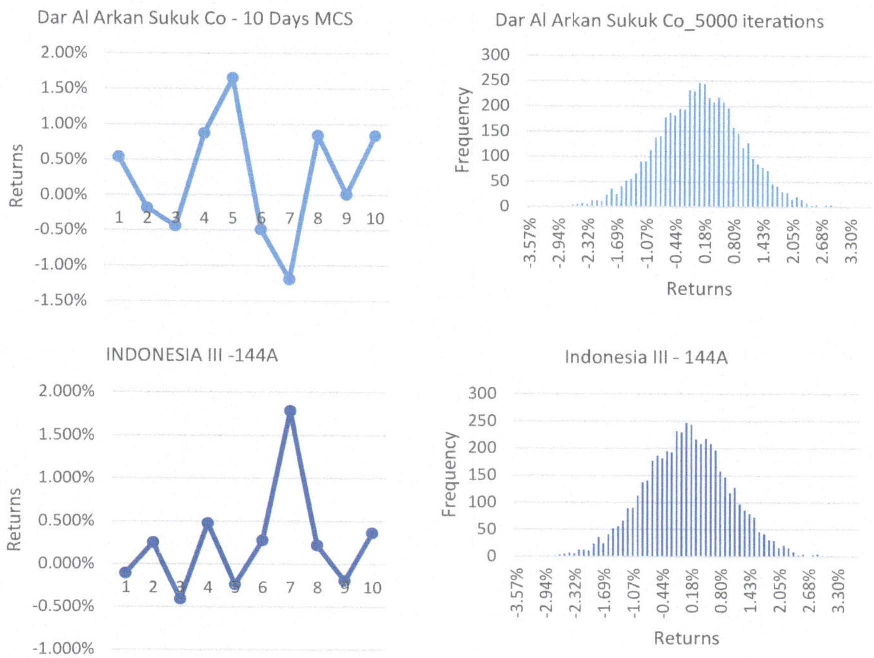

Fig. 17.6 Sukuk distribution in line chart and histogram

17.2.4 Comparing VaR Results of Historical and Monte Carlo Simulation

Comparison is, now, offered of both methods' results of VaR calculations in Historical and Monte Carlo simulations (MCS) as reported in Figs. 17.6 and 17.7. The worst expected loss of values in a day for *Sukuk* and bonds' portfolios are calculated by multiplying the worst daily returns of VaR estimates with a hypothetical portfolio value of $100,000. For example, historical simulation method shows a VaR of $900 for a portfolio of *Sukuk* issuance and a VaR of $480 for bonds' portfolio. This implies that one can expect the maximum daily loss on the market value of the *Sukuk* portfolio will not be larger than $900 and for bonds' portfolios will not be greater than $480 of its value at 99% of the time. It also means that there is a 1% chance the loss could be larger than those values (Table 17.7).

In the case of the MCS method, results show a VaR of $680 for a portfolio of *Sukuk* and a VaR of $340 for bonds' portfolios in VaR estimates of 10 days. Whereas, a VaR of $1,020 for a portfolio of *Sukuk* and a VaR of $540 for a portfolio of bonds in VaR estimates of (5000 iterations). Therefore, this suggests that the worst daily loss of *Sukuk* portfolio will not exceed $680 and $340 for bonds with the 99% confidence level in 10 days VaR estimates. In the second model of

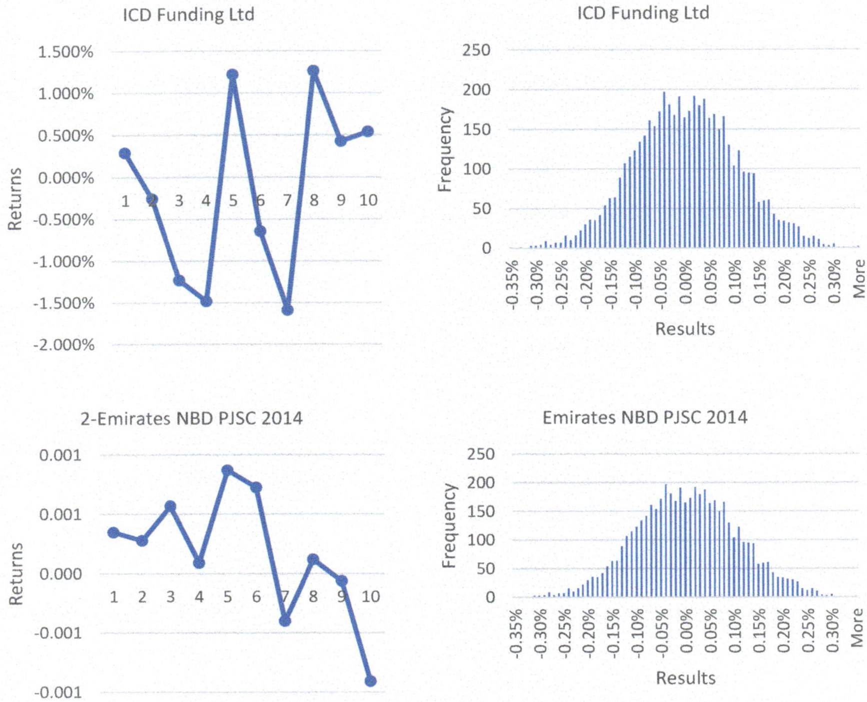

Fig. 17.7 Conventional bonds distribution in line chart and histogram

Table 17.7 Maximum loss of Sukuk and conventional bonds' portfolios

Method	VaR of Sukuk (%)	Loss of Sukuk portfolios	VaR of bonds	Loss of bonds portfolios	Change (%)
Historical simulations	−0.90	−$900	−0.48	−$480	47
Monte Carlo simulation:					
VaR of 10 days	−0.68	−$680	−0.34	−$340	50
VaR of (5000 replications)	−1.02	−$1,020	−0.54	−$540	47%

[a] VaR confidence level of 99%

[b] VaR Values are percentages of expected returns loss in holding period

(5000 iteration) MCS, the maximum loss in a day will not exceed $1,020 for a *Sukuk* portfolio and $540 for bonds, which means that there is a 1% chance the loss could be larger than these VaR estimates.

On the other hand, the historical simulation shows that the expected daily loss of *Sukuk* portfolios are greater than a portfolio of bonds with a value of 47%. Similarly, the results of Monte Carlo simulation show that the percentage change of both methods are close to the historical simulation method which highlights that the findings are robust when compared to each other. For example, the expected daily losses of *Sukuk* portfolios are higher than those of conventional bonds,' illustrating 50% in a 10-day holding period. Whereas, the second method shows that *Sukuk* have higher losses of 47% compared to conventional bonds. However, the slight differences apparent to both methods can be attributed to the extent to which returns on *Sukuk* and bonds diverge from normal presumptions, whereby, deviation from normality can lead to a different estimate of VaR when a normality assumption is dropped both in Historical simulation and the MCS methods. As illustrated in the above Table 17.6, *Sukuk* portfolios have a higher VaR risk level of expected daily losses than the conventional bonds. This highlight *Sukuk* as riskier than conventional bonds.

However, differences between *Sukuk* and conventional bonds risk level were tested using the F-test model by employing Minitab software. The results show that p-value is less than 0.01 with a 99% confidence level as presented in Fig. 17.8, which confirms that there are significance differences between the risk level of *Sukuk* and conventional bonds (see Appendix 4). Therefore, this results in a null hypothesis to be rejected, and, hence, accept the opposite. Therefore, the statement that *Sukuk* and bonds should have similar levels of risk were incorrect as revealed through the above figures, hence, a rejection of the null hypothesis, which illustrates no difference between *Sukuk* and conventional bonds, and the results support the alternative hypothesis that stated *Sukuk* are riskier than conventional bonds.

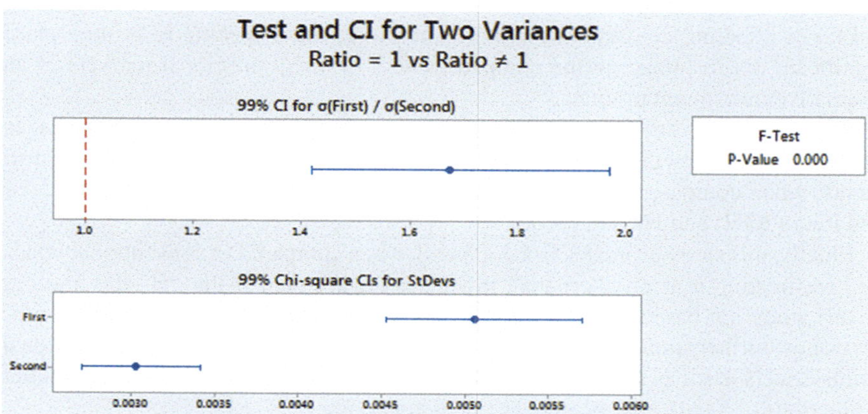

Fig. 17.8 F-Test results for Sukuk and conventional bonds

Furthermore, the study shows that *Sukuk* inherits higher market and credit risks than conventional bonds due to some restrictions that Shar'iah principles impose on *Sukuk* risk management. Also, other risks related to *Sukuk* are legal and regulatory risks specific to *Sukuk* may effect the *Sukuk* returns, and operational risks, which donot effect conventional bonds. Therefore, these risk factors place a major disadvantage on *Sukuk* competiveness in the global market as an alternative investment product.

17.3 Conclusion

Sukuk is an important instruments of an Islamic financial system, and normally, allow mobilisation of resources. This helps Islamic financial institutions to match their assets and liabilities. Whereas, the *Sukuk* market has diverged from initial *Sukuk* issuances by financial institutions to issuers ranging from infrastructure development, aircraft financing, socially responsible investing, *Takaful* sector, capital enhancement purposes, and so forth. Also, *Sukuk* encourages small investors to participate in Islamic financing and earn profits at the same time.

The uniqueness of *Sukuk* from its conventional counterparts has been a debatable issue among scholars and within relevant literature as an alternative to investment products. This study introduced a portfolio of *Sukuk* and conventional bonds to evaluate the risk level of Sukuk and conventional bonds. The results show that *Sukuk* portfolios have a higher VaR risk level of the expected daily losses than the traditional bonds in both Historical simulation and Monte Carlo simulation. Therefore, the empirical evidence reveals that *Sukuk* instruments are different to, and riskier than, conventional bonds. However, the study shows that *Sukuk* inherits higher market and credit risk than traditional bonds due to some restrictions that Shari'ah principles impose on *Sukuk* risk management. Also, the results confirm that these risks may be associated with other risk factors of *Sukuk*, such as, legal, regulatory, and operational risks, not affecting conventional bonds. Therefore, these specific risks may place significant disadvantage on the competitiveness of *Sukuk* in global markets as an alternative investment product.

There is little research regarding *Sukuk* compared to conventional products in literature. Therefore, this study fills the gap by examining risk levels of Sukuk instruments, when compared to conventional bonds. The findings reflect those of Cakir and Raei (2007) and Hassan (2006).

Finally, this study evaluates risks of *Sukuk* when compared to conventional bonds by investigating it as an alternative investment instrument. Although, the findings of this study are based on a reasonable sample of *Sukuk* and conventional bonds' portfolios, further studies including corporate and sovereign *Sukuk* and conventional bonds issuers, such as Qatar, Bahrain, Kuwait, and Saudi Arabia will produce better evaluations of *Sukuk* effects on investment portfolios.

Interesting aspects for future research include an examination and comparison of different industry sectors of *Sukuk* and conventional bonds in the Gulf states. Here, other methods of *Sukuk* risk evaluation may be applied using suitable software, since recent risk evaluation studies on *Sukuk* and bonds rely mainly on VaR Method analysis.

Appendices

Appendix 1

See Table 17.8.

Table 17.8 Main types of sukuk structures

Sukuk type	Characteristics
Murabaha (mark-up sale)	Usually used for purchasing products under an instalment sales contract. In this type of transaction, an asset is acquired by the purchaser (usually a bank); from a third party, at the demand of the originator. The product is then resold to the originator at an agreed mark-up for immediate or deferred payment in instalments
Istisna (Supply agreement)	Generally used in infrastructure and large developmental projects. In this type, the Islamic financial institution funds the project during its construction phase, whilst acquiring the title to that asset. Ownership is then passed on to the developer upon competition of the project
Salam (futures contract)	The buyer pays the seller the full price of a product, with the promise to be delivered at a future date
Ijarah (rental and lease agreements)	Based on a leasing scheme, the financing party purchases property, equipment or other asset desired by the originator and then leases it to the client for a rental fee. At maturity, the originator repurchases the underlying asset
Wakala (agency agreement)	One party (either the bank or client) serves as an agent to the originator undertaking transactions on his behalf
Mudaraba (partnership agreement)	A partnership agreement where the funds to finance a project are supplied by the provider of capital; while the entrepreneur offers labour and expertise. Profits ratios are agreed upon and are shared accordingly. However, in the case of loss, all losses are borne by the owner of capital; as the liability of the entrepreneur is restricted only to his time and effort
Musharakah (Equity partnership agreement)	Represents ownership of partnership equity. The financing party and originator contribute assets (cash or property) to a joint venture and share the generated profits according to predetermined ratios, whereas losses are split according to the respective capital contributions

Source Lackman (2015), Kammer et al. (2015, pp. 33–34)

Appendix 2

See Fig. 17.9.

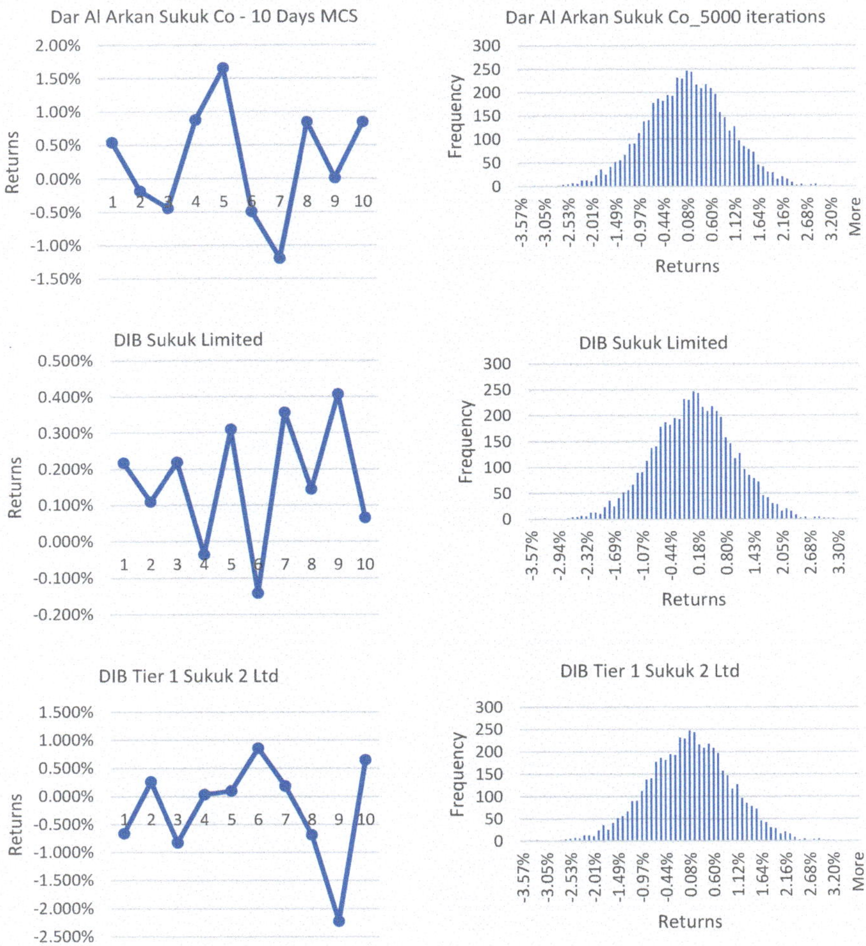

Fig. 17.9 Sukuk for 10 Day Monte Carlo simulation and (5000 iterations) tabulated in a histogram

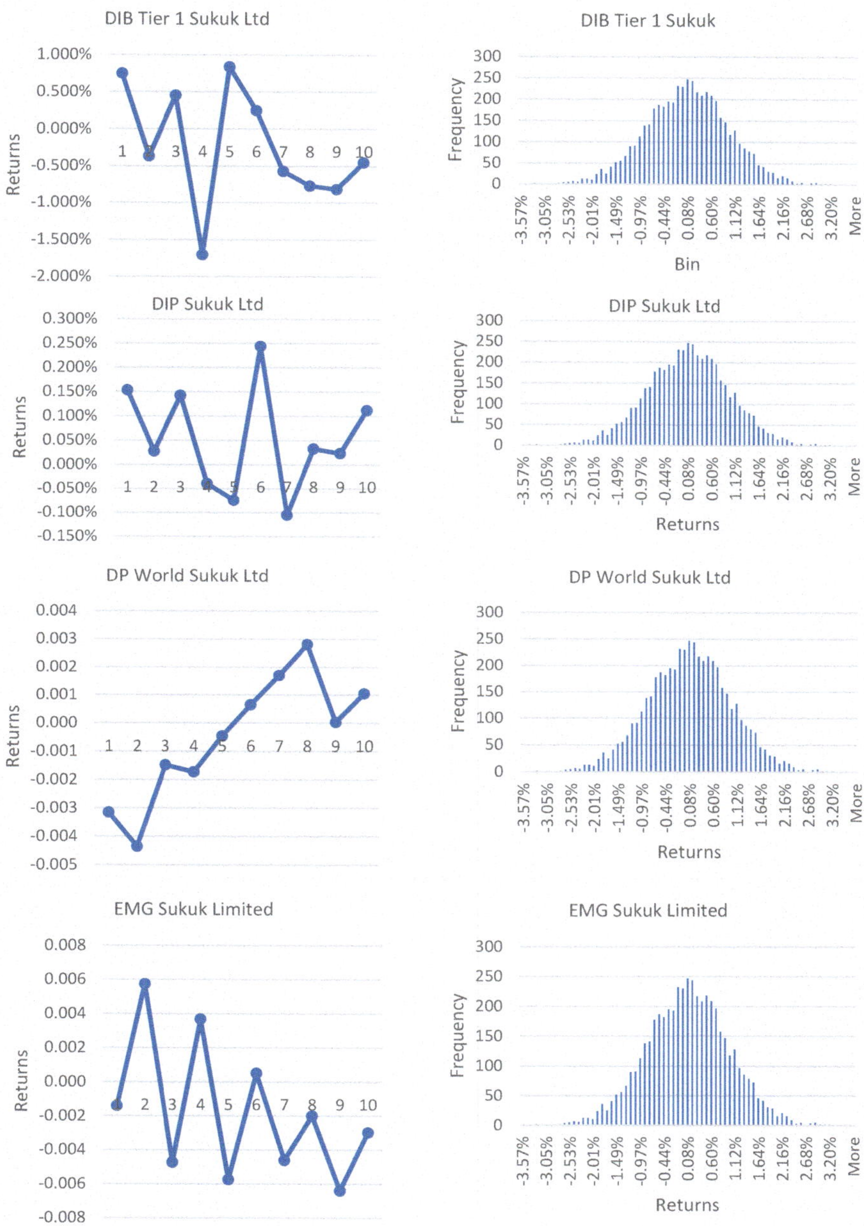

Fig. 17.9 (continued)

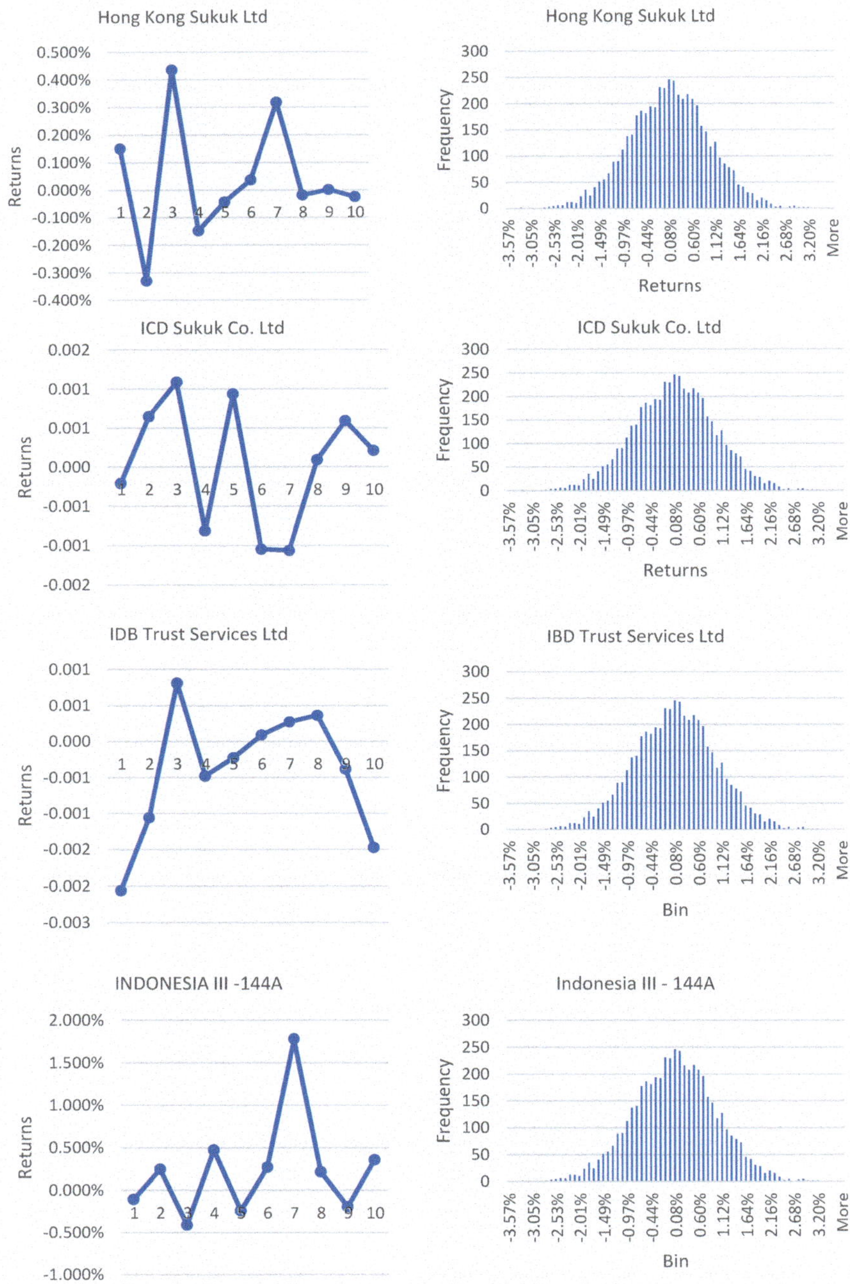

Fig. 17.9 (continued)

Fig. 17.9 (continued)

Appendix 3

See Fig. 17.10.

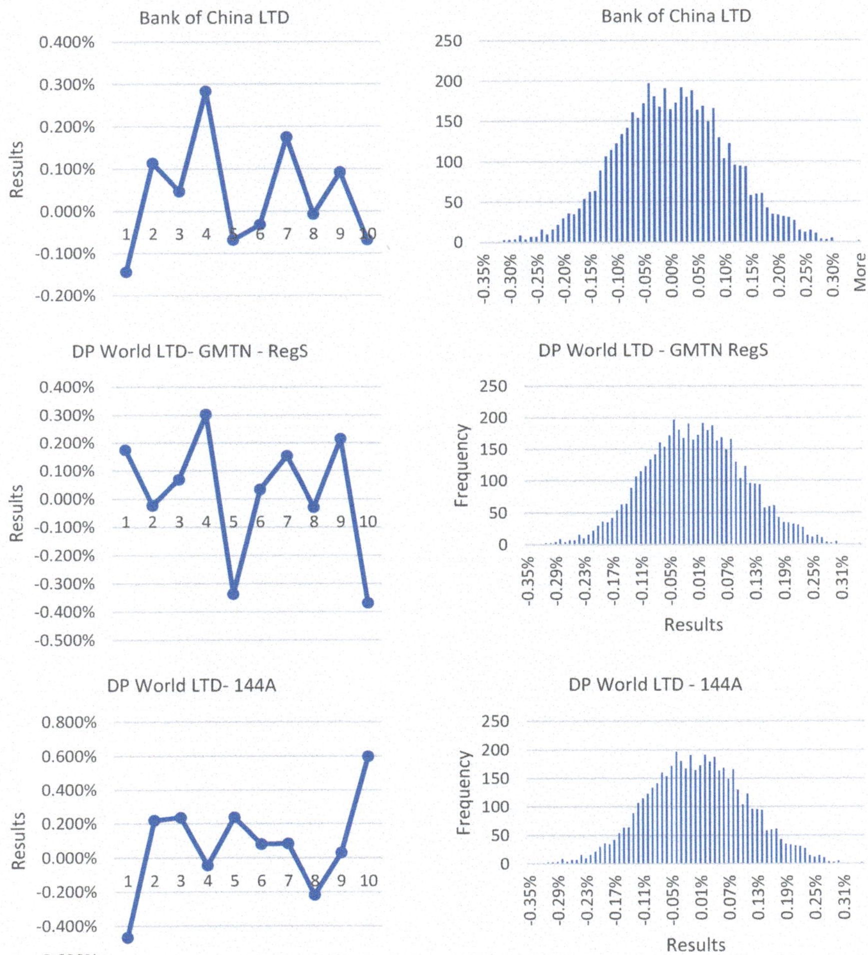

Fig. 17.10 Conventional bonds for 10 Day Monte Carlo simulation and (5000 iterations) tabulated in a histogram

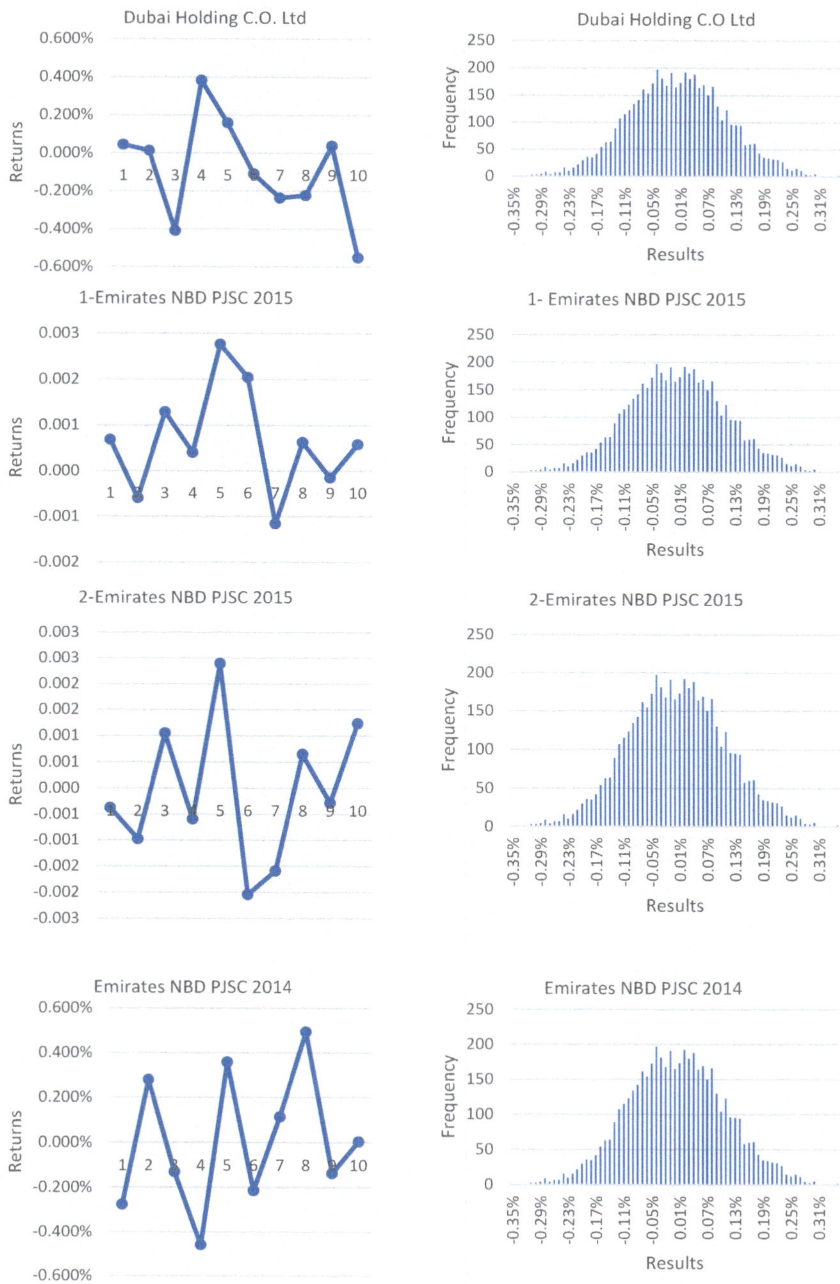

Fig. 17.10 (continued)

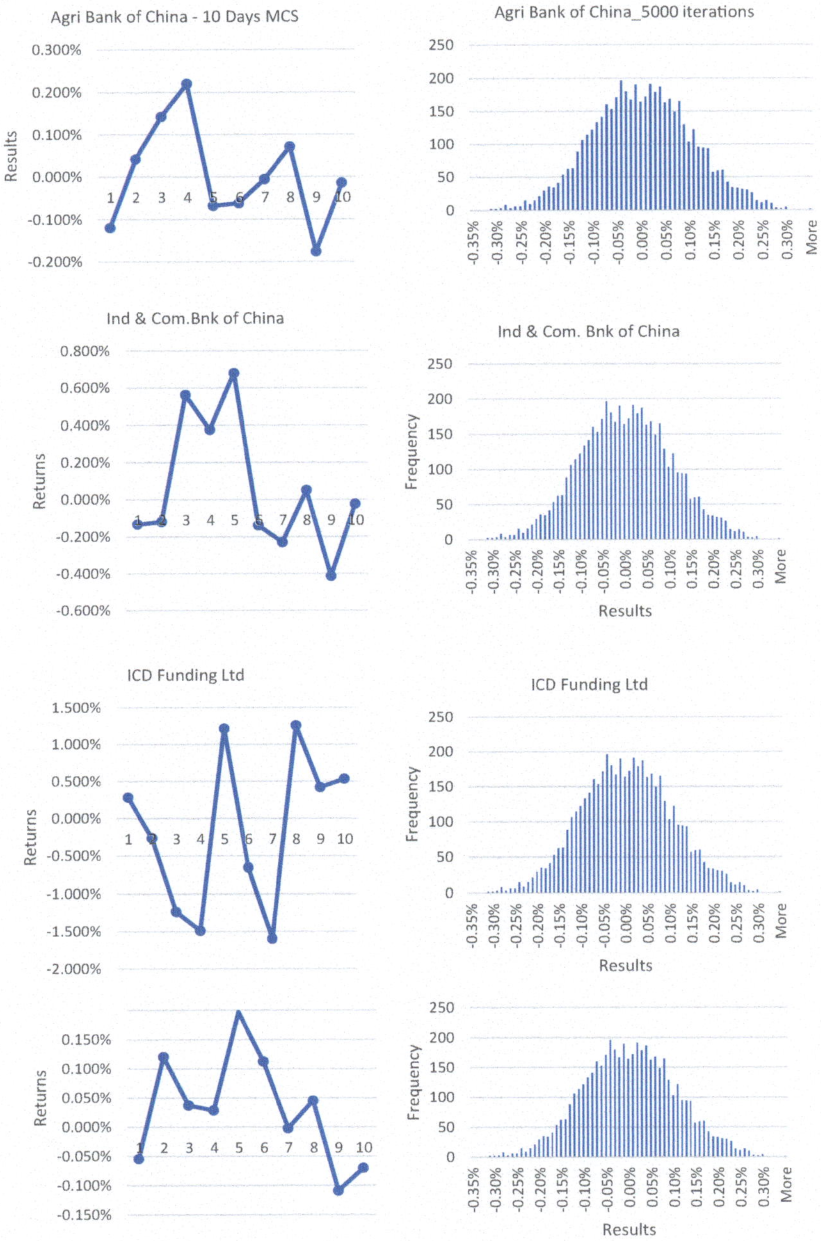

Fig. 17.10 (continued)

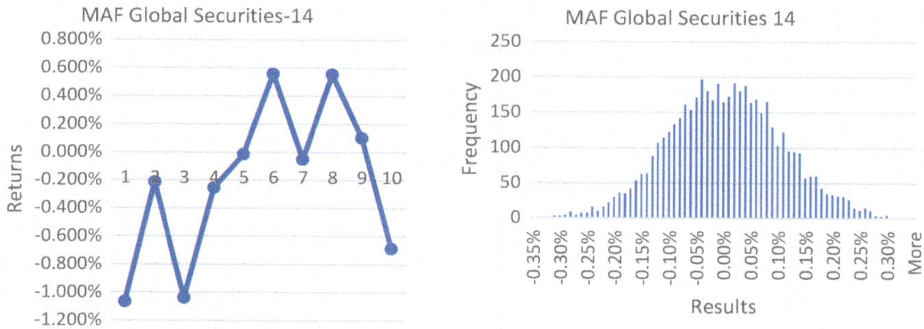

Fig. 17.10 (continued)

Appendix 4

See Table 17.9.

Table 17.9 Test analysis for sukuk and conventional bonds

Test and CI for Two Variances

Method

Null hypothesis	σ(First) / σ(Second) = 1
Alternative hypothesis	σ(First) / σ(Second) ≠ 1
Significance level	α = 0.01

Statistics

Sample	N	StDev	Variance	99% CI for StDevs
First	250	0.005	0.000	(0.005, 0.006)
Second	250	0.003	0.000	(0.003, 0.003)

Ratio of standard deviations = 1.673;
Ratio of variances = 2.799

99% Confidence Intervals

Method	CI for StDev Ratio	CI for Variance Ratio
F	(1.420, 1.971)	(2.017, 3.883)

(continued)

Table 17.9 (continued)

Test and CI for Two Variances

Tests:

Method	DF1	DF2	Test Statistic	P-Value
F	249	249	2.80	0.000

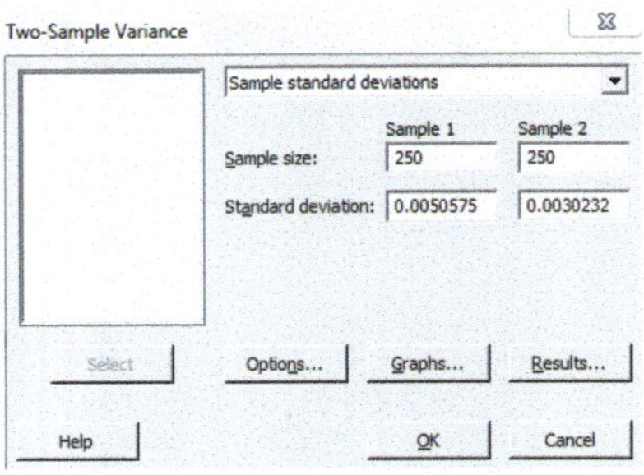

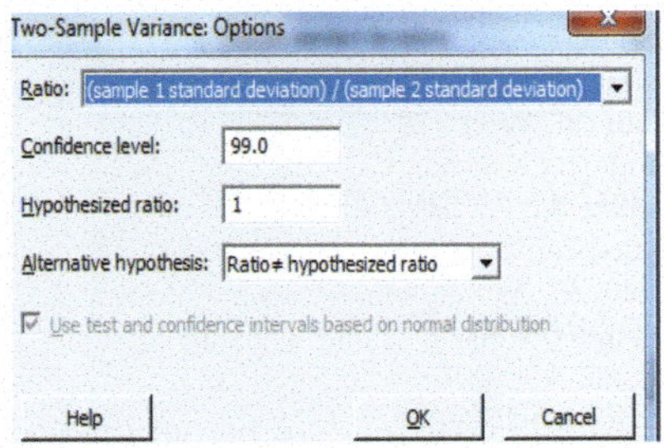

References

Abd Aziz, H., Chalabi, A., & Idris, U. (2016). Does Sukuk financing promote economic growth? An emphasis on the major issuing countries. *Turkish Journal of Islamic Economics., 3*(2), 63–73.

Abdullah, A., Jamaluddin, M. S. & Yazidi, A. S. (2014). Risk in funding infrastructure projects through Sukuk or Islamic bonds. *International Review of Management and Business Research.* 3 (2).

Accounting and Auditing Organization for Islamic Financial Institutions (AAOIFI) (2008). *Sukuk Shariah standards.* Retrieved May 14, 2017, from www.aaoifi.com.

Afshar, T.A. (2013). *Compare Sukuk (Islamic Bonds) with conventional bonds, Are they compatible?* Retrieved April 30, 2017, from http://www.jgbm.org/page/5%20Tahmoures%20A%20%20Afshar.pdf.

Ahmad, N. W., Bihari, N. F., Pain, N. R. I., Shah Shamar, W. S. (2015). Growth and prospect of Sukuk in Malaysian market: A review. In *Proceeding of the 2nd International Conference on Management and Mamola.* Retrieved March 20, 2017, from http://www.kuis.edu.my/icomm/2nd/download/IC%20021.pdf.

Ahmed, F., Ahmed, M., Hamedan, M., Kasi, A. S., & Khosi, A. A. (2016). A comparative study between Sukuk bonds and conventional bonds in Pakistan capital market. *International Journal of Multidisciplinary Research and Development, 3*(7), 6–11.

Ali, A. T., & Huayno, D. (2007). Risks of Sukuk structures: Implications for resource mobilization. *Thunderbird International Business Review, 49*(2), 203–223.

Al-Sayed, O. (2013). Sukuk risk: Analysis and management. *European Journal of Applied Social Sciences Research (EJASSR), 1*(3), 67–76.

Barakat, Z., & Youssef, A. (2009). Product analysis: Wa'ad. Islamic finance in practice issue three. Retrieved April 1, 2017, from http://www.ism.edu/images/stories/publications/IFP-Q1-2009-The-Structure-and-use-of-Waad.pdf.

Boutte, R., & El Mosaic, F. (2014). Sukuk and bond performance in Malaysia. *International Journal of Economics and Finance, 6*(2).

Bryman, A. (2001). *Social Research Methods* (1st ed.). Oxford University Press.

Bryman, A. (2008). *Social Science Research Methods* (3rd ed.). Oxford University Press.

Bryman, A. (2012). *Social Science Research Methods* (4th ed.). Oxford University Press.

Cakir, S., & Raei, F. (2007). *Sukuk vs. Eurobonds: Is there a difference in Value-at-Risk?.*
Creswell, J. W. (2003). *Research Design. Qualitative, Quantitative and Mixed Methods Approaches* (2nd ed.). Sage Publications.
Creswell, J. W. (2014). *Research Design. Qualitative, Quantitative and Mixed Methods Approaches* (4th ed.). Sage Publications.
Dowd, K. (2005). *Measuring Market Risk* (2nd ed.). Wiley and Sons Ltd.
Dusuki, W. A. (2013). *Islamic Financial System: Principles & Operations,* Kuala Lumpur, Malaysia: 2nd print, ISRA.
Essayed, E., Lee, E., & Tariq Ullah, K. (2014). Legal and regulatory issues in issuing Sukuk in South Korea lessons from developed countries' experience. *International Journal of Economics, Commerce and Management, 2*(7).
Funds at Work. (2010). *Shariah scholars—A network analytic perspective.* The Investment Industry's Strategy Consultant.
Godlewski, C., Turk-Arsis, R., & Weill, L. (2013). Sukuk vs conventional bonds: A stock market perspective. *Journal of Comparative Economics., 41,* 745–761.
Habib, F., Muhammad, M., & Sairally, B. S. (2015). *Islamic Capital Markets: Principles and Practices.* Kuala Lumpur. Malaysia: ISRA.
Hassan, A. (2006). *Islamic Features of a Sukuk.* Retrieved June 04, 2017, from www.meinsurancereview.com.
Heffernan, S. (2003). *Modern Banking in Theory and Practice.* Wiley.
Hussain, M., Shahmoradi, and Turk, R. (2015a). *An Overview of Islamic Finance.* IMF Working Paper, WP/15/120. Retrieved February 20, 2017, from https://www.imf.org/external/pubs/ft/wp/2015a/wp15120.pdf.
Hussain, M., Shahmoradi, & Turk, R. (2015b). An overview of Islamic finance. IMF Working Paper, WP/15/120.
IIFM. (2015). *Sukuk report: A comprehension study of the global Sukuk market.* Published November 2014: 4th Edition.
IIFM. (2016). *Sukuk report: A comprehension study of the global Sukuk market,* Published March 2014: 5th Edition.
Investinganswers.com. (2017). *Default risk.* Retrieved May 21, 2017, from http://www.investinganswers.com/financial-dictionary/bonds/default-risk-1313. Last accessed 26/03/2017.
Jobs, A.; Kunzel, P.; Mills, P. and Sy, A. (2008). *Islamic bond issuance—What Sovereign debt managers need to know.* IFM Policy Discussion Paper. Retrieved May 21, 2018, from https://www.imf.org/external/pubs/ft/pdp/2008/pdp03.pdf.
Kammer, A., Norat.M., Pinon, M., Prasad, A., Towe, C., & Zeidane, Z. (2015). *Islamic finance: Opportunities, challenges, and policy options: IMF discussion note.* Retrieved May 21, 2018, from http://www.imf.org/external/pubs/ft/sdn/2015/sdn1505.pdf. Last accessed 20/04/2017.
Kumar, R. (2011). *Research methodology: A step-by-step guide for beginners* (3rd ed.). Sage Publications Ltd.
Kunhibava, S. (2010). Derivatives in Islamic finance. International Shariah Research Academy for Islamic Finance (ISRA).
Lackmann, B. J. (2015). Types of Sukuk (Islamic Bonds) and history of Japanese company issuance. *Nomura Journal of Capital Markets., 6*(3), 1–20.
Mentel, G. (2013). Parametric or non-parametric estimation of value-at-risk. *International Journal of Business and Management, 8*(11), 103.
Meysam, S. (2013). Contractual structures and payoff patterns of Sukuk securities. *International Journal of Banking and Finance., 10*(2), 1–27.
Najeeb, S. F. (2013). Managing business and financial risks of Sukuk: An Islamic risk management perspective. *Journal of Islamic Business and Management,* 3(2).
NIST. (2013). Engineering Statistics Handbook: F-Test for Equality of Two Variances. Available: http://www.itl.nist.gov/div898/handbook/eda/section3/eda359.htm. Accessed Date: 02nd May 2017.
Obaidullah, M. (1998). *Financial engineering with Islamic options. Islamic economic studies.*

Obaidullah, M. (2009). Islamic risk management: Towards greater ethics and efficiency. *International Journal of Islamic Financial Services, 3*(4).
Parvees, T. (2015). *A compilation of contemporary Sukuk risks.* Retrieved May 21, 2018, from https://www.theinternationaljournal.org/ojs/index.php?journal=rjebs&page=article&op=view&path%5B%5D=4340&path%5B%5D=pdf.
Perignon, C., & Smith, D. R. (2008). *A new approach to comparing VaR estimation methods.* Retrieved January 03, 2017, from http://papers.ssrn.com/sol3/papers.cfm?abstract_id=981207&rec=1&srcabs=626682&alg=1&pos=2.
Salem, M. B; Fakfekh, M., & Hachicha, N. (2016). Sukuk issuance and economic growth: Tthe Malaysian case. *Journal of Islamic Economics, banking and Finance, 12*(2).
Saunders, M., Lewis, P., & Thornhill, A. (2009). *Research methods for business students* (5th ed.). Pearson Education Ltd.
Taoual, S. (2016). *A potential for stability and development in the GCC. economic discussion papers 2016–7. Kingston University, London.* Retrieved March 22, 2018, from http://eprints.kingston.ac.uk/34924/1/2016_007.pdf.
Ud Din, S. (2016). Conceptual and structural differences between conventional bonds and Islamic Sukuk. *Australian Journal of Business and Management Research New South Wales Research Centre Australia, 5*(5).
Usmani, M. T. (2008). *Sukuk and their contemporary applications.* AAOIFI Shariah Council, Bahrain.
Williams, C. (2007). Research methods. *Journal of Business & Economic Research., 5*(3), 65–71.
Zaidi, A. (2009). *Nature of risks present in Sukuk structures-rating agency perspective in Sukuk.* Sweet & Maxwell Asia.
Zulkhibri, M. (2015). *A synthesis of theoretical and empirical research on Sukuk.* Retrieved April 25, 2017, from www.sciencedirect.com; http://www.elsevier.com/journals/borsa-istanbul-review/2214-8450.

Alija Avdukic Ph.D. working is currently working as Associate Professor in Islamic Economics & Finance at Al-Maktoum College of Higher Education, UK. He earned his BA from Al-Azhar University (Egypt) and also BA from Damascus University (Syria); continued for Postgraduate Diploma in Islamic Studies from Al-Fatih Institute (Syria); MA in Islamic Economics, Finance and Management Gloucestershire University (UK) and Ph.D. in Islamic Political Economy and Finance from Durham University (UK). He is Deputy Director of MSc Islamic Finance program at University of Dundee; visiting faculty member for Master program in Islamic banking and finance for the joint program School of Economics, University of Sarajevo (Bosnia and Herzegovina) with University of Bolton (UK). He is also a senior research fellow at Ibn Rushed Centre for Excellence (UK). He is also a visiting research fellow of Durham Centre in Islamic Economics, Banking and Finance (UK).

Fawad Khaleel working as a Lecturer in Accountancy and Finance at Edinburgh Napier University, since 2015. He has a MA in Islamic Banking, Finance and Management and Ph.D. in Islamic Finance from Durham University (UK). His research currently focuses on the philosophy of critical accounting as an ontological authority to explore the epistemology of social, political and economic practices, within societal and institutional context. He is a Victorian explorer of contemporary socio-economic inefficiencies, with a focus on analytical epistemology.

Chapter 18
COVID-19 Pandemic and '*KITA JAGA KITA*': Appraisal of Social Responsible Practices of Islamic Banking Institutions in Malaysia

Noor Suhaida Kasri and Siti Fariha Adilah Ismail

The COVID-19 outbreak has caused unprecedented upheavals to the global economy at a scale never seen before in the history of humankind. While governments around the world grappled for the right panacea to address the socio-economic disruptions faced by their nations, the pandemic uncovered new outlook and opportunities. This inevitably compelled the global economies to revisit and reshape their thinking, re-prioritize, re-plan and start implementing initiatives that are more sustainable, resilient, and social in nature.

In this regard, banking system plays a vital role in strengthening and sustaining the economy of a country. In doing so, it must ensure that it facilities and supports the recovery measures as announced by its respective government for the survival of the nation particularly the bottom sector of the society during this challenging time.

Islamic banking institutions particularly are founded based on the rules and principles that are derived from the Quran and the Sunnah. Among the basic principles that Islam advocates is instilling social behaviour by doing good, being fair and just, respect, and care for others which assures upgradation of human morality and prosperity of people. Allah the Almighty mentions in the Quran, Surah An-Nahl (16:90), which means

> Indeed, Allah orders justice and good conduct and giving to relatives and forbids immorality and bad conduct and oppression. He admonishes you that perhaps you will be reminded' (Holy Quran website, 2022).

Meanwhile it was reported in a hadith narrated by Abu Hurairah (RAA) that the Prophet Muhammad (peace be upon him) said.

N. S. Kasri (✉)
INCEIF University, Jalan Tun Ismail, 50480 Kuala Lumpur, Malaysia
e-mail: noor-isra@inceif.org

S. F. A. Ismail
Maybank Islamic Bank, Dataran Maybank, Level 15, Jalan Maarof, Bangsar, 59000 Kuala Lumpur, Malaysia
e-mail: fariha.ismail@maybank.com

T. Azid et al. (eds.), *Wealth Management and Investment in Islamic Settings*,
https://doi.org/10.1007/978-981-19-3686-9_18

> Whoever relieves a believer's distress of the distressful aspects of this world, Allah will rescue him from a difficulty of the difficulties of the Hereafter. Whoever alleviates [the situation of] one in dire straits who cannot repay his debt, Allah will alleviate his lot in both this world and in the Hereafter. Whoever conceals [the faults of] a Muslim, Allah will conceal [his faults] in this life and the Hereafter. (The Comprehensive Book, n.d.).

The above spiritual decrees connote to the heavy social responsibility that Islamic banking institutions are shouldering as compared to its conventional counterpart. Nonetheless such responsibly adds value to the whole purpose of their establishment.

Based on the above premise, this paper un-earth the socially responsible banking practices of the Malaysian Islamic banking institutions during the COVID-19 pandemic. It showcases the unprecedented commitment of Islamic banking institutions in alleviating the people's hardship especially those from the bottom sector. The journey of these establishments articulates the importance of resilience, sustainability, inclusivity and strategic implementation that require balancing between supporting economic recovery and safeguarding the livelihoods of the people. These acts resonate the Malaysian communal COVID-19 campaign '*Kita Jaga Kita*' which means we take care of each other.

This paper adopts a qualitative research approach through the collection of secondary data from the internet. Through these data, innovative, impactful, and inspiring social responsible initiatives were found to be implemented by the Malaysian Islamic banking institutions during the pandemic. This paper has shortlisted five Islamic banking institutions which socio-economic contributions are deemed to be outstanding, inclusive and exemplary during this difficult moment. The five selected banks are Bank Islam Malaysia Berhad (Bank Islam), Maybank Islamic Berhad (Maybank Islamic), Alliance Islamic Bank Berhad (Alliance Islamic), CIMB Islamic Bank Berhad (CIMB Islamic) and Bank Muamalat Malaysia Berhad (Bank Muamalat). These humanity efforts and initiatives have lent support to the recovery measures introduced by the Government of Malaysia (GoM) and the Central Bank of Malaysia/Bank Negara Malaysia (BNM).

The analysis of the socially responsible practices of these Islamic banking institutions is timely as the global economies are searching for appropriate remedies in addressing the unprecedented scale of social and economic crisis caused by pandemic. Though the case studies are very much Malaysia-centric, the design and structures of these initiatives may trigger ideas, motivates, and build the required momentum to move on specially for Islamic banking industries worldwide.

This chapter is structured into five sections. Section 1 introduces the scope and perspective of the chapter. Section 2 describes the recovery measures announced by the GoM and the BNM respectively in their efforts to curb the impact of COVID-19. Section 3 is the lynchpin of this chapter where it appraises the socially responsible practices of the five selected Islamic banking institutions. While the focus of this section is on initiatives during the COVID-19 pandemic, there will be anecdotes on socially responsible initiatives undertaken prior to the pandemic. Finally, Chap. 4 concludes the chapter.

18.1 Malaysian Government and Bank Negara COVID-19 Economic Stimulus, Relief and Financing Packages

a. The Malaysian Government COVID-19 Economic Stimulus Packages

Since the COVID-19 pandemic outbreak, the Government of Malaysia (GoM) has unveiled in stages economic stimulus packages that cover short, medium, and long-term implementation. The progressive announcement has allowed the GoM to study and measure the impact of COVID-19 pandemic on the local economy. It enabled them to strategically plan on the most appropriate approach and implemented the most practical and affordable recovery measures that could cushion the adverse impact on the people and businesses.

The first economic stimulus package was unveiled by the GoM in February 2020, and by June 2020, three more packages were announced with the total value of RM315 billion (USD77 billion).[1] Though these measures were of temporary in nature, they have benefitted Malaysians during this tough time. These recovery packages cater not just individuals and households but also micro and small and medium enterprises (MSMEs) so to boost the economic activities and improve the country's gross domestic product (GDP) growth. These recovery packages were estimated to contribute to more than 3% of the country's 2020 GDP (The Star, 2020).[2]

In addition to these economic stimulus packages, in November 2020 the GoM has tabled the Budget for Year 2021 and the same has passed the policy stage at the Parliament. The proposed budget was acclaimed as the biggest budget ever which allocated RM236.5 billion (USD58 billion) for operational expenditure, RM69 billion (USD16 billion) for development expenditure, RM17 billion (USD4 billion) for COVID-19 fund and RM2 billion (USD491 million) for contingency savings (The Malaysian Reserve, 2020).

b. The Bank Negara Malaysia COVID-19 Relief Measures and Financing Packages

To compliment the economic stimulus measures issued by the GoM, the BNM has put in place several relief measures and packages to support MSMEs, SMEs and individuals particularly the Bottom 40 (B40) affected by the COVID-19 crisis. The following enumerates the range of relief measures, supporting facilities and financing packages offered by the BNM through its participating financial institutions:

a. ***Deferment of Loans/Financing to Individuals and SMEs***

In March 2020, BNM announced deferment of all loan/financing repayments to individuals and SMEs for a period of 6 months, effective from 1 April until 30 September, 2020. This offer is applicable to performing loans, denominated in Malaysian Ringgit,

[1] The exchange rate is based on BNM's rate on 27 November 2020 namely USD 1 = RM 4.07 (Bank Negara Malaysia, 2020a).

[2] For further details on the GoM stimulus and economic recovery packages, please visit https://www.pmo.gov.my/prihatin-economic-stimulus-package/ (Prime Minister Office of Malaysia, 2020) and https://penjana.treasury.gov.my/ (PENJANA, 2020).

and are not in arrears for more than 90 days as at 1 April 2020. Meanwhile for credit card facilities, individuals and SMEs were offered to convert their outstanding balances into a 3-year term loan with reduced interest/profit rates (Bank Negara Malaysia, 2020b).

b. ***Deferment and Restructuring of Loans/Financing to Corporations***

Corporations are also allowed to defer or restructure their loans/financing repayments in a way that would facilitate viable corporations to maintain jobs and swiftly resume their economic activities when their conditions gets better (Bank Negara Malaysia, 2020b).

c. ***Targeted Repayment Assistance***

Acknowledging the economic recovery remains challenging and persisted beyond the moratorium period, in October 2020, BNM introduced moratorium targeted extension and repayment flexibilities to assist the needy borrowers/customers depending on their financial circumstances. To implement this, over 2 million borrowers/customers were contacted and offered the repayment assistance by their respective banking institutions through calls, emails and mobile texts (Bank Negara Malaysia, 2020c).

As a result, there were more than 640,000 applications received, with about 98% of the applications approved. Out of which 40% of the applicants were given moratorium extension. These were unemployed individuals and affected businesses in sectors most hit by the COVID19. While the balance 60% received their instalments reduced. This allowed individuals from the B40 group as well as the SMEs to meet their payment obligations in quantum appropriate to their means and affordability (Bank Negara Malaysia, 2020e).

d. ***Agensi Kaunselling dan Pengurusan Kredit (AKPK)/Credit Counselling and Debt Management Agency***[3]

Individuals and SME borrowers/customers are able to seek assistance from APKK, an agency that is mandated by BNM to provide the necessary advice and assistance to them including communicating with their respective banking institutions for repayment assistance. The intermediation by AKPK, on a *pro bono* basis is vital particularly in cases where the borrowers/customers' applications for moratorium targeted extension got rejected or they are not comfortable with the financing repayment/payment terms proposed by their respective banks (AKPK, 2020a).

e. ***BNMTELELINK***[4]

[3] AKPK was established by BNM as part of a Consumer Protection Framework under BNM's 10-year Financial Sector Master Plan. AKPK offers financial services to individuals borrowers/customers but due to COVID-19, the services is extended to SMEs and micro-SMEs (AKPK, 2020b).

[4] BNMTELELINK is BNM contact point for public to refer their queries on matters pertaining to finance. (Bank Negara Malaysia, 2020f).

BNM closely monitors the practice of the banking institutions in responding and assisting their borrowers/customers. Tight timeframe is imposed on the banking institutions to respond to the targeted repayment assistance applications. They are given 5 days to respond to individual borrowers/customers and 14 days to SME borrowers/customers. Borrowers/customers who face difficulties in dealing or their banking institutions do not respond to them within the given timeline can directly contact and complain to BNM through BNMTELELINK at https://www.bnmtelelink@bnm.gov.my (Bank Negara Malaysia, 2020e).

f. ***Ease in Dealing***

Banking institutions have adopted several methods to ease the application process for example, simplifying the application steps, enabling online application as well as extending the branches' operating hours which includes weekends. For the repayment assistance application, the individual and SME customers/borrowers are not subjected to any processing fees/charges (Bank Negara, 2020e). Specially for B40s and MSMEs borrowers/customers who applied for targeted repayment assistance, those eligible would only need to inform their banking institutions of their choice of repayment without the need to submit any supporting documents (Bank Negara Malaysia, 2020g).

Meanwhile for the Medium 40 (M40) borrowers/customers who are registered with Bantuan Prihatin Nasional and who suffered depletion in their household incomes due to pandemic were also given flexibility through reduction of their monthly instalment amount. To secure such flexibility, they would need to submit to their banking institutions self-declaration that their income/household income have reduced (Bank Negara, 2020g). Ongoing engagement will continue to take place between them and their banking institutions to track the progress of their financial circumstances (Bank Negara Malaysia, 2020e).

g. ***Continuity of Financial Assistance***

While majority of borrowers/customers have resumed their monthly repayments/payments after the moratorium period expiration, they are still allowed to apply for targeted assistance throughout 2020 and into 2021, should there be a change in their circumstances that affected their payment ability. In response to these applications, their banking institutions are obliged to offer various forms of repayment assistance (Bank Negara Malaysia, 2020e).

h. ***Central Credit Reference Information System (CCRIS) Records***

Borrowers/customers who applied for repayment assistance under these COVID-19 relief measures will not have their arrears recorded on their CCRIS records (Bank Negara Malaysia, 2020e).

i. ***BNM Financing Facilities for SMEs and MSMEs***

BNM through its participating banking institutions continue to support sustainability of SMEs and MSMEs borrowers/customers during the challenging period through several financing packages. These financing facilities are tailored to the respective sectors and are opened from March till December 2020.[5]

In sum the scale of the relief measures particularly the targeted repayment assistance is an unprecedented initiative in the history of banking in Malaysia. The repayment assistance targeted approach demonstrated that relief measures can be extended in a more sustainable fashion thus instilling the required strength to the economic recovery. By adopting this strategic approach, banking sector can continue to assist borrowers/customers from numerous income groups, prioritising those from the B40 category, micro businesses as well as borrowers/customers affected by the GoM's movement restrictions (Bank Negara Malaysia, 2020e).

18.2 Social Responsible Practices of Malaysian Islamic Banking Institutions

The bold approach undertaken by the GoM and BNM through their economic stimulus packages and relief measures demonstrated the level of responsibility and accountability that these two key organs owed to the nation. Similar trait of responses is imitated by Islamic banking institutions in helping their customers and community wading this challenging period. This section highlights the journey of five Malaysian Islamic banking institutions which actions complimented the GoM and BNM economic recovery effort. These banks are Bank Islam, Maybank Islamic, Alliance Islamic, CIMB Islamic and Bank Muamalat. The choice of these establishments is due to the impact they made specially during the COVID-19 period through their product offerings and social-impact initiatives.

a. **Bank Islam Malaysia Berhad**

The COVID-19 outbreak has propelled Bank Islam to extend its Value Based Intermediation[6] (VBI) practices to a larger scale and reaching out to more underserved and underbanked segment of the society. In March 2020, BNM has selected Bank Islam to pilot the iTEKAD program. iTEKAD program was introduced by BNM as part of its measures to cushion the impact caused by COVID-19. It is a social finance support program offering the *asnaf* (deserving recipients of zakat) and the B40 household income group including the B40-owned micro-enterprises financial and technical solutions to enable them to generate sustainable income and becoming financially resilient (Bank Negara Malaysia, 2020j).

---

[5] For further details on the GoM stimulus and economic recovery packages, please visit https://www.bnm.gov.my/documents/20124/883228/Appendix.pdf/ecf3fed3-50d8-e5f1-c4e3-f0aa7ec0749d?t=1607521395787 (Bank Negara Malaysia, 2020h) and https://www.bnm.gov.my/covid19 (Bank Negara Malaysia, 2020i).

[6] VBI is an initiative launched by BNM in 2018 and through VBI, Islamic banking institutions are expected to create values and impacts to the economy, community and environment through their operations, activities and product offerings.

Henceforth in May 2020, Bank Islam launched the iTEKAD micro-financing programme and allocated RM5.3 million (USD1.3 million) which comprise of micro-financing facility and zakat (tithe) contribution. RM5 million (USD1.2 million) from the RM5.3 million (USD1.3 million) is sourced from BNM's Micro Enterprises Facility Fund while the balance, RM300,000 (USD73,7,10) is funded by Bank Islam's zakat fund. The micro-financing facility offers seed capital with an affordable micro-financing arrangement for eligible applicants (Malay Mail, 2020). It is offered at the rate of 4% per annum with minimum and maximum financing amount of RM5,000 (USD1,229) and RM50,000 (USD12,285) respectively and payment tenure between 1 to 5 years (Bank Islam, 2020a). Meanwhile zakat fund is used to facilitate the eligible *asnaf* recipients to purchase their required tools and equipment (Malay Mail, 2020).

To ensure the first phase of the programme is effectively rolled out, Bank Islam works together with the Federal Territories Islamic Religious Council (FT Religious Council) and SME Corporation Malaysia (SME Corp). Through their strategic synergy, the recipients are given structured entrepreneurship and financial management trainings conducted by SME Corp. These trainings enabled recipients to be exposed and gain awareness to the needed knowledge in managing an effective and sustainable businesses. The performance and success of the recipients are closely monitored by Bank Islam throughout the financing period (Malay Mail, 2020). The presence of FT Religious Council is crucial as in Malaysia, State Religious Councils are in charged with the administration and management of *zakat* properties including the selection and distribution of zakat to *asnaf*.

100 recipients are expected to benefit from iTEKAD program by the end of 2020. To enable iTEKAD program to continue and able to reach out to more deserving recipients, BNM will get iTEKAD program to be implemented by more Islamic banking institutions in collaboration with selected implementation partners like other state Islamic religious councils, agencies and non-governmental organisations. BNM also planned for iTEKAD program to optimise other Islamic social instrument namely cash waqf at the later stage (Bank Negara Malaysia, 2020j).

The introduction of iTEKAD program is followed by another similar microfinance program. In November 2020, Bank Islam launched BangKIT Microfinance programme with the aim to disburse RM20 million (USD4.9 million) using *Qard* (interest-free loan) for the benefit of 3,000 microentrepreneurs within a 5 years' time frame. The BangKIT Microfinance aids the shortlisted unbanked and underbanked microentrepreneurs to procure capital for their start-up business or business expansion and subsequently build a good credit record to facilitate their financings in the future. Like iTEKAD program, eligible micro-entrepreneurs will be provided with structured entrepreneurship training to educate them to grow their businesses sustainably. Financing amount as low as RM500 (USD123) to RM3,000 (USD737) is offered to start-up businesses and RM3,000 (USD737) up to RM20,000 (USD4,914) is offered for business expansion with a repayment period of between 6 months to 3 years (Bank Islam, 2020b).

Bank Islam is known among the Islamic banking fraternity to pioneer social-impact projects. Among its pronounced social-impact initiatives are the establishment of Menara Bank Islam and Sadaqa House. Menara Bank Islam project is a ground-breaking synergy between BIMB, FT Religious Council, Malaysian Hajj Pilgrim Fund Board (Lembaga Tabung Haji) and TH Properties Group of Companies. Such synergy resulted to the development of the Menara Bank Islam, a 34-storey Class A office built on 1.2 acres of waqf land owned by FT Religious Council at a cost of RM151 million (USD36 million) in 2011 (Chik, n.d.).

While Sadaqa House is an Islamic crowdfunding digital platform that Bank Islam launched in 2018 through its collaboration with Ethis Ventures Sdn Bhd. In its first phase, Sadaqa House has abled to raise contributions from the public and the same have been channelled to the following needy recipients:

- Heart Foundation of Malaysia (Yayasan Institut Jantung Negara (IJN)) which provided financial assistance to the selected IJN patients to undergo their heart surgery;
- Sultanah Bahiyah Foundation (Yayasan Sultanah Bahiyah (YSB)) and Technology Park Malaysia which funded the construction of fish drying cabins for fishermen community in Kedah, one of the northern states in Peninsula Malaysia; and
- Universiti Teknologi Malaysia (UTM) which funded the installation of solar system to aborigine's community in Malaysia (Bank Islam, 2018).

By the end of 2019, Sadaqa House has raised a total of RM368,621.59 (USD90,570). The funds have benefited 21 paediatric patients in IJN, 7 entrepreneurs under YSB and 13 houses under the UTM solar development project. Due to this achievement, in 2019, Sadaqa House was conferred the Best Social Financial Initiative 2019 award at the 5th Islamic Retail Banking Awards 2019 (Bank Islam, 2019).

Another commendable contribution of Sadaqa House is the use of its funds to finance the BangKIT Microfinance programme. At the initial stage of this program, Sadaqa House allocated RM2 million (USD491,400) which is targeted to benefit more than 200 microentrepreneurs, subject to the availability of funds. In addition to that, in November 2020, Sadaqa House organised *#KitaBantuKita* campaign which raised funds to help those badly hit by the third wave of the pandemic. This campaign featured 1:1 matching basis where for every RM10 (USD2.46) contribution made to *#KitaBantuKita* Campaign, Sadaqa House will add equivalent amount of RM10 (USD2.46) up to a maximum of RM500,000 (USD122,850) (Bank Islam, 2020b).

Prior to the *#KitaBantuKita* campaign, Bank Islam has contributed to various humanitarian and medical-related causes in combatting the COVID-19 pandemic. To name a few is its contribution of RM1.6 million (USD393,120) made together with its parent bank, BIMB Holdings Berhad (BHB) in March 2020. BHB contributed RM1 million (USD245,700) to #MusaadahCovid-19 Fund, a fundraising program initiated under the Prime Minister's Department (Religious Affairs) which provided relief to frontliners battling the COVID-19 outbreak. Bank Islam contributed the balance of RM600,000 (USD147, 420) through its corporate social responsibility vehicle, AMAL, that facilitated the following initiatives:

- Financial assistance to micro-entrepreneurs whose businesses were badly hit by the COVID19;
- Direct Relief Support Programme which supplied food and necessities to universities, orphanages, old folks' homes and homes for the disabled; and,
- Purchase of necessities and essential needs for hospitals and district health clinics (Bank Islam, 2020d).

In short, piloting iTEKAD program during the COVID-19 outbreak signifies the credibility and leadership of Bank Islam in the field of social-impact financing and initiatives. Being one of the founding members[7] of the VBI's Community of Practitioners (CoP),[8] Bank Islam has walked the talk and proven that VBI initiatives are implementable by Islamic banking community through strategic and effective coordination and networking among the relevant stakeholders.

b. **Maybank Islamic**

COVID-19 outbreak provides opportunity for Maybank Islamic to realise its ubiquitous 'Humanising Banking' motto. Maybank Islamic through Maybank Group's charity arm, Maybank Foundation, has spearheaded financial contributions and economic empowerment initiatives to the critical sector and needy community affected by the outbreak. In supporting the effort of the GoM to reduce the transmission of the COVID-19 virus, in March 2020, Maybank Foundation contributed RM4 million (USD982,800) through MERCY Malaysia's COVID-19 Pandemic Fund. The contribution is used to acquire the medical and related necessities and support required by the front liners and volunteers (Maybank Foundation, 2020a).

In line with the Standard Operating Procedure (SOP) of the Ministry of Health, the training programs conducted by Maybank Foundation through its R.I.S.E (Reach Independence & Sustainable Entrepreneurship) program[9] to the disabled and disadvantaged communities are conducted online. Participants' internet access and devices are provided by Maybank Foundation to ensure their attendance to the virtual training and learning are not disrupted during the COVID-19 pandemic. The regular trainings educate the participants on important topics related to business management and related skills. To develop their capacity building further, a structured mentoring system is run by the skilled Maybank volunteers that ensures effective implementation of the given knowledge and skills (Maybank Foundation, 2020b).

In October 2020, Maybank Islamic launched Malaysia's first ever Social Impact Deposit. The Social Impact Deposit is an Islamic Fixed Deposit (IFD-i) which is designed as a financial relief programme to render financial assistance to those who

[7] CoP founding members comprise of BIMB, Bank Mualamat, Agrobank, CIMB Islamic Bank Berhad and HSBC Amanah Malaysia Berhad.

[8] The establishment of CoP was to facilitate the adoption of VBI among the industry stakeholders and to lead by example in the VBI implementation.

[9] RISE program is designed to empower the financial standing and independence of the disabled and disadvantaged communities located locally and within the Asian region.

were economically affected by the pandemic. The recipients selected to benefit from this program includes Maybank Islamic' customers who are in dire need of financial assistance due to income loss or unemployed because of COVID-19 (Maybank Islamic, 2020).

This campaign is open to public and to participate, customers are required to make a 6 months IFD-i placement during the campaign period. The minimum placement amount is RM1,000 (USD245) in a single certificate, and the maximum placement amount is RM15 million (USD3.6 million) per customer (Maybank Islamic, 2020). The placement will earn them profit as per the prevailing board rate at time of placement. For every placement made during the campaign period, Maybank Islamic will contribute 0.3% p.a. to the Social Impact Assistance Account. The Social Impact Assistance Account is designated to provide interim financial relief to the selected recipients over a period of 6 months. An impact report will be made available on Maybank's digital banking platform, Maybank2U. The campaign is expected to end in December 2020 or upon reaching the campaign target set by the bank, whichever is earlier (Maybank Islamic, 2020).

With an asset base of RM240 billion (USD58 billion) as at end of September 2019, Maybank Islamic is Malaysia's biggest Islamic bank and by asset size, it is one of the top five Islamic banks in the world (RAM, 2020). Its pole position is a testament to its achievement in supporting the socio-economic growth of the country as aptly described by the then Maybank Chairman, Datuk Mohaiyani Shamsudin,

> As an organisation with a mission of humanising financial services, we have always ensured that our role goes beyond just driving economic growth for the country and region, but also in ensuring the well-being of our communities at all times, more so during critical moments such as the current Covid-19 situation which has stretched the resources of the country. (Maybank Foundation, 2020a)

c. **Alliance Islamic Bank Berhad**

Acknowledging the challenges brought by the COVID-19 pandemic, Alliance Islamic came forward to assist those in need. Leveraging on its *Shari'ah* compliant social crowd funding platform, SocioBiz, set up in 2019, Alliance Islamic launched campaigns to help financially disadvantaged individuals to raise funds for the purpose of starting or expanding a business or learning a new skill on earning a sustainable livelihood (Global Sadaqah, n.d.). Besides running campaigns to empower communities through entrepreneurship, SocioBiz also run campaign to assist Ministry of Health in tackling the challenges caused by COVID-19 (Global Sadaqah, n.d.).

In April 2020, Alliance Islamic together with the Association of Islamic Banking and Financial Institutions in Malaysia (AIBIM) launched on SocioBiz platform, the Emergency Relief Campaign dedicated to assist front-liners battling COVID-19 pandemic. Due to the significant increase of patients admitted due to the pandemic, two main hospitals in Klang Valley namely Hospital Kuala Lumpur and Hospital Sg Buloh as well as one hospital in Negeri Sembilan were selected for this campaign. A total of RM105,085 (USD25,819) has been raised under this campaign which fund was used to purchase and distribute the following equipment to these hospitals namely: PPE sets, face shields, shoe covers, sanitizer, heavy duty garbage bags, sterilized wrappers, adult raincoats, face masks, food packs, medical trolleys and tents (Global Sadaqah, 2020a).

To maximise the impact of its social crowdfunding platform, in April 2020 Alliance Islamic forged a new collaboration with Citrine Capital Sdn Bhd,[10] NGOhub[11] and Malaysian Global Innovation & Creativity Centre (MaGIC).[12] Through this new collaboration, a campaign was then launched on SocioBiz to help sustain the livelihood of the communities affected by COVID-19 (Global Sadaqah, 2020b). This campaign has raised a total of RM219,420 (USD53,911) which was then used to provide the affected B40 communities:

- The supply of 2167 grocery packages, each is enough to feed four persons for one week
- The supply of 6627 cooked food
- The supply of 10,000 protective hygiene essentials (in the form of 5000 face masks and 2000 hand sanitizers).

In addition to providing the above assistance, this campaign has supported the capacity of 11 social enterprises to extend their business runway by an average of 1.3 months, which includes continuous employment of 67 B40 employees and vendors. Through this campaign, 13,957 beneficiaries were supported which comprise of disadvantaged women, B40 batik artisans, low-income students, homeless people, indigenous people, B40 residents under the People's Housing Project and rural farmers (Global Sadaqah, 2020b).

In sum, Alliance Islamic's social impact projects during this challenging time have made tremendous impact to the needy individuals and businesses. These initiatives have enhanced the livelihoods of B40 communities affected by COVID-19 and reduced the risk of contracting virus among marginalised individuals. Essentially the initiatives have helped to increase the sustainability of social enterprises to continue conducting their businesses and indirectly continue retaining their B40 employees and vendors (Global Sadaqah, 2020b).

d. **CIMB Islamic**

In alleviating the hardship faced by the community, like its other brethren as mentioned earlier, in April 2020, CIMB Islamic Bank Berhad together with CIMB Bank Berhad (collectively referred to as 'CIMB' whenever relevant) launched a social-impact campaign through their charity crowdfunding portal, CIMB Cares. The campaign sought to help the underserved local communities and frontliners affected by the COVID-19 pandemic.

---

[10] Citrine Capital Sdn Bhd is a for-profit venture capitalist with the expectation of maximizing financial returns and positive societal impact. Its support is through the provision of financial capital and social innovation capital, aiming to propel them to the next level.

[11] NGOhub is an online and offline platform dedicated to enable, empower and serve NGOs.

[12] Malaysian Global Innovation & Creativity Centre (MaGIC) is an agency under the Ministry of Science, Technology and Innovation (MOSTI) mandated to spur the development and growth of technology adoption, and sustainable entrepreneurship ecosystem in Malaysia.

To maximise the impact of the fund raised, CIMB collaborated with 10 non-governmental organisations (NGOs) with strong grassroot expertise to help it connect with the underserved communities. The followings are the selected NGOs that assisted CIMB in distributing the urgent needs - food and hygiene provisions to the needy:

- The Budimas Charitable Foundation
- The Befrienders Kuala Lumpur
- Persatuan Penjagaan Kanak-Kanak Terencat Akal Johor Bahru
- Pure Life Society
- The Lost Food Project
- Al-Ikhlas Hope Society
- Kita Bantu Kita
- Pertubuhan Kebajikan Sedulur
- Project Wawasan Rakyat, and
- Persatuan Care Selangor (CIMB, 2020a).

To participate in this campaign, CIMB allowed its customers and non-customers to donate either directly via CIMB Cares, or by redeeming the customers' Banking or Credit Card Bonus Points online from April until end of June 2020. To make donation under the bonus points redemption, customers can redeem 4,000 bonus points for each RM10 (USD2.46) donation they would like to make. All donations were channelled, in full, directly to the participating NGOs with zero transfer fee (CIMB, 2020a).

In addition to the above, CIMB Islamic made 'offline contribution' by providing food supplies to a Centre for the Housing of the Poorest People (Pusat Perumahan Rakyat Termiskin ("PPRT")) community. The recipients include the participants of CIMB's annual entrepreneurial programme conducted together with Taylor's Education Group. A total of 300 families have benefited from this contribution (CIMB, 2020a).

Apart from the aforesaid initiative, CIMB has supported COVID-19 related initiatives through its charity arm, CIMB Foundation following its partnership with several NGOs namely:

- PERTIWI Soup Kitchen that provided meals to 2,000 underprivileged people.
- Pertubuhan Perkhidmatan Sosial dan Pembangunan Komuniti Daerah Gombak ("PSPK") (The Association of Services and Community Development of Gombak District) for its Breakfast On Us program that provided bread to 2,400 people.
- Program Perumahan Rakyat (PPR) (People's Housing Program) in Lembah Subang that provided grocery provisions benefited more than 80 underprivileged women and their families in Lembah Subang, with additional families in Kuala Lumpur, Penang, and Sabah (CIMB, 2020a).

Besides contributing via its own link as mentioned above, CIMB also contributed through the Government-Linked Companies (GLCs) Disaster Response Network

(GDRN). Under this network, CIMB supported various humanitarian and medical-related initiatives which includes the purchase of medical supplies, PPE and ventilators for the Ministry of Health. Through these social channels, by April, 2020, CIMB has reached and assisted approximately 29,000 people for a total value of more than RM2.4 million (USD589,680) (CIMB, 2020a).

Alongside these social efforts, in April, 2020 CIMB launched the CIMB COVID-19 Bereavement Support Programme for Individual Customers which grants financial assistance to their customers, or their immediate family member, in the unfortunate event of bereavement from COVID-19. A total of RM2 million (USD491,400) has been allocated by CIMB for this programme. This programme offers several financial support measures which includes:

- Cash contribution of RM5,000 (USD1,229) to defray the funeral expenses
- Cash contribution of RM2,000 (USD491) to pay for the outstanding bills incurred by the deceased
- A waiver of outstanding fees and charges owing to CIMB by the deceased customer
- Debts write-off on selected CIMB products of the deceased customer, subject to a cap (CIMB, 2020b).

In short, the partnership forged by CIMB with multi-backgrounds NGOs ensures the impact of its contributions reach and benefit as many underprivileged and marginalised communities. The various social initiatives and financial aid offered to the vulnerable communities as well as its own customers positions CIMB at the same rank with other leading banking institutions in fostering and promoting socially responsible practices particularly in the era of COVID-19.

e. **Bank Muamalat Malaysia Berhad**

COVID-19 pandemic has further increased the momentum of Bank Mumalat in giving back to the society though its social-impact initiatives. In September 2020, Bank Muamalat launched Jariah Fund, a crowdfunding platform for the purpose of raising funds for its selected social welfare projects. For the first phase, from September 2020 till March 2021, Bank Muamalat will be working with five identified NGOs, namely Yayasan Sejahtera, Yayasan Ikhlas, Yayasan Muslimin, The National Autism Society of Malaysia (NASOM) and Malaysian Association for the Blind (MAB). Acting as the Bank's charitable partners, the NGOs monitor the progress of the charitable campaigns running on its Jariah Fund platform (DRB-HICOM, 2020).

Several charitable projects have been identified to be part of the Jariah Fund campaigns. These projects include chilli cultivation, string hoppers sales project, educational projects for indigenous children and assistance to those affected by the COVID-19 Movement Control Order period (DRB-HICOM, 2020). Though it is just a month after the launch of these charitable campaigns, the amount collected for these campaigns have shown tremendous progress. For example, the campaign for the indigenous children education program and the campaign to purchase the required equipment for health patients have managed to secure the total expected amount totalling RM4872 (USD1,197) and RM7613 (USD1,871) respectively. While education development program under the MAB has collected more than 50% and the collection for economic empowerment program for single parent has reached almost 50% of the expected amount (Jariah Fund, 2020).

In addition to running the above campaigns, Bank Muamalat have assisted the communities by making several contributions via its Jariah Fund platform and its waqf vehicle, Wakaf Selangor Muamalat. Through its waqf vehicle, Bank Mualamat contributed RM369,200 (USD90,712) to 18 selected hospitals in 6 states in Malaysia[13] namely the Federal Territory, Selangor, Perak, Pahang, Kelantan and Sabah. These contributions have benefited the frontliners through the supply of the much needed equipment like syringe pump machines, N95 face masks and PPE (Wakaf Muamalat, 2020).

Wakaf Mualamat is Bank Muamalat's waqf vehicle. It was established in 2012 with the purpose of empowering and uplifting the community through the institution of waqf. The initiatives initiated under Wakaf Muamalat entails collaborative effort between Bank Mualamat with several State Islamic Religious Councils in co-managing the cash waqf fund via a Joint Management Committee (JMC). Its first collaborative partner was Perbadanan Wakaf Selangor (Selangor Waqf Corporation) the waqf arm for the Majlis Agama Islam Selangor (Selangor State Religious Council).[14] The success of their collaborative effort led other states to invite Bank Muamalat to collaborate on cash waqf management initiatives. Henceforth in 2017, Bank Muamalat collaborated with Perbadanan Wakaf Negeri Sembilan (Negeri Sembilan Waqf Corporation)[15] followed by Majlis Agama Islam dan Adat Istiadat Melayu Kelantan (Kelantan State Islamic Religious Council) (MAIK)[16] in 2018 and Majlis Agama Islam Kedah (MAIK) (Kedah State Religious Council)[17] in 2019. By the end of 2019, Wakaf Mualamat has collected RM26,737,824.47 (USD6.5 million), a 24% increase compared to 2018.[18] Through its JMC, Wakaf Muamalat has approved

---

[13] The hospitals that received the contributions from Waqf Selangor Mualamat are Hospital Sg Buloh, Selangor, Hospital Selayang, Selangor Hospital Selayang, Selangor, Hospital Kuala Lumpur, Kuala Lumpur, Hospital Serdang, Selangor, Hospital Raja Permaisuri Bainun, Ipoh, Perak, Hospital Kuala Krai, Kelantan, Hospital Tawau, Sabah, Hospital Duchess of Kent, Sandakan, Sabah, Hospital Tengku Ampuan Rahimah, Klang, Selangor, Hospital Sultan Haji Ahmad Shah, Temerloh, Pahang, Hospital Universiti Sains Malaysia, Kubang Kerian, Kelantan, Hospital Canselor Tuanku Muhriz, UKM Cheras, Kuala Lumpur, Pusat Perubatan Universiti Malaya, Kuala Lumpur, Hospital Tengku Ampuan Afzan, Kuantan, Pahang, Hospital Tanah Merah, Kelantan, Pusat Perubatan IIUM, Kuantan, Pahang, Hospital Kajang, Selangor and Hospital Raja Perempuan Zainab II, Kota Bharu, Kelantan (Waqf Muamalat, 2020).

[14] The collaboration between Bank Muamalat and Perbadanan Waqf Selangor led to the establishment of Waqf Selangor Muamalat.

[15] The collaboration between Bank Mualamat and Perbadanan Waqf Negeri Sembilan, the waqf arm for the Negeri Sembilan Islamic Religious Council led to the establishment of Waqf Negeri Sembilan Muamalat.

[16] The collaboration between Bank Muamalat and MAIK led to the establishment of Waqf MAIK Muamalat.

[17] The collaboration between Bank Muamalat and MAIKDA led to the establishment of Waqf Kedah Muamalat.

[18] Based on Bank Muamalat's 2018 Annual Report which reported the waqf fund collected by Waqf Selangor Muamalat was RM20,399,277.45 (USD5 million). Bank Mualamat through its

RM19,249,888.88 (USD 4.7 million) of which RM13,665,823.60 (USD3.3 million) has been disbursed to several health and education related wakaf projects (Bank Muamalat, 2019).

The above case studies have illustrated the unprecedented scale of socially responsible practices of Bank Islam, Maybank Islamic, Alliance Islamic, CIMB Islamic and Bank Muamalat. These initiatives have tremendously helped and motivated the community particularly those from B40 community to weather and rebuild their lives. Essentially the responsibility and concern shown through their socially responsible practices during this challenging period transcend the communal spirit and value as aptly epitomised by the COVID-19 communal motto: '*Kita Jaga Kita*/We Take Care of One Another'.

18.3 Conclusion

The COVID-19 pandemic has tested and is continuing testing the resilience of the global nation. It unveiled many valuable lessons for governments to take stock and revisit their existing approaches towards building a more sustainable and inclusive economy. This article narrated the journey of the GoM, the BNM and the Islamic banking institutions in Malaysia in implementing strategic and impactful recovery measures and financial assistance across a range of income groups. It unveiled how the pandemic has moved the Islamic banking industry to explore for a more impactful options to cater for the need of the vulnerable households specially the B40 category and micro businesses.

The unprecedented scale of the recovery measures and financial assistance offered evidenced that the Islamic banking institutions in Malaysia are well-equipped to respond to the demand of the domestic economy during the COVID-19 crisis. The strength and resilience of these banks are due to the large financial buffers built up over the years.[19] The measures and financial assistance have alleviated the challenges faced by the people and businesses specially in job preservation and business continuity (Bank Negara Malaysia, 2020k).

Essentially the social responsible practices depicted in these case studies highlighted the change in the mindset of the Islamic banking institutions in approaching and implementing Islamic social finance in a more meaningful way. It evidenced their willingness to embrace and internalise the spirit of *Maqasid al Shari'ah* (the objectives of *Shari'ah*) which envisions economic growth that is equitable, just, sustainable, and inclusive. Such COVID-19 pandemic could possibly be the avenue for Islamic banking institutions to take the lead in showcasing the wholesome value

---

Joint Management Committee approved RM5,791,271.15 (USD1.4 million) and RM11,100,844.20 (USD2.7 million) was disbursed on waqf projects (Bank Muamalat, 2018).

[19] As at the end January 2020, the Malaysian banking industry enjoyed excess capital buffers above the minimum regulatory requirement of RM119.7 billion (USD29 billion).

propositions of Islamic finance. Perhaps a post-COVID19 banking model for consideration by the global financial system that is built upon shared values of integrity, inclusivity, and sustainability.

References

AKPK. (2020a). Post Moratorium Guide. *AKPK*. Retrieved November, 20, 2020a from https://www.akpk.org.my/

AKPK. (2020b). Our Services. *AKPK*. Retrieved November 20, 2020b from https://www.akpk.org.my/

Bank Islam. (2018). *Bank Islam Launches Sadaqa House A Social Finance Initiative to Encourage Wealth Sharing.* [Immediate Release]. Retrieved November 12, 2020 from http://www.bankislam.com.my/home/assets/uploads/MEDIA-RELEASE-BANK-ISLAM-LAUNCHES-SADAQAH-HOUSE.pdf

Bank Islam. (2019). *Sadaqa House Bank Islam Diiktiraf Sebagai Inisiatif Kewangan Sosial Terbaik 2019.* [Immediate Release]. Retrieved November 10, 2020 from https://www.bankislam.com/wp-content/uploads/Siaran-Media-Sadaqa-House-Bank-Islam-Diiktiraf.pdf

Bank Islam. (2020a). *iTEKAD Microfinancing Program.* [Product Disclosure Sheet] Retrieved November 21, 2020a from https://www.bankislam.com/wp-content/uploads/PDS-iTEKAD-en.pdf

Bank Islam. (2020b). Bank Islam Expands Islamic Social Finance. [Immediate Release]. Retrieved November 28, 2020b from https://www.bankislam.com/wp-content/uploads/Media-Release-Bank-Islam-Expands-Islamic-Social-Finance-Agenda.pdf

Bank Islam. (2020d). *Bhb, Bank Islam Contributes Rm1.6 Million For COVID-19 Efforts.* [Immediate Release]. Retrieved November 28, 2020c from https://www.bankislam.com/wp-content/uploads/MEDIA-RELEASE-BHB-BANK-ISLAM-CONTRIBUTES-RM1.6-MILLION-FOR-COVID-19-EFFORTS.pdf

Bank Muamalat. (2018). *Annual Report 2018.* Bank Muamalat. Retrieved November 13, 2020 from https://www.muamalat.com.my/downloads/corporate-overview/annual/2018_Interactive.pdf

Bank Muamalat. (2019). *Annual Report 2019.* Bank Muamalat. Retrieved November 13, 2020 from https://www.muamalat.com.my/downloads/corporate-overview/annual/2019.pdf

Bank Negara Malaysia. (2018). *Implementation Guide for Value-based Intermediation.* Bank Negara Malaysia. Retrieved November 21, 2020, from https://www.bnm.gov.my/documents/20124/761682/Implementation+Guide+for+Value-based+Intermediation.pdf

Bank Negara Malaysia. (2020a). Exchange Rates. Retrieved November 28, 2020a, from https://www.bnm.gov.my/index.php?ch=statistic&pg=stats_exchangerates

Bank Negara Malaysia. (2020b). *Measures to Assist Individuals, SMEs and Corporates Affected by COVID-19.* [Press Release]. Retrieved November 19, 2020, from https://www.bnm.gov.my/index.php?ch=en_press&pg=en_press&ac=5018&lang=en

Bank Negara Malaysia. (2020c). *Transition to targeted repayment assistance* [Press Release]. Retrieved November 19, 2020b, from https://www.bnm.gov.my/index.php?ch=en_press&pg=en_press&ac=5125&lang=en

Bank Negara Malaysia. (2020d). The Shariah Advisory Council of Bank Negara Malaysia (the SAC) 30th Special meeting (revised on 16 October 2020c). *BNM*. Retrieved November 19, 2020c, from https://www.bnm.gov.my/index.php?ch=en_about&pg=en_sac_updates&ac=694

Bank Negara Malaysia. (2020e). *Targeted Repayment Assistance better serves borrowers' needs* [Press Release] Retrieved November 19, 2020, from https://www.bnm.gov.my/index.php?ch=en_press&pg=en_press&ac=5131l&lang=en

Bank Negara Malaysia. (2020f). *Establishment of Bank Negara Malaysia TELELINK 1–300–88-LINK.* [Immediate Release] Retrieved November 20, 2020, from https://www.bnm.gov.my/index.php?ch=en_press&pg=en_press&ac=693&lang=en#:~:text=BNMLINK%20and%20BNMTELELINK%20represent%20Bank,%2C%20fax%2C%20letter%20or%20email

Bank Negara Malaysia. (2020g). *Budget measures to assist individuals and SMEs affected by COVID-19.* [Immediate Release] Retrieved November 20, 2020, from https://www.bnm.gov.my/index.php?ch=en_press&pg=en_press&ac=5147

Bank Negara Malaysia. (2020h). Features of BNM's New and Enhanced Financing Facilities to Assist Malaysian SMEs. Retrieved November 18, 2020d, from https://www.bnm.gov.my/documents/20124/883228/Appendix.pdf/ecf3fed3-50d8-e5f1-c4e3-f0aa7ec0749d?t=1607521395787

Bank Negara Malaysia. (2020i). Measures to Address COVID-19 Impact. Retrieved November 18, 2020e, from https://www.bnm.gov.my/covid19

Bank Negara Malaysia. (2020j). Additional Measures to Further Support SMEs and Individuals Affected by the COVID-19 Outbreak. [Immediate Release]. Retrieved November 11, 2020, from https://www.bnm.gov.my/index.php?ch=en_press&pg=en_press&ac=5022&lang=en

Bank Negara. (2020k). *Measures to Assist Individuals, SMEs and Corporates Affected by COVID-19.* [Immediate Release]. Retrieved November 21, 2020, from https://www.bnm.gov.my/index.php?ch=en_press&pg=en_press&ac=5018&lang=en

Chik, M. N. (n.d.), Waqf Development: Islamic Banks–MAINs' Experience. Retrieved November 12, 2020, from http://www.kuis.edu.my/ircief/downloads/20170419/2-Waqf_Development-ustaz_nazri_chik.pdf

CIMB. (2020a). CIMB Partners grassroot NGOs to Accelerate Covid-19 Contributions for Front-liners and Underserved Local Communities. Retrieved November 15, 2020a, from https://www.cimb.com/en/sustainability/from-commitment-to-action/16-april-2020a/cimb-partners-grassroot-ngo-to-accelerate-covid-19-contributions-for-frontline.html

CIMB. (2020b). CIMB Covid-19 Bereavement Support Programme for Individual Customers. Retrieved November 15, 2020b, from https://www.cimb.com.my/en/personal/campaigns/covid-19/cimb-covid19-bereavement-support-programme.html

DRB-HICOM. (2020). Bank Muamalat Launches Jariah Fund. Retrieved November 13, 2020 from https://communique-drbhicom.com/2020/09/bank-muamalat-launches-jariah-fund/

Global Sadaqah. (n. d), Socio Biz Empowering Communities through Entrepreneurship. Retrieved November 13, 2020 from https://globalsadaqah.com/allianceislamic/

Global Sadaqah. (2020a). Emergency Relief for Front-liners Battling COVID-19. Retrieved November 13, 2020a, from https://globalsadaqah.com/campaign/sociobiz-covid19/

Global Sadaqah. (2020b). Social Enterprise Sustainability Initiative Report 2020b. Retrieved November 13, 2020b, from https://globalsadaqah.com/wp-content/uploads/2020b/09/SESI-Report-2020b.pdf

Holy Quran Website. (2022). Surah Nahl aya 90, English translation of the meaning Ayah. Retrieved March 3, 2022, from https://www.hati.my/the-pure-life-society/

Jariah Fund. (2020). Jariah Fund. Retrieved November 28, 2020, from https://jariahfund.muamalat.com.my/?page=1

Malay Mail. (2020). Bank Islam allocates RM5.3m for iTEKAD micro-financing programme. *Malay Mail.* Retrieved November 21, 2020, from https://www.malaymail.com/news/money/2020/05/14/bank-islam-allocates-rm5.3m-for-itekad-micro-financing-programme/1866196

Maybank Foundation. (2020a). Who We Are. Retrieved November 12, 2020a, from https://www.maybankfoundation.com/

Maybank Foundation. (2020b). Reach Independence & Sustainable Entrepreneurship (RISE). Retrieved November 28, 2020b, from https://www.maybankfoundation.com/index.php/our-impact/rise/rise-overview

Maybank Islamic. (2020). Frequently Asked Questions For The Social Impact Deposit. Retrieved November 12, 2020, from https://www.maybank2u.com.my/iwov-resources/pdf/personal/promotions/2020/faq_socialimpactdeposit.pdf

Prime Minister's Office of Malaysia Official Website. (2020). PRIHATIN economic stimulus package. Retrieved November 21, 2020, from https://www.pmo.gov.my/prihatin-economic-stimulus-package/

PENJANA. (2020). Building the economy together. Retrieved November 21, 2020, from https://penjana.treasury.gov.my/

RAM. (2020). *RAM Ratings reaffirms Maybank Islamic's AAA financial institution rating.* [Press Release]. Retrieved November 12, 2020, from https://www.ram.com.my/pressrelease/?prviewid=5269#:~:text=With%20an%20asset%20base%20of,the%20world%20by%20asset%20size

The Comprehensive Book. (n.d.), Sahih Muslim, Hadith Number 2667 Retrieved November 20, 2020, from https://sunnah.com/urn/2054270

The Malaysian Reserve. (2020). Budget 2021: Highlight of expenditures. The Malaysian Reserve.com. Retrieved November 20, 2020, from https://themalaysianreserve.com/2020/11/07/budget-2021-highlight-of-expenditures/

Wakaf Muamalat. (2020), Wakaf Updates. Retrieved November 13, 2020, from https://www.muamalat.com.my/wakafmuamalat/Berita-Wakaf/2020/sumbangan-wakaf-selangor-muamalat-untuk-membendung-pandemik-covid-19.html

Noor Suhaida Kasri Ph.D. is the Deputy Director, ISRA Research Management Centre of INCEIF University. She received her Doctor of Philosophy in Islamic Banking Finance and Management from University of Gloucestershire (in collaboration with Markfield Institute of Higher Education), UK. Her Master in Laws was from King's College of London. Her research interest is in law, regulation, social and ethical finance. She has written a number of research papers, articles and textbook chapters and presented in conferences globally.

Siti Fariha Adilah Ismail is an Executive at Shariah Centre of Excellence, Shariah Management, Maybank Islamic Bank. She received her bachelor degree in Islamic Jurisprudence (*Fiqh Wa Usuluh*) from Al Al-Bayt University, Jordan. She's currently doing her Master in Islamic Finance Practice (MIFP) at the International Centre for Education in Islamic Finance (INCEIF). Her recent article as co-writer entitled "Repayment moratorium in Malaysian Islamic banks" published by Islamic Finance News (IFN) and "Micro-takaful for B40 in Malaysia: Learning from the BIMA Experience" published by I-Fikr of ISRA.

Part IV
Waqf: An Ethical Investment

Chapter 19
Waqf as a Financing Tool and Its Role in Achieving SDGs and Foreseeing the Future

Eiman Ahmad Mohammad Khaleel Al Hashmi

Waqf is an Arabic word from the root *wa-qa-fa* which means to contain, stop, or preserve.[1]

Waqf is preserving a principal or an asset for the benefit of a philanthropic objective.[2] And what is meant by preserving an object is preserving it from ownership, so it cannot be sold, bought, gifted, nor inherited. Its usufruct and benefits are allocated for charitable and philanthropic purposes, which has the flexibility of either being dedicated for specific or general causes.[3]

Kahf (1998) defines *Waqf* as a productive operation that merges between saving and investments. Putting them in the form of a productive asset that increases the accumulation of capital for the purpose of continuous future output of services and cash flows. Sacrificing a present consumption opportunity for the sake of greater accumulation of productive capital bearing social benefits for the society.[4] *Waqf* is also characterized by its perpetual nature, it does not stop with the death of the person who built the *Waqf*. Therefore, *Waqf* is considered an exemplary for Sustainable Development.

The World Commission on Environment and Development (WCED) that introduced the concept of sustainable development and defined it as "development that

---

[1] Muhammad ibn Manzur, Lisan Al- 'Arab; Al-Fayoumy, Al-Misbah Al-Munir.

[2] Encyclopaedia of Islamic Jurisprudence, Kuwait Ministry of Awqaf and Islamic Affairs (201/23).

[3] Monzer Kahf, Financing the Development of Awqaf Property, (1998), retrieved from: http://www.iefpedia.com/english/wp-content/uploads/2009/11/Financing-the-Development-of-Awqaf-Property.pdf.

[4] *Ibid.*

E. A. M. K. Al Hashmi (✉)
Zayed University, Abu Dhabi, UAE
e-mail: dr.eimanalhashmi@gmail.com

T. Azid et al. (eds.), *Wealth Management and Investment in Islamic Settings*,
https://doi.org/10.1007/978-981-19-3686-9_19

meets the needs of the present without compromising the ability of future generations to meet their own needs."[5]

The Food and Agriculture Organization defined Sustainable Development as "the management and conservation of the natural resources base and the orientation of technological and institutional change in such a manner as to ensure the attainment and continues satisfaction of human needs for present and future generations".[6] Therefore, it may be concluded that achieving development is not limited to economic, but rather social and environmental which make the three pillars of Sustainable Development, economic development, social justice and environment preservation.

This chapter aims at investigating the capacity and flexibility of Waqf, and its ability to achieve advanced progress towards various SDGs. The challenges facing Waqf and hindering it from achieving its great potentials are analyzed and solutions and policy recommendations would be presented.

19.1 Concept of Sustainability in Islamic Economic Thoughts

If we were to contemplate about the Islamic economics thoughts and principles, we would notice that sustainability is the core value and principle upon which it is built. Allah-swt-says "He (Allah) brought you from the earth and settled you in it" (11:61). Some Shafi'i scholars say: settling us on earth implies the requirement of constructing and building a civilization. Which means that Allah has made it the duty of every human to contribute towards the continuous building of earth, generation after generation. This makes the wealth of the world a right for every person across times, with an embedded duty for each to not trespass on what is for another, which is confirmed by the Islamic teaching of balancing between consumption and expenditures whereby Allah (swt) Says: "And do not make your hand [as] chained to your neck or extend it completely and [thereby] become blamed and insolvent" (17:29). This can be extended to maintaining a balance between the ways we consumer and preserve the natural resources of all kinds.

Islam also teaches us the important of environmental sustainability, the Prophet (pbuh) said (There is none amongst the Muslims who plants a tree or sows seeds, and then a bird, or a person or an animal eats from it, but is regarded as a charitable gift for him). Hence a Muslim is required to preserve the natural balance of earth with all its creatures.

As for the social aspect, it materializes in social justice for all members of society. Allah (swt) Says: "Worship Allah and associate nothing with Him, and to parents

[5] (United Nations, 2000a, b) United Nations, Report of the World Commission on Environment and Development: Our Common Future, (2000), retrieved from: https://sustainabledevelopment.un.org/content/documents/5987our-common-future.pdf.

[6] Food and Agriculture Organization (FOA) Council (1989).

do good, and to relatives, orphans, the needy, the near neighbor, the neighbor farther away, the companion at your side, the traveler, and those whom your right hands possess. Indeed, Allah does not like those who are self-deluding and boastful" (4:36). And it is from the fair and impartial teachings of Islam that social justice is for every member of the society regardless of their race, ethnicity, or religion. In addition, it is the duty of the members of society to collaborate in eliminating poverty and hunger, and to provide water and sanitation for everyone. Sustainable development in Islamic teachings goes beyond material aspects, it covers moral, ethical, and behavioral aspects, which have direct impacts on achieving social justice and protecting human dignity.

19.1.1 Sustainability Development Goals

The leaders of 193 United Nations (UN) member countries came together in the United Nations Sustainable Development Summit that took place in September 2015 in New York. To inaugurate the new sustainable development goals that countries to work towards for the following fifteen years. The comprehensive and holistic nature of those goals gave it a key importance for each part of the global society, governments, and institutions to collectively work towards achieving them.

In January 2020, the Annual Meeting World Economic Forum took place in Davos under the title "Stakeholders for a Cohesive and Sustainable World". In which Mr. Badr Ja'far, the CEO of Crescent Enterprises said (The transfer of wealth of over 4 trillion dollars between the generations in the next 10 years out of which Islamic donations and charity work are estimated to contribute between 400 billion and 2 trillion dollars per year, which will stimulate growth and has great potentials to positively contribute to societies whilst achieving the SDGs at the same time).[7]

In the World Governments Summit 2016 that took place in Dubai, the SDGs were classified into six broad categories as follows:

1. Poverty and Inequality: Goals 1 and 10
2. Health, Education, and Gender: Goals 3, 4, and 5
3. Food, Water, and Energy: Goals 2, 6, and 7
4. Growth, Employment, and Innovation: Goals 8 and 9
5. Climate, Ocean, and Biodiversity: Goals 13, 14, and 15
6. Sustainable Consumption and Human Settlements: Goals 11 and 12

Having gone through the goals and their significance, analyzing the history of *Waqf* in Islamic civilization would make us realize its dynamic nature, and its roles that holistically covered the various needs of society. Therefore, operationalizing the *Waqf* industry to achieve development goals is pertinent and needs thorough strategic planning.

[7] https://www.albayan.ae/across-the-uae/news-and-reports/2020-01-23-1.3759124.

19.2 The Capacity of Waqf to Accommodate Advance Levels of SDGs

19.2.1 Waqf Aims at Ending Poverty in All Its Forms Everywhere

Achieving social justice among people is one of the key objectives of *Waqf*. It has an inherent ability to redistribute wealth and income through supporting its beneficiaries whether through financial returns or in-kind depending on the nature and purpose of *Waqf*. This enables the returns on *Waqf* assets and from its operations to be distributed on a large range of social groups such as the poor, the needy, students, indebted. etc. and part of the income is kept as a working capital for the *Waqf* to cover salaries of those working in it from the management to the general employees to ensure its operational sustainability. In addition, part of the retained earnings can be shared with the investors and shareholders.

Effective *Waqf* management is a key factor in eradication of poverty and providing employment opportunities for *Waqf* managers, governors, treasurers, and accountants, in addition to the job opportunities specific to the various *Waqf* purposes, such as teachers for Waqf schools, and doctors in *Waqf* hospitals, and nurses for *Waqf* elderly houses, construction workers for Waqf infrastructure projects, and farmers for *Waqf* farms, and so on.

In addition, Waqf helps reducing the concentration of wealth, as it removes from the concentration of wealth from the hands of the few to the benefits of the many. A leader may dedicate lands or real estates for the service of the society.[8]

This forms a way to redistribute wealth for generations to come, and this is supported by what Omar bin Alkhattab (raa) did when he was a Khalifah, he refused to divide the lands that were war tributes in Iraq. He relied on the verse in which Allah (swt) says: "And (the ones) who came even after them say, "Our Lord, forgive us and our brothers who went before us in belief, and do not set up in our hearts rancor towards (the ones) who have believed. Our Lord, surely You are Ever-Compassionate, Ever-Merciful" (59:10). Omar controlled the division of the tributes by the virtue of protecting the shares and the benefit of the lands for generations to come which would have otherwise been compromised had it been divided.

[8] Zakaria Al Ansari. Hashiyat Shaikh Sulaiman Al Jumal 'ala Minhaj Attalibeen [Shaikh Sulaiman Al jumal's notes on The Explanation of the System], vol. 3: 577; Mustafa Alsuyuti Alruhaibani. Matalib Uli Alnuha fi Sharh Ghayat Almuntaha [The Desires of the Intellects in an explanation of The Goal of The Denouement], vol.4, (1961): 278; Kuwait Ministry of Awqaf and Islamic Affairs. Encyclopedia of Islamic Jurisprudence, vol. 3, (2007): 107; Nazih Hammad. Mu'jam Al Mustalahat [The Dictionary of the Financial and Economic Terminologies in the Language of Jurist]s, (2008): 50.

19.2.2 *Waqf* Aims at Ending Hunger, Achieving Good Security and Improved Nutrition and Promote Sustainable Agriculture

Numerous texts from the Sunnah support this, Omar bin Al-Khattab (raa) received a land in Khaibar, and went to the Prophet (pbuh) and asked him, (Oh messenger of Allah, I have received a land in Khaibar, and I have never received something more precious to me than this, so what do you advise me to do with it?) the Prophet said: (You could preserve its capital and donate it (i.e. put it as Waqf)), and Omar established a *Waqf* with it, so that it cannot be bought or sold, nor gifted or inherited, and its produce was given to the poor, and relatives, and wayfarers, and so the land manger and the society benefitted from it.[9]

Abu Talha Al-Ansari (raa) came to the Prophet (pbuh) and he had a precious garden called (Bayraha'), he asked the Prophet what he should do with it to obtain rewards from Allah, the Prophet (pbuh) said (Make it a Waqf for you).[10] In addition, Othman bin Affan (raa) also made the well of Rumah a Waqf for the whole society to benefit from.

Historically, the Muslim ci]vilization was known for giving free food for those in need. This made it common to have restaurants that give out free food for those who cannot afford it (oftentimes knows as Tikia), such as Tikia Sultan Saleem, Shaikh Mohyi Addin in Demascus, Tikia near the Ibrahimi Haram (Cave of Patriarch), those Waqf restaurants have spread across the Muslim world especially near the Holy mosques (Makkah and Madinah). In contemporary times, various forms of feeding the hungry has been practiced such as food banks.

In addition, Waqf in Muslim civilization spreads into agriculture, which is highly connected to various other sectors of the general economy, and its prominent contribution to the production. Various scholars talked about the ways in which we can invest in agriculture through Waqf lands, utilizing a wide range of Islamic financial contracts such as lease (Ijara), and partnership contracts such as output sharing (Muzara'a), and corporative farming (Mugharasa and Musaqaa), which all operates to nourish and sustainably cultivates agricultural lands which will in turn ensure provision of food to the weakest social groups to fight hunger and poverty in a sustainable manner. Therefore, there is a need to direct the mangers of agriculture Waqf to the innovative solutions that may increase the efficiency and competitiveness of agriculture produce, as well as increase its resilience against climate changes in an eco-friendly manner, which will in turn enhance the food security, economic development, and the sustainable management of natural resources.[11]

---

[9] Imam Muslim ibn Al-Hajjaj, Sahih Muslim, Hadith No. 1632.

[10] Al Bukhari, Mohammed bin Ismail, Sahih Al Bukhari, Hadith No. 7050.

[11] FAO, IFAD and WFP (2014), The State of Food Insecurity in the World 2014. Strengthening the enabling environment for food security and nutrition.

19.2.3 *Waqf Ensures Healthy Lives and Promotes Well-Being for All Parts of Society*

Waqf has been successful in achieving records levels of health and wellness for people across all age groups. The wide range of hospitals (known as Bimaristan) is one of the key characteristics of the pivotal role of Waqf in Muslim civilization. Examples of which is Bimaristan Al-Muqtadiri, Bimaristan Al'udhadi in Baghdad, Bimaristan Al-Noori in Demascus, Bimaristan Al-Mansoori in Cairo, and Bimaristan Marrakech in Morocco. Muslims emphasized on the establishment of teaching hospitals as well as general and specialized hospitals including mobile clinics that would assist warriors in battlefields, and Waqf based hospitals in prisons, and ones specializing in illnesses such as Conjunctivitis, Leprosy, and neurological diseases. The Waqf in the medical sector went as far as establishing vast compounds with all the necessary attachments and services, in addition to the educational institutions that were established based on Waqf to develop human capital for medical studies, pharmaceuticals and biochemical engineering.[12]

When Ibn Jubair, a prominent Muslim scholar, went to Baghdad, he found a full street like a small city, knows as the Bimaristan Market, at its center if a mansion, surrounded by gardens and houses, all of which are Waqf properties, established to serve medical purposes, managed by doctors, pharmacists, and medical studies, and the expenses of which were sustained through the Waqf money that circulates widely in Baghdad.[13]

In addition, doctors looked after needy people, visiting them in their houses, and provide them with all the medicines and nutrition needed, and the number of patients that were taken care of and visited by doctors at any given points over two hundred poor person.[14]

Among the social roles conducted by the Bimaristan is looking after the patient even after their discharge, by providing for them what sustains them until they resume work and are able to sustain themselves.[15] In addition, to enhance the patients mental health, part of the Waqf budget was used to hire people who would talk next to the patients to provide mental emotional support for them which speeds up their recovery.

---

[12] Abd Allatif Al'abd Allatif, Athar Al-Waqf Fi Altanmiyah Al-Iqtisadiyah [The Impact of Waqf on Economic Development], The First Awqaf Conference, Mecca (2001), Umm Al Qura University.

[13] Al'andalusi, Mohammed bin Ahmed Jubair Tathkirah bil Akhbar 'an Ittifaqat Al Asfar, (2008), p. 176.

[14] *Ibid.*

[15] Abdullah Al Sadhan, Dawr Al-Waqf fi Bina' Al-haya Al-Ijtima'iyyah wa Tamasukaha [The Role of Waqf in Building the Social Life and its Coherence], The First Awqaf Conference, Mecca (2001), Umm Al Qura University.

19.2.4 Waqf in the Islamic Civilization Have Provided Free and Quality Education for All Parts of Society

The role of Waqf in education has been central in the Islamic civilization, Waqf contributed tremendously in establishing and sustaining schools, research centers, and libraries across the Muslim world, to the extent that almost every school and library had a Waqf dedicated to sustain it and provide its needed expenses. The comprehensive nature of Waqf allows for the equitable provision of quality education for all social classes.[16] It was reported by Ibn Jubair in Baghdad alone there were about thirty school, each has a mansion and a big building, the most famous of which was The Nithami School, which had Waqf real estates that were used to sustain the necessary working capital for its teachers and students, amounting to 15 thousand Dinar per month, and from it many Islamic scholars have graduated.[17]

Similarly, Ibn Khaldoun reported many examples of education Waqf in Baghdad, Kufa, and Basrah in Iraq the Cordoba in Spain, Kairouan in Tunisia, and Fes in Morocco, where various research centres were established, as well as in Cairo where great prosperity in the education sector was witnessed through Waqf institutions. Those great establishments date back to great initiatives such that of Salahuddin Al-Ayyubi, who established an agricultural land, with houses, shops, and schools to build self-sustaining systems, this system received the support of the proceeding leaders and state-heads, helping it grow to attract students, scholars, and scientists from the East to the West.[18]

The ruler Nureddin Mahmud Zengi have put significant efforts in further developing education Waqf, he established schools with a wide range of school of thoughts, and developed mechanisms to evaluate and monitor the sustenance of teachers, students, and the employees in general. In Al-Andalus, the School of Nasriyah was famous in Granada for its numerous Waqf properties. After the mosques of Granada, this school and education hub was the most prominent Waqf in Al-Andalus, Spain.[19]

Waqf supporter was not only limited to male leadrs, various female figures had significant contributions. Fatimah bint Muhammad Abdullah Al-Fehri built the Mosque of Kairouan in Fes, which is among the oldest Waqf by women in the West of the Muslim world, the Waqf developed to be a Mosque and a university. Another example was the Athrawia School which was established by Athra' who was Salahuddin Al-Ayyubi's niece, various prominent scholars and students of knowledge and scientists graduated from it, among which was Fatima bint Yahya Al-Maghami, who was famous for her knowledge and teaching.[20] In addition to the daughter of

---

[16] Baki Zahdi, Al-Waqf fi Al-Shari'ah Al-Islamiyyah [Waqf in Islamic Law], (1968), p. 42.

[17] Al'andalusi, Mohammed bin Ahmed Jubair Tathkirah bil Akhbar 'an Ittifaqat Al Asfar, (2008), p. 180.

[18] ibn Khaldun, Al Muqaddimah, *The Sciences are numerous only where civilization is large and sedentary culture highly developed*, (Dar Yu'rub,2004), 6/8.

[19] Muhammed Abdul Hameed Eisa, Tareekh Atta'leem fi Al Andalus [The History of Education in Andalusia], (Dar Al-Fikr Al-Arabi, 1982), p. 390.

[20] Abi Qassim Ibn Bashkawal, Al-Silah [The Link], Al-Khanji's Library (1955), vol.2, p. 694.

Faiz Al-Qurtobi, the wife of Abu Abdullah bin Etab, she was famous for learning science and literature, and she studied the interpretation of Quran (Tafseer), the Arabic language, poetry, and Fiqh, she travelled from Cordoba to Daniyah seeking knowledge form various scholars.[21] Other women also contributed in creating Waqf for early education to children, such as the Daughter of Al-Hazm, whose father used to teach the public and she would teach the children.[22]

Waqf libraries were an area of competition, whereby people used to compete to have central libraries for students of knowledge to benefit from, and Waqfs would be established to support the employees and researchers with all they need from finances and literature resources.[23]

Among the most prominent libraries was Dar Al-Hikma library, which was established in year 390 AH in Baghdad, it contained forty compartments, and a town hall. Other prestigious libraries include Alhukm Library in Al-Andalus which contained 300 thousand book, and Bani Ammar Library in Tripoli, which contained 1 million books, as well as other libraries across the Muslim world each with thousands of books.[24] Other historians including Will and Ariel Durant hat Al-Andalus had 70 public libraries, 20 of which are in Cordoba alone.[25] As for private libraries, some researchers report that it is beyond one may count and some of which was significantly large.[26]

19.2.5 The Role of Waqf in Caring for Woman and Its Role in Woman Empowerment

Woman are elevated in Islam, as the Prophet (pbuh) said (Woman are counterpart of men)[27] from which we understand the principle of fairness and equity between men and women in rights and obligations for each based on what matches their natural and biological design. Women have full ownership rights that enables them to own and transact in their properties as they will, therefore we see historically the wives of the Prophet (pbuh) established many Waqfs, such as Aisha, Umm Salamah,

---

[21] Abu Abdullah Mohammed bin Abdullah Al-Qada'ii Ibn Al-Abar, Al-Takmita Li-Kitab Al-Sila [The Continuation of The Book of Al-Silah], Dar Al-Fikr Printing, (1995), vol. 4, p. 251.

[22] *Ibid*, vol. 1, p. 287.

[23] Ibrahim bin Muhammed Al-Hamad Al-Mazini, Al-Waqf wa Atharuh fi Tashyeed Buniyat Al-Hadhara Al-Islamiyya [Waqf and its impact on building the structure of the Islamic Civilization], The Ministry of Awqaf and Islamic Affairs, 1999, p. 105.

[24] *Ibid*, pp. 161–157.

[25] Will and Ariel Durant, The Story of Civilization, *The Age of Faith,* vol. 4, (1950).

[26] Hamed Al-Shafi'i Diab, Al Kutub wa Al Maktabat fi Al Andalus [The Books and The Libraries in Andalusia], Dar Qiba' Publishing House, (1998), p. 110.

[27] Al-Tirmidhi, Muhammed bin 'Eisa bin Surah, Sunan Al-Tirmidhi (Aljami' Al-Saheeh), Dar Al Kutub Al Ilmiyah, 2002.

Umm Habiba, and Safiyya-raa-.[28] The Waqf of Zubaida in the year of 218 AH was known for the wells and other water sources that she established in Makkah, in addition to water storage units that were located between Makkah and Madinah.[29] Another example is the Waqf established by Shams Annahar, the servant of the Abbasid Khalifa Almuqtadi, which was established to support widows in the year of 492 AH,[30] and Fatimah Al-Fehri established Kairouan University and her sister Mariyam Al-Fehri established the Mosque of Al-Andalus.[31]

Perhaps the first women to manage Waqf properties was the wife of the Prophet (pbuh) Hafsa (raa), which was assigned by Omar bin Al-Khattab (raa) to manage his Awqaf after his passing.[32] Studies show that 25% of the Awqaf were established by women, and 14% were managed by women too, it was common in early 19th century Egypt for women to manage Waqf.

Women's role in establishing Waqf covered its various types, such as schools, hostels, hotels, restaurants, marriage support for the poor, building factories, gardens, wells, and infrastructure projects such as bridges and roads.

Waqf properties have also been known for catering for women privacy, whereby several Waqf properties were run by them exclusively with no men. Exampled of this include shops and markets for leasing jewelry, and ornaments and dresses for weddings, the poor would be able to borrow from it for their occasions. In Marrakech, a Waqf known as Dar Al-Daqqa was established, a refuge established for women who face issues with their husbands, they were allowed to stay there, and are provided with sustenance until the problems are resolved. Other forms of Waqf include Waqf Al-Anya (the dishes), which was established to help servants by giving them replacements in the case that they have broken any dishes from their house's properties to protect them from being beaten or harmed in any shape or form. In addition, Waqf of Milk was established by Salahuddin Al-Rumi where there was milk, as well as sugar water, and twice a week, women with young children would take what they need from the milk and sugar water. In the Quds, a Waqf called Al-Murabitat was established for women who migrated to Palestine but their male guardians passed away, they were allowed to stay and sustained in the Waqf until someone from their relatives comes to take them home. Other Waqfs were established to prepare the women for marriage, which was dedicated to providing poor women who want to

[28] Muhammad Abdullah Ahmed Al Qadahat, Ishamat Al-Mar'ah fi Al-Waqf wa Al'amal Al-Khairi Hatta Nihayat Alqirn Al-Thalith Al-Hijri [The Women Contribution in Waqf and Philanthropy], vol. 12, issue. 2, (2011), p. 140.

[29] Abi Abbas Shamsuddin Ibn Khalkan, Wafiyyat Al-A'yaan wa Anbaa' Abnaa' Al-Zamaan [The notables' mortality and the news of the sons of time], vol. 2, p. 314.

[30] Awdah, Weddah Rafe' Waqf Al-Mar'ah fi Dimashq fi Al-'Asr Al-Ayyubi [Women Waqf in Damascus in the Ayyubid Dynasty], Al Al-Bayt University, p. 12.

[31] Mufeed, Khadidja Al-Mar'ah wa Al-Waqf: Tajribah Maghribiyyah [Women and Waqf: A Moroccan Experience], Journal of Waqf, issue. 10, 2006, pp. 164–165.

[32] Fatimah Hafith, Ru'yat Al-Dawr Al-Hadhari Majallat Al-Wa'i Al-Islami [Journal of Islamic Awareness], Ministry of Awqaf and Islamic Affairs, issue 325, (2002), p. 55.

marry but cannot afford it, they would borrow all their needs from jewelry, ornaments, and dresses. Furthermore, Waqf for training and skill development for women were also common, which helps them in developing and refining skills that they can use to work and earn from it.[33]

19.2.6 The Role of Waqf in Ensuring Availability and Sustainable Management of Water for Irrigation and Sanitation for All

Islam commands us to enhance water availability as it is a crucial natural resource without which a society cannot exist. It is frowned upon anyone who deprives wayfarers of water, the Prophet—pbuh—said (There are three persons whom Allah will not look at on the Day of Resurrection, nor will he purify them and theirs shall be a severe punishment. They are:

- A man possessed superfluous water, on a way and he withheld it from travellers.
- A man who gave a pledge of allegiance to a ruler and he gave it only for worldly benefits. If the ruler gives him something, he gets satisfied, and if the ruler withholds something from him, he gets dissatisfied.
- And man displayed his goods for sale after the 'Asr prayer and he said, 'By Allah, except Whom None has the right to be worshipped, I have been given so much for my goods,' and somebody believes him (and buys them). The Prophet then recited: "Verily! Those who purchase a little gain at the cost of Allah's Covenant and their oaths." (3:77).[34]

When there was a drought and the water lacked in the early years of Islam, the Prophet—pbuh-immediately incentivized those who are able to buy the Well of Ruma, whereby he—pbuh—said (He who purchases the Well of Ruma and offers its water to Muslims free of charges will be granted paradise),[35] Othman bin Affan-raa—bought the well and kept it as Waqf.

Continuous efforts throughout the Muslim civilization have been taken to provide water to the travelers, society and general public. This was done through various methods and water sources, such as wells, springs, lakes, and water channels to ensure access for all. A good example for this is the spring established by Zubaida, the wife of Haroon Arrasheed, who hired engineers to construct a channel under the rocks to transfer water from Hunain to the Mecca Harem (covering a distance of over

[33] http://iswy.co/e16l9t.

[34] Al Bukhari, Sahih Al Bukhari, Book 42: Distribution of Water, Hadith 2358, In-book reference: Book 42, Hadith 7 English translation: Vol. 3, Book 40, Hadith 547.

[35] Ahmad 524, in Hadith Encyclopedia.

25 km). Such efforts were seen in the Quds in Palestine, where many wells were also put as Waqfs for everyone to benefit from, in addition to most of the Islamic cities such as Cairo, Cordoba, and the west of the Muslim world.[36]

19.2.7 Ensuring Access to Affordable, Reliable, Sustainable, and Modern Energy for All

Energy takes a central role in human life, and its preservation is highly guarded in Islam. The Prophet—pbuh—said (Muslims have common share in three (things). grass, water and fire).[37] This implies that the general society has a right over those three things, and that no one party should have the absolute monopoly or control over them such that they have the ability to deprive others of it. For grass, it applies to the farms and agricultural produce, for water, it includes the rivers, springs, and other natural water sources, and for fire, it includes all the energy sources such as fire wood, coal, and natural gas.[38] Therefore, Waqf played a central role in providing energy and ensuring suitable infrastructure for it such as street lights for travelers, orphanages and elderly nursing houses, and providing warmth during winter.

The energy sources have evolved with the technological evolution especially sustainable and alternative energy sources. Some Waqf institutions adopted solar energy to provide energy for remote areas that have no access to the grid. However, those initiatives are thus far limited and needs significant attention, especially that it has great potentials in addressing key issues of poverty, and availability of clean water and energy. The adoption of renewable energy would be a structural transformation in the fight against poverty and unemployment. Therefore Waqf institutions should take more active steps towards the deployment of renewable energy, developing the necessary infrastructure, and building the institutional framework that would ensure its sustainability, as well as conducting the research needed in order to provide energy sustainability and with the least possible costs.

19.2.8 Developing Social Capital and Building Resilient Infrastructure

Waqf have had profound impact on the development of social capital, it was the bases upon which many schools, universities, hospitals, mosques, libraries, farms, parks,

[36] 'Ashoor Sa'eed, Buhuth fi Tareekh Al-Islam wa Hadharatih [Reseaches in the Islamic History and Civilization], Dar 'Alam Al-Kutub, (1987), p. 214.

[37] Imam Abi Dawud, Sunan Abi Dawud, Book 24, Hadith 3477, In-book reference: Book 24, Hadith 62, English translation: Book 23, Hadith 3470.

[38] https://www.dorar.net/hadith/sharh/79474.

orphanages, elderly houses, special needs, restaurants, and overall comprehensive facilities that satisfies social needs.

Similarly, Waqf played an important role in infrastructure developments such as roads, bridges, digging wells, water reserves, pit stops for travelers, public toilets, graveyards, and guest houses to cater for the poor, needy, and travelers.

It is undeniable that building a comprehensive and diverse social capital contributes to economic development and reduces unemployment, and an equally strong infrastructure helps providing the suitable environment for domestic and foreign direct investments, which would lead to increase in production, financial and current accounts, and consequently economic growth.[39]

19.2.9 Contribution of Waqf to Achieving Sustainable Industrialization

Waqf has supported the growth of various industries, such as weapons, pharmaceuticals, papers, mats, perfumes, chandeliers, and producing construction material such as wood, concrete, glass, and marbles.[40]

Comprehensive industries and production lines were established and sustained through Waqf, an example is the Ministry of Awqaf of Egypt that has established companies and factories such as Delta Sugar Company, and Samanoud company for fabrics, in addition to buying shares and taking part in stimulating manufacturing companies of metals, foods, and diaries. In the United States, Sara Islamic charity establishment invested 60% of their portfolio in manufacturing industries of food, agriculture, fabrics, pharmaceuticals, and advanced technologies.[41] Despite earlier contributions of Waqf in various industries, such initiatives seem to be rare and limited today. Therefore, steps need to be taken by Waqf institutions to contribute to the industrial revolution and to help nourish the supply to fulfill the needs of our societies.

---

[39] Ahmed Malawi, Dawr Al-Waqf fi Attanmiyyah Al-Mustadama [The role of Waqf in sustainable development], The Third Awqaf Conference, Saudi Arabia (2010), p. 11.

[40] Abd Allatif Al'abd Allatif, Athar Al-Waqf Fi Altanmiyah Al-Iqtisadiyah [The Impact of Waqf on Economic Development], The First Awqaf Conference, Mecca (2001), Umm Al Qura University, pp. 117–118.

[41] *ibid.*

19.2.10 *Waqf* Promotes Peace and Security Mentally, Socially, and Economically

Allah (swt) Says "Those who spend their wealth [for the sake of Allah] by night and by day, secretly and publicly—they will have their reward with their Lord. And no fear will there be concerning them, nor will they grieve" (2:274).

Waqf helps spreading social and mental safety, as well as solidarity and unity among the various classes of society, whereby the rich would help the poor by providing them with opportunities, as well as charities that would suffice the hungry. This protects the society from social destruction that is greed, selfishness, envy, conflicts, and hate, which in turn reduces crime rate and transgression on others property that is usually a result of wide-spread poverty and deprivation.

Waqf helps spreading social peace through increasing economic growth, and attaining economic sufficiency in providing the resources needed for the society and allocating them efficiently, providing employment opportunities and achieving balance between individuals' needs and society's demands, market stability would be achieved with the increase in investments in agriculture, industries, and trading.

The role of Waqf in achieving security can also be seen in its contribution in fighting hunger by establishing restaurants and feeding the poor, and fighting thirst by providing water for drinking and sanitation to those who have no access to it, and fighting unemployment by enhancing institutional structures and their role, and fighting illiteracy by building schools and universities, and financing academic and scientific research, fighting against diseases by building and supporting hospitals and developing the pharmaceutical industry as well as medical research and development, fighting against transgression and theft by providing humanitarian aid to those in need, and benevolent loans to the poor and those in need, lastly, fighting homelessness by providing guest houses to those who seek refuge. The Prophet (pbuh) said: (Seek your weak for me. For indeed your sustenance and aid is only by your weak).[42]

19.2.11 *Waqf* Helps in Protecting Freedom, Justice, and Human Dignity

Islam came with significant social reforms, it promoted freeing the slaves in active initiatives to abolish slavery and protecting human dignity, the Prophet—pbuh—said

[42] Al-Tirmidhi, Sunan Al-Tirmidhi (Aljami' Al-Saheeh), Hadith 1702, In-book reference: Book 23, Hadith 33, English translation: Vol. 3, Book 21, Hadith 1702.

(Free the captives, feed the hungry and pay a visit to the sick)[43] and Imam Malik said that people should free the captive even if they have to bear the expenses.[44]

The concept of freedom in Islam goes beyond freeing the slaves and captives, it extends to include all layers of society, including the poor, needy, illiterate, elderly, and the indebted, this is because moral and emotional limitations constricts an individual from reaching their full potentials as a productive member of society.

19.2.12 *The Environmental Role of Waqf*

Islam teaches us to preserve the environment with all its components from animals, plants, water, air, soil, and natural demographics, it was narrated by Mu'ath bin Jabal, that the Prophet (pbuh) said (Be on your guard against three things which provoke cursing: easing in the watering places and on the thoroughfares, and in the shade (of the tree).[45] Allah Has warned to exclude from His mercy those who cause pollution by disposing of waste in water from wells, rivers, and natural resources, as well as disposing of waste on roads and vicinities, this is held in high regards by Islam for what it implies from protecting life under the seas and above land for a better life for humanity, the Prophet (pbuh) said (Whoever has land should cultivate it himself or give it to his (Muslim) brother gratis).[46]

Today, we are living in a highly polluted environment, the climate balance is distorted, which puts higher responsibility on governments to preserve the environment. Waqf institutions need to contribute to this responsibility, the Prophet (pbuh) said (There is none amongst the Muslims who plants a tree or sows seeds, and then a bird, or a person or an animal eats from it, but is regarded as a charitable gift for him).[47] Waqf money can be used to support recycling and waste processing, extending water sanitation and drainage systems in the country, and developing and supporting renewable energy sources in order to minimize carbon emissions destroying the atmosphere.

[43] Al-Bukhari, Sahih al-Bukhari, Hadith 3046, In-book reference: Book 56, Hadith 252, English translation: Vol. 4, Book 52, Hadith 282.

[44] Ibn Al-'Arabi, Abu Bakr Muhammed bin Abdullah, Ahkam Al-Quran [The Rulings of the Quran], (88/1); Abi Hayyan Al-Andalusi, Muhammad bin Yusur Tafseer Al-Bahr Al-Muheet [The exegesis of the sea ocean], (5/8).

[45] Imam Abi Dawud, Sunan Abi Dawud, Book 1, In-book reference: Book 1, Hadith 26, English translation: Book 1, Hadith 26.

[46] Al-Bukhari, Sahih al-Bukhari, Hadith 2340, In-book reference: Book 41, Hadith 21, English translation: Vol. 3, Book 39, Hadith 533.

[47] Al-Bukhari, Sahih al-Bukhari, Hadith 2320, In-book reference: Book 41, Hadith 1, English translation: Vol. 3, Book 39, Hadith 513.

19.2.13 Conserving and Protecting the Environment, Oceans, Biodiversity, and the Ecosystem

Waqf may contribute to this area through the development of electronic platforms that would raise and spread awareness regarding the harms and negative impacts of pollution of all types, and the importance of cooperation and collaborations between government and private sectors in fighting against climate change. This can be done through organizing of waste disposition and management channels, fighting against deforestation. Therefore, Waqf institutions can develop initiatives and programs for this purpose, and assist in moving towards a green economy that uses clean and renewable sources of energy and avoid fossils of all kinds. Waqf can also establish vertical farms and other types of sustainable farming that would assist in attaining food sufficiency. In addition, Waqf can also establish and support researchers in clean waters and sanitation to ensure access to all. While the aforementioned is on domestic levels, Waqf can support international initiatives through establishing Waqf investment funds that supports fights against climate change and protection of environment, biodiversity, and the ecosystem.

19.2.14 Sustainable Consumption, Production Patters, and Sustainability Cities and Human Settlements

Islamic economic thought is principled upon sustainable development, which makes Waqf by nature a tool that is used for sustainable development, aiming to create economic balance between consumption and expenditure, and the avoidance of prodigality and excessive production which would lead to inefficient allocation of resources and consequently increased waste levels.

This can be achieved through sustainable management of natural resources, and effective waste management that would minimize it, recycles it, and dispose of it in the best ways possible, as well as enhancing the consumption practices in buying, using, and producing. This can be achieved through raising awareness using Waqf platforms and communication networks to its importance and incentivizing the society to adopt consumption practices that are in line with sustainable development goals. The role of the Waqf electronic and media platforms is to spread the knowledge of sustainable cities and its embedded practices that provides a holistic and comprehensive coverage for sustainability in all its aspects.

19.3 Recommendations for Operationalizing Waqf to Achieve SDGs

i. **Creating institutional framework to manage all charitable and Waqf activities**

While individual efforts in establishing Waqf initiatives make great contributions, they cannot stand against contemporary challenges, making it subject to inability to scale and sustain operations needed to achieve sustainable development goals. Therefore, it is pertinent to create an institutional framework for Waqf, which would ensure its long term sustainability, organization, and long term strategic plans that would be developed and implemented in the light of the evolving trends, needs, and technological solutions, all of which will in turn enable scalability, efficiency, and enhances profitability and self-sufficiency of the Waqf.

ii. **Developing a management system for Waqf institutions**

The availability of financial resources is not the sole factor to achieve development, human capital is the true engine of growth. While other resources such as technologies and natural resources evolve with time, it is the human capital, with its dynamic nature, which brings all those resources to use through the development of operations and systems that matches the available resources to the needs of the time. Human capital encompasses management and production processes, innovation, and social, political, and economic systems, which holds the key to economic development.[48]

A strong management system for Waqf institutions has two main components. First, designing a comprehensive and detailed organizational structure tailored to the nature and goals of the underlying Waqf institution. Second, developing an overseeing governance framework that would ensure transparency and efficiency of Waqf operations.

Second, establishing a strategic plan to guide the Waqf operations in the short and long run, by providing periodic data and statistics either through government agencies, or through research centers dedicated to developing strategic plans for Waqf institutions.

iii. **Independence of Waqf institutions**

The independence of Waqf institutions is undoubtably a crucial element of success, to ensure that the Waqf institution operates in its complete authority independent from political pressures that would undermine its authority and managerial as well as financial independence. Therefore, a Waqf institutions should operate as an independent legal entity, one that is independent from the person establishing the Waqf and its beneficiaries. Dr. Abdessalam Al-'Ebadi says (It is the financial and managerial

[48] Mash'hoor, Ni'mat Abdullatif Al-Zakah Al Usus Al-Shari'yiah wa Al-Dawr Al-Inmaa'iy wa Al-Tawzee'iy [The Zakah: legal foundation and the development and distribution role], (1993), p. 126.

independence that Waqf institutions have that provides Waqf institutions the protection from being merged and lost in the state and government properties, and it is what provide it protection against transgression by using Waqf properties for matters that are not within the scope conditioned by the Waqf establishers (i.e. Waqif).[49]

It is worth mentioning that the government of Dubai adopted Waqf institutions' independence, whereby his excellency Shaikh Mohammed bin Rashid Al-Maktoum, he Vice President and Prime Minister of the United Arab Emirates, issued a license for the first Waqf institutions, which states that the non-for-profit Waqf institutions shall be self-financed through its income generating activities and the management of the Waqf should work on investing its revenues in its dedicated activities domestically and internationally. Those Waqf institutions are independent legal entities that have financial and managerial independence that are governed by the Waqf regulations of Dubai, and it can expand its operations through establishing branches and different offices in the Emirates of Dubai after securing the respective clearance and authorization from the institutions' management.[50]

The government plays a legislative and governance role and its interference in Waqf operations should be through legal channels, it has the authority to hold the managers and trustees of Waqf accountable. Several lessons can be derived from the experience of developed economies regarding institutional independency, some of which are as follows:

a. The importance of partnership, interaction, and cooperation between individuals, institutions, civil society, and Waqf. This network provides the channels and access for the Waqf to provide the suitable and needed social services.
b. The individual's freedom in volunteering and contributing to social services and matching their desire to contribute to the needs of the Waqf operations.
c. The importance of developing and implanting standard operating procedures that would mitigate any potential risks of working and volunteering in social services.
d. Protecting the rights of the Waqf establisher (Waqif), the Waqf beneficiaries, and the Waqf in general.[51]

On the other hand, Dr. Al-'Ebadi stated that financial and managerial independence of the Waqf company may have its disadvantages. It may prevent Waqf institutions from getting the government support that is accessible to other government-linked institutions especially from the managerial assistance. This lack of support might hinder the progress of the Waqf sector and the legislative development that provides

---

[49] Al- 'Ebadi, Abdussalam Dawood, Al-Mu'assasah Al-Waqfiyyah Al-Mu'asirah, Ta'seel wa Tatweer [The Waqf corporation, its origin and development], The Second Conference of Islam and its Contemporary Challenges, (2007).

[50] Emirates News Agency, "Awqaf & Minors Affairs Foundation" issues the first license to Waqf institution, 8th May 2020, retrieved from: http://wam.ae/ar/details/1395302687629.

[51] Al-Ashqar, Usamah Omar, Tatweer Al-Mu'assasah Al-Waqfiyyah Al-Islamiyyah fi Daw' Al-Tajribah Al-Khayriyyah Al-Gharbiyyah [Developing the Islamic Waqf Institution in the light of the western philanthropic experience], (2012), Dar Al-Nafa'is for Publishing and Distribution, pp. 151–152.

it with the suitable environment needed across time, as well as access to the needed human capital. These drawbacks may be amplified if the Waqf is inherently inefficient, operationally weak, or not optimally productive.[52] Therefore, the active role of a government is important for the legislative aspects of Waqf, its protection, governance, as well as development. Such as legislations that prohibit family Waqf, or those imposing taxes on Waqf funds.

i **Reviewing Waqf Laws by issuing Laws and Legislations to govern Waqf institutions' operations and jobs**

Reviewing and issues laws and legislations are critical to ensure the Waqf institutions are provided with a supportive regulatory environment for them to thrive throughout varying and evolving times. Fiqh scholars and legal authorities need to review the current laws and remove legislations that act as hindrance for the Waqf institutions form achieving their development goals, such as the laws that prohibit family Waqf, or those that impose tax on Waqf funds. Reviewing the laws would enable and empower the Waqf establishers to achieve their targets and goals beyond the traditional and classical form of Waqf towards more innovative forms that have been approved by Islamic Fiqh Academies such as Waqf of usufruct, and Waqf of rights such as commercial brands,[53] trademarks,[54] copy rights and patents.[55]

ii. **Forming an advance information and communication management system, aiming to educate citizens, and spread the culture of Waqf**

Journalism and media have a great impact on people and social behaviors, beliefs, point of views, opinions, personalities, crystalizing thoughts, and developing narratives. This is specifically relevant to today, where media platforms of all its types made the world a much smaller place, with news dispatching and spreading from east to the west within seconds. Therefore, Waqf institutions should utilize the communication and media platforms to spread awareness on Waqf and its operations.

It is important for each Waqf institution to have its own communication department, to take part in raising the awareness regarding the Waqf legality, and its role in development. Bringing together the potentials and capacities of contemporary times that would bring about the benefits of Waqf in fulfilling the needs of the society, enhancing the sense of unity and humanity, cooperating towards the developing of minds and skills to fight against poverty and unemployment, and achieving advanced levels of sustainable development goals.

---

[52] Al- 'Ebadi, Abdussalam Dawood, Al-Mu'assasah Al-Waqfiyyah Al-Mu'asirah, Ta'seel wa Tatweer [The Waqf corporation, its origin and development], The Second Conference of Islam and its Contemporary Challenges, (2007).

[53] Muhammed Husni Abbas, Al-Tashrei' Al-Sina'iy [Industrial Legislation], (1967), Dar Al-Nahdha Al-Arabiyyah, p. 165.

[54] Mustafa Kamal Taha, Mabadi' Al-Qanoon Al-Tijari [Principles of Commercial Law], (1962), Dar Al-Ma'arif, p. 456.

[55] Al-Nahee, Salahuddin Al-Wajeez fi Al-Milkiyyah Al-Sinaiyyah wa Al-Tijariyyah [Brief about industrial and commercial property], (1983), Dar Al-Furqan, p. 60.

iii. **Connecting persons in charge of Waqf with the noble goals of Waqf institutions and materializing this connection operationally**

This can be done through the following[56]:

i. Setting governance and auditing tools to hold the Waqf management accountable on their performance, preventing it from underperforming to ensure its success and growth.
ii. Setting standards for choosing suitable managers and making it competitive based on the type of investment and Waqf standards.
iii. Linking managers remunerations with certain Key Performance Indicators (KPIs), such that the remunerations are a ratio of the financial revenues of the Waqf money.

19.4 Conclusion

This chapter have included several main conclusions:

i. Waqf in Islamic history and civilization have set great examples in achieving high levels of sustainable development in various aspects of life, education, healthcare, social, housing, services, economic, political, military, energy, infrastructure, food security, water and sanitation, renewable and affordable energy, as well as manufacturing and scientific innovation.
ii. Today, we are in dire need for developing a strategic plan the mobilized Waqf and utilizes it in fighting against poverty and hunger, and to spread justice across all levels and groups of our societies. It is pertinent to direct Waqf towards building health and education institutions, as well as developing and implementing plans to use Waqf to provide access to water and energy for all.
iii. Historically, Waqf has taken special care of women and children. Many were dedicated to provide educational classes to widowed, divorced, orphaned, and poor women who had no support. Waqf provided its beneficiaries beyond basic needs, it also provided women with skills and opportunities for them to be active and productive members of society.
iv. Activating and utilizing Waqf resources has great potentials in solving water shortages and provides access to those who have none. Through advance technologies and channels, remote villages may gain access to clean water. In addition, strategies can be put in place to utilize renewable and sustainable energy sources. Artificial intelligence may also be used to assist in eradicating poverty, illiteracy, and diseases.

---

[56] (Hadbaoui & Ghanem, 2013) Hadbaoui, Asma; Ghanem, Hadjar Dawr Al-Waqf fi Tahreek'Ajalat Al-Tanmiya: Isti'radh ba'dh Al-Namathij Al-Waqfiyyah Al-Najiha [The role of Waqf in rolling the wheel of development: presenting successful Waqf examples], (2013), The Second International Conference on not-for-profit Islamic Finance, p. 8.

v. Waqf in Islamic civilization had a direct role in stimulating manufacturing linked to the needs of the beneficiaries. Although in contemporary times this is limited to the classical and traditional forms of Waqf which may not be feasible and efficient. Therefore, Waqf institutions have the responsibility to utilize the technological advancements to enhance manufacturing and production which matches the cotemporary needs of the beneficiaries.

vi. Waqf achieves great financial and moral objectives, as it enhances social justice, and redistribution of revenues and wealth, as well as fulfilling basic needs to various levels of society who are in dire need such as poor, indebted, homeless, widows, and orphans. It provides security on individual as well as societal level in financial and moral dimensions. Waqf also protects human dignity, and gives the poor and needy freedom from financial, intellectual, and mental limitations.

vii. In order for Waqf to achieve advance levels of sustainable development goals, Waqf needs to operate within an advance and independent institutional framework which governs all the Waqf activities, this would enable the utilization of advance tools and technologies and transfer of knowledge from developed economies that can enhance the Waqf operations and management.

viii. It is critical for the Shari'ah scholars to review Waqf laws and legislations and remove laws that hinder the Waqf form achieving its developmental goals. Such as laws prohibiting the establishment of family Waqf, and ones that impose tax on Waqf funds. Therefore, enhancing and adjusting Waqf regulations would assist Waqf establishers to achieve their desired goals.

Bibliography

Abbas, M. H. (1967). *Al-Tashrei' Al-Sina'iy [Industrial Legislation]*. Dar Al-Nahdha Al-Arabiyyah.

Abi Hayyan Al-Andalusi, M. b. (2001). *Tafseer Al-Bahr Al-Muheet [The exegesis of the sea ocean]*. In S.A. Maujood, S.A. Mu'wadh, Z.A. Al-Nooqi & A.A.-N. Al-Jamal (Eds.) (1st ed.). Dar Al-Kutub Al-Ilmiyyah.

Al Bayan. (2020). Jalsah Tastatli' Dawr Al-Qitaa' Al-Khairiy bi Tahqeeq Al-Istidama fi Al-Aswaq Al-Nashi'ah [Looking into the role of the philanthropic sector in acheiving sustainability in developing markets]. Davos, Switzerland. Retrieved from https://www.albayan.ae/across-the-uae/news-and-reports/2020-01-23-1.3759124.

Al Bukhari, M. b. (1979). *Sahih Al Bukhari*. In M.A. Khateeb (Ed.) (1st ed.). Al Maktabah Assalafiyah.

Al Haythami, A. i. (1986). *Majmau' Al-Zawa'id wa Manba' Al-Fawa'id [The Collection of the Appendages and Source of Benefits]*. In Al-'Iraqi, & I.H. Al-Asqalani (Eds.) Al-Ma'arif Corporation.

Al Qadahat, M. A. (2011). Ishamat Al-Mar'ah fi Al-Waqf wa Al'amal Al-Khairi Hatta Nihayat Alqirn Al-Thalith Al-Hijri: Dirasah Tatbeeqiyyah 'ala Tareeq Al-Hajj Al-Iraqi ('Ain Zubaidah) wa Tawfeer Al-Khadamat bi Mecca [The Women Contribution in Waqf and Philanthropy]. *King Faisal University Scientific Journal, 12*(2).

Al Sadhan, A. b. (2001). Dawr Al-Waqf fi Bina' Al-haya Al-Ijtima'iyyah wa Tamasukaha [The Role of Waqf in Building the Social Life and its Coherence]. *The First Awqaf Conference* (pp. 213–243). Umm Al Qura University.

Al'abd Allatif, A. A. (2001). Athar Al-Waqf Fi Altanmiyah Al-Iqtisadiyah [The Impact of Waqf on Economic Development]. *The First Awqaf Conference* (pp. 91–135). Mecca: Umm Al Qura University.

Al'andalusi, Mb. (2008). *Tathkirah bil Akhbar 'an Ittifaqat Al Asfar [The Reminder of the News about Consensus of Travels]*. Dar Al Suwaidi Publishing House.

Al-Ashqar, U. O. (2012). Tatweer Al-Mu'assasah Al-Waqfiyyah Al-Islamiyyah fi Daw' Al-Tajribah Al-Khayriyyah Al-Gharbiyyah [Developing the Islamic Waqf Institution in the light of the western philanthropic experience] (1 ed.). Dar Al-Nafa'is for publishing and distribution.

Al-'Ebadi, A. D. (2017). Al-Mu'assasah Al-Waqfiyyah Al-Mu'asirah, Ta'seel wa Tatweer [The Waqf corporation, its origin and development]. *The Second Conference of Islam and its Contemporary Challenges*. Amman Message.

Al-Hanbali, I. R. (1996). *Fath Al-Bari fi Sharh Sahih Al-Bukhari*. In T. A. Muhammed (Ed.) (1st ed.). Dar Aljawzi.

Al-Mazini, I. b.-H. (1999). *Al-Waqf wa Atharuh fi Tashyeed Buniyat Al-Hadhara Al-Islamiyya [Waqf and its impact on building the structure of the Islamic Civilization]*. Ministry of Awqaf and Islamic Affairs.

Al-Nahee, S. (1983). *Al-Wajeez fi Al-Milkiyyah Al-Sinaiyyah wa Al-Tijariyyah [Brief about industrial and commercial property]* (1st ed.). Dar Al-Furqan.

Al-Qadoomu, E. S. (2016). *Awqaf Al-Nisaa' wa Ishraqatiha Al-Hadariyyah [Women Awqaf and its civilization radiance]*. Retrieved from Islam Way http://iswy.co/e16l9t.

Alruhaibani, M. A. (1961). *Matalib Uli Alnuha fi Sharh Ghayat Almuntaha [The Desires of the Intellects in an explanation of The Goal of The Denouement]*. Almaktab Al-Islami.

Al-Tirmidhi, M. b. (2002). *Sunan Al-Tirmidhi (Aljami' Al-Saheeh)*. In A. b. Shakir (Ed.). Dar Al Kotob Al Ilmiyah.

Ansari, Z. A. (n.d.). *Hashiyat Shaikh Sulaiman Al Jumal 'ala Minhaj Attalibeen [Shaikh Sulaiman Al jumal's notes on The Explanation of the System]*. Dar Alfikr.

Awdah, W. R. (n.d.). *Waqf Al-Mar'ah fi Dimashq fi Al-'Asr Al-Ayyubi [Women Waqf in Damascus in the Ayyubid Dynasty]*. Al Al-Bayt University.

bin Hanbal, I. A. (1969). *Musnad Al Imam Ahmed bin Hanbal [Predicate of Imam Ahmed bin Hanbal]*. In S. Al-Arna'ut (Ed.) Al Risalah Corporation.

Bin Manzur, M. b. (n.d.). *Lisan Al-'Arab [The Arab Lexicon]* (1 Ed.). Dar Sadir.

Diab, H.A.-S. (1998). *Al Kutub wa Al Maktabat fi Al Andalus [The Books and The Libraries in Andalusia]* (1st ed.). Dar Qiba' Printing, Publication, and Distribution House.

Dorar. (2018). *Al-Mawsoo'ah Al-Hadeetha [The new Encyclopedia]*. Retrieved from Al-Dorar Al-Sunniyyah: https://www.dorar.net/hadith/sharh/79474.

Durant, W., & Durant, A. (1950). *The story of civilization* (Vol. IV). Simon & Schuster.

Eisa, M. A. (1982). *Tareekh Atta'leem fi Al Andalus [The History of Education in Andalusia]*. Dar Alfikr Al-Arabi.

Emirates News Agency. (2018). *"Al-Awqaf wa Shu'oon Al-Qasr" Tamnah Tarkheesan li Awwal Mu'assasah Waqfiyyah ["Awqaf & Minors Affairs Foundation" issues the first license to Waqf institution*. In M. Al-Sumaiti, A. Al-Mokhtar, & W. Al-Ruhaibi (Eds.). Retrieved from Emirates News Agency http://wam.ae/ar/details/1395302687629.

FAO, IFAD, WFP. (2014). *The State of Food Insecurity in the World 2014. Strengthening the enabling environment for food security and nutrition*. Rome: Food and Agriculture Organization of The United Nations. Retrieved from http://www.fao.org/3/a-i4030e.pdf.

Gulf News. (2020, January 23). *UAE launches initiative to teach coding to 5 million youngsters*. In S. Saseendran (Eds.). Retrieved from Gulf News https://gulfnews.com/uae/uae-launches-initiative-to-teach-coding-to-5-million-youngsters-1.69211653.

Hadbaoui, A., & Ghanem, H. (2013). Dawr Al-Waqf fi Tahreek'Ajalat Al-Tanmiya: Isti'radh ba'dh Al-Namathij Al-Waqfiyyah Al-Najiha [The role of Waqf in rolling the wheel of development: presenting successful Waqf examples]. *Al-Mu'tamar Al-'lmiy Al-Duwaliy Al-Thani Hawl Dawr Al-Tamweel Al-Islamiy Ghair Ribhi [The Second International Conference on the Role of not-for-profit Islamic Finance]*. Blida: Encyclopedia of Islamic Economics and Finance.

Hafith, F. (2002). Ru'yat Al-Dawr Al-Hadhari. *Majallat Al-Wa'i Al-Islami [Journal of Islamic Awareness]* (325).
Hammad, N. (2008). *Mu'jam Al Mustalahat [The Dictionary of the Financial and Economic Terminologies in the Language of Jurists]*. Damascus: Dar Al-Qalam.
Ibn Al-Abar, A. A. -Q. (1995). *Al-Takmita Li-Kitab Al-Sila [The Continuation of The Book of Al-Silah]*. In A. A.-S. Al-Harras (Ed.) Dar Al-Fikr Printing.
Ibn Al-'Arabi, A. B. (n.d.). *Ahkam Al-Quran [The Rulings of the Quran]*. In M. A.-Q. Ataa (Ed.). Dar Al-Fikr for Printing and Publishing.
ibn al-Hajjaj, M. (1954). *Sahih Muslim* (1st ed.). In M. F. Abdulbaqi (Ed.). Dar Ihya' Al Kutub Al 'Arabiyah.
Ibn Bashkawal, A. Q. (1955). *Al-Silah [The Link]*. In A.-S. E. Al-Attar (Ed.). Al-Khanji's Library.
Ibn Khaldun, A. A. (2004). *Al Muqaddimah [The Introduction]*. In A. M. Al-Darwish (Ed.). Dar Ya'rib.
Ibn Khalkan, A. A. (n.d.). *Wafiyyat Al-A'yaan wa Anbaa' Abnaa' Al-Zamaan [The notables' mortality and the news of the sons of time]*. In E. 'Abbas (Ed.). Dar Al-Thaqafah.
Imam Abi Dawud, S. a.-S. (2015). *Sunan Abi Dawud*. Dar Al-Kutub Al-'lmiyyah.
Kahf, M. (1998). Financing the Development of Awqaf Property. *Seminar on Development of Awqaf.* Kuala Lumpur: Encyclopedia of Islamic Economic and Finance. Retrieved from http://www.iefpedia.com/english/wp-content/uploads/2009/11/Financing-the-Development-of-Awqaf-Property.pdf.
Kuwait Ministry of Awqaf and Islamic Affairs. (2007). *Encyclopedia of Islamic Jurisprudence*. Kuwait Ministry of Awqaf and Islamic Affairs.
Malawi, A. I. (2010). Dawr Al-Waqf fi Attanmiyyah Al-Mustadama [The role of Waqf in sustainable development]. *The Third Awqaf Conference: Al-Waqf Al-Islami, Iqtisad, Idarah, wa binaa' Hadarah [Islamic Waqf, the economy, management, and building of a civilization]* (pp. 3–21). Saudi Arabia: Islamic University of Madinah.
Mash'hoor, N. A. (1993). *Al-Zakah Al Usus Al-Shari'yiah wa Al-Dawr Al-Inmaa'iy wa Al-Tawzee'iy [The Zakah: legal foundation and the development and distribution role]*. Beirut: Al-Mu'assasah Al-Jami'iyyah Li Al-Dirasat wa Al-Nashr wa Al-Tawzee'.
Mufeed, K. (2006). Al-Mar'ah wa Al-Waqf: Tajribah Maghribiyyah [Women and Waqf: A Moroccan Experience]. *Journal of Awqaf* (10), 165–164.
Sa'ati, Y. M. (1988). *Al-Waqf wa Buniyat Al-Maktaba Al-Arabiyyah: Istinbat Al-Mawrooth Al-Thaqafi [Waqf and the structure of the Arabic Library: Deduction of the cultural heritage]*. Riyadh: King Faisal Centre for Research and Islamic Studies.
Sa'eed, '. (1987). *Buhuth fi Tareekh Al-Islam wa Hadharatih [Reseaches in the Islamic History and Civilization]* (1st ed.). Dar Alam Al-Kutub.
Taha, M. K. (1962). *Mabadi' Al-Qanoon Al-Tijari [Principles of Commercial Law]*. Dar Al-Ma'arif.
United Nations. (2000a). *Report of the World Commission on Environement and Development: Out Common Future*. Canada: United Nations. Retrieved from https://sustainabledevelopment.un.org/content/documents/5987our-common-future.pdf.
United Nations. (2000b). *Report of the World Commission on Environment and Development: Out Common Future*. Canada: United Nations. Retrieved from https://sustainabledevelopment.un.org/content/documents/5987our-common-future.pdf.
Zahdi, B. (1968). *Al-Waqf fi Al-Shari'ah Al-Islamiyyah [Waqf in Islamic Law]*. Dar Alnahda Al-Arabiya.

Dr. Eiman Ahmad Mohammad Khaleel Al Hashmi is currently an assistant professor in college of humanities and social science, Zayed university—UAE. She received her PhD with first class honors with distinction in "Investment of zakat and its role in development of the Islamic world" from Cairo University, Dar Aloluom college, (Egypt) with excellent with highest honor (2012). Eiman published *a book titled "The provisions of Zakat and its latest developments: A contemporary scientific study* " and a number of papers in referred Journals, including;" *How to eliminate* *poverty by Zakat,. Difference of contemporary Fiqh council's resolutions on zakat fund investment is a diversity difference or antagonism difference. Fiqh councils between the agreement and disagreement, images of contemporary usury transactions* and participated in a range of forums on Islamic economics and finance. She also presented various academic as well as research-based papers at several national and international conferences. Her research activities are currently, *Waqf* (endowment), *Maqasid al-Shari'ah* (legitimate purposes), *Zakat*, Islamic *shari'ah.*

Chapter 20
Blended Finance and the Role of *Waqf* Bank: Shaping the SDGs in Indonesia

Gunawan Baharuddin and Bayu Taufiq Possumah

Since adopted by the General Assembly of the United Nations in September 2015, the Sustainable Development Goals have been accepted by Indonesia. The government has demonstrated strong commitment and initiatively responded in programs such as linking most of the SDGs targets and indicators to the national mid-term development plan (RJPMN), capitalizing on the SDGs' strong convergence. During the first three years of SDG implementation, Indonesia ranked 98th out of 149 countries in terms of overall SDG performance, with a score or value of 54.4 out of 100.[1] According to the report by the BPS, Indonesia has achieved 49 and 18 unfinished agenda out of 8 goals, 18 targets and 67 indicators of MDGs. Among these accomplishments are the achievement of universal primary education, the promotion of gender equality and the empowerment of women, and the reduction of child mortality, while the unfinished agenda includes eradicating extreme poverty and hunger, maternal mortality rates, combating HIV/AIDS, malaria, and other diseases, and ensuring environmental sustainability (for example forest cover, CO_2 emission, rural drinking water, affordable sanitation), and global partnership for development.[2]

According to the International NGO Forum on Indonesian Development (INFID) report, citizen's perceptions towards socio-economic inequality were still high. INFID's survey in 2017 in 34 provinces concluded that the inequality index increased from 5.6 to 6% in 2018. This means, the community considers that there are inequalities in six out of 10 areas of inequality. The three highest sources of inequality in the

[1] SDG Index and Dashboard Global Report, Country Profiles, July 2016 by Bertelsmann Stiftung and Sustainable Development Solutions Network.
[2] www.bps.go.id.

G. Baharuddin
Universitas Pancasila Indonesia, South Jakarta, Indonesia

B. T. Possumah (✉)
Institut Agama Islam Tazkia, Bogor, Indonesia
e-mail: btaufiq@gmail.com

T. Azid et al. (eds.), *Wealth Management and Investment in Islamic Settings*,
https://doi.org/10.1007/978-981-19-3686-9_20

three underdeveloped regions are income, job opportunity, and property ownership. However, it should be acknowledged that Indonesia's ranking in the implementation of the SDGs went up one level from 100 to 99 with the difference in scores still relatively low at 62.8 according to the SDGs index by the Bertelsmann Stiftung and the Sustainable Development Solutions Network.

Indonesia has actually aligned the national development priorities with the SDGs agenda and integrated them further into national and sub-national development plans, allocated budgets consistently, and adjusted them to the local context. It is estimated that globally, around 3–5 trillion USD is needed to achieve the SDGs. Discovering an innovative solution to finance inclusive and sustainable development programs is a must. For example, to finance infrastructure projects in the medium terms target, Indonesia needs around 37 billion USD. More than 40% of these financing needs are expected to be included in the government budget, but the remainder will be financed by state-owned enterprises and the public–private sector. Based on this, the Waqf's role is critical, particularly in 2018, when it is estimated that the potential of waqf assets in Indonesia has reached IDR 2,000 trillion, and the potential of waqf money has reached IDR 188 trillion per year.

The remaining structure of this paper divided into four sections after Introduction as the first. The second section will discuss about blended finance and what are the principles to implement it. Then followed by the third section which explain further how the Waqf Bank works. The most important section comes after attempted to draw the model of waqf bank in Indonesia, where blended finance is being used to achieve the Sustainable Development Goals (SDGs). And the last section as the closing section is conclusion.

20.1 Blended Finance and Its Principles

Blended finance, as defined by the Organization for Economic Cooperation and Development (OECD), is the strategic use of development finance to mobilize additional finance for sustainable development in developing countries.[3] Blended finance is a strategy used by donors to mitigate risk, rebalance risk–reward profiles, and achieve development impact by combining or aligning official development finance or philanthropic funds with private capital.[4] Apparently, term of blended finance is relatively new, but in some way this kind of system has been applied for years. Some Development Finance Institution (DFIs) can argue that their daily operational

---

[3] Organization for Economic Cooperation and Development (OECD), "Making Blended Finance Work for the Sustainable Development Goals," January 29, 2018, 13, http://www.keepeek.com/Digital-Asset-Management/oecd/development/making-blended-finance-work-for-the-sustainable-development-goals_9789264288768-en#.WoHxtujwbcs.

[4] IFC, *Annual Report 2016: Experience Matters* (Washington, DC: IFC, 2016), http://www.ifc.org/wps/wcm/connect/bf1bfb0b-216b-4cde-941b-dd55febe9d3a/IFC_AR16_Full_Volume_1.pdf?MOD=AJPERES.

in a form of blended finance i.e. the Overseas Investment Cooperation (OPIC) and International Finance Cooperation (IFC).

In order to mobilized private capital for social development, blended finance is one approach to do the transform but some aspects must be underline regarding deployment, implementation, limitation, and barriers for examples incentives for the private sector.[5] Accordingly, blended finance is not the main thing for development, rather it is an alternative instrument and approach for either commercial and social development internationally and locally.

Adopting the OECD DAC Principles in this philanthropic theme will provide a clear definition as well as a five-point checklist to ensure that blended finance meets accepted quality standards and has an impact. These are the principles: (1) Connect the use of blended finance to a development rationale. Before deploying blended finance, development objectives and expected outcomes should be defined. They should be mutually agreed upon and accepted by all parties as a critical foundation for the deployment of blended finance. The overarching goal of using blended finance is to increase the availability of sustainable, market-based solutions for development financing needs. (2) Create blended finance to increase commercial finance mobilization. Development finance in blended finance should make commercial finance more accessible in order to maximize total financing for development outcomes. (3) Adapt blended finance to the local environment. Development financial services should be used to guarantee that blended finance supports local development needs, priorities, and capacities. Blended finance can help meet local development goals by allowing for the capital investment of businesses that support local consumers and encourage productive employment. (4) Concentrate on effective collaboration for blended finance. The goal of blended finance is not just to change the motivations of commercial or development actors, but rather to discover attractive investment opportunities that generate both development and commercial returns and therefore can be endorsed by commercial finance. (5) In order to ensure public accountability and results, stay updated on blended finance. Its deployments should be scrutinized on the core principle of clear results frameworks, measuring, reporting on, and communicating on financial flows, commercial returns, and development results to enhance transparency on the essential use and return on investment of development finance.

20.2 Waqf Bank: How It Works?

There is no particular term and condition in the Quran about what is the shari'ah condition and how to implement the waqf itself. One of the reason this shall be done by the Muslim is because the Prophet Muhammad Peace Be Upon Him has given examples on how to manage waqf where the assets remain in the hands of their

[5] Savoy, C. M. and Milner, A. N. (2018). Blended Finance and Aligning Private Investment with Global Development: Two Sides of the Same Coin. A Report of the CSIS Project on Prosperity and Development and the Royal Embassy of Denmark. Centre for Strategies & International Studies.

owners, but the benefits are felt by the ummah in need. The initial instruction of waqf management was begin when the Prophet (PBUH) allowed Umar bin Al Khattab to organize a waqf asset to generate benefits from the production output to be given to people who need it and did not enrich himself. In this story implies a principle that correlate with Justice principle (*'adalah*) in good governance.

In this article, the issue of waqf bank is floored with the intention that the management of waqf assets can be more professional both in terms of accountability or management so that the potential contained in this waqf can be a large source for Muslims empowerment and also to keep this assets of waqf continues to grow and develop.

The objective of waqf bank is twofold. One of the intention to the establishment of waqf bank is for humanity mission that contribute to the public beneficial in order to enhance the life of poor people and also to improve the micro enterprises. Technically, the initial capital of waqf bank is sourced from cash waqf from investments of generous Muslims. Then, the invested cash waqf is organized as follows in general:

- The investment instrument is designed in such a way, which is of course based on sharia compliance and with the knowledge of the sharia supervisory institution. Waqf investors are also given an explanation of the benefits of cash waqf. If this is done transparently, cash waqf will be very attractive to waqf investors (wakif).
- The generated Profits will be distributed back into the waqf bank for assets accumulation.
- Particular amounts of money distributes for poor people donation to help them for daily consumptions (this scheme is one of the connection bridge between waqf and the achievement of SDGs targets).
- Another amounts om money are sent to the micro enterprises in order to develop their business.

In essence, fundamental principles of good governance are *amanah* (trusted), *'adalah* and *syura* which adjusted and applied in the foundation of Islamic management system (Iqbal & Lewis, 2009). In the context of waqf, the committee of *syura* is illustrated as board of directors. To be highlighted, the *mutawalli* (trustee) obliges to provide full responsibility to the stakeholders. Hisham (2006), Cajee (2007) identify that stakeholders for waqf institutions are the donators, organization's CEOs, policy makers, beneficiaries and public community in general. In purpose to make sure that all the Islamic values are implemented in the waqf management system, those supervisors are called as *Hisbah* or Judge (*qadhi*) (Iqbal & Lewis, 2009). The judge has the authority to appoint, supervise and even to change *mutawalli* if the judge found that there was something wrong in the managerial process of waqf funds by the *Mutawalli*. However, the judge cannot revoke the *mutawalli's* license just because of complaints from other parties, unless there is sufficient evidence. Another institution that can also be appointed as a supervisor is the Sharia Auditor team.

As mentioned earlier that the *mutawalli* is not responsible to Allah alone but also to other peoples. The form of responsibility to Allah is not like the form of responsibility to humans, but this still can be done and measured through consistency of the shari'ah implementation. Cutt and Murray (2000) state that the origin of law, the form of transparency among the humans is in the shape of information presentation include the analysis on facts and how its evaluation. Therefore, in this context, a transparent report from *mutawalli* allows to provide understanding to the users how good the shari'ah values implemented in the management of waqf assets.

Along the history of Islam, Waqf was one of the instrument that play a vast role in the Islamic socio-economic system, especially during the caliph of Ottoman (1517–1924). This shows that in the past, waqf had been used as a development instrument so this should be a strong reason to review the possibility to include waqf as one of the important variables in economic development policies. If regulations or policies can be formulated to regulate and provide a strong foundation in waqf management nationally, it is not impossible that the assets of waqf are transferred to the next generation, which will have positive economic implications in the aspect of distribution, consumption, production including savings either in micro or macro perspectives.

Continuity on waqf means that once an asset donated for waqf, the status will be permanent and no one can change its status. Therefore, this asset cannot be sold, transferred or liquidated. At this point of view, it can be concluded that there are three definitions that correlated with the term of perpetuity. Firstly, after declaration made by the donors, the waqf asset will be legally bound automatically. Secondly, waqf has no limits including time. Thirdly, the principal of waqf must be permanent forever. Therefore, although the value of assets can be reduced, its benefit must be maintained and even increased.

20.3 Modelling Waqf Bank Based Blended Finance for SDGs in Indonesia

In this case, the *Waqf Bank-based blended finance* considered is one of the most appropriate schemes to be applied, since the sustainability institution is a must. Where only the yield is used for business activities and the principal is not taken. Basically, this scheme of Waqf consists of 4 parts. First, *Sinking funds.* Funds received by institutions and must be spent on a program. Second, *endowment funds.* Funds received by an institution and managed for eternal needs, without time limits. Usually used for long-term investments. Third, *the revolving fund,* used for rolling programs. In general, this type of fund is used for loans and business capital, where Fund channels get a share from funds distributed. The last is *a mixed fund*, which combines three previous funds.

Waqf bank based blended finance is considered the same as Public–private partnership or partnership between government and private sector. Also called a combination of philanthropic and private financing (philanthropy-private partnership). As an innovation, *Waqf bank based blended finance* is a model of impact investment and Crowdfunding to mobilize public capital for long-term investments. In this case is including optimizing international funds that are committed to SDGs (potential funds

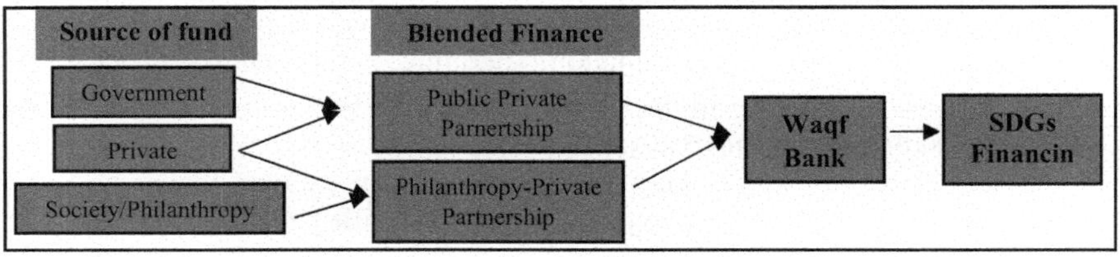

Fig. 20.1 Waqf Bank model

that can be collected with worldwide blended finance schemes is around USD 12 trillion). The SDGs financing gap is symptomatic of a business model gap. Impacts can be used as a bank business models and generate revenues starting point for Waqf. This can reduce costs, risk certain addresses issues and catalyse public private sector solutions (Fig. 20.1).

In Indonesia for example, an agreement signed between UN Environment and BNP Paribas, was a historic MOU to work together and channel private financing of at least 10 billion USD by 2025 from global capital markets to large-scale sustainable and climate-resilient projects in new economic power area. This sustainable financing facilities aims to provide a platform for private sector to engage with public stakeholders and civil society by offering models of SDG-based projects that are feasible to their global customers. The first of these facilities, the Tropical Landscapes Finance Facility (TLFF), which was established in Indonesia, to support the government in reducing deforestation and restoring degraded land.

The application of *Waqf bank based blended finance* in Indonesia in the initial stages needs to be focused on fulfilling social funding sources that have characteristics of removing income inequality and can spur economic growth. By establishing financial institutions such as Waqf Banks, the existence of blended finance will be able to cover part of the funding needs of the social infrastructure sector especially education and health facilities such as schools and hospitals worth USD 392 million by the end of 2019. The government can develop *Waqf Bank based blended finance* schemes and other philanthropic funds to support SME projects with cluster patterns (industrial sector, plantation, fisheries, etc.). This is also the nascence of new entrepreneurs or new start-ups.

Notably, exposure to sources of finance for the MSME sector has remained limited. According to 2015 Indonesian banking statistics, only 17.75% of total bank loans were distributed to the UMKM sector. This situation also demonstrates that the above sector still requires more financial assistance. MSMEs, in fact, play a critical role in driving regional and national economies. This sector has proven its strength and resilience as the spine of Indonesia's economy during the crisis; additionally, this sector absorbs 97% of the total workforce, significantly lowering the unemployment rate, and able to contribute 60% to GDP (GDP). In short, MSME is a strategy for public engagement in which Waqf Bank and MSME can work collaboratively to drive the economy, principally for the weaker sections of society.

In depth, waqf can be set as a powerful instrument with extensive benefits in the context of social security. Why social security? Because in general, social security covers the assistance to the fulfilment of daily needs and social insurance on the potential risk in the future (for examples: chronic ills, accident at the workplace, elderly, unemployment or losing a job). The core idea of this social security discourse is departed from the realization of state's responsibilities to provide an ultimate services for the people towards sudden matters such as primary needs, poverty, disease, illiteracy and elder period. The social security system in the developed countries have been developed extensively and even become the important element for the economic cycles where the source of funds generated from the tax of their citizens. In Switzerland or other Scandinavian countries for instance, the government imposes high tax for those who earns fixed salary up to 25%. In return, the government provides free education, health care facilities, integrated public transportation for everyone. In contrast, social security systems in the developing countries are still underdeveloped where less generated income from tax side is one of the causes. This because the majority income of the peoples are still low.

In Islam, social security becomes the government's obligation for the people at lease to cover their minimum standard of living and provide assistance for everybody who requires. These kind of obligations are contained in the method of "*Tasharruful imam 'ala a' ra'iyyah manutun bi al Malahat*" which means that a leader's visions are depend on the public interests. Therefore, social security policies shall be directed as the tools to attain people's prosperity. At the individual level, everyone in the society must helps those who need to live a decent life by fulfilling their basic needs. In order to implement this policy, the assistance can be directed towards financial and moral assistance schemes. The financial assistance aims to enable the poor to reach the limit of 'financial independence' or 'prosperity'. This is where the urgency of Waqf in meeting these needs.

The *Waqf bank-based blended finance* approach in alleviating income inequality is a type of fortune at the bottom of the pyramid approach (Prahalad & Hart, 2002) and creating shared values (Porter & Kramer, 2011) which provide confidence that the unification of social and economic goals is likely very possible. This effort really needs support and collaboration from various parties, both domestic and international. The support including preparation and development of blended finance regulation, technical assistance, grants, guarantees, soft loans, evaluation and formulation of policies and others. Therefore, the SDGs can be used as a liaison between the Waqf and the achievement of the *Maqhasid sharia*, such as Preservation of religion (hifz al-din), life (hifz al-nafs), intellect and reason (hifz al-aql), lineage (hifz al-nasb) and wealth (hifz al-mal).

20.4 Conclusion

Blended finance is a critical different strategy to organizing new sources of funding for the SDGs while also dispatching public funds to attract private sector participation.

Blended finance is the way how to use public capital or Islamic philanthropic sources would be used to significantly raise direct investment in order to achieve the SDGs. Blended finance enables for-profit and non-profit entities to participate alongside each others and achieving their own goals (social impact, financial return, or a blend of both). In this study we propose waqf as one of source of fund to be included in the blended finance model, to initiate alternative investment possibilities in developing countries such as Indonesia, leading to greater development impact, particularly for SMEs and the poor. Hopefully, this study may contribute to practical discussion on how to maximize the potential of waqf fund and it's institution through blended finance model for SDGs.

References

Cajee, Z. A. (2011). Revitalising the institution of awqaf in developing the community. In M. Kahf, & Siti-Mashitoh (Eds.), *Essential reading in contemporary waqf issues* (pp. 323–349). Kuala Lumpur: Cert Publications.

Cutt, J., & Murray, V. (2000). *Accountability and effectiveness evaluation in non-profit organizations*. Routledge.

Iqbal, Z., & Lewis, M. K. (2009). *An Islamic perspective on governance*. Edward Elgar Publishing.

Porter & Kramer. (2011). Creating shared values. *Harvard Business Review,* January–February 2011.

Prahalad, C. K., & Hart, S. L. (2002). The fortune of the bottom of pyramid. *Revista Eletrônica de Estratégia & Negócios, 26*, 54–67.

Yacoob, H. (2006). *Waqf accounting in Malaysian state Islamic religious institutions: The case of Federal territory SIRC*. Unpublished masters dissertation, International Islamic University Malaysia, Kuala Lumpur.

Gunawan Baharuddin He teaches political islamic economics, islamic economic system, and islamic social finance. As a lecturer at the Universitas Pancasila, He was also involved in several group researchers at the faculty of economics and business and was appointed as the coordinator of an international program. He earned a Master's Degree in Islamic Economics from Universiti Kebangsaan Malaysia (2012) and his Doctorate in islamic Economics from the Academy of Islamic Studies, Universiti Malaya, Malaysia (2021). In 2021, Dr. Gunawan with his other colleagues established the Indonesia Waqf Institute (IWI) and ran several seminars in order to enhance public literacy of waqf and other social islamic finance.

Bayu Taufiq Possumah is a PhD in Islamic economics at the Institute of Islamic Civilization (Hadhari), Universiti Kebangsaan Malaysia (UKM) in 2013. He is a former researcher at Institut Islam Hadhari and the Research Center for Islamic Economics and Finance (EKONIS) UKM also as former senior lecturer of Financial Economics at University Malaysia Terengganu (UMT). Currently he serves as senior lecturer at Institut Tazkia Indonesia and appointed as Director of Indonesia Waqf Institute (IWI). He has presented papers at many international and local conferences, including the Islamic Banking, Accounting and Finance Conference, International Workshop of Islamic Economic and Finance Theory, World Universities Zakat Conference, Malaysia Finance Association Conference, and World Conference on Islamic Thought and Civilization. His paper "Economic Distribution in Islam: Virtues and Philosophical in Nature" was awarded Best

Performance Award (Gold) in the 5th International Symposium on Islam, Civilization, and Science (ISICAS 2014) in Kyoto University Japan, the paper later published as a book Bank *Waqf*.

Chapter 21
Waqf Contributions for Sustainable Development Goals: A Critical Appraisal

Omar Kachkar and Marwa Alfares

The 2030 Agenda for Sustainable Development are endorsed by world leaders in September 2015 in the United Nations headquarters in New York. The agenda featured 17 Sustainable Development Goals (SDGs) consisting of 169 targets. These targets are grouped into five themes: finance, information and communications technology (ICT), capacity building, trade, and systemic issues, presented below in Fig. 21.1.

The SDGs are intended to encourage policymakers across the world to achieve concrete targets for 2015–2030 and to meet a range of other objectives. Such objectives include poverty alleviation, improving healthcare and education in addition to other economic, social, and environmental objectives (World Bank Group report, 2017; the United Nations, 2015).

However, financing the above SDGs requires mobilization huge financial resources. According to the McKinsey Global Institute (MGI) report (2017), every year through 2035, the world needs around $3.7 trillion to invest in the necessary infrastructure such as roads, railways, ports, airports, power, water, and telecoms to support economies in order to keep up with the projected GDP growth. Such needs could increase further by up to $1 trillion annually (Woetzel et al., 2017).

In Organisation of the Islamic Cooperation (OIC) countries, finding the necessary funds to finance SDG development projects is even more serious and urgent. This is due to the fact that the majority of OIC countries are considered among the emerging markets and developing economies (EMDE) including OIC countries in Asia and sub-Saharan Africa. In other words, OIC countries have been for years

O. Kachkar (✉)
Ibn Haldun University, Ordu cad. F-05 Blok No. 3, Başakşehir, Istanbul 34480, Turkey
e-mail: omar.kachkar@ihu.edu.tr

M. Alfares
Istanbul Sabahattin Zaim University, Bulvar Istanbul Sitesi, Block DA, Dara 41, Başakşehir, Istanbul 34480, Turkey
e-mail: alfares.marwa@std.izu.edu.tr

T. Azid et al. (eds.), *Wealth Management and Investment in Islamic Settings*,
https://doi.org/10.1007/978-981-19-3686-9_21

Fig. 21.1 UN 17 SDGs. *Source* https://sustainabledevelopment.un.org/sdgs

facing accumulated deficits in providing for the overall infrastructure development in particular for basic utilities of poverty alleviation healthcare and education as will be elaborated in the coming discussion. Lack of financial resources has seriously hindered the ability of these countries to exploit their full development potential (Woetzel et al., 2017). The following section will analyse the status quo of four of the key SDGs in OIC member states. Namely, poverty alleviation, healthcare, education and infrastructure, these sectors correspond to the UN SDG 1, SDG 3, SDG 4 and SDG 9 respectively.

Poverty alleviation: Poverty alleviation is the first SDG and one of the most significant indicators of development situations in nations. Unfortunately, poverty in OIC countries constitutes a major challenge for development efforts. According to the 'poverty line' criteria, that was introduced by the World Bank in 1990, it is determined as earning an average of $1.25 of daily income per person. The objective of the poverty line is to track poverty across nations (World Bank, 2014). Overall, OIC countries, have witnessed a remarkable improvement in poverty alleviation efforts. Over a period of two decades, the total number of poor people fell from 369 million in 1990 to about 322 million in 2011. Despite such remarkable improvements, poverty in OIC countries is still very high. It is estimated that around 500 million poor persons are living in OIC countries with less than $2 a day or below the national poverty line (SFC Report, 2017). Even when the progress is compared to counterparts countries, poverty in OIC countries is higher as illustrated in Fig. 21.2.

In 1990 poverty in non-OIC, countries were 3.61 times more than poverty numbers in OIC counterpart. In 2011, the percentage shrank to 1.99 times more. While the number has been cut into half during the period from 1990 to 2011, the number slightly improved in OIC which remained within 300 million. The number has been improved in 2017 to 241 million, out of approximately 700 million

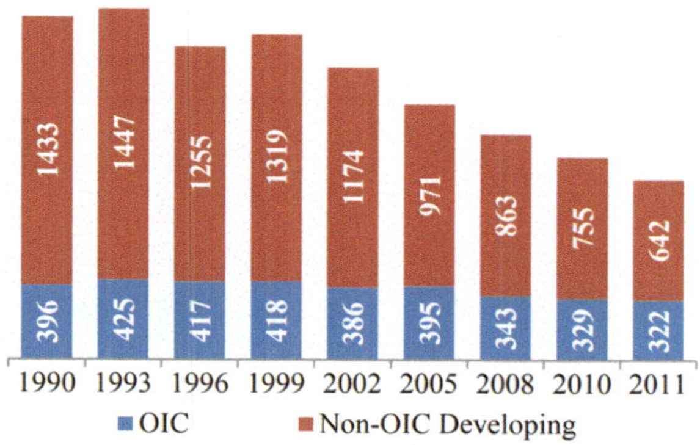

Fig. 21.2 Poverty in OIC and non-OIC countries. *Source* SESRIC staff calculations based on World Bank, PovcalNet, COMCEC and SESRIC Technical Report (2015)

(COMCEC Report, 2019). In 1990, while 22% of the world's total poor lived in OIC countries, in 2011 OIC countries were home to over one-third (33.1%) of the world's total poor in 2011 (SESRIC & COMCEC Report, 2015; Haneef et al., 2015). On average, Muslim majority countries have been characterized with high poverty levels due to a severe income disparity, lower literacy rates relative to Muslim minority countries, low percentage of enrolment ratio in primary education, less health expenditure, less improved portable water, low life expectancy, low human capital, weak governments (Shaikh et al., 2017).

Healthcare: despite the improvements on many fronts, many efforts are direly needed in this sector. Since 1990, mother and child mortality rates have remarkably declined with 44% and 52% respectively. However, many OIC countries have missed the Millennium Development Goal 5 (MDG 5) MDG4 targets of aims at reducing three-quarters in maternal mortality and two-thirds child mortality respectively by the end of 2015. Consequently, populations of many OIC countries in particular in South Asia and Sub-Saharan Africa suffer serious difficulties in accessing proper health care services due to "the lack of adequate and sustainable financial resources, poor health infrastructure and insufficiently trained health workforce." (OIC Health Report, 2017). Despite all the improvements, health care situations in OIC countries are far behind counterparts in non-OIC countries as in the illustrations below.

As shown in Fig. 21.3 life expectancy has significantly improved in all OIC countries. Upper middle groups live longer in comparison to low-income countries. However, life expectancy in all OIC countries, and all groups live shorted than counterparts in non-OIC countries. Similar observations are clear in the mortality rate under five and the maternal mortality ratio (Figs. 21.4 and 21.5).

Education: in respect to education as the fourth goal of the SDGs, the situation in OIC countries does not seem in a good shape particularly in comparison to non-OIC countries. As illustrated in Fig. 21.6, average government spending on education as a ratio of GDP remained less compared to non-OIC countries.

The spending in 2004 was slightly better compared to non-OIC countries but in 2014 the spending on education considerably decreased from 4.1 to 3.5 and

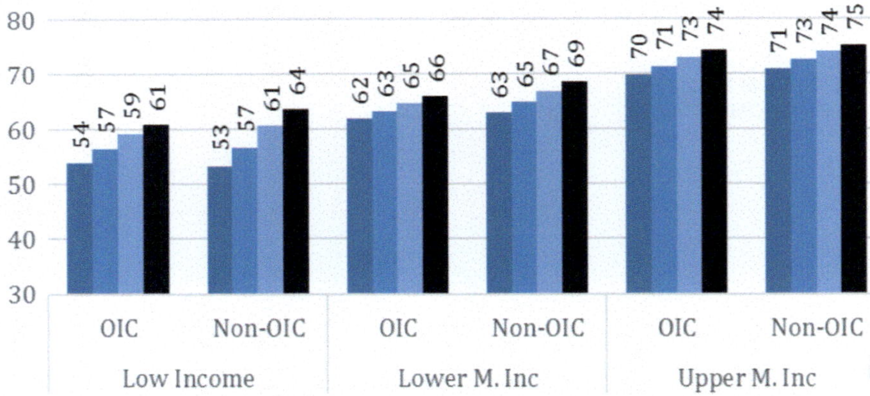

Fig. 21.3 Life expectancy at birth last 20 years. *Source* (COMCEC, 2019; Ahmed, 2019) http://www.comcec.org/en/wp-content/uploads/2019/04/2-OIC-Presentation_Access-to-Health-Services-1.pdf

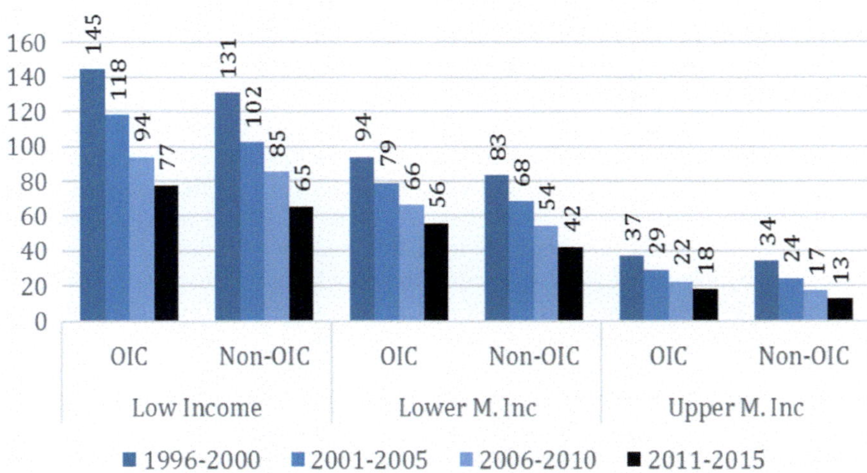

Fig. 21.4 Mortality rate under 5 (per 1000 births). *Source* (COMCEC, 2019; Ahmed, 2019) http://www.comcec.org/en/wp-content/uploads/2019/04/2-OIC-Presentation_Access-to-Health-Services-1.pdf

consequently become much less than the spending of other groups namely, non-OIC countries which reached in 2014 approximately 4.8 of their GDP. Likewise, the government spending per student is less in OIC countries compared to other groups as illustrated in Fig. 21.7.

Despite the impressive achievements, according to the figures above, OIC countries are lagging behind other countries in non-OIC countries, let alone developed countries.

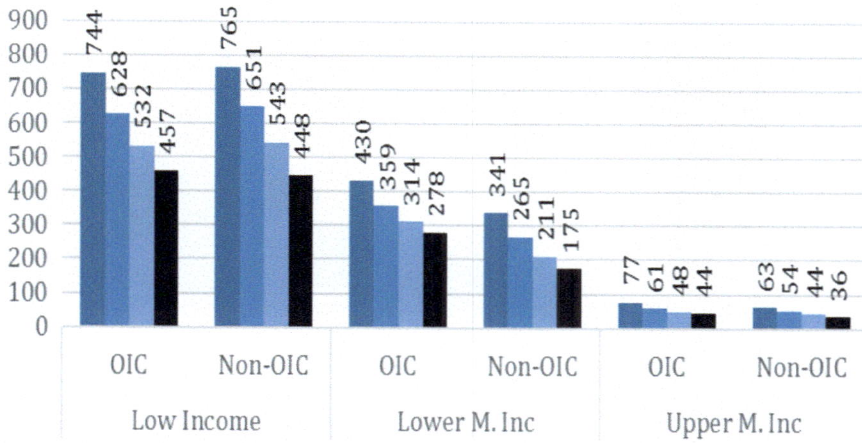

Fig. 21.5 Mortality ratio (per 100,000 births). *Source* (COMCEC, 2019; Ahmed, 2019) http://www.comcec.org/en/wp-content/uploads/2019/04/2-OIC-Presentation_Access-to-Health-Services-1.pdf

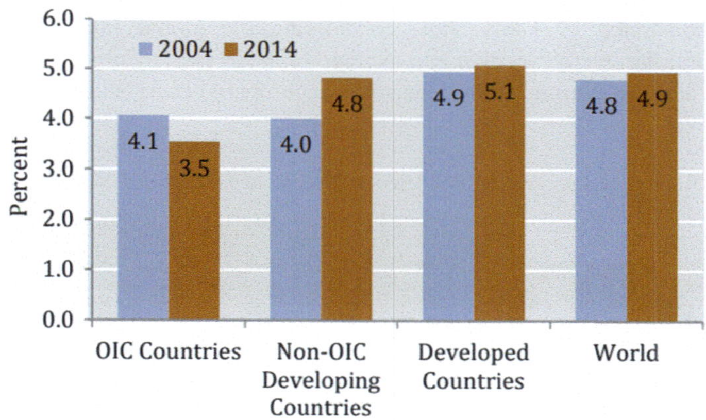

Fig. 21.6 Government spending on education as a percentage of GDP. *Source* (BAĞCI, 2019) https://www.sesric.org/imgs/news/1584_PRESENTATION_SESRIC_EN.pdf

Overall, member countries of the Muslim world have a very long road ahead to achieve the developmental goals. Lack of funds constitutes a major obstacle to achieve those goals in particular in the three sectors highlighted earlier, i.e. poverty alleviation, health care, and education. Islamic social finance represents a great opportunity to assist in bridging the funding gap and hence shoulder great responsibility that is currently born solely by governments in many Muslim World.

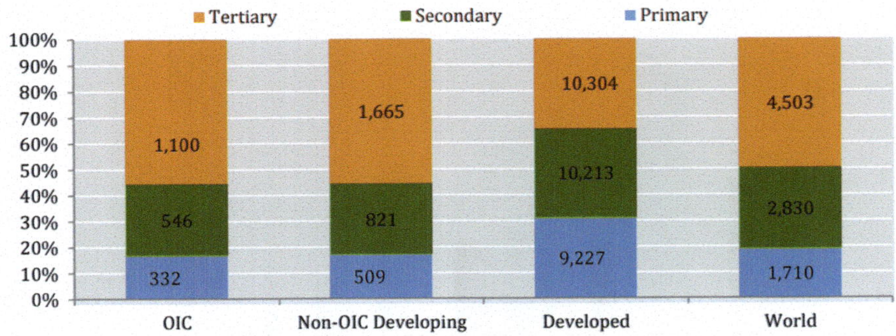

Fig. 21.7 Government spending on education per student. *Source* (BAĞCI, 2019) https://www.sesric.org/imgs/news/1584_PRESENTATION_SESRIC_EN.pdf

Infrastructure development: to understand the seriousness of the developmental challenges within OIC members, illustrative Table 21.1 provides an illustration of the latest figures on the situation of infrastructure development in OIC countries. The following table provides a comparison between OIC member countries with non-OIC developing countries in infrastructure ranking.

As demonstrated in Table 21.1, considering the global ranking of overall infrastructure, the overall median and average rank for OIC members is lower than the counterpart developing economies with 88 compared to 81 and 84 compared to

Table 21.1 Rankings in infrastructure progress, OIC and counterpart developing countries

	All developing economies, except for OIC members				OIC members			
	Highest rank	Lowest rank	Average rank	Median rank	Highest rank	Lowest rank	Average rank	Median rank
Overall infrastructure	26	139	82	81	2	140	84	88
Roads	19	139	81	84	1	140	83	86
Railroad infrastructure	16	108	64	63	13	107	68	70
Port infrastructure	7	139	83	85	3	140	80	81
Air transport infrastructure	6	140	82	83	2	139	84	86
Available airline seat km/week, millions	2	140	82	85	5	136	77	72
Electricity supply	17	138	79	79	10	140	90	103
Mobile telephone subscriptions/100 population	8	140	74	78	2	136	73	85
Fixed telephone lines/100 population	7	137	76	74	22	140	95	98
Global Competitiveness Index	14	122	70	71	14	140	88	97

Source: World Bank, based on the World Economic Forum's 2016 Global Competitiveness Report.
Note: Data are available for only 38 of the 57 OIC members. OIC = Organization of Islamic Cooperation. 1 = highest-ranked; 140 = lowest ranked.

Source (International Bank for Reconstruction and Development; the World Bank, 2017)

82, respectively. Except for port infrastructure, availability of airline seats, and slightly the mobile telephone subscription, the average ranking of OIC members are lower in roads, railroad infrastructures, electricity supply, and other sectors. It is believed that in the largest 13 economies only an estimated of approximately USD 1.6 trillion deficit in infrastructure investment during 2016–2040a (COMCEC, 2019).

21.1 Islamic Social Finance

Islamic social finance represents a great potential source of funding to support Sustainable development projects in the Muslim World. Islamic social finance is the Islamic version of social finance. Social finance shares many features with the Islamic economic system including Islamic financial instruments. Many of these features are among the intrinsic components of Islamic social finance that has recently emerged as one of the potential instruments to address the widening gap in financing sustainable development projects. Islamic social finance enjoys an array of financial instruments for funds mobilizing for social impact projects. These instruments, including zakah, awqaf, sadaqah cooperative takaful, and not-for-profit microfinance (IRTI Islamic Social Finance Report, 2017) these instruments have played a crucial role in providing for the basic needs of Muslim communities throughout Islamic history and contributed tremendously in providing public facilities and rendering basic services and consequently reduces the burden on the government budget and increases public spending. The following section will examine the institution of waqf as a fundamental component of Islamic social finance.

21.1.1 Overview of Waqf and Cash Waqf

Waqf is considered among the highest forms of charity in Islam. The institution of waqf has played a vital role in enhancing the welfare of Muslim communities and in providing for basic social services for the Muslim communities including education, healthcare. Most infrastructure projects were taken care of by waqf that includes roads, bridges, mosques, schools, libraries, and hospitals (ISRA, 2012). Recently, in the midst of the discussions on the socio-economic development in the Islamic World many voices started to call for the revival of *waqf* and to include it in the development strategies and poverty alleviation efforts (Ahmed, 2004; Khan, 2012; Kahf, 2002). To this effect, the Islamic Development Bank is actively promoting research on *waqf* and has established for this purpose a *waqf* development fund. Furthermore, recent initiatives by the bank have been directed towards establishing a *waqf* development bank (Economic and Social Commission for Western Asia (ESCWA), 2012).

Traditionally, most *waqf* deeds were assigned for properties to generate specific benefits for specific beneficiaries. There was no risk of exposing the corpus of *waqf* to any risk of loss. In the era of Imam Zufar, the ideal use of cash *waqf* was to be invested in profit and loss sharing businesses (*mudhrabah*) which was the common practice at the time. This suggestion of investing cash *waqf* in *mudhrabah* was no so practical (Nadwi & Kroessin, 2013).

Cash waqf is one of the sustainable innovation in Islamic social finance that can significantly contribute in mobilising funds for achieving the SDGs. Cash waqf has its roots in the Islamic history. Notable, during the Ottoman era, cash *waqf* used to be invested in a common transaction known as *Istiqlal*. *Istiqlal* transactions used to be performed through three stages; a sale contract between the borrower and the *waqf* institution followed by a lease contract and ended with a purchase back contract. In more details, according to *Istiqlal* transactions, the borrower would sell his house to the *waqf* and obtain in return the capital he needed. The borrower would ask the *waqf* for permission to stay in his house. This permission would be granted to the borrower according to a rental contract. So, the borrower would sell his house and rent it to stay in it. Now after about one year, the borrower would return the capital and his house would be returned to him in a purchase contract. Total rents collected from such transactions would constitute the annual profit of cash *waqf*. After the deduction of management expenses, the collected revenues would be then channelled to the charitable purposes as stipulated in the endowment deed (Cizakca, 2011).

This practice of cash *waqf* was initially limited to Ottoman Empire, however, it was eventually spread to other Muslim countries and it had been approved in Egypt, Iran as well as in the Indian sub-continent at the beginning of the twentieth century (Cizakca, 2013).

To sum up, the institution of *waqf* was established as early as the days of the prophet (PBUH) and continued to cater for the various social services throughout Islamic History. Cash *waqf*, in particular, has evolved during the days of the Ottoman Empire and recently it has started to revive in the realization of its flexibility in particular in terms of liquidity.

21.1.2 Waqf Sukuk: The Practical Implementation of Cash Waqf

Overview of waqf sukuk

Among the recent concepts in the realm of Islamic capital market and Islamic bonds is the concept of waqf sukuk (endowment bonds). Waqf Sukuk is the outcome of merging Islamic bonds with the concept of waqf. AAOIFI defines sukuk as: "certificates of equal value representing undivided shares in ownership of tangible assets, usufructs and services or (in the ownership of) the assets of particular projects or special investment activity" (AAOIFI, Shari's standard No. 17, 2008,

p. 307). As such waqf Sukuk can be defined as certificates that represent waqf assets, such assets can be either fixed assets like properties and buildings, movable assets like money, planes and cars or intangible assets such as copyrights and patent royalties (Naqqasi, 2012).

At this juncture, it is worth noting that waqf sukuk are categorised into two types, the first type is the purely charitable waqf sukuk that generates no income to the sukuk holders, even though that the waqf project generates income, however, the income is designated to be channelled to the beneficiaries. As far as the researcher is aware, so far there has been no such sukuk issued under this category. Nonetheless, serious efforts are currently undergoing to issue such sukuk in collaboration between Awqaf New Zealand, ISRA consultancy and the Islamic Solidarity Fund for Development (ISFD) of the Islamic Development Banks (IsDB). (See Appendix A for the structure of awqaf New Zealand and the awqaf farms) The New Zealand project aims to generate income from the waste products of the Qurbani sheep. The other category is the hybrid waqf and commercial model. This category often generates a stream of income to the sukuk holders. Numerous examples can be pointed out on this category most notably the King Abdul Aziz Waqf in Saudi Arabia that developed a multiplex of high towers called Zam Zam Tower located near al-Harem in Mekkah. Under this project, a 24 year reversionary ground lease was awarded to the developer according to the concept of Build–Operate–Transfer (BOT). Whereas the land belonged to the waqf); the building was owned by the developer while the manfa'ah (usufruct)—the right to stay in the building—was sold to the sukuk investors. In some ways, the structure is similar to a time-share vacation facility with a fraction of ownership in the lease. However, the most striking feature is that intifa' sukuk was used instead of normal ijarah sukak because the Saudi laws do not allow foreign ownership of the real estate in Makkah and Madinah. Thus, the concept of waqf played a major role in overcoming this obstacle. (ISRA, 2012) the example of the pure waqf sukuk with no income to the sukuk holders is In New Zealand, the Awqaf.

21.1.3 *Waqf Contributions to Achieving SDGs: Selected Cases*

This section will highlight the contribution of waqf institutions in Turkey with a special focus on two main institutions, namely, The Humanitarian Relief Foundation (İnsan Hak ve Hürriyetleri), (IHH) and The Turkish Diyanet Foundation (The Diyanet vakfı). Additionally, the discussion will shed some light on activities of one of the leading institutions in the Muslim World that has made great advances in the development, promotion, and replication of the model of Waqf in its member as well as non-member states, i.e. the Islamic Development Bank (IsDB). The discussion will analyze the waqf projects and activities of two of IsDB subsidiaries, the Islamic Solidarity Fund for Development (ISFD) and Awqaf Properties Investment Fund (APIF).

21.1.3.1 Case One: Waqf Contributions to SDGs in the Republic of Turkey

In Turkey, Waqf activities date back to the era of the Ottoman empire. According to Orbay (2014), the Waqf system was seen in many ways as the backbone of the Ottoman empire where Waqf provided a range of services from education, health, to social projects. Currently, the General Directorate of Foundations (GDF), Vakiflar Genel Müdürlügü in Turkish, that was established in 1924, is responsible to oversight all 52,000 waqfs in Turkey of which many dates back to the times of the Ottoman Empire. The properties managed by GDF include iconic structures such as Blue Mosque and Grand Bazar of Istanbul. It is estimated that 3,500 foundations have been restored by GDF. Awaqf contribution to the local economy reached around TL 2.5 billion www.vgm.gov.tr/home-page.

Activities of GDF in 2018 included the provision of financial and non-financial support to thousands of people within the republic of Turkey and outside Turkey. Table 21.2 summarises GDF activities in 2018.

Within the scope of this study, this discussion will focus on activities of two of the biggest waqf institutions in Turkey namely, The Humanitarian Relief Foundation (İnsan Hak ve Hürriyetleri), (IHH) and The Turkish Diyanet Foundation (The Diyanet vakfı).

The Humanitarian Relief Foundation (İnsan Hak ve Hürriyetleri), (IHH)

IHH is waqf foundation for humanitarian relief (see Appendix B), it was set up by a group of concerned volunteers during the Bosnian Civil war in 1992. Shortly after

Table 21.2 GDF activities in 2018

Activity	No. of beneficiaries	SDGs
Scholarships	20,000 students	4 QUALITY EDUCATION
Financial support	5,000 orphans and handicapped people	1 NO POVERTY
Food packages	20,315 families each month in Turkey	2 ZERO HUNGER
Hot food	2,000 people in Istanbul	2 ZERO HUNGER
parcels of food packages	26,000 to families outside Turkey	2 ZERO HUNGER

Source (IsDB, 2019)

that in 1995 to be precise, the foundation became an official organization with its headquarters in Istanbul, Turkey. The aim of providing humanitarian aid to any part of the world in times of natural disasters. The IHH has grown its branches over the last twenty-five years of history to reach communities in five different continents. In 2019, the Foundation provided its services to more than 24 million people in over 80 countries around the world. It operates 1363 projects in 10 sectors as illustrated in Table 21.3. Revenues gathered from donations are invested and the proceeds are used to support its activities. In generating revenue, the foundation organizes panels, concerts, auction activities and other revenues to be obtained from the foundation's assets.

IHH has significantly contributed to the overall welfare of communities within Turkey and outside Turkey. Its activities included construction of new schools, orphanages, training, mosques, clinics, water wells and other cultural projects.

Currently, the IHH is active in Syria in providing shelter and dignified livelihood to the refugee community displaced by the civil war. With coordination from 10 different centres, the IHH through its Container Cities project hosts more than 150 thousand people. In these centres, the IHH provides support among other things food, clothing, shelter, and education. The foundation ensures the education of children does continue through the provision of education services in 43 schools and one university. In addition, the foundation ensures the protection of the welfare of the orphans who deserve additional care is such a dire situation. Base on their statistics, they provide aid to more than 10,000 orphans in these facilities on a monthly basis.

In 2007, the IHH launched its cataract campaign named "If you can see, they should too" to provide such medical assistance to thousands of people in Africa. The IHH established its eye hospital in the capital of Niger–Niamey in 2014. The IHH aimed at doing eye surgery of 6000 patients within a 5 years period in a country like Niger where cataract is a major source of blindness due to the desert nature of the topography. The sustainability of this project goes beyond the laudable gesture of helping people regain their sight. The IHH in cooperation with specialists from Turkey, do provide training programs to local doctors in a quest to improve and develop their capabilities.

In other countries of Africa such as Chad, Ghana, Mali, Guinea, Niger, Cameroon, Sierra Leone, Benin, Sudan, Ethiopia, Somali, Tanzania, Kenya, and Zimbabwe, the IHH through its Wells projects has built and is building thousands of wells to provide drinkable water to local communities. The base of their official figures, the IHH over a twenty years period has constructed 8369 wells in 37 countries. As basic as it may seem, the life impact of such a project is immense as the availability of safe drinkable water is key to the social and economic development of communities.

In addition to the above-named projects, the IHH is active too in Gaza through its established office since 2009. In Gaza, the foundation runs an Orphanage, delivering food aid, winter aid, financial assistance, Ramadan iftar meals, Eid

Table 21.3 IHH projects in 2019

No.	Expenditure	Amount in Turkish Lira (TL) (₺)	Percentage (%)	SDGS
1	Food security	188.799.105	35.77	2 ZERO HUNGER
2	Education	26.846.440	5.09	4 QUALITY EDUCATION
3	Health	48.175.902	9.13	3 GOOD HEALTH AND WELL-BEING
4	Protection	141.961.012	26.90	16 PEACE, JUSTICE AND STRONG INSTITUTIONS; 5 GENDER EQUALITY; 2 ZERO HUNGER
5	Shelter	22.533.682	4.27	15 LIFE ON LAND; 1 NO POVERTY
6	Non-food aid	70.143.434	13.29	15 LIFE ON LAND
7	Water, sanitation and hygiene	19.839.466	3.76	6 CLEAN WATER AND SANITATION
8	Culture	8.472.158	1.61	15 LIFE ON LAND
9	Agriculture	277.887	0.05	1 NO POVERTY
10	Search and rescue	767.046	0.15	15 LIFE ON LAND

Source IHH Annual Report (2019)

activities with rams etc. the IHH is one foundation with much admiration both within and outside Turkey with series of accolades both local and international for its work in building sustainable communities where the potential of all and sundry can be realized in the most dignified manner possible.

The Turkish Diyanet Foundation (The Diyanet Vakfı)

TDF is seen as one of the most established and influential institutions in Turkiye. Established in 1975 its headquarter is located in Ankara and legally it is under the supervision of the General Directorate of Foundations (Saad et al., 2017). Aside from the provision of humanitarian aid the Diyanet Vakfı also plays a very important role in terms of education, health, and organizing of cultural events. The Foundation provides its services to beneficiaries inside Turkey and abroad, especially to Muslim communities in Europe including, Holland, Belgium, Germany. Aid activities ranges from professional and training classes to teaching new languages and other vocational courses in addition to providing religious education. The Foundation furthermore, supported the poor families with medicine, hospital bills, and other healthcare support.

The foundation owns a series of schools and hospitals where approximately 9,472,505 people benefited from the services provided by these medical centres (Saad et al., 2017). When it comes to education, The Turkish Diyanet Foundation (TDF) formed a property education unit in 1994 (Saad et al., 2017). With regard to this, the foundation facilitates the quality and easy access to education in Turkish universities and Imam-Hatip High Schools. Additionally the Foundation also offer in-kind allowances to non-Turkish students. In particular students the Eastern bloc such as Mongolia, Turkmenistan and the like. TDF sponsors brilliant but needy students abroad to various universities for higher education in the field of Theology, Philosophy and other social science-related courses. The Foundation shows very significant support to education and research with an expenditure of 167.321.089,15 TL in 2019 as in Table 21.4.

Table 21.4 Turkish Diyanet Foundation expenditure for the year 2019 in Turkish Lira

Sector	Amount	SDGs
Education and research	167.321.089,15	
Social services	324.903.193,17	
Charity and volunteer	315.789.624,97	Not specified
Culture, art, sports	19.723.438,80	
Other	105.595.477,19	

Source https://tdv.org/tr-TR/kurumsal/mali-bilgiler-2/

21.1.3.2 Case Two: Islamic Development Bank (IsDB)

Since its inception, IsDB has been one of the leading institutions in the Muslim world in promoting waqf and supporting waqf properties. Through its subsidiaries, IsDB provide development assistance to OIC as well as to non-OIC member countries. The following discussion will underscore the waqf projects of two of IsDB subsidiaries and their contributions in line with SDGs.

Islamic Solidarity Fund for Development (ISFD-IsDB)

The ISFD is one of the waqf funds and development arms of the Islamic Development Bank (IsDB). ISFD was established in as a waqf fund in 2005 in during the IsDB's extraordinary Islamic conference held in Makkah on 30 May 2007 in Dakar, Senegal (https://isfd.isdb.org).

The Fund targets a principal capital of US$10 billion, in the form of a Waqf (i.e. Endowment). Its major source of the fund comes from a voluntary contribution from its member countries. Through co-financing, the funds are used to finance projects that improve the lives of the poor in its member countries. The fund has achieved significant milestones in its activities since its inception. About 80 percent of ISFD projects are allocated in the less developed member countries (IsDB, 2018a, b). Since its inception, from 2008 to 2017, a total of 117 projects have been approved, with a valued of US $2.8 billion in 33 member countries. ISFD's contribution in those projects stood at US $734.22 million. The sectoral distribution of the total approved projects is depicted in Fig. 21.8 (ISFD Annual Report, 2017), within the context of SDGs, SDG 1&2 on poverty and hanger, ISFD spent a total of US $238.59 m, on projects related to agriculture and rural development, followed by education with expenditure of 201.09 m, energy with US $64.15 m, finance, US $75.40 m, health (US $99.0 m), transport with US$ 28.00 m, water & sanitation US $5.00 m and other projects with US $22.00 m. Table 21.5 depicts all ISFD projects with corresponding SDGs.

ISFD Islamic microfinance programs

In line with the ISFD efforts to combat poverty and enhance the welfare of poor communities, numerous microfinance projects were supported by ISFD. The support has been channelled through the Microfinance Support Programme, the Vocational Literacy Program, and other individual projects. Several member countries have benefited from ISFD support including, Mauritania, Niger, Senegal, Sierra Leone, Kazakhstan, Kyrgyzstan Tajikistan, and Benin. (ISFD, 2017). In Sudan, microfinance projects is among the successful stories of such microfinance programs sponsored by ISFD. A recent program was jointly supported by IsDB and other partners. The total value of the project was approximately US$63.5 million, ISFD contributed with US$3 million and IsDB provided US$14.45 million. The program targeted seven groups:

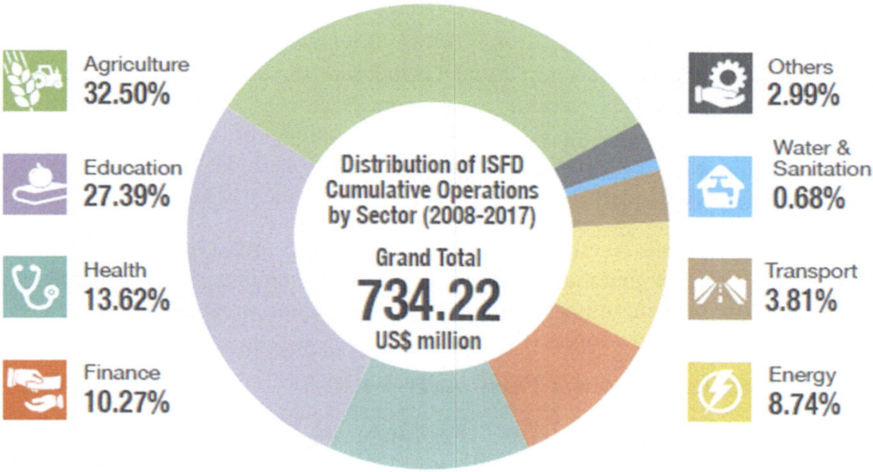

Fig. 21.8 Sectoral distribution of ISFD projects 2008–2017. *Source* (ISFD Annual Report, 2017)

Table 21.5 ISFD projects 2008–2017. In US$ million

Sector	Amount	SDGs
Agri. and Rural Develop.	238.59	1 No poverty; 2 Zero hunger; 11 Sustainable cities and communities; 9 Industry, innovation and infrastructure
Education	201.09	4 Quality education
Energy	64.15	7 Affordable and clean energy
Finance	75.40	15 Life on land
Health	99.99	3 Good health and well-being
Transport	28.00	9 Industry, innovation and infrastructure; 11 Sustainable cities and communities
Water & Sanitation	5.00	6 Clean water and sanitation
Other	22.00	Not specified
Total	**734.22**	

Source ISFD Annual Report (2017)

1. micro-entrepreneurs,
2. female heads of households,
3. unemployed graduates,
4. skilled labourers,
5. micro-entrepreneur start-up projects,
6. deprived rural productive families and
7. active disabled people.

As part of Sudan's Islamic financial system, all the microfinance provided to clients was based on murabaha, that is a Shari'ah-compliant mode of financing. Beneficiaries of the microfinance program reached approximately 56,000 clients, about 51% of them are women (ISFD, 2017).

Awqaf Properties Investment Fund (APIF-IsDB)

In addition to the ISFD, the IsDB hosts the Awqaf Properties Investment Fund (APIF). APIF was inaugurated in 2001 with total subscriptions of US$50 million paid by IsDB along with nine other institutions. APIF key mandate is to finance waqf project that can potentially generate income in particular commercial and residential real estate properties in a Shriah compliant mode of financing. APIF provides financing to waqf institutions and charitable organizations in both member and non-member OIC states and helps them to achieve their mandate www.isdb.org/apif. As illustrated in Fig. 21.8, by the end of 2019, APIF has approved 54 in the fields of education, relief, religious and waqf education, youth empowerment and health care. The supported projects operate in 29 countries totaling up to US$ 1.19 billion. IsDB's contribution has been approximately US$ 256 including US$ 180 million from APIF and the remaining is from the beneficiaries www.isdb.org/apif (Fig. 21.9).

These projects have been essential in empowering less fortunate communities and assisting in the provision of education, better health delivery, more job opportunities, and turned idle assets into income-generating assets capable of improving their livelihood. Over the last five years, an average of five projects have been approved annually by APIF. In 2019, four projects were approved with a funding total of $12 million. Table 21.6 shows the details of the approved projects.

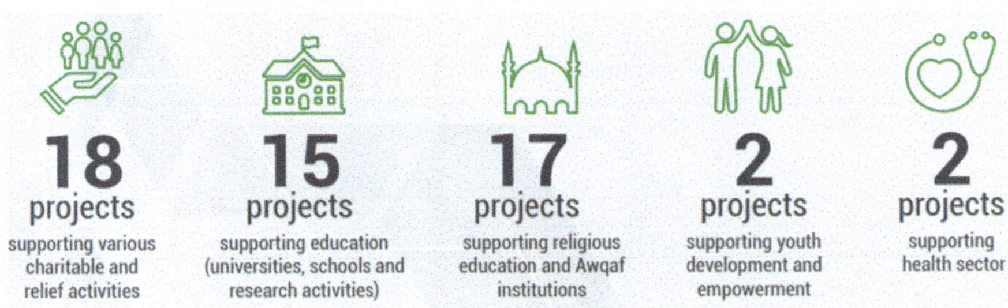

Fig. 21.9 APIF projects. *Source* APIF Annual Report (2019)

Table 21.6 List of APIF projects approved in 2019 (all figures are in $ millions)

No.	Project name	APIF	IsDB Line	Beneficiary & Others	Total
1	Construction of a Commercial and Residential complex in Dakar - Senegal for the benefit of the Daras	50.5	10.70	4.00	20.20
2	Construction of a Waqf Medical Commercial Complex in Tripoli, Lebanon In Favor of Islamic Medical Association	2.75	2.75	2.48	7.98
3	Purchase of Properties in the United Kingdom to be used as Waqf for the Mercy Mission, United Kingdom	1.60	1.60	1.11	4.31
4	Construction of a Mixed-Use Commercial Center in Columbus, Ohio, USA to be Used as a Waqf for Abubakar Asiddiq Islamic Centre Inc.	2.20	2.20	1.64	6.04
Total amount		12.05	17.25	9.23	38.53

Source (APIF Annual Report, 2019)

In reference to SDGs, in collaboration with organizations, APIF support projects that ultimately contribute to various Sustainable Development Goals (SDGs) of Education (SDG No. 4) Healthcare (SDG No. 3), Poverty Alleviation (SDG No. 1), Women Empowerment (SDG No. 10), and others (APIF Impact Report, 2019). Table 21.7 provides a snapshot on the Impact projects that have been funded fully or partially by APIF (APIF Impact Report, 2019).

Table 21.7 List of impact projects funded fully or partially by APIF

Waqf Beneficiary Institutions	Number of Long-Term Beneficiaries	Total Numbe of Beneficiaries	Proportion Funded by Waqf	Other/Notes	SDGs
IsDB-BISEW (Bangladesh)	7,000 completed IT and vocational training and placed in jobs; all other beneficiaries are in long-term-oriented programs	43,000	Full	92% job placement for program graduates, many in life-changing career jobs	4, 8, 10, 17
Fujairah Welfare Association (UAE)	6,000 empowered via vocational training, workshops, and Productive Families Program	9 Million	Partial	50,000 annual sponsorships (orphans, students, families, special needs); and many one-time spot interventions	1, 4, 8, 10, 11, 17
Towfiq Welfare Society (Somalia and Kenya)	20,000 orphans, students, and instructors supported	400,000	Partial	Operate social infrastructure institutions, including 7 schools and 1 university with its hospital	1, 3, 4, 8, 11
High Authority of Waqf (Senegal)	12,500 students in the major daras (Quranic schools) to benefit	12,500	Partial	64 daras (Quranic schools) to be supported	4, 8, 17

Source (APIF Impact Report, 2019)

21.2 Challenges Encountering Full Employment of Waqf in SDGs

The presentation of the aforementioned studies evidently show the great potential of waqf contributions in development projects, particularly in key SDG sectors. Namely in poverty alleviation, infrastructure, health and education projects. However, it is believed that optimal benefit of waqf sector is far from being fully utilised in the socio-economic development efforts of Muslim countries. For instance in the Kingdom of Saudi Arabia, a study conducted by 'the Investor for Securities' revealed that approximately 54% awqaf in the kingdom is idle land (Economies of Waqf Report, 2018).

Many challenges are encountering the full exploitation of waqf. These challenges include legal, administrative, financial, and other challenges. The following Table 21.8 elaborates on the various challenges of full employment of waqf in socio-economic development.

From the theoretical perspective, many of the challenges above are attributed to one key issue revolves around the 'principle-Agent problem' (Zeni & Sapuan,

Table 21.8 Summary of challenges to full employment of waqf in socio-economic development

Legal	Administrative	Financial	Human capital & manpower	Political	Others
- Lack or absence of proper legislations and laws, - Unregistered Waqf properties - Illegal acquisition and occupation of waqf properties - Weakness of registration system of waqf - Slowness in settling disputes	- Poor management and administration - Bureaucracy - Centralization of waqf administration and mismanagement	- limited sources of funds - lack of capital fundraising	- Low education for the practitioners - Inadequate manpower - Lack of integrity and qualification of Mutawalli - Lack adequate managerial and administrative knowledge - Lack of organizational and administrative competency	- Political interference in the appointment of the institutions' administrators - Possibilities of power misuse in waqf properties	- Non-strategic place of waqf property - Unproductive *waqf* assets - Lack of public awareness - Lack of Shari'ah and advisory board - Little or no trust or confidence - Lack of development initiatives - Lack of information and code of governance

Source Hasan and Siraj (2016), Ahmad (2019), AZGANIN (2019), Mohamad et al. (2012), Ismail et al. (2014), Azmi et al. (2014)

2018). This problem arises a when "there is a conflict of interest between the agent and the principal, which typically occurs when the agent acts solely in his/her own interests. The separation of the "ownership" (principal) and the 'control' (agent) in principal-agent relationships creates the grounds for potential conflict of interests between the two parties". (The Corporate Finance Institute, 2022).

In waqf, the principle-agent problem is more evident from the waqif (waqf founder) trustee side as well as from the trustee-beneficiary side. Many researchers have highlighted the conflict of interest between the principal and trustees as an underpinning challenge in waqf management (Htay & Salman, 2015; Ibrahim & Ibrahim, 2013). The issue of the principle-agent problem is multiple in waqf because the ownership of waqf properties has been a controversial issue among Shari'ah scholars a long time ago. As perceived by imam Abu Hanifah and Malik, the ownership remains with the waqf. On the other hand, Imam al-Shafi, Hanabilah scholars and Imam Abu Yusuf and Muhamamd from Hanafi school of thought believe that ownership of the waqif is ceased over the waqf asset. Imam Ahmad believes that ownership settles with the beneficiaries (Abdullah, 2020; Amin, 1994).

From the practical perspective, a closer look at the challenges highlighted in Table 21.5 reveals that a critical challenge has been for long time is the lack of funds and financial resources. Ironically, many contemporary writings emphasize the important role of waqf in economic development, these writing particularly point out to cash waqf a source of fund to mobilize funds for development projects, however, it should be emphasized that waqf could be a source of fund only when principal waqf properties and/or funds are efficiently invested to generate income to channel to beneficiaries and may be any surplus can be used to create new waqf. In other words, without actual funds and donations from the public and institutions, waqf becomes void and useless. Eventually, what really matters for the development of current existing waqf properties or for the creation of new waqf projects is the amounts of funds collected from individuals and institutions.

Now going back to the fundraising, a key challenge facing fundraising efforts revolves around the lack of trust and faith in waqf management (reference). Based on previous negative experiences of individuals as well as by institutions has resulted in a trust crisis'. This crisis in fact is the result of several reasons. On top of these reasons is the mismanagement of waqf properties, corruption, inefficiency, and lack of transparency. In turn, these reasons boil down to political interference, lack of competency by waqf managers, management staff, nazirs and mutawallis of waqf properties.

At this juncture, it is believed that a robust waqf governance framework is essential to address the mismanagement issues and transparency of practices and operations of waqf institutions and properties. Only then waqf can have the chance to prosper again and to regain the lost trust among the public (Zeni & Sapuan, 2018). Thus, hard work and serious effort must be exhorted to enhance transparency and to restore the trust in waqf among the public and the institutions. To this effect, AAOIFI has already released the seriousness of the governance in waqf institutions, accordingly, AAOIFI has issued its waqf governance standard 2018. The standard emphasizes in paragraph no. 12 "Different organs of governance and the management have to strive to enhance confidence and trust which are vital to the sustainability of the Waqf's operations." Therefore, AAOIFI asserts that the objective behind issuing the standard is to "provide the core principles of governance as applicable to Waqf and prescribes the principles-based guidance on the institutional and Shari'ah governance. These include the specific considerations for the setup of Waqf, the key responsibilities and principles for establishing terms of reference of different organs of Waqf, including the proposed organs, guidance on internal control, policies and procedures, guidance on transparency and disclosures" A summary of the good governance indicators is provided in Table 21.9.

As can be clearly observed from the above in the table, the items underscored in the table relate to the five pillars of waqf governance, four of them are traditionally mentioned in corporate governance namely: accountability, fairness, transparency, and responsibility in addition to one pillar specific to Islamic institutions that is Shari'ah compliance. It is worth noting that, many of the items highlighted in the table are clearly expressed as indicators of waqf good governance, in contrast, quite a good number of the items have been deduced by the author from the standard as indicators of good governance.

Table 21.9 Waqf good governance indicators (AAOIFI waqf governance standard 2018)

Policies • Shari'ah compliance policy • Risk management policy • Investment policy • Disclosure and transparency policy; • Policy for stakeholders' relationship • Conflict of interest policy • Whistle-blowing policy • Document archiving policy • The policy of receiving comments and observations and complaints and addressing them • Policy of communication with the media • Information security policy • Human resources policy • Appointment policy (silent)	**Committees** • Audit committee • Shari'ah supervisory • Executive committee • Investment committee • Governance committee • Nomination and remuneration committee
Controls • Shari'ah compliance control • Internal audit • External audit • Internal Shari'ah audit (the standard is silent on external Shari'ah audit)	**Transparency and disclosure** • Disclosure and transparency policy • Shari'ah annual report • Annual/semi-annual reports • financial reporting • external audit report

Source AAOIFI waqf governance standard 2018, developed by the author

21.3 Conclusion and Recommendations

Islamic social finance with all its components of mainly, zakah, waqf, charity and al-qardh al-hasan has come to the spotlight recently as a potential source of funds to close the funding gaps in financing and achieving the UN-mandated SDGs for 2030. The majority of countries in the Muslim world are in desperate need of funds. Waqf is one of the potential institutions that can be leveraged on in order to tackle the socio-economic challenges. However, it must be emphasized that waqf as an intermediary that must be supported by the public and institutions to raise the required funds. However, the necessary public trust has been seriously damaged due to discouraging experiences of previous and existing waqf management in addition to some other legal and administrative issues. Thus, several challenges need to be overcome to regain the lost trust and a lot of hard work is required to revive the waqf institution and its vital role. A robust waqf governance framework (WGF) is fundamentally significant to be developed and implemented. Such WGF should be part of a more comprehensive Waqf Promotion Plan (WPP) that includes as well establishing waqf ecosystem with a solid waqf infrastructure. Recommended components of a Waqf Promotion Plan (WPP) are listed below:

1. Enforcing waqf-friendly laws and regulations through a robust legal framework on waqf that is direly needed to offer clear guidelines on and to regulate the establishment, management, governance, and investment of waqf properties, assets and institutions.
2. Establishing the waqf Infrastructure via creating the relevant supporting institutions, includes
    - Training centres to address the lack of skilled workforce in waqf sector and
    - Research academies to contribute in strategic plans and other waqf-related issues
3. Raising awareness among the public as well as among institutions on waqf significance in the socio-economic development
4. Providing political support through enforcing certain policies and incentives in the form of government grants, and tax incentives to waqf potential contributors from individuals and institutions.

Appendix A

Cash Waqf Sukuk Structure of Awqaf Farms

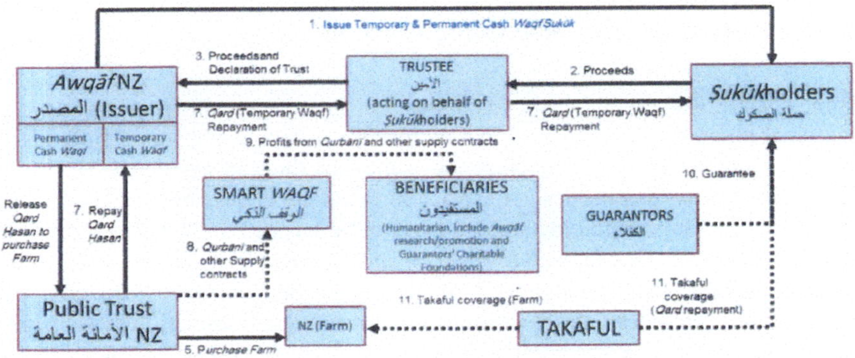

Source https://cibfmbrunei.com/wp-content/uploads/2017/05/Smart-WAQF-BIIS-August-2017-v3.pptx

Appendix B

IHH Waqf Deed

Vakfın Adı : İnsan Hak ve Hürriyetleri ve İnsani Yardım V.

Vakfedenler : Mahmut Savaş, Fehmi Bülent Yıldırım

Vakfın Amacı : Nerede olursa olsun sıkıntıya düşmüş, felakete uğramış, savaş, tabi afet vb. sebeplerle mağdur olmuş, yaralanmış, sakat kalmış, aç yada açıkta kalmış zulme uğramış bulunan tüm insanlara gerekli yardımı ulaştırmak ve bu insanların temel hak ve hürriyetlerinin ihlal edilmemesi için gerekli tüm girişimleri yapmak amacıyla vakıf senedinde belirtilen faaliyetlerde bulunmaktır.

Vakfın İkametgahı : İstanbul

Vakfın Tescil Kararını Veren Mahkemenin Adı Karar Tarihi ve Nosu : Eyüp Asliye 2. Hukuk Mahkemesinin 29/12/1995 gün, E: 1995/632, K: 1995/799 sayılı kararı

Vakfın Mal Varlığı : 15.500 Alman Markı nakit

Vakfın Organları : Mütevelli Heyet, Yönetim Kurulu

Türk Medeni Kanunu Hükümlerine göre kurulan vakıflar hakkındaki tüzüğün 13. maddesi gereğince ilan olunur. 6176/1-1

Source https://www.ihh.org.tr/en

References

AAOIFI, Shari's Standard. (2008). AAOIFI, Shari's Standard no 17 (2008). Shariah Standard (17) Investment Sukuk. Retrieved from http://aaoifi.com/ss-17-investment-sukuk/?lang=en

Abdullah, M. (2020). Classical waqf, juristic analogy and framework of Awqaf doctrines. *ISRA International Journal of Islamic Finance, 12*(2), 281–296. https://doi.org/10.1108/IJIF-07-2019-0102

Ahmed, H. (2004). Role of Zakah and Waqf in poverty alleviation (Occasional Paper No. 8). Islamic Research and Training Institute, Islamic Development Bank, Jeddah.

Ahmad, M. (2019). An empirical study of the challenges facing zakat and waqf institutions in Northern Nigeria. *ISRA International Journal of Islamic Finance, 11*(2), 338–356. https://doi.org/10.1108/IJIF-04-2018-0044

Ahmed, T. (2019). State of access to health services in the OIC and lessons learnt from the selected case studies. *Presented at the 13th Meeting of the COMCEC Poverty Alleviation Group*, Ankara, 4 April 2019.

AIPF Impact Report. (2019). The development impact of the awqaf properties investment fund. Retrieved from https://www.isdb.org/apif/sites/apif/files/2020-03/APIF%20Impact%20Report%20%28English%20Version%29.pdf

Amin, H. A. (1994). Idarah wa Tathmīr Mutamallakat al-Awqaf. IRTI, Jeddah.

APIF Annual Report. (2019). Retrieved from https://www.isdb.org/sites/default/files/media/documents/2020-06/APIF%20ANNUAL%20REPORT%202019%20%28ENGLISH%29_0.pdf

Azganin, H. (2019). Redevelopment of idle Waqf property through financial technology: Case of Malaysia. *The International Revue of Entrepreneurial Finance, 2*(1), 42–58.

Azmi, N., Muhamad, S., & Kamarudin, M. (2014). Challenges in developing the waqf properties: The study on state Islamic religious council in Kelantan. *International Journal of Management Sciences, 3*(7), 487–490.

BAĞCI, K. (2019). Education and scientific development in OIC countries 2016. Retrieved from https://www.sesric.org/imgs/news/1584_PRESENTATION_SESRIC_EN.pdf

Cizakca, Murat. (2011). The waqf, its contribution and basic operational structure. PowerPoint presentation: INCIEF. Retrieved from http://www.iqra.org.my/slide/Iqra%20Waqf%20101.pptx

Cizakca, Murat. (2013). The new waqf law prepared by IDB/IRTI and the Kuwait Public Foundation: A critical assessment. Fourth draft of the paper submitted at the PNB Paribas-INCEIF Centre for Islamic Wealth Management Inaugural Colloquium on Dec. 19th, 2013, Kuala Lumpur.

COMCEC. (2019). Infrastructure financing through Islamic finance in the Islamic countries. Retrieved from https://sbb.gov.tr/wp-content/uploads/2019/06/Infrastructure-Financing-through-Islamic-Finance-in-the-OIC-Member-Countries.pdf

COMCEC Report. (2019). CCO brief on poverty alleviation. Retrieved from http://www.comcec.org/en/wp-content/uploads/2016/05/CCO-POV-ENG-v2-1.pdf

Corporate Finance Institute. (2022). What is a principal-agent problem? Retrieved from https://corporatefinanceinstitute.com/resources/knowledge/other/principal-agent-problem/

Economies of Waqf Report. (2018). Retrieved from https://waqef.com.sa/site_books_show.php?show=540

ESCWA. (2012). *Arab forum: "Towards a new welfare mix: Rethinking the roles of the state, market and civil society in the provision of basic social services" Beirut*, 19–20 December 2012. https://www.unescwa.org/sites/default/files/event/materials/arab_forum_towards_a_new_welfare_mix_rethinking_report_e.pdf

Haneef, M. A., Pramanik, A. H., Mohammed, M. O., Amin, M. F. B., & Muhammad, A. D. (2015). Integration of waqf-Islamic microfinance model for poverty reduction: The case of Bangladesh. *International Journal of Islamic and Middle Eastern Finance and Management*.

Hasan, R., & Siraj, S. (2016). Complexities of waqf development in Bangladesh. *Journal of Emerging Economies & Islamic Research, 4*(3), 17–26. https://doi.org/10.24191/jeeir.v4i3.9093

Htay, A. N. N., & Salman, S. A. (2015). Theoretical concepts of good governance practices for waqf (Islamic endowment) institution. In *The 3rd International Proceedings on Management, Leadership, and Governance Conference 2015 (ICMLG 2015)*. New Zealand: Auckland.

Ibrahim, D. B., & Ibrahim, H. B. (2013). Revitalization of the Islamic trust institution through corporate waqf. Retrieved March, from http://www.internationalconference.com.my/proceeding/icber2013

IHH Annual Report. (2019). Retrieved from https://ihh.org.tr/public/publish/0/135/ihh-yillik-rapor-2019—en-121220.pdf

International Bank for Reconstruction and Development/The World Bank. (2017). Mobilizing Islamic finance for infrastructure public private partnerships.

IRTI Islamic Social Finance Report. (2017). The Islamic Research and Training Institute (IRTI). Retrieved from https://www.researchgate.net/publication/325698377_IRTI_Islamic_Social_Finance_Report_2017/link/5b1ed117a6fdcc69745bf23a/download

IsDB. (2018a). Islamic development bank ordinary capital resources financial statements and independent auditor's report for the year ended 31 December 2018a. Retrieved from https://www.isdb.org/sites/default/files/media/documents/2019-09/IsDB%20OCR%20FS%20YE18(19406019_1).PDF

IsDB. (2018b). Islamic development bank ordinary capital resources financial statements and independent auditor's report for the year ended 31 December 2018b. Retrieved from https://www.isdb.org/sites/default/files/media/documents/2019-09/IsDB%20OCR%20FS%20YE18(19406019_1).PDF

IsDB. (2019). Enhancing waqf assets and Islamic banking in Turkey. Retrieved from https://www.isdb.org/case-studies/enhancing-waqf-assets-and-islamic-banking-in-turkey

ISFD Annual Report. (2017). Retrieved from https://isfd.isdb.org/EN/publications/Documents/Annual%20Reports/ISFD%20Tenth%20Annual%20Report%201438%20-1439%20(2017).pdf

ISFD. (2017). Success stories series: No. 7 (May 2017). Retrieved from https://isfd.isdb.org/EN/Documents/ISFD-funded%20Microfinance%20Projects.pdf

Ismail, C., Muda, S., & Hanafiah, N. (2014). Challenges and prospects of cash waqf development in Malaysia. *Journal of Basic and Applied Scientific Research,* 4(2), 340–348.

ISRA. (2012). *Islamic financial system: Principles and operations*. International Shari'ah Research Academy for Islamic Finance (ISRA).

Kahf, M. (2002). Financing community Islamic activities and preserving the Muslim public properties in North America. Retrieved March February 6, 2015, from monzer.kahf.com

Khan, F. (2012). Waqf: An Islamic instrument of poverty alleviation—Bangladesh Perspective Thoughts on Economics (Vol. 22, No. 03). Retrieved from https://catalog.ihsn.org/citations/25102

Mohamad, N., Abdul Kader, S., & Ali, Z. (2012). Waqf lands and challenges from the legal perspectives in Malaysia. In *IIUM-Toyo Joint Symposium 2012. Sustainable Built Environment: Lesson Learned from Malaysia and Japan*. Retrieved from https://www.semanticscholar.org/paper/WAQF-LANDS-AND-CHALLENGES-FROM-THE-LEGAL-IN-Mohamad-Kader/0ea5ccc6206aa6824ad86834c44053a336b787f7

Nadwi, M.A., & Kroessin, M. (2013). Cash waqf: Exploring concepts, jurisprudential boundaries and applicability to contemporary Islamic microfinance. Islamic Relief Worldwide (Working Paper Series No. 2013-0x). Birmingham, UK.

Naqqasi. (2012). Retrieved from http://iefpedia.com/arab/wp-content/uploads/2011/12/Mohd-Negasiqatar.pdf

OIC Health Report. (2017). Organisation of Islamic Cooperation Statistical, Economic and Social Research and Training Centre for Islamic Countries. Retrieved from https://www.sesric.org/files/article/590.pdf

Orbay, K. (2014). Waqf institutions (charitable endowments). Turkish Cultural Foundation.

Saad, N. M., Kayadibi, S., & Hamid, Z. (2017). The contribution of waqf institutions in Malaysia and Turkey in improving the socio-economic conditions of society. *Turkish Journal of Islamic Economics, 4*(1), 1–29.

SESRIC & COMCEC Report. (2015). Measurement of Poverty in OIC Member Countries.

SESRIC Technical Report. (2015). Measurement of Poverty n OIC Member Countries. Retrieved from https://www.researchgate.net/publication/313442033_Measurement_of_Poverty_in_OIC_Member_Countries

SFC Report. (2017). Social financing: A Shari'ah compliant model. Soyan Financial Consultancy.

Shaikh, S. A., Ismail, A. G., & Mohd Shafiai, M. H. (2017). Application of waqf for social and development finance. *ISRA International Journal of Islamic Finance, 9*(1), 5–14. https://doi.org/10.1108/IJIF-07-2017-002

Shariah Standards AAOIFI. (2018). Waqf Governance Standard. Retrieved from https://aaoifi.com/governance-standard13-waqf-governance/?lang=en

The United Nations. (2015). The UN 2030 Agenda for Sustainable Development. Retrieved from https://sustainabledevelopment.un.org/content/documents/21252030%20Agenda%20for%20Sustainable%20Development%20web.pdf

Woetzel, J., Nicklas, G., Mischke, J., Kamra, Z. P., & Palter, R. (2017). Bridging global infrastructure gaps. McKinsey Global Institute, McKinsey & Company. Retrieved from https://www.mckinsey.com/business-functions/operations/our-insights/bridging-global-infrastructure-gaps

World Bank. (2014). Knowledge in development note: Measuring global poverty. Retrieved from http://bit.ly/1vUPbSJ

World Bank Group Report. (2017). Mobilizing Islamic finance for infrastructure public private partnerships. Retrieved from http://documents.worldbank.org/curated/en/898871513144724493/pdf/122039-WP-P159471-12-12-2017-11-42-45-MobilizingIslamicFinanceforInfrastructurePPPsFINAL.pdf

Zeni, N., & Sapuan, N. (2018). Revitalizing waqf governance: A theoretical perspectives. *International Journal of Advanced Biotechnology and Research (IJBR), 8*(3), 305–311.

Omar Kachkar earned his PhD in Business Administration (Islamic Finance), from IIUM Malaysia. MA. Islamic Banking & Financ from University of Loughbrough UK. Excellent background on *Shari'ah*, Islamic Economics, Banking & Finance in both academic and industry. Reviewer of several International Journals specialized in Islamic finance. Registered *Shari'ah* Advisor at Securities Commission Malaysia. Registered curriculum external reviewer in the ministry of higher education Oman. Associate of Association of *Shari'ah* Advisors in Islamic Finance—ASAS. *Shari'ah* Advisor, Trainer and a researcher in *Shari'ah* and Islamic finance. During employment with ISRA, Omar supervised and coordinated several translation projects with IRTI (IsDB Institute), IFSB and AAOIFI. He additionally translated the book of Mufti Taqi Usmani 'Introduction to Islamic Finance' from English into Arabic. Currently, Omar is an assistant professor at Ibn Haldun University in Istanbul in the Department of Management.

Marwa Alfares is currently a PhD candidate at Istanbul Sabahattin Zaim University in Islamic Economics and Finance. She holds a Master's degree from the University of Malaya in Kuala Lumpur. She has an excellent background in Islamic law with excellent command of the Arabic and English languages. Marwa is equipped with excellent research skills. Her research interests include *Waqf*, *Zakah*, social finance, Green *Sukuk*, alternative finance, and Credit Guarantee.

Part V
Special Issue

Chapter 22
A Path Towards Success for Muslim Households: Wealth Management and *Shari'ah* Rulings

Toseef Azid, Othman Ibrahim Altwijry, Osama Rewashadeh, and Nasim Shirazi

After many initiatives were taken by the different countries towards Islamic finance and opened several Islamic financial institutions, then many products were launched for the Muslim households to manage their wealth by following the rules and regulations of *shari'ah* (Islamic jurisprudence) (Shahar et al., 2017). Moreover, the advanced technology also supported households to assess and forecast the pricing risk under the umbrella of *shari'ah* (Fernández, 2021). Therefore the number of opportunities has been increased for them to invest in the different products launched by the Islamic financial institutions (IFI). This enabled more households to involve in more financial activities which are *shari'ah* compliant.[1] In the past, it has been observed that most of them were reluctant to invest in the different investment plans that the conventional financial institutions offered. The steps taken by the Islamic financial industry provided them more opportunities to be engaged in various economic activities. It is worthwhile to note that all of these activities are permitted by the *shari'ah*, for example, no interest (*riba*), no gambling (*maysir*), and not extraordinary *gharar* (uncertainty) (Rianto et al., 2019). It is also important to note that the form and substance of every product the IFI offers must be fulfilled the objective of *shri'ah* (Ebrahim & Abdelfattah, 2021). Although IFI opens a few avenues, significant instruments offer a reasonable profit to their client, such as *shira'kah,*

[1] "https://www.salaamgateway.com/story/islamic-finance-starts-at-home-not-at-the-bank-says-university-head-and-financial-management-coach-d retrieved on 12th February 2022 (Islamic Finance Starts at Home not at the bank, says university head and financial management coach Dr Murniati Mukhlisin reported by Yosi Winosa)".

T. Azid (✉) · O. I. Altwijry · O. Rewashadeh
College of Business and Economics, Qassim University, Buraydah, Saudi Arabia
e-mail: toseefazid@gmail.com

N. Shirazi
College of Islamic Studies, P.O. Box 34110, Doha, Qatar

T. Azid et al. (eds.), *Wealth Management and Investment in Islamic Settings*,
https://doi.org/10.1007/978-981-19-3686-9_22

mudharabah, murabaha, ijara istisna, salam, etc. (Kumar, 2014). All these are asset-based or assets-backed and have been proved more resilient during the financial crises of 2008 and 2009 (Farooq & Zaheer, 2015).

It is also observed that before the establishment of the Islamic financial industry, most Muslims were not very much keen to get benefits from employer-based retirement benefits because almost all of them are based on interest, which is not permitted in the system of Islam. However, after establishing and developing the Islamic financial industry, they felt comfortable. They had confidence in the Islamic financial institutions, and they moved from employer-based retirement plans to contribution plans which gave them more control over their investment and finance (Hughson & Wahdy, 2019). This is because they feel that these products are more valid and reliable from the Islamic point of view. Furthermore, it also gives them a sense of psychological, social, and economic security. They also feel that the Islamic financial system is more resilient because its transactions are asset-based/backed instead of based on interest (Ashraf et al., 2015).

As observed in the different financial crises, the high rate of debt based on interest is more volatile and has a lot of risk for clients (Minsky, 1992). Minsky further explained the different types of non-government borrowers as:

> Minsky argued that a key mechanism that pushes an economy towards a crisis is the accumulation of debt by the non-government sector. He identified three types of borrowers that contribute to the accumulation of insolvent debt: hedge borrowers, speculative borrowers, and Ponzi borrowers. The' hedge borrower' can make debt payments (covering interest and principal) from current cash flows from investments. For the "speculative borrower", the cash flow from investments can service the debt, i.e., cover the interest due, but the borrower must regularly roll over, or re-borrow, the principal. The "Ponzi borrower" (named for Charles Ponzi, see also Ponzi scheme) borrows based on the belief that the appreciation of the value of the asset will be sufficient to refinance the debt but could not make sufficient payments on interest or principal with the cash flow from investments; only the appreciating asset value can keep the Ponzi borrower afloat. (Hagberg, 2021, p. 71).

Availability of funds for the *shari'ah* compliant products and development of new financing approaches enhanced the investment opportunities among those clients who are willing to invest in the *shari'ah* compliant products. Consequently, it increased their income and enabled them to plan for their smooth path of consumption (Islamic Finance and Wealth Management Report June 29, 2021, Alpen Capital and Alpen Capital Advisors, Dubai).[2]

Islamic financial institutions are in the process of innovations that should not replicate those offered by their conventional counterparts (Lewis, 2008). Their innovations invite their clients to be engaged in those financial activities which are *Shari'ah* compliant, whereas simultaneously, their research and development department is analyzing the response of their clients (Ismail, 2019). After the mid-2000s, economic volatility was observed due to the conventional financial institutions' financial innovations. These financial opportunities created an understanding that less risk is not always good. Conversely, more risk is not always bad, and consequently, households

[2] https://argaamplus.s3.amazonaws.com/86f171a0-dcdc-4a26-b7f1-35345c16f250.pdf retrieved on 13th February, 2022.

prefer more risk to getting the higher expected utility (Dynan, 2009). However, this was not the case in the Islamic financial industry. Their innovations and development of the new products did not create the understanding mentioned above. Because they offer those products that are asset-based/backed and have no extraordinary risk, they are more stable, not leading to high volatility, and give more economic and psychological security to their clients. For example, *shirakah* and *mudharabah*, the instruments of IFI are based/baked on assets and based on profit sharing, are more resilient than the interest-based instruments. Therefore expanded financial opportunities by the Islamic financial institutions are neither carrying more vulnerability nor threat for the concerned households. Due to asset-based/backed instruments, the households did not observe a large swing in their wealth (BelouafI, 2014).

On the other hand, if there is more access to credit based on interest, it leads to an unexpected swing in the wealth of the households. For example, during the recent financial crises, it has been proved that the high degree of borrowing surged asset prices (especially the housing price) were highly unsustainable. In resultant, more debt ultimately reduced the prices at an unexpected level. This factor was not healthy for the economies and eventually had a bad impact on households' wealth (Dynan, 2009).

Lending is another essential feature of Islamic society, which is based on the concept of brotherhood. A loan is always benevolent, whereas all other financial transactions are asset-based/backed, leading to the system's stability (Sadr, 2015). Generally, the savings of Muslim households are only for the investment either he will invest himself or supply these funds based on partnership, i.e., *shirakh* or *mudharabah*. Otherwise, he cannot keep his savings with him because there is a deduction of 2.5% every year in terms of *zakat* (a religious duty). This is a unique case that one can see in the saving behavior of Muslim households. It is worth noting that Muslim households must follow the basic injunctions of shari'ah during wealth management and investment (Farooq, 2014).

22.1 *Shari'ah* Maxims and Their Application in Finance

All the maxims are derived from the holy *Qur'an* and the practices of Prophet Muhammad (PBUH). The most important aspect is the intention. It is derived from a famous hadith of the prophet (PBUH):

> Acts are judged by intentions (Bukhari; Sahih Hadith no, 1)

Intention and motivation play a fundamental rule in the eyes of *shari'ah*. The validity of any act is based on intention and motivation. For example, if sellers know that in the sale transaction of grapes, the buyers will extract wine out of them, this contract will be invalid. Or, if in the sale of weapons, sellers know that buyers will use them against Muslims, then this sale will be invalid. Allah (SWT) says in chapter 5 verse 2:

Help one another in righteousness and piety, but help not one another in sin and rancor (5:2)

It depends upon the objective and intentions; if the objective is unlawful, the action will also be unlawful. Muslim households should be aware of the other party's intention during the contract of wealth management. If he has any contract for his financial matters and if he knows that his funds will be used for those activities that are not permitted by the shari'ah, he should not sign that contract. The intention of the action changed the status of doers. For example, before ending the year, if a person gives a gift to someone from his zakatable assets and intends to avoid the payment of *zakat*, then this gift is not valid. If anyone gives a gift and donation with specific objectives, its nature will change, and it will be considered a sale contract, not a gift or donation. In the contract of *mudharabah*, if all the profit is for the fund supplier, it will be considered a loan contract is bearing interest. If all the profit is for the worker, it will be regarded as a benevolence loan (*Qard-Hassan*).

Similarly, preferred shares are not allowed because these are hybrid, i.e., having profit plus bearing pre-determined interest. The form and substance of any transaction should fulfill the objective of *shari'ah* (*Maqasad al-Shari'ah*). Another example is the deposits in the bank, i.e., Imam Kasani described the nature of deposits as:

If a deposit was in a money form, and the trustee uses it, then, *wadi'ah* (deposit) will change into a loan transaction. Any income drawn from its use will accrue to the custodian of deposit, i.e., the debtor (banks in present-day times). If the depositor permits its use as his agent, then the contract will be treated as an agency contract. The custodian of deposit may charge his fee as an agent (*wakalah al istismar*; investment agent in present-day terms). But if he allows him to use it based on profit and loss sharing, then the contract will be converted into *Mudharabah* contract (cited from Mansoori, 2012, p.21).

In this case, the position of the depositor is as a creditor, and the bank's position is as a debtor. Therefore any benefit that the bank gives to the creditor is *riba*. As Prophet (PBUH) said:

Every loan that entails benefit is riba.

It is a worthwhile phenomenon that there is one transaction of *Qard-Hassan* (goodly loan) between followers of Islam and Allah (SWT). As the Quran mention in chapter 64 in verse as 17:

If you give Allah a goodly loan, He will increase it for you several folds and will forgive you (64:17).

And in chapter 73 in verse 20:

Establish regular prayer and give regular charity and give Allah Qard Hasan (73:20).

Maududi explains the nature and significance of goodly loan (*Qard Hassan*) in *Tafhim ul Qur'an* as:

How Generous and Beneficent is Allah that if a man spends the wealth granted by Himself in His way, He calls it a loan Himself, provided that it is a good loan, that is, a loan which is given with a pure intention, without any selfish motive of winning reputation and renown, or of doing a favor to somebody, but only for the sake of Allah's approval and to win His good-will and rewards. Allah makes two promises in this regard:

(1) That He will repay it, increasing it manifold.

(2) That He will also give from Himself the best reward for it.

All those activities in the process of wealth management should also be under the principle of *shari'ah*, known as "sadd al-dharai" (blocking means to some evil; anything that has some benefit but the end is unlawful). The validity/invalidity of some transactions are based on intentions and motivation, for example, *Bay' al-Inah* (buying back at less price), Bay'*bi al-Wafa*[3], and organized *Tawarruq*.[4] Therefore, any household cannot increase/manage its wealth by using these lawful instruments if its end result is unlawful.

As Prophet (PBUH) said,

> Harm and retaliation by the harm is not allowed (Bayhaqi; al. sunnan al –kubra, Hadith no. 12099)

It is a guideline for the Muslim Households that they are not allowed to initiate any activity of harm and not in the response of any harm. Whatever the situation, no one should suffer during any activity that is the same for the financial transaction. For example, if the assets of another person are damaged due to the action of someone, the victim should not retaliate in his response. The Law of inhibitions (*hajr*) is also applicable if someone is not capable of disposing of or properly transacting his assets or if it harms others. The one significant cause is as:

> *Safah* or prodigality

Verse 4 of chapter *Nisa* presents the cause of *safah*:

> And make trial of orphans, till they reach the age of marriage. If then you find sound judgment (rushd) in them, then, release their property to them. (4:6)

Mansoori (2012; p. 67) stated: "*Safah*, in Islamic law, refers to the disposition of a person in his property, contrary to its dictates of the intellect and *shari'ah* by spending it without righteous purpose. It means squandering and using more of it than necessary, despite the persistence of one's intellect in reality. A *safih* undertakes financial transactions carelessly and in a manner that a prudent person is likely to avoid." He further added: "The *Shafi'i* Jurists maintain that *rushd* is the maturity of actions, not only about financial matters but also in the matter(s) of din" (Mansoori 2012; p. 67). Therefore if any household has some *safih* under his supervision, then this is his responsibility to manage his wealth according to the verdict of *shari'ah*.

---

[3] " This is a transaction in which a person, in need of money, sells a commodity to a lender on the condition that whenever the seller wishes, the lender (the buyer), would return the purchased commodity to him upon surrender of the price. The reason for its designation *wafa* is promise to abide by the condition of returning the subject matter to the seller, if he too surrenders the price to the buyer. Like *bay al-inah*, this too is a legal device for *riba*" (Mansoori 2012, p. 26).

[4] "*Tawarruq* is a transaction whereby a person who is in need of money, buys a commodity on credit from certain person, and then sells it in the market on cash at a price less than the one at which he purchased from its owner" (Mansoori 2012, p. 44).

It is also recommended that profit without the liability of loss be considered *riba*. Hadith of Prophet (PUBH) is:

> Entitlement to profit depends upon liability for loss (Bayhaqi; al. sunnan al –kubra, Hadith no. 10880)

And also, someone cannot sell that commodity that is not under his possession. Hadith of Prophet (PBUH) is:

> Do not sell what you do not have (Bayhaqi; al. sunnan al –kubra, Hadith no. 10559)

And at the end, the benefit of society supersedes the benefit of any individual.

> Public interest takes precedence over individual interest (This maxim is based on the doctrine of *Maslahah Mursalah*)

It is observed from the above discussion that *shari'ah* has given the clear cult verdict on the management of wealth and investment. It also guides if someone possesses the wealth of a minor or *safih* then how he will manage the wealth of minor.

22.2 Debt and Muslim Households

In the conventional economics literature, one can see a lot of discussion about different dimensions of debt, whether this debt belongs to a household or corporation. Economic theory suggests a positive association between education plus more young people population and rate of household's debt, i.e. if there are more educated and young individuals in the economy, then there is a high rate of debt (Dwyer et al., 2011). However, as mentioned above, in the Islamic system, debt is only in the form of a benevolence loan because an additional amount more than principle is not permitted. Moreover, Islamic economics suggests that zero interest and zakat implementation enhance capital circulation. Consequently, more economic activities will take place, positively impacting households' wealth (Azid, 2005). It is also worthwhile to note that there have been more financial innovations in the Islamic financial industry even during the last three decades. Still, there is not too much demand for debt as observed in the conventional financial market (Dynan & Kohn, 2007). At present, there is an excellent opportunity for Muslims to invest their savings in the different schemes that Islamic financial institutions offer. Because Muslim households are confident that most of the financial instruments offered by IFI are asset-based/backed thus, there is a very oblique chance of unsustainability in their projects. In this respect, Islamic financial institutions play a significant role (Myers & Hassanzadeh, 2013).

Another factor that plays a significant role in the process of wealth management that is the pattern of Muslim consumption. Allah (SWT) guides believers neither to be miser nor extravagant. As it is mentioned in chapter 25 verse 67 of Qur'an:

> and those who, when they spend, are neither extravagant nor miserly, and it (i.e., their spending) is moderate in between (the two extremes) (25:67)

Therefore, the variations in the different economic factors have no influence, which one can observe in conventional economies. For example, if the prices of the assets are increasing due to some inflationary pressures, it has not a significant conventional wealth effect on the behavior of these asset owners. The increase in capital gain does not peruse them to increase consumption or investment. As observed in the conventional system, if consumers do not have sufficient funds, they will borrow from the financial institutions. In return, they will pay interest to them, whereas interest has no room in the Islamic system (Al-Jarhi 2017). It is also advisable for Muslims not to spend more because they should be altruistic towards their descendants. As it is observed from one of Hadith of Prophet (PBUH).

> Sa'ad reported: "The Prophet, peace and blessings be upon him, visited me while I was ill in Mecca". I said, "I have some wealth. May I donate all of it?" The Prophet said, "No." I said, "Half of it?" The Prophet said, "No." I said, "A third of it?" The Prophet said, "Yes a third, but this is still too much. That you leave your inheritors wealthy is better than leaving them dependent, begging for what people have. Whatever you spend on them is charity for you, even the morsel you feed to your wife." (Ṣaḥīḥ al-Bukhārī 5039).

The only point that we have to be emphasized is that borrowing is not appreciated in the culture of Islamic society. On the other hand, if Muslims are wealthy, they have to pay zakat (an obligatory duty) and other charities and give benevolent loans to the needy members of society. Therefore in this way, they will get the reward from Allah (SWT). Hadith of Prophet about the reward on giving the benevolence loan is as:

It was narrated from Anas bin Malik that the Messenger of Allah (PBUH) said:

> On the night on which I was taken on the Night Journey (Isra), I saw written at the gate of Paradise: 'Charity brings a tenfold reward, and a loan brings an eighteenfold reward.' I said: 'O Jibril! Why is a loan better than charity?' He said: 'Because the beggar asks when he has something, but the one who asks for a loan does so only because he is in need. (Sunan Ibn Majah, Vol3, Book 15, Hadith 2431

Riba is not permitted where charity is rewarded by Allah (SWT). Qur'an says in chapter 2 verse 276 about interest and charity in this way:

> Allah will deprive usury of all blessing, but will give increase for deeds of charity: For He loveth not creatures ungrateful and wicked. (2:276)

Let's compare the conventional financial system with the Islamic financial system. It will be clear that there will not be too much demand for the debt with the increase in the price of assets because investment through interest-based funds is not permitted. Therefore borrowing will not increase, even in the case of high growth of financial innovations. However, it is well recognized that the growth of these innovations is not as high as in their conventional counterparts, and simultaneously there are fewer chances of moral hazards and adverse selection in the Islamic system.

22.3 Path of Success and Household's Behavior

However, in the Islamic system, the success of anyone depends on the success of both of his lives, i.e., worldly life and life hereafter. As a Muslim, one has to manage how to spend in the way of Allah (SWT) and how to look after his family and offspring. Therefore the concept of wealth management is entirely different than the conventional wealth holder. It is assumed that there is more stability in Islamic society if individuals spend more in Allah's way (SWT). The expansion of benevolence loans and charity leads to smooth consumption across different segments of the society, which will mitigate the gap of inequality (Ayuniyya et al. 2017). Therefore, benevolence loans have been more appreciated in the system of Islam. Also, relaxing in the return time has more reward than the charity as mentioned in the following saying of Prophet (PBUH).

> Buraydah (may Allah be pleased with him) said: I heard the Messenger of Allah (blessings and peace of Allah be upon him) say: "Whoever gives more time to a debtor who is in difficulty will have (a reward) equivalent to giving that amount in charity for each day." Then I heard him say: "Whoever gives more time to a debtor who is in difficulty will have (a reward) equivalent to giving double that amount in charity for each day." I said: I heard you, O Messenger of Allah, saying that whoever gives more time to a debtor who is in difficulty will have (a reward) equivalent to giving that amount in charity for each day, then I heard you say whoever gives more time to a debtor who is in difficulty will have (a reward) equivalent to giving double that amount in charity for each day. He said: "For each day he will have (a reward) equal to giving that amount in charity before the time for repayment of the debt comes, then if the time for repayment of the debt comes and he gives him more time, for each day he will have (a reward) equivalent to giving double that amount in charity. (Imam Ahmad 22537)

Through the transfer of payments from the higher-income group to the lower-income group, the aggregate marginal propensity to consume out of current aggregate income will increase, which positively impacts the level of employment. This will increase the sustainability of the economy because the sensitivity of consumption of the poor income group is more than the higher income group (Azid, 2005).

As one can see that the Islamic financial industry is growing rapidly, it is better for IFI to guide the recipients of funds about their use and how they manage their wealth over the life cycle. Simultaneously, lenders or charity givers may also play the role of wealth manger and guide them on how to spend this amount. For example, the instrument of *murabaha* or diminishing *musharakah* increases the capacity of the Muslims to purchase the homes without being involved in the interest. It is worth noting that these transactions are not as risky as we have observed in the conventional financial market. The clients of Islamic Financial Institutions are not paying debt services which are sometimes artificially very high (Hayat & Malik, 2014). However, as a true believer, this is a client's responsibility to understand his religious commitments and try to meet these obligations. There are fewer chances to expose the clients of Islamic Financial Institutions to more risk and the loss of property because of these institutions' solid and sound system. It is also a blessing that there is a minimum possibility for greater access to credit in the Islamic financial industry, therefore less chance to more risk. Also, Muslim investors will not invest in those products which are showing unexpectedly high returns. For example, the mortgage boom of pre-2008–09 is the best example of how greater access to credit has put the household at greater risk (Dynon 2009). During this period, it was also observed that low-income households were allowed to become homeowners or purchase larger homes with very low or without down payments (Mayer et al., 2009). In the beginning, the rate of interest was very low and then it was matched with the market rate, which boosted their installments and led to the negative amortization. However, this is not the case in the transactions of the Islamic financial industry, especially in the housing market. Because both parties are sharing in the assets and if there is any issue, it is necessary for both parties to share their financial responsibilities as per contract (Al-Maddah 2017).

In both cases, the wealth holders are earning the reward from Allah (SWT); either they are paying charity or giving benevolence loans to their fellows, or they are investing in the products of Islamic financial institutions. Allah (SWT) says in chapter 2 verse 280:

"And if the debtor is in a hard time (has no money), then grant him time till it is easy for him to repay," "but if you remit it by way of charity, that is better for you if you did but know" [*al-Baqarah* 2:280].

This arrangement of benevolence lending is very much appreciated in this system. It is not a predatory lending practice, and it plays a vital role in creating confidence among the members of society and participants of the market. It creates aggregate demand, which positively impacts growth, productivity, and employment. In the Islamic system, both fund suppliers and demanders are comfortably involved in the participatory investment. In contrast, the lending and delinquency rate will be very low because of Islam's ethical and moral teachings. In the case of *Murabahah* or diminishing *Mushrakah,* there is a minimum chance of foreclosure. Consequently, it does not lead to the negative impact of home finances observed during the recent financial chaos in most countries that issued conventional interest-based loans. In this context, the innovation of *Murabahah* and *Musharakah* mitigates the risk to households. It also has a positive spillover effect across households, and expanding funds supply has no adverse outcome in the housing market. On the other hand, Islamic Financial Institutions are not allowed to misinterpret the products they are launched (Sekreter, 2013).

22.4 Household Assets and Islamic Financial Institutions (IFI)

If we see the asset side of Muslim households' balance sheets, we can see some major changes after the development of the Islamic financial market. First, Muslims have new opportunities to take funds from these institutions. Second, they can plan about their retirement saving and other savings in the profit-loss products of IFI and widespread holding of *sukuk* (Islamic bonds). Third, because of the business nature of IFI, the products are less volatile. These financial innovations gave great exposure to Muslim households, which mitigated their risk of having funds with them without investing or depositing in the current accounts of the conventional bank. It has been observed that this financial innovation of IFI accentuated the financial behavior of Muslim households (Wahyuni, 2012).

Muslim households are also paying zakat (obligatory religious duty on their idle assets) and charity; in most Muslim countries, banks are also receiving this zakat and then disbursing them among the poor segments of the society in an organized manner. Historically it has been observed that several Muslim households are also investing under the item of *waqf* (Islamic trust) (Shaikh et al., 2017). However, the financial innovation of the Islamic financial market made it comfortable for Muslim households to invest in the products these institutions launched. These all are less risky because of their nature, i.e., asset-based/backed. These steps allow households to invest in the financial activities of IFI on a profit-loss sharing basis or *murabahah* or *Ijara* basis. Chapter 2 verse 278–279 of *Qur'an* describes as:

> O you who have believed, fear Allah and give up what remains [due to you] of interest, if you should be believers. And if you do not, then be informed of a war [against you] from Allah and His Messenger. But if you repent, you may have your principal - [thus] you do no wrong, nor are you wronged. (2:278-79)

22.5 Conclusion

During the past four decades and particularly since the mid-1980s, a lot of expansion has occurred in the Islamic financial market, which allowed Muslim households to invest in Islamic-based products. This has also opened the door of future investment and expanded the opportunity to spend more in the way of Allah (SWT). These opportunities lead them towards success in this world and life hereafter. Consequently, this is mitigating their risk in this life and life hereafter. This also significantly impacts the welfare of the whole Muslim community. The growth of house financing among the Muslim community has jumped dramatically during the past decades, increasing the saving rate of Muslim households. Because before the proper development of the Islamic financial market, Muslim households were not fully exposed to these instruments and reluctant to deal with the conventional banking system, i.e. believers were not feeling comfortable dealing with the interest-based system.

However, it is still too early to guess the impact of IFI on the behavior of Muslim households because different religious schools have different opinions about Islamic financial instruments and products. And also still this market is not fully developed. However, we expect that Muslim households' exposure to IFI will increase their interest in their products and feel more comfortable. Likewise, regulators and *shari'ah* boards are learning step by step about the functioning of the IFI and getting the vivid lesson from the different cases of financial institutions. Therefore, they are issuing the rules and regulations that are more precise and supporting under the umbrella of shari'ah related to institutions and their clients. In addition, regulators and *shari'ah* boards have their deep eyes on the volatility of the wealth of households.

However, better outcomes can be achieved if there is an appropriate balance between the proper regulations and better-informed households, i.e., leads to more benefits and greater opportunities for households and IFI. Both appropriate regulations and well-informed households will avoid harmful transactions.

References

Al-, M. (2017). An economic theory of Islamic finance. *ISRA International Journal of Islamic Finance, 9*(2), 117–132.

Al-, F. A. (2017). Islamic finance and the concept of profit and risk sharing. *Middle East Journal of Entrepreneurship, Leadership and Sustainable Development, 1*(10), 89–95.

Ashraf, S., Robson, J., & Sekhon, Y. (2015). Consumer trust and confidence in the compliance of Islamic banks. *Journal Financial Services Marketing, 20*, 133–144. https://doi.org/10.1057/fsm.2015.8

Ayuniyya, Q., Pramanik, A. H., Saad, N. M., & Ariffin, M. I. (2017). The comparison between consumption and production-based Zakat distribution programs for poverty alleviation and income inequality reduction. *International Journal of Zakat (IJAZ), 2*(2), 11–28. https://doi.org/10.37706/ijaz.v2i2.22

Azid, T. (2005). The concept and nature of labor in Islam. *Review of Islamic Economics, 9*(2), 93–124.

BelouafI, A. (2014). *Islamic finance and financial stability: A review of theoretical literature*. Working Paper Series, EI/WP/2014/3, Islamic Economic Institute, King Abdul Aziz University, Jeddah, Saudi Arabia.

Ebrahim, A., & Abdelfattah, T. (2021). The substance and form of Islamic finance instruments: An accounting perspective. *Journal of Islamic Accounting and Business Research, 12*(6), 872–886. https://doi.org/10.1108/JIABR-10-2019-0200

Dwyer, R. E., McCloud, L., & Hodson, R. (2011). Youth debt, mastery, and self-esteem: Class-stratified effects of indebtedness on self-concept. *Social Science Research, 40*(3), 727–741. https://doi.org/10.1016/j.ssresearch.2011.02.001

Dynan, K. E. (2009). Changing household financial opportunities and economic security. *Journal of Economic Perspectives, 23*(4), 49–68.

Dynan, K. E., & Kohn, D. L. (2007). The rise in U.S. household indebtedness: Causes and consequences. In C. Kent, & J. Lawson (Ed.), *The Structure and the Resilience of the Financial System: Proceedings of a Conference* (pp. 84–113). Sydney: Reserve Bank of Australia.

Farooq, M. (2014). Islamic wealth management and the pursuit of positive-sum solutions. *Islamic Economic Review, 22*(2), 99–124. https://doi.org/10.12816/0008097

Farooq, M., & Zaheer, S. (2015). *Are Islamic banks more resilient during financial panics?* IMF working Paper, WP/15/41, Research Department and Strategy, Policy, and Review Department, Washington, DC, USA.

Fernández, S. S. (2021). *Islamic Fintech*. Oxfordshire, UK: Routledge.

Hagberg, L. (2021). *Digital phenomenology: Proving digital philosophy and post-Keynesian economics*, BOD, Stockholm, Sverige.

Hayat, U., & Malik, A. (2014). *Islamic Finance: Ethics, Concepts, Practice*. Charlottesville, USA: CFA Institute Research Foundation.

Hughson, H., & Wahdy, M. R. (2019). *Planning an Islamic Retirement Investments, accounts, and shari'ah compliance, The Assembly of Muslim Jurists of America 16th Annual Imams'* Conference

held at Houston, United States. Retrieved February 12, 2022, from https://www.amjaonline.org/wp-content/uploads/2019/04/Planning-an-Islamic-Retirement-Hughson-_-Wahdy.pdf.
Ismail, A. G. (2019). *Innovation, Islamic Finance and Economic Development*. IESTAC Working Paper Series, Working Paper No 16, Islamic Studies and Thought Centre, Malaysia.
Kumar, R. (2014) Islamic influence (Chap. 10). In R. Kumar (Ed.), *Strategies of Banks and Other Financial Institutions: Theories and Case*. Amsterdam, Holland: Elsevier.
Lewis, K. M. (2008). In what ways does Islamic banking differ from conventional finance? *Journal of Islamic Economics, Banking and Finance, 4*(3), 9–24.
Mansoori, M. T. (2012). *Shari'ah maxims modern applications in Islamic finance*, 2nd edn. Shari'ah Academy, International Islamic University, Islamabad.
Mayer, C., Pence, K., & Sherlund, S. M. (2009). The rise in mortgage defaults. *The Journal of Economic Perspectives, 23*(1), 27–50.
Myers, T. A., 7 Hassanzadeh, E. (2013). *The Interconnections Between Islamic Finance and Sustainable Finance*. Manitoba, Canada: The International Institute for Sustainable Development.
Minsky, H. P. (1992, May). *The Financial Instability Hypothesis*, Working Paper No. 74 (pp. 6–8). NY, USA: The Jerome Levy Economics Institute of Bard College.
Rianto, H., Olivia, H., & Siregar, S. (2019). Islamic family financial management. *Proceeding International Seminar on Islamic Studies, 1*(1). Indonesia.
Sadr, K. (2015). *Qard Hasan* financing in Islamic banks. *ISRA International Journal of Islamic Finance, 6*(2), 1–14. https://doi.org/10.12816/0019261
Shahar, W. S. B., & Puad, N. B. M. (2017). The historical development of Islamic banking. In *Proceeding of the 4thInternational Conference on Management and Muamalah (ICoMM 2017)*. e-ISBN: 978-967-2122-15-9503.
Shaikh, S. A., Ismail, A. G., & Shafiai, M. H. M. (2017). Application of waqf for social and development finance. *ISRA International Journal of Islamic Finance, 9*(1), 5–14.
Sekreter, A. (2013). Importance of transparency in Islamic finance. *Journal of Business, 2*(2), 47–50.
Wahyuni, S. (2012). Moslem community behavior in the conduct of Islamic bank: The moderation role of knowledge and pricing. *Procedia—Social and Behavioral Sciences, 57*, 290–298. https://doi.org/10.1016/j.sbspro.2012.09.1188

Toseef Azid, Ph.D. is professor of Economics at College of Business and Economics, Qassim University, Saudi Arabia and International Visiting Scholar, Economics Department, Wayne State University, Detroit, Michigan, USA (2017). He holds PhD in Economics from University College of Wales, Aberystwyth, UK. He received Fulbright Award as Scholar in Residence where he worked on a research project on "Economics of Middle Eastern Countries". His research focuses on technological change, development Economics, labour economics, Islamic economics and Islamic finance. His recent books as co-editor entitled "Labour in an Islamic Setting: Theory and Practice" and "Social Justice and Islamic Economics: Theory, Issues and Practice" published by Routledge, UK, "Corporate and Shari'ah Governance in the Muslim World: Theory and Practice" published by Emerald, UK and "Economic Empowerment of Women in the Islamic World: Theory and Practice" published by World Scientific Publications, Singapore.

Othman Ibrahim Altwijry, Ph.D. is Assistant Professor in the College of Business and Economics, Qassim University, Saudi Arabia. He holds his Ph.D. in Islamic Banking and Finance from International Islamic University, Malaysia (2013). He got his Bachelor of Islamic Law/*Shari'ah* from Qassim University (2003), Master of Science in Islamic Banking and Finance from International Islamic University, Kuala Lumpur, Malaysia (2010). He presented several papers in the international conference held in the different parts of the world. His papers are published in peer reviewed international journals. Two of his papers won second prize in the International conference held in Malaysia and Dubai.

Osama Rewashadeh, Ph.D. is Associate Professor at University of Qassim College of Business and Economic and Director of AACSB Office (CBE). He has earned his bachelor's degree at Poona University (1994, India), his master's degree at M.S Baroda University (1996 India) and Ph.D. at University of Rajasthan (2001 India).He has more than 13 Academic research publications; also given invited International conference talks. His Interest research is funded by the corporate finance, credit management and Banking and non-banking systems. He possesses a wealth of knowledge in financial theory of teaching and applications in college classroom, acquired by attending seminars and workshops. He is the Director of the AACSB Office in CBE and serves in many committees (Director of financial program, and Director of Curriculum development Committee , and Revising and developing Curriculum etc.) He published in National and International peer reviewed journals also serving as international advisor of academic journals.

Nasim Shirazi, Ph.D. is a professor at the College of Islamic Studies (CIS), Hamad bin Khalifa University, Doha. Before joining CIS, he was working as Lead Economist and Acting Manager, Islamic Economics & Finance Research Division, IRTI, Islamic Development Bank. Previously, he worked Deputy Dean (Suleyman Demirel University, Almaty), Dean, Director Research and Director General, International Institute of Islamic Economics (IIIE), International Islamic University Islamabad (IIUI), Pakistan. Professor Shirazi served as a professor at International Islamic University Malaysia as well. He holds a Ph.D. in Economics from IIIE, IIUI. He has designed, developed, and taught courses at the graduate and post-graduate levels in Economics, Finance, Islamic Economics, and Decisions Sciences at the National and International Universities. With more than 76 publications, Professor Shirazi is well respected for his research in development economics, public finance, and Islamic.